Post-Wall German Cinema and National History

Studies in German Literature, Linguistics, and Culture

Post-Wall German Cinema and National History

Utopianism and Dissent

Mary-Elizabeth O'Brien

CAMDEN HOUSE

Rochester, New York

First published 2012
by Camden House

Camden House is an imprint of Boydell & Brewer Inc.
668 Mt. Hope Avenue, Rochester, NY 14620, USA
www.camden-house.com
and of Boydell & Brewer Limited
PO Box 9, Woodbridge, Suffolk IP12 3DF, UK
www.boydellandbrewer.com

ISBN-13: 978-1-57113-522-3
ISBN-10: 1-57113-522-7

Library of Congress Cataloging-in-Publication Data

O'Brien, Mary-Elizabeth, 1959–
    Post-wall German cinema and national history: utopianism and dissent /
Mary-Elizabeth O'Brien.
        p. cm.
    Includes bibliographical references and index.
    ISBN-13: 978-1-57113-522-3 (hardcover : alk. paper)
    ISBN-10: 1-57113-522-7 (hardcover : alk. paper)
    1. Motion pictures — Germany — History — 20th century. 2. Motion
pictures — Political aspects — Germany. 3. Germany (East) — In motion
pictures. 4. Politics in motion pictures. 5. Utopias in motion pictures.
6. Nostalgia in motion pictures. I. Title.
    PN1993.5.G3O25 2012
    791.43'65843087—dc23
                                                                            2011047357

This publication is printed on acid-free paper.
Printed and bound in Great Britain by
CPI Antony Rowe, Chippenham and Eastbourne.

For my husband, Joseph Chautard

Contents

Acknowledgments   ix

Introduction   1

1:   Amnesia, Nostalgia, and Anamnesis as Reactions to
the *Wende*   23

2:   In the Shadow of the Wall: Political Oppression and
Resistance in the GDR   99

3:   The Wild West and East of Eden: The Red Army Faction
and German Terrorism   173

4:   History Lessons: The Enduring Appeal of Utopianism
and the Specter of Violence   253

Epilogue   297

Works Cited   305

Index   331

Acknowledgments

MANY INDIVIDUALS AND ORGANIZATIONS have helped me to complete this book. I owe a substantial debt of gratitude to Stephen Brockmann and Shirley Smith for reading the entire manuscript and providing insightful comments that allowed me to refine my arguments at crucial stages in the writing process. I would like to thank the two anonymous readers for their exacting criticism that proved indispensible in making revisions. Laura McGee spent countless hours with me watching movies, attending podium discussions, and debating issues in contemporary German cinema, for which I am deeply grateful. Ruth Cape and Karin Hamm-Ehsani discussed important issues at length, offered valuable suggestions, and encouraged me when I needed it the most. I have profited greatly from conference panels where I could debate my ideas, and I would especially like to thank John Blair, Muriel Cormican, Owen Evans, Rick McCormick, Gabriele Mueller, and James Skidmore for their input. Thanks are due to my students who have shared my passion for German cinema and allowed me to experiment with new ideas in the classroom. Research on this book would not have been possible without access to the library at the Hochschule für Film und Fernsehen Konrad Wolf. I am indebted to the librarians, director Lydia Wiehring von Wendrin, and Kirsten Otto, who provided expert advice, found numerous articles and important references for me, helped locate photographs, and welcomed me with a smile and assistance throughout my sabbatical and frequent research trips. Renate Göthe provided guidance and innumerable newspaper articles. Ulrike Rollnik and Susanne Reiser tirelessly furnished a steady stream of DVDs. I would like to thank Dieter Jaeger for giving me permission to publish the beautiful photograph for the book's cover. For their help in obtaining photographs, I am grateful to Peter Latta at the Filmmuseum Berlin-Deutsche Kinemathek, Hiltrud Schulz at the DEFA Film Library, and Manja Meister at DEFA Spektrum. Working again with Camden House has been a pleasure. I am grateful to editorial director Jim Walker for his openness to this topic and helpful suggestions. Managing editor Ryan Peterson, production editor Jane Best, and copyeditor Sue Innes provided meticulous copyediting and careful preparation of the manuscript. Skidmore College offered funding and a yearlong sabbatical leave, which allowed me uninterrupted periods of time for research and writing. I am grateful to Dean of the Faculty Muriel Posten, Dean of the Faculty Beau Breslin, Vice President for Academic Affairs Susan Kress, and Associate Dean Paty Rubio for their steadfast support. I would like to thank Courtney Ross for her generous sponsorship of my research via the Courtney and Steven Ross Chair in Interdisciplinary Studies. Finally, I would like to thank my husband, Joseph Chautard, because without his constant support, encouragement, and occasional gentle nudge, this book would never have come to fruition.

Introduction

> As the "people of the centre" in every sense of the term, the Ger-
> mans are more intangible, more ample, more contradictory,
> more unknown, more incalculable, more surprising, and even
> more terrifying than other peoples are to themselves: — they
> escape definition, and are thereby alone the despair of the French.
> It is characteristic of the Germans that the question: "What is
> German?" never dies out among them.
>
> — Friedrich Nietzsche, *Beyond Good and Evil*

ON 3 OCTOBER 1990 THE COLD WAR officially ended on German soil.
With the demise of the German Democratic Republic and the emergence of a unified state in the form of the Federal Republic of Germany,
not only the Cold War but in some ways also the Second World War
faded into history. The fall of the Berlin Wall and unification allowed the
postwar era to take on the contours of a completed historical period that
occupies the immediate past and provides an epochal buffer zone between
the present and the Third Reich. The year 1989/90 marked a profound
shift in international relations and allowed the postwar era to supersede
the Third Reich as the defining moment in recent German history. The
signing of the 4+2 treaty implied that the international community had
formally pardoned Germany and, to more cynical minds, had lifted its
sentence of postwar division as retribution for the atrocities committed
under National Socialism. International approval of plans for unification
implicitly paved the way for a redefinition of Germany as a reasonably
contrite former combatant and morally acceptable modern state. But how
can a divided country whose common jingoist, genocidal past has rendered nationalism deeply suspect begin to conceive of itself as a viable and
future-oriented unified nation?

Divided Germany, more than any other country, marked the battle
lines between the competing superpowers. In official rhetoric, the FRG
imagined itself as a prosperous, peace-loving democracy repelling the Bol-
shevist threat and pitted against the rival GDR, which in turn saw itself as
the showcase of the socialist planned economy and the bulwark against
capitalism's fascist legacy. Little of the GDR's political and social institutions, artistic heritage, everyday culture, and value systems, or even material goods and architecture survived the unification process, which some
critics have labeled an annexation.[1] In the last twenty years the physical

changes have at times overshadowed the mental gymnastics necessary for the two Germanys to merge into one. The Berlin Wall was dismantled, statues of Marx, Engels, and Lenin were toppled from their pedestals and carted off to oblivion, and the Palace of the Republic was closed and left to decay on public display. The names of streets, squares, municipalities, and states changed as cities all over the former GDR became huge construction sites. Berlin in particular with its sea of massive cranes became a city destroying and reassembling itself in a nearly frantic search for a new postwar, post-Wall, some might even argue post-history, identity. The decision to move the capital from Bonn to Berlin intensified debates about whether unified Germany was moving backward or forward, reverting to a historical nationalism that led to world war or simply returning to the traditional seat of government that signaled Germany's normalization.[2] The refurbishing of the Reichstag with a reflective glass dome signifying a more thoughtful, open political process, coupled with the transformation of no-man's-land surrounding Potsdamer Platz into the shimmering steel and glass facade of a shopping arcade and entertainment center, exemplify in concrete terms several of the most persistent, if contested, aspects of the Berlin Republic's self-image: democratic political representation, a free market economy, the promise of prosperity and amusement, and a balance between preserving memory and living in the present.

The term *Vergangenheitsbewältigung*, originally referring to the psychological work of a nation coming to terms with its immediate past of a horrific, nearly incomprehensible fascist dictatorship, has taken on new meaning in the Berlin Republic. With the collapse of the GDR, a radical shift has taken place in what constitutes the immediate past. 1989 has replaced 1945 as designating the primary caesura of recent German history. This shift reflects what Hayden White has described as the essential mechanism by which we distinguish historical epochs, namely a shift in moral regimes.[3] Since 1945 the single most important historical question posed by academics, policy makers, and the general public has been: what led Germany on the barbarous path to National Socialism, world war, and genocide? And while this issue continues to play a major role in the collective imagination and notions of German identity both at home and abroad, other questions have started to garner more intense scrutiny. With 1989 as the new guidepost, increased attention has been focused on Germany's postwar division, the legacy of the Stasi police state, the '68 student movement, and the rise of homegrown terrorism in the sixties and seventies. Underlying much of these discussions is a sense that without the familiar leftist-rightist standoff, in which two equally strong opposing ideological agendas vied for the public's allegiance, if not its heart, the nation lacks orientation and suffers from the loss of a system that for all its defects provided forty years of stability and clear-cut choices. Since the GDR failed from within, Marxism has been discredited to such an extent that there is relatively little public support for the Left Party, the official successor to the Socialist Unity Party of Germany (SED), which ruled the GDR for forty years.[4] As long as the GDR existed, Germans in both the East and the West could take solace in the notion that there was at least an attempt to bring about a utopian vision of Germany as an alternative to individualistic, alienating, and consumer-driven capitalism. And despite the reality of a generally conservative unified Germany (governed for all but seven years by the Christian Democratic Union), this dream of a socialist alternative continues to be a strong undercurrent in the Berlin Republic. Comments made by acclaimed West German poet and essayist Hans Magnus Enzensberger are emblematic of this stance. In a 2008 interview with *Spiegel* magazine, Enzensberger admitted that he has not completely given up on the basic tenets of Marxism: "In my toolbox I still find a crowbar or two from Mr. Marx's workshop that seem usable to me. It just seems to me that the famous revolutionary subject is in short supply." Enzensberger continues to believe in the utopian ideal of changing the world:

> Whoever doesn't dream about this, you have to feel sorry for them. It is no coincidence that there is not a party program in which social justice isn't evoked on every page. To be sure, no one knows exactly what that means. But the belief that such a thing could exist won't die out, although there has never been anything like it in the ten thousand year history of humanity, and although everyone knows that extreme injustice takes place in this world. It starts already with the fact that one person is beautiful and the other ugly, one healthy and the other sick. Nonetheless, a wonderful characteristic of our species is that it does not want simply to accept injustice, even if every false prophet takes advantage of our dreams.[5]

Despite Marxism's collapse in the GDR and throughout the Soviet bloc, Enzensberger refuses to give up hope of finding a political solution to economic disparity and individualistic self-interest.

Especially in the realm of cultural production, one routinely encounters this popular discourse that pits a majority obsessed with conformity, consumption, and forgetting against a minority that mourns the loss of a common utopian drive to establish an egalitarian society on German soil and relentlessly tries to keep the dream alive. A renewed interest in the unrealized promise of socialism in the GDR and the misguided utopianism of the Red Army Faction (Rote Armee Fraktion, RAF) are only two examples of the current and widespread desire for political idealism. What is striking about today's utopianism is that it is often accompanied by a growing cynicism that such political ideals — however desirable — are not obtainable. Acknowledging the dream as a dream and the existence of false prophets does not mean that the dreamer necessarily wants to stop dreaming.

Twentieth-century German politics was rampant with utopian visions of a perfectible world. From the extremes of both right and left, political ideologies arose that promised to solve all social ills and create a harmonious social order, meaningful work, a restored national pride via a higher purpose, and a munificent welfare state. National Socialism proffered a *Volksgemeinschaft* (people's community) of healthy, racially pure Aryans who would work toward a common good in a social-welfare state and restore Germany's status among the nations. Marxism vowed the formation of a classless society where each citizen would contribute and develop according to individual talents and needs. National Socialism and Marxism were utopian (Gr. *ou* = no, *topos* = place) in the sense that they envisioned a world beyond the here and now, and if this no place, nowhere were ever to materialize, it would require a radical transformation of reality.[6] Both ideologies, despite their obvious aberrations and without implying that they are the same thing, were deeply utopian, promising the racially select/enlightened an ideal state, yet they ultimately ended in totalitarianism. For divided Germany in the aftermath of the Second World War, the imperative to rectify the atrocities of the Third Reich, in essence to get it right, to establish righteous ideals that would lead to a just social order, was (and in many ways continues to be) a common priority. For the East, this came in the form of a communist government that did indeed provide work and social services to its citizens but also erected the Iron Curtain and developed the most expansive surveillance system known to mankind.

Despite all its failings, the GDR is routinely depicted in the media today as a noble experiment gone wrong, implying that if the bureaucrats had just gotten it right, social justice would have prevailed. In the West the drive to get it right resulted in a return to constitutional government and capitalism, a system that seemed to many in the first postwar generation to resemble the pillars that supported National Socialism. The '68 student revolution and the left-wing terrorism of such groups as the RAF galvanized the nation. Their opposition to the status quo has been valorized not only as a corrective to a petrified conservative regime but also as evidence that German resistance is not an oxymoron and that the German people learned from their recent history to resist tyranny.[7] In unified Germany, mainstream politics adheres to democratic principles and the persistent utopian visions of the radical right and left remain on the fringe. Yet this drive toward an idealized solution to injustice is exceedingly resilient in the popular imagination. While there is nearly universal consensus in Germany that National Socialism was a mistake of biblical proportion, the verdict on Communism is more ambivalent, since as Enzensberger noted, the belief that a utopian form of social justice could exist will not die out. Rather than imagining futurist realms, German intellectuals look increasingly to the divided country's recent past as a way to imagine an alternative world. Since 1989 a growing number of writers, filmmakers, and cultural critics have turned their attention to the postwar period to see where the nation went wrong as it tried to rectify the mistakes of an even deeper past.

While some observers have characterized unification as the mindless act of a somnambulant nation, mechanically returning to the familiar, others still have questioned what exactly was keeping the two German states apart after the end of the Cold War. Former chancellor Willy Brandt suggested that with the fall of the Wall the two halves could now grow together.[8] Faced with an uncertain future, Helmut Kohl promised that "through a common effort we will soon succeed in transforming Mecklenburg-West Pomerania and Saxony-Anhalt, Brandenburg, Saxony, and Thuringia once again into blossoming landscapes, in which it is worthwhile to live and work."[9] Brandt and Kohl's use of nature metaphors implied that unification was a natural process. Their status as former and present chancellors representing both the SPD and CDU lent their statements a certain validity and a sense of common public will in the West.

Although politicians like Brandt and Kohl openly embraced unification, many prominent Western intellectuals were decidedly against such a move. Nobel Prize Laureate Günter Grass was among the strongest opponents of unification, arguing that German people must learn from the history of the Third Reich that a unified German nation-state posed a threat to peace. Grass contended in 1990:

> Auschwitz speaks against every trend born of manipulation of public opinion, against the purchasing power of the West German economy — for the hard currency of Deutschmarks even unification can be acquired — and yes, even against the right to self-determination granted without hesitation to other peoples, Auschwitz speaks against all this, because one of the preconditions for the terrible thing that happened was a strong, unified Germany. . . . We have every reason to fear ourselves as a unit. Nothing, no sense of nationhood, however idyllically colored, and no assurance of late-born benevolence can modify or dispel the experience that we the criminals, with our victims, had as a unified Germany. We cannot get around Auschwitz. And no matter how greatly we want to, we should not attempt to get around it, because Auschwitz belongs to us, is a permanent stigma of our history — and a positive gain! It has made possible this insight: Finally we know ourselves.[10]

Whereas Grass advocated a self-imposed division to guarantee that German dominance would never again produce such barbarity, novelist Martin Walser took a diametrically opposed view and argued for national self-determination despite the horrific crimes committed under National Socialism. As early as 1977 Walser defended the notion of national sovereignty, declaring: "We have to keep the wound called Germany open" and maintaining that Germany should be allowed to determine its own path:

> The existence of these two countries is the product of a catastrophe whose causes can be known. I find it unbearable to let German history — as badly as it proceeded in recent times — end as a product of catastrophe. . . . I refuse to participate in the liquidation of history. Within me another Germany still has a chance. Namely, one whose socialism is not imposed by a victorious power but is allowed to develop completely on its own; and one whose development toward democracy is not restricted to stumbling along according to the capitalist crisis rhythms.[11]

Walser's 1998 acceptance speech upon winning the Peace Prize from the German Book Trade, however, contained his most controversial formulation on the relationship between national identity, national history, individual conscience, and collective guilt. Walser's polemic against an institutionalized memorializing of the Holocaust unleashed a furious public outcry.[12] Lamenting that Auschwitz was being used by certain intellectuals as a "moral bludgeon" and rallying against the "never-ending representation of our disgrace" in the media, he contended that the history of the Holocaust was being instrumentalized for political purposes, including the attempt to deny the validity of German national identity in the present.[13] Walser's arguments that a constant collective commemoration of the Holocaust ultimately absolved the individual from any personal responsibility for the past, and that the focus on suffering allowed Germans to identify with the victims rather than accept affinity with the perpetrators, were largely lost in his provocative and often ambiguous formulations. Using the same starting point as Günter Grass, Martin Walser came to the opposite conclusion, asserting: "What we did in Auschwitz, we did as a nation, and for that reason this nation must persist."[14]

The weight of German crimes against humanity during the Third Reich made expressions of German nationalism and patriotism socially unacceptable in the Cold War era. Only in recent years has there been a cautious move toward expressing pride and love of country. Even before the 2006 World Cup, when Germans took to the streets adorned in their national colors and demonstrated pride in their country while acting as good hosts to the world, there were indications that German politicians were guardedly addressing patriotism. In the context of the guiding culture (*Leitkultur*) debate in 2000, in which politicians deliberated on whether Germany possessed a set of specific values and norms to which immigrants should conform,[15] Joschka Fischer, foreign minister and Green Party leader at that time, admitted: "In Germany, you wave the flag and at a certain point you arrive at the remembrance of Auschwitz.

You try to be a patriot here, you love your country, you accept the heritage, and then you discover you cannot love the heritage. So it is always a broken patriotism born of a broken history."[16] Four years later love of country continued to be seen as highly problematic. In his acceptance speech as federal president, Horst Köhler caused a sensation when he openly declared: "I love our country. . . . Patriotism and cosmopolitanism are not opposites, they determine each other. Only he who respects himself respects others too."[17] In a speech at the CDU party congress in December 2004, where Angela Merkel was endorsed as the party's candidate for chancellor, she spoke of Germany as a "community of 80 million people with a common destiny" and "love of one's own country."[18] Merkel sought to differentiate between patriotism, which implies duty-bound participation in civic life and collective self-respect, and nationalism, which sets one group against another. Merkel argued that "Living as a responsible community, granting a sense of security and safety, learning loyalty and dependability, being aware of one's ancestry and roots — from these one develops a feeling for one's home country."[19]

Nation building is by definition always incomplete, a project constantly under negotiation, but the events surrounding the fall of the Wall and unification have brought the question of what it means to be German to the forefront of political debates and cultural production with a growing sense of urgency. Telling stories about a shared past, establishing foundation myths, and finding commonalities of experience are pivotal steps in the construction of national identity. When Germans turn to twentieth-century history, they are immediately confronted with a form of nationalism in the Third Reich that led to world war and genocide. As such, the National Socialist past demonstrates Germany's greatest failure and as a cautionary tale remains an essential part of the national grand narrative. Looking at the more recent past of postwar division from 1945 to 1989 and seeking positive role models that could engender pride and love of country, one is struck by a recurring storyline that pits valiant individuals against an unjust, corrupt government. Seen from the present, with the collapse of the GDR a foregone conclusion and the '68 generation now featured among the country's most influential leaders, these David and Goliath stories about resistance supply strong identification figures and provide the plotlines for a national narrative that ends in self-determination. The central aim of this book is to demonstrate that the German cinema has provided a forum for this national narrative in which utopianism and dissent in the postwar period emerge as a prominent model for post-Wall German identity.

History is not merely an objective past reality just waiting to be uncovered but is always mediated and given significance as a constructed narrative. Historians, whether working in print or on film, assemble the past into a coherent and meaningful story through narration, the conscious act of selection, arrangement, and control. Despite historiography's demands for scientific objectivity and empirical evidence, narrating history necessitates at least some element of imagination, for as Hayden White has so convincingly argued:

> How else can any past, which by definition comprises events, processes, structures, and so forth, considered to be no longer perceivable, be represented in either consciousness or discourse except in an "imaginary" way? Is it not possible that the question of narrative in any discussion of historical theory is always finally about the function of imagination in the production of a specifically human truth?[20]

Imagination is of central importance, because beyond rendering verifiable facts and chronology, recounting the past as a narrative is based on conventions that give the illusion of an inherent cohesiveness and purpose to what happened. Narrative emplotment is a construct that gives meaning to the random flow of events and allows us to draw a moral lesson from historical situations that are not intrinsically tragic, comic, romantic, or satirical.[21] Our penchant for history "in the form of well-made stories, with central subjects, proper beginnings, middles, and ends, and a coherence that permits us to see 'the end' in every beginning," as Hayden White maintains, "arises out of a desire to have real events display the coherence, integrity, fullness, and closure of an image of life that is and can only be imaginary."[22]

This desire for the past to be presented as coherent, meaningful, and concluded finds expression not only in the realm of history as an academic discipline but also in mainstream cinema, where the history film promises viewers much the same agenda plus the benefits of immediacy, vivid audio-visual effects, and a keen potential for identification and emotional involvement. Even more than textbooks, history films use imagination to render the past as if it were unfolding before our very eyes. Apart from creating sets and costumes, filmmakers fabricate dialogs for which there is scant documentary evidence, invent, delete, or combine figures to approximate certain historical truths, collapse time to conform to the convention of a two-hour feature film, and juxtapose events in a manner that can imply cause and effect when in reality no such causal relationship existed. History films tend to focus on individuals (rather than institutions, masses, or processes), and therefore personal problems are often conflated with historical problems to such an extent that the solution to one seems to be the solution to the other. What the history film sacrifices in accuracy and complexity, it gains in predictable plot arcs that chart history in familiar ways as romance, tragedy, or comedy. The role of human agency, coincidence, interpersonal processes, movements, and ideas in determining the outcome of historical events can be skewed by the dramatic constraints. There are history films that consistently work against the dominant paradigm outlined here. Films associated with art cinema, for example, challenge viewers by refusing to grant the type of narrative closure offered in mainstream cinema and draw attention to the artistic edifice to question history as a well-made story that ends in resolution rather than doubt.[23] Rather than privileging one over the other as more fruitful to the study of history on film, or buying in to the binary that pits commodity against art,[24] it is important to see mainstream and art cinema as varying degrees along a spectrum of approaches to history and recognize that cinematic conventions have a history of their own that deserves investigation.

Historians like Robert Rosenstone and Robert Topin have made significant strides in their efforts to convince the history profession that feature films have validity beyond their status as artifacts and can offer compelling depictions of history. Rosenstone contends that the history film functions according to a set of conventions and practices and that the "world of history on screen is one worth attending to, one that can render an important past, do a kind of history that is complex enough so that we must learn how to read it."[25] Noting that accuracy and empirical evidence are not the only measuring stick for historical significance, Topin claims that the history film "can arouse emotions, stir curiosity, and prompt viewers to consider significant questions."[26] Feature films can provide the kind of immediacy and affective investment in the outcome of personalized stories set in the past to inspire spectators to ponder historical problems long after the screen fades to black.

A brief note on the term *history film* is in order. The genre of history film, as I use it in this book, refers first and foremost to narrative feature films set in the past that are based on actual historical events and persons or are a completely fictionalized portrayal of events that could have happened during a specific historical period. This may seem tautological, but this common sense definition is important because it encompasses the ever narrower sub-genres such as the biopic (depiction of an exemplary person's life or a pivotal period therein), docudrama (a hybrid genre that incorporates both documented historical events and a fictionalized dramatic framework), epic (large scale productions that depict monumental historical events through spectacle), or costume drama (a period piece notable for recreating the look and ambience of the past through costumes and set design). In contrast to historians who seem eager to define the genre in its broadest sense and advocate for the notion that these films contribute to a critical discourse on history, film scholars have been somewhat hesitant to use the term history film or even historical drama as an overarching genre designation. In their important studies of film genre published in 1999 and 2000 respectively, Rick Altmann's *Film/Genre* and Steve Neale's *Genre and Hollywood* offer scant attention to the history film as a major genre and single out only the biopic and epic for analysis.

Both Altmann and Neale maintain that genre refers to more than simply a set of films that share formal characteristics or common material, and they support a more comprehensive stance that considers genre as a network, in which the expectations of producers, directors, audiences, advertisers, and critics all contribute to an ever-changing practice. According to Altmann, genre is distinguished by a continuous process of transformation, which entails a messy course of articulation, disruption, and renewal rather than a comfortable, smooth evolution. He summarizes:

> Genres are not only formal arrangements of textual characteristics; they are also social devices that use semantics and syntax to assure simultaneous satisfaction on the part of multiple users with apparently contradictory purposes. That is, genres are regulatory schemes facilitating the integration of diverse factions into a single unified social fabric. As such, genres operate like nations and other complex communities. Perhaps genres can even teach us about nations.[27]

Altmann suggests that the study of genre can reveal much about the nation because both seek to integrate competing discourses and agendas into "a single unified social fabric." Genre films draw on a system of conventions structured according to cultural values. They are recognizable formulas, open to almost endless variation and subject to change over time, but they retain some aspect of familiarity that makes them comprehensible as part of a system. Because genre films are based on familiar outlines shaped and reshaped by collective memories and a common cultural heritage, they are uniquely suited to an investigation of national identity.

In recent years, the term *heritage cinema* has been applied to a wide array of German history films set in the twentieth century.[28] The term was first introduced in Britain to describe a genre of costume films made during the 1980s and 1990s that constructs and reinforces a nostalgic view of the country's past. British heritage films are most often set in the Regency and late Victorian eras and feature upper- or middle-class protagonists who inhabit bucolic landscapes and meticulously decorated interiors. They demonstrate punctilious attention to historically accurate costumes, props, and sets, a fixation on authenticity that Richard Dyer has referred to as a museum aesthetic.[29] Primarily based on English literary adaptations by such canonical authors as Jane Austen and E. M. Forster, heritage films focus on the themes of privilege, wealth, power, inheritance, manners, social codes, family dynamics, and romantic desire. Characterized by a style long associated with art-house cinema (a slow-paced lingering camera, minimalist editing with a preponderance of long and medium shots, a highly stylized mise-en-scène, an episodic narrative lacking goal-oriented action) yet without overly auteurist signatures, these films made the crossover to mainstream audiences and were successful at the box office in Britain and abroad. Packaging English heritage for global consumption, these films were marketed as an integral part of the heritage and tourist industries that sought to preserve and sell a specific version of British history.

Heritage cinema was initially seen as a cultural product of Thatcherism, advocating a restoration of Britain's former prestige, wealth, dominance, and class distinctions. Such films depicting an alluring vision of the past stood in strong contrast to the contemporary circumstances of rising unemployment, ethnic and racial diversity, evolving sexual norms and gender identities, and competing definitions of what it means to be British. Andrew Higson, a leading authority in the field, argues that heritage films seek to "reclaim sites of social consensus against the grain of historical trauma."[30] According to Higson, this genre tends to privilege the visual over the narrative; the camera lingers on beautiful costumes, props, and landscapes in a manner that does not advance the narrative or comment on the characters' emotional state. More importantly, the excessive attention to the image purportedly obliterates the potential for political challenges that could surface at the narrative level. Higson maintains that "the past is displayed as visually spectacular pastiche, inviting a nostalgic gaze that resists the ironies and social critiques so often suggested narratively."[31] He claims that spectacle competes with and routinely wins over the narrative as the central tool audiences use for interpretation: "even those films which develop an ironic *narrative* of the past end up celebrating and legitimating the *spectacle* of one class and one cultural tradition and identity at the expense of others through the discourse of authenticity, and the obsession with the visual splendours of period detail."[32] Higson's thesis that visual splendor anesthetizes audiences, turning them into enraptured, passive observers incapable of thinking critically, has been met with significant criticism. Claire Monk has noted that Higson's remarks not only privilege the visual over narrative in an art form that operates on both levels; they also assume a monolithic approach to the spectator position and a belief that the image commands more seductive power than the word.[33]

In the context of German films, Lutz Koepnick has advocated for the term heritage cinema for post-Wall films dealing with German-Jewish relations in Nazi Germany, arguing that it reflects "post-unification cinema's drive for consensus." Koepnick notes that some caution should be applied:

> To be sure, the German heritage film should not be understood as the product of some sinister intentionality or coherent program. . . . Many of the films discussed here not only explore possible meanings of national history from "below"; they also reclaim sites of German-Jewish reciprocity against the grain of historical traumas. In many of these films what remains of the past is not the disconcerting memory of trauma, but rather the image of intuitive understanding, harmonious community, and ethnic consensus.[34]

Koepnick identifies a series of films that reveal "scopic rapture" and

> turn the history of Jews in modern German culture into an occasion
> for the spectacular display of heritage properties. Paradoxical though
> it may seem, they present the past, not only as a site of violence and
> trauma, but also of precious properties and valuable assets, of splen-
> did decors and richly textured signifiers of pastness.[35]

The term heritage film may be warranted to characterize the set of films
Koepnick has identified, which try to recover and preserve an unknown
or underappreciated heritage, in order to establish a positive legacy that
bolsters national self-worth in the face of nearly overwhelming collective
shame for the past and also to foster a social value in the present that
promotes multicultural understanding and acceptance. Whether we consider heritage film a genre, a sub-genre, a production trend, or a cycle, it
is a critical construct that works best for a limited set of films with similar thematics, stylistic devices, discourses, and functions as social practices
capable of addressing the needs of diverse stakeholders. Heritage film
thus does not adequately reflect the variety of films under investigation in
this book. If we take history films about terrorism as an example, Christopher Roth's *Baader*, Volker Schlöndorff's *Die Stille nach dem Schuss*,
Andreas Dresen's *Raus aus der Haut*, and Uli Edel's *Der Baader Meinhof Komplex* are distinguished by different aesthetic choices and offer different answers to the question of whether aspects of domestic terrorism
constitute a precious historical legacy that merits preservation. Claire
Monk has convincingly argued that "heritage-film criticism has become
as effective a commodity in the academy as heritage films have been in
the cinema."[36] Looking to the past for a history worthy of preservation
is a prominent feature of historical inquiry, but it is certainly not the only
one. Another strain of historical work demystifies accepted views of the
past. Still another explores the trauma, suffering, and mistakes of the past
that need to be remembered for the sake of the victims and functions as
a cautionary tale to guide behavior in the present. It is not my goal here
to provide a definitive taxonomy of history films. My interest is to explore
how films made since 1989 treat the history of divided Germany, whether
there is a dominant practice, and whether contested histories have found
their way into cinema. My study adopts a broad approach and follows
Robert Rosenstone's notion that "what makes a film historical is its willingness to engage the discourse of history — that is, the facts, the issues,
and the arguments raised in other historical works."[37] Thus in addition
to history films set in the recent past with plots that take place between
approximately 1967 and 1989, I will end my study by also addressing
films set in the present day with characters who intensely scrutinize the
course of German history in order to locate a workable legacy for their
lives today.

In *Post-Wall German Cinema and National History* I study the genre of history film as a set of texts and a discursive network that can tell us something about the German nation, past and present. Monumental historical changes require reflection, and because of the capacity of motion pictures to tell compelling stories about the past, the cinema has provided fertile ground for debates about postwar German history. Whether one considers commercially successful popular motion pictures, intellectually challenging auteurist films, or event-television films, media representations of national history reveal a great deal about how a shared understanding of the past is integral to constructing a sense of collective identity in the present. My study investigates history films made in Germany from 1989 to 2009 that interrogate postwar German history, and I argue that the cinema provides an important public forum, where different notions of German history and national identity can be consumed, negotiated, and contested. Adopting an approach that is attentive to both textual analysis and sociohistorical context(s), I am interested in what individual films have to say about the recent past and how the relationship between cinema, historiography, political and artistic debates, and public opinion contribute to the ongoing nation-building project. To capture the variety of influences and give expression to dominant and countervailing voices involved in this process, I survey history films' discursive networks via publicity material, trade-press reviews, history books, parliamentary debates, podium discussions at the movie theater, and web-based materials.

In this book I look specifically at recent German films to explore how utopianism and political dissent have shaped post–Second World War German history and the construction of national identity after unification in 1990. In chapter 1 I study films that depict the *Wende* (turn of events) using the themes of amnesia, anamnesis, and imprisonment to problematize the notion of a collective memory of the momentous events that took place in 1989. In chapter 2 I target films that present the GDR as an *Unrechtstaat*, a fortified prison state replete with police surveillance, scarcity, censorship, and the lack of basic freedoms. In chapter 3 I focus on films about the Red Army Faction or Baader-Meinhof Gang, which illustrate the crushing effect of National Socialism on the '68 generation as well as their rebellion against the excesses of capitalist consumer paradise. In chapter 4 I consider films set in the present that look to the past for guidance and formulate the notion of "creative chaos" as a strategy to protest against the loss of utopian dreams. My goal is to analyze exemplary films in the context of their production, exhibition, and reception in order to elucidate the persistence of certain models and formulas for postwar history. My selection of films includes a wide range of history films made over the last two decades: box office hits, modest films with small audiences, and television films that attracted millions of viewers. I include motion pictures that won artistic acclaim as well as those that failed to gain critical or public approval. This variety is important to gauge which conventions are repeated and circulated, to identify which storylines are resilient, and to determine whether there is a resistant popular practice. At issue here is the overriding question: to what extent do these films contribute to the master narrative that legitimates the existence of the German nation state?

In the last twenty years the German film industry has undergone significant changes: structurally with the privatization of the GDR's state-run film production company DEFA (Deutsche Filmaktiengesellschaft), financially with the growth of government subsidy boards and increased TV sponsorship of cinema productions, and, of course, technically with digital filmmaking, the development of DVDs, and the shift toward web-based viewing formats. The definition of cinema as an institution needs to reflect these changes, and we must acknowledge above all that films are watched not only in movie theaters, museums, and collective venues but also by individuals in their own individual space. Based on this broader understanding of how viewers access and manage their consumption of films, I analyze motion pictures intended for release in movie theaters, those planned for a premiere run in the theater and subsequent television broadcast, and also those exclusively produced for television. In nearly every case, the films I treat are available in commercial release for sale as DVDs in Germany.

At the turn of the millennium Eric Rentschler identified a prevalent approach to filmmaking in unified Germany that strived for common ground and building consensus over uncomfortable and provocative challenges to the status quo. Apart from the "offbeat voices and less reconciled visions" of directors like Tom Tykwer, Fatih Akin, Rosa von Praunheim, Ulrike Ottinger, and Harun Farocki, who made "less visible films with a historical ground, a post-national sensibility and a critical edge," Rentschler argued that the vast majority of German film productions in the nineties consisted of light fare meant to please and placate audiences.[38] This trend toward uncomplicated story lines with agreeable resolutions was all the more prominent if one compared German cinema of the nineties with that of the seventies. Rentschler applauded New German Cinema directors such as Alexander Kluge, Rainer Werner Fassbinder, Werner Herzog, and Wim Wenders, who in the seventies "interrogated images of the past in the hope of refining memories and catalysing changes."[39] By contrast Rentschler saw contemporary German cinema as lacking "oppositional energies and critical voices" leading to a "cinema of consensus."[40]

If we limit our scope to mainstream cinema, then Rentschler's remarks hold true for much of the nineties, if not today as well. The vast majority of films made in Germany over the last two decades do not challenge viewers with open, innovative narrative forms, and they do not pose difficult or disturbing questions. However, the same can be said of the seventies even during the heyday of New German Cinema, when directors like Fassbinder and Herzog were greeted with critical acclaim abroad but largely ignored at home. The overwhelming majority of German cinemagoers in the seventies were drawn primarily to conventional home-grown fare and increasingly to Hollywood productions.[41] Another area of contention would be that Rentschler does not address the films made from 1989 to 1992 at the DEFA studios.[42] In this brief period when the entrenched bureaucracy with its institutionalized system of self-censorship was being dismantled, leaving sufficient funding available for experimentation, a new generation of DEFA filmmakers (born around 1949) made unconventional and thought-provoking films that failed to find an audience. Films by directors like Jörg Foth, Peter Kahane, and Herwig Kipping fell into the so-called *Wendeloch* (the hole created by the turn of events in 1989).[43] Their aesthetic and political rebellion against accepted dogmas, however, deserves to be included among the "oppositional energies and critical voices" Rentschler locates largely in the West. Finally, I think it is important to stress that there are contemporary German filmmakers such as Christian Petzold, Sylke Enders, Christoph Hochhäusler, Andreas Dresen, and Hans Weingartner, to name just a few, who contribute to what I will call a cinema of consciousness that challenges the status quo and addresses pressing social problems without proposing simple solutions. What separates these young directors most distinctly from the auteurs of New German Cinema is that they are much more likely to embrace in a selective fashion certain aspects of popular mainstream cinema to capture their audience.

Social critic Klaus Theweleit provocatively suggested in 1995 that the brutality of twentieth-century German history was so traumatic that it precluded the very existence of anything one could rightly call German film. Germans, he argued, were incapable of producing a self-critical national cinema, because of their distorted relationship to their own history: "We 'see' nothing we could render in film, because we cannot see ourselves as part of the German violence unleashed in this century and its effects. We cannot appreciate our bodies and thus we cannot acknowledge them."[44] Although Theweleit's statement is worthy of rumination for its ability to challenge established notions of the relationship between film and history, it does not adequately portray the current state of affairs in the German motion-picture industry. Since the fall of the Berlin Wall, German filmmakers have focused their sights on German history with varying degrees of intensity and success. Contemporary German films display a wide variety of approaches to postwar history. Some exhibit conciliatory gestures and others demand revision of accepted truths, but they all participate in a discourse that tries to make sense of the past and its effect on the present.

For a few hours at least, motion pictures can bring history to life again, resurrecting the dead and bygone times with such immediacy that it feels as if we are transported back in time. Alison Landsberg has coined the term "prosthetic memory" to describe how mass media can allow people to experience a past that they have not lived as if it were a vivid memory. She poses the idea that "the experience within the movie theater and the memories that the cinema affords — despite the fact that the spectator did not live through them — might be as significant in constructing, or deconstructing, the spectator's identity as any experience that s/he actually lived through."[45] According to Landsberg, cinema can transform history from an objective accounting of the past that remains distant because it happened to other people to an artificial experience that has all the markings of the real: a physical response, a visual and auditory record, and an affective encounter that can be recalled, even though the events never actually happened to the viewer. Experiencing history at an emotional, somatic level as if it were memory allows viewers to identify with people from the past and empathize with them to such an extent that they feel related despite the divisions of time, space, and social conditions. Landsberg's premise is that an intensification of affect will lead to greater empathy, because spectators put themselves into the other's emotional state. She considers empathy "instrumental in articulating an ethical relation to the other" and argues that empathy generated from prosthetic memories can lead to "social responsibility as well as political alliances that transcend race, class, and gender; . . . it becomes the basis for mediated collective identification and the production of potentially counterhegemonic public spheres."[46] There is much to commend in Landsberg's approach. Identification and emotional involvement can indeed help audience to feel the type of horror, despair, ecstasy, and hope experienced by people in other times. However, how does prosthetic memory work with movies that subvert realism, block identification, and problematize affective experience? In my opinion, Landsberg privileges affect as the key to empathy and social responsibility. She thus neglects to address how motion pictures also convey knowledge, demand reasoning skills, and require evaluation of situations, ideas, relationships, and motivations. Attention to immediacy, identification, and empathy is important, but as I argue in this book, feature films also operate on the cognitive level. Not only the typical debates captured in dialogs, also narrative structures alert viewers to pivotal historical concepts such as causality and consequence. Therefore, I would like to expand Landsberg's notion of prosthetic memory to include a discussion of how history films help viewers to comprehend the dynamics of chance, agency, and passivity that play an equally important part in historical understanding.

In his 1949 acceptance speech as the first president of the Federal Republic, Theodor Heuss recognized one of Germany's contradictory qualities that might hinder the development of a new national identity. Heuss remarked: "Strange German people, full of great tensions, where the subaltern stands next to ingenious speculative rambling, where petit bourgeois stands next to great romanticism."[47] This tension is evident in contemporary German cinema. The films discussed in this book reflect a fundamental dilemma that has captured the popular imagination in unified Germany and has played out in various modes, ranging from the media blitz commemorating the fortieth anniversary of 1968 to the cinema's ongoing fascination with the GDR and the RAF. Mediated engagements with postwar history make clear that the general public has lost faith in the type of political utopia that engendered twentieth-century dictatorships and terrorism but doggedly continues to long for a collective solution to society's imperfections. Confronted with a national history of two dictatorships fuelled by grandiose plans for social engineering, this longing for idealism often wavers between cynicism and naïve faith, creating a nearly schizophrenic mindset. Wavering between disappointment with failed utopian experiments and a relentless desire to strive for the perfect society, the cinema looks to the immediate past to find a way out of the quandary and forge a shared destiny for the future.

Notes

[1] Noted social and political theorist Jürgen Habermas, for instance, referred to Chancellor Helmut Kohl's push for a speedy unification as a calculated "annexation" of the GDR. Habermas was dismayed that the unification process was led by a narrow reading of two articles in the Basic Law written specifically to deal with postwar division of Germany. Kohl's process favored Article 23, which allowed for the accession of German territory, over Article 146, which would have required a constitutional assembly. Habermas maintained that the FRG undertook "an annexation, which dishonestly evades one of the essential conditions for the founding of any nation of state-citizens: the public act of a carefully considered democratic decision taken in both parts of Germany. This act of foundation can only be carried out consciously and intentionally if we agree not to accomplish unification via Article 23 of the Basic Law (which governs the accession of 'other parts of Germany')." Jürgen Habermas, "Yet Again: German Identity; A Unified Nation of Angry DM-Burghers?" *New German Critique* 52 (1991): 95–96.

[2] For a discussion of the debate around normalization in unified Germany, see Mitchell G. Ash, "Becoming Normal, Modern, and German (Again?)," in *The Power of Intellectuals in Contemporary Germany*, ed. Michael Geyer (Chicago: U of Chicago P, 2001), 295–313, and Stuart Taberner and Paul Cooke, eds., *German Culture, Politics, and Literature into the Twenty-First Century: Beyond Normalization* (Rochester, NY: Camden House, 2006).

³ Hayden White, *The Content of the Form: Narrative Discourse and Historical Representation* (Baltimore: Johns Hopkins UP, 1990), 23.

⁴ The Socialist Unity Party of Germany (Sozialistische Einheitspartei Deutschlands, SED) existed from 1946 to 1990 and was reorganized as the Party of Democratic Socialism (Partei des Demokratischen Sozialismus, PDS) from 1990–2005. In 2005 it merged with the Electoral Alternative for Labor and Social Justice (Wahlalternative für Arbeit und Soziale Gerechtigkeit, WASG) and adopted the name Left Party (die Linkspartei) and later simply The Left (die Linke). Of the 622 members of the seventeenth session of the German Bundestag, seventy-six members represent The Left. Statistics are available at The German Bundestag, http://www.bundestag.de/htdocs_e/bundestag/members17/bygroup.html.

⁵ "In meinem Werkzeugkasten finde ich nach wie vor die eine oder andere Brechstange aus der Werkstatt des Herrn Marx, die mir brauchbar scheint. Nur an dem berühmten revolutionären Subjekt scheint es mir zu hapern. . . . Wer nicht davon träumt, kann einem nur leid tun. Es ist ja kein Zufall, dass es kein Parteiprogramm gibt, in dem nicht auf jeder Seite die soziale Gerechtigkeit beschworen wird. Zwar weiß niemand genau, was damit gemeint ist. Aber die Vorstellung, dass so etwas existieren könnte, ist nicht totzukriegen, obwohl es etwas Derartiges in der zehntausendjährigen Geschichte der Menschheit noch nie gegeben hat, und obwohl jeder weiß, dass es auf der Welt extrem ungerecht zugeht. Das fängt schon damit an, daß der eine schön, der andere hässlich, der eine gesund und der andere krank ist. Trotzdem ist es ein schöner Zug unserer Spezies, dass sie die Ungerechtigkeit nicht einfach resigniert hinnehmen will, auch wenn jeder falsche Prophet sich unsere Träume zunutze macht." Markus Brauck and Matthias Mattusek, "'Phantastischer Gedächtnisverlust:' Gespräch mit dem Schriftsteller und einstigen Marxisten Hans Magnus Enzensberger," *Spiegel Online,* 3 Nov. 2008, http://www.spiegel.de/spiegel/0,1518,587872,00.html.

⁶ See Richard Saage, *Utopieforschung: Eine Bilanz* (Darmstadt: Primus, 1997), 148–56. For a historical overview of utopia from the Renaissance to the twentieth century, see Frank E. Manuel and Fritzie P. Manuel, *Utopian Thought in the Western World* (Cambridge, MA: Belknap, 1979).

⁷ Former student rebel and Green Party politician Joschka Fischer summarized his generation's attempt to separate itself from National Socialism via protest: "But even in rebellion, one could not wipe the filth of the fatherland from one's boots. One was always caught in a web called Germany, and so the basic political feeling of my generation, the 68ers, can be described in simple terms as: disgusted." The German original: "Aber selbst in der Rebellion wurde man den Dreck des Vaterlandes nicht von den Stiefeln los. Immer wieder verfing man sich in einem Gespinst, welches Deutschland heißt, und so läßt sich das politische Grundgefühl meiner Generation, der 68er, mit schlichten Worten beschreiben: zum Kotzen." Joschka Fischer, "Identität in Gefahr!" in *Grüne Politik: Eine Standortbestimmung,* ed. Thomas Kluge (Frankfurt am Main: Fischer, 1984), 28–29.

⁸ Willy Brandt is frequently quoted as having said "Jetzt wächst zusammen, was zusammengehört" (now that which belongs together can grow together) at the historic rally in front of the Schöneberg city hall on 10 November 1989. Timothy Garton Ash examines the apocryphal nature of this statement and the process by which it came to mark the *Wende.* See Timothy Garton Ash, ed.,

Wächst zusammen, was zusammengehört? Deutschland und Europa zehn Jahre nach dem Fall der Mauer: Vortrag im Rathaus Schöneberg zu Berlin, 5. November 1999, Schriftenreihe der Bundeskanzler-Willy-Brandt-Stiftung 8 (Berlin: Bundes-kanzler-Willy-Brandt-Stiftung, 2001).

[9] "Durch eine gemeinsame Anstrengung wird es uns gelingen, Mecklenburg-Vorpommern und Sachsen-Anhalt, Brandenburg, Sachsen und Thüringen schon bald wieder in blühende Landschaften zu verwandeln, in denen es sich zu leben und zu arbeiten lohnt." Helmut Kohl, "Fernsehansprache von Bundeskanzler Kohl anlässlich des Inkrafttretens der Währungs-, Wirtschafts- und Sozialunion, 1. Juli 1990," Konrad Adenauer Stiftung, http://www.helmut-kohl.de/index.php?msg=555.

[10] Günter Grass, "Writing after Auschwitz (1990)," in *Two States — One Nation?*, trans. Krishna Winston and A. S. Wensinger (New York: Harcourt Brace Jovanovich, 1990), 122–23.

[11] "Wir müssen die Wunde namens Deutschland offenhalten . . . Daß es diese zwei Länder gibt, ist das Produkt einer Katastrophe, deren Ursachen man kennen kann. Ich halte es für unerträglich, die deutsche Geschichte — so schlimm sie zuletzt verlief — in einem Katastrophenprodukt enden zu lassen. . . . Ich weigere mich, an der Liquidierung von Geschichte teilzunehmen. In mir hat ein anderes Deutschland immer noch eine Chance. Eines nämlich, das seinen Sozialismus nicht von einer Siegermacht draufgestülpt bekommt, sondern ihn ganz und gar selber entwickeln darf; und eines, das seine Entwicklung zur Demokratie nicht ausschließlich nach dem kapitalistischen Krisenrhythmus stolpern muß." Martin Walser, "Über den Leser — soviel man in einem Festzelt darüber sagen soll," in Martin Walser, *Ansichten, Einsichten: Aufsätze zur Zeitgeschichte*, vol. 11 of *Werke*, ed. Helmuth Kiesel and Frank Barsch (Frankfurt am Main: Suhrkamp, 1997), 569 and 571.

[12] For an analysis of Walser's speech "Die Banalität des Guten" and his novel *Ein springender Brunnen*, see Stephen Brockmann, "Martin Walser and the Presence of the German Past," *German Quarterly* 75, no. 2 (2002): 127–43.

[13] Martin Walser, "Experiences with Composing a Sunday Speech," in *The Burden of the Past: Martin Walser on Modern German Identity. Texts, Contexts, Commentary*, ed. and trans. Thomas A. Kovach and Martin Walser (Rochester, NY: Camden House, 2008), 91 and 89. Walser uses the term "Moralkeule" and speaks of "die unaufhörliche Präsentation unserer Schande." See Martin Walser, "Erfahrungen beim Verfassen einer Sonntagsrede," Deutsches Historisches Museum, Lebendiges virtuelles Museum Online, http://www.hdg.de/lemo/html/dokumente/WegeInDieGegenwart_redeWalserZumFriedenspreis/index.html.

[14] "Was wir in Auschwitz begangen haben, haben wir als Nation begangen, und schon deswegen muß diese Nation weiterbestehen als Nation" "Wir brauchen eine neue Sprache für die Erinnerung: Das Treffen von Ignatz Bubis und Martin-Walser," *Frankfurter Allgemeine Zeitung*, 14 Dec. 1998.

[15] In his book *Europa ohne Identität* (Munich: Bertelsmann, 1998) Bassam Tibi, a professor of political science in Göttingen, coined the term "Europäische Leitkultur" to designate the values and norms prevalent in the European cultural community. In the fall of 2000, CDU parliamentary leader Friedrich Merz introduced

the term *Leitkultur* into the public debate to suggest that there was a clear set of German cultural values and norms associated with constitutional patriotism and a national identity rooted in the European Union. According to Merz, immigrants who wished to live in Germany should adhere to these core values. For a collection of contemporary opinions on patriotism and core values, see Norbert Lammert, ed., *Verfassung, Patriotismus, Leitkultur: Was unsere Gesellschaft zusammenhält* (Hamburg: Hoffmann & Campe, 2006).

[16] Quoted in Roger Cohen, "Call for 'Guiding Culture' Rekindles Political Debate in Germany," *New York Times*, 5 Nov. 2000.

[17] "Ich liebe unser Land. . . . Patriotismus und Weltoffenheit sind keine Gegensätze, sie bedingen einander. Nur wer sich selbst achtet, achtet auch andere." Horst Köhler, "'Das sind neue Gründerjahre': Köhler-Rede im Wortlaut," *Spiegel Online*, 23 May 2004, http://www.spiegel.de/politik/deutschland/0,1518,301109,00.html.

[18] Angela Merkel spoke of Germany as a "Schicksalsgemeinschaft von 80 Millionen Menschen" and of "Liebe zum eigenen Land." Quoted in Christian Reiermann, "Wie Angela Merkel ihre wichtigste Rede vorbereitete: Zwischen Reformdebatte und patriotisch-pathetischer Tünche," *Welt Online*, 5 Dec. 2004, http://www.welt.de/print-wams/article119007/Wie_Angela_Merkel_ihre_wichtigste_Rede_vorbereitete.html.

[19] She said: "Verantwortungsgemeinschaft leben, Geborgenheit und Halt geben, Treue und Verlässlichkeit lernen, sich seiner Herkunft und Wurzeln bewusst sein, daraus entwickelt sich ein Gefühl für Heimat." Quoted in Silke Fredrich and Anja Wunsch, "Parteichefin entschlossen: Merkel; 'Alles für Wachstum, Arbeit, Wohlstand,'" *RP Online*, 6 Dec. 2004, http://www.rp-online.de/politik/deutschland/Merkel-Alles-fuer-Wachstum-Arbeit-Wohlstand_aid_71166.html.

[20] White, *The Content of the Form*, 57.

[21] See Hayden White, *Metahistory: The Historical Imagination in Nineteenth-Century Europe* (Baltimore: Johns Hopkins UP, 1973).

[22] White, *The Content of the Form*, 24.

[23] David Bordwell defines art cinema as "a distinct mode of film practice, possessing a definite historical existence, a set of formal conventions, and implicit viewing procedures." According to Bordwell, art cinema is organized around the principles of realism and authorial expressivity, which result in a conscious visual style, an alienated protagonist, psychological ambiguity, and an open narrative that precludes resolution. David Bordwell, "The Art Cinema as a Mode of Film Practice," in *The European Cinema Reader*, ed. Catherine Fowler (London: Routledge, 2002), 94.

[24] In 1981 Steve Neale identified the binary between Hollywood mainstream cinema and European art cinema as a strategy to cultivate a distinctly European film industry and film culture. He advocated looking at art cinema's "sources of finance, its modes and circuits of production, distribution and exhibition, its relationship to the state, the nature of the discourses used to support and promote it, the institutional basis of these discourses, the relations within and across each of these elements, and the structure of the international film industry." Neale

concluded that art cinema is a brand-recognition strategy developed to capture a distinct market share exploiting the "discrimination between art and industry, culture and entertainment, meaning and profit." Steve Neale, "Art Cinema as Institution," in Fowler, *The European Cinema Reader*, 103 and 119.

[25] Robert A. Rosenstone, *History on Film / Film on History* (Harlow, UK: Pearson Education 2006), 2. For further analyses of the history film by historians, see Mark Carnes, ed., *Past Imperfect: History according to the Movies* (New York: Henry Holt, 1995); Steven Mintz and Randy W. Roberts, eds., *Hollywood's America: United States History through Its Films*, 4th ed. (Malden, MA: Wiley-Blackwell, 2001); and Marnie Hughes-Warrington, *History Goes to the Movies: Studying History on Film* (London: Routledge, 2007). For studies by scholars in film studies and humanities, see also Robert Burgoyne, *Film Nation: Hollywood Looks at U.S. History* (Minneapolis: U of Minnesota P, 1997); Marcia Landy, ed., *The Historical Film: History and Memory in Media* (New Brunswick, NJ: Rutgers UP, 2001); and David Eldridge, *Hollywood's History Films* (London: I. B. Tauris, 2006).

[26] Robert B. Toplin, *Reel History: In Defense of Hollywood* (Lawrence: UP of Kansas, 2002), 1. Toplin provides a useful overview of current scholarship on the history film in chapter 5, 160–77.

[27] Rick Altmann, *Film/Genre* (London: British Film Institute, 1999), 195. See also Steve Neale, *Genre and Hollywood* (London: Routledge, 2000).

[28] See Lutz Koepnick, "Reframing the Past: Heritage Cinema and Holocaust in the 1990s," *New German Critique* 87 (2002): 47–82; Lutz Koepnick, "'Amerika gibt's überhaupt nicht': Notes on the German Heritage Film," in *German Pop Culture: How "American" Is It?*, ed. Agnes Mueller (Ann Arbor: U of Michigan P, 2004), 191–208; and Jaimey Fischer, "German Historical Film as Production Trend: European Heritage Cinema and Melodrama in *The Lives of Others*," in *The Collapse of the Conventional: German Film and Its Politics at the Turn of the Twenty-First Century*, ed. Jaimey Fisher and Brad Prager (Detroit: Wayne State UP, 2010), 186–215.

[29] Richard Dyer, "Feeling English," *Sight and Sound* 4, no.3 (1994): 16–19.

[30] Andrew Higson, *English Heritage, English Cinema: Costume Drama since 1980* (Oxford: Oxford UP, 2003), 119.

[31] Higson, *English Heritage*, 109.

[32] Higson, *English Heritage*, 80. Emphasis added.

[33] See Claire Monk, "The British Heritage-Film Debate Revisited," in *British Historical Cinema: The History, Heritage and Costume Film*, ed. Claire Monk and Amy Sargeant (London: Routledge, 2002), 176–98.

[34] Koepnick, "Reframing the Past," 51–52.

[35] Koepnick, "Reframing the Past," 49.

[36] Monk, "The British Heritage-Film Debate Revisited," 182.

[37] Robert Rosenstone, "Film Reviews," *American Historical Review* 97, no. 4 (1992): 1138. See also Hughes-Warrinton, *History Goes to the Movies*, 191.

[38] Eric Rentschler, "From New German Cinema to the Post-Wall Cinema of Consensus," in *Cinema and Nation,* ed. Mette Hjort and Scott Mackenzie (London; Routledge, 2000), 275. Rentschler names here eighteen directors who are "exceptions to the rule."

[39] Rentschler, "Post-Wall Cinema of Consensus," 263–64.

[40] Rentschler, "Post-Wall Cinema of Consensus," 263 and 264.

[41] Rentschler emphasizes that New German Cinema "constituted a potent mythical construction, replete with a heroic historical narrative driven by hero-directors, an international co-production of domestic supporters and foreign enthusiasts which played an essential role in the legitimation and continuing existence of an otherwise unpopular minor cinema." Rentschler, "Post-Wall Cinema of Consensus," 261. Despite acknowledging this mythic construction, Rentschler uses New German Cinema to gauge the potential of today's cinema to challenge viewers and as a measure of quality.

[42] Rentschler singles out Heike Misselwitz as one of the "explorers of darker provinces" and mentions "the recalcitrant remnants of DEFA with their reflections on a lost world and an uncommodious new situation" without naming or analyzing their films. Rentschler, "Post-Wall Cinema of Consensus," 275.

[43] For an excellent analysis of the DEFA films that fell into the so-called *Wendeloch*, see Laura Green McGee, "'Ich wollte ewig einen richtigen Film machen! Und als es soweit war, konnte ich's nicht!' The End Phase of the GDR in Films by DEFA Nachwuchsregisseure," *German Studies Review* 26, no. 2 (2003): 315–32.

[44] "Wir 'sehen' nichts, was wir in einem Film wiedergeben könnten, weil wir uns nicht sehen können als Teil der auslöschenden deutschen Gewalt in diesem Jahrhundert oder als deren Resultate. Wir können unsere Körper nicht anerkennen und also auch nicht erkennen." Klaus Theweleit, *One + One: Rede für Jean-Luc Godard zum Adornopreis* (Berlin: Brinkmann & Bose, 1995), 52.

[45] Quoted in Robert Burgoyne, "Prosthetic Memory/Traumatic Memory: *Forrest Gump* (1994)," in *The History on Film Reader*, ed. Marnie Hughes-Warrington (London: Routledge, 2009), 138.

[46] Alison Landsberg, *Prosthetic Memory: The Transformation of American Remembrance in the Age of Mass Culture* (New York: Columbia UP, 2004), 21.

[47] "Seltsames deutsches Volk, voll der größten Spannungen, wo das Subalterne neben dem genial spekulativ Schweifenden, das Spießerhafte neben der großen Romantik steht." Theodor Heuss, quoted in Volker Kronenberg, "Patriotismus in Deutschland: Eine Nation auf der Suche nach sich selbst," *Die politische Meinung* 421 (Dec. 2004): 31.

1: Amnesia, Nostalgia, and Anamnesis as Reactions to the Wende

Forgetting, I would even go so far as to say historical error, is a crucial factor in the creation of a nation, which is why progress in historical studies often constitutes a danger for [the principle of] nationality. Indeed, historical enquiry brings to light deeds of violence which took place at the origin of all political formations, even of those whose consequences have been altogether beneficial.

— Ernest Renan, "What is a Nation?"

NINETEENTH-CENTURY FRENCH PHILOSOPHER Ernest Renan suggested that the violence and traumatic events upon which nations are formed must be forgotten if unity is ever to take hold among competing factions that make up the whole. Forgetting past transgressions constitutes a logical step for bringing former adversaries together. Such willful amnesia allows rival groups to establish a clean slate from which to build a common future. Such a simple agenda, however, is fraught with difficulties. At stake is not merely what should be forgotten, but who chooses, and what criteria the past will be judged by. If social accord requires the mindful elimination of past conflict, what happens to the principles of justice, responsibility, and *Wiedergutmachung*, the straightforward German word for reparations that literally means making things good again? Can a nation afford to forget past crimes and wrongs, and won't they simply return in symbolic forms and in very concrete disputes that demand attention? Nation building, like writing history, requires equal parts of remembering and forgetting, but acknowledging this truism does little to solve the inherent problems of dealing with a collective past. Part of the quandary is that amnesia and anamnesis are solutions to competing agendas; the former works toward unanimity by erasing all evidence of conflict (hence its related term, amnesty[1]), and the latter strives for truth and reconciliation by exposing areas of dispute.

During the *Wende*, the transitional period between the collapse of the GDR in 1989 and the beginning of a unified FRG in 1990, the task of forgetting was not undertaken equally by the former East and former West. In the euphoria unleashed by the opening of the inner German border, the majority of Easterners were eager to shed the historical weight of forty years and do as the popular cigarette advertisement suggested and "Test the West." Discarding material goods and acquiring Western products was a widespread phenomenon that signaled a willingness to expunge the old and adopt the new. Household goods, clothing, and an array of everyday objects quickly ended up in junk piles littering the streets. Cultural ethnologist Ina Merkel concludes: "It was not until years later that GDR citizens realized that when they discarded their belongings, they had also rid themselves of their memories and biographies."[2] In the aftermath of unification, the swift assimilation of Easterners into the Federal Republic seemed to necessitate the removal of all vestiges of a communist past. The federal government contributed to an erasure of the GDR from collective memory well beyond the practical necessity of dismantling the former state's political and military apparatus as a precondition of German unity. It fostered the exchange of elites from West to East in nearly all realms of social interaction: politics, economics, the judiciary, media, and academe.[3] It also made decisions that changed the face of Eastern cities, divesting them of the GDR's symbolic identity by disassembling its monuments and renaming its geography. The GDR national anthem, flag, emblem, uniforms, and holidays were summarily abolished. Bank account numbers, license plates, and passports were suddenly invalid. This process of forced amnesia occurred with such rapidity that it seemed to many that their own sense of self was being eliminated with the last remnants of their customary old world.[4] In tandem with state-sponsored acts that led to a forgetting of the GDR, the privatization of state industries and discontinuation of common consumer products meant that the familiar aspects of daily life were largely gone. The national project of collectively forgetting the Eastern way of life has left its mark on many individuals, who feel their past has been unfairly deemed worthless, and on a unified nation that is now beginning to question whether this blanket rejection of everything generated by the GDR was too hasty. What was lost in the annexation of the East?

French conceptual artist Sophie Calle explored exactly this question of what was lost in her installation "The Detachment / Die Entfernung," first shown at the Galerie Arndt in Berlin in 1996. Calle was intrigued by the hasty removal of GDR monuments, memorial plaques, insignia, and street signs in East Berlin, which left the city riddled with voids yet marked by obvious traces of the erasure process. Her project was to document the original via archival images, photograph the current absence, and record people's memories of these sites in an effort to recapture the collective memory of the GDR. Calle describes her efforts as follows: "To record this process, I visited places from which symbols of GDR history have been effaced. I asked passers-by and residents to describe the objects that once filled these empty spaces. I photographed the absence and replaced the missing monuments with their memories."[5] The catalog accompanying the exhibition is framed by an old GDR map of East Berlin that prominently locates the monuments (and renders West Berlin as a blank space), archival photographs, postcards depicting the absence of GDR iconography, texts of people's memories, and an outline of the Berlin senate's plans for monument removal and redesign.

Calle's project illustrates Maurice Halbwachs's seminal notion that lived space is central to group identity formation and that memory is constructed in a social and spatial context. Collective memory is reflected and produced through relationships to objects and places. According to Halbwachs, "every collective memory unfolds within a spatial framework." He explains, "We recapture the past only by understanding how it is, in effect, preserved by our physical surroundings. It is to space — the space we occupy, traverse, have continual access to, or can at any time reconstruct in thought and imagination — that we must turn our attention."[6] The connection between memory and the environment becomes even stronger when the physical space is destroyed. Traumatic and extraordinary events that demolish communal space are significant, "because they occasion in the group a more intense awareness of its past and present, the bonds attaching it to physical locale gaining greater clarity in the very moment of their destruction."[7] "The Detachment" examines how memories of the GDR are closely related to the places where these memories were formed and the removal of such national symbols can have a profound effect on how people view the past and themselves. It also highlights that individuals recall the past in often contradictory ways, an insight Halbwachs readily conceded in his study *Collective Memory* (1925). In "The Detachment," there is no unified, homogeneous memory of the monuments, let alone a single view on the transformation of society. The responses reveal that collective memory, while based on shared space and common experiences, is multifaceted and multivalent. It is a process that must be negotiated and that evolves through collective acts such as narration. Calle, for example, asked a group of people to describe the GDR state emblem that was once located on the facade of the Palace of the Republic and removed after unification, leaving an empty circle. The responses varied widely, ranging from dreadful to beautiful to innocuous. The insignia and its absence evoked for all the participants, regardless of their ideological standpoint, a sense of shared fate and collective identity:

> There was a coat of arms on it. The circular frame contained a stalk of barley, a hammer and a pair of dividers made of some precious metal, copper I think. I found it dreadful * Of course, it was beautiful! What you could read into it, you can't read into our new order. As you see, it is empty now * . . . It was well-balanced. It was logical. It was German. We had seen it so often that we didn't even question it. It looked rather good. It didn't bother us * . . . The empty frame now refers to the situation in general. I don't think we need to preserve and reconstruct everything. We could just leave things as they are. As traces. Rather than make way for Coca-Cola signs * There's

a resistance in that hole. In my mind it's still there. Like a ghost, I
see it there * There were a pair of dividers. Dividers making circles:
the perfect form. The instruments of utopia have now disappeared.
All that's left is the utopia, but an empty one. We only see the void.[8]

Collective memories interact with personal memories and include not just
traces of what happened but also unrealized dreams and neglected possibilities. The missing symbol of the GDR thus becomes the representation
of socialism's lost utopia.

Amnesia is the loss of memory due to a traumatic injury, brought
on by a physical or mental shock. The gap in memory can be selective,
forgetting what has become useless, disturbing, or too difficult to accom-
modate. Collective amnesia functions in much the same way. If we listen
to the memories preserved in "The Detachment," we hear a fairly common complaint that collective amnesia of the GDR was imposed on the
inhabitants from the outside. One respondent laments: "The whole situation makes you feel like your home is being remodeled. The problem
is that decisions which affect the entire design and climate of the city
are made by people who have not previously lived here. It's really about
the Wessis not wanting to leave anything for us."[9] This comment carries resentment over Western hubris, but it also reflects the dislocation of
an entire nation of seventeen million people who did not pack up their
bags and physically migrate but nonetheless gave up their citizenship and
joined an intact social system of some fifty-four million people with unfamiliar political, economic, and cultural practices. Instead of migrating to
the West, Easterners stayed home in a place that many felt had become
a foreign country (hence the common joke at the time: "We emigrated
without leaving"). The West came to the East via a comprehensive institutional transplant that made home seem strange and changed without its
inhabitants' input.

In the first decade after its official demise, the German Democratic
Republic unexpectedly began to flourish as a popular trend in unified Germany. By the turn of the millennium, it had reached the point of being
a fad. As if resurrected devoid of political content and manifest primarily
in its material culture and rituals of daily life, the GDR was suddenly hip
and gave rise to a phenomenon called *Ostalgie*, a nostalgia for the former East. Jana Hensel's *Zonenkinder* (Zone children, 2002) and Claudia
Rusch's *Meine freie deutsche Jugend* (My free German youth, 2003), two
popular memoirs chronicling teenage life in the waning years of socialism,
competed for the public's attention with coffee-table books such as *Das
dicke DDR Buch* (The big GDR book, 2002) and the trendy board games
Stalinallee and *DDR Ferner Osten* (GDR Far East).[10] *Ostalgie* parties,
where teenagers dressed up in the uniforms of the Free German Youth
(FDJ) and danced to GDR rock bands such as the Phurdys, were all the

rage. In the summer of 2003, four *Ostalgie* variety shows flooded the airwaves, offering television audiences a chance to reminisce (or wonder) about such exotic artifacts of Eastern daily life as Trabant autos, Vita-Cola, Young Pioneers, and even that little green man from Eastern traffic lights, the *Ampelmann*.[11]

Nostalgia (*nostos* = return home, *algia* = longing) is the desire to return home and revisit a time and place where one belonged to an intact community with a shared history. It is an ambiguous response to the passing of time, because it mourns loss and displacement while nursing the hope of recovery. Nostalgia is an unreachable goal, and the sentiment works on the feelings of existing at the crossroads of time, a path that promises to lead backward but can never reach its target. But why has Germany undergone a nostalgia for the East, a system often described as an *Unrechtsstaat*, a fortified prison state replete with police surveillance, scarcity, censorship, and the lack of basic freedoms?[12] It is important from the start to differentiate between various forms of nostalgia: the enjoyable consumption of retro products, the viewing of lighthearted motion pictures that reconstruct the past as a happy place where one belonged, and the viewing of films that express a sense of loss over a vanished world and disappointment with the present. Buying reissued familiar name-brand food items from your childhood or wearing retro clothing tend to be appealing, because these small acts conjure up a time that is irretrievably gone but can be fleetingly recouped in a mixture of product and fantasy. A film such as *Sonnenallee* (Sun Alley, Leander Haußmann, 1999) is a more complex cultural artifact, which speaks to viewers on many levels. It is an appealing coming-of-age story, a winning comedy, and one of the first motion pictures to look at the GDR from the perspective of someone who was generally satisfied with his friends, family, and community. Much of the impulse behind *Ostalgie* as seen in films like *Sonnenallee* is the attempt to overcome the individual's loss of legitimacy and value in a denigrated common past.[13] By contrast, *Good Bye, Lenin!* (Wolfgang Becker, 2003), which is treated in depth in this chapter, represents a more ambivalent approach to *Ostalgie*. It simultaneously celebrates and ridicules efforts to resurrect the GDR via its material goods, but it also expresses bereavement over the loss of utopian ideals. Moreover, its self-reflective, ironic narrative framework and its unabashed joy at rewriting history encourage contemplation about the subjective factors operating in historiography and the political motivations behind media manipulation.

Should the GDR be understood as real-existing socialism, a failed experiment, repressive totalitarianism, or a welfare dictatorship? Depending on one's answer, the popular fascination with everyday life in the GDR, especially rituals and texts that celebrated a happy, fulfilling life in the SED state, could be met with approval, bewilderment, or outrage. Already in the nineties, many critics in both East and West dismissed

Ostalgie as merely the domain of naive romantics, party loyalists, or capitalist entrepreneurs seeking a market niche. Others deemed this nostalgia for the good old days irresponsible, because it failed to recognize the GDR's human-rights violations and the suffering of its victims. In 1999 anthropologist Daphne Berdahl rallied against the notion that *Ostalgie* was "merely" restorative desire or escapism. She argued that such dismissals and ridicule were "part of a larger hegemonic project to devalue Eastern German critiques of the politics of re-unification." Allegations that *Ostalgie* trivialized history represented broader "struggles over the control and appropriation of historical knowledge, shared memories, and personal recollections."[14] Berdahl had conducted numerous interviews with Easterners throughout the nineties and was among the first scholars to advocate for taking *Ostalgie* seriously as a significant cultural practice. She maintained that it served different functions in different social groups, but it was fundamentally about asserting aspects of collective memory that had not been acknowledged:

> *Ostalgie* represents loss, belonging, solidarity, and a time that differentiates *Ossis*. Still others find the products of *Ostalgie* appealing as reminders of the daily hardships they have overcome through the collapse of socialism. *Ostalgie*, in all its various forms, thus does not entail an identification with the former GDR state, but rather an identification with different forms of oppositional solidarity and collective memory. It can evoke feelings of longing, mourning, resentment, anger, relief, redemption, and satisfaction — often within the same individuals.[15]

Berdahl regarded *Ostalgie* as a form of resistance and a means to counter the dominant discourse, which characterized the GDR's consumer goods, lifestyles, and ideals as substandard or passé.

Writing at the same time as Berdahl, cultural ethnologist Ina Merkel argued along the same lines that *Ostalgie* revealed prevalent social attitudes. Whereas Berdahl attributed to *Ostalgie* the potential to resist hegemonic power structures, Merkel saw it primarily in terms of its ability to satisfy emotional needs in a period of enormous social upheaval. In her extensive study on GDR consumer culture, *Utopie und Bedürfnis* (Utopia and need, 1999), Merkel maintained that the consumption of retro eastern products was not evidence that post-Wall consumers wanted to reestablish the SED regime or that they had idealized the political world of the past. She cautioned "that even a retrospectively romanticized view should not be seen as longing for the past system but rather for the daily experiences that cannot be repeated, for the long lost tastes, colors, and forms."[16] Merkel noted that the rapid course of events resulting in the collapse of the GDR, the currency union, and the dismantling of local industries meant that "there was no phase of reflection, mourning, or farewell, which to some extent is taking place now. In the face of all the existing changes, the objects still available ensure a certain continuity in the private realm and offer the space to retreat and reflect."[17] Following Halbwachs's concept that objects play a crucial role in identity formation and that one only recognizes their importance once they are gone, Merkel advanced the idea that *Ostalgie* afforded a type of psychological anchor in a world of constant change. Holding on to physical reminders of the past gave consumers access to feelings of certainty and stability they associated with such objects.

As early as 1991 cultural critic Andreas Huyssen recognized that the unstable conditions in the East could easily lead to the development of "a nostalgic GDR identity that feeds on the hazy beautification" of the past. Huyssen pointed out that nostalgia for the East could also be extremely appealing to many Western intellectuals, because they clung to an idealized vision of the GDR. He reasoned: "The abstract need for a potentially utopian space, an 'other' of capitalistic Germany, led to the continued hold of the official GDR on the West German left's imagination, however subliminal it may have been."[18] In subsequent studies, prominent scholars such as Paul Cooke, Barbara Mennel, Julia Hell, and Johannes von Moltke among others have expounded upon the ways in which Western leftists have embraced nostalgia for the GDR (and for political activism in the FRG from 1968 through the eighties) or *Westalgie*. The GDR functions for these Westerners as a projection screen for their own socialist values that have been maligned by the collapse of the Soviet Union and all the Warsaw Pact countries.[19]

From this brief outline it is clear that *Ostalgie* serves a multitude of functions. It validates a former way of life, reaffirms personal and communal identity, legitimizes a socialist political agenda, and provides amusement and distraction.[20] Much of the journalistic and scholarly work that analyzes the cultural preoccupation with the GDR past focuses on the notion of nostalgia, which obscures the fact that looking at history is not always about wanting to return or longing for restoration because the past was somehow better. In her groundbreaking study on nostalgia in post-communist Eastern Europe, Svetlana Boym offers a paradigm that opens up the discussion to other possibilities and takes into account the conflicting desires embodied in the term nostalgia. Boym differentiates between two approaches to the past: restorative and reflective nostalgias. "Restorative nostalgia," she writes, "puts emphasis on *nostos* and proposes to rebuild the lost home and patch up the memory gaps. Reflective nostalgia dwells in *algia*, in longing and loss, the imperfect process of remembrance." Boym explains: "Restorative nostalgia manifests itself in total reconstructions of monuments of the past, while reflective nostalgia lingers on ruins, the patina of time and history, in the dreams of another place and another time."[21] Boym's work is extremely useful because it points to the necessity of expanding our understanding of what precipitates the nearly obsessive return to history and memory.

Building on Boym's observations, I would like to suggest that we look beyond nostalgia and examine how the last twenty years are also characterized by various attempts at *anamnesis*, the drive to remember what has been forgotten because the unexplored past stands in the way of moving on.[22] Looking at the past is not always an attempt to *recover* lost treasures; it can also be an enterprise to *uncover* painful and disturbing traumas that need resolution. Memory can be the means by which one passes judgment on the past. In the case of collective crimes, memory is an essential vehicle for the type of resolution that requires individuals and society to confess, assign guilt, endure punishment, and offer absolution. Following the *Wende*, many things were forgotten — both trivial and monumental. A systematic reckoning has not taken place, and thus there is a persistent return to the past to salvage what was valuable and to expose injustice and human suffering. Jacques Derrida has observed that without engaging in anamnesis to address an earlier trauma, one will be locked in a relationship to the past that obscures the future.[23] Derrida notes: "To think memory or to think anamnesis, here, is to think things as paradoxical as the memory of a past that has not been present, the memory of the future — the movement of memory as tied to the future and not only to the past, memory turned toward the promise, toward what is coming, what is arriving, what is happening tomorrow."[24] Interestingly, Derrida's comments on the future-past correspond to conclusions made recently by cognitive neuroscientists. A group of researchers working at the Royal Holloway University of London discovered that physical damage to the hippocampus region of the brain can lead to amnesia, and those patients suffering from such amnesia cannot imagine future events. They are confined to a perpetual present. Scientist Narender Ramnani asserts that "memories are there to help us use past events to shape future events or future plans."[25] Researchers found evidence that amnesiacs could not envision the future because they suffered from a deficit of spatial acuity: "The patients' imagined experiences lacked spatial coherence, consisting instead of fragmented images in the absence of a holistic representation of the environmental setting."[26] Neuroscientific discoveries that the ability to remember the past is directly linked to the ability to imagine the future and that memories are formed in a spatial context substantiate the theoretical reflections of such prominent thinkers as Derrida and Halbwachs. Whether one looks to the natural sciences or to philosophy, it is clear that anamnesis is an essential step in the process of constructing the future.

The forces of forgetting and remembering in post-Wall German culture reflect an epochal shift that was nearly unfathomable in its rapidity and disruption of certainties.[27] The Cold War order reflected relatively stable antagonisms that divided the world into clear-cut zones of influence. The

Berlin Wall marked that dividing line between two opposing systems. From the moment the Wall fell, the legitimacy of the GDR and Germany's postwar division was called into question. With the masses demonstrating for change in autumn 1989, followed by the opening of the inner-German border, the fate of the GDR was, for a short period of time at least, uncertain. The country was faced with difficult choices. Should the GDR reform itself into a more humanitarian form of socialism, should the two states unite, or should the GDR develop on a completely different path? While demonstrators had changed their signs reading "we are the people" to "we are one people," unification was not a foregone conclusion among all constituencies in the GDR. The Central Round Table, a group of GDR human rights activists, politicians, and representatives from the church, workers' unions, and artists met in Berlin from 7 December 1989 to 12 March 1990 to discuss new elections, the dismantling of the Ministry for State Security, and the formulation of a new constitution centered on human rights and a federalist union with the FRG. The Central Round Table was working under the assumption that in the event of unification a constitutional assembly would be established according to Article 146 of the Basic Law, which stipulated: "This Basic Law, which is valid for the entire German people following the achievement of the unity and freedom of Germany, shall cease to be in force on the day on which a constitution adopted by a free decision of the German people comes into force."[28] For Chancellor Helmut Kohl and his CDU-backed government, however, the line of action was clear and indisputable. German unification would be decided by an election, and no constitutional assembly would take place. The vote for unification ultimately won, but this move reintroduced with a new urgency the most contested and unresolved debate of the postwar era: the problem of whether a German nation-state after National Socialism was politically and morally justified.

As long as the two Germanys existed, it was possible for each to view the other as primarily responsible for the crimes of fascism, warmongering, and genocide. The GDR unequivocally accepted the official definition of National Socialism formulated by Georgi Dimitroff in 1935, which identified fascism as "the open, terroristic dictatorship of the most reactionary, the most chauvinistic, the most imperialistic elements of finance capitalism."[29] As an explicitly anti-capitalist form of government, the GDR saw itself as free from the stigma of National Socialism and attributed to the FRG the sole responsibility for the legacy of the Third Reich. The Federal Republic in turn saw itself as a democratically elected, pluralistic form of government and viewed its commitment to democracy as well as its policy of reparations to Holocaust victims as contrition for past crimes against humanity. The FRG located guilt in the GDR, which continued in its eyes to function as a totalitarian state upheld by secret police, the suppression of political dissent, and a fortified border. Without a German alter ego, a unified nation-state would have to reformulate its concept of guilt for the past.

Some critics considered the specter of nationalism a serious threat and feared that the mistakes of the past could be repeated in a unified Germany. Tragically, the rise of right-wing nationalism and violence in the early nineties seemed to validate the worst fears of a fascist mindset lurking just beneath the surface and waiting to be released. Between 1990 and 1991, violent offenses increased more than fivefold, with 1,483 racially motivated crimes against foreigners registered in Germany.[30] Attacks on foreigners and race riots in Hoyerswerda in September 1991 and Rostock in August 1992 soon escalated to arson and murder. In Mölln in November 1992, neo-Nazis threw Molotov cocktails at two houses occupied by Turkish immigrants, killing a woman and two girls. In May 1993 in Solingen, two women and three girls of Turkish descent burned to death in a neo-Nazi arson assault. The wave of xenophobic violence unleashed in Germany was an alarming beginning for the new state. Scholars attributed hatred and violence against foreigners to a variety of causes, including disorientation because of the social upheaval of unification, perceived economic threats posed by foreign guest workers and asylum seekers, and a renewed desire for ethnocultural homogeneity in the face of globalization.[31]

Politicians continued to debate the origins of National Socialism and its reemergence in contemporary right-wing extremism, but they placed a new emphasis on coming to terms with GDR history as part of a redefinition of the unified German state. The Bundestag established two special Enquete commissions to investigate the legacy of the GDR, and the titles given to these commissions already set the agenda for understanding the GDR as the inheritor of the historical legacy of fascism. The first Enquete Commission was entitled "Treatment of History and Consequences of the SED-Dictatorship in Germany," and the second was called "Surmounting the Consequence of the SED-Dictatorship in the Process of German Freedom." By defining the GDR primarily as a dictatorship and looking for ways to assign guilt for past crimes, in some ways the very question of a possible German authoritarian mindset was transferred from the deeper past of the Third Reich to the closer past of the GDR. If the reasons behind communist totalitarianism could be identified and blame assigned, then unified Germany would be given a green light. Paul Cooke has rightly argued that in the aftermath of unification "the GDR seemed to be functioning as a kind of Saidian 'Other,' that is as a historical space through which the FRG could self-reflexively distance itself from the whole of Germany's dictatorial legacy and thereby confirm its democratic credentials."[32] Narratives, both historical and fictional, that exposed the authoritarian roots of the GDR past could create a unitary national memory and function as means to legitimize the new polity.

Notably, the Bundestag never felt the need to reexamine West German history as part of its project of coming to terms with the postwar past. Selectively forgetting half the nation's past, the sole area of historical work would lie in the East. The questions asked in the nineties were not necessarily how people had lived but how the SED regime had perpetrated injustices and human-rights abuses. The stated purpose of this project would be to integrate forty years of GDR history into the collective memory of a unified nation-state, and the starting point was to substantiate the state's violence against its citizens. When the masses stormed the Berlin headquarters of the Ministry for State Security (MfS) on 15 January 1990, they unearthed indisputable evidence of abuse. The sheer magnitude of the surveillance apparatus erected by the MfS, commonly known as the Stasi, boggles the mind. Journalist John Koehler asserts that in 1989 the Stasi employed 102,000 full-time officers and noncommissioned personnel. By reviewing the secret files, researchers have been able to identify 174,000 informers (Inoffizielle Mitarbeiter, IMs), who were recruited to spy on their fellow citizens. Koehler estimates that if one adds together the number of officers, full-time informants, and part-time collaborators, the result would be "nothing short of monstrous: one informant per 6.5 citizens." The zeal with which the Stasi compiled information on GDR citizens resulted in roughly six million secret files in a nation of seventeen million inhabitants.[33] Beyond foreign espionage, the secret police were responsible for domestic surveillance of political dissidents, outspoken writers and intellectuals, oppositional groups that found a safe haven in the church, and various discontented factions. Their charge as "sword and shield" of the SED party was to collect information on any possible challenge to the system and quell opposition through a variety of tactics, including discrediting campaigns, spreading a culture of distrust, threats both veiled and open, interrogation without legal representation, and imprisonment without trial in secret prisons such as the notorious detention center at Hohenschönhausen on the outskirts of Berlin.[34] One group targeted for intense scrutiny was those who expressed the wish to emigrate to the West or who were suspected of planning an illegal border crossing. The GDR denied its citizens the basic right to leave the country, criminalizing unauthorized trespass of the state's frontier, referred to as *Republikflucht* (fleeing the republic), as an act of treason punishable by two years in prison.

A reckoning with the GDR will ultimately have to deal with its inner contradictions, its noble social-welfare accomplishments and its brutal repression of opposition. With its promise of material security, work, education, and health care on the one side and its enforcement of conformity, obsessive paranoia toward disagreement, and forceful denial of basic human rights on the other side, the GDR functioned as a caring homeland for some and a prison state for others. The GDR in retrospect will inevitably be haunted by this dual legacy. Looking to the cinema, one finds a public forum to explore the incompatible aspects of history and to imagine how they have affected individual lives. Cinema approaches this ambiguity with stories that use amnesia to draw our attention to what has been forgotten.

The films under discussion in this chapter center on the *Wende*, the turn of events in 1989–90 that led to the collapse of the SED regime; they address the GDR as absence. *Berlin Is in Germany* (2001), *Führer Ex* (2002), and *Good Bye, Lenin!* (2003) thematize amnesia and anamnesis in narrative tropes involving imprisonment, thereby enacting the dilemma of national guilt and responsibility for a collective past. Whereas early documentary films about the GDR's punitive treatment of its disaffected citizens were largely "distinguished by a clear victim/victimizer dichotomy,"[35] these three feature films wrestle with the question of guilt and innocence in a more nuanced and ambivalent manner. They present characters who are imprisoned for trying to escape from the GDR and thus miss out on the events surrounding the *Wende*. *Berlin Is in Germany* and *Führer Ex* are based loosely on the real-life experiences of men who were incarcerated for attempting to defect, were released into an unfamiliar post-Wall Berlin, and refashioned themselves to survive in a transformed Germany. *Good Bye, Lenin!*, by contrast, tells a fictional story about a family torn apart by the father's escape to the West and a mother confined to the prison house of memory, who wakes up in an unknown world. In each case, the characters experience a form of amnesia and search for a lost home, selectively forgetting aspects of their personal past as a necessary step in the process of remembering a common history.

Berlin Is in Germany and *Führer Ex* share a highly negative view of the GDR as a dictatorial prison state with nothing worth recouping except family and friendship. They both present protagonists, who attempt to free themselves from a restrictive life behind the Wall but in the process ironically end up in the even more controlled confines of a penitentiary. The decision to leave the GDR places the figures in a situation where they are forced to use violence, but, as I will argue, this resistance to totalitarianism renders them morally righteous and exonerates them from existential guilt. The GDR state is held responsible for violence, and once freed from the grips of an inhumane system, these individuals are poised to integrate into unified Germany. *Good Bye, Lenin!*, by contrast, is a mixture of what Svetlana Boym has labeled restorative and reflective nostalgias, granting nearly equal attention to the rebuilding of home and to the acknowledgment of irretrievable loss. Becker's film highlights the postmodern preoccupation with ruptures, discontinuities, and absences in order to question the master narrative that sees the period 1989–90 as the inevitable triumph of capitalism over Communism. Taken together, these films about remembering the GDR assign guilt to a state that needs to be forgotten or to be remembered as something it never was but could have been.

Fig. 1.1. Still from Hannes Stöhr's Berlin Is in Germany *(2001).
Photo courtesy of Arne Höhne Presse + Öffentlichkeit.*

Berlin Is in Germany

Filmed in twenty-eight days on a modest budget, *Berlin Is in Germany* was Hannes Stöhr's debut feature film and his final graduation project at the German Film and Television Academy Berlin (Deutsche Film-und Fernsehakademie Berlin, dffb). The idea for this updated version of an East German Rip van Winkle came from real life. A probation officer related to Stöhr the remarkable but true story of ex-convicts from the GDR, who only knew about the fall of the Wall from television and returned home after a decade in prison to a completely unfamiliar world. Stöhr made a short film on this topic, but he envisioned a full-length feature film. Significant financial and logistical support for this project came from an unlikely source: two competing public television stations. The established Western Second German Television (Zweites Deutsches Fernsehen, ZDF) and the smaller East German Broadcasting Brandenburg (Ostdeutscher Rundfunk Brandenburg, ORB) decided to join forces in a historic move to fund the East Wind television film series about recent developments in the new German federal states and Eastern Europe.[36] *Berlin Is in Germany* premiered at the Berlin Film Festival in the Panorama series on 8 February 2001 and was released in German cinemas nine months later on 1 November 2001, where it reached an audience of 117,023 viewers in its first year.[37] Despite its limited success at the box office, the film made the rounds at international film festivals and won several prestigious awards, including the Audience Prize at the Berlin

Film Festival, the Studio Hamburg Young Talent Award, and the German Film Critics Prize for best motion picture. Stöhr's film then opened the East Wind series on 9 March 2003 in a simultaneous broadcast on ORB and ZDF. The critical response was overwhelmingly positive, with Philipp Bühler from the *Berliner Zeitung* claiming: "This could be the definitive East-West story," and Wolfgang Hamdorf from *Film-Dienst* suggesting that it "belongs to the most touching human films about East and West living together or meeting each other, about the crashes and upheavals in the new Germany."[38]

Berlin Is in Germany is a tragi-comedy about ex-convict Martin Schulz, who was convicted of murder while attempting to flee the GDR in 1989 and sentenced to life in prison.[39] The verdict was reduced to manslaughter after the *Wende*, and he was released in 2000. Hoping to recover some semblance of his former life, Martin pushes forward with optimism and sanguinity in the face of nearly insurmountable challenges. His wife Manuela is living with another man, his son Rokko does not know he exists, and he cannot find a skilled job. Martin dreams of becoming a taxi driver and creating a stable life so that he can establish a solid relationship with his son and win back his wife. Adapting to life in the new capital city with the help of his old friends, Martin seems on his way back to normalcy when he learns that an ex-con cannot apply for a taxi license. Robbed of his modest dream, he begins a downward spiral and is arrested on false charges. The film ends like a modern-day fairy tale with Martin's second release from prison swathed in renewed optimism that he can make it this time.

Despite its absurdist premise of a guiltless murderer and its ending reminiscent of a Grimms' fairy tale replete with wish fulfillment and the triumph of moral justice, *Berlin Is in Germany* has its roots in the bizarre reality of post-Wall Germany. Hannes Stöhr interviewed inmates from the Brandenburg penitentiary who had been incarcerated during the GDR and discharged completely unprepared for the changes in unified Germany. While the men's real lives were too tragic for his purposes, the director did draw on their stories to write the screenplay and form the composite figure of Martin. Stöhr relied heavily on these prisoners' memories for his film, since he was born in the Swabian village of Hechingen-Sickingen in 1970 and only moved to Berlin at the age of twenty-five in 1995. After performing civil service in the field of psychiatry, Stöhr studied European law, English, and Spanish from 1991 to 1993 at the University of Passau. He received an Erasmus scholarship to study in Santiago de Compostela, Spain, and traveled extensively through Central and South America. He then studied scriptwriting and directing from 1995 to 2000 at the dffb under such notable directors as Volker Schlöndorff, Helke Misselwitz, Mike Leigh, and Wolfgang Becker. Stöhr also worked for periods as a street performer, juggler, actor, circus performer, film projectionist, light technician, cutter, and director's assistant before becoming an independent screenwriter and director. His fascination with the law and the circus give this film a unique tone, lending humor to the serious dilemmas facing a man who has no frame of reference to cope with the post-communist world order.

As *Berlin Is in Germany* opens, time is out of sync. Suffering a form of social amnesia brought on by the fact that he has been in prison for over a decade, Martin missed out on the collapse of the GDR as well as the invention of mobile phones, Berlin's metamorphosis into an immense construction site, and the extensive migration resulting from the opening of German borders. From the first shot in the Brandenburg penitentiary on the historic night of 9 November 1989 to the moment Martin rides past the new chancellery as a free man in the daylight of 2000, the past intrudes upon the present in a restless, fragmented manner, constantly shifting between scenes in the prison and those of the ex-con traveling on the train back home to a place that no longer exists. At the outset, a title informs the viewer that the story begins in the GDR past. In the dark green glow of history, a guard makes his nightly rounds, is alerted to the momentous events by the clanking noises coming from the prisoners' cells, and quickly turns on the radio to hear the news. As the announcer reports on the historic border opening, a second title appears over a black background stating that eleven years later twenty inmates still remain incarcerated and that Martin Schulz will be released today. Thus while the radio announcer's voice from 1989 continues to describe in detail the opening of the iron curtain on that fateful night, the viewer is cast into the present on the day Martin is discharged in 2000. This oscillation between past and present is linked to the crossing of spatial borders. In his first appearance on screen, Martin adopts a pose that will characterize his position throughout much of the film: he stands patiently waiting for the massive prison gates to open and grant him passage. He also waits dutifully at an unmanned gate until he realizes that no one will come to authorize his transit, and there is nothing preventing him from simply going underneath the barrier arm. Once on the train, Martin is yanked back to prison like a yoyo in time, reliving his release and then finding himself back in the compartment, staring out of the window as the whirling green countryside turns into a sea of construction cranes that fill the Berlin skyline. Martin's journey is less about geographic sites than about the landscape of memory. Traveling through a tunnel that leads from the prison to freedom, this man with no memory of the last decade undergoes a rebirth parallel to that of the nation. Hannes Stöhr considered this amnesic condition as central for an understanding of the present state of Germany, commenting that: "only someone like Martin Schulz can come to Berlin and perceive the changes in recent years with naive eyes. He functions as a mirror for the city, he makes visible the changes we have all experienced."[40] The coordinates of Martin's time travel are the penitentiary and the new chancellery, the former prison state of the GDR and the recently constructed, united Federal Republic. When Martin sees the buildings housing the democratically elected government, he stops reliving his past and becomes firmly planted in the present. He has arrived in a new world where the old "Berlin, capital of the GDR" and "West Berlin, FRG" are now simply a place called "Berlin, Germany." The GDR past is forgotten because it has no value for the present, a point visualized best in Martin's gesture of making paper airplanes out of his useless East Germany money.

The Berlin Martin enters is *unheimlich*, both familiar and strange, and his survival depends upon his ability to forget the past and negotiate his way in an altered reality. Martin's only possessions when he leaves prison — a television, identification card, driver's license, and wallet full of GDR money — are useless relics from the past and symbolize his impending struggles in unified Germany. He must overcome a virtual understanding of reality via television images, refashion his identity to conform to a different social environment, establish the authority necessary for free mobility, and gain sufficient monetary resources to succeed in the new economic order. Martin is poorly equipped for his journey and relies heavily on his television, his one source of information about the world outside that moved forward while he stood still. Clutching his portable television as he walks across Alexanderplatz and carrying it with him whenever he moves, Martin may be knowledgeable about high-tech consumer products like Tamagotchi virtual pets and Game Boys, but he is unprepared for the complexities of buying a subway ticket from an automat, let alone finding a decent job and housing. While Martin wanted to flee to the West in 1989, he is not prepared for it in 2000 and must learn to adapt to the new circumstances under capitalism. As his friend Peter instructs, there is an established pecking order in the West: "First in line are the locals, then Giuseppe, then Achmed, and at the end is Zoni from the East," and the bottom line is: "You got nothing, you are nothing."[41]

Like the ever-changing capital city, Martin is embarking on a new life, but his old friends serve as role models of the winners and losers in the transition to capitalism. Peter, the self-designated "Zoni," who cannot find a permanent job and tries to commit suicide, is nearly a cliché of the so-called *Jammerossi* (complaining easterner). Crying as he relates to Martin how he tried to work on a construction site in Stuttgart but was constantly treated as a second-class citizen, Peter is downtrodden and emasculated.[42] He lacks the necessary skills to become independent, failing at every job he gets, and suffering from the cold, harsh conditions under capitalism as illustrated in his last job as an ice man carting around frozen food. Sitting outside the public telephone booth, flipping through the want ads and drinking beer, Peter is a caricature of the clueless new-comer to capitalism and functions as a foil for Martin and an example not to follow. But even Peter starts to adapt to the new environment, buying a mobile phone and paying Martin back his debt. By contrast, the Russian ex-convict Viktor never breaks from his past behavior and the vicious cycle of crime. After his release from prison, Viktor becomes a sex-shop owner, dreams of the perfect bank heist, and engages in a shady trade that smacks of child pornography, which ultimately sends him back to prison. Viktor's unsavory ventures in the underbelly of capitalism as a pimp and pornographer result in renewed incarceration and serve as a cautionary tale for Martin to stay on the narrow path and not fall into recidivism. Viktor's redeeming quality is his pronounced sense of honor among thieves; he turns himself in so that Martin can go free. Here too Stöhr has created a rather clichéd figure, the criminal with a heart of gold, but Viktor's quirky sense of humor and his keen awareness that he will most likely never break this pattern of crime make him a sympathetic, if rather one-dimensional, character. The Cuban taxi driver Enrique, a foreigner from one of the last bastions of Communism, is ironically the most successful at adaptation. As a man employed in a stable job with an intact nuclear family, he demonstrates that integration is possible.[43] Martin follows Enrique's positive example and decides to become a taxi driver because this profession offers him the best chances of regaining social status, respectability, and a steady income needed to be the head of his family again.

It is not surprising that Martin, a man imprisoned for crimes resulting from an attempted illegal border crossing, chooses a profession that will give him the freedom to roam unfettered. Indeed, we see him on count-less vehicles moving through the city, on the train, subway, and street-car, but he is most at home when driving Enrique's Mercedes Benz taxi. When Martin drives the taxi through Berlin, his joy is not based merely on unrestricted movement; the route he takes symbolizes the mastery of GDR history. Martin steers his way past the East Side Gallery, the last remnant of the Berlin Wall transformed from a fortified political border that kept ordinary citizens under lock and key into a public art work. He also drives past the twin towers of the Frankfurter Tor, once the entrance to the Stalinallee erected as a monument to the Soviet dictator and now the guidepost to the trendy neighborhood of Friedrichshain. By choosing this path and not one in the Western part of town, Martin seems to relish the transformation of the East, the shedding of its socialist identity, rather than his newfound ability to travel to unknown destinations. The frequent references to modes of transportation are nearly over-determined. Mar-tin repeatedly stares at the jumbo jets flying overhead, his estranged wife Manuela works as a travel agent, and a hand-made airplane adorns her front door. References to border crossings are equally abundant. Martin is constantly asking for admittance, standing at the prison gates, ringing the bell to his former wife and son's home, and waiting to get in to see the stripper Natasha. When he starts to integrate into this new world, he becomes the gate keeper, inviting newspaper reporters into his hotel room and granting customers access to the strippers. The significance of free travel to the collapse of the GDR cannot be underestimated. As author Christoph Hein summaries in succinct fashion: "The mere announcement permitting citizens previously outlawed foreign travel swept a state out of the world."[44] Despite the fact that Martin tried to escape the GDR, travel to foreign realms no longer interests him, since the city itself has changed and cast off its former identity. He even jokes with Manuela that the constant sound of airplanes is enough to convince him that travel should be made illegal again. The liberty to go wherever he wants in an open city and the freedom to see his son is enough for Martin, and he is content to move within these confines.

When Martin first arrives back in Berlin, he finds himself homeless, sleeping in a barren, cell-like hotel room or in the back of a sex shop, and constantly looking for direction. The famed television tower on Alexanderplatz looming over the city becomes a point on the historical compass to orient Martin. This former symbol of GDR national pride and modernity has become a nostalgic icon for the newly hip Mitte district and a visible reminder that the center of Berlin has shifted eastward, returning to its historic origins. No matter where Martin looks, the TV tower dominates the horizon and appears so often that one might consider it a main character in the film. The ambiguity embodied in this object that haunts nearly every scene, its ability to function simultaneously as a reminder of the past and as a monument to the resilience of the present to adapt to change, makes it an appropriate metaphor for the spirit of the Berlin Republic. Thus it is only fitting that Martin and Manuela find themselves *inside* the TV tower as they study a map of post-unification Berlin. Martin's dream of becoming a taxi driver requires him to learn new names for familiar old streets. In order to master the geography of a new Germany, Martin undergoes a process that involves at least as much forgetting as remembering. Manuela summarizes: "You are fit in the East. All you have to do is forget the old names."[45] This selective amnesia in regard to East German history is a prerequisite for economic and emotional survival.

Although Martin is able to forget the geography of the past with a little coaching, his own personal history proves more difficult to repress. Like the number 214 etched in the window next to Martin as he rides the tram and studies the city map, a ghost-like reminder of his incarceration for unauthorized attempt to emigrate in violation of paragraph 214, the past continues to haunt the present. As a convicted felon, he is barred from getting a taxi-driver's license and is forced to lie to potential employers to explain the eleven-year void in his work history. Most importantly, there are three competing versions of Martin's personal history in the GDR. The first version is clearly a lie. When Western dinner guests ask Martin where he was in the turbulent days of autumn 1989, he tells them he was a simple soldier forced by a corrupt and crumbling government to man a tank and wait for orders to shoot at protestors on Alexanderplatz. This vivid account of being a pawn in an inhumane regime is not completely fictional, but it is actually Peter's experience. Martin does not merely steal his friend's personal history and claim it as his own; he rewrites it to portray himself as a rebel, who stood up to authorities and refused to follow orders blindly. In contrast, the second version is rendered as a flashback lit in the green glow of history and based on Manuela's memories: in the spring of 1989 she and Martin are planning to escape to the West but are exposed by the building manager, who finds their hiking equipment hidden in the cellar. When this party loyalist confronts Martin and reminds him that fleeing the republic is a felony, Martin pushes the old man, who falls to his death. According to this version, Martin lashed out in the heat of an argument, and the resulting death was an unintentional accident that occurred while his back was turned. Finally, the third version is told by a policeman, who reads from official trial transcripts and the coroner's report, both of which testify that the building manager suffered massive injuries because Martin beat him to death in an act of premeditated murder.

Various commissions of the German federal government have made a case for cultural institutions and the media to inform the public about GDR history in the belief that a consciousness of past misdeeds will lead to purification of the polity. If an acknowledgment of personal and collective guilt is indeed a necessary condition for the moral and political rebirth of Germany, then Stöhr's film does not provide the definitive model of vicarious remorse. What *Berlin Is in Germany* does offer is a story that underscores the ambiguity of guilt, the exigency of amnesia, and the necessity of overcoming a sense of victimization. In particular, this film illustrates that narrating a personal and, by extension, national history is never value-free. Whereas West Germans are spared the soul searching inherent in the system change, East Germans are forced to examine their individual and collective past. If the GDR was a corrupt, inhumane, and criminal system, then are ordinary citizens criminals who must accept collective responsibility for past injustices? Stöhr's film posits this uneasy question, and the fact that his main character was imprisoned for mysterious circumstances surrounding an illegal escape only serves to highlight that complicity is never black and white. In the face of Western scrutiny, East German history becomes a story of the little man's courageous resistance against state tyranny, but this grand narrative is exposed as a fabrication. Equally suspect is the state-sanctioned version that posits the ordinary citizen as a vicious assailant. Although there is never clarity over which version is true, the flashback depicting an accidental death is given the most validity, since it is the only one in which the viewer sees the events taking place rather than merely hearing someone's account. Hannes Stöhr maintains that he wanted the problem of guilt to remain ambiguous, stating: "the question of the factual chain of events is left open. How do I judge it? I personally believe Martin's version of its being an accident, but I can't answer the question definitively. Perhaps it happened differently, and he intentionally murdered the building manager like the medical records suggest."[46] Although Stöhr argues that viewers must decide the truth, he has stacked the deck in Martin's favor by providing only one visible representation of the events in Manuela's flashback. The validity of this version is strengthened by the fact that immediately after Manuela has finished telling her story, Martin wakes up from a bad dream, and while he says nothing, this is the first indication that he may be troubled by guilt and remorse. The lighting and color scheme also contribute to the authenticity of Manuela's account. When she begins her story, she is dressed in orange in her bright orange-red bedroom, but in the flashback events are colored in the green tint of history, and when Martin awakens he is bathed in the blue of twilight, closer to the dreary past than the vivid present and reminiscent of the color scheme dominating the opening scenes in prison. As it stands, Martin's violent action is the result of unfortunate circumstances, and, by analogy, GDR history becomes the accident of birth, a force beyond the individual's control.

Martin is a highly sympathetic figure who functions so clearly as a mirror for the changes in Germany that the manner in which he deals with his past carries symbolic weight as a paradigm for the nation. Several newspaper film critics recognized early on that Jörg Schüttauf's masterful performance helped to convince the audience to accept Martin's deadly use of force as morally just and see the story as a parable of the good-hearted underdog who triumphs over evil. As Wolfgang Hamdorf puts it, Schüttauf's portrayal is "so convincing that the script's plot twists depicting the hero in an exceedingly haunting flashback as an 'innocent murderer,' who in effect 'only' killed an extortionist block warden, seem superfluous."[47] According to Kerstin Decker, Schüttauf played Martin "with such simplicity, proletarian ruggedness, directness and gentle reservation" that "we recognize ourselves in the other. This recognition is the opposite of what one calls 'social criticism.'"[48] This flattering mirror reflecting a collective identity without blemishes borders on a "cinema of consensus" as outlined by Eric Rentschler. Along these lines, Gunnar Decker argues that without Jörg Schüttauf's tour de force, "one could chop *Berlin Is in Germany* to pieces as one of the many mediocre films that immediately drop their chosen topic as soon as it starts to hurt. Films that place the audience's pleasure above the uncomfortable things they have to tell."[49] As appealing as Jörg Schüttauf's performance and the underdog storyline are, the nearly universal reading of this film as a national parable necessitates further inquiry. Regardless of the mitigating circumstances, Martin killed a man, and the loss of human life is a crime of immense magnitude that requires reflection. Martin, however, suppresses all memory of his participation in the event. He speaks about it only when he is arrested, at which time he vehemently proclaims his innocence.

Released in 2000, Martin is a stigmatized outsider, an average guy who just happened to have lived in the GDR and was caught up in circumstances beyond his control. His initial crime was planning to escape to the West, so that his guilt in manslaughter is mitigated by his original intention to reject the SED regime. If we take Martin as a stand-in for the entire GDR population, then this sympathetic figure, who lashed out against a representative of the oppressive state, is innocent of complicity in the system.[50] Ordinary people like Martin must forget responsibility for past wrongs in order to live in the present. The system itself was the crime and once its former citizens adapt to the new capitalist system, rebuild their personal relationships and elective affinities, and overcome their sense of victimization, they will be fit to enjoy the promise of prosperity and freedom in the FRG.

What does this FRG look like in 2000? *Berlin Is in Germany* addresses the negative aspects of unification — the rise in unemployment, prostitution, and crime; hatred of foreigners and discrimination against Easterners; disillusionment and homelessness — but these serious social problems come across as largely transitional phenomena, which can be surmounted by reestablishing strong family ties and overcoming a deeply rooted sense of victimization. The GDR is presented as a prison state with little worth remembering other than family and friends. Martin is mistakenly arrested and confronts the police investigator with his own accusations, condemning the man for continuing to uphold a totalitarian state. When he learns that the policeman is actually a Westerner from Bremen, Martin has his own *Wende* that allows him to escape the past. For it is only when Martin stops seeing himself as a permanent victim of the SED state that he can he move on — reconstruct his life, repair his personal relationships, and embark on a new career path.

As Berlin adapts to its status as the capital of a unified Germany, its distinctiveness as the site of national identity becomes a prominent theme. What is obvious to his eleven-year-old son Rokko is a new lesson for Martin. In his English homework notebook, Rokko affirms his personal and national identity with simplicity and clarity: "I am a boy from Berlin. Berlin is in Germany." The GDR refused to accept the term "East Berlin" and insisted on calling the city "Berlin, capital of the GDR" to emphasis the socialist state's legitimacy as the rightful heir to power. Martin learns from his son that these rules no longer apply. And yet the fact that this declaration of national identity is rendered in a foreign language indicates that what it means to be German in 2000 has changed radically since 1989. Berlin is characterized by a multi-ethnic population, and its inhabitants have migrated here in recent years from different countries and speak different languages. The reporter from the *Berlin News* has a distinctly American accent and writes for a German-language paper with an English title. The Russian ex-convict Viktor, the Cuban taxi driver Enrique, the French dinner guest Pierre, not to mention the Swabians Wolfgang and his college friend, all seek a home in this constantly changing city. The prostitute Natasha, however, is a woman of multiple Eastern European ethnic origins, who best exemplifies the prevalent hybrid identity in the post-communist, globalized new millennium. Although she masquerades as a Russian because this is a fantasy in sexual tourism that sells particularly well, her real name is Ludmila, and she is most recently from Vienna. Her mother is from Macedonia, her father is from the Ukraine. She was born in Belgrade, grew up in Zagreb, and then went to Vienna, before moving to Berlin as a foreign-exchange student. The limits of multi-cultural acceptance are demonstrated, however, when Martin suggests that Viktor change his name to Thorston so that he can fit in better.

For Martin, the only things worth saving from the GDR are personal relationships. He reconnects with his old friends Peter and Enrique, and the three simple working men reestablish the camaraderie and support system long associated with socialism. Reaping the benefits of a collective without ideological baggage or state coercion, they have gained from their past the experience of solidarity that will help them master the present. Martin also makes every effort to reconstitute his family, and when he needs them the most, his wife and son stand by him. Beyond that, the past is forgotten to make room for the present. As if drinking from the waters of Lethe, Martin seems to forget his own culpability in a fellow human being's death and also the former regime's power over him. He leaves prison the second time around as neither victim of the system nor perpetrator of a crime. Falsely accused, he is redeemed, and the Russian takes the blame for an unspoken offense. Considering Martin's everyman quality and the film's fairytale-like resolution of conflicts, *Berlin Is in Germany* lends itself to a reading as a parable for the GDR. Crimes were committed, but the blame does not lie with the people, who were held in a system not of their own making. Many tried to escape, others were forced to man the tanks, but the culpability for untold wrongdoings belongs to the foreign power that set it all in motion, the former Soviet Union. Apart from metaphorically assigning guilt and exonerating the innocent, *Berlin Is in Germany* concludes with an image of its hero driving off into a future as a free man who seems to have what it takes both personally and socially to make it in a capitalist, democratic unified Germany.

Fig. 1.2. Screenshot from Winfried Bonengel's Führer Ex *(2002).*

Führer Ex

Violence against foreigners and the specter of right-wing extremism in post-unification Germany are alluded to briefly in Hannes Stöhr's tragi-comedy *Berlin Is in Germany*. Right-wing rowdies shout racial slurs and threats at the black Cuban Enrique. Martin and Enrique answer xenophobia with a definitive show of force, beating up the racists and implying that a strong hand can quickly overcome this new phenomenon. By contrast, neo-Nazism is at the center of Winfried Bonengel's *Führer Ex,* and this tragic film locates the origins of xenophobia and right-wing extremism firmly in the German Democratic Republic. *Führer Ex* is based loosely on the real-life experiences of Ingo Hasselbach, a young punk in the GDR who was imprisoned for rebelling against the communist state, became a prominent neo-Nazi leader after the *Wende,* and in a dramatic move left the scene, renounced right-wing violence, and published his autobiography, *Die Abrechnung: Ein Neonazi steigt aus* (The reckoning: a neo-Nazi exits; English title: *Führer Ex,* 1993). Although *Führer Ex* was Bonengel's debut feature film, it was honored with an invitation to compete at the Venice Film Festival and premiered there on 31 August 2002. The film was released in German cinemas on 5 December 2002, where it suffered an extremely poor box-office showing, reaching a mere 32,763 viewers in its first full year.[51]

Winfried Bonengel was born in Werneck, Bavaria, in 1960 and moved to France in 1985 to study directing at the ESRA Film Academy in Paris. Upon completion of his studies in 1989, he began working as a director's assistant in French television and in the theater. In the nineties, Bonengel's work in Germany focused exclusively on documentary films about right-wing extremism.[52] His television documentaries on the growing neo-Nazi movement since unification, *Wir sind wieder da* (We are back, 1991) and *Eine unheilige Allianz* (An unholy alliance, 1992), were followed by the highly controversial film *Beruf Neonazi* (Occupation neo-Nazi, 1993), a documentary featuring Munich-based neo-Nazi leader Bela Ewald Althans. *Beruf Neonazi* premiered in Potsdam and was scheduled to be released in German cinemas in late November 1993, but the film's distribution was repeatedly interrupted and delayed because of protests and government intervention. In particular, a scene in which the neo-Nazi Althans stands in the gas chamber at Auschwitz and declares the Holocaust to be a lie caused an uproar in Germany. The lack of an authoritative voice-over denouncing Althans as a Holocaust-denier and the absence of any expert testimony that could offer a counter position were seen as evidence that Bonengel had either knowingly or unwittingly provided neo-Nazis with a platform to disseminate their racist views.[53] The controversies surrounding *Beruf Neonazi* hindered Bonengel from obtaining financing for *Führer Ex*, and it took him nearly seven years to find a producer (Laurens Sträub) who was willing to support the screenplay he had written together with Hasselbach. Bonengel had met Hasselbach in 1991 during the filming of *Wir sind wieder da* and had been instrumental in his exit from the neo-Nazi scene, including cowriting his autobiography, *Die Abrechnung*. For the feature film they decided to fictionalize much of Hasselbach's story in the form of a buddy film and concentrate on the personal conflicts that motivate the two protagonists to embrace and then reject membership in a neo-Nazi organization.

Führer Ex centers on the friendship between the sensitive Heiko and the hardened Tommy, who are both part of the punk scene in the GDR in the late 1980s. Tommy is arrested for burning the national flag and returns home from prison a changed man with SS tattoos. He tries to convince his friend that Nazis are the ultimate dissenters, but Heiko is unimpressed. They decide to escape over the Wall in the hope of making it to Australia. Caught in the act of fleeing the republic, they are sent to prison, where Tommy immediately joins the ranks of old-Nazis, and Heiko tries to make it on his own. After Heiko is brutally raped, he decides to join the Nazis for protection. The two plan to break out of prison, but only Tommy succeeds, and he lands in Bavaria shortly before the *Wende*. Following a gap of six months, Tommy returns to find his best friend completely changed. Heiko is now a leader in the infamous Weitlingstrasse neo-Nazi headquarters in East Berlin. After participating in a violent attack, Tommy decides to leave the scene for good, and Heiko is ordered to kill his best friend. The two confront each other, and friendship wins over ideology, but Tommy is beaten to death by right-wing thugs. The final shot follows a second gap in time and shows a normal-looking Heiko walking down a crowded street, alluding to his successful exit from the neo-Nazi scene.

The opening title sequence juxtaposes a distinctly punk outlook on national identity and the carefully fashioned self-image the GDR tried to project, an image that conveyed the socialist state's victory over the past, rising from the ruins of a devastating war to establish its dominion over German history. A jarring punk rendition of the GDR national anthem, "Auferstanden aus Ruinen" (Arisen from the ruins), performed by the band MIA accompanies a sweeping panorama of news footage in the faded color palate of a bygone era, featuring the hallmarks of socialist realist architecture and historiography: the palace of the republic, the television tower on Alexanderplatz, and the Stalinallee from the fountain on Strausbergerplatz to the Frankfurter Tor, the triumphant unveiling of the colossal Ernst Thälmann monument, and finally a paternalistic, smiling Erich Honecker patting a child on the head. The title sequence then segues to the two main protagonists pissing on Honecker's photo in the newspaper *Neues Deutschland*. Heiko and Tommy are punks who protest against the system in mostly symbolic terms like pissing on the SED First Secretary's image, but from the start it is clear that their pranks will ultimately harm them and not the system, since Heiko ends up soiling his own tennis shoes instead of the newspaper.

Indeed, Heiko and Tommy direct their aggression against themselves in an attempt to opt out of the system. They engage in self-mutilation, breaking each other's hands and arms, to avoid having to go to work, a fairly common practice among punks and hooligans, but one that was combated with the full resources of the state.[54] The GDR considered citizens who refused to work *asocial*, and under paragraph 249 of the penal code criminalized anyone who "infringed upon the public order by avoiding regular work." Law historian Inga Markovits points out that asocial behavior in the GDR was a serious offense and could lead to dire consequences: "Capital crimes aside, asocial behavior was more harshly punished than any other offense in East Germany. In 1988, *Asoziale* made up 24.46% of the East German prison population, two and a half times more than those convicted of 'border crimes' and by far the largest group of those behind bars in the GDR."[55] Heiko and Tommy's refusal to work, although motivated by sheer boredom and a youthful desire to play, becomes a political act in a society where the guaranteed "right to work" is actually the "duty to work." Fearing categorization as social parasites, they risk permanent bodily injury just to enjoy the freedom of being on their own for a short period of time.[56]

The desire to be free from the constraints of bourgeois norms and to act autonomously motivates the teenagers to create a rooftop oasis.

Located high above the city of Berlin, removed from the boredom and restrictions of everyday life, the rooftop is a private refuge where Heiko and Tommy dream about being somewhere else. Australia becomes for the teenagers a utopian possibility, an exotic far-off place where they imagine one can roam freely. Stuck in the GDR, they want to separate themselves from the majority of people who simply conform and fit in. By listening to punk music and sporting work boots, leather jackets laden with buttons, and unruly hairdos, they protest against the regimentation of life in the GDR. Other than hanging out in a punk bar that offers the same type of autonomous space as their rooftop, their activities are mostly provocative defiance rather than serious delinquency. Tommy harasses an old man in a wheelchair, the two boys jump on a row of cars, and they climb a fence and hang out on a soccer field. Their deviation from the norm seems rather harmless and typical of adolescent behavior, but since the GDR views alienation as a Western problem stemming from capitalistic labor practices, these alienated outsiders represent a threat to the very essence of the state. Tommy crosses the line when he burns the GDR flag. Now his symbolic lashing out against authority has turned into a political act of dissent that is immediately discovered (in an unconvincing twist of fate) and that will result in his imprisonment for "public vilification of the state" (öffentliche Herabwürdigung) in violation of paragraph 220 of the penal code.

In both the GDR and the FRG, punks were a marginal group in the eighties.[57] Despite their small numbers, they stood out as extreme nonconformists who rejected socialist utopianism as much as mainstream capitalist self-satisfaction. With their collective anthem "no future" and their affinity to things broken, deteriorated, and discarded, punks gave voice to a pessimistic world outlook that called for a dogged survival mentality. What separated them most clearly from other disenfranchised groups was their anti-utopian view that the world could not be saved and that one must learn to live in the rubble. Hardcore punks rejected the rosy optimism of leftists on both sides of the Wall who believed in the possibility of creating an equalitarian society. Punks, however, shared with groups like squatters and autonomists the "hope of creating a living space — be it in youth centers or occupied houses — in which they could develop in a self-determined and 'autonomous' fashion."[58] Alternative youth groups were bound by a common desire "to prevail over an intensely experienced sense of loneliness, boredom, fear and powerlessness" that often expressed itself in violence.[59]

According to Ingo Hasselbach, in the GDR in the eighties the line between hippie, punk, and skinhead was not always clear-cut. As declared opponents of the status quo, members of the various groups socialized and respected each other to some extent. As a young boy, Hasselbach was fascinated by a group of hippies who lived near his grandmother in

Prenzlauer Berg. These long-haired, free-living outsiders who had no interest in work or bourgeois values were the epitome of rebellion in the seventies. In the eighties, he was more attracted to the punks, because of their aggressive stance. He started sporting conspicuous green pants, a spiky hairdo, and a jacket with slogans familiar from the West German autonomist scene ("Destroy what destroys you" and "No power for no one") as well as those directed specifically at the GDR ("You are free when no one is watching you"). Together with his punk friend Freddy (a model for the figure of Tommy), Hasselbach rebelled by spray-painting the anarchy symbol and swastikas without really understanding the latter's significance.[60] The conflation of anarchy and National Socialism may have seemed like a logical move for teenagers who simply wanted to provoke and shock the authorities. For the government, however, the use of swastikas in public spaces was tantamount to treason, because it betrayed the fundamental belief that socialism had conquered the German past. The GDR defined itself at its most basic level as an anti-fascist state and considered the establishment of a socialist planned economy as evidence that it had overcome the fascist legacy that continued to mar the FRG. Punks like Hasselbach, who spray-painted swastikas and adopted National Socialist symbols, registered their hatred of the system by breaking one of the country's most sacred taboos. Bonengel does not depict this scene in his film because it would contradict his portrayal of Heiko and Tommy as innocent misfits who become victims of the system. Whereas the figure of Tommy goes to jail for burning the national flag, Hasselbach was arrested in November 1987 for shouting "The Wall has to go!" and sentenced to a year in Rummelsburg penitentiary. In prison he became familiar with neo-Nazis, but he insists that the prison mindset — deadening one's emotions and becoming completely hardened to any affective connection to others — was more important than ideology in his conversion to right-wing extremism.[61]

Punks seem almost destined to become obligatory stock figures in motion pictures about the GDR in the late eighties, because they demonstrate in highly visible and auditory terms the historic clash between a repressive regime that demanded conformity and a youth that refused to be molded into compliant wards of the state. From *Die Stille nach dem Schuss* (The calm after the shot, English title: *The Legend of Rita*, dir. Volker Schlöndorff, 2000) and *Wie Feuer und Flamme* (Like fire and flame, English title: *Never Mind the Wall*, dir. Connie Walther, 2001) to the television film *Das Wunder von Berlin* (The miracle of Berlin, dir. Roland Suso Richter, broadcast on 27 January 2008 on ZDF), punks are depicted as sympathetic underdogs, who stand up to authority and refuse to blend in and integrate into the system.[62] With their provocative clothing and hairstyles, loud music and underground concerts, and refusal to live and work in conventional ways, punks were easy prey for the Stasi.

They routinely paid for their "asocial behavior" with police harassment or a stint in prison.[63]

Bonengel's film argues that the GDR radicalized its already marginal youth groups by overreacting to the teenagers' relatively innocuous adolescent rebellion. When Tommy returns from prison, he exhibits a harsher exterior and looks more like a skinhead than a punk. Before being arrested he already sported a bomber jacket and the steel-tipped boots typical of skinheads, but now he has a closely shorn haircut and displays both an SS tattoo on his arm and a bobbed wire tattoo on his neck, an escalation of the more common leather collar worn by punks to signal their unwilling bondage to the establishment. Most importantly, he professes a newfound belief that the Nazis are the only true nonconformists in the socialist state. Tommy's transformation from a punk to a Nazi sympathizer is presented as a reaction to the restrictive environment. The GDR is depicted as a prison state that creates its own opposition. When asked how it was in prison, Tommy replies: "Well, like everywhere else in the GDR, just a bit narrower."[64] Tommy's remarks are somewhat clichéd but set the stage for viewing the system as responsible for the reversion into right-wing extremism. The protagonists are depicted as innocent victims, who cannot control the situation and only react to a world not of their making. Tommy and Heiko are extremely limited in their options, and the more they protest about being confined behind the Wall, the more they are subjected to the gravitational pull of the neo-Nazis. When they are incarcerated for *Republikflucht*, the rebels are exposed to a hostile environment where they have few options beyond association with right-wing extremists if they want to survive.

One area that makes the punks especially vulnerable to the neo-Nazis is their early socialization in homophobia and repression of feelings as essential components of conventional male identity. Confusion over gender roles and inexperience with sexual activity belong to adolescent development, but from the start Heiko is hypersensitive to these issues. His very first line in the film is a question to Tommy about whether he has ever thought about doing something with a woman other than sleeping with her. Considering that the teenagers are shown pissing together, their conversation establishes an intimacy and also their roles in the relationship: Heiko is the naive, innocent one, and Tommy is the more experienced, dominant one his friend looks up to. Even in the "normal" everyday life of the GDR, definitions of masculinity and appropriate behavior for men are important for Heiko's sense of identity. Notably, he lives with his single mother, and the absence of a father-figure means that he has no positive male role model and thus turns to his friend for acceptance and approval (Tommy appears to be in the same situation, but there are no specific references to his family life). Heiko's naiveté about women is coupled with a pronounced homophobia that is repeatedly associated with Tommy. When talking to friends about Tommy's imprisonment, one boy comments: "Your friend probably doesn't know any more whether he is a man or a woman."[65] Heiko is deeply distressed by the idea that his best friend would be forced to engage in homosexual activity, and immediately following this conversation Beate makes a pass at him. When he hesitates, she asks him if he is gay. He confesses that he is a virgin, and Beate takes the lead, so that Heiko can successfully engage in sexual intercourse. In order to prove his newfound masculine identity, Heiko sends the imprisoned Tommy Beate's underwear — as well as his mother's lingerie. After Tommy returns from prison, Heiko asks to see his friend's gunshot wound, and so Tommy obliges and drops his pants. With his finger pressed against the wound located on Tommy's ass, Heiko is surprised when his mother walks into the room. He protests: "Mama, it isn't what you think."[66] Heiko's unspoken fear that his mother thinks he is a homosexual is unfounded, but he tells her twice (earlier he insisted that he was not wearing her missing underwear) that despite appearances he is not moved by homoeroticism. Heiko does not know how to express his feelings for Tommy and has difficulty differentiating between affection and sexual desire.

In the exclusively male environment of prison, definitions of masculinity become essential to Heiko's understanding of who he is. His worst fears become real when he is brutally raped in the shower room. When Heiko screams for Tommy's help, his best friend calls on fellow inmates to help him break down the shower room door. Tommy saves Heiko, and the other prisoners beat the rapist, leaving the perpetrator a bloody victim on the bathroom floor. Tommy consoles Heiko saying: "You are not the only one this has happened to," if not a confession that he too was raped, then at least an acknowledgement that this is not Heiko's fault and that many men have been victims of sexual violence in prison. Faced with the threat of further rape and humiliation, Heiko breaks down and joins the group led by the old Nazi Friedhelm Kaltenbach. Earlier Tommy had tried to convince Heiko to revise his negative opinion of Nazis: "These feeble-minded Nazis are the only ones in this country who offer resistance. They don't put up with anything from the filthy Communists. They are men."[67] Tommy's remarks are not merely political; they are deeply personal. In a world of constant threats to one's wellbeing and one's understanding of masculinity, the Nazis are presented as the only viable option, because they are considered "real men." Kaltenbach later tells Heiko that he is proud of him for stabbing a second potential rapist because he has learned the most important lesson in life: "Never let yourself be pulled down" (sich niemals unterkriegen lassen). This father-figure reinforces the classical stereotypes of hyper-masculinity with value placed on physical strength, power, aggressiveness, courage, hardness, inflexibility, and the rejection of homosexuality.

Being in prison makes Heiko's desire to belong to the dominant group more acute than under normal conditions, but this fictional depiction strongly resembles the findings from current research on neo-Nazism in Germany. Sociologist Christine Wiezorek conducted interviews with young men in prison and questioned them about their reasons for joining the neo-Nazi movement. In particular, group membership and the notion of maintaining one's status and position vis-à-vis authority were seen as attractive. Twenty-two-year-old Rolf, born in the GDR and the product of a broken home, was imprisoned four times as a youth for various offences, including violence against foreigners. Rolf summarized his motives for being in the right-wing extremist scene:

> I just wanted to belong for once to the stronger mass and simply acted accordingly, dressed that way and such. Well, my worldviews, they weren't yet like they are now, in the extremist realm they are now. It was quite simply this feeling of belonging, simply being cool, and belonging, to hang out with these people and to swig a beer together and such, you know, consume alcohol, and that kind of shit. Anyway, in that way I sort of slipped into the right-wing scene. . . . That there are people around who are working in the underground, and despite a ban don't let themselves be pulled down ("so nicht halt jetzt unterkriegen lassen"), and I thought that was good, and so I could identify with that.[68]

The idea of never allowing oneself to be subjected to another man's power and hyper-masculine posturing are, according to political scientist Michael Kohlstruck and ethnologist Anna Verena Münch, significant factors that influence young men's decision to join right-wing extremist groups. Young recruits view these groups as attractive because they offer membership in a primarily male collective with straightforward definitions of manliness and power. Kohlstruck and Münch argue:

> The masculine style is distinguished by the cultivation of a specific image of manliness, a type of traditional masculinity, which is characterized by a danger-seeking, dominating, and body-conscious demeanor. Along with the disruptions in the order of everyday life, an offensive demonstration of power and an aggressive physicality, two specific mindsets are typical for masculine scenes: they link their autochthon orientation (territorial behavior etc.) with a general xenophobia, and they combine an emphasis on masculinity with a decided hostility toward unmanliness.[69]

Even before they enter prison, Heiko and Tommy live in a world without strong and positive adult male role models. The GDR seems populated by weak and repellent men, because the only ones shown on the screen are a helpless elderly man in a wheelchair, a petty bourgeois conformist in a tracksuit washing his beloved Trabi, two slimy middle-aged men gawking at Beate, and an overweight policeman, who cannot catch Tommy and cowardly shoots him from behind. The women, by contrast, are sexually emancipated, if not outright aggressive. Both Beate and Heiko's mother sleep with multiple partners and seem to have little need for men outside of sex. Beate sleeps with both Heiko and Tommy and follows her sexual and violent impulses with equal zeal. Notably, the only act of violence depicted in the GDR (outside prison) is initiated by a woman. When Beate notices that a middle-aged man has been staring at her, she taunts him by exposing her breasts and then starts punching and kicking him. Heiko watches, but Tommy steps in and unleashes his pent-up hostility, kicking the man long after he is incapacitated. Beate and Tommy's violent outburst exemplifies Hannah Arendt's famous axiom "violence appears where power is in jeopardy."[70] Beate perceives a loss of power over her body and sexuality, and Tommy protests a loss of power to the adult world that locked him away in a cell and continues to keep him captive behind the Wall.

On the pendulum of power that fluctuates between anarchy and order, Heiko and Tommy swing between the two extremes, depending on their circumstances. When they are relatively safe in their normal lives, they preach anarchy under the autonomist rubric "no power for no one." However, once they find themselves in prison and a true state of anarchy threatens, because no one has complete control and everyone is vying for power in a raw struggle for survival, then they are desperate for the concept of order. In *Führer Ex*, Communism and National Socialism are competing ideologies that not only vie for the adolescents' allegiance but also function as a distorted mirror for each other. Heiko and Tommy reject the GDR value system and seem oblivious to the slogan on the prison wall claiming: "order, cleanliness, and discipline are strictly the rule here."[71] In a double irony, the GDR prison does not deliver on this pledge, and the boys turn to the Nazis because they promise exactly the kind of order the communists cannot provide. Although Heiko is initially hesitant, he becomes a zealous neo-Nazi convert. Tommy, by contrast, is at heart an anarchist who has no interest in submitting to any order. He is pragmatic, aligning himself first with the Nazis for protection and then with the communists by becoming a Stasi informant so that his best friend will be released from solitary confinement. Tommy's one golden rule is friendship, and he will do what it takes to help his friend. Once he is free in a Germany without a wall, Tommy reverts back to his old ways of anarchy. In the neo-Nazi headquarters after the *Wende*, Tommy may applaud Heiko's fanatic speech about never letting anyone pull them down again ("sich nicht unterkriegen lassen"), but he has no interest in submitting to a hierarchical order. Heiko informs him: "Order and discipline rule in this house. . . . Everyone has to become subordinate. This applies to you too, clear?"[72] Tommy wants nothing to do with a regulated lifestyle and has to be dragged from his bed and forced to work in this new regime that is starting to look like the old one.

Führer Ex does not provide a simple ideological and historical comparison between the Third Reich and the GDR. It does not, for instance, examine the continuity of criminalization of asocials from Nazi Germany to the GDR. What it does argue is that the GDR was a dictatorship like the Third Reich, and that these two German historical regimes shared certain basic social values and also a style of demonstrating political power over their subjects. Historian Gordon Charles Ross has analyzed right-wing extremism in the GDR in the 1980s and concludes that this group espoused a set of beliefs long associated with the German nation: "What did the GDR right-wing extremists understand by 'Germanness'? In their view, being 'German' meant being hard-working, productive, orderly, clean, disciplined, and strong. Values such as strength and power, national pride, discipline, order, and the heroism of the German soldier in the Second World War were idealized."[73] Along with an appreciation of order, discipline, and hard work, the GDR is shown to be the inheritor of Nazi Germany's perfected manipulation of its subjects through coercion and appeasement. The long arm of the Stasi reaches even into the darkest and most remote corner of the state. In ever narrower confines — a cell in a prison in a prison state — Heiko has reached the end of the line and begins to drift into insanity. The Stasi officer uses Heiko's suffering to manipulate his friend Tommy. Standing in front of the obligatory Honecker portrait, the Stasi officer tries to cajole Tommy with a cup of real coffee and flattery, telling him he is intelligent and acknowledging his point of view: "You shouldn't think that you are the only one. There are a great many dissatisfied young people who see problems in our country and want to change things."[74] When these strategies do not produce the desired compliance, the Stasi officer screams at Tommy to look at him. This violent outburst followed by controlled rage has the intended effect of making Tommy stiffen in fear and brace himself in anticipation of punishment. The Stasi officer's demonstration of controlled rage resembles Heiko's controlled hysterical performance as a neo-Nazi leader. Tommy's reaction to Heiko's power posturing is relaxed and approving because this rage is directed at "the red mob on the street." The rather sedate symbols of power in the GDR, the party insignia button in the Stasi officer's lapel and the Honecker portrait on the wall (which present clear historical echoes of the Gestapo with their party insignia and Hitler portrait), become full-blown requisites in the neo-Nazi headquarters. Heiko wears a brown shirt, swastika arm band, and leather strap across his chest, his hair is slicked down and perfectly parted, and he stands in front of the Nazi war flag. Most notable is the shift to severe (if overdone) lighting, where Heiko is lit from below, creating the menacing high contrasts typical of horror films.

Führer Ex has a significant void in time from the opening of the Wall in November 1989 to late May 1990, when Tommy returns to Berlin. The amnesic gap falls exactly in the in-between period when the GDR was no longer fully autonomous but had not yet completely vanished. Half a year, in which monumental changes took place, is missing, so that the transition of the GDR from a sovereign state to a part of the FRG simply happens. There is no historical memory of the Round Table discussions, the first free elections in the GDR in March 1990, and the signing of the treaty on monetary, economic, and social union on 18 May 1990, paving the way for currency reform and unification. Concomitantly, the two main protagonists undergo a state of unconsciousness, forgetfulness, and unseen evolution that stands in strong contrast to the very visible political and social changes taking place in the country. The void in time between the GDR's collapse and the emergence of a unified Germany is simultaneous with the rise in right-wing extremism, Heiko's conversion to neo-Nazism, and Tommy's reversion to anarchy with a propensity for Western values.

Tommy escapes from prison in late 1989 and ends up in Bavaria, where he sleeps through the fall of the Wall in a drunken stupor. Tommy experiences a form of amnesia and is oblivious to the historical moment, but the television playing near his bed captures the event. The Bundestag is shown celebrating the historic fall of the Wall by singing the national anthem, the third verse of Heinrich Hoffmann von Fallersleben's "Das Lied der Deutschen" (1841). Bundestag members sing about "Unity and law and freedom for the German fatherland. Let us all strive for that in brotherhood . . .," but they are interrupted by a crosscut to GDR prisoners singing the same song. The prisoners, however, revert to the notorious first verse and official anthem under Hitler: "Germany, Germany above all, above everything in the world. When always, for protection, we stand together as brothers."[75] While Tommy slumbers in a blissfully innocent state of unconsciousness, the past and present battle over definitions of German brotherhood. On the one side is law and freedom, and on the other is nationalism and defense. In the six months that follow the *Wende*, neither the political process nor the characters' psychological development find their way to the screen, because amnesia is a fundamental component in this story about forgetting the GDR politically and personally.

Heiko has most obviously become a neo-Nazi zealot, but Tommy has changed too. During the amnesic gap both Tommy and Heiko have forgotten the GDR and their former identity in the prison state. Tommy arrives at the Weitlingstrasse in a vintage Ford Escort Ghia and parks in front of McDonalds. Thus associated with the American consumer goods promised under capitalism, Tommy enters neo-Nazi headquarters as Friedhelm Kaltenbach's voice off-screen denounces these newfound consumerist fantasies as deadly and unworthy: "What can this society offer us? Discotheques? Corruption? Unemployment? AIDS? Drugs? Bombs? There is nothing this state can entice us with."[76] Tommy's association with Western capitalist goods after his extended stay in the FRG and Kaltenbach's rejection of just such a way of life reiterates the film's central premise that neo-Nazism has its roots in the East.

Many film reviewers criticized *Führer Ex* for concentrating almost exclusively on the protagonist's personal motivation for joining the neo-Nazis and thus neglecting to address the importance of political ideology. Cristina Nord, film critic for *taz*, considered Bonengel's film to be over-determined and clichéd. She was especially disappointed that Heiko's psychological development from a brutalized inmate forced to join the neo-Nazis to a convicted leader of the radical right after the *Wende* was missing from the film. In her opinion:

> It has the side-effect that *Führer Ex* shifts some of the responsibil-ity on to the GDR system. Because the East German authorities did not know how they were supposed to respond to the rebel-liousness of young men other than with repression. According to this thesis, they drove them into the arms of the Nazis. Let's not forget the single mother with a successful career, who carries on with various lovers, instead of taking care of her son: How could one not become right-wing?[77]

Along the same lines, Katja Nicodemus, film critic for *Die Zeit*, argues that the story of neo-Nazis is a crucial aspect of contemporary life and needs to be told. However, she faults Bonengel with the same tactic that marred his previous film, *Beruf Neonazi*: he fails to take a stance. Accord-ing to Nicodemus, *Führer Ex* illustrates the young men's indeterminate rage against the system and authority in all its guises as well as the state's overzealous response that helped to create its own dissidents. She con-cedes that life in prison is hardly conducive to soul searching, but notes that the ideological aspect of a conversion to right-wing extremism is a glaring omission. She writes: "Traumatic experiences like a gay rape in the shower room or months in solitary would certainly not make a young person already filled with impotent rage any more affable, but the actual politicization does not seem to take place in prison. It is precisely the conversion of indeterminate rage into ideological supercharge, the really suspenseful moment, peripeteia, and breaking point of such a genre film that is swallowed up in the script by a big black vacuum-like ellipse." The problem Nicodemus sees is that this storyline shifts responsibility from individual choice to circumstances: "In this way, the responsibility for the turn to the extreme right is diverted to a rather daring alliance: a youth spent in the restrictive GDR, the slightly dubious lifestyle of a mother, who presents her offspring with a conga line of changing foreign lovers instead of a father, as well as gay repression in prison."[78] Both Nord and

Nicodemus fault the film for its stereotypical depiction of male aggression and its gender bias against sexually active mother figures. Their primary point of contention is that the lack of psychological development means that the rise of neo-Nazism in the GDR is attributed to the repressive state authority, and thus a structural problem that will somehow disappear with the collapse of Communism. Their criticism has validity if we keep in mind that neo-Nazism is also prevalent in the West and developed over the decades in a completely different political environment.

Winfried Bonengel justified the logic of his screenplay based on his extensive research on the neo-Nazi movement in Germany. Despite many reviewers' strong desire for *Führer Ex* to uncover evidence that young men became violent neo-Nazis because of strong ideological convictions or that they were seduced by the power of propaganda and indoctrination, Bonengel claims that their motivations are often much more simple and mundane. The vast majority of young men in the radical right movement joined up for personal reasons. The character of Heiko is based to a large extent on Ingo Hasselbach's experiences and those of many of his comrades in the National Alternative (Nationale Alternative, NA). According to Hasselbach, Heiko represents a typical development of a young man from maltreated social outsider to angry, violent insider. Based on his brutal prison experiences, Heiko sees no other viable choice for survival than to join the dominant group. Bonengel defends the void in psychological development, stating: "I refrained from showing his further career in this group because the decisive step is that after his prison experiences he sees no other way, even though in the beginning he found being a Nazi completely absurd. If he wants to survive, he needs these people." For Bonengel it was important to show "that there are emotional reasons why people become Nazis. It is like in a sect. If I compliment someone enough, he starts to feel good, and thus is more easily manipulated. Indoctrination only comes afterward, and therefore it plays a role only relatively late in the film."[79]

In a review for the *Stuttgarter Zeitung*, Ruppert Koppold considered Heiko's decision to join the neo-Nazis unconvincing because it was motivated either by a single event (his rape and solitary confinement) or not displayed at all. Koppold rejected the film's narrative reliability as history, because if one accepted its premise one would be forced to conclude "in the end that anyone at any time can become a neo-Nazi and again at any time can be 'denazified.' One can hardly call that enlightenment."[80] Koppold's statement reveals less about Bonengel's film than about a widespread but unspoken fear that National Socialism could resurface in Germany at any time. It is easier to reject the film than to accept its implication: given the right circumstances, anyone could become a Nazi. Admittedly, *Führer Ex* suffers from problems ranging from an often simplistic if not Manichaean view of good and evil and excessive clichés to a melodramatic musical score that does not suit the punk theme. Moreover, its claim to be based on historical events and its obvious fictionalization of Hasselbach's life in ways that overdetermine the protagonists' innocence mar the film. However, there are several aspects of *Führer Ex* that make it an especially relevant contribution to the current discourse on German national identity and that make it extremely disturbing. If the viewer accepts Bonengel's take on history, then the GDR was a dictatorship, neo-Nazism too closely resembles both past and present familiar definitions on what it means to be German, and anyone could become a neo-Nazi. These deeply troubling ideas, in my opinion, are at the root of much of the criticism lodged against the film and contributed significantly to its poor showing at the box office. If we examine how *Führer Ex* compares to other recent motion pictures about right-wing extremism and how historians, political scientists, and sociologists view the rise of neo-Nazism among youth, then a pattern emerges that puts Bonengel's film squarely in mainstream trends in both artistic and sociological assessments of this disturbing phenomenon.

Führer Ex follows a now familiar storyline, whereby a sympathetic teenage boy from a broken home is drawn into the orbit of neo-Nazis by personal circumstances and eventually triumphs over the situation to liberate himself from their influence. Similar narratives that concentrate primarily on the troubled personal lives and problematic social milieu of young men who turn to right-wing extremism can be found in the feature films *Kahlschlag* (Clean sweep, Hanno Brühl, 1993, WDR), *Platzangst* (Claustrophobia, Heike Schober and René Zeuner, 2003), and *Kombat Sechzehn* (Combat sixteen, Mirko Borscht, 2005) as well as in the documentary *Stau — jetzt gehts los!* (Bottleneck — now it's moving!, Thomas Heise, 1992).[81] All of these films emphasize the emotional suffering, masculine crisis, and lack of a familial and social support system that drive teenage boys into the arms of right-wing extremist gangs. In *Kahlschlag* sixteen-year-old Robin, son of a divorced mother and absent father, joins a skinhead gang after being attacked by a group of Turks, but he decides to distance himself from the scene after witnessing the beating of a Turkish girl. Now considered a traitor, Robin becomes the victim of right-wing violence. *Platzangst* is based on a true story about sixteen-year-old Martin, the son of an absent father in a small town in Brandenburg, who joins up with skinheads because they offer the acceptance and sense of belonging he desperately needs. When Martin falls in love with the Russian girl Marina, he is forced to choose between the gang and the foreign girl. Although the film ends without a clear resolution of the dilemma, Martin loves Marina, and the film tips in favor of the couple. In *Kombat Sechzehn* sixteen-year-old Georg moves with his father from Frankfurt am Main to Frankfurt an der Oder after his parents' divorce. Lonely in a new town without his old friends and disqualified from competing in a Taekwondo league because of his relocation, Georg joins a group of skinheads and lets out his aggression in street fighting. After the group attacks an innocent bystander, and Georg and his friend Thomas refuse to give the notorious curb kick, they become victims of a beating but eventually free themselves from the gang. In the documentary *Stau — jetzt gehts los!* Thomas Heise interviews five neo-Nazi teenagers from Halle-Neustadt, who pose for the camera and present their racist and jingoist views in a highly provocative manner. Heise also examines their personal circumstances and social environment and reveals the extent to which these frightened young boys are looking for approval and recognition in a hostile world.

Helke Sander's black comedy *Dazlak-Skinhead* (1997) offers a somewhat different plot twist but a comparable redemption of the right-wing extremist. A feminist, a skinhead, and a black German end up together on a bizarre road trip to Oberfranken, Bavaria, and along the way a series of prejudices are revealed to be unfounded. Dazlak (Turkish for skinhead) is introduced as a drunken, vulgar, and violent young man responsible for driving his own car into a gully and destroying the car of the woman who saved him. Later it is revealed that he was not drunk but swerved to avoid hitting a deer. Despite appearances, this rather sympathetic figure from Rostock, who listens to skinhead music and adopts this fashion style, is not a raging hooligan but a talented pâtissier. Dazlak learns to fit in with people from different backgrounds — in contrast to the petty bourgeois, prejudiced Bavarians — and he even wins the girl in the end. None of these films about skinheads and the neo-Nazi youth did well at the box office, but they deal with the question of guilt and redemption in such a similar manner that they represent a dominant discursive practice.[82] These films depict the protagonist's development from an innocent and vulnerable young man in a hostile environment to a violent perpetrator who awakens to the evil of his chosen path and finds the inner strength to change himself. This narrative frames neo-Nazism as a bad choice good people make in bad circumstances. It celebrates the healing power of love and friendship that can awaken individuals to evil and lead them to redemption.

This conventional cinematic narrative corresponds to a large extent with trends in sociological studies on right-wing extremism in Germany. Beginning in the 1980s, sociologists began to focus extensively on extremist attitudes instead of political affiliations in the FRG. The SINUS study published in 1981 marked a significant shift in sociological research "characterized by an expansion of the term right-wing extremism, which was no longer limited to political behavior and ideology but rather encompassed also the attitudes of the population."[83] Studies on violence against foreigners since unification paint a nearly uniform picture of the perpetrators: 90 percent were men under the age of 25, more than 62 percent had a secondary general school certificate (Hauptschulabschluß),

90 percent of the attacks were carried out by groups, and more than 90 percent of violent incidents were not motivated by political ideology.[84] In contrast to expectations that these violent offenders were motivated by political convictions or were acting on orders of a politically organized group with a specific agenda, researchers have found that this is not the case in most crimes committed against foreigners and those designated as weak outsiders. Instead they have concluded:

> The motivation of offenders is dominated by a masculine presentation of strength and superiority, mixed with a sometimes quite open but more often latent and diffused hatred of everything foreign to them and that deviates from their norms. The ostensive political content of their use of violence is rather minor, just as the everyday activities in the clique are hardly distinguished by serious political calculations.[85]

The fact that these young men are average and routinely carry out violent attacks that are not clearly linked to a readily recognizable aberrant political party is a troubling conclusion, because then it is nearly impossible to separate oneself from such individuals and place such acts in a distant category of deviance. If these teenagers are rather average, come from average families, and live in an average economic milieu, then right-wing extremism is much closer to home than one might like. Psychologist Klaus Weber has formulated this issue in exceedingly provocative terms by questioning whether the very term "right-wing extremism" does not function as a distancing mechanism for people "to feel they bear no resemblance to this and show themselves to be 'good people' in comparison to those who are 'extreme' and thus false."[86] Weber argues that it is important to recognize that this youth phenomenon is heavily influenced by an "adult world full of anti-Semitism, racism, and *völkisch* national propaganda." Violence against foreigners and outsiders has to do "with social relations in which for decades all parties in the 'middle' have claimed that WE have too many asylum seekers in our country, WE suffer from social freeloaders (or as Mr. Clement calls those receiving Hartz-IV: parasites), and WE have to promote those willing to perform and leave the others to their fate."[87]

Despite the criticisms of newspaper reviewers, *Führer Ex* does offer a perspective on youth membership in neo-Nazi groups that is consistent with much recent research conducted by historians, political scientists, and sociologists, and also with findings supported by the Federal Office for the Protection of the Constitution (Bundesamt für Verfassungsschutz). However, the film participates not only in the public discourse on the causes for a revival of neo-Nazism but also in an equally contentious discourse on the GDR as a prison state. Within this context, *Führer Ex* functions as part of a meta-narrative about recent German history that has serious consequences for a common understanding of individual guilt and state culpability in the exercise of violence. Bonengel presents the GDR as a repressive state and the neo-Nazi youth as victims of circumstances. According to this logic, the victim of an unjust system becomes the perpetrator of another unjust system in order to survive. Bonengel concludes: "It is about the perversion of a victim who becomes a perpetrator . . . He is a very fascinating character: extremely sensitive and vulnerable as well as extremely ready to use violence."[88] More emphatically than in *Berlin Is in Germany*, *Führer Ex* portrays the GDR as a prison state where individuals do not have complete freedom to make choices. And just as in Hannes Stöhr's film, we have here protagonists who are led into violence precisely because they decide to leave the GDR illegally. Their decision to commit the crime of *Republikflucht*, to reject the GDR dictatorship and yearn for freedom, lends them a naive quality that tends to exonerate them morally as righteous individuals who fought the system. Like Martin, Heiko and Tommy are judged to be victims of a totalitarian system, and their violent behavior is rendered as a reaction to their loss of freedom. Moreover, despite the allure of group membership in the neo-Nazi scene, both Heiko and Tommy eventually see the evil of violence and make a conscious decision to distance themselves from it.

Bonengel's emphasis on the limited choices his protagonists have means that he missed out on an opportunity to explore the part of Hasselbach's autobiography that connects the rise of neo-Nazism to a much broader phenomenon: the search for political utopianism and the fatal attraction of violence to obtain a better world. Hasselbach admits that being a member of the neo-Nazi scene was like taking a drug; it afforded an emotional euphoria that was missing from everyday life. As a neo-Nazi he belonged to a group that sanctioned and even encouraged the release of pent-up anger in violent acts against outsiders. It also provided an ideological mission that promised a utopian vision of a purer world. Hasselbach concludes that his choice to join a neo-Nazi organization could easily have taken on a different flavor had he lived in the Federal Republic. As a teenager he was fascinated by the Red Army Faction:

> For years I procured everything about the RAF that I could get my hands on. Actually, I had dreamed of becoming a terrorist, and my concept of such a life was rather romantic. I considered terrorists idealists who fought for a better and more just world. During my time in GDR prisons I saw myself constantly as a victim of an unjust and authoritarian state that committed violence against me. Violence became an everyday thing for me: violence was committed against me, and I committed violence. Admittedly, I was not conscious of the point in time when I turned from being a victim into a perpetrator.[89]

Fig. 1.3. Still from Wolfgang Becker's Good Bye, Lenin! *(2003). Photo © and by permission of The Kobal Collection, WDR, X-Filme, and Conny Klein.*

Hasselbach's amnesia about his own development from a victim to a perpetrator and the largely unexplored connection between right-wing violence and left-wing terrorism are noteworthy gaps in his personal history that could illuminate aspects of the broader national history. These voids are, however, indicative of how painful it is to see oneself as responsible for brutality and how compelling a romanticized notion of violence can be for some people, if it is framed as a necessary tool to bring about a better world.

Good Bye, Lenin!

It seems rather incredible that thirteen years after unification one of the most popular German films would be a fairy tale about bringing the GDR back to life. Yet millions flocked to see the story of a committed socialist who slept through the 1989 revolution in a coma, and her son, who recreated the GDR in her bedroom to spare her the shock of seeing her dream crushed. *Good Bye, Lenin!*, directed by Wolfgang Becker with a screenplay cowritten by Becker and Bernd Lichtenberg, was greeted with mixed reviews when it premiered at the Berlin Film Festival on 9 February 2003.[90] The moviegoing public, by contrast, was enthralled with the film and rushed to sold-out performances when it went into general release on 13 February. *Good Bye, Lenin!* achieved a level of popularity that is extremely rare among German films. With 6,439,777 viewers in Germany, it joined the ranks of international blockbusters in 2003, with audiences figures comparable to those of films such as *Lord of the Rings III: The Return of the King, Pirates of the Caribbean: The Curse of the Black Pearl, Matrix Reloaded,* and *Catch Me If You Can.*[91] Released in seventy countries around the world, the film had estimated gross earnings of more than 79 million dollars.[92] It also won around thirty national and international awards, including the German Film Prize for best motion picture, direction, editing, music, production design, actor, and supporting actor, and the European Film Prize for best motion picture, screenplay, and actor.

Prior to *Good Bye, Lenin!* Wolfgang Becker had made only three films for the cinema, but his work was greeted with numerous artistic awards and a growing number of viewers. Born in Hemer, Westphalia in 1954, Becker studied Germanistics, History, and American Studies at the Free University Berlin from 1974 to 1979. He then studied filmmaking at the German Film and Television Academy (dffb) from 1980 to 1986. While still a student at the film academy, Becker worked with many of the great directors of German cinema. In 1982 he was Istvan Szabo's directorial assistant on the television film *Katzenspiele* (Cat games).[93] In 1983 he was a camera assistant on Hans W. Geißendörfer's *Ediths Tagebuch* (Edith's diary) and in 1984 a cameraman on Alexander Kluge and Hans-Jürgen Syberberg's *Feuertheater* (Fire theater) as well as on Helma Sander-Brahms's *Alte Liebe* (Old love). He directed and wrote the screenplay for his graduation film, *Schmetterlinge* (Butterflies), based on the eponymous short story by British writer Ian McEwan. This black-and-white film about a nineteen-year-old, Andi, who witnessed a little girl's accidental drowning, is told in intermittent flashbacks, which reveal that the "witness" is far from an innocent bystander. Andi actually led nine-year-old Kaja to the desolate canal region promising she could find butterflies. Tragically, the canal turns out to be a grungy industrial area where young men torture animals, dilapidated buildings bear swastika graffiti, and Andi sexually abuses Kaja under a bridge as a thunderous train roars overhead. After the little girl runs away and falls down, Andi hovers over her unconscious body before tossing her toy into the canal. The child's death is never shown, and the viewer is left with the image of an emotionally detached and likely murderer playing soccer alone, oblivious to the suffering he has caused. *Schmetterlinge* won the Student Academy Award, the Golden Leopard at Locarno, and the Saarbrücken Prime Minister's Award at the Max Ophüls Film Festival. Without the aid of a distributor, Becker brought the film to the cinema on his own.

Becker's first full-length feature film, *Kinderspiele* (Child's play), for which he also wrote the screenplay, premiered on 29 June 1992 in Munich and was broadcast on the Arte television station on 6 May 1994. Like his graduation film, this production received important awards, including the German Film Critics Prize and the Adolf Grimme Prize. *Kinderspiele* takes place in West Germany in the early sixties and continues the theme of abused children. Eleven-year-old Micha comes home from the last day of school with one of the best report cards in his class and news that he can start secondary school in the fall, but his parents are unimpressed. His father is an erratic, foul-tempered mason foreman, who routinely beats his son. His mother cares little for her eldest child, favoring his younger brother, and she eventually abandons Micha and his father. Micha acts as an intermediary between his parents, rewriting their letters in the hope that his mother will return, but his creative deceit is to no avail. Micha looks to the heavens for help, even though he knows that many stars no longer exist, and all he sees is the remnant of something that has long been extinguished. His best friend Kalli teaches him about sex, stealing, and how to throw a knife. Child's play leads to tragedy when the victim of violence becomes the perpetrator. Cornered and brutally beaten by his irate father in the coal-filled cellar, Micha instinctually defends himself and unknowingly kills his father with a hammer. Covered in coal dust and tears, this abandoned and abused child whose future was so bright ends up in a bubble bath that can never wash away his trauma.

Das Leben ist eine Baustelle (Life is a construction site, English title: *Life Is All You Get*, 1997), cowritten by Becker and Tom Tykwer, earned largely positive reviews and a strong box-office showing with 488,488 tickets sold in its premiere run. It also won several important awards, including Special Mention at the Berlin Film Festival, the German Film Critics Award, and the German Film Prize in Silver for best motion picture. In stark contrast to the typical romantic comedies of the nineties that feature successful, middle-class thirty-year-old yuppies in Munich suffering from an identity crisis and lack of love, Becker's black comedy is set in a working-class milieu in Berlin. The main protagonist, Jan Nebel, is a sympathetic anti-hero, whose life seems to consist of one disaster after another. He gets caught in an anarchist riot, is arrested, loses his job in a slaughterhouse, finds his father dead, face down in a bowl of ravioli, and learns he might have HIV. The one bright spot is that he falls in love with the street singer Vera, who mysteriously leaves his bed every night. The film's German title, literally "Life is a construction site," refers to the provisionary, indeterminate nature of the city and its inhabitants' lives. Akin to the theme of a generation drifting through the world not knowing where it is headed, the film is characterized by an episodic structure and open-ended narrative. Becker's three early films illustrate several prominent themes that return in *Good Bye, Lenin!*: a fascination with broken families, the stars in far-off space, creative deceit, unexpected revelations, and the inevitable comedy accompanying life's most tragic moments.[94]

Good Bye, Lenin! is a tragi-comedy about the Kerner family, which spans more than a decade, from summer 1978 to October 1990. The film opens with grainy home movies of the family vacation, but the primary action begins a short time later in the Kerner's Berlin apartment. While eleven-year-old Alex and his sister Ariane watch the televised launch of Sojus 31, where GDR cosmonaut Sigmund Jähn becomes the first German in outer space, the Stasi interrogate Christiane Kerner about her husband's defection to the West. After a mental breakdown Christiane devotes herself completely to her children, teaching, and socialist activism. Eleven years later, in the autumn of 1989, Christiane suffers a massive heart attack after seeing the police beating peaceful demonstrators and arresting her son. She wakes up from an eight-month coma with amnesia and in such a fragile condition that Alex decides to spare her the shocking news about the collapse of socialism and recreate the GDR in her bedroom. Alex's hilarious attempts to turn back the clock culminate in a fictionalized newscast suggesting that the fall of the Wall was actually the triumph of Communism over capitalism. The film ends, as it began, with home movies that feature Christiane surrounded by her children happily posing for the camera.

Good Bye, Lenin! is less concerned with an accurate historical picture of political developments than with the loss of utopian ideals and the reconstruction of national identity. What this film shares with various forms of *Ostalgie* is a profound sense of loss, but unlike the more sensational television shows that celebrate GDR material culture while conveniently neglecting its totalitarian legacy,[95] Becker's film takes a nuanced approach to socialism's checkered past. It shows a much more ambivalent picture of GDR life than the lighthearted comedy *Sonnenallee* or the gloomy punk drama *Wie Feuer und Flamme*.[96] Indeed, its main focus is the transitional period surrounding the collapse of the Berlin Wall and unification. While films like *alaska.de* (Ester Groneborn, 2000) and *Vergiß Amerika* (Forget America, Vanessa Jopp, 2000) depict a post-Wall Eastern dystopia, Becker's film is a bittersweet farewell to the GDR that wavers between hope and sadness.[97] *Good Bye, Lenin!* pokes fun at the frenzied attempts to reconstruct Eastern consumer products as a means to preserve and validate the ideal of a state that no longer has a material, political, or geographic existence. Yet, it also mourns the missed opportunity of the GDR, the utopian aspirations that were never truly brought to fruition. *Good Bye, Lenin!* is a response to recent history that constantly shifts strategies: alternately ridiculing futile attempts to recapture a bygone era and wallowing in regrets over irretrievable loss, and then celebrating the power of imagination to create the past we need for the present.

Memory, more than history, is the central concern in this film. At stake is the ability to remember not merely a series of past events but more importantly the traces of wishes and hopes. Because Christiane cannot remember her immediate past, Alex is forced to recall what it was about the former GDR that is worth preserving. The things that Alex remembers are his mother's activism, her attempts to make constructive criticism, her love of homeland, and her steadfast belief that a better world is possible. With his mother playing the leading role in his memories of the GDR, it becomes a community where people helped each other and a childhood state that provided unconditional love, wellbeing, and security. Two aspects of reminiscence play a pivotal role in bringing these memories to life: ruins and mediated reality.

The modern ruins of Tacheles set the stage for Alex and Lara's first date, providing not only hauntingly beautiful scenery but also a public space that celebrates the transition between past and future.[98] Originally built in 1907 as a shopping arcade, the building covered an entire city block and served various functions over the years, even after much of it had been destroyed by bombs during the Second World War.[99] Tacheles was originally scheduled for demolition in February 1990, but after the fall of the Wall it suddenly became a squatter's colony and the site of underground nightclubs, avant-garde art studios, and impromptu performance space. Rising from the ruins of history, this dilapidated arcade-turned-bohemian-cultural-center became a memorial site to the creative potential of change. Located in the historic city center but existing on the borders of time, Tacheles embodied the hope for alternatives to either Western or Eastern lifestyles. As Alex and Lara sit on the edge of a furnished room and the camera pulls back to reveal the skeletal remains of the building, Alex reflects in a voice-over on how the broken-down past is a catalyst for the future: "The winds of change blew right into the ruins of our republic. Summer came, and Berlin was the most beautiful place on earth. Everything was imaginable. Everything was possible. We had the feeling of being in the middle of the world. Where something was finally moving. And we were moving with it. . . . The future lay unknown in our hands, unknown and full of promise."[100] This twentieth-century ruin functions as a physical testimony to the nation's historic wounds as much as its desires. With its scars and absences on display, Tacheles promotes contemplation on what was and what could be. Rather than rendering this state of flux as horror, *Good Bye, Lenin!* presents it as the liberation of imagination. In the void created by the death of the GDR and the not-yet birth of the unified FRG, anything seems possible. Along with the setting and camera work, the soundtrack reveals the emancipatory utopian dimension of the void. Alex and Lara are seen talking, but their voices are swallowed up by the lingering music, so that the audience is compelled to imagine their conversation, just as the characters are imagining their open future of endless possibilities.

After the Berlin Wall turns into historical debris, Alex becomes an archeologist of memory, recovering traces of the past and imbuing them with meaning. Having grown up in the so-called *Mangelgesellschaft* (society of scarcity), he is well-equipped to deal with scarcity and shortages. Alex puts into practice the culturally learned skills that ethnologist Ina Merkel has identified as typical for GDR citizens who were schooled in adapting to shortages and thus developed a heightened versatility. Merkel notes that these cultural practices "refer not only to limitation and frugality, the clever handling of resources, but also at least as much to enjoyment and creativity."[101] Relentlessly digging around in trash barrels, scouring flea markets, and exploring abandoned flats in search of the artifacts of GDR daily life, Alex attempts to salvage something from his past that has significance for the present. In the most telling example, he rummages through piles of broken-down furniture to find his mother's savings, in essence searching for value in the discarded objects of a bygone era. This quest, however, can uncover painful truths, as when Ariane tears away at the kitchen cupboards to find hidden meaning, her father's unread letters Christiane buried behind the facade of everyday life. Memory work can be devastating when the discovery confirms a loss that cannot be easily mended, the loss of one parent and the betrayal of another.

Alex's obsession with finding authentic GDR products to serve as props for his staging of the past is essential to the plotline, but it also mirrors the much larger cultural phenomenon of *Ostalgie*. In the East, local consumer goods were generally considered substandard to Western products, which functioned as the ultimate measure of consumer satisfaction and status.[102] However, after the system collapsed, GDR products were suddenly desired and became a source of security, if not pride, in a shared past. In the face of economic recession, rising unemployment, and second-class status in the West, Easterners found in everyday objects a physical reminder of a world that had vanished, a world in which the individual had meaning and the collective existed.[103] Precisely the mundane aspects of GDR products were seen as positive. Historian Paul Betts has noted that "there was little variety of goods and little brand-name competition; many of the products introduced in the consumer rush of the '60s stayed in production until 1989 with little or no change in content or form. Regardless of how monotonous this may have been, the aesthetics of sameness was crucial in shaping the GDR's collective memory."[104] Betts goes so far as to argue: "material dreams of the good life prompted the 1953 uprising, the 1961 construction of the Wall, and, of course, its dramatic dismantling a generation later. Indeed, it was the consumer dreams born amid pain and privation — like that in the West during the depression — that eventually crowded out more traditional socialist concerns."[105] If consumerism played such a prominent role in the political upheaval of 1989, then it is only fitting that it should also be the vehicle for criticizing the course of post-unification history. *Ostalgie* works to reestablish individual value in the face of a maligned common past.

Just like the *Spreewald* pickles Christiane craves that have disappeared from the store shelves because they are not economically viable, so too are individuals like the former school principal Klapprath and the elderly neighbor Herr Ganske discarded as useless in the new Berlin Republic. Klapprath laments that back then "We were all valuable people."[106] Alex's project to find relics of a departed quotidian world can be seen as a heroic effort to restore value to the lives and ideals that were pushed aside in the rush to unification. Recovering old familiar items of everyday life from the garbage and recycling them is empowering because it acknowledges the traces of a lost home and community that have nearly been expunged from collective memory.

Alex's archeological work can also be seen as carrying on his mother's legacy. Christiane was never a mindless follower of the SED regime. Although her colleagues considered her overzealous and perhaps naive in her unbending idealism, she did routinely criticize the products of the socialist state. This might seem like a minor lashing out, since she did not protest against the more obvious manifestations of human-rights abuses (until the night she saw policemen beating protesters and ordered them to stop). Moreover, Christiane's critique was always once removed, since she literally gave her voice to others, dictating witty critiques of shoddy products only to have others sign their name to the complaint. Frau Schäfer, for example, twice signed her own name to a complaint Christiane had composed. The right to complain and offer suggestions via written petitions was guaranteed in the GDR constitution, but Christiane's satiric jabs about the poor quality of goods produced in the Workers-and-Farmers-State cut the GDR's self-image to the quick. The planned market economy was supposed to produce according to the needs of the workers, but as Christiane observed: "If it is our fault that our body sizes do not comply with the fulfillment of the plan, comma, please accept our apologies. Period. If such is the case, comma, we will try in the future to be smaller and squarer. Period. With socialist greetings. — Hanna Schäfer."[107] Christiane focused on material culture as a vehicle of protest. Alex follows her example, and so the tradition of small steps against authority emerges as a counter-narrative to the prevailing history of a nation of conformists too afraid to speak out against injustice at any level.

One of the most poignant scenes in Becker's film is when Christiane makes her way to the street for the first time and enters into a surreal world that makes no sense to her. The first thing she sees in the elevator is a swastika and obscene graffiti before encountering Westerners with their strange possessions, piles of junk littering the streets, an improvised used-car lot, and a series of advertising billboards, including one promising to "fulfill every special wish" and another revealing the fragmentary slogan "conquer the East." Christiane stares in wonder at the unfamiliar surroundings just as a helicopter carrying a huge, partially dismounted statue of Lenin flies through the sky over Karl-Marx-Allee. Seen from his coattails upward, a book in one arm, the other arm extended outward, and set against a blue sky filled with fluffy clouds, Lenin soars toward the camera, which then circles around Christiane, so that it looks as if the legendary revolutionary is saying his last farewell to her personally before being carted off to oblivion. The lofty utopian ideals of Communism are redirected to the earthy desires of capitalism. The carefully staged setting reminds the viewer that along with consumption come such threats as a resurfacing of National Socialism, pornography, planned obsolescence, and a constant bombardment of advertisements.

In 1990 time is out of sync, depicted as either speeded up beyond the normal rhythms of everyday life or slowed down to the point of inertia. The extraordinary speed with which life was changing during the *Wende* is reflected in several scenes by using time-lapsed photography. Alex is shown in fast motion riding his moped, Alex and Dennis zip around town in their delivery van at a quickened pace, and the nightly traffic is accelerated to such an extent that it looks like a moving neon painting. On Alexanderplatz time even marches in the wrong direction. The world clock with its cylindrical orbiting planets spins around backward so that the hours retreat as Alex collects material remnants of the past. By comparison, time frequently slows down to almost a complete standstill. When Christiane collapses after witnessing her son's arrest and when she sees Lenin flying through the air, time moves in a jerky slow motion, as if the camera were registering her shudder at the death of a utopian belief.

There are several locations where the past continues to exist undisturbed by the passing of time. The abandoned apartment Alex and Lara find is like sleeping beauty's castle, a fairy-tale place time has forgotten. When Hungary opened its borders to Austria in May 1989, its owner, like many East Germans, took advantage of the opportunity and left everything behind. Apart from the accumulated mail, a fine coating of dust, and the overgrown vines covering the balcony, nothing has changed. The ironing board stands ready to use, the electricity and telephone still work, and, most importantly, the cupboards are filled with the GDR products Alex has been so desperately seeking. The apartment is a respite from the hectic world of constant change, but it lends the past a fairy-tale quality, as if it were a place where wishes come true. This refuge also suggests that the GDR was a *niche society*, a term coined in 1983 by Günter Gaus, the FRG's first official diplomatic representative to the GDR. Gaus used the term to designate how the vast majority of GDR citizens found some personal freedom by retreating to a private realm.[108] According to Gaus, the majority paid lip service to official rhetoric in the public realm, but in private niches among friends and family in such places as allotment gardens and dachas, people could speak their mind. Whereas the former owner intentionally left the GDR to escape from the narrow confines of a niche,

Alex and Lara gladly return to it periodically because they need a niche to protect themselves from being overwhelmed by capitalism's unending stimulus and restless pace.

Christiane's bedroom becomes another space frozen in time, but unlike the abandoned apartment, it is manufactured to simulate the intact world of the past. At Christiane's birthday celebration Alex enacts the yearly ritual to honor his mother and tries to demonstrate that home and community continue to exist. He gathers friends and family for gift giving and speeches, but Klapprath's appeal to Christiane, "Stay just the way you are," and Herr Ganske's wish "that everything would return to what it once was," reveal a profound longing for a past that made sense and was populated by idealists who held everything together.[109] The sweet Young Pioneer song, "Our Homeland," performed by Christiane's former pupils, is an echo from Alex's childhood home movies. It conjures up images of the lost *Heimat* that transcends any specific region, if not time itself. According to the song, home is everywhere; it can be found in all the towns, cities, fields, forests, and animals of the earth. The one thing that binds it all together is the people: "We love the beautiful homeland, and we protect it, because it belongs to our people."[110] The collective evoked in the song is only fleetingly reconstructed and quickly falls apart in the face of Western commercialism. When a massive Coca-Cola banner intrudes upon the idyll, the older generation breaks into the Free German Youth song "Build." This song, written in the aftermath of the Second World War, encouraged the new generation to build socialism one brick at a time. In 1990 the young people are distracted or simply not interested in the old people's song and its call to "Build, build, build, new German youth, build. For a better future we are erecting the homeland."[111] Preserving the *Heimat*, an intact community where one is valued, is only possible in the ephemeral realm of memory.

Along with ruins, the media function as a tool to remember the GDR. Unlike physical artifacts that carry traces of a lost home and its ideals, photographic evidence attests to the manipulability of images and their inability to convey the whole story about the past without contextualization. *Good Bye, Lenin!* embeds various film material as a means of preserving the past, incorporating personal memory via home movies and public memory via archival footage. In nearly every case where embedded film material is used, it is accompanied by a self-reflective commentary. Alex's voice-over is from the vantage point of the present and provides ironic observations that are only possible with the benefit of memory and hindsight. It also supplies necessary information to fill in narrative gaps, and personal insights to help viewers glean the story's moral lesson. The commentaries he writes for Dennis to read on the fictional *Aktuelle Kamera*, by contrast, are bold lies to convince Christiane that GDR socialism continues to thrive and is actually realizing its promise.

The film opens with faded home movies taken at the family's dacha in the summer of 1978 and is accompanied by the lullingly somber piano music composed by Yann Tiersen. Robert's voice is heard from off-screen, and this doting father encourages his children to perform for the camera. The happy childhood scenes from bygone days, including a shot of Alex in his junior rocket-builder T-shirt in front of the famous television tower on Alexanderplatz, are then rendered in a red-tinted sepia. These dated family photographs flow in and out of the title sequence, which features vintage postcards of East Berlin. The camera moves into the structures represented on the postcards in accordion-like fashion, constantly revealing yet another monument, as if to illustrate the multitude of facades erected to uphold the GDR's official public image. The postcards — with their images of public sites on the front and private, unseen messages on the back — highlight the intersection of national and individual histories. This notion is reinforced as the faded home movies segue into a television newscast of the Soyuz 31 space mission and then into news that Alex's father has fled to the West. Individual and national biographies overlap but keep their separate shapes.[112] In a voice-over Alex remarks: "On 26 August 1978 we had reached world-class status. Sigmund Jähn, citizen of the German Democratic Republic, was the first German to fly into outer space. However, for our family everything went south on this day."[113] The voice-over is especially telling because it demonstrates how the idyllic image of a happy family integrated into their socio-political environment (at least photographically) is deceiving. The fact that the mother is conspicuously missing from the home movies before her husband's defection insinuates that the "memory" of an intact nuclear family is perhaps not as reliable as the authentic looking, home-made images and sentimental music might suggest. From the very start, *Good Bye, Lenin!* works with multiple layers of meaning that refer to different stories that are simultaneously being told. The family was intact before the father departed, as the images suggest; conversely, the family was alienated as illustrated through the father's disembodied voice and the mother's absence. Alex's voice-overs function throughout the film as a means to provide distance and reveal alternative explanations, even if they are not free of subjectivity.

Whether personal memory or public history, the past is a moving target, and the power to tell the story determines its contours, with deceit a common tool for survival (and, if we are to believe this film, a necessary tool for love). With the SED state regulating all forms of media, freedom of speech was severely restricted in the GDR. The public was acutely aware of the fact that official rhetoric did not always correspond to the reality of real-existing socialism. Conversely, learning to read between the lines became a national hobby. Writers and filmmakers routinely used metaphors and creative wording with double meanings to reach a public that knew how to decipher coded critiques of social conditions. As a product of this society, Alex understands how to maneuver through the minefield of sights and sounds. The power of the state to deceive its citizens by recording events through a restricted lens is thus not without its limitations. In the autumn of 1989 Alex exposes the GDR as a Potemkin village. Archival footage shows Honecker and Gorbachev presiding over a military parade to commemorate the fortieth anniversary of the GDR. In a voice-over Alex comments ironically that "a gigantic gun club was giving its final performance."[114] Even in the past, without the benefit of knowing how history will turn out, Alex sees through the public show to its rotten core. When told that his mother has been invited to the evening's celebrations in the Palace of the Republic, he bitingly remarks: "They'll all be standing around celebrating themselves, all the old geezers."[115]

Just as the communist block was notorious for airbrushing dissenters out of the picture and manipulating collective memory, Alex begins to use the media to create a simulacrum of reality capable of deceiving his mother. His fictional *Aktuelle Kamera* news reports are hilarious attempts to shelter his mother from the truth, as for example when he tries to justify the Coke sign outside her window. Masquerading as a reporter in their home-made newscasts, Dennis announces that international courts have finally settled a patent dispute verifying that Coke was originally a GDR recipe stolen by the West. But Alex's growing obsession with creating an alternate reality starts to be more about his own insecurities than about his mother's health, and his tactics begin to resemble those of the state "protecting" its citizens against Western propaganda. In recognition of the malleability of historical truth, he concedes: "Truth is a dubious affair."[116] Alex's rewriting of history to explain a present that intrudes upon his mother's waking dream leads him to follow an agenda remarkably similar to that of the former GDR apparatchik. He uses the media to suit his own agenda, mobilizing everyone he can to play act for the good of the mother(land). Yet in this humorous and often compelling drama, where the family is a synecdoche for the nation, it is out of love for his mother and her ideals that Alex looks to the stars and imagines a past he can be proud of. Alex creates a what-if scenario that reflects a willful lie and a deep-rooted wish, a maneuver that film scholar Roger Hillman has fittingly termed "history in the subjunctive mood."[117] As a counter to the historical amnesia represented by his mother, Alex writes the history he would have liked to experience and argues that this shared fiction is the most satisfying and the most authentic foundation for the united German nation.

The tangle of lies is never one-sided, and individual memory conveyed as family history is no more reliable than national recall via the media. Christiane Kerner lied about her husband's *Republikflucht*, not merely to the Stasi but to her own children. Her devotion to the GDR, what Alex calls her marriage to the socialist fatherland, is thus suspect as a survival technique conceived as much out of desperation as out of conviction. While she is seen as a truth-teller, writing poignant and witty letters complaining about shoddy products, giving voice to the powerless, she is imprisoned by her own mendacity. Trying to live with the deception that her husband's flight to the West was abandonment for another woman rather than a politically motivated decision is unbearable and ultimately results in her first, self-induced, coma in a psychiatric hospital. Christiane's carefully constructed self-image as a committed socialist earned her "the fatherland's Order of Merit in Gold and appreciation for extraordinary service in the construction and development of a socialist social order."[118] This mask, however, crumbles when she witnesses a public display of police brutality. She can no longer maintain the pretense, and the trauma of acknowledging state oppression sends her into her second, life-threatening, coma. A year later at the family's dacha Christiane finally tells the truth. She knew all along that Robert was defecting, and she did not have the courage to endure the likely repercussions of trying to emigrate. She feared that if she applied for an exit visa the state would take away her children. So she lied to them and to herself. She confesses to Alex and Ariane: "I didn't go. That was the biggest mistake of my life. I know that now. I, I lied to you. Please forgive me."[119] This painful revelation shifts the guilt for the family's breakup from the absent father to a deceitful, frightened mother. It also requires a reevaluation of the relationship between the individual and the state, because if Christiane's zeal was partially a survival tactic, how much of her support for socialism as a model citizen lent respectability to a corrupt, oppressive state? The perennial question of whether one can live a good life in a bad system is now flavored by regret, since she admits that she lived a public life that was untrue to her personal desires.

Is Christiane's bedroom a museum to safeguard a precious and fragile history or a prison cell to isolate and contain dangerous memories capable of destroying the present? This dichotomy is at the core of the debate regarding the *Wende*. The inexorable 79 square meters of the GDR surviving in a historical void forces viewers to see the absence and consider a meaningful and coherent explanation — for as Benedict Anderson maintains: "All profound changes in consciousness, by their very nature, bring with them characteristic amnesias. Out of such oblivions, in specific historical circumstances, spring narratives."[120] In order to reinterpret the contested territory of GDR history, *Good Bye, Lenin!* uses the tropes of amnesia and absence to provide the necessary distance and empty space where imagination can freely conceive another version of the past. Learning to forget, as Friedrich Nietzsche has reasoned, is just as important as learning to remember, because:

There is a degree of sleeplessness, of rumination, of the historical sense, which is harmful and ultimately fatal to the living thing, whether this living thing be a man or a people or a culture. To determine this degree, and therewith the boundary at which the past has to be forgotten if it is not to become the gravedigger of the present, one would have to know exactly how great the *plastic power* of a man, a people, a culture is; I mean by plastic power the capacity to develop out of oneself in one's own way, to transform and incorporate into oneself what is past and foreign, to heal wounds, to replace what has been lost, to recreate broken moulds.[121]

Amnesia, the inability to remember, is directly linked to amnesty, and if one is ever to heal from past traumas one must learn to forgive and forget. While Christiane proves too weak to adapt, Alex refuses to let the past be, in Nietzschean terms, "the gravedigger of the present." He willfully forgets the past as he remembers it and invents his own version of history to suit his present needs. Using fantasy to create the type of perfect world both he and his mother desire, Alex taps into the plastic power necessary to transform what has been lost into something he wants to believe is real.

Christiane's amnesia allows Alex that distance to imagine a different master narrative for Germany. In his hands, the peaceful revolution is literally a remake, a cinematic reconstruction of one of recent history's most memorable newscasts: the fall of the Wall on 9 November 1989. The throngs climbing up on the Berlin Wall are no longer the downtrodden Easterners freeing themselves from a repressive totalitarian regime. They are now asylum-seeking Westerners who are fed up with the rise of neo-Nazi parties, finally recognize their hollow existence in a consumer-driven market economy, and yearn for socialist ideals. Alex remakes history so that the *Wende* is actually the triumph of Communism over capitalism. For Alex, this fictionalized version of history is more real than anything that transpired in reality, because it records the unrealized dreams of a future that never arrived. And in this sense *Good Bye, Lenin!* participates in reflective nostalgia, for while it sanctions the desire to retrieve the irretrievable, it acknowledges the impossibility of a homecoming to an intact past. The cost of recovery is high, for while Alex is able to reclaim his absent father, it is only at the cost of his mother, since Christiane's impending death activates Robert's return home. Moreover, Alex must accept the revelation that his mother deceived him, so that his ideal image of her as selflessly dedicated to her children and the socialist fatherland has serious cracks in it.

But the film's final irony is lost on Alex. He professes his mother's undying belief in socialism and the GDR: "The country my mother left was a country she believed in. And that we let survive until her last breath. A country that in reality never existed like this." He maintains: "My mother outlived the GDR by exactly three days. I think it was right that she never learned the truth. She died happy."[122] His contention is ironic, since his mother did not die in ignorance. Lara told Christiane the truth so that she could recognize the final "newscast" on the opening of the Wall as a "loving lie" Alex tells to himself as much as to her. The text he writes for his childhood hero — who may or may not be a simple taxi driver with a remarkable resemblance to the cosmonaut — is accompanied by archival footage that puts a new spin on a familiar story. New First Secretary Sigmund Jähn delivers a compelling, if unlikely, self-critique of the GDR: "We know that our country is not perfect. But what we believe in has inspired people around the world time and again. Perhaps at times we have lost sight of our goals, but we have rethought things. Socialism does not mean walling yourself in. Socialism means to approach others, to live with others. Not just to dream about a better world but to make it come true."[123] Casting a knowing glance at her starry-eyed son, Christiane lets him believe his fictional version of history because it helps him cope with an unappealing present.

Good Bye, Lenin! is the most successful unification film made to date, garnering both popular and critical acclaim. But what exactly makes it a hit? Beyond an appealing cast, evocative music, and slick production values, the tragi-comedy genre offers the audience an emotional roller coaster with many points of identification to frail and flawed yet endearing human beings. GDR history framed as a family drama personalizes the story in readily recognizable and ever popular formulas. But what sets *Good Bye, Lenin!* apart from recent fare is that it criticizes both sides of the political spectrum, taking equal aim at the crushing effect of the communist state and the excesses of capitalist consumer paradise.[124] Whereas the GDR is depicted as a repressive state (for example, the Stasi visit to the Kerner home, the brutal arrest of demonstrators, and the sabotage of Christiane's career for being overzealous), the West is presented as suffering from *affluenza*, the widespread disease of overconsumption, exhaustion, and indebtedness caused by the relentless pursuit of the capitalist dream.[125] The most chilling line of the film must certainly be college dropout Ariane's deadpan refrain: "Thank you for choosing Burger King."[126] The colonization of the East, so poignantly depicted in "Wessi" Rainer's fascination with Eastern (read Middle Eastern!) dance, the exotic other ("Ossi" Ariane dressed as a belly dancer), and even Rainer's home tanning salon to darken his colonial skin, must surely resonate with viewers who find the reality of today's Western capitalism at least as disturbing as that of yesterday's Eastern Communism. Christiane's disorientation as she sees Lenin flying through the heavens and riding off into the sunset is not only palpable; it is contagious. What happened to the dream, the noble goal of creating a more just and egalitarian state on German soil?

Good Bye, Lenin!'s success in Germany can be attributed in part to its topicality. Becker's film delves into nostalgia and amnesia as inherent components in the development of nationhood, that shared sense of identity found in a common history and culture, and it suggests alternative national narratives. It may be ironic that at a time when the nation-state seems to be losing much of its validity, the "belated German nation" produces a blockbuster film imagining the recovery of a long-lost national unity.[127] However, national identity is far from dead; it is a vital factor for ordinary people all over the world, and this film defines nation in largely positive terms.[128] Moreover, idealism is essential to the future of any nation; there has to be a value system that envisions what that nation wants to become as much as what it is.

The conclusion of *Good Bye, Lenin!*, while characterized by deep loss, still has a glimmer of hope that may account for its universal appeal. Faced with an existential crisis, Alex does not turn to his real father but to his idealized father image, the cosmonaut Sigmund Jähn. Even after the death of the GDR, the idealism represented in the dream of reaching the stars has such resilience that it simply refuses to end up in the dustbin of history. *Good Bye, Lenin!* ends with a return to the faded archival images and the grainy, overexposed home movies that opened the film. Is it a coincidence that the last thing we see is Christiane as she sets the automatic timer, directs the last shot, and assembles a narrative that features a loving parent celebrating fantasy surrounded by her happy children looking up to her in adoration? What nation would not want to see itself in this picture of childlike wonder, safety, and imaginative play? While it may not be a viable political strategy in itself, imagination and the remembrance of ideals are essential to the construction of national identity.

In 2003 *Good Bye, Lenin!* became a prominent topic for film critics, cultural observers, and even politicians. On the evening of 3 April 2003 Becker's film reached a milestone in the annals of German politics. For the first time in history, members of the Bundestag went together to the movies. On the invitation of Minister of Culture Christina Weiss, over 200 members of parliament representing all the political parties collectively watched *Good Bye, Lenin!* at the International Kino in the Karl-Marx-Allee, which had been the premiere cinema in the former GDR. This ceremonial act was staged and paid for by X Film Creative Pool to promote its own production, but also to encourage lawmakers to provide more extensive subsidies to the German film industry.

Writing for *Neues Deutschland*, the former SED party newspaper, Gunnar Decker maintained: "Becker's film is an offering of reconciliation to the Germans — and they understand it as such. Because one must acknowledge the GDR, if one wants to bury it properly. . . . *Good Bye, Lenin!* is also a sad film. It shows inescapable death and departure. But it is never hopeless, never cynical or indifferent. Therein lies its poetic magic."[129] In an article for *Tagesspiegel* Kerstin Decker suggested that a true unification was finally taking place in the cinema thirteen years after the political reality: "*Good Bye, Lenin!* is in fact a funerary film for the GDR. And that is important. Because no one has buried it yet, there was no farewell, it was suddenly just gone like the Spreewald pickles in Alexander's grocery store, from one day to the next. The cinema is making up for something for which there was no time in reality."[130] Decker describes, perhaps better than any other contemporary critic, how this film participates in a discourse of recovery — not the history of a perfect state but the memory of a communal hope that a better world was possible. She argues that this film is socially relevant because it "is the reconciliatory laying to rest of the utopia of the GDR — and this utopia was in a certain sense more real than its laughable, military, petty bourgeois, obdurate reality. To be sure, utopia was hard to grasp, but it was in the books we read, in a lot of music, in many films — and eventually it had a definite political name: Gorbachev. The utopia of the GDR has been the great undead of the last thirteen years."[131] Finally laying to rest the utopian dreams of the GDR is important, because it restores dignity to the people who lived decent lives there. Decker concludes: "After the *Wende* we ex-GDR citizens became ugly. A people made up of lily-livered hypocrites crippled by dictatorship. Regardless of what mirror we looked in, it was always the same face. And now this film shows a different one, in focus. It is this recognition of a truth that enchants people and makes them applaud."[132] Decker's remarks are indicative of how *Good Bye, Lenin!* can fulfill the emotional needs of different viewers in equally appealing ways. It offers validation for those who seek legitimization that people lived worthy lives in the GDR and a projection screen for those who desire the preservation of a utopian socialist agenda. Ending with a death and an imminent birth, the film reassures us that life goes on, and with the return of the father, it implies that some lost things can be recovered. Most important, the film's self-reflective irony encourages spectators to view the world from dual perspectives at the same time, mourning the passing of an era in which a perfectible world was believed to be achievable, while simultaneously celebrating the fantasy that universal ideals survive and can come true.

Remembering, Forgetting, and Forgiveness

The trauma of being held against one's will, punished with confinement for trying to escape, and forced to choose between self-preservation and injury to others results in amnesia. Recovering traumatic memories involves a process that largely exonerates the individual and implicates the system. This scenario is the basic plotline for the films under discussion, and it also forms the general coordinates for assigning guilt in an emplotment of GDR history. *Berlin Is in Germany, Führer Ex*, and *Good Bye, Lenin!* employ different generic conventions and are set apart by very different tones. However, they all use tropes of amnesia and imprisonment to expose the inherent malevolence of a political regime that kept its citizens under lock and key behind a wall. In each case, a memory lapse is predicated on a violent history that is in many ways simply incomprehensible. Characters are caught in circumstances beyond their control, and their initial efforts to free themselves result in physical violence, psychological pain, and incarceration. Martin, Heiko, Tommy, Christiane, and Robert plan to flee the GDR illegally, and this act of defiance sets events in motion. Denied the right to self-determination and freedom of movement, Martin lashes out against the system's representative, Heiko and Tommy turn aggression inward through self-mutilation, and Christiane falls into a catatonic state. In their failed attempts to defect, they are caught in a web of violence — as victims who turn into perpetrators of aggression, control, and forms of deceit that mimic the methods used by the state they rejected.

Recovering memory, both personal and collective, takes different forms in each film, but it is never complete or fully transparent. Martin tries out three possible memoryscapes for his personal history, and while there is no certainty as to which version is true, the one that posits his being involved in an accidental killing is given the greatest credence. Martin's strategy for dealing with a collective past is simply to forget it — forget the old names for places and forget the state's hold over him, so that he can have a clean slate. In contrast to Martin, Christiane's personal memory work is much more painful, because she attributes volition to her actions, accepting that she made a mistake and asking for forgiveness. Despite her son's best efforts, Christiane regains collective memory of the historical changes in 1989–90, but in a manner obscured from the audience. Lara tells her the truth behind a glass door that allows the viewer to see but not hear her moment of recovery. Heiko is never shown contemplating his past with any great deliberation. His transformation in prison from a punk to a reluctant neo-Nazi follower is depicted as a practical choice based on imminent threats. The subsequent amnesic states encompassing both his conversion to a neo-Nazi zealot and his return to normalcy are left unexplored. The lack of reflection about personal responsibility and the psychological shifts that occur as Heiko changes location imply that guilt lies in the environment, outside the individual.

Martin and Heiko learn to separate the past from the present, effectively breaking the ties that bind them to the GDR. At the end of *Berlin Is in Germany* and *Führer Ex* the protagonists are shown moving on, both literally and figuratively. As the recurring melody composed by Florian Appl plays in the background, Martin leaves the jailhouse unaccompanied and shuts the door, closing a chapter in his life. He walks toward the camera, which follows him from feet to head as he moves forward. The camera pulls back in a smooth crane shot to reveal Martin walking alone on an empty street. The perspective is limited, showing the ever-smaller figure of Martin walking down the middle of a narrow street, with only the fenced-off concrete sidewalks visible. Even as the camera slowly pulls up higher, exposing the first floors of tall buildings lining the street, the horizon is obscured by trees and more buildings in the distance. A taxi moves into the frame from behind Martin and stops so that he can get in. The Latin beats of the band Sonido Tres playing "El pobre tipo" (Poor Guy) are superimposed on the main melody and eventually take over. This song about a poor guy everyone disparages, who cannot change the past and must put it behind him, epitomizes Martin's approach. Since the song is associated with the Cuban taxi driver Enrique, it reassures the audience that his friend is driving Martin into his future, a world whose horizon is greater than the one the viewer is left with.

In much the same way as Martin is saved from the confines of prison and his past, Heiko experiences salvation through his friend's sacrificial death. The neo-Nazi Heiko with his slicked-back, perfectly parted hair, and black jacket cradles Tommy's dead body, leans back against the wall, and screams "no" as the overblown melodramatic violin music swells. In a sweeping crane shot, the camera rises from Tommy's corpse past the nearly comatose Heiko over the rooftop into the pitch-black sky. It is as if Tommy's spirit were ascending into heaven, thereby freeing his friend from the clutches of the neo-Nazis. In a blunt cut, the last scene features Heiko dressed in a plaid red shirt, his hair fashionably unruly, looking like any normal young man as he walks down the street toward the camera. The slightly blurred medium shot of his undulating body as he moves through a crowd is briefly brought into focus just as the music transitions to MIA's punk song "Alles neu." Heiko, now shown in a close-up, is effectively moving forward devoid of a social context. The film ends in a freeze-frame that captures half his face, and the credits roll by as MIA's song promises "alles wird wie neu sein" (everything will be like new). Finally free from both the GDR and right-wing extremism, he is poised to start a new life unencumbered by the past.

Good Bye, Lenin! has a dual ending that highlights conflicting desires and ambivalence toward the past. The first ending takes place on the rooftop where Alex, his family, and friends have gathered to take their leave of Christiane and the GDR. In a home-made rocket prominently bearing the GDR national emblem, Alex sends his mother's ashes up into the heavens, an act that defies the legal statutes of both the former GDR and the FRG. This ambivalent gesture, mourning the passing of the GDR and simultaneously resisting its authority, characterizes much of the film's stance. Following archival footage of Sigmund Jähn in his space capsule and faded images of bygone days in Berlin that appear like snapshots from memory, Christiane and a group of children, including Alex and Ariane, appear in an old home movie. In a voice-over, Alex comments that his mother believed in his fictional construct and that the GDR remains "a country that in my memory will always be associated with my mother."[133] Conflating the memory of his beloved mother with the flawed GDR, Alex suggests that they both failed to live up to some expectations but are deserving of respect and devotion. In the film's second ending, Christiane stands behind a camera, sets the automatic timer, and directs the last shot (paradoxically captured by some unseen camera). *Good Bye, Lenin!* concludes with Christiane in the role of director-star of a collective fantasy and Alex in the role of adoring son, an image that stops in a freeze frame. Unlike Martin and Heiko, Alex does not completely sever his ties to his mother and the GDR and is not shown moving on into the future. For Alex, the past remains like a photograph, a sentimental, admittedly staged image frozen in time that can summon up the memory of his wishful dreams.

The main characters are sympathetic individuals who become victims of a totalitarian regime that leaves them little choice but to inflict pain on themselves and others. In the end, Martin, Heiko, and Christiane are absolved of their guilt. Martin receives a formal pardon, Heiko obtains a new lease on life, and Christiane's family forgives her and grants her final wish. For these protagonists, renunciation of the GDR resulted in a ruptured personal history. Out of sync with the rest of the East German populace, their amnesia and memory work draw attention to the broader social transformations that have taken place and the things that have been forgotten. As the titles of all three films indicate, these stories are not just about individuals but also about the nation and its ruptured collective history. *Berlin Is in Germany, Führer Ex,* and *Good Bye, Lenin!* suggest these ruptures can be healed. Martin and Heiko go forward into an unknown but promising future, and Alex mourns the death of his mother and the GDR in a way that allows him to retain positive memories while conceding their mistakes and indisputable passing. *Berlin Is in Germany* and *Führer Ex* have no nostalgia for the past. They depict the GDR as a totalitarian state with nothing worth remembering except personal relationships. If anything, these two films can be seen as countering the *Ostalgie* wave that concentrates on pleasant memories and obscures the equally important memory of political dissent and dissatisfaction. Stöhr's and Bonengel's films refocus attention on the violence committed by the SED regime against the entire populace by refusing them the basic right to leave. Guilt lies squarely with the system that was intrinsically unjust. *Good Bye, Lenin!* is much more sympathetic to the GDR as a failed experiment, yet it too acknowledges the existence of political oppression and the high cost paid by the entire family for the father's defection.

All three films present the GDR as a prison state and populate it with individuals who wanted out and tried to escape. These figures of active resistance to totalitarianism provide the models of positive collective identity and a shared past necessary to build a common future. The protagonists possess such sympathetic and representative qualities that their personal stories can easily be read as a parable for the nation. In this national narrative, composed of nearly equal parts fact and fiction, a variety of good people resisted, were punished by a pernicious government, but eventually triumphed to free themselves and topple the regime. Amnesia and anamnesis become important components in this narrative, articulating dissatisfaction with the past and the present, acknowledging absence, and addressing unresolved issues of guilt. These motion pictures stress the value of mourning, letting go of the past, acknowledging its usefulness, blemishes, and irretrievability.

Notes

[1] In the aftermath of the Peloponnesian War and the revolt against the Thirty Tyrants, the ancient Greeks conceived of amnesty as a means to eradicate civil strife among the survivors. The amnesty they proposed mandated a forgetting of past offences so comprehensive that the mere mention of earlier wrongs resulted in the death penalty. See Faustin Z. Ntoubandi, *Amnesty for Crimes against Humanity under International Law* (Leiden, The Netherlands: Martinus Nijhoff Publishers, 2007), 15–16.

[2] East Germans initially discarded GDR consumer products after the currency reform of 1990 and eventually returned to familiar Eastern products in the course of the nineties. See Ina Merkel, "From Stigma to Cult: Changing Meanings in East German Consumer Culture," in *The Making of the Consumer: Knowledge, Power and Identity in the Modern World*, ed. Frank Trentmann (Oxford: Berg, 2006), 257.

[3] Some 20,000 managers and aides transferred from the old federal states to the new ones to oversee the development of political parties after 1990. See Jennifer A. Yoder, *From East Germans to Germans? The New Postcommunist Elites* (Durham: Duke UP, 1999), 20. Nearly three-fourths of academics in the GDR lost their positions at universities, with the result that only 104 of the 1,878 professors employed in the new federal states hailed from the former GDR. See Paul Cooke, *Representing East Germany since Unification: From Colonization to Nostalgia* (Oxford: Berg, 2005), 3.

[4] Historian Stefan Wolle asserts: "Many former GDR citizens feel deeply wounded by the handling of history. They see their own biographies put into doubt by the radical critique of GDR reality. For years or even decades they worked for this state without taking advantage of privileges. Many of them believed with their whole heart in the perfecting of socialism. Today they feel betrayed and disappointed." The German original: "Doch viele ehemalige DDR-Bürger fühlen sich durch den Umgang mit der Geschichte tief verletzt. Sie sehen durch die radikale Kritik an der DDR-Realität ihre eigene Biographie in Zweifel gezogen. Jahre oder sogar Jahrzehnte haben sie für diesen Staat gearbeitet, ohne dafür Privilegien in Anspruch zu nehmen. Manche von ihnen haben ehrlichen Herzens an eine Verbesserung des Sozialismus geglaubt. Heute fühlen sie sich betrogen und

enttäuscht." Stefan Wolle, *Die heile Welt der Diktatur: Alltag und Herrschaft in der DDR, 1971–1989*, 2nd ed. (Munich: Econ Ullstein, 2001), 21.

[5] The introductory remarks are unpaginated. The dual-language text includes the same passage in German: "Um diesen Vorgang zu dokumentieren, suchte ich Orte auf, von denen Symbole der DDR-Geschichte entfernt worden sind. Ich bat Passanten und Anwohner, die Gegenstände zu beschreiben, die einst diese leeren Stellen füllten. Ich fotografierte die Abwesenheit und ersetzte die fehlenden Monumente durch die Erinnerung an sie." Sophie Calle, *The Detachment / Die Entfernung* (Berlin: G + B Art International, 1996), n.p.

[6] Maurice Halbwachs, *The Collective Memory*, trans. Francis J. Ditter and Vida Yazdi Ditter (New York: Harper & Row, 1980), 140.

[7] Halbwachs, *Collective Memory*, 131.

[8] Calle, *The Detachment*, 26–27. "Ein Wappen war da drin. In dem Kreis waren eine Gerstenähre, ein Hammer und ein Zirkel, aus edlem Material gemacht, Kupfer glaube ich. Ich fand das ziemlich gräßlich * Na klar war das schön! Man konnte darin sehen, was man jetzt in der neuen Gesellschaftsform nicht mehr sieht. Wie Sie sehen, steht das sowieso leer * . . . Es war sehr ausgewogen. Es war logisch. Es war deutsch. Wir haben es so oft gesehen, daß wir es nicht mehr in Frage stellten. Es sah ziemlich gut aus. Es hat uns nicht gestört * . . . Der leere Rahmen ist jetzt ein Verweis auf die gesamte Situation. Ich finde nicht, daß man immer alles erhalten und rekonstruieren muß. Man kann die Dinge auch einfach belassen, wie sie sind. Als Spuren. Statt nur noch Coca-Cola Reklame aufzuhängen * Da ist ein Widerstand in diesem Loch. In meinem Kopf ist es ja noch da. Ich kann es dort sehen, wie einen Geist * Das war ein Zirkel. Zirkel ziehen Kreise. Die vollkommene Form. Die Werkzeuge der Utopie sind nun verschwunden. Was bleibt, ist die Utopie, aber eine leere. Man sieht nur die Leere." Calle, *Entfernung*, 26–27. The asterisks separate comments from different speakers.

[9] Calle, *The Detachment*, 11. "Die ganze Situation gibt dir das Gefühl, daß die Heimat umgebaut wird. Das Problem ist, daß nun Leute über den ganzen Bau und das Klima in der Stadt entscheiden, die vorher nicht hier gelebt haben. Es geht doch darum, daß die Wessies uns gar nichts lassen wollen." Calle, *Die Entfernung*, 11–12.

[10] See for example, *Stalinallee: Ein Spiel auf Ehre und Gewissen: Für 2–6 Spieler* (Berlin: Karl-Marx-Buchhandlung Kundel & Lenzner, 1999); *DDR Ferner Osten: Würfelrallye und Ratespiel mit "Ach, Ja!" Effekt*. Autorenkollektiv Eike Bochmanny und Peter Zehrt (Berlin: Inkognito, no date); Jana Hensel, *Zonenkinder* (Reinbek bei Hamburg: Rowohlt, 2002); *Das dicke DDR Buch* (Berlin: Eulenspiegel, 2002); and Claudia Rusch, *Meine freie deutsche Jugend* (Frankfurt am Main: Fischer, 2003).

[11] The television shows included *Die Ostalgie-Show* (ZDF, 17 Aug.), *Ein Kessel DDR* (MDR, 22 Aug.), *Meyer & Schulz — die ultimative Ost-Show* (SAT. 1, 23 and 30 Aug.), and *Die DDR Show — von Ampelmann bis zum Zentralkomitee* (RTL, 4 episodes starting 3 Sept.). Novelist Alexander Osang argued that GDR history told by means of its consumer products and celebrity biographies obscures the human dimension of material culture, resulting in the dehumanization of Easterners, because "the borders between East guest and East product are

blurred" (Die Grenzen zwischen Ostgast and Ostprodukt sind fließend). Alexander Osang, "Zu Gast im Party-Staat," *Der Spiegel*, 8 Sept. 2003, 212. Peter Hoff characterizes this phenomenon as a further indication of Western colonization of the East: "It was a West show about the exotic East" (Es war halt eine West-Show über den exotischen Osten). Peter Hoff, "Der ultimative Ost-Zoo: Nicht nur ein Fernsehabend im Zeichen der (N)Ostalgie," *Neues Deutschland*, 25 Aug. 2003.

[12] For various interpretations of the GDR, see Mary Fulbrook, *Anatomy of a Dictatorship: Inside the GDR, 1949–1989* (Oxford: Oxford UP, 1995); Klaus Schroeder, *Der SED-Staat: Partei, Staat und Gesellschaft, 1949–1990* (Munich: Carl Hanser, 1998); and Konrad H. Jarausch, *Dictatorship as Experience: Towards a Socio-Cultural History of the GDR* (New York: Berghahn, 1999).

[13] See Muriel Cormican, "Thomas Brussig's Ostalgie in Print and on Celluloid," in *Processes of Transposition: German Literature and Film*, ed. Christiane Schönfeld and Hermann Rasche, Amsterdamer Beiträge zur neueren Germanistik 63 (Amsterdam: Rodopi, 2007), 251–68.

[14] Daphne Berdahl, "'(N)Ostalgie' for the Present: Memory, Longing, and East German Things," *Ethnos: Journal of Anthropology* 64, no. 2 (1999): 205.

[15] Berdahl, "(N)Ostalgie for the Present," 203.

[16] Merkel writes, "daß sich selbst ein retrospektiv verklärender Blick nicht als Sehnsucht nach dem vergangenen System verstanden wissen will, sondern nach nicht mehr wiederholbaren Alltagserfahrungen, nach verloren gegangenen Geschmäckern, Farben und Formen." Ina Merkel, *Utopie und Bedürfnis: Die Geschichte der Konsumkultur in der DDR* (Cologne: Böhlau, 1999), 401. It is worth noting that Ina Merkel was a founding member of the Independent Women's Union and a participant in the historic Round Table discussions during the *Wende*. Das Unabhängige Frauenverband (UVF) was officially founded on 3 December 1989 and a congress was held on 17 February 1990 to establish the organization's statutes and program. For original documents, including flyers, protocols, and interviews, see the website DDR 1989/90 Documente, http://www.ddr89.de.

[17] "Das Ende der DDR kam fast über Nacht. Nach der Währungsunion hatte sich die Produktkultur schlagartig verändert. Die Ereignisse überschlugen sich und die Zeit raste dahin. Es fehlte eine Phase der Besinnung, der Trauer und des Abschieds, die jetzt teilweise nachgeholt wird. Die noch vorhandenen Gegenstände sichern im privaten Bereich über die ganzen stattgehabten Umbrüche hinweg eine gewisse Kontinuität und bieten Rückzugs- und Besinnungsräume." Merkel, *Utopie und Bedürfnis*, 401.

[18] Andreas Huyssen, "After the Wall: The Failure of German Intellectuals [1991]," in *Twilight Memories: Marking Time in a Culture of Amnesia* (New York: Routledge, 1995), 43.

[19] See for example Paul Cooke, *Representing East Germany since Unification*, 105 and 160. Cooke provides convincing analyses of Oskar Roehler's *Die Unberührbare* (The untouchable woman, English title: *No Place to Go*, 2000) and Becker's *Good Bye, Lenin!* as examples of Westalgie. See also Andrew Plowman, "Westalgie? Nostalgia for the 'Old' Federal Republic in Recent German Prose," *Seminar: A Journal of Germanic Studies* 40, no. 3 (2004): 249–61; Julia Hell and Johannes von Moltke, "Unification Effects: Imaginary Landscapes of the Berlin Republic,"

Germanic Review 80, no. 1 (2005): 74–95; and Barbara Mennel, "Political Nostalgia and Local Memory: The Kreuzberg of the 1980s in Contemporary German Film," *Germanic Review* 82, no. 1 (2007): 54–77.

[20] The literature on *Ostalgie* is extensive, but the following selection offers important insights: Claudia Sadowski-Smith, "Ostalgie: Revaluing the Past, Regressions into the Future," *GDR Bulletin* 25 (1998): 1–6; Norbert Kapferer, "'Nostalgia' in Germany's New Federal States as a Political and Cultural Phenomenon of the Transformation Process," in *Political Thought and German Reunification: The New German Ideology*, ed. Howard Williams, Colin Wight, and Norbert Kapferer (New York: St. Martin's, 2000), 28–40; Martin Blum, "Remaking the East German Past: Ostalgie, Identity, and Material Culture," *Journal of Popular Culture* 34, no. 3 (2000): 229–53; and Anna Saunders, "Normalizing the Past: East German Culture and Ostalgie," in Taberner and Cooke, *German Culture, Politics, and Literature into the Twenty-First Century*, 89–103.

[21] Svetlana Boym, *The Future of Nostalgia* (New York: Basic Books, 2001), 41. Unfortunate typos like "Karl Liebknecht had made a speech here [at the Berlin castle] proclaiming a German Socialist Republic on November 9, 1919 (sic)" (183) and "On October 7, 1990 (sic) the palace held an official celebration of the 50th (sic) anniversary of the foundation of the GDR just at the time when Easterners were escaping en masse via Czechoslovakia and Hungary" (188) mar Boym's interesting study of post-Wall Berlin. Moreover, they make the reader acutely aware of the unreliability of memory.

[22] The term anamnesis originates from Greek (*anamimneskein*) and refers to the process of remembering. It is commonly used by medical professionals to refer to a patient's personal medical history and is used as a diagnostic tool.

[23] Jacques Derrida observes that trauma survives in a discursive positioning that demands attention and persists until remembered and addressed: "When the discourse *holds* in some way, it is at once because it has been opened up on the basis of some traumatizing event, by an upsetting question that doesn't let one rest, that no longer lets one sleep, and because it nevertheless resists the destruction begun by this traumatism." Jacques Derrida, *Points: Interviews, 1974–1994*, ed. Elisabeth Weber, trans. Peggy Kamuf & Others (Stanford, CA: Stanford UP, 1995), 381.

[24] Derrida, *Points*, 383.

[25] "Amnesia Patients Stuck in Present," *BBC News*, 15 Jan. 2007, http://news.bbc.co.uk/go/pr/fr/-/2/hi/health/6263421.stm.

[26] Demis Hassabis, Dharshan Kumaran, Seralynne D. Vann, and Elanor A. Maquire, "Patients with Hippocampal Amnesia Cannot Imagine New Experiences," *PNAS* 104, no. 5 (2007): 1726.

[27] Michael Schindhelm coined the term *Verschwindigkeit* (verschwinden = to disappear, Geschwindigkeit = speed) to describe the speed with which things were disappearing after 1989. Schindhelm writes: "Disappearance-velocity, as one could describe the phenomenon of these losses, produces nostalgia. It is a growing protest reaction based on the asymmetry of time. On the one side, it feeds an incessant longing for a lost or rather stripped, irrevocable past and on the other side skepticism about a terroristic future that decrees

life be continuous change. . . . Alienation from the social environment leads to alienation from time." The German original: "Verschwindigkeit, so könnte man das Phänomen dieser Verluste beschreiben, produziert Nostalgie. Sie ist eine aus der Asymmetrie der Zeit aufkeimende Protestregung und nährt einerseits eine ins Nichts unwiderruflich verlorener beziehungsweise abgestreifter Vergangenheit gehende Sehnsucht und andererseits die Skepsis gegenüber einer terroristischen und das Leben als ständige Veränderung dekretierenden Zukunft. . . . Die Entfremdung von der sozialen Umwelt führt auch zur Entfremdung von der Zeit." Michael Schindhelm, "Der Terror der Zeit: Warum die Nostalgie um sich greift — in Ost wie in West," *Die Zeit*, 31 Oct. 2001.

[28] Konrad Jarausch and Volker Gransow, *Uniting Germany: Documents and Debates, 1944–1993* (Oxford: Berghahn, 1994), 190.

[29] Georgi Dimitroff defined fascism as the "offene terroristische Diktatur der reaktionären, am meisten chauvinistischen, am meisten imperialistischen Elemente des Finanzkapitals." Quoted in Georg Klaus and Manfred Buhr, *Philosophisches Wörterbuch*, 2 vols. (Leipzig: VEB Bibliographisches Institut, 1964), 1:363.

[30] David Kaufman, "The Nazi Legacy: Coming to Terms with the Past," in *Modern Germany: Politics, Society and Culture*, ed. Peter James (New York: Routledge, 1998), 126.

[31] See Wolfgang Kühnel, "Hitler's Grandchildren? The Reemergence of a Right-Wing Social Movement in Germany," in *Nation and Race: The Developing Euro-American Racist Subculture*, ed. Jeffrey Kaplan and Tore Bjørgo (Boston: Northeastern UP, 1998), 148–74.

[32] Cooke, *Representing East Germany since Unification*, 28.

[33] John O. Koehler, *Stasi: The Untold Story of the East German Secret Police* (Boulder, CO: Westview, 1999), 8–9. See also A. James McAdams, *Judging the Past in Unified Germany* (Cambridge, UK: Cambridge UP, 2001), 55–87.

[34] The entire area around Hohenschönhausen was cordoned off from the public and literally a blank space on city maps. For a history of the prison, see Peter Erler and Hubertus Knabe, *Der verbotene Stadtteil: Stasi-Sperrbezirk Berlin-Hohenschönhausen*, 2nd ed. (Berlin: Jaron Verlag, 2005). For first-hand accounts by prisoners, see Hubertus Knabe, ed., *Gefangen in Hohenschönhausen: Stasi-Häftlinge berichten* (Berlin: List Ullstein, 2007).

[35] Marc Silberman, "Post-Wall Documentaries: New Images from a New Germany?" *Cinema Journal* 33, no. 2 (1994): 32.

[36] The East Wind series was first conceived in 1997 by then CEO of ORB Hansjürgen Rosenbauer, and production work began in 1999 under the joint direction of Annedore von Donop (ZDF) and Cooky Ziesche (ORB/RBB). East Wind premiered a total of twelve films in 2003, 2004, and 2006 on ZDF and ORB/RBB. On 1 May 2003 ORB and Sender Freies Berlin, SFB, were merged to form Rundfunk Berlin-Brandenburg, RBB (Broadcasting Berlin-Brandenburg). RBB is one of nine stations that form the Arbeitsgemeinschaft der öffentlich-rechtlichen Rundfunkanstalten Deutschland, ARD (Consortium of Broadcasting Institutions of Germany) also known as Das Erste (Channel One). See Lena Bodewein, "In der Zeitmaschine: Mit *Berlin is in Germany* starten ORB und

ZDF die zwölfteilige Ostwind Reihe," *Der Tagesspiegel*, 9 Mar. 2003; Steffen Grimberg, "In einem fremden Land: Mit *Berlin is in Germany* starten ORB und ZDF ihre ambitionierte Filmreihe 'Ostwind,'" *taz*, 9 Mar. 2003; Frank Kaspar, "Entlassen in eine fremde Freiheit: Die außergewöhnliche Filmreihe 'Ostwind' dokumentiert den Wandel nach dem Fall der Mauer: *Berlin is in Germany* (ZDF/ ORB)," *Frankfurter Allgemeine Zeitung*, 8 Mar. 2003; and Helmut Ziegler, "Aus dem Schlamm: ORB und ZDF starten das Projekt Ostwind mit dem Film *Berlin is in Germany*," *Berliner Zeitung*, 9 Mar. 2003.

[37] Statistics are available at the German Federal Film Board (Filmförderungsanstalt, FFA), http://www.ffa.de.

[38] Philipp Bühler claimed: "Dies hier könnte die endgültige Ost-West-Geschichte sein," and Wolfgang Hamdorf suggested that it "gehört zu den menschlich ergreifendsten Filmen über das Zusammenleben bzw. Zusammentreffen von Ost und West, über Abstürze und Umbrüche im neuen Deutschland." See Philipp Bühler, "Wiedergänger von Franz Biberkopf: Eine Parabel über Ost und West und ein sehr guter Film: *Berlin is in Germany* von Hannes Stöhr," *Berliner Zeitung*, 1 Nov. 2001, and Wolfgang Hamdorf, "*Berlin is in Germany*," *Film-Dienst* 22 (23 Oct. 2001): 22.

[39] Paragraph 213 of the GDR penal code outlawed illegal border crossing and carried a penalty of two years' imprisonment for standard cases. Paragraph 214 outlawed disturbance of state and social activities and was usually evoked in reference to unauthorized attempts to emigrate to the FRG. See entries for "Republikflucht" and "Strafrecht" in *DDR Handbuch*, ed. Bundesministerium für innerdeutsche Beziehungen, 2nd rev. ed. (Cologne: Verlag Wissenschaft & Politik, 1979), 908–9 and 1063.

[40] In an interview Stöhr remarked: "Nur einer wie Martin Schulz kann nach Berlin kommen und die Veränderungen der letzten Jahre mit naiven Augen wahrnehmen. Er wirkt auf die Stadt sozusagen wie ein Spiegel, er macht die Veränderungen sichtbar, die wir alle erlebt haben." *Berlin is in Germany*, Presseheft, n.p. n.d.

[41] "Erst kommen die Einheimischen, dann der Giuseppe, dann der Achmed, und zum Schluss da kommt der Zoni" and "Haste nüscht, biste nüscht." Film dialogue. *Berlin is in Germany* [2001], dir. Hannes Stöhr, DVD (Berlin: Absolut Medien, 2003).

[42] David Clarke argues that the collapse of the *GDR* resulted in the symbolic emasculation of East German men like Peter and that after he is released from prison, "Martin's mission during the rest of the film is to regain his masculinity by reestablishing his status as breadwinner, father and husband." David Clarke, "Representations of East German Masculinity in Hannes Stöhr's *Berlin is in Germany* and Andreas Kleinert's *Wege in die Nacht*," *German Life and Letters* 55, no. 4 (2002): 438. See also Owen Evans, "Taking Stock of the *Wende* on Screen: Michael Klier's *Ostkreuz* and Hannes Stöhr's *Berlin is in Germany*," *German as a Foreign Language* 1 (2006): 60–75.

[43] Nick Hodgin maintains, "Whatever the specifics of his desires, it is in Martin's *umlernen* (relearning) that the key to his success lies; mental miscegenation is offered as a guiding principle for success in modern Germany." Nick Hodgin,

"*Berlin is in Germany* and *Good Bye Lenin!* Taking Leave of the GDR?" *Debatte: Review of Contemporary German Affairs* 12, no. 1 (2004): 33.

44 "Allein die Ankündigung, den Bürgern die bisher verwehrten Auslandsreisen zu erlauben, fegte einen Staat aus der Welt." Christoph Hein, "Dritte Welt überall. Ostdeutschland als Avantgarde der Globalisierung: Wo das Kapital flieht, kommt der Nationalismus zurück," *Die Zeit*, 30 Sept. 2004.

45 "Im Osten bist du fit. Du musst bloss die alten Namen vergessen." Some things remain the same: "Left, clutch; middle, brake; right, gas. Like in the East" (Links Kupplung, Mitte Bremse, rechts Gas. Wie im Osten). Film dialogue.

46 Stöhr states: "Die Frage nach dem tatsächlichen Tatverlauf bleibt offen. Wie will ich das beurteilen? Ich persönlich glaube Martins Version vom Unfall, aber ich kann die Frage nicht abschließend beantworten. Vielleicht war es auch anders, und er hat den Hausbuchverwalter vorsätzlich umgebracht, wie es das medizinische Gutachten nahelegt." *Berlin is in Germany*, Presseheft.

47 Schüttauf is "so überzeugend, daß die Wendungen des Drehbuchs, den Helden über eine mehr als gespenstische Rückblende als 'unschuldigen Mörder' darzustellen, der eigentlich 'nur' einen erpresserischen Blockwart im Affekt umgebracht hat, überflüssig erscheinen." Hamdorf, "*Berlin is in Germany*," 22. Kathrin Wesely also describes Schüttauf's performance as so sympathetic that his guilt is secondary: "The question of why he did time is pushed into the background and is not answered until later on." (Die Frage, weshalb er gesessen hat, rückt in den Hintergrund und wird erst viel später beantwortet.) Kathrin Wesely, "Anrührendes Porträt eines Ossies, der nach zehn Jahren Knast in die ihm fremde Welt entlassen wird," *Schwäbisches Tagblatt*, 3 Nov. 2001.

48 Schüttauf played Martin, "mit einer Einfachheit, proletarischen Ungeschlachtheit, Direktheit und zärtlichen Zurückhaltung zugleich" that "Wir erkennen uns im anderen. Dieses Erkennen ist ungefähr das Gegenteil von dem, was man 'Sozialkritik' genannt hat." Kerstin Decker, "Staatsende, letzter Akt: Hannes Stöhrs melancholische Komödie um einen herzensguten Ex-Knacki, *Berlin is in Germany*," *Der Tagesspiegel*, 1 Nov. 2001.

49 "So könnte man *Berlin is in Germany* abhacken als einen der vielen mittelmäßig gemachten Filme, die das selbstgestellte Thema sofort fallen lassen, wenn es anfängt weh zu tun. Filme, die das Wohlgefallen des Kinobesuchers über das stellen, was sie an unangenehmen Dingen zu erzählen haben." Gunnar Decker, "Wege durchs Labyrinth: *Berlin is in Germany* von Hannes Stöhr," *Neues Deutschland*, 1 Nov. 2001.

50 Martin is repeatedly equated with such legendary figures as Simplicissimus, Franz Biberkopf, and Robinson Crusoe. See Bühler, "Wiedergänger von Franz Biberkopf"; Decker, "Staatsende, letzter Akt"; Thomas Winkler, "Leise Überraschungen: Ein bisschen staunend und ein bisschen zurückgelehnt; In Hannes Stöhrs Film *Berlin is in Germany* spielt Jörg Schüttauf einen DDR-Bürger, der zehn Jahre nach dem Fall der Mauer aus dem Gefängnis entlassen wird," *taz*, 31 Oct. 2001; Eberhard von Elterlein, "*Berlin is in Germany*: Du sollst du selbst bleiben," *Die Welt*, 1 Nov. 2001; and Helge Hopp, "Die Heimat kann sehr kalt sein: Mit *Berlin is in Germany* starten ZDF und ORB ihre Filmreihe 'Ostwind,'" *Die Welt am Sonntag*, 9 Mar. 2003.

[51] Statistics are available at http://www.ffa.de.

[52] Since 2002 Bonengel has worked exclusively in television directing episodes of the forensic drama *R.I.S. — Die Sprache der Toten* (Sat. 1) and telenovellas *Schmetterlinge im Bauch* (Sat. 1), *Verliebt in Berlin — Annas Rückkehr* (Sat. 1), and *Anna und die Liebe* (Sat. 1).

[53] A thirty-minute segment of *Beruf Neonazi* was broadcast in a Spiegel TV documentary on the Vox television channel on 19 February 1994. David Bathrick provides an exhaustive review of the controversies surrounding this film and concludes that despite the lack of an all-knowing authoritative voice-over, Bonengel's film is far from neutral or positively disposed to neo-Nazi rhetoric. See David Bathrick, "Anti-Neonazism as Cinematic Practice: Bonengel's *Beruf Neonazi*," *New German Critique* 67 (1996): 133–46. See also John E. Davidson, "Overcoming Germany's Past(s) in Film since the Wende," *Seminar: A Journal of Germanic Studies* 33, no. 4 (1997): 307–21.

[54] In Connie Walther's teenage love story, *Wie Feuer und Flamme* (2001), the punk Capitan also engages in self-mutilation to avoid work.

[55] Inga Markovits, "Two Truths about Socialist Justice: A Comment on Kommers," *Law & Social Inquiry* 22, no. 3 (1997): 861–62.

[56] See Jan C. Behrends, Thomas Lindenberger, and Patrice G. Poutros, eds., *Fremde und Fremd-Sein in der DDR: Zu historischen Ursachen der Fremdenfeindlichkeit in Ostdeutschland* (Berlin: Metropol, 2003), and Sven Korzilius, "*Asoziale*" und "*Parasiten*" im Recht der SBZ/DDR: Randgruppen im Sozialismus zwischen Repression und Ausgrenzung (Cologne: Böhlau Verlag, 2005).

[57] In reference to the FRG, Andreas Wirsching cites the following statistics from the 1985 Schell Youth Study: 0.3% of the surveyed youth designated themselves punks, 0.2% as squatters, 0.4% as rockers, and 1% as alternative. Even in the broader category of anti-nuclear power movement, only 3.2% of the surveyed youth counted themselves in these ranks. Andreas Wirsching, *Abschied vom Provisorium, 1982–1990* (Munich: Deutsche Verlags-Anstalt, 2006), 399.

[58] Youth groups display the "Hoffnung, sich einen Lebensraum zu schaffen — seien es Jugendzentren oder besetzte Häuser — in denen sie selbstbestimmt und 'autonom' sich entfalten können." Monika Reimitz, Wolfgang Thiel, and Hans-Jürgen Wirth, "Muß denn Leben Sünde sein? Notizen, Assoziationen und Interpretationen zu Gesprächen mit Hausbesetzern und Punks," in *Zwischen Resignation und Gewalt: Jugendprotest in den achtziger Jahren*, Marlene Bock, Monika Reimitz, Horst-Eberhard Richter, Wolfgang Thiel, and Hans-Jürgen Wirth (Opladen: Leske + Budrich, 1989), 26.

[59] The various groups were bound by "die Überwindung von intensiv erlebter Einsamkeit, Langweile, Angst und Ohnmacht.'" Reimitz et al, "Muß denn Leben Sünde sein?" 28.

[60] Ingo Hasselbach and Winfried Bonengel, *Die Abrechnung: Ein Neonazi steigt aus* (Berlin: Aufbau Taschenbuch 2001), 16 and 35.

[61] Hasselbach, *Die Abrechnung*, 26 and 30–31.

[62] In contrast, punks and autonomists of the Federal Republic do not carry the same symbolic weight in historical dramas about the West, perhaps because their

quarrel with society was more marginally registered as a fringe phenomenon. Nonconformist youth in the FRG did not routinely land in prison for failing to work or wearing unusual clothing but more likely for engaging in armed confrontation with the police. Their dispute with authority took on a much more active and violent form than in the GDR and was characterized by young people routinely throwing rocks, shattering windows, building barricades, and committing arson. Police in full riot gear responded by beating protestors and using water canons and teargas to subdue the crowds. For a rather romanticized version of the eighties punk and *Autonomen* in the FRG, see for example Gregor Schnitzler's comedy, *Was tun, wenn's brennt* (What to do in case of fire, 2002). Documentary films dealing with punks in the GDR include *Flüstern und schreien* (Whisper and scream, dir. Dieter Schumann, 1988) and *Ostpunk — Too Much Future* (dir. Carsten Fiebeler and Michael Boehlke, 2006).

[63] See Ronald Galenza and Heinz Havemeister, eds., *Wir wollen immer artig sein: Punk, New Wave, HipHop, und Independent-Szene in der DDR, 1980–1990*, rev. ed. (Berlin: Schwarzkopf & Schwarzkopf, 2005), and Michael Boehlke and Henryk Gericke, eds., *Too Much Future: Punk in der DDR*, rev. ed. (Berlin: Verbrecher Verlag, 2007).

[64] "Na, wie überall in der DDR, nur ein bisschen enger." Film dialogue, *Führer Ex* [2002], dir. Winfried Bonengel, DVD (Munich: Universum Film, 2003).

[65] "Dein Freund weiß wahrscheinlich schon gar nicht mehr, ob er Mann oder Frau ist." Film dialogue.

[66] "Mama, das ist nicht so, wie du denkst." Film dialogue.

[67] "Diese schwachsinnigen Nazis sind die Einzigen, die in diesem Land Widerstand leisten. Die lassen sich nichts gefallen von Dreckskommunisten. Das sind Männer." Film dialogue.

[68] "Ich wollte halt auch wieder einmal zu den, der stärkeren Masse halt hinzugehören und habe mich halt dann demzufolge auch so gegeben, so gekleidet und so, ja. Na ja, meine, meine Weltansichten und so, die waren eigentlich noch nicht so, jetzt so, in dem extremen Bereich, wie sie jetzt so sind. Das war aber ganz einfach nur dieses Zugehörigkeitsgefühl, einfach cool zu sein, und so mit dazugehören, ja, mit bei, bei den Leuten zu stehen und dort ein Bierchen zu saufen und so, und halt Alkoholkonsum, und so der ganze Scheiß. Tja, so bin ich halt teilweise in die rechte Szene gerutscht. . . . Dass es irgendwo Leute gibt, die im Untergrund arbeiten und, äh, sich trotz des Verbotes und so nicht halt jetzt unterkriegen lassen, und das fand ich schon gut, und demzufolge konnte ich mich damit auch identifizieren." Quoted from Christine Wiezorek, "Rechtsextremismusforschung und Biografieanalyse," in *Moderner Rechtsextremismus in Deutschland*, ed. Andreas Klärner and Michael Kohlstruck (Hamburg: Hamburger Edition, 2006), 248–49.

[69] "Der maskuline Stil ist geprägt von der Kultivierung eines bestimmten Männlichkeitsbildes, eines Typs traditioneller Männlichkeit, der durch ein Risiko suchendes, dominierendes und körperbetontes Auftreten charakterisiert ist. Neben den Ausbrüchen aus der Ordnung des Alltags, einem offensiven Machtgebaren und einer aggressiven Körperlichkeit sind zwei bestimmte Mentalitätskomplexe typisch für maskuline Szenen: Sie verbinden ihre autochthone Orientierung

(Territorialverhalten usw.) mit einer allgemeinen Fremdenfeindlichkeit, und sie kombinieren die Betonung von Männlichkeit mit einer dezidierten Feindseligkeit gegen Unmännlichkeit." Michael Kohlstruck and Anna Verena Münch, "Hypermaskuline Szenen und fremdenfeindliche Gewalt: Der Fall Schöberl," in Klärner and Kohlstruck, *Moderner Rechtsextremismus in Deutschland*, 309.

[70] Hannah Arendt, *On Violence* (New York: Harcourt, Brace & World, 1970), 56.

[71] "Ordnung, Sauberkeit und Disziplin sind hier strengst Regeln." Film text.

[72] "Hier im Haus herrscht Ordnung und Disziplin. . . . Hier muss sich jeder unterordnen. Das gilt auch für dich, klar?" Film dialogue.

[73] Gordon Charles Ross, "The Swastika in Socialism: Right-Wing Extremism and Militant Nationalism in the GDR," in *East Germany: Continuity and Change*, ed. Paul Cooke and Jonathan Grix, German Monitor 46 (Amsterdam: Rodopi, 2000), 84.

[74] "Du musst doch nicht denken, dass du der Einzige bist. Bei uns gibt's eine ganze Menge unzufriedener junger Menschen, die Probleme in unserem Land sehen und etwas verändern wollen." Film dialogue.

[75] The Bundestag members sing: "Einigkeit und Recht und Freiheit für das deutsche Vaterland! Danach lasst uns alle streben brüderlich," followed by the prisoners, who sing: "Deutschland, Deutschland über alles, über alles in der Welt, wenn es stets zu Schutz und Trutze brüderlich zusammenhält." Film text.

[76] "Was kann uns die Gesellschaft noch bieten? Diskotheken? Korruption? Arbeitslosigkeit? AIDS? Drogen? Bomben? Es gibt nichts, womit dieser Staat uns locken kann." Film dialogue.

[77] "Das hat den Nebeneffekt, dass *Führer Ex* dem DDR-System einige Verantwortung zuschiebt. Weil die ostdeutschen Autoritäten nicht wussten, was sie dem Aufbegehren der jungen Männer außer Repression entgegenhalten sollten, so die These, trieben sie sie in die Arme der Nazis. Nicht zu vergessen die allein erziehende, beruflich erfolgreiche Mutter, die es mit diversen Liebhabern treibt, statt sich um den Sohn zu kümmern: Wie sollte einer da nicht rechts werden?" Cristina Nord, "Scheitel und Falte im rechten Winkel: Nah dran an der Exploitation; Winfried Bonengels Spielfilmdebüt *Führer Ex* will zeigen, wie aus einem jungen, unpolitischen Mann ein strammer Nazi wird," *taz*, 5 Dec. 2002.

[78] "Traumatische Erlebnisse wie eine schwule Vergewaltigung im Duschraum und monatelange Einzelhaft werden einen ohnehin schon mit ohnmächtiger Wut gefüllten jungen Menschen zweifellos nicht umgänglicher machen, doch die eigentliche Politisierung scheint im Gefängnis nicht stattzufinden. Genau das Umschlagen von der unbestimmten Wut in die ideologische Aufladung, eigentlich spannender Punkt, Peripetie und Bruch eines solchen Genrefilms, verschluckt das Drehbuch in einer dicken, schwarzen, staubsaugerhaften Ellipse." The problem she sees is that this means that: "Einer recht gewagten Allianz wird auf diese Weise die Verantwortung für den Ultrarechtsdrall zugeschoben: Der Jugend in der engen DDR, dem leicht lotterigen Lebenswandel einer Mutter, die ihrem Sprössling statt des Vaters eine Polonaise wechselnder ausländischer Liebhaber vorsetzt sowie der schwulen Repression im Knast." Katja Nicodemus, "Die unbestimmte Wut auf alles: Winfried Bonengels *Führer Ex* gelingt das Kunststück eines unpolitischen Neonazi-Films," *Die Zeit*, 5 Dec. 2002.

[79] When Heiko finds himself in prison, it becomes clear "dass er für sich keine andere Möglichkeit sieht, als sich einer Gruppe anzuschließen. Ich habe darauf verzichtet, seine weitere Karriere innerhalb dieser Gruppierung zu zeigen. Denn der entscheidende Schritt ist, dass er nach seinen Erfahrungen im Gefängnis keinen anderen Weg mehr sieht, obwohl er es am Anfang vollkommen absurd findet, Nazi zu sein. Wenn er überleben will, braucht er Leute. . . . Mir geht es darum zu zeigen, dass es emotionale Gründe sind, warum Leute Nazis werden. Das ist wie in einer Sekte. Wenn ich jemandem genügend Komplimente mache, wird er sich wohl fühlen und ist damit leichter manipulierbar. Danach erst kommt das Indoktrinieren, und deswegen spielt es im Film erst relativ spät eine Rolle." Cristina Nord, "Das Leben besteht aus Klischees: Warum das Indoktrinieren keine Rolle spielt; Ein Gespräch mit dem Regisseur Winfried Bonengel," *taz*, 5 Dec. 2002.

[80] "Am Ende ist es so, dass jeder jederzeit zum Neonazi werden und sich auch jederzeit wieder 'entnazifizieren' kann. Nein, Aufklärung kann man das nicht nennen." Ruppert Koppold, "Das kann doch jedem passieren: Winfried Bonengels *Führer Ex*," *Stuttgarter Zeitung*, 5 Dec. 2002.

[81] The television film *2 ½ Minuten* (Rolf Schübel, 1997, ZDF) also concentrates on the personal and social factors that lead to violence against foreigners, but it does not provide an awakening that results in a renunciation of such behavior. Schübel's film is a reconstruction of an actual event that happened in a Berlin train. Three Turkish boys and two German girls were taking the train to Alexanderplatz, where they wanted to go to a disco. A group of six German boys entered the train and in the two and a half minutes between stations a fight ensued that resulted in three German boys being injured; one died of stab wounds days later. Schübel begins his film with the fight and in a series of flashbacks explores the lives of the protagonists who will clash on that fateful night. The Turkish youth who wielded the knife was acquitted of charges and the incident was deemed self-defense. The notoriously brutal murder of sixteen-year-old Marinus Schöberl in Potzlow in 2002 by brothers Marcel and Marco Schönfeld and their friend Sebastian Fink has served as the background for two documentaries: *Zur falschen Zeit am falschen Ort* (At the wrong place at the wrong time, Tamara Milosevic, 2005) and *Der Kick* (The kick, Andres Veiel, ZDF Theaterkanal edition, 2006). In contrast to Kohlstruck and Münch's study, which attributes Schöberl's murder largely to hyper-masculine attitudes, Veil, using two actors playing over twenty roles, explores in a starkly minimalist presentation the personal, social, economic, and historical background that contributed to this tragedy. Compare Kohlstruck and Münch, "Hypermaskuline Szenen und fremdenfeindliche Gewalt," 302–36 and Andres Veiel, *Der Kick: Ein Lehrstück über Gewalt*, 2nd ed. (Munich: Goldmann, 2008).

[82] *Kahlschlag* was broadcast on the Westdeutschen Rundfunk (WDR) television station in 1993 and is available in DVD. *Kahlschlag* [1993], dir. Hanno Brühl, DVD (Remscheid: Kinder- und Jugendfilmzentrums, 2005). *Platzangst* was a student film by Heike Schober and René Zeuner, who studied at the Hochschule für Film und Fernsehen "Konrad Wolf" Potsdam-Babelsberg. It premiered on 3 April 2003 under the distribution of the filmmakers and sold 13,143 tickets. *Kombat Sechzehn* premiered on 20 January 2005 at the Saarbrücken Film

Festival, where it won the prestigious Max Ophüls Prize. Despite this auspicious beginning, it sold only 11,430 tickets at the box office. It is available in DVD. *Kombat Sechzehn* [2005], dir. Mirko Borscht, DVD (Berlin: Indigo, 2009). *Stau — jetzt gehts los!* premiered at the Duisburg Film Festival on 11 November 1992 and is available for rental. *Stau: jetzt gehts los* [1992], dir. Thomas Heise, VHS (Bonn: Landesfilmdienst Nordrhein Westfalen, 1993). *Dazlak-Skinhead* premiered on 25 October 1997 at the International Film Festival in Hof but did not find a distributer. It was first broadcast on 27 August 2002 on Bavarian Broadcast (Bayrischer Rundfunk, BR). It is available in DVD. *Dazlak-Skinhead* [1997], dir. Helke Sander, DVD (Essen: Sunny Bastard, 2007). Statistics are available at http://www.ffa.de.

[83] "Sie ist durch eine Erweiterung des Rechtsextremismusbegriffs gekennzeichnet, der nicht mehr auf politisches Handeln und Ideologieproduktion begrenzt wird, sondern nun auch Einstellungen in der Bevölkerung umfasst." Andreas Klärner and Michael Kohlstruck, "Rechtsextremismus: Thema der Öffentlichkeit und Gegenstand der Forschung," in Klärner and Kohlstruck, *Moderner Rechtsextremismus in Deutschland*, 19.

[84] Statistics quoted in Kohlstruck and Münch, "Hypermaskuline Szenen und fremdenfeindliche Gewalt," 302–3 and Andreas Klärner, "'Zwischen Militanz und Bürgerlichkeit:' Tendenzen der rechtsextremen Bewegung am Beispiel einer ostdeutschen Mittelstadt," in Klärner and Kohlstruck, *Moderner Rechtsextremismus in Deutschland*, 45.

[85] "Die Motivation der Täter wird dominiert durch maskuline Präsentation von Stärke und Überlegenheit, gemischt mit einem manchmal ganz offenen, häufig aber eher verborgen-diffusen Hass auf alles, was ihnen fremd ist und von ihrer Norm abweicht. Der vordergründig politische Gehalt ihrer Gewaltausübung ist eher gering, ähnlich wie auch die alltäglichen Aktivitäten in der Clique kaum von ernsthaftem politischen Kalkül geprägt sind." Quoted from Kohlstruck and Münch, "Hypermaskuline Szenen und fremdenfeindliche Gewalt," 303.

[86] Such terms as right-wing extremism allows, "daß diejenigen, die dies jeweils postulieren, sich frei von jeglichem Bezug dazu empfinden und als 'Gutmenschen' auf diejenigen zeigen, die eben 'extrem' und damit falsch seien." Klaus Weber, "Sozialpsychologie des Rechtsextremismus," Rechtsextremismus bei Jugendlichen: Symposium Dokumentation, 8 May 2005, 31. http://www.kjr-m.de/publikationen/pdf/rechtsextremismus2005.pdf.

[87] Weber writes that youth are influenced by "die Erwachsenenwelt voll von Antisemitismus, Rassismus und völkisch-nationaler Propaganda." Violence against foreigners and outsiders has to do "mit den gesellschaftlichen Verhältnissen, in denen seit Jahrzehnten von allen Parteien der 'Mitte' behauptet wird, WIR hätten zu viele Asylanten im Land, WIR würden unter Sozialschmarotzen (oder wie Herr Clement Hartz-IV-Empfänger nannte: Parasiten) leiden und WIR müssten die Leistungswilligen födern und die anderen ihrem Schicksal überlassen." Weber, "Sozialpsychologie des Rechtsextremismus," 32 and 33.

[88] "Es geht um die Perversion des Opfers, das zum Täter wird . . . Er ist ein sehr spannender Charakter: extrem sensibel und verletzlich sowie extrem gewaltbereit." Alexia Angelopoulou, "Nun ist Schluss mit diesem Thema: Mit *Führer Ex*

hat Regisseur Winfried Bonengel seinen ersten Kinofilm abgedreht," *Stuttgarter Nachrichten*, 5 Dec. 2002.

[89] "Über Jahre hinweg hatte ich mir alles über die RAF besorgt, dessen ich habhaft werden konnte. Eigentlich hatte ich immer davon geträumt, Terrorist zu werden, und meine Vorstellungen von einem Leben als ein solcher waren eher romantischer Art. Ich hielt Terroristen für Idealisten, die für eine bessere und gerechtere Welt kämpfen. Während meiner Zeit in DDR-Gefängnissen sah ich mich stets als Opfer eines ungerechten und autoritären Staates, der Gewalt auf mich ausübte. Gewalt wurde für mich zu einer alltäglichen Sache: Auf mich wurde Gewalt ausgeübt, und ich übte Gewalt aus. Der Zeitpunkt allerdings, an dem aus mir als "Opfer" ein "Täter" geworden war, war mir nicht bewußt geworden." Hasselbach and Bonengel, *Die Abrechnung*, 117. For further references to the RAF, see also 118 and 133.

[90] Before the film's premiere there were positive reviews, such as Nikolaus von Festenberg, "Sandmännchen rettet die DDR: Wolfgang Beckers wunderbare Kinophantasie *Good Bye, Lenin!* wehrt sich mit viel Ironie gegen den unerbittlichen Lauf der Geschichte," *Der Spiegel*, 3 Feb. 2003, 120, and Evelyn Finger, "Die unsinkbare Republik: Wolfgang Beckers Tragikomödie *Good Bye, Lenin!* kennt viele Arten von Gelächter," *Die Zeit*, 6 Feb. 2003. By contrast, Anke Westphal lamented that the film was "nothing more than an attempt to make an ass out of the public" (nichts Anderes als eine Publikumsverarschung). She was especially disturbed by the idea that Christiane was outed as a fake, who only adopted socialist zeal to survive after her husband's defection. See Anke Westphal, "Was unterging, taucht nicht mehr auf: *Good Bye, Lenin!* von Wolfgang Becker legt heiter Distanz ein — das macht traurig," *Berliner Zeitung*, 8 Feb. 2003. Daniel Haufler found that the film did not balance comedy and tragedy well and often fell into overly sentimental melodrama. Haufler also criticized the cinematography as clichéd and reminiscent of television fare. See Daniel Haufler, "Die DDR ist eine Baustelle: In Wolfgang Beckers Wettbewerbsbeitrag *Goodbye, Lenin!* wird der sozialistische Osten Deutschlands neu erfunden," *taz*, 10 Feb. 2003.

[91] In Germany in 2003, viewer numbers were 6,594,748 for *Lord of the Rings III*, 5,897,793 for *Pirates of the Caribbean*, 4,773,455 for *Matrix Reloaded*, and 3,473,003 for *Catch Me If You Can*. By the end of 2004, *Good Bye, Lenin!* reached 6,574,961 viewers in Germany. Statistics are available at http://www.ffa.de.

[92] For worldwide grosses, see Box Office Mojo, http://www.boxofficemojo.com/movies/?page=main&id=goodbyelenin.htm.

[93] In the eighties, Hungarian director Istvan Szabo worked extensively in the German motion picture industry. He is perhaps best known for directing three German-language films, all starring Klaus Maria Brandauer: *Mephisto* (1981), *Oberst Redl* (Colonel Redl, 1985), and *Hanussen* (1988).

[94] Along with his work as a director and screenwriter, Becker cofounded with Tom Tykwer, Dani Levy, and Stefan Arndt the highly successful production company X-Film Creative Pool. Since 1997 he has also taught direction at the dffb, the Film Academy in Ludwigsburg, and the Art Academy for Media in Cologne. In 2010 Becker began filming *Ich und Kaminski*, based on Daniel Kehlmann's novel of the same name and starring Daniel Brühl. It is slated for release in 2012.

[95] *Die DDR Show* (RTL) did include a segment on political oppression that seemed rather out of place in the upbeat variety-show format. Following a piece on the Lipsi dance craze in the fifties, moderator Oliver Geissen interviewed Erika Riemann, who as a fourteen-year-old in 1945 had disfigured a portrait of Stalin by drawing a bow on his moustache in red lipstick. She spent eight years in Bautzen, Sachsenhausen, and Hoheneck prisons for this childhood prank.

[96] Comedies dealing with the end of the GDR and reunification include *Go Trabi Go* (Peter Timm, 1991), *Wir können auch anders* (We can do it differently, English title: *No More Mr. Nice Guy*, Detlev Buck, 1993), *Adamski* (Jens Becker, 1994), *Helden wie wir* (Heroes like us, dir. Sebastian Peterson, 1999), whereas dramas include *Das alte Lied* (The old song, dir. Ula Stöckl, 1992), *Apfelbäume* (Apple trees, dir. Helma Sanders-Brahms, 1992), *Herzsprung* (Heart leap, dir. Helke Misselwitz, 1992), *Stilles Land* (Silent country, dir. Andreas Dresen, 1992), and *Der Brocken* (The Brocken, English title: *Rising to the Bait*, dir. Vadim Glowna, 1992). For recent studies on unification films, see Leonie Naughton, *That Was the Wild East: Film Culture, Unification, and the New Germany* (Ann Arbor: U of Michigan P, 2002), and Elizabeth Mittman, "Fantasizing Integration and Escape in the Post-Unification Road Movie," in *Light Motives: German Popular Film in Perspective*, ed. Randall Halle and Margaret McCarthy (Detroit: Wayne State UP, 2003), 326–48. Even the horror genre has used German reunification as its premise with *Das deutsche Kettensägenmassaker: Die erste Stunde der Wiedervereinigung* (The German chain saw massacre: The first hour of reunification, dir. Christoph Schlingensief, 1990). For an analysis of unification horror films, see Randall Hall, "Unification Horror: Queer Desire and Uncanny Visions," in Halle and McCarthy, *Light Motives*, 281–303.

[97] Earlier post-unification Eastern dystopias that feature disenfranchised youths include *Ostkreuz* (Eastern cross, dir. Michael Klier, 1991), *Jana und Jan* (dir. Helmut Dziuba, 1992), and *Engelchen* (Little angel, dir. Helke Misselwitz, 1996).

[98] Wolfgang Becker discusses how the actual ruin was unsuitable for filming and therefore had to be rebuilt on a sound stage. For details, see *Good Bye, Lenin!* [2003], dir. Wolfgang Becker, DVD (Hamburg: Warner Home Video, 2003). Janet Stewart presents an excellent analysis of Tacheles in the framework of post-unification architectural debates. See Janet Stewart, "Das Kunsthaus Tacheles: The Berlin Architecture Debate of the 1990s in Micro-Historical Context," in *Recasting German Identity: Culture, Politics, and Literature in the Berlin Republic*, ed. Stuart Taberner and Frank Finlay (Rochester, NY: Camden House, 2002), 51–66. For photographs and interviews with artists from the period immediately following unification, see Andreas Rost, *Tacheles: Alltag im Chaos; Ein Fotobuch*, interviews by Annette Gries and Heinz Havemeister (Berlin: Elefanten Press, 1992), n.p. Several artists complain that the creative chaos of the period often developed into aggression and violence rather than the peaceful utopia envisioned in Becker's film. See in particular the interviews with Ilona Sommerfeld, Ludwig Eben, and Leo.

[99] The Friedrichstrassen-Passage and subsequent Wertheim department store went bankrupt in 1908 and 1914 respectively. In 1924 it underwent major renovations to add a large storage cellar and glass dome. In 1928 the electric company AEG took over and opened the House of Technology as a marketing and exhibition

space for new products and technologies. In 1936 it was the historic site of one of the world's first television broadcasts, sending images of the Berlin Olympic Games. During the Nazi period it housed various party organizations, including offices of the German Work Front, Central Land Office, the SS, and, after 1943, French prisoners of war. Despite being severely damaged in bombing raids during the Second World War, the building continued to be used in the Soviet Occupational Zone and later in the GDR. In 1948 it housed the Free German Federation of Trade Unions, a storage unit for the National People's Army, various small businesses, and a cinema. For a brief history of the building, see Rost, *Tacheles: Alltag im Chaos*, n.p. and the Tacheles website, http://www.tacheles.de.

[100] "Der Wind der Veränderung blies bis in die Ruinen unserer Republik. Der Sommer kam und Berlin war der schönste Platz auf Erden. Alles war denkbar. Alles war möglich. Wir hatten das Gefühl im Mittelpunkt der Welt zu stehen. Dort, wo sich endlich etwas bewegte. Und wir bewegten uns mit. . . . Die Zukunft lag ungewiss in unseren Händen, ungewiss und verheißungsvoll." Michael Töteberg, ed., *Good Bye, Lenin! Ein Film von Wolfgang Becker: Drehbuch von Bernd Lichtenberg, Co-Author Wolfgang Becker* (Berlin: Schwarzkopf & Schwarzkopf, 2003), 38–39.

[101] ". . . verweisen nicht nur auf Beschränkung und Genügsamkeit, den klugen Umgang mit Resourcen, sondern mindestens ebenso stark auf Genuß und Kreativität." Merkel, *Utopie und Bedürfnis*, 14.

[102] GDR psychiatrist Hans-Joachim Maaz notes: "There was nothing that could beat the fetish value of western goods. Empty western beer or cola cans were placed as ornaments on the shelves of the wall unit, plastic bags bearing western advertisements were bartered, western clothes made the man. Real shortages and inferior merchandise in our country, and the surplus of items and quality luxuries in the West were the emotional background for a neverending and never-satisfied spiral of consumption." Hans-Joachim Maaz, *Behind the Wall: The Inner Life of Communist Germany*, trans. Margo Bettauer Dembo (New York: W. W. Norton, 1995), 86.

[103] Collecting GDR memorabilia and buying reissued GDR consumer products can be seen as attempts to relive the past at the surface level. The most extreme case, however, was Frank Georgi's plan in 1993 to build a GDR theme park at a former army camp near Prenden where visitors would relive Communism for the price of an entrance ticket. Upon arriving, visitors would sign up for a specific time limit and not be allowed to leave until the time had passed. They would exchange Western currency for Eastern currency, shop in nearly empty stores, and drive around in Trabants within a barbed wire radius filled with guard towers. Visitors would be observed and possibly arrested by Stasi agents if they made anti-system remarks, although jail sentences would be measured in hours rather than years. "Stalins Rache: Ein Berliner Konzertveranstalter will, hinter Mauer und Stacheldraht, eine Mini-DDR bauen; Ossi-Park," *Der Spiegel*, 18 Oct. 1993, 88–89.

[104] Paul Betts, "The Twilight of the Idols: East German Memory and Material Culture," *Journal of Modern History* 72, no. 3 (2000): 754.

[105] Betts, "Twilight of the Idols," 762.

[106] "Wir waren alle wertvolle Menschen." Töteberg, *Good Bye, Lenin!*, 68.

[107] "Wenn wir schuld daran sind, mit unseren Körpergrößen der Planerfüllung nicht nachkommen zu können, Komma, bitten wir dies zu entschuldigen. Punkt. In diesem Fall werden wir uns bemühen, Komma, in Zukunft kleiner und viereckiger zu werden. Punkt. Mit sozialistischem Gruß. — Hanna Schäfer." Töteberg, *Good Bye, Lenin!*, 85.

[108] See Günter Gaus, "Nischengesellschaft," in *Wo liegt Deutschland: Eine Ortsbestimmung* (Hamburg: Hoffmann & Campe, 1983), 156–233. Mary Fulbrook provides an excellent analysis of the concept of a *Nischengesellschaft*. She concludes that the term best describes the brief period from Honecker's assumption of power in 1972 to 1975. See Fulbrook, *Anatomy of a Dictatorship*, 129–50.

[109] Klapprath tells her: "Bleib wie du bist," and Herr Ganske wishes: "dass alles wieder so wird, wie es mal war." Töteberg, *Good Bye, Lenin!*, 73.

[110] The children sing "Und wir lieben die Heimat, die schöne / Und wir schützen sie, weil sie dem Volke gehört, / Weil sie unserem Volke gehört." From "Unsere Heimat," composed by Hans Naumilkat with a text by Herbert Keller. Film text.

[111] The song, also known as "Jugend erwach!" (Youth awaken), was composed by Reinhold Limberg. The refrain is "Bau auf, bau auf, bau auf, bau auf, neue deutsche Jugend, bau auf. Für eine bessere Zukunft richten wir die Heimat auf."

[112] Jennifer Kapczynski reads the film's opening differently. She argues that Becker's "nostalgic aesthetics" reify "the central concern of *Good Bye, Lenin!* as the intersection of personal and national memory, staging the attachment to nation as a complex bond." Becker's attention to visual authenticity leads him to adopt "a style that engages in the very fetishization of history that his film questions." While I find Kapczynski's reading compelling at several levels, I contend that the voice-over and commentaries throughout the film highlight the fact that the personal and national are not the same thing and that the incongruity between sights and sounds requires the viewer to distinguish between the ideal and the real. Compare Jennifer Kapczynski, "Negotiating Nostalgia: The GDR Past in *Berlin Is in Germany* and *Good Bye, Lenin!*" *Germanic Review* 82, no.1 (2007): 83, 86, and 87–88.

[113] "Am 26. August 1978 waren wir auf Weltniveau. Sigmund Jähn, Bürger der Deutschen Demokratischen Republik, flog als erster Deutscher ins All. Mit unserer Familie aber ging es an diesem Tag so richtig den Bach runter." Töteberg, *Good Bye, Lenin!*, 8–9.

[114] ". . . ein überdimensionierter Schützenverein seine letzte Vorstellung gab." Töteberg, *Good Bye, Lenin!*, 17.

[115] "Da stehen sie alle rum und feiern sich selbst, die ganzen alten Säcke." Töteberg, *Good Bye, Lenin!*, 20.

[116] "Wahrheit [ist] nur eine zweifelhafte Angelegenheit." Töteberg, *Good Bye, Lenin!*, 78.

[117] Roger Hillman, "*Goodbye Lenin* (2003): History in the Subjunctive," *Rethinking History* 10, no. 2 (2006): 221–37.

[118] Christiane earns "den vaterländischen Verdienstorden in Gold und Würdigung außerordentlicher Verdienste beim Aufbau und bei der Entwicklung der sozialistischen Gesellschaftsordnung." Töteberg, *Good Bye, Lenin!*, 15.

[119] "Ich bin nicht gegangen. Das war der größte Fehler meines Lebens. Das weiß ich jetzt. Ich, ich hab euch belogen. Verzeiht mir bitte." Töteberg, *Good Bye, Lenin!*, 110.

[120] Benedict Anderson, *Imagined Communities: Reflections on the Origins and Spread of Nationalism*, rev. ed. (London: Verso, 1991), 204.

[121] Friedrich Nietzsche, "On the Use and Disadvantages of History for Life," in *Untimely Meditations*, ed. Daniel Breazeale, trans. R. J. Hollingdale (Cambridge: Cambridge UP, 1983), 62. The German original: "*Es giebt einen Grad von Schlaflosigkeit, von Wiederkäuen, von historischem Sinne, bei dem das Lebendige zu Schaden kommt, und zuletzt zu Grunde geht, sei es nun ein Mensch oder ein Volk oder eine Cultur.* Um diesen Grad und durch ihn dann die Grenze zu bestimmen, an der das Vergangene vergessen werden muss, wenn es nicht zum Todtengräber des Gegenwärtigen werden soll, müsste man genau wissen, wie gross *die plastische Kraft* eines Menschen, eines Volkes, einer Cultur ist, ich meine jene Kraft, aus sich heraus eigenartig zu wachsen, Vergangenes und Fremdes umzubilden und einzuverleiben, Wunden auszuheilen, Verlorenes zu ersetzen, zerbrochene Formen aus sich nachzuformen." Friedrich Nietzsche, "Vom Nutzen und Nachtheil der Historie für das Leben," in *Unzeitgemäße Betrachtungen II: Vom Nutzen und Nachtheil der Historie für das Leben* [1874], vol. 1 of *Sämtliche Werke: Kritische Studienausgabe*, 15 vols., ed. Giorgio Colli und Mazzino Montinari (Munich: Deutscher Taschenbuch Verlag, 1980), 250–51.

[122] "Das Land, das meine Mutter verließ, war ein Land, an das sie geglaubt hatte. Und das wir bis zu ihrer letzten Sekunde überleben ließen. Ein Land, das es in Wirklichkeit nie so gegeben hat." He maintains: "Meine Mutter überlebte die DDR genau drei Tage. Ich glaube, es war schon richtig, dass sie die Wahrheit nie erfahren hat. Sie ist glücklich gestorben." Töteberg, *Good Bye, Lenin!*, 131 and 129.

[123] "Wir wissen, dass unser Land nicht perfekt ist. Aber das, woran wir glauben, begeisterte immer wieder viele Menschen aus aller Welt. Vielleicht haben wir unsere Ziele manchmal aus den Augen verloren, doch wir haben uns besonnen. Sozialismus, das heißt, sich nicht einzumauern. Sozialismus, das heißt auf den anderen zuzugehen, mit dem anderen zu leben. Nicht nur von einer besseren Welt zu träumen, sondern sie wahr zu machen." Töteberg, *Good Bye, Lenin!*, 127.

[124] This film is also unique because of its advertising blitz that includes several web sites featuring video and audio clips, various downloads, an on-line game, and a chat room. These web sites even provide links for Spreewald pickles, Coca-cola, and Mercedes that seem to be a vital part of the expanded filmic experience rather than mere commercials and feed on (rather than criticize) product fetishism. See the official web site in Germany at *Good Bye, Lenin!*, http://www.79qmddr.de/ and http://www.sonyclassics.com/goodbye/flash.html.

[125] *Affluenza* was produced by John De Graaf and Vivia Boe and hosted by Scott Simon. A coproduction of KCTS/Seattle and Oregon Public Broadcasting (OPB), it aired as a PBS documentary on 15 Sept. 1997. See the accompanying text: John De Graaf, David Wann, and Thomas H. Naylor, *Affluenza: The All Consuming Epidemic* (San Francisco: Berrett-Koehler Publishers, 2001).

[126] "Vielen Dank, dass Sie sich für Burger King entschieden haben." Töteberg, *Good Bye, Lenin!*, 30 and 90.

127 Stephen Brockmann, who has written about the notion of national identity in contemporary German literature and literary debates, made this point earlier in a larger context: "the triply 'delayed' Germany of the 1990s was unified as a nation at precisely the moment when the concept of nation itself as a primary political category was coming into question as a result of economic globalization processes that seemed increasingly to render national governments impotent." Stephen Brockmann, *Literature and German Reunification* (Cambridge: Cambridge UP, 1999), 166–67.

128 Benjamin R. Barber, *Jihad vs. McWorld* (New York: Ballantine Books, 1996), and Samuel P. Huntington, *The Clash of Civilizations and the Remaking of World Order* (New York: Simon & Schuster, 1996), while often characterized by hyperbole and a lack of specificity, do address the equally powerful drives toward atomization and homogenization on the international stage and point to cultural identity as a potential source of conflict in the post-cold-war scramble for power. Edward W. Said delivers a scathing and compelling critique of Barber and Huntington's work for ignoring the complexity of identity and positing simplistic oppositions (for example, the oddly unified but poorly defined "Western" civilization against monolithic Islam). Said suggests that identity, including national identity, is a set of interlocking positions that shifts according to setting, time, and emphasis. See *Professor Edward Said in Lecture: The Myth of the "Clash of Civilizations"* (Northampton, MA.: Media Education Foundation, 1998).

129 "Beckers Film ist ein Versöhnungsangebot an die Deutschen — und diese verstehen es auch so. Denn man muss die DDR anerkennen, wenn man sie richtig beerdigen will. . . . *Good bye, Lenin!* ist auch ein trauriger Film. Er zeigt das unausweichliche Sterben und den Abschied. Aber nie hoffnungslos, nie zynisch oder gleichgültig. Darin besteht der poetischer Zauber." Gunnar Decker, "Vielfalt statt Einfalt: Zum Ost-West-Kinoerfolg von *Good Bye, Lenin!*" *Neues Deutschland,* 8 Mar. 2003.

130 "*Good Bye, Lenin!* ist in der Tat ein DDR-Begräbnisfilm. Und das ist wichtig. Denn es hatte sie ja keiner begraben, da war kein Abschied, sie war plötzlich einfach nur weg wie die Spreewald-Gurken in Alexanders Kaufhalle, von einem Tag auf den anderen. Das Kino holt nach, wozu in Wirklichkeit keine Zeit war." Kerstin Decker, "Das wahre Ende der DDR: Wolfgang Beckers wundersame Komödie *Good Bye, Lenin!*," *Der Tagesspiegel,* 28 Feb. 2003.

131 "Denn dieser Film ist zugleich die versöhnende Grablegung der Utopie der DDR — und diese Utopie war doch in gewissem Sinne immer wirklicher als ihre lächerliche, militante, kleinbürgerliche, verstockte Wirklichkeit. Die Utopie war zwar schwer fassbar, aber sie war in den Büchern, die wir lasen, in mancher Musik, in manchen Filmen — und irgendwann hatte sie einen genauen politischen Namen: Gorbatschow. So war die Utopie der DDR die große Untote der letzten dreizehn Jahre." K. Decker, "Das wahre Ende der DDR."

132 "Nach der Wende waren wir Ex-DDR-Bürger hässlich geworden. Ein diktaturgekrümmtes Volk aus Duckmäusern. Egal in welchen Spiegel wir sahen, immer dasselbe Gesicht. Und nun zeigt dieser Film ein anderes, scharf gestellt. Es ist wohl dieses Wiedererkennen einer Wahrheit, das die Menschen zu Beifall hinreißt." K. Decker, "Das wahre Ende der DDR."

133 "Ein Land, das in meiner Erinnerung immer mit meiner Mutter verbunden sein wird." Töteberg, *Good Bye, Lenin!,* 131.

2: In the Shadow of the Wall: Political Oppression and Resistance in the GDR

THE PORTRAYAL OF GDR HISTORY in motion pictures made since 1989/90 has sparked lively debates in the trade press, in nationally renowned newspapers and magazines, and among leading cultural and political figures. Commentators have repeatedly and often passionately questioned who has the right to tell the history of the GDR, Easterners or Westerners? Those who lived through it and can vouch for the authenticity of their story based on eyewitness experience or those who never took part in the events and therefore have the distance to look back on history and reflect upon it objectively? Without falling into the trap of essentialism that would privilege one voice over another based on some perceived innate truth (or arguing that history can only be told by contemporaries), it is important to note that in the Berlin Republic the position of former GDR citizens is structurally inferior to that of Westerners, and that the debate about a filmmaker's place of origin is fundamentally about this inequality. Contentious film reviews in the trade press are symptomatic of the larger debates over the emerging GDR memory landscape.

Already at the time of the unification process, then Minister of the Interior Wolfgang Schäuble stated for the record that the West did not view the East as an equal partner but more as the prodigal son returning to the fold under the protection of the righteous father. Schäuble maintained:

> My dear citizens, what is taking place here is the accession of the GDR to the Federal Republic, and not the other way around. We have a good *Grundgesetz* (Basic Law), which has proved its worth. We will do everything for you. You are welcome to join us. We do not wish callously to ignore your wishes and interests. However, we are not seeing here the unification of two equal states. We are not starting again from the beginning, from positions that have equal rights. The *Grundgesetz* exists, and the Federal Republic exists.[1]

Entering into the union as the wayward state, the GDR and its citizens were given and accepted the mandate to shed their sovereignty and identity and adopt Western standards. This process of assimilation is far from over, and the distance between Easterners and Westerners continues today. Apart from the social and economic inequalities that separate

them, there is a crucial difference of opinion over how the federal government, commemorative sites, research institutions, and the general public
should remember the GDR. And while the lines of disagreement do not
run parallel to an easily drawn East-West division, contending opinions of
the GDR range from an oppressive dictatorship replete with party dominance, omnipresent secret police, relentless suppression of dissent, and a
nearly impenetrable fortified border to a relatively normal, modern state
that afforded its citizens stability and security in the form of guaranteed
work, housing, and social welfare as well as promoting a sense of camaraderie and at least a modicum of individual fulfillment.

Even after the German Bundestag established two Enquete Commissions (reports published in 1995 and 1999) to investigate the legacy
of the GDR, there is still no consensus on how to deal with the past
adequately.[2] On 9 May 2005 then Federal Commissioner for Culture
and Media (Bundesbeauftragte für Kultur und Medien, BKM) Christina
Weiss appointed a team of experts to devise a concept for organizing in a
decentralized fashion a historical alliance to analyze the SED dictatorship.
Under the chairmanship of Martin Sabrow, professor of history at the
University of Potsdam and director of the Center for Contemporary Historical Research, the so-called Sabrow-Commission published its findings
in spring 2007 amid growing controversy. Their primary recommendation
was for the consolidation of nationwide efforts into three main categories: "authority-society-opposition," "surveillance and persecution," and
"division and border." This threefold structure was envisioned as a practical solution to the current inefficiency, expense, and inability to oversee
the various public and private agencies undertaking projects related to
the memory of the GDR. For example, the commission outlined practical concerns about coordinating commemorative sites such as the former
headquarters of the Ministry for State Security in the Normannenstrasse
and the Stasi prison at Hohenschönhausen, in order to facilitate dialogue
and work within the parameters of limited federal financial support. One
of their more controversial suggestions was to coordinate these autonomous memorial sites under the authority of the Federal Commissioner
for the Records of the Ministry for State Security of the Former GDR
(Bundesbeauftragte für die Unterlagen des Staatssicherheitsdienstes der
ehemaligen Deutschen Demokratischen Republik, BStU). Merging the
management of such sites might foster efficiency but it would sacrifice
autonomy, a point of contention among those who, like Hubertus Knabe,
argued that history cannot be centrally organized as if it were part of an
SED planned market economy.[3] Equally contentious was the recommendation that the BStU continue to manage the Stasi files and delay the
eventual transfer of these files to the Federal Archive for the foreseeable
future. The BStU was originally given a limited period of oversight of the
Stasi files to allow affected individuals and scholars access to materials that

would normally be closed to public access for up to thirty years to protect privacy rights. At stake in the proposed transfer is the issue of privacy rights for individuals and information rights for the general public.

Beyond recommending the coordination of public and private institutions, the Sabrow Commission studied the current level of historical awareness and concluded that it was inadequate and divisive. Their findings show that nearly twenty years after unification the general public cannot agree on how to view the GDR past: there is "a divided perception of GDR history in the East and West, which in the old federal states is considered only marginally a part of pan-German history."[4] They felt strongly that the government should act "to counter a threatening 'islandization' of GDR history in the historical consciousness and to embed the GDR into an integrated inner-German history between 1945 and 1990 in the European and global context."[5] The majority of experts on the committee argued that there needs to be a paradigm shift away from "the priority currently given to public documentation about state repression to the more neglected areas of resistance and assimilation, ideology and party rule, as well as everyday life under the dictatorship."[6] In particular, they saw the need for scholarly work that explores how everyday activities helped sustain the SED regime. Comparing the status of research on the GDR to that on National Socialism, the commission maintained that both areas suffered from the same shortcomings: the research "does not adequately make visible the everyday manner in which the system functioned and the daily negotiation of individual free space to make decisions, nor is it sufficiently attentive to the important role of behavior and responsibility of individuals for the power of dictatorship."[7] Human-rights activist, writer, and film director Freya Klier, herself a target of the Stasi, published a minority report that strongly contested the recommendation to move the focus away from the state and its power apparatus. Klier writes: "The pillars of the collapsed dictatorship do not simply march at memorial sites — they sit in the Bundestag, in the media, in schools and on numerous committees in our democracy. And they never get tired of polishing up their unjust state as democratic in retrospect and making it look good in the public memory."[8] One of the most important tasks facing the country, according to Klier, is to teach recent history to a younger generation who is completely overstimulated by media input and for whom the GDR is as distant as ancient Rome. She suggests that young people have to be given a sensory experience of state repression, as is possible in the memorial site at Hohenschönhausen prison, in order to appreciate fully what people under a dictatorship are capable of doing to each other.

The Sabrow Commission acknowledged that the media play a decisive role in disseminating an image of the GDR that influences how the public views history and national identity. They warn that there has been "in the last few years a growing trivialization of the GDR as a political system especially in the media, which in recent times increasingly involves attempts of historical revisionists to negate its dictatorial character and disrespect its victims."[9] The wave of *Ostalgie* manifest in films, television variety shows, memoirs, and merchandising as well as attempts by former GDR officials to underestimate their own culpability impede a serious reckoning with the past. Mentioning specifically the ability of a film like *Das Leben der Anderen* to promote interest in the GDR among Western audiences, the experts called for more attention to the ways in which media contribute to the development of historical consciousness.

As the discussion about the GDR memory landscape is transferred to the realm of motion pictures, the problem of how to represent the SED regime most accurately is ultimately intertwined with questions about genre, identification, the relationship between the imaginary and the real, and the possibilities and limitations of cinema to convey a truthful and comprehensive picture of history.

Because genre films are based on familiar characters and plots that guarantee predictable results, they are ready-made formulas for talking about human existence that have a significant impact on the interpretation of history. The melodrama, for example, offers a different worldview than the historical epic, the docudrama, or the comedy. Working within the parameters of classical narrative cinema, filmmakers who present the personal dilemmas of individuals impacted by political events largely beyond their control often turn to the generic conventions of the melodrama. While this genre fulfills audience expectations for identification with appealing characters and offers an emotionally gratifying experience that helps viewers to understand what oppression feels like, it tends to ascribe the turn of historical events to personal motivations. Denunciation and imprisonment are often motivated by jealousy and greed, implying that human-rights violations are not a structural fault of dictatorship but the failing of emotionally weak but politically powerful individuals. With its standard figure constellation of economically, politically, and socially dominant villains exploiting weaker but morally superior prey, ordinary citizens come across as victims rather than complicit in the system. The docudrama fairs no better in respect to its generic limitations. Docudramas concentrating on the machinations of powerful figures in the public arena, who make decisions affecting the entire society and the course of history, often fail to address the everyday life of exemplary ordinary people. The docudrama can give individuals too much credit for events that arise from social circumstances at a particular moment in time. Historical epics with their ambitious scope must still pare down the amount of action covered in order to fit the conventional timeframe of a few hours or even of a multiple segmented serial. By trimming the plot one risks lapsing into clichés, and collapsing time can lead to the erroneous conclusion that certain events happened simultaneously or as a consequence of unrelated acts. Comedies with their lighthearted tone can trivialize historical suffering and lead to a normalization of dictatorship that excludes any acknowledgement of the authoritarian structures. In this brief overview, it is obvious that no one genre is completely adequate to the task of capturing the complexity of lived history, and that the formal conventions of storytelling pose serious challenges to those who try to illuminate the past though the lens of fiction. If motion pictures, like history books, require us to imagine at least some aspect of how past events fit together into a logical story with a clear moral lesson, then a series of dilemmas arise that can never be solved definitively. How do audiences differentiate between fact and fiction? What facts are sacred and should not be manipulated for the sake of aesthetic expediency? And are there emotional truths that can best be explained through falsification or distortion of verified reality?

This chapter will begin with an overview of DEFA films made in the transitional period from the GDR to a unified Germany, from 1989 to approximately 1992. These films are often said to fall into the so-called *Wendeloch*, the hole that existed after the fall of the Wall when neither East German nor West German audiences had much interest in watching motion pictures about the collapse of the GDR. I then study three motion pictures in greater depth, because they exemplify developments in the GDR memory landscape at three distinct historical junctures and tell us at least as much about the past as about the present: *Die Architekten* was filmed immediately following the revolution of 1989, *Das Versprechen*, in the mid nineties when unification had become reality, and *Das Leben der Anderen*, in the new millennium as a new generation is emerging for whom the GDR is not lived experience. Their attempts to portray life in the GDR and their critical reception reveal much about how the legacy of the socialist state has developed in the public imagination over nearly two decades. These three films also correspond to a great extent to the three categories of memory outlined in the Sabrow Commission's report published in 2007: "authority-society-opposition," "division and border," and "surveillance and persecution." While none of them treat one area of the SED regime exclusively, they do place more emphasis on different features. *Die Architekten* focuses attention on the relationship between "authority-society-opposition" and the way in which hope for a better future was constantly extinguished and rekindled; *Das Versprechen* examines the heartbreak of families and an entire people separated by the "division and border" mandated by the Cold War; and *Das Leben der Anderen* deals with the destruction of individual lives by a pervasive system of "surveillance and persecution." The final section of this chapter is devoted to recent television films about the GDR. The line between film and television financing is becoming ever grayer. Television stations are increasingly providing funding for films that premiere first in cinemas and are later broadcast on television. Federal and state film boards originally set up to finance motion pictures are now also funding television films. Moreover, the sheer number of audience-share figures for television films, in some instances over ten million viewers, means that many more people are viewing history on television than in the cinema. When one also factors in DVD sales, the sheer number of viewers who watch films outside the cinema is important to consider when trying to gauge the impact of media on the public's perception of history. Finally, this chapter ends with an examination of whether the cinema and television approach history with much the same stance or whether there is a discernible difference in their modes of inquiry.

Das Wendeloch

In the months leading up to the fall of the Berlin Wall and the collapse of the German Democratic Republic, filmmakers were already beginning to explore the seedier side of life under Honecker's real-existing socialism. Among the first to deal with the authoritarian aspects of the GDR were veteran DEFA directors such as Frank Beyer, Heiner Carow, Roland Gräf, and Ulrich Weiß, as well as the younger generation making their first independent feature films, such as Jörg Foth, Peter Kahane, and Herwig Kipping.[10] These early films made during or shortly after the *Wende* at the DEFA studios concentrate on the disillusionment and despair of individuals who no longer have the strength to fight against the persistent corruption, bureaucratism, surveillance, and repression in the GDR. Collectively they mourn the loss of a utopian vision to create a democratic, just, and classless society.

Jörg Foth's *Letztes aus der Da Da eR* (The last from the Ge De aR, 1990) and Herwig Kipping's *Das Land hinter dem Regenbogen* (The land beyond the rainbow, 1992) are avant-garde productions that eschew the conventions of classical narrative cinema with its reliance on realism, psychological development of characters, and resolution of conflicts.[11] Instead these directors make use of parable in a dreamlike fantasy world and employ Brechtian alienation effects and haunting imagery to depict the GDR as an absurd state of existence. Foth and Kipping's films are highly original and deviate significantly from the socialist realism favored by the DEFA studios, even in the eighties. Foth turned to the traditions of political cabaret, poking fun at past and present conditions with an infectious irreverence that is, however, laden with an underlying sadness that such lofty ideals could go so wrong. By contrast, Kipping's semi-autobiographical tale is a nightmare vision of collectivism, heavily influenced by Russian masters Tarkovsky and Dovzhenko.

Fig. 2.1. Still from Jörg Foth's Letztes aus der Da Da eR *(1990).*
Photo © and by permission of DEFA Spectrum and Thomas Plenert.

Poets Steffen Mensching and Hans-Eckardt Wenzel wrote the script
for *Letztes aus der Da Da eR* based on their traveling musical cabarets.
They play themselves as the clowns Meh and Weh, who are released from
prison and embark on a journey to Paris, or paradise.[12] Renowned author
Christoph Hein appears early on as the garbage man who delivers the
clowns from the prison of the GDR to the garbage dump of post-Wall
Germany. Hein voices the sentiment of many intellectuals who fought for
serious reforms in the GDR but were unprepared for its sudden collapse
and the unmitigated acceptance of the FRG that followed. He laments:
"The general stupidity drowns me. When I saw my country dying, I
sensed that I loved it. I bear the grief that the Roman patricians bore in
the fourth century. I feel an unbeatable barbarity rising from the ground.
I hope to be dead before it tears everything away. I have always tried to
live in an ivory tower but a sea of shit is crashing onto its walls."[13] In
a series of satirical songs and sketches the two clowns make their way
through various stations of the GDR and the new world of the FRG:
piercing each other with medals for their contributions to socialism until
they collapse from the pain, rowing through a dead river brewing with
chemicals singing about all the folks who went to the West while the
boatman repeats the lyrical refrain "everything is completely in vain," and
walking through the slaughterhouse of capitalism as cattle are hit on the
head, tremble helplessly, and are butchered. At the film's conclusion the
clowns find themselves in a tranquil graveyard enjoying the peace and
quiet until they are caught up in a hypnotic display of German patriotism

Fig. 2.2. Still from Herwig Kipping's Das Land hinter dem Regenbogen *(1992). Photo © and by kind permission of Dieter Jaeger.*

from the buildings surrounding them. The red-gold-black flag flying from every balcony and the growling German Shepherds put them into such a trance that they end up kneeling on the ground, barking like dogs, and bowing to the inevitable.

Das Land hinter dem Regenbogen, written and directed by Herwig Kipping, is a surreal vision of communist dictatorship that takes place in 1953 in the fictional village of Stalina. From the opening scenes, where life-sized dolls hang from the trees, a white witch cradles a snake that winds itself around a ruined cross, red and black smoke rises from enormous chimneys towering over the dilapidated village, and men kill and skin a rabbit as a blindfolded child plays hide and seek — all set to Gustav Mahler's ethereal music — it is clear that symbolic imagery takes precedence over plot. The story is told through the eyes of two children, the ten-year-old boy called Rainbow-maker, whose grandfather is the devoted Stalinist mayor of the village, and the eerily beautiful little girl Marie, who sings nursery rhymes and recites enigmatic verses. The children dream of utopia but play in a forest that is as beautiful and as wicked as any imagined by the Grimm brothers. The boy's father, grandfather, and the chairman of the farm collective are all socialists who fight over power using common methods of tyranny, including assassination, denunciation, banishment, and indoctrination of the youth as informants. Life in this grotesque vision of the GDR in the fifties consists mostly of marching in parades, giving speeches, getting drunk, having sex, killing animals, and praying to Stalin. Although Kipping's village is an imaginary place, there are direct references to the GDR: Walter Ulbricht's photograph graces the building that serves as both SED party headquarters and a brothel. After the death of their god-like leader, the inherent brutality of the regime bursts out into the open. The revolt of the 17 June 1953 is depicted in apocalyptic tableaus of fiery destruction that end in the grandfather's being crucified on a black-red-gold stake and crying out "Stalin, why have you forsaken me?" Despite the destructive force of extreme political idealism, the hope of finding utopia is inexplicably resilient. The film ends with the entire village, including the children, marching out into the wasteland past the lonely Karl Marx monument in search of the land beyond the rainbow.

In contrast to Foth and Kipping's experimental work, Roland Gräf's *Der Tangospieler* (The tango player, 1991), Heiner Carow's *Verfehlung* (The mistake, 1992), and Frank Beyer's *Der Verdacht* (Suspicion, 1991) are mainstream productions by seasoned directors based on well-known literary texts, and they star popular actors. These three films are indebted to the DEFA tradition of realism and focus on the everyday lives of individuals who are subjected to the arbitrary power of the socialist state. The main characters are complex figures; they do not seek to change the system through active protest, but when they are robbed of their freedom and self-determination, they must choose between conformity and defiance.

Der Tangospieler, based on Christoph Hein's eponymous novel and starring Michael Gwisdek, is a calm and confident film about the unwitting dissident Hans-Peter Dallow. Sentenced to twenty-one months in prison for playing the piano at a cabaret where students sang a tango maligning the state, Dallow experiences momentary paralysis and cannot sign his name on his release papers as the film opens. Leaving prison in early 1968, the former historian wants nothing more to do with his profession or the piano. He is a mere shell of his former self and wants only to be left alone to ponder the injustice done to him. Schulz and Müller, the laughable Laurel and Hardy type Stasi officers who show up on his doorstep and promise restitution of his position at the university if he will become an informant, are all the more frightening for the banality of their power. Never fully liberated from his wrongful imprisonment, Dallow floats through his life, passive and unable to forget the past. In a rare moment of rage he attacks the judge who sentenced him unfairly but falls short of killing him. Dallow has become so distant in his personal relations and political beliefs that he is numb to the news that Soviet tanks have violently crushed the Prague Spring. Despite his attempts to maintain a position as an outsider, he eventually surrenders himself to the system in a moment of opportunism. When an unsuspecting colleague tells students that it is unthinkable that Soviet and GDR troops would ever invade Czechoslovakia and that the news must be Western propaganda, he is fired and replaced by the formerly disgraced history teacher, Dallow. Ironically, it is another trivial mistake, naively questioning a story that seems ludicrous but is actually true, that lands the colleague in much the same kind of trouble as Dallow faced by playing the piano and that exemplifies the arbitrary nature of power in the SED state. Upon his triumphant return to the university, Dallow waves happily to the dimwitted Stasi man Müller, suggesting that collaboration is the price he has paid for his rehabilitation and promotion. The cost is nothing less than his identity, for the film ends on the same note it began: Dallow is unable to make his arm work and sign his name legibly on his new employment papers.

Heiner Carow's *Verfehlung* is the counterpart to *Der Tangospieler*, because here the main character, the fifty-year-old widowed cleaning woman Elisabeth Bosch, lashes out against the representative of the SED state and kills her oppressor. The film features Angelica Domröse, famous for her starring role in Carow's DEFA classic *Die Legende von Paul und Paula* (The legend of Paul and Paula, 1972). Thus the naive but strong-willed Elisabeth, who insists on grabbing on to her chance for happiness, seems like the logical development of the free-spirited but doomed Paula. Based on a short story by Werner Heiduczek, *Verfehlung* concerns a love affair destined for tragedy because of the inner-German border in late 1988 and early 1989. Jacob, a widowed dockworker from Hamburg, visits relatives in the decrepit East German village of Bubenau and falls in love with Elisabeth, but the political division of the two German states prevents them from being together. The two secretly meet in a friend's apartment in East Berlin, but when Jacob comes to Bubenau without a visa to celebrate publicly his engagement to Elisabeth, the town's mayor, who is also in love with her, has his rival arrested and deported. In a purely personal vendetta, the scorned mayor uses his position of authority to ruin the lives of Elisabeth's children. Son Hans is loyal to the regime but is suddenly denied his appointment as a foreign correspondent in Damascus, while son Holger, who takes part in the oppositional church movement, is carted off to a psychiatric hospital. The film culminates in the carnivalesque atmosphere of the 750th anniversary of the village, where the mayor gives an impassioned speech espousing socialism's successes while farm women do a can-can dance down the main street and masked villagers walk through a fun-house hall of mirrors. The carnival reveals the surreal and distorted nature of the SED regime and fulfills its function as the fleeting overturn of established power structures when Elisabeth kills the mayor after he tries to rape her. Elisabeth's rebellion on the eve of the revolution is ultimately self-destructive, forcing her to go from the petty and restrictive cage of the GDR to an even smaller prison cell in united Germany.

Frank Beyer's *Der Verdacht*, with a screenplay by Ulrich Plenzdorf based on Volker Braun's *Die unvollendete Geschichte* (Unfinished story,

1975/1988) and starring Michael Gwisdek, continues this trend. *Der Verdacht* is set in the GDR in the seventies and is about the absurd lengths to which the party went in order to preserve the illusion of consensus. Karin, the daughter of a high-ranking party official, is given an internship in the state-run newspaper, where she must prove her partisanship as a prerequisite for admission to the university. Her father insists that she break up with her boyfriend Frank because the young man has "plans," a rather vague category of anti-social behavior that is eventually identified as *Republikflucht*. The daughter bows to the pressures of her parents and the state, breaking off their relationship, but she is fired from her job and relegated to the status of menial worker. When Frank attempts to commit suicide and lies in a coma, the truth comes out, that the only evidence against him is that a friend who defected wrote him a letter encouraging him to leave — a letter Frank never received. Beyer prefigures Frank's suicide attempt and the theme of petty bourgeois acquiescence to social pressures by having Karin and Frank attend a performance of the controversial cult classic *Die neuen Leiden des jungen W.* (The new sorrows of young W.), but the director also creates critical distance to the topic through self-reflectivity by having Ulrich Plenzdorf, the author of both the drama and this film's script, prominently seated in the theater behind Karin and Frank. Like other DEFA directors from this period, Beyer also inserts surreal episodes in his realistic narrative, rendering Karin's misgivings in fantastic dreams that reveal the absurdity of the system. Frank's recovery, the family's remorse, and Karin's return to her lover do not represent a comfortable and reassuring return to normalcy, since Frank has no memory of the events. When he laughs at the story the nurses told him that he supposedly tried to kill himself over a failed escape attempt and betrayal and puts his arms around his girlfriend, her awkward smile and searching look speak volumes for the suppressed history lying just below the surface.

These dark, retrospective films with characters who suffer from ailments ranging from disillusionment to madness appeared in cinemas at the same time as lighthearted comedies such as *Go Trabi Go* (Peter Timm, 1991), its sequel *Das war der wilde Osten* (That was the Wild West, Wolfgang Büld and Reinhard Klooss, 1992), *Superstau* (Super traffic jam, Manfred Stelzer, 1991), and *Wir können auch anders* (*No More Mr. Nice Guy*, Detlev Buck, 1993). These road movies, which explore the culture clash when East meets West in a post-cold-war world, started a comedy wave that culminated in two films based on scripts by Thomas Brussig, *Sonnenallee* and *Helden wie wir* (Heroes like us, Sebastian Peterson, 1999). The box office hit *Sonnenallee* in particular caused an uproar for portraying the GDR as a normal state, where teenagers go to extraordinary lengths to get pop music, everyone just wants to fit in, and it seems completely acceptable for a young man to stylize himself as a rebel and rewrite history in order to win over a beautiful girl.

One of the most popular genres used to explore the impact of the Wall on the lives of individuals has been the melodrama. Margarethe von Trotta's *Das Versprechen* (The promise, 1995), a highly emotional story of a couple who continued to love each other despite living on opposite sides of the Berlin Wall, was the first film to deal with German division from 1961 to 1989. *Wie Feuer und Flamme* a teenage love story set in the punk scene in 1980s East Berlin, likewise relies on the forced separation of lovers to portray the division of the two German states. A love triangle is at the center of *Der rote Kakadu* (The red cockatoo, Dominik Graf, 2006), where a group of young people in Dresden in 1961 try to follow their dreams but run into trouble with the law for playing forbidden Western rock-and-roll music and writing decadent poetry. They must decide to stay or flee before the borders are fortified.

Television films such as *Nikolaikirche* (St. Nicholas Church, Frank Beyer, 1995), *Der Tunnel* (The tunnel, Roland Suso Richter, 2001), *Zwei Tage Hoffnung* (Two days of hope, Peter Keglevic, 2003), *Die Luftbrücke — Nur der Himmel war frei* (The Berlin air lift — Only the heavens were free, Dror Zahavi, 2005), and *Die Mauer — Berlin '61* (The Wall — Berlin 1961, Hartmut Schoen, 2006) are largely docudramas that center on the most well-known crises as told through the eyes of sympathetic characters. These made-for-television movies were remarkably popular and reached an audience of millions.[14]

Die Architekten

Just three days shy of the fortieth anniversary of the German Democratic Republic and a month before the Berlin Wall fell, director Peter Kahane began filming *Die Architekten* (The architects) based on a script by Thomas Knauf. *Die Architekten* concerns a young man's crumbling dream of building a utopian urban landscape and was intended as a radical critique of contemporary conditions. However, by the time it premiered on 27 May 1990 at the last Feature Film Festival of the GDR, it had become a dirge to the vanishing socialist state.[15] Although the script was approved in December 1988 and production authorization was granted in April 1989, filming was repeatedly delayed and began only on 3 October 1989, with the final shooting completed on 16 January 1990.[16] In the tumult of the *Wende* Kahane decided at first to make changes in the script to keep pace with the emerging political transformations, but the speed and scope of these changes were too vast to overcome. Eventually he recognized that *Die Architekten* was not a film about the present but a history film about the recent past. Kahane noted: "We tried to be in sync with the time, and we were always chasing after it. We filmed demonstrations and vigils and suddenly something else would become important. Then we made the decision that this would become a historical film,

Fig. 2.3. Still from Peter Kahane's Die Architekten *(1990).*
Photo © and by permission of DEFA Spectrum/Christa Köfer.

ending in the spring of 1989."[17] According to the director, the decision
to go back to the original script meant that there would be a shift in
tone rather than extensive plot modifications: "Earlier the images and
music were supposed to make clear that despite his defeat Daniel would
continue to fight with even greater radicalism. That was our desire and
also our way of experiencing the tragic and nonetheless encouraging
ourselves. After the people of this country changed our society with just
such radicalism, the hope was fulfilled. What remains is to tell about our
losses."[18] In the period leading up to the peaceful revolution of 1989,
filmmakers and audiences alike were ready for a more open and analyti-
cal look at present-day circumstances. Kahane recalled that "the time of
being indirect was over for us. We wanted to call things what they were,
we wanted to see the Wall on film, to show a departure and experience
the whole misery of people who were cheated out of one of the most
important things — their hopes — . . . and the absurdity of a political
system which did not let its own people become active and because of
that had to collapse."[19]

Peter Kahane was born in 1949, the year the GDR was founded.
His career was marked by the same overblown tutelage in the DEFA studios that his character Daniel faces in the field of architecture. Like his

compatriots in this last generation of East German directors, the so-called *Nachwuchsregisseure*, Kahane was only entrusted with his own project as a full-fledged director in 1988, just shy of his fortieth birthday. He applied three times to the Hochschule für Film und Fernsehen Konrad Wolf in Babelsberg-Potsdam before being accepted and completing his studies between 1975 and 1979. He worked as an assistant director until 1983. Only after proving himself as a junior director in 1985 with the coming of age/buddy film *Ete und Ali* (Ete and Ali, 1985) and the subsequent teenage love story *Vorspiel* (Prelude, English title: *Prepared for Love*, 1987) was Kahane given the position of director in 1988. His first proposal for a film about the relationship between communists and Jews in a French internment camp during the Second World War was not approved, because it did not conform to the prevailing concept of antifascism. *Die Architekten* was his first independent feature film under DEFA. Kahane felt growing frustration with the system that kept him at bay: "I always had the feeling, and so did nearly all my colleagues in my age group, that they wouldn't let me enter into this country. I longed for nothing more eagerly than to take part in the GDR. I wanted finally to arrive and not always have the feeling that somehow they were making me stand outside on the doorstep."[20] According to Kahane, this was a common experience for the entire middle generation of GDR citizens, who grew up believing in the idealism of building a perfect society but were always relegated to the sidelines as powerless observers: "We were probably the last generation that took seriously the public challenge to join in and participated the least . . . Thus we got caught in the discrepancy between demands and possibilities — our age-group, just as old as this country. But they didn't really want us. They disparaged us as young talent, as apprentices."[21]

The middle generation's pressing desire to utilize its untapped creativity and contribute to a better society is the central theme of *Die Architekten*. Daniel Brenner, a 38-year-old architect who has never realized a single original project, is given the opportunity to assemble his own team and design a business and cultural center for a new housing development on the outskirts of Berlin. Emboldened by this rare chance to create a livable space on a human scale, Daniel devotes himself fully to the project, neglecting his family to such an extent that his marriage crumbles and his wife and daughter defect to the West. Ultimately faced with the unbridgeable gap between the ideal and the practical, Daniel's team is forced to make so many concessions that their final design is devoid of any imagination and looks like every other dreary city center in the GDR. The team falls apart, but Daniel continues to make compromises in the hope that some glimmer of his design will come to fruition. While government officials celebrate Daniel's debatable achievements with meaningless awards to uphold a facade of success, he ends up alone and collapses from exhaustion and defeat.

It is remarkable that this film script was ever approved, because its critique of architecture cuts to the core of one of the most cherished myths in the GDR: namely that the socialist state was built on the ruins of National Socialism and that the reconstruction of the country based on humanistic principles wed to modern technology would free the worker from fascist ideology. From its very inception the GDR saw itself as a phoenix born from the ashes of destruction as immortalized in the first line of the national anthem: "risen from the ruins and facing the future" (Auferstanden aus Ruinen und der Zukunft zugewandt). The building metaphor signaling the need for a collective renewal of society was so central to the state's identity that the term *Aufbau* (construction) lent its name to the premiere publishing house in the GDR, the literary epoch of *Aufbauliteratur* or reconstruction literature from 1945 to 1953 dedicated to promoting antifascist, socialist values, and to the relentlessly repetitive refrain from the FDJ anthem admonishing East German youth to build up the new state ("Bau auf, bau auf, bau auf, bau auf, Freie Deutsche Jugend, bau auf !"). The propaganda value of architecture to make the emerging state's power visible in concrete terms was not lost on officials like Walter Ulbricht, as both the success and the failure of the Stalinallee building project so poignantly demonstrate. The grandiose neo-classical facades of the workers' palaces in the Stalinallee constructed in the fifties were meant to be commensurate with the workers' decisive role in the socialist state. The SED considered the fact that the 17 June 1953 uprising originated largely on the street dedicated to the memory of the Soviet leader as an especially painful failure and a betrayal of enormous proportions by the immature and ungrateful workers.[22]

The GDR constitution guaranteed housing, and in the sixties the government began to construct large housing complexes made of prefabricated materials (*Plattenbaugebiete*) that dominated the urban landscape and were known for their monotony, poor craftsmanship, and isolating properties.[23] *Die Architekten* focuses on the failures of this building program, which resulted from economic shortages and an entrenched official policy that forced architects to follow conventional methods. Daniel's team takes seriously the *16 Principles of Urban Planning* drafted in the early fifties and based on Soviet models, including the mandate that "the city is in structure and architectonic form the expression of the political life and national consciousness of the people."[24] These young men and women want to create through architecture a close-knit community in which the residents can enjoy a sense of belonging. Daniel reasons: "Therefore it's less about expensive facades and much more about comfortable rooms. Passageways, squares, streets with human proportions. Full of diversity. Where people meet and don't get lost, as is now the case. Only if we hold to this principle will the people of our city have a sense of wellbeing and recognize the city as home."[25] One of their greatest challenges is to ensure architectural variety, not merely to provide people with alternatives that best fit their lifestyle but also so that each place has a unique quality. Half in jest, the group concedes: "Only those who can choose have . . . feelings for the homeland."[26] In the heated context of the *Wende,* as hundreds of thousands of GDR citizens were marching in the streets demanding free elections among other things, the use of the word *wählen* meaning both "to choose" and "to vote" reflects the growing desire for more than just a livable physical environment but also for democratic processes and self-determined nationhood. Without being able to differentiate one neighborhood from another, the local from the regional or national, one cannot expect people to feel connected to their immediate environment. Paradoxically, it is by acknowledging and fostering difference on the micro level that one can engender similitude on the macro level. Taken to its ultimate extreme the collective essence of socialist life would require that every neighborhood and every city look alike in order to guarantee equal access and distribution of assets, but the young architects argue that equality does not have to mean monotony.

In the late eighties the gigantic prefabricated housing developments throughout the GDR were surrounded by social and commercial spaces that dwarf the inhabitants and stifle interaction. Cookie-cutter buildings made of the same concrete facades stood facing vast empty, treeless squares. The cheerless surroundings contributed to an overwhelming sense of alienation in the population. The architects envision building a completely different urban setting, one that provides variety, visual surprise, smaller proportions to promote coziness and contact, and a sense of belonging that will stem the flow of GDR citizens escaping to the West. Their imaginative designs include a Vietnamese restaurant, a hexagon-shaped ice cream shop, a rooftop playground, a department store with fresh air instead of air conditioning, glass-topped buildings, and comfortable open spaces for socializing, where art and nature coexist in harmony. Construction foreman Franziska, like her namesake Franziska Linkerhand, the idealistic young architect from Brigitte Reimann's eponymous novel, marvels that they are poised to create a whole new GDR architecture.[27] Unfortunately, despite their hard work the plans never get past the conceptual stage. The bureaucrats reject their designs as completely unrealistic. Not only are there serious shortages of construction materials, but the industrial plants are unwilling to alter manufacturing techniques to make the necessary materials, because such changes would endanger their fulfillment of production quotas. Equally important is that the bureaucrats want no risk taking and insist upon conformity to the tried and true methods, which naturally will result in the same uniform development that already exists everywhere in the country.

What the architects recognize and the bureaucrats refuse to acknowledge is that the dreary blocks of uniform housing, devoid of individuality and any sense of joy in living, are reflected in the lives of those who must inhabit this cold environment. In the numbing atmosphere of a housing development without any common space for entertainment, companionship, and intellectual stimulus, Daniel's wife Wanda has lost all sense of herself. Her isolation and lack of identity are illustrated by her constant staring into the mirror or off into empty space and by the fact that she is often filmed alone in the frame looking lost and without purpose. Wanda hits rock bottom one evening as she sits helplessly on the floor watching the mindless variety show "Ein Kessel Buntes" on television. Over the ridiculously cheerful love song performed by GDR singing stars Monika Hauff and Klaus-Dieter Henkler, Wanda's quiet weeping is barely perceivable. When Daniel finally notices his wife, the former med. student is astonished at how low she has sunk: "Look what I'm watching. . . . I'm turning into an idiot here. . . . I'm becoming a mouse . . . turning more and more into a mouse. A little, gray mouse. I no longer experience anything."[28] Unlike Daniel who is engrossed in difficult but rewarding work, Wanda has no outlet for her creativity and in the end refuses to accept this vegetative, purposeless state of existence.

Daniel is oblivious to his wife's suffering and suggests merely changing the channel. Indeed, Daniel's detachment is visualized through his position vis-à-vis Wanda; he is repeatedly shown bending over his work with his back to her. When Wanda tries to express her deep-seated feeling of worthlessness, he dismisses it as her inability to find the right dress to wear. The more Daniel tries to placate Wanda, the angrier she becomes, because he fails to acknowledge the problem. Finally she breaks down and shouts: "Stop making fun of me, you macho! You don't care how I'm doing. You don't even notice all the things I do so that you can work in peace. . . . Leave me alone. Leave me. And from now on I'm going to do my own thing. My own thing!!!"[29]

Wanda's charge of chauvinism is not an isolated incident. Indeed, sexist attitudes toward women are shown as pervasive. The rhetoric afforded to promoting gender equality and the family, officially defined in the GDR as "the smallest cell of society" (die kleinste Zelle der Gesellschaft), is contradicted by the chauvinist attitude toward women and their role as mothers first and foremost. When Daniel introduces his team of seven samurai, director Wieschala sarcastically remarks that he can only see three heroes since the other four are women. In response to Franziska's retort that women obviously do not count under socialism, Wieschala adopts a paternalistic tone: "I have no doubt that you women are highly qualified architects. But you yourselves know that especially among young women there are . . . contradictions between engagement in work and family planning."[30] Franziska fires back that she has a solution and hands the stunned director a condom. Despite this timely and biting come back, the very real pressures on women to do double duty as mothers and workers are not met with commensurate support. Faced with numerous delays and compromises, the young trainee Barbara quits when she becomes pregnant. Some women are encouraged never even to enter into their chosen careers because they are not capable of juggling family and professional responsibilities. Trained architect Renate admits that she never practiced her profession, because she was convinced that a single mother could not do the job. The fact that she has internalized the prevailing sexist attitudes becomes readily apparent when Renate explains why she is now working in an archive: "I never was an architect. My male colleagues convinced me anyway that as a single mother one can't be both. So based on my own wish I was promoted to here."[31]

Ironically, the proposed sculpture, "Family in Stress," reflects the status of Daniel's own marriage, but he seems more intent on producing a socially meaningful artwork than restoring his broken relationship with his wife. The sculpture depicting a faceless mother, father, and child hurrying off into different directions was intended as an acknowledgment that the conditions for a harmonious domestic life were not yet met under real-existing socialism. The artist's insistence on placing the sculpture in front of the grocery store reflects the economic aspects of this discord and the pressure that shortages in the planned economy put on families and personal relationships. The bureaucrats reject the sculpture out of hand. Construction director Adam states publicly:

> With all due respect for the originality of the works — these suggestions in their present condition are unacceptable. What does "Family in Stress" mean and for whom are we supposed to erect this memorial? Have you seriously debated this with the sculptors? Comrade Brenner, I think you all have landed in a dead end. A "Family in Socialism" is an important theme — such a group sculpture is thinkable. The portrayal of stress cannot be the concern of engaged socialist artists.[32]

Much more problematic than the sculptures are the extravagant designs that force the central planners to think outside the box. Reminiscent of Khrushchev's admonishment to "my dear expensive architects," which signaled the shift to mass, prefabricated housing, director Adam demands that the team follow standard building methods in place since the sixties. Strict adherence to conventional architectural styles is part and parcel of the government's attempts to preserve the dominant power structures — in concrete if need be.

Daniel seeks out his mentor Professor Vesely to help save the project. Not surprisingly, the eighty-year-old architect who helped reconstruct the GDR after the Second World War lives on Strausberger Platz in one of the workers' palaces built in the fifties. Proud of his contributions to the monumentalism glorifying the communist state, Vesely encourages Daniel to stop fighting the central planners and learn to compromise. As he puts his arm around Daniel's shoulders and looks out the window onto Karl-Marx-Allee (the former Stalinallee), Professor Vesely relishes the authority embodied in architecture: "Building is politics, the portrayal of power. Every house tells a tale . . . intentionally or unintentionally. Of wealth or thrift, dreams or despair, economics, technology, and of course the taste, good or bad, of the customer."[33] The entrenched nature of power in the GDR is made clear shortly after this meeting, when Daniel takes Renate and her son for a drive through the city on a gray, wintry day. Despite the fact that Daniel has a newly constituted family, they cannot provide him with the sense of belonging he so desperately desires, because the physical environment continues to alienate its inhabitants. In a long, lingering shot from Daniel's car, the camera follows the Berlin Wall while a children's chorus sings the ironically cheerful folksong "Unsere Heimat, das sind nicht nur die Städte und Dörfer" (Our homeland is not just the cities and villages). The song continues as the view from Daniel's car changes but never offers any solace: the never-ending gray facade of the Berlin Wall that blocks the view and restricts movement to a narrow strip is followed by long shots of the highway, where faceless people in tiny cars just like Daniel's buzz past industrial plants like drones. Daniel's car is dwarfed as it enters a massive prefabricated housing development typical of the Marzahn district and approaches the hive-like skyscraper towering so high that the camera cannot capture it in its entirety. There is no escape from the uniformity that turns people into insignificant creatures.

Photographer Martin Bulla, who joined the team because he believes in lost causes, is the most critical voice among them and the first to leave when their plans are rejected. Early on he warned the other architects that their reluctance even to imagine anything out of the ordinary was just a form of self-censorship that saved the authorities the trouble of restraining them. Unlike Daniel, Martin refuses to accept the official system of tutelage that keeps ordinary citizens in their place, because: "At 39 I want finally to be an adult."[34] Now that the central planners have stripped their design of originality he warns: "We should quit before they slay us with the waterwheel of uniformity. Now we have to fight even for the title 'socialist work collective.' There's nothing more they fear than a collective of people who are united. They are hard to govern."[35] Martin's admonition reflects a remarkable insight into the mindset that eventually toppled the regime, but his artwork is even more sensitive. Martin's black and white photographs reveal the bleak urban landscape, where both old and new buildings show the signs of neglect and a lack of imagination. History is recorded physically on these architectural surfaces as scars. Most disturbing, however, are his portraits of men and women who epitomize the idea of lives not led because of the stifling atmosphere of conformity. With their careworn faces, vacant expressions, and dead eyes, these people

exist as mere shells without joy or passion. Far from illustrating the positive hero dedicated to building the socialist state, who perseveres against
all obstacles and retains his optimism and partisanship, these ordinary
citizens are resigned and defeated. Daniel studies the unsettling portraits
that record in minute detail the human cost of unfulfilled dreams and
recognizes his ex-wife's despondent face. He turns toward the camera and
sees Martin watching him with a photographer's probing eye. Set against
a white background and captured in the same close-up as in the other
portraits, Daniel's sad and helpless expression poignantly demonstrates
that he too has joined the hopeless masses.

Together with the frozen moments captured in Martin's photographs, there are several references to the passage of time as out of sync
with interior yearnings. In the first sequence introducing the Brenner
family, Daniel's daughter Johanna paints colorful and imaginative houses
in a lush green environment, while Daniel meticulously sketches an exact
replica of a fossil and Wanda daydreams alone in the next room. The
unencumbered fantasy of youth is lost on the older generation, which has
learned to endure the petrified societal and personal relationships inherent in the stagnating environment of the GDR in the late eighties. When
Wanda stares at herself in the mirror, all she sees is time ravaging her
face and, more importantly, her unexplored inner reaches. This untapped
potential is the price one must pay in order to buy into the system, since
socialism's utopian vision requires the renunciation of current individual
desires for the promise of future fulfillment for all.[36] Wanda finally breaks
with Daniel and decides to move to the West, because she has lost all
hope that a day of gratification will ever come. She asks Daniel: "Why
should I live here? Simply because I was born here? I need more. I want
to find myself again. In work, in the way that people interact with me and
that I interact with others. But I . . . I don't find myself anywhere."[37]
Refusing to let time simply pass her by, Wanda displays the courage Daniel lacks, and thus she leaves the country, risking the uncertainty of a new
life in the West.

Die Architekten broke numerous taboos and deviated substantially
from the socialist realist principles that still largely governed DEFA productions in the eighties. In Kahane's film the requisite depiction of partisanship was inverted, since the party officials and high-ranking bureaucrats
are revealed to be overly cautious reactionaries intent on maintaining the
status quo. The young skilled workers who eschew party membership are
the revolutionary driving force in society. The approved film script openly
stated that in the last decade many talented young people had defected to
the West or had been imprisoned for something as simple as participating in a sit-in against the demolition of a church. Even the Stasi, known
in the parlance of everyday life as "the firm" and "sneak and peek," was
not immune and was addressed in metaphoric language that leaves little

to the imagination. Winfried decries the situation: "They put a cuckoo in our nest . . . Naumann, the firm's perfumed nightmare. Promoted out of every department for incompetence. Daniel, you have to do something." Daniel calmly responds: "Oh, that's crazy. Your mistrust is absurd. Even if he is a cuckoo — we don't have anything to hide."[38] In the completed film all figurative language is dropped and the architects call the Stasi by name and talk about how people in the church are forming a movement and protesting.

The Berlin Wall and the border between West and East Germany were generally taboo and rarely graced the screen in DEFA productions. A notable exception was Roland Gräf's film *Die Flucht* (Escape, 1977), where the problem of highly skilled workers leaving the country is depicted in an unusually open fashion. The main character, a dedicated physician who cannot conduct important medical research in the East and thus intends to flee to the West, decides to stay for love and a second chance in his career. While *Die Flucht* presents the main character, Dr. Schmith, as a compassionate figure whose motives for leaving the GDR are altruistic, the film still shows the limits of DEFA productions in the late seventies. It seems as if the very thought of fleeing the republic was a transgression that precluded rehabilitation and reintegration into society. The physician is harassed by the coyotes he originally hired to take him over the border and under duress agrees to make the illegal crossing, only to be thrown from the speeding car and killed. Thus despite the film's critical look at GDR society, it literally eliminates from the picture a troublesome individual who does not fit easily into the schema of good and evil. By contrast, in *Die Architekten* Wanda is a sympathetic character who defects to the West with her daughter in a desperate act to save herself. The departure scene where Wanda and Johanna say good-bye to Daniel at the Friedrichstraße train station in front of the *Tränenpalast* (palace of tears), where in reality families and friends enacted tearful leave-taking on a daily basis, was unique and marked a radical shift in DEFA censorship policies in 1988–89. *Die Architekten* was also exceptional for showing the Brandenburg Gate surrounded by the Wall and a Western observation platform. In this scene, Daniel desperately pulls open his jacket to expose his sweater so that his daughter will recognize him from her platform in the West, but the gesture to assert his individuality is futile and ends only with his humiliation and despair. The scene at the Brandenburg Gate was originally intended as the film's finale and was supposed to exhibit Daniel's resolve to continue the good fight, as illustrated in the last stage direction, which called for a silent reaffirmation of his commitment: "His face shows pain — but also energy."[39]

This optimistic conclusion might have come across as plausible if we consider several important scenes that were cut after the *Wende*. The most startling difference between the approved script of 17 July 1989 and the film completed after the fall of the Wall is that Kahane and Knauf initially had Daniel joining the SED. Daniel consults with his mentor Professor Vesely, who suggests that the architect needs to join the party if he really wants to change things. Daniel refuses: "Sure, first the party and then careerism. That won't work precisely because the instruments with which I can acquire power and influence are exactly *the* instruments which will destroy me and my ideas."[40] And yet without explanation Daniel makes an about-face and assimilates. The stage directions read: "Daniel becomes a candidate for the SED, Zahlke hands him his candidacy card, the by-laws, and a bouquet of flowers." Director Wieschala expresses his surprise that the architect has joined the party, and Daniel boldly warns him: "From now on you will be surprised even more often."[41] The conversion of a reluctant hero to the party was a standard plot twist in socialist realist literature and may well have contributed to the approval of this film script in the GDR. However, it is questionable whether audiences in 1988 and 1989 would have been reassured by a film that spent over an hour portraying despair and hopelessness and then concluded with less than five minutes of familiar clichés.

Peter Kahane readily conceded that by the time his film hit the cinemas history had passed them by, and what once seemed spectacular in its radical critique was eclipsed by a much more astonishing revolutionary reality. Furthermore, he noted that the timing of the premiere in early June 1990 was unfortunate, since it fell in the period when most East Germans were changing their currency to West Marks. Preoccupied with the uncertainties of the pending economic union, his intended audience was not interested in watching a film about the collapse of their state.[42] Nor apparently were Western audiences interested in the unfamiliar conditions in the GDR. The film was shown in empty theaters. A reviewer for the *Frankfurter Allgemeine Zeitung* suggested that Kahane should have either changed the plot to reflect the political upheaval surrounding the *Wende* or written a more general story to appeal to a wider (read Western) audience.[43] The critical reception of *Die Architekten* in the GDR press was largely positive and the vast majority of reviewers saw the film as an important document of the time. Writing for *Junge Welt*, Peter Claus maintains: "As an immediate reflection on the collapse of old GDR structures, the film has without a doubt great significance in my opinion, also as a document — about a country at its end."[44] Roland Herold insists in his review for the *Sächsisches Tageblatt*: "For me Kahane's film is among the most unsettling documents in the DEFA productions. . . . It seems completely out of the question to take in this film in a detached fashion. For the first and perhaps for the last time something like the process of mastering the past is being carried out. A look back, an honest accounting, an answer perhaps to the question of many frightened people whether what happened was the right thing."[45] Most Eastern commentators appreciated the authenticity of the story and the manner in which it captured the prevalent spirit of the time as wavering between hope and disillusionment.[46] Nearly all GDR reviewers saw the film as coming too late to fulfill its intended function as an aid for audiences to recognize social problems and encouragement that change was possible. Cinema in the GDR, Birgit Galle argued in the former SED party organ *Neues Deutschland,* functioned at its best as a unique opportunity to voice dissatisfaction in the highly restrictive public sphere. Galle states that the entire society needed such forums as cinema, "needed, that means above all counter arguments to the continuous agitation of the time. Back then and still yesterday filmmakers wanted to give their opinion, to register their opposition to the dangerous obstinacy of official ideology."[47] Axel Seitz in the *Norddeutsche Zeitung* posed the most provocative question: "Is it the unwanted look backward into our past or the one forward that sees no value in such films?"[48] In mid-1990, evoking the memory of a familiar but bygone world must have inevitably brought with it questions about the desirability of the present and trepidation about an undefined future.

Rather than focusing exclusively on the more obvious manifestations of the police state, such as the Stasi, censorship, imprisonment, and fortified borders, *Die Architekten* emphasizes the mindset that led to the GDR's downfall. The SED state collapsed from the inside because it encouraged an exaggerated form of stability that resulted in stagnation and a system of tutelage that constantly treated the populace as immature. The party's insistence on adherence to outdated and inefficient norms had a crushing effect on precisely those individuals who craved admittance into the system. Ironically, it was the idealistic middle generation who wanted nothing more than to function as a workable cog in the wheels of power, who sought the promise of socialism to unleash their creativity and grant them a sense of purpose, who became alienated and left, succumbed to defeatism, and eventually helped topple the regime.

Das Versprechen

When Margarethe von Trotta's *Das Versprechen* (The promise) opened the Berlin Film Festival on 9 February 1995, it was highly anticipated as the first feature film to address the German misery of division in a story spanning the entire duration of the Berlin Wall.[49] The film centers on Sophie and Konrad, two young lovers who attempt to escape the GDR in 1961 through the sewer canals. Only Sophie makes it to the West because Konrad trips over his shoelaces at the precise moment that a troop transport comes upon the manhole cover. He promises to catch up with her but circumstances repeatedly prevent him from joining her in the West. Despite the fact that in the next twenty-eight years they can only see each other four times, they have a child together and continue to love each other. With a script co-written by von Trotta and Peter Schneider, two

Fig. 2.4. Still from Margarethe von Trotta's Das Versprechen *(1995).*
Photo courtesy of Stiftung Deutsche Kinemathek.

prominent representatives of the '68 generation of student radicals who
had vigorously criticized the West German state but were far from promoting a blanket acceptance of the GDR's real-existing socialism, the
film had the potential to be an evenhanded depiction of the historical
divide between the two systems, albeit from a Western perspective. In
particular, Schneider's famous declaration in *Der Mauerspringer* (The
Wall jumper, 1982), that it would take longer to dismantle "the wall in
the head" than any physical barriers, suggested to many that the film
would shed light on the ideological schism between East and West.[50]
Moreover, since von Trotta was known for her ability to depict monumental historical events in terms of their effects on individual lives,
the story of unfulfilled love and the forced separation of a family was
immediately seen as a synecdoche for the fate of the German nation
after 1945. Despite, or more likely because of, the expectation that von
Trotta would deliver the definitive portrayal of the Wall, *Das Versprechen* was harshly reviewed in the press.

No stranger to the ire of German film critics, von Trotta was attacked
for, among other things, not having the right national pedigree to direct
the quintessential epic film on German postwar division. *Der Spiegel* magazine was especially vitriolic in its depiction of von Trotta as a somewhat
obtuse and self-serving ex-patriate:

> When the GDR collapsed Margarethe von Trotta was living in Rome and seemed to have justifiably turned away from the German miseries perhaps forever. It took the impetus of an Italian producer, who suggested a Wall film to her, before she recognized the arrogating magnitude of the task. At first she hesitated. However, after two additional films in Italy, she grabbed onto the Wall story completely, as is her style, in order to make it her own. Now she sits enthroned, an all-German concerned mother hen like never before.[51]

In an equally contentious interview with the director and co-scriptwriter published in *Die Tageszeitung*, Peter Schneider summarized: "Margarethe is always attacked because she was not here but in Rome when the idea was developed; they dispute her right to make such a film."[52]

Considering von Trotta's complex personal and intellectual background, it is perhaps not too surprising that critics questioned the extent to which her films are German. She has long acknowledged that she sees herself as an outsider, homeless and illegitimate, and thus particularly drawn to German history and identity politics: "I look for my family because I never had one and for my home because while I indeed grew up here and follow what happens here, at the same time I always have the feeling: this is not my country."[53] Born in Berlin in 1942, the illegitimate daughter of German painter Alfred Roloff and Baltic aristocrat Elisabeth von Trotta, who was born in Moscow but became a displaced person after the 1917 revolution, Margarethe von Trotta was stateless until 1964 when she married German citizen Jürgen Moeller. During her studies in Paris she fell in love with the movies and especially the works of Alfred Hitchcock, Ingmar Bergman, and French new-wave directors. Not only was it her inclination to seek inspiration in Anglo-American, Swedish, and French rather than German cinema; she had been living in Italy for seven years before she moved in 1994 to Paris, where she still resides today. Von Trotta's fascination with fractured identity and characters who seek their opposite in order to become complete is rendered in her films as an agonizing process often ending in madness and suicide or at the very least betrayal and imprisonment. These stories are often set against the most contested arenas of twentieth-century German history: the ideological battles waged between the socialist and communist parties and the assassination of Rosa Luxemburg and Karl Liebknecht, the motivations for terrorist action by the Red Army Faction and their subsequent incarceration in isolation torture, the systematic genocide of the Jews under National Socialism and the women's protest in the Rosenstraße, and most recently the inner-German spy system that preyed upon its victims via Stasi Romeos.

Numerous critics complained that von Trotta focused too much attention on the political repression in the GDR and exploited simplistic clichés.[54] The *Spiegel* article was particularly malicious in its comment that "without a doubt beyond reproach is the political correctness: German finger-pointing cinema par excellence for all the knowledge-hungry people in all the Goethe Institutes of the Third World."[55] Perhaps what actually disturbed these critics is that *Das Versprechen* is not so much about political oppression in the GDR and consumerism sustained by a fascist legacy in the FRG as about separation, the separation of lovers because of political decisions beyond their control, and about the imposed division of Germany by the postwar victors. An overwhelming sadness about the inability to affect change permeates the film, and it is this version of the past, I would argue, that many critics could not accept as the national history of Germany. Von Trotta's choice of melodrama as the appropriate genre for rendering the story of the Wall as an act beyond an individual's control was particularly apt because, as Thomas Elsaesser has rightly argued, the melodrama "records the failure of the protagonist to act in a way that could shape the events and influence the emotional environment, let alone change the shifting social milieu," and by extension, the political milieu.[56] The mere coincidence of Konrad's missing out on the chance to escape because of his untied shoelaces was a plot twist that some reviewers rejected outright. Comparing the character motivation in Christa Wolf's novel *Der geteilte Himmel* (Divided heaven, 1963) to *Das Versprechen*, Jörg Magenau applauded Wolf's novel because: "There too a couple is separated by political circumstances, but Manfred's escape to the West takes place after wrestling for a long time about the correct, better life. Christa Wolf leaves no doubt that remaining, as Rita decides to do, was the better choice even though she is uncertain, filled with contradictions and conflicts . . . Konrad remains in the East because he tripped over an untied shoelace. An unfortunate coincidence replaces what had been a conscious decision for Christa Wolf."[57] Leaving aside the question of whether remaining in the GDR and accepting the Wall as a necessary sacrifice was the right choice, Magenau has conveniently forgotten that the film and the novel take place in different time periods. What Magenau fails to acknowledge is that Wolf's characters part ways before the Wall was even built, and the vast majority of GDR citizens who woke up to the fortified border on 13 August 1961 did not have the option of making a conscious decision to stay or leave without risking imprisonment or death. Even an attempt to flee the country was a crime against the state, punishable by imprisonment. Anyone caught in the act of an illegal border crossing faced armed guards authorized to shoot to kill. Margarethe von Trotta and Peter Schneider see their story as ambiguous and repeatedly question the extent to which their characters are governed by outside forces or motivated alternately by fear, daring, complacency, ambition, and idealism. However, they stress that these characters have limited options in a Germany whose sovereignty is itself limited. *Das Versprechen* depicts

German national history and identity as subject to exterior forces. It is exactly the collective powerlessness of the German people to determine their own national borders, to ensure freedom of movement and association that, while difficult to accept, ultimately defined postwar German history until the *Wende*.

A montage of black and white historical footage outlining the Cold War battle lines in the early 1960s opens *Das Versprechen*. An accompanying voice-over sets up the film's central theme that by 1961 Germany was already divided into two distinct nations: "So began one of the strangest experiments in history. A people who were once consumed by the delusion of dominating the world gradually turned into two peoples. And soon the Wall was the only thing that perpetuated the illusion that a mere wall separated the Germans."[58] Images of cold-war warriors John F. Kennedy, Nikita Khrushchev, Walter Ulbricht, Willy Brandt, and Lyndon B. Johnson are followed by footage of the more or less nameless masses who helped build, defend, escape, protest, and mourn the Wall. Shots of construction workers laying the bricks and mortar are juxtaposed to the now-famous images of GDR soldier Conrad Schumann throwing down his rifle as he jumps over the barbed wire, 77-year-old Frieda Schulze climbing out of her apartment window and falling to the ground, and numerous men and women staring in disbelief, crying, and waving handkerchiefs over the newly erected border.

Das Versprechen thus shares with many of von Trotta's other films the use of embedded documentary material to comment on how individuals learn about and confront history and contemporary political events. As young schoolgirls Marianne and Juliane watch a documentary about Nazi atrocities and become physically sick to learn about their national heritage in *Die bleierne Zeit* (Leaden time, English title: *Marianne and Juliane*, 1981). In *Rosa Luxemburg* (1986), the revolutionary lies paralyzed on her bed weeping after she learns of her lover's death on the frontline, while newsreel footage of brutal carnage, desolate battlefields, and war widows fills the screen to the accompaniment of frantically pulsating violins, as if to imply that the wheels of history have driven over her body. However, in contrast to *Die bleierne Zeit, Rosa Luxemburg, Rosenstraße* (2003), and *Die andere Frau* (The other woman, 2004), which are nonlinear narratives about German history characterized by flashbacks and framed narratives, *Das Versprechen* is relentlessly chronological. The asynchronic editing techniques used in von Trotta's other historical dramas to comment on the relationship between the past and the present, between memory and the act of remembrance, are missing here.[59] In contrast, the narrative in *Das Versprechen* marches forward in an unwavering straight line and never affords the main characters or the viewers the opportunity to reflect on the past via editing.

Far from being a stylistic anomaly, the chronological editing and prominent use of documentary material in *Das Versprechen* are inextricably linked to von Trotta's concept of the relationship between individuals and historical forces. The film's linear structure suggests that the course of modern German history was largely governed by outside forces as a reaction to the country's earlier imperialistic war mania. The superpowers' agreement to determine Germany's postwar fate, shown in the handshake between Kennedy and Khrushchev, is underscored by the opening voice-over contending that the decision to build the Wall was made by the Soviet Union in cooperation with the capitalist West: "The Soviet Union held the copyright on the idea and its implementation, and West German companies delivered the barbed wire."[60] The characters who must negotiate their lives in a land held captive as a pawn in the game between the superpowers have few options. Cowriter Peter Schneider maintains that what interested him was not the machinations of world leaders who make history writ large but the lives of ordinary people, who must act within a narrow strip of freedom. Schneider poses the question: "What does history do to individuals whom it has to a certain extent taken hostage? The principle of chance is obviously part of it. Does Konrad stay in the East because of a ridiculous misfortune — because in the decisive moment he tripped over his shoe laces? How does the pair deal with this chance happening; indeed, is it actually chance?"[61]

Embedded news footage becomes an important instrument for reflection on individual resolve that is challenged by overwhelming might. The use of well-known documentary material situates the fictional story within a historical context, but it is the highly conspicuous manner in which it is inserted into this story that halts the narrative flow and beckons contemplation. Sophie, Konrad, Barbara, and Harald learn about historic events from watching television and must act or react to a world not of their making. In her aunt's West Berlin villa Sophie watches a newscast about the now legendary tunnel, which allowed twenty-six people from East Berlin to escape to the West in 1962.[62] Her passionate interest in the fate of the escapees is juxtaposed to her aunt's apathy and highlights the West's patent indifference to the plight of East Germans. In an East Berlin classroom Barbara, Harold, and some twenty students watch on television a Western news report showing Soviet tanks crushing the Prague Spring in 1968 and drawing parallels to the 1953 workers' revolt in the GDR and the Hungarian Uprising of 1956. The devastating news that socialism with a human face met its limits at the end of a Soviet rifle inspires Barbara and Konrad to engage in civil disobedience. They don black armbands and a photograph of Dubcek, staging a silent protest to mourn the death of a dream. In 1981 during the commemorative ceremonies marking the twentieth anniversary of the Wall, Sophie and Konrad watch television shows from rival German states offering conflicting versions of history. Sophie sits in her Kreuzberg apartment crying as she watches GDR news featuring an impressive military parade and extolling the efforts of the countless troops "to ensure the invulnerability of our borders and our territory."[63] At the same time Konrad is in his office watching a West German television report about human-rights protests in West Berlin and also the fictional account of Harold posing as the crucified Christ with the number 20 painted on his chest. The television reports draw attention to the public aspect of shared media images that transcend the Wall and unite Germans on both sides, despite all efforts by the GDR government to isolate itself from the West. The effectiveness of both Eastern and Western propaganda is, however, highly questionable. In the battle of the loudspeakers, for example, the message falls on deaf ears. While dueling loudspeakers on each side of the border try to influence citizens in the competing system, an old man sets up a ladder near the Wall in West Berlin and waves to a girl and older woman at the window in the East. In the midst of ideological warfare this divided family is oblivious to the rhetoric and merely does what it can to reconstitute itself, if only for a fleeting moment.

The relentless march of history illustrated in the documentary footage is juxtaposed to frozen personal time. From the opening scene, where the hand of a woman waving a handkerchief is suddenly rendered motionless and becomes the backdrop for the opening credits, to the final shot of the film, a close-up of Sophie's sad face, slightly out of focus and motionless, the course of exterior events is repeatedly arrested by intense emotional reactions. The incongruity between remote societal circumstances and personally significant feelings highlights, but never quite resolves, the question of whether the main characters are subjects or objects of history. In their first appearance on screen Sophie and Konrad seem frozen in time as they slow dance, while the entire auditorium around them appropriately bops to "Rock around the Clock." While the Prague Spring is in full motion outside, the young lovers run up the staircase in their hotel with the steady cam capturing their magnetic pull in one continuous shot over three flights of stairs. Accompanied by the overblown musical track with its excessively sentimental horns and strings, which allows no diegetic noise into their acoustically sealed private world, the steady cam follows them in spiraling movements, catching up to the lovers and then beckoning them upward in a dance of seduction with each other and with the camera. When the historical events in 1989 finally bring about what people in 1961 had passionately desired, it is too late for the characters to move in sync with time.[64] The former lovers are no longer the same people. Sophie's frozen image reflects their uncertain futures and, by extension, the fate of the German nation in late 1989.

In this film the possible actions and reactions to the division of Germany are reflected in the opposite personalities of the two main

characters. Konrad's diffidence and quiet resignation stand in stark contrast to Sophie's self-assured bravado. This figure constellation — pairing
a sensitive, passive individual with a practical, assertive one in a powerful
but ultimately doomed symbiosis — is familiar to viewers of von Trotta's
earlier films *Schwestern oder die Balance des Glücks* (Sisters or the balance
of happiness, 1979), *Die bleierne Zeit* (1981), and *Heller Wahn* (Sheer
madness, 1983). In *Das Versprechen* the existence of the Wall magnifies
the opposing tendencies.

Konrad Richter is the more passive, unworldly individual, who seems
at first to be a mere object acted upon by stronger forces. Sophie has to
alert him that it is time for their escape and later that Soviet tanks have
entered the Czechoslovakian capital. She is the one who figures out that
there are identical lanterns on different squares, enabling their reunion in
Prague. He is the dreamer and scientist who is more engrossed in romantic sentiments and complex mathematical equations than practicalities.
When faced with the full force of the state's paternalistic power over him,
Konrad remains inactive to the point of immobilization. Interrogated by
the Stasi, he neither betrays his friends nor protests the harsh treatment:
he simply remains silent. During their training as border guards, Harald
refuses to be indoctrinated and accept the command to shoot escapees,
but Konrad merely gives his brother-in-law a knowing look and keeps
rank. Although he initially takes it stoically when his father slaps him
across the face for trying to flee the country, Konrad eventually lashes out
against his father, a committed socialist, and the authoritative system he
represents. In the sheltered realm of the home, Konrad refuses to accept
the party line and shouts: "First I have to let myself be walled in because
I live in a better country. And then I have to let my father denounce me
because I want to get away from this better country."[65] Silent immov-
ability toward state officials and more honest and emotional outbursts
toward father figures continue to be his strategy. When a party representative hands Konrad a petition in support of the Soviet action in Prague,
he quietly refuses to sign it. Alone on the rooftop with his mentor Professor Lorenz, Konrad chastises the older man for signing the petition and
argues that such behavior is a cowardly crime that makes tyranny possible.
This conversation, in particular, illustrates that Konrad is acutely aware of
his ability to make certain choices, even in a one-party state.

Konrad's restricted existence in the GDR is repeatedly visualized in
images of entrapment. The prisons that individuals create for themselves
and those imposed by society are ever-present in Margarethe von Trotta's
films. In *Das Versprechen* Konrad is often framed by bars, railings, glass
doors, and windows that hinder his movement. He is trapped in a telephone booth when his father calls the Stasi to turn him in, cornered behind
a glass door and blocked from exiting the hotel by a Russian soldier during the Prague uprising, and forced to wait behind a glass door at the East

Berlin train station while his son crosses the border. Even when Konrad makes love to Sophie in Prague, he is filmed from behind the bars of a brass bed. On the night the Wall comes down, he is shown at work walking along an embankment of windows set against an eerily lit swimming pool and then on the balcony of his apartment. When his son leads him to the Bornholmer Bridge to meet Sophie, Konrad seems ill prepared to deal with this newfound freedom of movement and simply stops in his tracks.

As the years go by Konrad conforms more to societal pressures and finds a comfortable niche for himself and his new family. In a heated conversation with Sophie twenty years after his failed escape attempt, Konrad argues that he was never completely free to make his own decisions but found a way to survive and even prosper: "I had to learn to adjust to the life that was available to me."[66] Conformity in everyday life often manifests itself in small gestures that are never quite black and white. For example, when Alex gives his half-sister Lena an exotic stuffed panda bear and stirs up desires that can never be fulfilled, Konrad sneaks into her room at night and paints the toy to match the local brown bears in a degrading act of acquiescence but also in a tender way that a father would shelter his daughter. In a similar manner, he tries to convince Barbara to leave the GDR, because her husband is at his wit's end, fulfilling the Stasi officer's directive to rid the country of troublesome dissidents but also voicing his own opinion, because he cares for his sister and brother-in-law. It is, however, in a conversation with his son Alex that Konrad steps over the line toward denial and self-delusion. Stylizing himself as an intrepid idealist, he tells his son: "Remaining here — that was a daring move, an adventure. We wanted to build something completely new."[67] Perhaps recognizing the half-truth of his statement with its obvious trace of official rhetoric, Konrad admits that unlike Sophie he felt at home in the GDR and had valid reasons for wanting to stay. Perhaps the boldest move Konrad ever makes to assert himself is at the Olympic Stadium, when he literally inserts himself into the picture, joining a group of Japanese tourists taking a photograph with Sophie. This valiant effort to win Sophie's heart is followed by an even more courageous act to preserve his relationship with his son. Threatened with the prospect of never seeing Alex again, Konrad attacks the Stasi officer Müller, and his life falls apart like a house of cards. The consequences of Konrad's violent assault on the system are staggering and result in his losing everything he holds dear: his career, social status, family, and home.

Sophie Sellmann, by contrast, is a doer, impatient and quick to judge, because she sees the world in absolute terms. The generation conflict evident in Konrad's disputes with his father and Professor Lorenz takes on a more bitter form in Sophie's case, because she believes her stepfather was responsible for her father's suicide in prison. Sophie considers her mother's marriage to this man as a clear choice of him over her, and she refuses to make any concessions. Although the details of her father's imprisonment are never revealed, it seems as if Sophie has idealized him as a martyred resister and inherited his defiant nature. Her uncompromising attitude is readily apparent in her confrontations with Konrad, both in Prague and later at the Olympic Stadium. The lovers question each other's actions and ask whether each could have behaved differently. Sophie refuses to see Konrad's unwillingness to come to the West as anything more than a personal decision motivated by ambition and complacency. She cannot tolerate his blaming his circumstances on chance or political pressure: "At some point you have to proclaim your life as your own, even if it merely happened to you."[68] Taking action, however, does not necessarily bring happiness or even resolution. Sophie admits that she left the GDR but she is not sure that she has arrived anywhere yet. Despite the personal freedom and economic opportunities available in the West, she does not feel at home there. It is only in the optimistic air of the Prague Spring, where she can enjoy "democracy plus socialism" as well as an emotionally and sexually fulfilling relationship, that Sophie can envision finally reaching a spiritual home. However, just as the promise of the West as the land of plenty proved to be empty, so too does the promise of socialism with a human face fail to be fulfilled. Sophie reacts with anger and impetuousness, instinctively lashing out at the armed soldiers, which results in her being arrested and separated once again from Konrad.

The contrasts between Sophie and Konrad are marked by their costumes, which leave no doubt as to their different natures. Sophie's ardent personality is visualized in red costumes that denote her passion and vitality, beginning with her red dress at the high school dance and ending with her red coat in the closing scene of the film. Equally striking is Sophie's affinity to black and white clothing, including her checkered coat, her polka-dot hair ribbon, her knitted hat, her minidress in Prague, and the dress she wears when she takes Alex to the border crossing. In addition, nearly every piece of furniture and wall covering in her Kreuzberg apartment is black and white, hinting that she sees the world in these absolute terms. For Sophie there is no moral gray area, things are either right or wrong, people are either strong or weak. Konrad, by contrast, appears throughout the film in muted dark colors of gray, brown, and black, which are never too far removed from his military uniform. Apart from his white shirts, occasional striped patterned clothing, and dull maroon accents, he wears red only once. In Prague he dons a thin red tie when dancing with Sophie and his new Czechoslovakian colleagues, indicating that her active nature has vitalized him.

Von Trotta does not give complete credence to either Konrad's stance that life just happened to him or to Sophie's opinion that she carved out her own life based on sheer determination. It is the interchange between the public and the private, the sociopolitical milieu into which one is cast, and the conscious personal choices one makes that shape the course of each individual life and ultimately the contours of the social order. Kristie A. Foell has aptly noted that: "paradoxically, each appears more 'innocent' if s/he is a passive object acted upon by the forces of history, a melodramatic hero/ine tied to the railroad tracks of the historical process, as it were. By contrast, to the extent that each has actively chosen his or her own fate, each is responsible for the couple's separation, for the lack of closure in the melodramatic narrative."[69] Von Trotta's steadfast reliance on some of the more obvious components of the melodrama — a prominent, often intrusive musical score, extreme sentimentality, the aesthetically pleasing rendition of pain, domestic conflict amid societal pressures — stands in stark contrast to her refusal to offer narrative closure. The traditional family melodrama, with its emphasis on domestic discontent, female suffering, and the eventual reaffirmation of patriarchal familial structures, has long relied on exposing social contradictions only to deny them as driving factors in favor of character motivation and adaptation. In melodrama, the need for change is generally directed inward to the character and not outward to social institutions, such that characters adjust themselves to the system rather than look for ways to change their collective reality. Von Trotta's incomplete familial reunion of a bridge ending in a freeze-framed still image casts doubt on the feasibility and desirability of reestablishing the status quo. This incongruity between adherence to genre conventions and a denial of the expected resolution in reassuringly familiar images makes *Das Versprechen* a difficult film to process.

One of the most problematic aspects of this film is that von Trotta is especially skilled at translating the sentimental into powerful cinematic terms that totter between emotionally touching and overblown kitsch. In a scene worthy of Douglas Sirk, von Trotta stages a classic example of melodrama's rendering of unfulfilled female desire as glamorous and beautifully painful. Learning that Konrad did not show up for the escape she had planned, Sophie, dressed in a bright red taffeta ball gown, long white gloves, and glimmering jewelry, her lips bright red, and crying her eyes out, lies prostrate with grief on a sleek black-and-steel modern couch in front of a prominent, sparkling abstract design on the wall. The camera slowly pans in a half-circle around her lovely form, until it comes to a close-up of her tear-stained face. Abandoned in the midst of splendor and wealth, Sophie is the icon of female desire for love and sexuality left unsatisfied. In a crosscut to Konrad sitting upright in his bunk at night while his fellow soldiers sleep, the camera continues to arch around its parallel victim and the circle of despair is complete. Swathed in the blue-gray light of the GDR barracks and facing a cold, barren future without his beloved, Konrad quietly weeps in a pose reminiscent of the poet doomed to military service from Herbert Maisch's Nazi-era classic *Friedrich Schiller: Der Triumph eines Genies* (1940).

With its exaggerated costume details, stylized lighting, intimate camerawork focused on capturing the characters' suffering in minutiae, and nearly overpowering musical score, *Das Versprechen* seeks to elicit an emotional reaction using such heavy-handed methods that one wonders whether the attention to artifice is intentional. According to director Jutta Brückner, melodramatic excess is a staple of von Trotta's filmmaking and is used to make the viewer uncomfortably aware of the fact that social reality is created and not a natural phenomenon completely beyond human agency: "Images of interiors almost always have *too much*, too much significance in the details, in the aesthetic construction, to allow anyone to live life here effortlessly. A realism, which nearly cites itself, shows the weight of things and attitudes that smother people. . . . [Characters] observe each other in a light that is meticulous and has this touch of *too much*, imparting upon the realistic ambience an aura of inexplicable significance."[70] In *Das Versprechen* the excessive details are not merely evident in highly emotional signifiers such as Sophie's red bow functioning as a reminder of unfulfilled love or Konrad's untied shoe laces indicative of the disjointed condition of the separate German states. They are found in the license plate with the letters B-RD on the first American-made car the escapees see in the West signaling their arrival in the promised land, the pub sign *Zur Insel* on the West Berlin side of the Wall that has turned the city into an island, the cracked mirror as Soviet tanks roll into Prague and destroy the idealistic vision of socialism, and the child's ball mysteriously returned every time it ventures over the Wall, highlighting the ridiculous nature of the man-made border. If the reviews published in newspapers are any indication of the public reception, then for some viewers the exaggerated details appear as clichés, which disturb absorption in the film's events, and for others they are extremely moving elements that do not create the distance necessary for critical evaluation. Rarely do they function as artificial constructs that lead to contemplation on how society is built upon consensus and can be changed.

Apart from the main characters, Konrad and Sophie, who chose to live either with the SED dictatorship or outside it, there are secondary characters who actively protest from within and try to reform society. Konrad's sister Barbara and her husband Harald, for example, are dissidents who stage peaceful protests and suffer the consequences of imprisonment and expatriation. Barbara is a minister in a church where parishioners can voice dissatisfaction and carry out nonviolent campaigns against the establishment. Historically, the church was one of the few open forums in the GDR and functioned as a refuge for dissidents. The Monday night prayer services, like the one Barbara holds, developed into the peaceful, candle-lit demonstrations that eventually toppled the regime. Although Harald does not share Barbara's religious faith, he is equally convinced that engaged civil protest will result in a better system of democratic socialism. Harald's publicity stunt, posing as the crucified Christ at the Wall, lands him in prison and eventually sees him expatriated from the GDR. When Harald arrives at the Zoo train station in West Berlin, he is disoriented by the homeless, prostitutes, and punks loitering aimlessly amid wanted posters for RAF terrorists. Unlike Sophie, Harald has no desire to embark on a new life in the West, and cast out alone, without his wife and without any prospects, he makes his way back across the border to East Berlin. In no-man's-land on the boundary between the two German states, GDR border guards order him to stop or they will shoot, orders Harald had earlier refused to give. Now without hope he walks toward the armed soldiers, knowingly committing suicide.

Perhaps what separates von Trotta's film most distinctively from more recent ones is that it doggedly reminds the viewer that Germans on both sides of the Wall share the legacy of the Third Reich. Whereas the GDR adopted Georgi Dimitroff's famous definition of fascism as the "terrorist dictatorship of the most reactionary, chauvinistic and imperialistic elements of finance capitalism" and saw itself as the properly cleansed socialist state championing anti-fascism, the FRG likewise considered itself to be a thoroughly denazified, reformed democratic republic destined to defend the German nation against human-rights abuses under Communism. *Das Versprechen* reveals the irony of national myth-making on both sides on the Wall. The GDR and the FRG believe that their alter ego is the sole inheritor of National Socialism's historical guilt. However, both states perpetuate authoritarian attitudes and refuse to look below the surface to investigate the ways in which the Third Reich continues to influence the present. Konrad's mentor Professor Lorenz, for instance, decided to stay in the East because former Nazis took over positions of authority in the West, indicating a seamless transition from National Socialism to Western capitalism. This notion is picked up again in scenes depicting Sophie working in her aunt's fashion salon, which is located in a high-rise overlooking the Europa Center. The haute couture outfits modeled for a select group of perfectly coifed women in fine suits with matching hats and accompanied by a white poodle epitomize the vain and idle pastimes of the rich. As John Blair has astutely argued, the Emperor Wilhelm Memorial Church — "left incompletely repaired as a reminder of the Third Reich and WWII — appears rather prominently behind Sophie's aunt as she narrates her fashion show, insinuating that there is a problem in paradise, that consumption, fashion, etc. are being used to suppress memory."[71] Von Trotta's exposure of the ugly premise hiding beneath the seductive surface of West Germany's economic miracle is matched by her biting criticism of totalitarian practices in the GDR. For example, when Konrad's sister Barbara is arrested for political dissent, her father is denied the right to attend her trial. As a devoted communist, Herr Richter (alias Mr. Judge) is shocked to learn that in the GDR there is not even a pretense at justice. Richter is outraged because in Nazi Germany his own parents were at least allowed to attend his trial, but when he openly makes the comparison, he is threatened with arrest, because uncovering any evidence contrary to the GDR's carefully crafted anti-fascist image is strictly taboo. Even the least sympathetic character, the Stasi officer Müller, demonstrates how the notion of the GDR's rectifying the horrors of the past was a deeply satisfying and highly idealistic myth at the heart of postwar German national identity. After watching educational films about the Nazis as a child, Müller dreamed of joining the Stasi, because he believed that supporting the GDR would help rectify the atrocities of the Second World War. Being confronted with documentary footage of the war and holocaust was a decisive generational experience that Müller shared with rebellious sisters Marianne and Juliane from von Trotta's *Die bleierne Zeit*. Like these Western activists, a feminist journalist fighting for abortion rights and a RAF terrorist, the Easterner Müller justifies his activities in the secret police as the logical outcome of a collective national past. He asserts that he was motivated by emotion and political idealism: "I developed such a . . . hatred — I desperately wanted to do something so that it never happened again."[72]

From the opening voice-over stating that postwar division was imposed on Germany as punishment for the crimes committed during the Second World War to the scene at the Olympic Stadium built in 1936 to glorify and legitimize the Third Reich in the international arena, *Das Versprechen* demonstrates that one cannot separate the German past from the present. Speaking to a group of Japanese tourists (who bear their own historical guilt as former imperialists), Sophie reveals the connection: "Without the many Germans cheering Adolf Hitler, there would have been no Second World War, no Soviet occupation in middle and Eastern Europe . . . and no Wall in Berlin." Margarethe von Trotta acknowledges that this idea is difficult to sell because "Germans always see themselves as victims of history, not as subjects. They always endure everything, lamenting. Yet what we are living today is the consequence of our own history. That is the thing that is easily forgotten."[73]

Das Versprechen is in many ways a hard sell. It does not give viewers an easily identifiable position as morally clean winners of German history or of the Cold War. Nor does it end on a happy note with the resolution of conflicts and the joyous restoration of the nuclear family. There is no emotionally fulfilling embrace between Konrad and Sophie but rather an arrested moment in the in-between. Von Trotta's choice of using the border crossing at the Bornholmer Bridge rather than the scenes at the Brandenburg Gate or Checkpoint Charlie is decisive, for this location highlights that the coming together of the two German nations is now possible, but the crossing is a journey that has just begun. The family meets in the no-man's-land between the two states and their future is uncertain. The division of Germany, like that of this exemplary family, has been so disruptive that it is impossible to visualize Konrad, Sophie, and Alex in the same frame, let alone see the bigger picture of a unified people. The bittersweet smile frozen on Sophie's slightly out-of-focus face reflects both the pain of historical losses and the resilient hope for reconciliation in the future.

Das Leben der Anderen

In the opening scene of *Das Leben der Anderen* a young man is being interrogated at Hohenschönhausen prison for crimes against the state. When he protests his innocence, Captain Gerd Wiesler reveals the perverse logic of a dictatorship against which there is no defense: "So you believe that we simply incarcerate upstanding citizens on a whim? . . . If you think our humanistic state capable of such a thing, then we would be right to arrest you for no other reason than that."[74] In the next scene Wiesler uses the tape of this interrogation to teach young recruits at the Ministry for State Security (MfS) standard cross-examination techniques. After a student questions whether it is humane to grill a suspect for forty hours straight, Wiesler conspicuously marks a cross next to his name in the seating chart. The omnipresent surveillance system upholding the SED dictatorship is directed against its opponents and supporters with equal force and works precisely because the irrational fear of being secretly watched is constantly substantiated as real. In a masterful use of Orwellian double-think, Wiesler demonstrates that no one is beyond suspicion and there is no safe refuge against the eyes and ears of Big Brother in the GDR of 1984.

Made by newcomer Florian Henckel von Donnersmarck, *Das Leben der Anderen* was heralded in the film branch as an unexpected masterpiece by a first-time director and brought this 33-year-old film student international acclaim. Born in Cologne in 1973, von Donnersmarck already had an impressive résumé, having spent his childhood in New York, Berlin, Frankfurt am Main, and Brussels before studying Russian in Leningrad and then political science, economics, and philosophy at Oxford. After winning a competition for an internship with Sir Richard Attenborough to work on the film *In Love and War* (1996), he studied direction at the Munich Academy for Television and Film (Münchner Hochschule für Fernsehen und Film, HFFM). As a student he made several well-received shorts, including *Dobermann* (1999), which won the Max Ophüls Award, and *Der Templer* (2002), before writing, directing, and coproducing *Das Leben der Anderen* as his graduation project from the HFFM. This debut film was showered with highly coveted awards, including the Bavarian Film Prize, the German Film Prize, the European Film Prize, and the Oscar for best foreign-language film. The accolades were all the more surprising considering the

Fig. 2.5. Still from Florian Henckel von Donnersmarck,
Das Leben der Anderen *(2006). Photo © and by permission of*
The Kobal Collection, Creado Film, BR, and Arte.

film's modest origins: it was shot in thirty-eight days on a moderate budget of 1.8 million Euros.[75] However, from the start von Donnersmarck had grand designs for his work, and the film's genesis has now taken on nearly mythic proportions. The idea was conceived for a classroom training exercise in the very first semester of his film studies. Listening to Beethoven's Moonlight Sonata and wondering how he could complete the fourteen treatments he had been assigned as homework, he was reminded of Lenin's contention that he could not listen to Beethoven's Appassionata Sonata because "it affects your nerves, makes you want to say stupid, nice things, and stroke the heads of people who could create such beauty while living in this vile hell." However, if Lenin intended to bring about a revolution he would have "to hit them on the head without any mercy."[76] Von Donnersmarck was inspired by this idea and envisioned a man wearing headphones, spying on his enemy but forced to listen to beautiful music and thus cast into a moral dilemma between following his political ideology or his aesthetic yearnings.[77] It took eight years before this idea came to the screen, but von Donnersmarck's tenacity paid off, since he was able to engage a remarkable team of actors, including Ulrich Mühe, Sebastian Koch, Martina Gedeck, and Ulrich Tukur, as well as cameraman Hagen Bogdanski and composer Gabriel Yared. From its premiere on 23 March 2006 to the end of December 2006, *Das Leben der Anderen* sold 1,678,572 tickets in Germany, making it the fourth most popular German film of the year, although still far short of Tom Tykwer's star-studded mega-hit *Das Parfum: Die Geschichte eines Mörders* (Perfume: The history of a murderer, 2006) with 5,480,675 viewers.[78]

Set in East Berlin in 1984, *Das Leben der Anderen* is a tale of loyalty, betrayal, and the power of art to awaken the soul. Part melodrama, part thriller, and part historical drama, the story revolves around the notion that individuals can change. As the film opens, hard-line MfS officer Gerd Wiesler is ordered to conduct surveillance on playwright Georg Dreyman, because of false charges of sedition. Wiesler quickly learns that Minister Bruno Hempf wants to discredit Dreyman so that he can continue to sexually exploit the writer's lover, actress Christa-Maria Sieland. Motivated by righteous indignation, Wiesler breaks all the rules, secretly entering into Dreyman's life and protecting him from the long arm of the law. The more Wiesler watches and listens, the more he becomes enamored with the playwright's life, with poetry, music, physical affection, and love, until he is willing to defy his long-held beliefs and act against the state. The committed socialist Dreyman likewise undergoes a transformation and illegally publishes, in the Western press, an essay critical of the regime. Despite Wiesler's attempts to shield the couple, he cannot help Sieland, who becomes an informant, betrays her lover, and subsequently commits suicide. Wiesler saves the playwright but is suspected of complicity and demoted to the lowest rank. After the *Wende*, Dreyman learns about Wiesler's intervention and dedicates his novel, *The Sonnet of a Good Person*, to the former Stasi officer.

Captain Gerd Wiesler, played by the late actor Ulrich Mühe, starts out as a coldly calculating, highly disciplined officer whose devotion to "the firm" is beyond question. Zipped up tightly in his gray, perfectly symmetrical parka and living alone in an apartment with no more human warmth than a cell, Wiesler's entire existence is defined by renunciation of desire in the service of the state. His encounter with Georg Dreyman and Christa-Maria Sieland shatters the carefully constructed belief system that gave credence to his ruthless behavior. As an interrogator who coerces ordinary citizens into denouncing others and as a teacher in the MfS academy training a new generation of spies, Wiesler sees himself as a loyal soldier fighting to protect a good society. Fully invested in his identity as the "sword and shield of the party," he accepts that the ends justify the means. He eschews any sense of elitism, joining the rank and file in the cafeteria, because "socialism has to start somewhere."[79] In contrast to the zealous romantic Wiesler, the highest ranking representatives of the SED dictatorship are self-serving egotists, who display no interest in socialist ideals, let alone art or morality. The men who regulate the nation's cultural life are power-hungry careerists without scruples. Lieutenant Colonel Anton Grubitz and his former boss, Minister of Culture Bruno Hempf, are petty opportunists who seek personal gratification and take sadistic pleasure in torturing their prey. Grubitz plays with an underling careless enough to tell a joke about Erich Honecker, and Hempf torments Sieland with public praise as her unsuspecting lover watches in bewilderment. Once the ascetic Wiesler discovers that Hempf has abused his power to pursue selfish goals, and in particular sexual conquest, he decides to act. Rather than recognizing the inherent inhumanity of a political system that obsessively observes its citizens and curtails basic freedoms, Wiesler is motivated by his distaste for corruption and sexual exploitation. He does not question the need for surveillance or strict controls on liberty to uphold the social order and reign in dissidents; instead Wiesler rejects the unfair use of such legitimate political tools for corrupt purposes.

Like Wiesler, playwright Georg Dreyman, code-name "Lazlo," is a steadfast believer in socialism, but unlike the Stasi officer Dreyman is able to combine political commitment, art, and intimacy. Dreyman is the rarest of animals, a conscientious, politically engaged writer who is interesting enough to be read in the West. With his rumpled brown corduroy suit, boyish good looks, and charming manner, he comes across as a sympathetic, quietly confident, and authentic individual. Far from being either a mouthpiece of the party or a disgruntled agitator, he criticizes the GDR in acceptable doses and firmly believes that people are capable of goodness and change. It is only after the suicide of his best friend, theater director Albert Jerska, who had been blacklisted for seven years, that Dreyman loses faith and stops writing. Inspired by Sieland's decision to reject Hempf, he resolves to act against the state and publish an essay about suicide in the GDR in *Der Spiegel* magazine. Dreyman's act of dissent is naive on several levels. He does not see that his actions have consequences for himself and others, and that his daring move could send Sieland down a spiral of destruction ending in her suicide. Another unforeseen casualty is his own art, since he is unable to write anything for six years, from the time of her death in March 1985 until two years after the *Wende*. It is only after reading his Stasi files in 1991 and learning of Wiesler's intervention and Sieland's duplicity that Dreyman returns to his earlier idealism and writes the novel *The Sonnet of a Good Person*.

Both Wiesler and Dreyman share a deep commitment to the GDR and believe that they are contributing in their own way to a better world. They remain loyal to the ideals of socialism and challenge state authority only in order to preserve these values and reform the system from within. However, in their personal lives the two men could not be more different from each other. Whereas the Stasi officer has no close relationships and spends his free time alone watching television, the playwright enjoys intimacy in his friendships and a full social life characterized by enjoyable activities such as music, dancing, parties, and meaningful conversations. The contrast between the two is revealed most aptly in their chosen environments, with Wiesler's bleak prefabricated high-rise apartment swathed in the cold colors of gray and blue juxtaposed to Dreyman's turn-of-the-century apartment filled with art and sunshine, and bathed in warm colors. (Von Donnersmarck follows here the same visual coding that von Trotta used in *Das Versprechen* to differentiate the GDR from the FRG.) The relationship between the men begins in the theater, where Dreyman reigns, unaware of the intrigue secretly brewing, and Wiesler establishes the power of his authoritative gaze. Armed with binoculars, Wiesler starts out as an objective observer of Dreyman's play but soon becomes a voyeur; he is enthralled with the actress Sieland and the drama unfolding offstage between Hempf, Dreyman, Sieland, Hauser, and Grubitz. In the course of his investigation, Wiesler seems to fall in love with Dreyman at least as much as with Sieland, if not more. In his one-sided relationship with the couple, Wiesler starts to emulate Dreyman, sneaking into his apartment, stealing his volume of Brecht's poetry, and literally placing himself in the other man's position vis-à-vis his lover. After listening to Sieland pleading for Dreyman to hold her, Wiesler sits in the attic with his eyes closed, hugging the back of his stool and fantasizing that he is part of the scene taking place in the apartment below. Wiesler also hides in the doorway with the typewriter just as Dreyman had when Sieland came home from a rendezvous with Hempf. The Stasi officer's attempt to insert himself into the life of others is not limited to adopting their relative positions. Wiesler acts like a stage manager, outlining the apartment in chalk as if blocking the movements of actors on a stage. He then begins to determine the outcome of events, as if he were writing the script of Sieland and Dreyman's life. Like a benevolent puppeteer he manipulates Dreyman to go outside and learn of Sieland's adultery, and he uses his knowledge of Sieland's circumstances to persuade her to return to her lover. In the end, Wiesler takes on the role of dramatist, replacing Dreyman (who has now become an essayist) as the creative voice of the film. Wiesler transforms life into fiction and writes an imaginary play, instead of composing an accurate surveillance report, in order to mask Dreyman's seditious activities.

Christa-Maria Sieland, the object of their mutual affection, rarely finds the strength to assert her will and become an active subject. From her first appearance on screen until her last, she is the object of Wiesler's controlling gaze and specular desire. First seen on stage as a prophet who falls unconscious from the weight of her vision, she continues to be moved by forces beyond her control. Sieland's status as object is made evident most notably in the scene where Wiesler manipulates Dreyman to go outside and witness proof of her infidelity. Hidden in the attic, Wiesler watches on a monitor as Dreyman hides in a doorway and watches an unsuspecting Sieland, and so both men observe undetected the drama that Wiesler has written for the actress. Sieland lacks self-confidence and is easily manipulated by powerful men to do their bidding. Intelligent, beautiful, and talented, she nonetheless relies on tranquilizers to make life bearable and allows herself to be seduced by Hempf, because she believes that prostituting herself is the only way she can pursue her chosen profession. In contrast to Dreyman, who still believes in socialism and the capacity for change, Sieland recognizes that in the GDR artists are beholden to those in power and the system demands its pound of flesh. She accuses Dreyman of simply closing his eyes to the fact that he has sold himself for art as much as she has, because they live in a country where the regime decides who can act, direct, and write and what pieces will reach the public. Like Jerska, Sieland needs the theater and an audience to be complete, and so it is not merely because of her pangs of conscience over informing on her lover but also the fact that she is bereft of any hope of ever setting foot on stage again that she kills herself. Just as Jerska's death motivated Dreyman to act, Sieland's sacrificial death becomes the catalyst for Wiesler's redemption.

While the male characters accept the risks involved in being honorable and remain true to their beliefs, the female characters succumb to threats and are rewarded with special privileges. Women, like next-door neighbor Frau Meineke and Christa-Maria Sieland, are easily manipulated. They surrender to the power exerted on them and make choices that uphold the surveillance state. Both women are reluctant to participate in clandestine activities but are silenced by preferential treatment such as a guaranteed place at the university for her son or a promised career on the stage. The gendered pattern of active male-passive female is linked to the subject-object of the gaze so familiar to audiences trained in the generic conventions of classic Hollywood melodramas from the forties and fifties. When Frau Meineke attempts to assert herself and secretly watches Wiesler through the peephole of her apartment, he immediately confronts her and threatens her family if she insists upon appropriating the gaze. Before the audience ever sees Frau Meineke, the camera adopts her point of view as she looks out her peephole at the Stasi men who are planting surveillance devices across the hall in Dreyman's apartment. Framed by a mask device placed in front of the camera to create the circular frame of the peephole, a frontal medium shot captures Wiesler leaving Dreyman's apartment from Frau Meineke's unique vantage point. The audience first sees Frau Meineke in a close-up as she leans against the door to get a better look at the drama unfolding. Each time the camera captures her point of view, the mask device marks the shot as distinctly hers. However, a close-up of the peephole from outside her apartment and a brief changing in lighting when she blinks, is followed by a final masked frame that shows Wiesler looking straight into the camera and proceeding toward her door. After he recognizes that she has been surveilling him, the masked frame disappears and is replaced by an unobstructed high-angled shot of Wiesler walking toward her door, a frontal medium shot of him facing her apartment, and finally a low-angle shot of him knocking on her door. A trembling Meineke lowers her eyes when confronted by Capitan Wiesler who looks directly at her and reestablishes his dominance and visual authority.

In her seminal article on female spectatorship, Mary Ann Doane notes that when traditional gender roles associated with spectatorship are reversed, the female voyeur "poses a threat to an entire system of representation," because "there is always a certain excessiveness, a difficulty associated with women who appropriate the gaze, who insist upon looking."[80] Throughout the film Christa-Maria Sieland remains the object of collective male desire, routinely put on display and watched intensely by Hempf, Wiesler, Dreyman, and Grubitz. Only once is she depicted as openly looking; she runs into the street and turns to look directly into the camera as a truck crashes into her. Sieland's intense gaze is a conscious decision to assert female autonomy, which ends in self-destruction. Although Albert Jerska also kills himself, his death takes place conspicuously offscreen. Sieland's suicide, by contrast, is the turning point in the film and signals the demise of the GDR. Her brutal death visualizes political victimization in the GDR and is essential to the storyline. However, once Dreyman learns the truth of Sieland's betrayal and Wiesler's intervention, she becomes the perpetrator and the Stasi officer the victim. It seems that for the men to become heroes, the slaughter of a sacrificial lamb is required, and since Sieland is weak and pusillanimous, her death is acceptable in narrative terms.

Von Donnersmarck's film presents a spectrum of artists who believe in the claims of socialism and want to stay in the GDR to help create a better society but are impeded by the party. Jerska is blacklisted for signing his name to a petition reminiscent of the one that many artists and notables signed in protest of Wolf Biermann's notorious expatriation in 1976. Despite the fact that he has been banned from the theater and lives in a shabby room in a cramped communal apartment, Jerska refuses to go to the West, where his reputation would allow him to find work easily. He is destroyed in the end by a system where no one is who he seems to be. When Dreyman is surprised by his friend's newfound cynicism, Jerska replies: "Perhaps back then that was the false Jerska: friendly and filled with human kindness because of the powerful fodder of success . . . which I had thanks to the magnanimousness of the bigwigs."[81] The journalist Paul Hauser is the rebellious successor of Jerska, and like the older man he vocally attacks the corrupt representatives of the regime. A stint in Hohenschönhausen prison has not frightened him into submission; indeed it has emboldened him to speak out against injustice. When Hempf unwittingly quotes Stalin's infamous phrase that the writer is the engineer of the soul, it is Hauser who draws attention to the phrase's origin and hints that the minister has an affinity to the former Soviet dictator. It is also Hauser who publicly denounces the director Schwalber as a Stasi mole and forces Dreyman to take sides, telling his friend: "You are such a pathetic idealist that you are almost a bigwig. Who do you think destroyed Jerska? Exactly those kind of people: informants, traitors, and conformists! At some point you have to take a position, otherwise you are not a human being."[82]

Jerska's suicide is a catalyst for Dreyman and ironically also for Wiesler. Jerska's final gift to his friend, the music for "The Sonata of a Good Person," inspires these two idealists on opposite sides of the power line to act against a corrupt regime in order to become morally good people. Upon learning of Jerska's death, Dreyman begins to play the haunting sonata on the piano, while Sieland silently stands by her man and Wiesler listens on his headphones in the attic above. Fascinated by these strange and compelling sounds, the Stasi officer is caught up in the artists' world, mesmerized by their creativity and intense emotional life. The characters are connected not only by the music but also by the camera movements and editing. The camera travels around Wiesler in an arc and in the next shot the same movement follows Dreyman and Sieland to complete the circle, as if embracing the three characters and allowing the surveillant to share in his targets' sorrow and philosophical reflections. Dreyman unknowingly addresses Wiesler when he comments on the relationship between art and politics: "I'm always reminded of what Lenin said about the Appassionata: 'I cannot listen to it, otherwise I would not see the revolution through to its end.'" Dreyman is convinced that art can humanize and inspire people to be good. He asks: "Can someone who has heard this music, really heard it, still be a bad person?"[83] The answer to this rhetorical question is offered shortly thereafter, when Sieland tells Wiesler (in the guise of a theater enthusiast) that he is indeed a good person.

The power of art is a leitmotif that runs throughout the film. Von Donnersmarck cites not only Soviet leaders Stalin and Lenin but also German poets Bertolt Brecht and Wolfgang Borchert to express a belief in art's ability to stir the deepest reaches of the soul. During his surveillance duties Wiesler is introduced to a completely new realm of emotion and contemplation via literature and music. Attracted by this unknown world of artistry and the life of others, Wiesler steals a volume of Brecht's poetry from Dreyman's apartment. Lying on his couch reading "Remembering Maria A.," Wiesler hears Dreyman's voice as if the playwright were speaking to him directly as he recites the first stanza of the poem:

> It was a day in that blue month September
> Silent beneath a plum tree's slender shade
> I held her there, my love so pale and silent
> As if she were a dream that must not fade.
> Above us in the shining summer heaven
> There was a cloud my eyes dwelt long upon
> It was quite white and very high above us
> Then I looked up, and found it had gone.[84]

While Wiesler remains engrossed in Brecht's poem and Dreyman's voice, the camera slowly rises above him to replicate the poem's spatial relationship of bodies located beneath and aloft. Like the poetic I who remembers a fleeting feeling symbolized in the cloud rather than the actual woman he once loved, Wiesler admires Sieland from afar and at times seems more captivated by the notion of love than by the real woman. Just like her near namesake Maria A., Christa-Maria is rendered as silent and pale, most notably in the scene where she stands in a milky white nightgown quietly watching over Dreyman as he performs the "Sonata of a Good Person." When she meets her death and disappears from the picture, Sieland is likewise wrapped in a white robe decorated with golden stars hinting at the celestial bodies of Brecht's poem. Immediately following her death in Dreyman's arms, the camera shifts to a traveling shot of barren trees set against a dreary sky, evoking the lamentful passing and disembodiment of the female lover that ultimately frees the poetic I from the miasma of love.

Although there are no overt references to Brecht's plays, the title of this sonata closely resembles *The Good Person of Szechwan* and alludes to one of Brecht's most persistent themes: the dilemma of wanting to be good in a world not yet ready for goodness. While Brecht's good person Shen Te tries to make moral choices and treat her fellow human beings with kindness and charity, circumstances prevent her from doing so without putting her own existence at risk. It is impossible to survive in an unjust world and remain a good person. In many of Brecht's plays, a willingness to die becomes the touchstone by which to gauge whether one is good or not. *Mother Courage*'s mute Kattrin drumming on the rooftop to warn the villagers of the approaching enemy, or the young comrade in *The Measures Taken* who willingly accepts death to save the revolution are only two examples of what Marc Silberman has described as Brecht's attraction to "the idea of redemption through the negation of self."[85] In *Das Leben der Anderen,* the topos of death as the price for goodness is not reflected in the main characters Dreyman and Wiesler, who succeed in doing the right thing without being caught and severely punished. Instead the negation of self is the female lead's fate; Sieland succumbs to pressures exerted by a morally bankrupt regime and commits suicide. In her first appearance on screen, she is seen on stage in the role of Marta from Dreyman's play *Visions of Love*. This seer who suffers visions and falls unconscious in front of a factory conveyer belt evokes comparison to Brecht's Joan Dark in *Saint Joan of the Stockyards*, who battles corruption on behalf of Chicago workers on the eve of the Great Depression. Whereas Shen Te and Joan Dark are caught in a tragic bind and either are left helpless or must die for a cause, Sieland fails to measure up. She prostitutes herself to a party boss, anesthetizes herself with drugs, and sells out her lover twice to survive.

What separates the heroes in *Das Leben der Anderen* most significantly from those found in Brecht's plays is that the filmic characters act as individuals doing good (or bad) deeds in secret. The men transform themselves in the hope of creating a better society, but they lack the courage or conviction to challenge the system openly, defiantly, and transform society as a whole. Sieland is victimized by powerful men and too weak to fight against oppression. Rather than finding the strength to do good in an evil world, she directs aggression inward and escapes the system through self-negation. In stark contrast, Brecht's heroes routinely acknowledge that individual acts of kindness merely uphold the status quo and that real social change demands collective action. In her last words ("Take care that you leave the world not just as good people but that you leave behind a good world") Joan Dark advocates a complete over-throw of the establishment, because: "Only violence helps where violence reigns."[86] These sentiments could not be further from those presented in von Donnersmarck's film. Jerska, Dreyman, and Wiesler do not reject socialism as the most just political ideology, nor do they endorse the idea of overthrowing the system. Instead, they fight corruption embodied in unsympathetic officials and seek to reform the system surreptitiously from within. In *Das Leben der Anderen* individual acts of goodness and the sacrificial life of another seem to be sufficient ingredients to cause revolu-tionary change. The two main heroes remain true to their ideals but suffer no tragic fate; the required self-sacrifice is performed by a woman dressed in white who vanishes like Maria A., and the revolution takes place effort-lessly offscreen as if the inevitable result of their individual choices. The only reference to the coming upheaval is a newspaper headline trumpet-ing Gorbachev's election as General Secretary of the Communist Party of the Soviet Union. Four years and seven months (11 March 1985 to 9 November 1989) are swallowed up in the cut from Gorbachev's image to a conveyor belt in the MfS mail room and a muffled radio report announcing the historic opening of the Berlin Wall. The surprising lack of any visualization of the 1989 revolution suggests that political change was the logical consequence of private deeds rather than collective action. The apparent effortlessness with which the GDR collapsed implies that the corrupt state was toppled by countless small acts of defiance that took place unobserved in the hidden space that connects Wiesler's world. The seamless editing results in a historical void that proves necessary to maintain Wiesler and Dreyman's integrity as honorable men (especially in light of their complicity in Sieland's death) and to mask the incongruity between their own secretive resistance and the nation's open defiance of government control.

The transition from the GDR to a reunified Germany also takes place in a historical void, with the Stasi workers silently walking out of the door on the left, followed by a stage curtain opening up to the single figure on the right and the insertion of the date to indicate that two years have passed. Returning to the same theater where Wiesler first encountered Dreyman and to the same play, *Visions of Love*, the new circumstances are reflected in the production and in the audience. Dreyman, who once occupied the lofty position of playwright in his own private loge, now sits in the orchestra seats with a sleek new dark haired and silent beauty at his side. On stage, Christa-Maria Sieland has also been replaced by a black actress dressed in a white toga, who delivers her lines in a poetic monotone voice on a minimalist, highly stylized, black and white stage. The theatrical realm that once served as a communal forum for public (if highly ambiguous) debates comes across as elitist entertainment in a world without grey tones and with no room for nuance. The resulting loss of utopian ideals is voiced by the film's most unsympathetic character but still rings true. Hempf laments to Dreyman: "What should one write about in this FRG: there is nothing left to believe in and nothing left to rebel against. It was nice in our little republic. Many people are just now starting to understand that."[87]

It is telling that the former playwright Georg Dreyman embraces a completely new genre for his post-Wall reckoning with the past, for in writing a novel he acknowledges no need for actors, directors, a public stage, or an audience. This choice of genre makes the suffering of Sieland and Jerska seem secondary, since these actors on the stage of history are transformed into figures whose lives are mediated through the lens of a narrator's authorial view. Moreover with its dedication to *HGW XX/7*, the novel, which inherently exposes the relationship between the individual and society, becomes a reflective piece directed at an audience of one: HGW, alias Hauptmann Gerd Wiesler. By rejecting the theater with its communal aspect as an outdated remnant of a GDR past that required a public display of dissent, Dreyman's turn to the interior dialogue mandated by separate individuals reading a novel in private implies that unified Germany is marked by consensus. However, even in a nation bound by a shared condemnation of the SED dictatorship, the utopian vision of socialism still survives. The fact that the film concludes with Wiesler buying Dreyman's novel in the Karl Marx Bookstore in the former Karl-Marx-Allee speaks volumes for the persistence of political utopianism despite its rocky history in twentieth-century Germany.

This final move reiterates an ironic stance toward socialism that is prevalent in the film and in contemporary German cinema in general. Von Donnersmarck uses thinkers like Lenin, Marx, Borchert, and Brecht to validate Marxism's admirable goals of seeking social justice, but the filmmaker refuses to engage the full magnitude of their revolutionary ideology. Rather than arguing in favor of radicalism's call for a systemic change in the distribution of wealth, *Das Leben der Anderen* distills the ideas of these philosophers and poets down to the question of individual morality, a value easily integrated into Western capitalism and ultimately antithetical to Lenin and Brecht's intentions. In *Das Leben der Anderen* the GDR was run by self-serving, power-hungry officials who designed a security system that allowed them to exploit others. The state apparatus tapped into the sincere idealism of people like Wiesler and turned them into efficient robots, demanding nothing less than the renunciation of desire. Viewing the GDR as an experiment gone wrong, the film refuses to give up on socialism's core idea of humanism. When Dreyman sits at his desk writing an essay on the loss of hope, the song "Stand in the middle of the rain," based on a poem by Wolfgang Borchert, plays in the background and beckons him to believe "and try to be good."[88] The idea of being good in a bad world resonates throughout the film, but the pivotal transformation that occurs is depicted as personal and not systemic. In the final scene, the former representative of a repressive state buys *The Sonnet of a Good Person* and confirms that the book was intended for him because he is indeed a good person capable of change. The implication is that individual morality somehow led to political change, certainly not the Marxist ideal of collectivizing the means of production, indeed the exact opposite, but a single good person's actions resulted in shared change nonetheless. The return to capitalism and individualism as the dominant values takes place via a historic peaceful revolution never depicted on screen, a tacit acknowledgment that the selective adoption of Marxist ideology is a paradox that cannot undergo the scrutiny of closer examination.

More than any other film in recent years, *Das Leben der Anderen* stimulated a heated debate in Germany about the Stasi legacy. On 14 March 2006, one day before the film's gala premiere, Minister of Culture Bernd Neumann invited the entire German Bundestag to a special performance of the movie.[89] On the same day, an open-podium discussion took place to debate the future of the area surrounding the former Stasi prison at Hohenschönhausen, a memorial site now dedicated to teaching about the persecution of political resisters in the GDR. The quarantined area, appearing as a blank space on Berlin city maps during the GDR and cordoned off from the public eye, contained office space for the Ministry of State Security and provided housing for many MfS officers and their families. Officials at the memorial site, including its current director Hubertus Knabe and former inmates now serving as tour guides of the prison facility, proposed the installation of four commemorative plaques on surrounding buildings to mark their function in the "Communist dictatorship." Unexpectedly, nearly 200 former MfS officers showed up in force to confront the victims, protesting the use of the term "Communist dictatorship" and declaring their innocence of all crimes. Former prison guards claimed that there were no human-rights violations on their watch, and they decried the fact that their prior workplace had been turned into a "chamber of horror." In a bizarre twist of logic, the last commandant of the prison, ex-Stasi General Siegfried Rataizik, went so far as to suggest that former inmates were falsifying history and denigrating the good name of loyal servants of the state. Rataizik complained bitterly about the former prisoners who now serve as museum guides: "They depict themselves as victims and declare us [former MfS employees] to be the perpetrators."[90] The victims of the Stasi, many subjected to isolation torture and other forms of psychological terror during years of incarceration, were shocked by the open attack of their former oppressors and also by the silence of Cultural Senator and PDS party member Thomas Flierl, who witnessed the harassment but did nothing to defend them. Flierl's only response was to recommend that a dialogue between victims and Stasi officers would help to illuminate the past.

Hubertus Knabe refused to allow von Donnersmarck to film in the prison because the storyline heroized a Stasi officer who became enlightened and converted. Since there was no evidence that such a case ever happened, Knabe considered the film a falsification of history that insulted the memory of those who suffered at the hands of the Stasi. According to Knabe, "the victims council rejected it categorically because their experience with the state security was diametrically opposed." It would be unacceptable to allow the crew to film "in a place where people suffered and which they would perhaps recognize in the cinema, to misuse as a backdrop for a film that handles the past in such a casual manner."[91]

Prominent writers Wolf Biermann, Thomas Brussig, Jana Hensel, and Anne Funder published essays on the relationship between the film and the reality of life in the GDR. The initial and current federal commissioners for the Stasi files, Joachim Gauck and Marianne Birthler, voiced their opinions in interviews as did the vice president of the Bundestag, Wolfgang Thierse. Joachim Gauck was moved by the film and exclaimed enthusiastically: "Yes, it was like that!" He conceded that it was unlikely that there had ever been a Stasi officer like Wiesler, "but a feature film is not contemporary documentation, it can treat history in a freer manner."[92] Like Gauck, Marianne Birthler was highly skeptical that there was a historical precedence for a Stasi officer risking his career and potentially his freedom to protect ordinary citizens, but she argued: "Perhaps the film is more about the longing for such a thing. *Das Leben der Anderen* demonstrates in an insistent fashion how even in a rather unbloody dictatorship like the late GDR people were limited and were robbed of their trust in their fellow men."[93] Along these same lines, former GDR dissident Wolf Biermann was impressed with von Donnersmarck's film: "The basic story in *Das Leben der Anderen* is crazy and true and lovely — which means utterly sad. The political sound is authentic, the plot moved me."[94] Biermann acknowledged that some aspects of the story and setting seemed inaccurate, but this was of little consequence in the end. The decisive thing for Biermann was that the film put a face on the unknown Stasi officers who hounded him for years and continue to haunt his memories. In particular, the figure of Lieutenant Colonel Anton Grubitz, played by actor Ulrich Tukur, fascinated him: "This strong character actor finally lent to the ideologically encrusted silhouette in the grotto of my mind a human mug, behind which even the rest of the face becomes visible. Thus the formulaic villains of my life finally experienced an authentic concretion, with which I can recognize in every desolate human face how all the colors between black and white are illuminated."[95] Noting that Alexander Solzhenitsyn's slim novel, *One Day in the Life of Ivan Denisovich*, did more to sensitize the world to the plight of political prisoners in Soviet gulags than any multivolume historical account detailing all the atrocities committed under Stalin ever could, Biermann maintained that fiction can reveal important historical truths. Recognizing that the emotional world conjured up in the cinema can resonate with audiences in a way that dry facts never will, he contended: "Sometimes a work of art has more documentary evidentiary value than documents whose truth is doubted — in any event by perpetrators but even more painfully by quickly bored viewers."[96] Biermann's stance was reiterated by civil-rights activist and BStU administrator Tobias Hollitzer, who argued that motion pictures are important because they allow audiences to become emotionally engaged with a past they never experienced: "Despite all the objections one could raise about details or from a scientific perspective, films like *Das Leben der Anderen, Nikolaikirche*, and even *Der Tunnel* are important moments of national civic education. They build a bridge between the part of the country that experienced the communist dictatorship firsthand and the part that cannot imagine it with any exactitude."[97]

Objections to the film focused on von Donnersmarck's choice of a Stasi officer as the hero and on the fact that he wrapped up a complex political reality in the guise of a personal love story. Rüdiger Suchsland writes: "That is the curious thing about this film: the surveillance the film describes and uses to expose the true nature of the surveillance state is driven by the purely personal motive of jealousy and not by political motives. . . . Henckel von Donnersmarck invents the Stasi good person and one wonders where this need for exoneration comes from that is satisfied in this kind of scenario?"[98] Because this film has a visual code that looks historically accurate, and it draws the viewer, like Wiesler, emotionally into the life of others, it has the potential to be a powerful, if not *the* representative version of the GDR past in the minds of many Germans. The ramifications are potentially far-reaching if we concentrate on the notion of a shared national past in which the perpetrator turns into a victim. GDR historians Stefan Wolle, Günter Jeschonnek, and Jens Gieseke have criticized the film in categorical terms as a dangerous falsification of history that could have serious consequences. Writing for *Deutschland Archiv*, a journal originally dedicated to GDR research and now focused on recent German history, Günter Jeschonnek contends that von Donnersmarck "places his audience under tutelage and releases them with a historical lie."[99] Jan Schulz-Ojala, film critic for *Tagesspiegel*, sees a growing trend evident not only in *Das Leben der Anderen* but also in

Der Untergang (Downfall, Oliver Hirschbiegel, 2004) and *Der freie Wille* (Free will, Matthias Glasner, 2006), a "peculiar trend in a society that seems to be defining itself anew in this century. The Germans: for several years now the former nation of perpetrators likes to present itself, sometimes with a scientific pitch and sometimes through the media, as mass victims."[100] As a national narrative, *Das Leben der Anderen* shifts culpability for the SED dictatorship's crimes from the Stasi rank and file to the informants they coerced. The implications of this shift in focus are significant, because, as Schulz-Ojala argues, von Donnersmarck's film "transforms a perpetrator into a tragic figure, a victim of circumstances, a good person — and at the same time basically humanizes the attendant apparatus."[101] Although *Das Leben der Anderen* received a myriad of international prizes and was almost universally praised as an extremely well-crafted film, many critics contended that it failed as a reflection of history. Singling out the Oscar for best foreign-language film as an indicator of how the film was too Hollywood and too consensus-driven, many writers claimed that it lacked a specifically German touch. Citing again Schulz-Ojala: "*Das Leben der Anderen* plays in the gloomy, musty old bygone GDR, but it has something undeniably American in its insistence on formal perfection seen in every image and its mainstream-oriented extreme emotional absorption."[102] Indeed it was the film's very aesthetic accomplishment, emotionally laden storyline, potential for identification with sympathetic characters, and mainstream qualities that made it highly suspect as a useful guide to history.

Affect or Accuracy?

What is the best approach to the GDR memory landscape, affect or accuracy? Can motion pictures give audiences a more vivid, and thus more truthful, rendering of the past exactly because they distort facts and manipulate emotions? Does it matter if audiences are left to their own resources to differentiate between fact and fiction? These issues are especially relevant now as a generation is emerging for whom the GDR is not lived experience. The results of a recent study confirm the serious state of affairs in public education. Nearly half of Berlin's high-school students believed the GDR was not a dictatorship and over 70 percent thought the Wall was built by either the West Germans, the Soviets, the Americans, or all the Allies together. Students complained that their teachers never got past the Third Reich in history class and that they learned about the GDR from films like *Sonnenallee* and *Good Bye, Lenin!*[103]

If we take a look at the history films that have flooded the airwaves since fall 2007, high-school students may not be getting an accurate picture from television, either. Between September 2007 and April 2008, seven television films about GDR history flooded the airways and reached millions of German viewers. Beginning in September, *An die Grenze* (To the border, dir. Urs Egger, 7 Sept. 2007 Arte/ZDF) was followed in rapid succession by *Prager Botschaft* (Prague embassy, 23 Sept. 2007, RTL), *Die Frau vom Checkpoint Charlie* (The woman from Checkpoint Charlie, dir. Miguel Alexandre, 28 Sept. 2007, Arte/ARD), *Heimweh nach drüben* (Homesickness for over there), dir. Hajo Gies, 3 Oct. 2007, MDR), and *Die Todesautomatik* (Death automat, dir. Nikolaus Stein von Kamienski, 26 Nov. 2007, ZDF). The trend continued with *Das Wunder von Berlin* (The miracle of Berlin, dir. Roland Suso Richter, 27 Jan. 2008, ZDF) and *12 heißt: Ich liebe Dich* (Twelve means I love you, dir. Connie Walther, 16 April 2008, ARD). The audience shares for these television films are staggering in comparison to the average cinema numbers, with figures ranging from nearly 3 ½ to 11 million viewers, numbers that movie theaters can only dream of. Three films exemplify current trends and give us different views of the past regarding victimization and agency. While all seven films are about state repression, a few venture into the gray areas of history, where the lines between complicity and resistance are not as precise as one might like. The immense popularity of certain television films suggests, however, that a national history of clear-cut perpetrators and empowered victims appeals best to the public.

Die Frau vom Checkpoint Charlie, directed by Miguel Alexandre and starring Veronika Ferres, was by far the most popular television event, a two-part special that reached more than ten million viewers each night.[104] Advertised as a real-life historical drama, it is about a mother victimized by the socialist state, who eventually triumphs over all obstacles to gain her freedom and right to self-determination.[105] The film is based loosely on the life of Jutta Gallus, who was caught trying to flee the GDR in 1982 and sentenced to three years' imprisonment for attempting to cross the border illegally. Gallus was deported to the FRG but forced to leave her children behind. Once in West Berlin she protested at Checkpoint Charlie for four years before the GDR finally allowed her two daughters to join her in the West. Although the director stressed that his film was painstakingly researched, he maintained that it is not a docudrama about Gallus but rather a more universal story based on historically verifiable events that happened to many different people. There are numerous freely invented, melodramatic plot twists that serve to heighten the viewer's emotional response. For example, on the very day that protagonist Sara Bender is supposed to wed her fiancé Peter Koch, she learns that her father, who lives in West Germany is seriously ill, but she is denied a visa to visit him in the hospital before he dies. Not only the impediment to familial wellbeing but also the figure of Peter Koch is completely fictional. Whereas the real-life Gallus planned her escape with her boyfriend, the fictional Sara falls prey to Peter, a Stasi Romeo who betrays her. There are so many fictional vignettes that it becomes increasingly difficult to

Fig. 2.6. Screenshot from Miguel Alexandre's
Die Frau vom Checkpoint Charlie *(2007).*

believe that any one person could have possibly experienced them all, and
the film starts to resemble a telenovella — if not a modern-day telling
of the trials of Job. For example, the Gallus children actually lived with
their biological father in their childhood home while their mother was in
prison, and both girls became television stars. However, in Alexandre's
film they are forced out of ballet class and communal activities, sent to
an orphanage, and then placed in a foster family loyal to the SED regime.
In the world of television, Peter lies to Sara's children, telling them that
their mother has died in a car crash and encourages the girls to let their
foster parents adopt them. And when Peter's boss at Stasi headquarters
announces that they have received orders to assassinate Sara, Peter vol-
unteers to carry out the orders. However, this is only a ruse, since he
warns her of the impending danger in the best tradition of popular melodrama. While these fictional events demonstrate the state's brutal treatment of its citizens and a pervasive intrusion into family life, they also
shift the story from an individual account to a universal chronicle of all
the GDR's crimes. Sara Bender thus stands for all the people who resisted
the SED regime, refused to be bent into subjugation, and won by sheer
determination. Since she must also fight against the FRG's cold-hearted
bureaucracy and unwillingness to endanger the precarious East-West
détente, Sara becomes the embodiment of national civic courage, a pan-
German national hero fighting to reunite her family — and by extension,

the country. This representative quality can also be seen in the depiction of the two male leads, cold-war warriors on opposite sides of the battle for political supremacy and for Sara's heart. On the one side is deceitful GDR patriot and Stasi officer Peter Koch, and on the other, enlightened libertarian and photographer Richard Panter. This Westerner with a camera who can see more than others and can capture images is the ultimate cinematic hero. As if this is not enough, he also exemplifies the global citizen: he was born in Switzerland, raised in Shanghai, and holds both an American and a diplomatic passport!

Perhaps not too surprisingly, the public came back for more, with even higher ratings on the second night, and the critics lambasted the film as "Edutainment," "a maudlin pity-party, and a dull and grinding tearjerker."[106] Although the film delivered visual authenticity by means of costumes and set designs, the exaggerated narrative emplotment and overly sentimental approach contributed to a simplistic black-and-white world of good and evil. Kerstin Decker astutely argues that television films like *Die Frau vom Checkpoint Charlie*

> are less a mirror of the GDR than a mirror of contemporary television aesthetics. They are ideological products . . . and therefore dishonest, because of their pandering to the public. Because they don't expect the public to be capable of any intellectual challenge that goes beyond differentiating between black and white, good and evil. No nuances, no dissonance. It's legitimate when a soap opera says: I am a soap opera. When it says: I am a representation of history, it becomes embarrassing.[107]

Die Frau vom Checkpoint Charlie creates a past with clear-cut perpetrators and empowered victims, history-light that shies away from the complexities of human motivation. Despite its focus on female suffering, tearful departures, and prolonged separations, the film stops short of showing anything too disturbing, such as prison conditions. It adheres to the contours of what Eric Rentschler has called a cinema of consensus that avoids difficult issues and seeks common ground. With its stoic heroine determined to overcome all adversity, the film does not delve too deeply into such messy feelings as loneliness, betrayal, and desperation. Instead, it filters out the harshest elements of a government that is both oppressive and apathetic, and offers up a soothing version of the past, in which victims overcome the powers that be. Human-rights activist Friedrich Schorlemmer has suggested that *Die Frau vom Checkpoint Charlie* is more than simply an attempt by television filmmakers to reassure viewers that the past has been mastered. Schorlemmer criticized the film because it depicts the GDR as if it were a place governed exclusively by terror and "gives the impression that one must be reminded of this over and over, so as to kill the GDR again and again, to make it illegitimate, and to warn people at the same time against today's political leftists, who allegedly have not distanced themselves enough from such practices."[108] Indeed, the GDR depicted here has no redeeming values and is criminalized in a much more overstated fashion than in *Berlin Is in Germany* or *Führer Ex*. In such an exaggerated form, it is either laughable or monstrous, a preposterous and iniquitous regime that deserved to be slain. As Schorlemmer reminds us, such a view of the past leaves little room for a rehabilitation of Marxism and the legacy of real-existing socialism in today's political arena.

An die Grenze, directed by Urs Egger, sets a different tone. Rather than portraying heroic resisters who champion freedom in sensational ways, *An die Grenze* aims for a more nuanced depiction of GDR history, from the perspective of a border guard.[109] Screenwriter Stefan Kolditz drew upon his own experience as a border guard and claimed that his script was realistic but not autobiographical. The main character, Alex, starts out in 1974 as a naive young man who voluntarily signs up for military service, because he wants to defy his prominent father and demonstrate that no one deserves special privileges under socialism. In the GDR Border Troops Alex comes of age, losing his illusions and learning to think for himself. As an experienced soldier warns him, in this transitional zone at the border "you discover who you really are," and the lessons are hard ones.[110] While officers teach recruits about idealistic notions of military honor, duty, and camaraderie, everyday life in the barracks is brutal — with senior conscripts hazing new recruits in violent and humiliating ways. Alex is dismayed by the discrepancy between patriotic rhetoric declaring socialism's inherent humanism and the installation of automatic firing devices along the border. On his first patrol, Alex dutifully faces westward to defend the homeland against imperialism but is admonished to turn around and recognize that his job is to face eastward and shoot at fellow countrymen trying to escape. Indeed the external enemy's only acts of aggression are symbolic, heckling him to desert and blasting rock-and-roll to herald the seductive power of the West.

As the title of Egger's film implies, *An die Grenze* is about movement, not stasis, and the dividing line has surprisingly porous edges. Recruits are taught that there is a sharp ideological divide between East and West and that the fortified inner-German border is necessary to ensure world peace. They are traumatized to learn that the so-called "anti-fascist protective barrier" is actually designed to keep East Germans in rather than foreigners out, but they do not view the West as a viable alternative. Instead they consider the competing societies equally undesirable and foresee no escape from the system. One soldier remarks: "Here there are lies, over there complacency and over-indulgence — and in between, no alternative."[111] It is highly unlikely that in the mid-1970s these naive young soldiers would have considered Western lifestyles complacent and

Fig. 2.7. Screenshot from Urs Eggers's An die Grenze *(2007).*

over-indulgent. Rather than reflecting common sentiments at the height of the cold-war era, this statement better encapsulates a contemporary attitude that there is no viable alternative to capitalist consumerism and widespread political apathy or pessimism. The fate of the GDR is embodied best in political officer Captain Dobbs, an emasculated old man whose wife is openly cheating on him. This relict is an idealist who believes in the nobility of service to the state but is incapable of upholding his authority or engendering loyalty and in the end commits suicide. Like Captain Dobbs, the old GDR leaders, who may have once been inspired by lofty ideas, lost their power to rule and could not earn their subjects' support. Screenwriter Stefan Kolditz considered the utopianism of figures such as Alex and Captain Dobbs essential aspects of telling GDR history: "If the notion of utopia is not included in the discussion, then in retrospect the GDR remains the insipid idea of idiotic functionaries."[112] The emphasis placed on the conflict between utopian ideals and the brutal enforcement of compliance sets *An die Grenze* apart from *Die Frau vom Checkpoint Charlie* and makes it, despite its shortcomings, a history film worthy of rumination on where exactly the borders between right and wrong, utopia and reality were set and where they should ideally be placed in the world today.

In *An die Grenze*, the border is a space of precarious balance, in which nature persists in all its beauty and danger. In the buffer zone of no-man's-land, the camera lingers on images of animals roaming freely, oblivious to the arbitrary human constraints imposed on the natural world. With its unspoiled vistas of forests and lakes, the borderland offers respite from regimented army life. Alex flees here to rendezvous with his girlfriend Christine and to express doubts about real-existing socialism. In contrast to the physical border between the two German states, the border between loyalty and betrayal is anything but clear-cut. When Christine asks Alex to help her brother Knut escape, the young soldier must decide whether he will remain loyal to his country or to his own moral compass. He must choose between upholding his sworn duty to defend socialism and *looking* the other way when Knut crosses the border. Indeed the act of looking is central to Alex's development. The young man is the object of the state's multidirectional gaze; in an early scene he sits in front of the ubiquitous portrait of Erich Honecker while being interviewed by army recruiters whose backs face the camera. Christine plays a pivotal role in Alex's enlightenment: she gives him a camera to fulfill his dream of becoming a photographer and opens his eyes to the injustice of a system that walls in its citizens. Functioning as his conscience, she poses the crucial question: "If you don't have a choice, how do you know if you are on the right side?"[113] Finally, looking and making indelible images propels the narrative. A photograph motivates Knut's escape over the Wall, since he illegally took a photo of the automatic firing devices installed at the border and sent it to a Western human-rights organization.

Perhaps the weakest aspect of this screenplay is that in its zeal to present a soldier's perspective, it ends up rewriting history so that GDR citizens escape unharmed while border guards die. In contrast to the documented history of the Wall, where hundreds of civilians died trying to escape the GDR,[114] we have here a scenario where an officer commits suicide and two border guards are killed on duty. The shooting is based loosely on the notorious incident of border guard Werner Weinhold, who killed two fellow guards while deserting and defecting to the West in 1975, but it leaves the impression that border guards were victims and not perpetrators. Similar to *Das Leben der Anderen*, an SED functionary has misgivings and secretly helps resisters. In both films the resistance is based on personal motivations and takes place in a manner that has little or no negative consequences for those involved and never challenges the status quo.

The final film, *12 heißt: Ich liebe Dich*, directed by Connie Walther, is based on a true incident so incredible that it reads like a fairy tale. Dissident Regina Kaiser was arrested in 1981 on charges of treason, and Uwe Karlstedt was the Stasi officer who interrogated her for eight months in Hohenschönhausen prison. During this time, the dissident and her interrogator fell in love, but this did not stop him from preparing the evidence that was used against her at trial and resulted in her being sentenced to three years in the notorious women's prison at Hoheneck before being deported to West Berlin. After the fall of the Wall, Regina and Uwe found each other, fell in love again, and married. Their life was the material for a documentary film and a joint memoir.[115] In Walther's film the names are changed, but the story follows the memoir closely. Dissident Bettina Kramer is arrested and sent to Hohenschönhausen, where she is interrogated by Stasi officer Jan Kohlfeld. During the months of interrogation Bettina falls in love with Jan and invents the code words 11 and 12 — there are 11 letters in the German phrase "du bist schön" (you are beautiful) and 12 in "ich liebe dich" (I love you). A decade after the GDR collapsed, Bettina and Jan have moved on with their lives. She is working as a tour guide at the former prison and Jan has become an accountant, but when they meet again, they fall in love — to the dismay of their families and victims' associations.

Much of Walther's film takes place in Hohenschönhausen, where the daily life of political prisoners is degrading. Stripped of her clothes, her dignity, and even her name, Bettina becomes Prisoner 770 and is subjected to isolation and disorientation to make her more pliable. She is kept in solitary confinement in an 8-foot by 10-foot cell with guards routinely turning on the light, waking her, and looking through the peephole. The only conversations she has other than interrogation are limited to the guards shouting "Face the wall, eyes down!" Bettina admits that she looks forward to meeting with her interrogator, because he is her only human contact, but the film never examines the motivation behind her emotional attachment. It does not judge her or explore the possibility that she is suffering from the Stockholm Syndrome; rather it treats love as a nonrational phenomenon, against which there is no defense.

Jan is perhaps the more interesting figure because he is *not* an idealist who believes in socialism or that the ends justify the means. Jan is an opportunist who wants to advance his career, and while he loves Bettina, he never tries to save her. He simply does his job and retains his sense of purpose. Jan is a fairly sympathetic figure, a family man who takes care of his wife and child, and a good officer who follows orders. He is not the cliché of a power-hungry Stasi officer who stands around barking orders or intimidating suspects. But he is also not a hero who becomes enlightened, like Alex in *An die Grenze* or Captain Wiesler in *Das Leben der Anderen*. Jan never questions what he is doing; he never comes to an epiphany. He does not recognize the dictatorial aspects of the regime or his own culpability in making sure an unjust system keeps working like a well-oiled machine. He remains a normal, average guy who "is happy when his boss is happy."[116] *12 heißt: Ich liebe Dich* employs a motif common to many recent films, in which the woman functions as the man's conscience (for example in *An die Grenze* and *Das Wunder von Berlin*). After Bettina is fired from her position at the prison memorial site because of her love affair with a former Stasi officer, she flares up at Jan and pronounces his moral duty: "Obviously you are not responsible for the GDR political system, but you are for your own decisions."[117] After he acknowledges that she is right and accepts responsibility for his own actions, the two quickly reconcile. The film ends on a positive note, implying that Jan can help Bettina heal the wounds of the past. *12 heißt: Ich liebe Dich* was sharply criticized by eight victims associations representing some 200,000 former political prisoners. These groups demanded that the television station take the film off the air. As a compromise, the station broadcast Bettina Renner's documentary *In den Fängen der Stasi* (In the Clutches of the Stasi) after the feature film. Hubertus Knabe, the director of the memorial site at Hohenschönhausen prison, criticized the film because he could find no evidence that the story was true. In his opinion, a love story between a prisoner and a Stasi officer trivialized the real suffering experienced by those incarcerated for political dissent.[118]

Comparing cinematic productions to television, it is clear that television outsells the cinema by millions of viewers. This discrepancy may well be attributed to the ease of watching a show on the couch in the evening or the relatively inexpensive nature of public broadcasting in contrast to the costs of attending the movie theater. However, the magnitude of these disparate audience figures compounded by the different accents found in television and cinematic films warrant contemplation. If market shares are any indication of what the German public wants, then it follows that audiences want history remodeled into something they can live with. Many historical truths are simply too brutal, too complicated, too hard to accept. History-light is easier to bear than collective bad memories. If we take *Die Frau vom Checkpoint Charlie*, *An die Grenze*, and *12 heißt: Ich liebe Dich* as elements in a national narrative, then the coordinates of history translate into a melodrama with multiple happy endings. Victims like Sara were apolitical individuals who wanted the right to self-determination. Unrelenting in their opposition to state tutelage, they possessed the willpower needed to win their freedom. Soldiers like Alex were morally conscientious individuals who believed they were doing the right thing and refused to follow orders blindly, so that the only deaths at the border were those of guards. Even Stasi officers like Jan were normal people who just did their job and had a soft spot in their heart. The past is behind us if victims like Bettina forgive the perpetrators and redeem them through love. Since the fall of the Wall, the melodrama has been the most common genre for depicting GDR history, and recent television movies continue this trend, so personal relations still motivate political choices. Seen through the lenses of unification, one can understand why melodrama with its prolonged suffering, gallant rescues, and just rewards and punishment is appealing for a national narrative. Taken together, what these recent television films offer are either empowered victims who prevail over an unjust government or blurred lines between victim and perpetrator in a plea for understanding, forgiveness, and reconciliation.

By contrast, *Die Architekten, Das Versprechen,* and *Das Leben der Anderen* are far from the often simplistic feel-good movies about the GDR that have flooded the air waves recently. All three films delve into the emotional cost of staying true to one's belief system and feature heroes who retain hope despite enormous pressure exerted on them by a ruthless state authority. Kahane's *Die Architekten* is about an entire generation's losses and specifically the emotional toll paid by idealists who try to live up to socialism's compelling rhetoric of creating a better world but are crushed by a bureaucracy that demands conformity. Von Trotta's *Das Versprechen* illustrates the losses of an entire people who are held captive by political forces beyond their control and the painful choices made by individuals faced with limited options. Von Donnersmarck's *Das Leben der Anderen* explores the idealism on both sides of the GDR political divide, the forces of state authority and the ultimately stronger force of artistry, that together fight for morality. While this last film focuses on the transformation of a Stasi officer and implies that he is a victim of circumstances, it does not shy away from showing the cost in human lives for defying the SED dictatorship, especially in its depictions of suicides. What these three films share is the belief that the GDR was a good idea gone bad. In each of these films, the betrayal of good people by a political system that promised the closest thing to paradise on earth and delivered a hellish dictatorship is all the more bitter, since the resisters remained committed socialists at heart. In their own way, Daniel Brenner, Sophie Sellmann, Konrad Richter, Gerd Wiesler, and Georg Dreyman believe in the perfectibility of society and never lose faith in the shared project of fostering a humane and egalitarian Germany.

Notes

1 Quoted in Cooke, *Representing East Germany since Unification*, 4.

2 The first Enquete Commission, "Treatment of History and Consequences of the SED-Dictatorship in Germany" (Aufarbeitung von Geschichte und Folgen der SED-Diktatur in Deutschland), collected testimony and documents from 1992 to 1994. The second Enquete Commission, "Surmounting the Consequences of the SED-Dictatorship in the Process of German Freedom" ("Überwindung der Folgen der SED-Diktatur im Prozeß der deutschen Freiheit"), worked from 1995 to 1998.

3 Hubertus Knabe, "Das Aufarbeitungskombinat: Merkwürdige Vorschläge zur Neuorganisation des DDR-Gedenkens," *Die Welt*, 8 May 2006, in *Wohin treibt die DDR-Erinnerung: Dokumentation einer Debatte*, ed. Martin Sabrow, Rainer Eckert, Monika Flacke, Klaus-Dietmar Henke, Roland Jahn, Freya Klier, Tina Krone, Peter Maser, Ulrike Poppe, and Hermann Rudolph (Göttingen: Vandenhoeck &

Ruprecht, 2007), 191. Further references to this work are given using the abbreviation *DD* and the page number.

4 "Hierzu zählen aus Sicht der Kommission insbesondere — eine nach Ost und West geteilte Wahrnehmung der DDR-Geschichte, die gerade in den alten Bundesländern nur sehr bedingt als Teil der gesamtdeutschen Geschichte verstanden wird." "Die Empfehlungen der Expertenkommission zur Schaffung eines Geschichtsverbundes 'Aufarbeitung der SED-Diktatur.'" *DD*, 20.

5 "Nicht weniger wichtig ist es, einer drohenden 'Verinselung' der DDR-Geschichte im Geschichtsbewußtsein entgegenzutreten und die DDR in eine integrierte deutsch-deutsche Geschichte zwischen 1945 und 1990 im europäischen und globalen Kontext einzubetten." *DD*, 22.

6 The Sabrow commission was concerned about "eine gegenwärtige Vorrangstellung der öffentlichen Dokumentation staatlicher Repression gegenüber derjenigen von Widerstand und Anpassung, Ideologie und Parteiherrschaft sowie von Alltag in der Diktatur, die als Wirkungsmechanismen deutlich unterbelichtet bleiben." *DD*, 21.

7 Comparing the status of GDR research to that on National Socialism, the commission lamented that both suffered from the same inadequacies: "daß sie die alltägliche Funktionsweise des Systems und die tägliche Aushandlung individueller Entscheidungsspielräume nicht ausreichend sichtbar zu machen und dem Stellenwert des Verhaltens und der Verantwortung des einzelnen für die Macht der Diktatur nicht hinreichend gerecht zu werden vermag." *DD*, 32.

8 "Die Stützen der untergegangenen Diktatur marschieren ja nicht nur in Gedenkstätten auf — sie sitzen im Bundestag, in den Medien, in Schulen und vielfältigen Gremien unserer Demokratie. Und sie werden nicht müde, ihren Unrechtsstaat im Nachhinein demokratisch aufzupolieren und in der öffentlichen Erinnerung zu glätten." Freya Klier, "Sondervotum," *DD*, 44.

9 The commission recognized "eine in den letzten Jahren zunehmende und insbesondere medial vermittelte Trivialisierung der DDR als politisches System, mit der gerade in jüngerer Zeit vermehrt Versuche einer geschichtsrevisionistischen Negierung ihres Diktaturcharakters und einer Verächtlichmachung ihrer Opfer einhergehen." *DD*, 20.

10 In addition, Egon Günther, who left the GDR in 1978 to work in the West, returned to the DEFA studios to direct *Stein* (1991), based on a script he cowrote with Helga Schütz. The story follows the life of Stein, a renowned actor who exiled himself to his remote villa after the Soviet invasion of Prague in 1968 and fell into a state of delusion bordering on madness. Stein harbors social misfits, but not renegade Soviet soldiers, and only makes his way to Berlin in 1989 to find a young girl he hopelessly loves. *Stein*, like most films made at the DEFA studies during this period, lapses into a surreal mode when Stein finds himself in the tumult of the revolution and hypnotizes a policeman to avoid arrest. For an overview of films produced by DEFA from the *Wende* until the studio stopped production in 1992, see Daniela Berghahn, "East German Cinema after Unification," in *German Cinema since Unification*, ed. David Clarke (London: Continuum, 2006), 79–104, and Naughton, *That Was the Wild East*, 206–34.

[11] Ulrich Weiß's *Miraculi* (1992) and Andreas Höntsch *Der Straß* (Rhinestone, 1991) also belong to this trend of surreal visions.

[12] For a detailed study of the clown persona in the political theater and songs of these popular cabaret artists, see David G. Robb, "Wenzel & Mensching: A Carnivalesque Clowns' Act Spanning the GDR and United Germany," *German Studies Review* 23, no. 1 (2000): 53–68.

[13] "Die allgemeine Dummheit ertränkt mich. Als ich mein Land krepieren sah, spürte ich, daß ich es liebte. Ich empfinde die Trauer, die die römischen Patrizier im vierten Jahrhundert empfanden. Ich fühle eine heillose Barbarei aus dem Boden aussteigen. Ich emphoffe [sic], krepiert zu sein, bevor sie alles mit sich gerissen hat. Ich habe immer versucht in einem Elfenbeinturm zu leben; aber ein Meer von Scheiße schlägt an seine Mauern." Steffen Mensching and Hans-Eckardt Wenzel, *Letztes aus der Da Da eR*, DEFA-Studio für Spielfilme, "Nachwuchsgruppe," Prokuktionsleitung: Manfred Renger, unpublished film script, 19 Mar. 1990, Version D I/5, 24–25. The film dialogue is slightly different and notably includes a line not found in this version of the filmscript: "Die halbe Nation ist irre und die andere nicht ganz bei Groschen" (Half the nation is crazy and the other half is not quite with it). Compare *Letztes aus der Da Da eR* [1990], dir. Jörg Foth, DVD (Amherst, MA: DEFA Film Library, 2009).

[14] See Sven Felix Kellerhoff, "Millionenquoten für Geschichte: Historische Ereignisse als Rahmen von fiktiven Dramen werden zum Erfolgsrezept deutscher Filmemacher," *Die Welt*, 22 Mar. 2006.

[15] At the 1990 Feature Film Festival of the GDR *Die Architekten* won a special prize and the best supporting actor award for Wolfgang Greese. In the first week of June 1990 the film also opened the Festival of New German Film in Potsdam. Finally, it enjoyed a gala performance at the International cinema in Berlin on 21 June 1990 and went into general release the next day. See Bundesarchiv-Filmarchiv, ed., *Filmobibliografischer Jahresbericht 1990 (und Überläufer)* (Berlin: Henschel Verlag, 1994), 23–24 and 575, and Bärbel Dalicow, "Traurige Feste: Festival des jungen deutschen Films in Potsdam," *Filmspiegel* 15 (1990): 15.

[16] In the press packet for *Die Architekten*, Peter Kahane notes that filming began on 3 October 1989, which is echoed in Regine Sylvester's report on events during production. The German Federal Film Archive dates the filming as beginning on 2 October 1989 and completed on 16 January 1990. In subsequent interviews Kahane recalls beginning the filming in September of 1989. Compare "Gespräch mit dem Regisseur Peter Kahane," in *Die Architekten: Presseinformation* (Berlin: Progress Film-Verleih, n.d.), 4; Regine Sylvester, "Leidenschaft und Überlebenskämpfe: Drehreport über den neuen DEFA-Film *Die Architekten* von Thomas Knauf (Autor), Peter Kahane (Regie), Andreas Köfer (Kamera)," *Filmspiegel* 9 (1990): 4; Bundesarchiv-Filmarchiv, *Filmobibliografischer Jahresbericht 1990 (und Überläufer)*, 23; and "'Eine Abbildung der Realität in ihrer Härte:' Ein Gespräch mit Peter Kahane über seinen Film *Die Architekten*," *Filmkunst und Gesellschaftskritik — Sozialethische Erkundungen, Film & Theologie* 7, ed. Walter Lesch, Charles Martig, and Joachim Valentin (Marburg: Schüren Verlag, 2005), 189.

[17] "Wir haben versucht, auf die Höhe der Zeit zu kommen, und wir hechelten immer hinterher. Wir haben Demonstrationen und Mahnwachen gedreht und

schon wieder wurde anderes wichtig. Dann faßten wir einen Entschluß: das wird ein historischer Film, er endet im Frühjahr 1989." Sylvester, "Leidenschaft und Überlebenskämpfe," 5.

[18] "Früher sollte durch Bild und Musik klarwerden, daß Daniel trotz seiner Niederlage mit viel größerer Radikalität weiterkämpfen wird. Das war unser Wunsch und auch unsere Art, Tragisches zu erleben und uns trotzdem immer wieder Mut zu machen. Nachdem die Menschen in diesem Land mit eben dieser Radikalität unsere Gesellschaft verändert haben, hat sich eine Hoffnung erfüllt. Es bleibt, über unsere Verluste zu erzählen." Sylvester, "Leidenschaft und Überlebenskämpfe," 5.

[19] "Die Zeit der Indirektheiten war für uns vorbei. Wir wollten die Dinge beim Namen nennen, wollten im Film die Mauer sehen, wollten eine Ausreise zeigen und das ganze Elend derer erleben, die um eine der wichtigsten Sachen betrogen wurden — um ihre Hoffnungen. . . . Von der Absurdität eines politischen Systems, das seine eigenen Leute nicht aktiv werden läßt und daran zugrunde gehen muß." Quoted in McGee, "'Ich wollte ewig einen richtigen Film machen!,'" 326.

[20] "Ich hatte immer das Gefühl, und das hatten meine Kollegen in meinem Alter fast alle, man läßt mich nicht rein in dieses Land. Ich wollte eigentlich nichts sehnsüchtiger als mitmachen in der DDR, ich wollte endlich ankommen und nicht immer das Gefühl haben, die lassen mich irgendwie draußen vor der Tür." Dietmar Hochmuth, "Eine Suche ohne Ende: Gespräch mit Peter Kahane; Interview, 1993," in *DEFA NOVA: Nach wie vor? Versuch einer Spurensicherung*, ed. Dietmar Hochmuth (Berlin: Freunde der deutschen Kinemathek, 1993), 115.

[21] "Wir waren wahrscheinlich die letzte Generation, die die öffentlichen Aufforderungen zum Mitmachen für voll nahm und die am wenigsten daran teilhatte . . . So gerieten wir in den Widerspruch zwischen Anspruch und Möglichkeit — unser Jahrgang, immer so alt wie dieses Land. Doch man hat uns nicht wirklich gewollt. Man hielt uns als Nachwuchs, als Lehrlinge klein." Klaus Maihorn, "Mutiges Menetekel — zu spät," *Wochenpost*, 6 Jul. 1990.

[22] See Werner Durth, Jörn Düwel, and Niels Gutschow, *Architektur und Städtebau der DDR*, 2 vols. (Frankfurt am Main: Campus, 1998), 1:162–93, and Bruno Flierl, *Gebaute DDR. Über Stadtplaner, Architekten und die Macht. Kritische Reflexionen, 1990–1997* (Berlin: Verlag für Bauwesen, 1998), 12–33.

[23] Despite these negative aspects, the *Plattenbaugebiete* were highly coveted housing areas, because they offered indoor plumbing, central heating, and modern kitchens and bathrooms. For an account of how prefabricated housing units were considered a privilege among many social groups, see György Konrad, "Rückblick auf die Beglückung," in *Glück, Stadt, Raum in Europa, 1945 bis 2000*, ed. Romana Schneider and Rudolf Stegers (Basel: Birkhäuser, 2002), 9.

[24] "Die Stadt ist in Struktur und architektonischer Gestaltung Ausdruck des politischen Lebens . . . und des nationalen Bewußtseins des Volkes." Durth et al., *Architektur und Städtebau der DDR*, 1:173.

[25] "Und deswegen geht es weniger um teure Fassaden, als vielmehr um angenehme Räume. Passagen, Plätze, Straßen mit menschlichen Proportionen. Abwechslungsreich. Auf denen man sich trifft und nicht verliert, wie es jetzt meist ist. Nur wenn wir uns daran halten, werden sich die Leute in unserer Stadt wohlfühlen

und sie als Heimat annehmen." Thomas Knauf, *Die Architekten*, DEFA Studio für Spielfilme, Gruppe "Babelsberg," Produktion: Herbert Ehler, Unpublished film script, 17 Jul. 1989, D II /8, 31. There are slight differences between the film dialogue and the film script that do not affect the meaning. Compare *Die Architekten* [1990], dir. Peter Kahane, DVD (Berlin: Icestorm Entertainment, 2005). Further references to this film script are given using the abbreviation *Ar* and the page number.

[26] "Nur wer wählen kann, der hat . . . Heimatgefühle!" *Ar*, 32.

[27] DEFA director Lothar Warneke brought *Franziska Linkerhand* to the screen in his film *Unser kurzes Leben* (Our short life, WDR, 1981). Brigitte Reimann's life was the subject of two television documentaries, Katharina Schubert's *Ich habe gelebt und gelebt und gelebt: Die DDR Schriftstellerin Brigitte Reimann* (I lived and lived and lived: The GDR author Brigitte Reimann, WDR, 1990) and Ulrich Kasten's *Ich liebe, mein Gott — ich liebe: Das kurze Leben der Brigitte Reimann* (I love, my God, I love: The short life of Brigitte Reimann, ORB, 1999), as well as Markus Imboden's bio-pic starring Martina Gedeck, *Hunger auf Leben* (Hunger for life, MDR, 2004).

[28] "Guck mal, was ich sehe. . . . Ich verblöde hier. . . . Ich werd' zur Maus . . . ich werde immer mehr zur Maus. Zu einer kleinen, grauen Maus. Ich erlebe nichts mehr." *Ar*, 52–53.

[29] "Hör auf, mich zu verhöhnen. Du Macho! Dir ist es doch egal, wie es mir geht, du merkst noch nicht mal, was ich alles mache, damit du in Ruhe arbeiten kannst. . . . Laß mich in Ruhe. Laß mich. Und von nun ab mach ich nur noch meins. Meins!!!" *Ar*, 54.

[30] "Ich zweifle nicht daran, daß Sie hochqualifizierte Architektinnen sind. Aber Sie wissen selbst, daß es gerade bei jungen Frauen . . . Widersprüche gibt zwischen dem Engagement für die Arbeit und der Familienplanung." *Ar*, 26.

[31] "Architekt bin ich nie gewesen. Meine männlichen Kollegen jedenfalls haben mir eingeredet, daß man als alleinstehende Mutter nicht beides sein kann. Also bin ich auf eigenen Wunsch hier heraufbefördert worden." *Ar*, 23.

[32] "Bei allem Verständnis für Originalität der Arbeiten — aber diese Vorschläge sind in der vorliegenden Art unakzeptabel. Was heißt 'Familie im Streß' und für wen sollen wir dieses Denkmal aufrichten. Habt ihr das mit den Bildhauern ernsthaft erwogen? Genosse Brenner, ich glaube, ihr seid da in eine Sackgasse geraten. Eine 'Familie im Sozialismus' ist ein wichtiges Thema — eine solche Gruppenplastik ist denkbar. Darstellung von Stress kann nicht das Anliegen von engagierten sozialistischen Künstlern sein." *Ar*, 77–78.

[33] "Bauen ist Politik, Machtdarstellung. Jedes Haus erzählt von Verhältnissen . . . ungewollt oder gewollt. Von Reichtum oder Sparsamkeit, von Träumen oder Hoffnungslosigkeit, von Ökonomie, Technologie und natürlich von gutem oder schlechtem Geschmack der Auftraggeber." *Ar*, 93–94.

[34] "Mit 39 möchte ich endlich erwachsen sein." *Ar*, 81.

[35] "Wir sollten aufhören, bevor man uns mit der Wasserwaage der Gleichförmigkeit erschlägt. Jetzt müssen wir sogar noch um den Titel 'Kollektiv der

sozialistischen Arbeit' kämpfen. Dabei fürchten sie doch nichts mehr als ein Kollektiv von Leuten, die sich einig sind. Die kann man schwer regieren." *Ar*, 80.

[36] Klaus Finke examines in greater detail the depiction of time in regard to socialism's demand for renunciation of current desires in *Die Architekten*. See Klaus Finke, "Utopie und Heimat: Peter Kahanes Film *Die Architekten*," *DEFA-Film als nationales Kulturerbe?* Beiträge zur Film- und Fernsehwissenschaft 58, ed. Klaus Finke (Berlin: Vistas, 2001), 53–60.

[37] "Warum soll ich hier leben? Nur, weil ich hier geboren wurde? Ich brauch' mehr, Ich will mich wiederfinden. In der Arbeit, in der Art, wie man mit mir umgeht und wie ich mit anderen umgehen kann. Aber ich . . . ich find' mich nirgendwo wieder." *Ar*, 84–85.

[38] Winfried decries the situation: "Da haben sie uns einen Kuckuck ins Nest gesetzt . . . Naumann, der parfümierte Alptraum des Betriebes. Aus jeder Abteilung weggelobt wegen Unfähigkeit. Daniel, du mußt was unternehmen." Daniel responds: "Ach, Unsinn. Euer Mißtrauen ist albern. Und selbst wenn er ein Kuckuck ist — wir haben doch nichts zu verbergen." *Ar*, 45.

[39] Stage directions read: "Er öffnet seinen Mantel, hält ihn aufgeschlagen, wie ein Exhibitionist und verharrt in dieser Pose. Schließlich wird ihm sein sonderliches Gebaren bewußt. Wir sehen Daniel von hinten vor dem Brandenburger Tor. Wind weht ihm in den Rücken. Schließlich dreht er sich um — dem Zuschauer zu. Sein Gesicht zeigt Schmerz — aber auch Energie" (He unbuttons his coat, holds it open like an exhibitionist, and holds this pose. Finally he becomes aware of his strange behaviour. We see Daniel from behind, in front of the Brandenburg Gate. Wind blows at his back. Finally he turns round — toward the viewer. His face shows pain — but also energy.) *Ar*, 143.

[40] "Klar, erst Partei und dann die Karriere. Das geht aber schon deshalb nicht, weil die Mittel, mit denen ich mir Macht und Einfluß verschaffe, eben auch *die* Mittel sind, die mich und meine Ideen kaputtmachen." *Ar*, 140.

[41] Stage directions read: "Daniel wird Kandidat der SED, Zahlke überreicht ihm die Kandidatenkarte, das Statut und einen Blumenstrauß" and Daniel warns Director Wieschala: "Du wirst dich von nun an noch häufiger wundern." *Ar*, 141 and 142.

[42] Even in the first half of 1990, GDR cinemas sold 40 percent fewer tickets than during the same period in 1989. Beyond the shock of entering into a new world, GDR viewers were also faced with economic changes in the film industry that made going to the movies in mid-summer 1990 a much more costly endeavor than just months earlier, especially after East German cinemas were reorganized as Kino-GmbH on 1 July 1990. Whereas a movie ticket in June 1990 cost between 1 and 1.5 East Mark, by 1991 the same ticket cost 6 DM. Dieter Wiedemann, "Wo bleiben die Kinobesucher? Daten und Hypothesen zum Kinobesuch in der neuen deutschen Republik," in *Medien der Ex-DDR in der Wende*, ed. Peter Hoff and Dieter Wiedemann, Beiträge zur Film- und Fernsehwissenschaft 40 (Berlin: Vistas, 1991), 81.

[43] MZ., "Mauern für die Phantasie: *Architekten* beim nationalen DDR-Filmfestival in Ost-Berlin," *Frankfurter Allgemeine Zeitung*, 6 Jun. 1990.

[44] "Als unmittelbare Reflexion des Niedergangs der alten DDR-Strukturen aber hat der Film, meine ich, zweifellos einen großen Wert, auch als Dokument — über ein Land an seinem Ende." Peter Claus, "Wunden eines 'Versagers': Ab heute in den Kinos; *Die Architekten*, ein DEFA-Film von Peter Kahane und Thomas Knauf," *Junge Welt*, 21 Jun. 1990.

[45] "Kahanes Film gehört für mich zu den erschütternsten Dokumenten der DEFA-Produktion. . . . Diesen Film unbeteiligt zu konsumieren, scheint völlig ausgeschlossen. Zum ersten und vielleicht vorerst auch zum letzten Male wird so etwas wie eine Vergangenheitsbewältigung betrieben. Ein Rückblick, eine ehrliche Bestandsaufnahme, eine Antwort vielleicht auch auf die Frage vieler Verängstigter, ob das, was geschehen, richtig gewesen ist." Roland Herold, "Die verratene Generation: Erster DEFA-Film nach der Wende; Peter Kahanes *Architekten*," *Sächsisches Tageblatt*, 29 Jun. 1990.

[46] See Marlene Köhler, "Kommt jetzt die unterhaltsame und gut erzählte DEFA-Film-Geschichte? Zu ersten Eindrücken vom 6. Spielfilm-Festival der DDR," *Mitteldeutsche Zeitung*, 29 May 1990; Cornelia Resik, "*Die Architekten*," *Sächsische Zeitung*, 13 Jul. 1990; Heide Gossing, "Begrabene Träume: *Architekten*, neuer DEFA-Film von Peter Kahane," *Ostsee Zeitung*, 6 Sept. 1990; Dk. "Die vergessenen *Architekten*: Mehr als Trafo-Stationen und Einheitsblocks durften sie nicht bauen; Die Defa setzte den Architekten des Sozialismus ein filmisches Denkmal," *Sächsische Zeitung*, 17 Nov. 1990.

[47] "Gebrauchen, das meint doch vor allem die Gegenargumentation zur damaligen Daueragitation. Damals und gestern noch wollten Filmemacher ihre Meinung sagen, Widerspruch anmelden zur gefährlichen offiziellen Ideologiestarre." Birgit Galle, "Hier zartes Klopfen, dort hartes Hämmern — aber wer wird es hören: Zu den DEFA-Premieren *Die Architekten* und *Karla*," *Neues Deutschland*, 23 Jun. 1990.

[48] "Ist es der nicht gewünschte Blick zurück in unsere Vergangenheit oder schon der nach vorn, der für solche Filme nichts übrig hat?" Axel Seitz, "Wen provoziert diese Leere? Auf der Leinwand gesehen: *Die Architekten*," *Norddeutsche Zeitung*, 4 Jul. 1990.

[49] A limited showing in Leipzig in late October 1994 allowed the film to be nominated as the official German submission for the best foreign-language feature film at the 67th Oscar ceremony. The reception in Leipzig was much the same as at the premiere in Berlin, a mixed reaction with some viewers praising the film's emotional impact and others considering it kitsch. See Gisela Hoyer, "Liebesgeschichte in Mauer-Schatten: Trottas neuer Film *Das Versprechen* unterwegs nach L.A. in Leipzig voraufgeführt," *Leipziger Volkszeitung*, 29/30 Oct. 1994.

[50] "Die Mauer im Kopf einzureißen wird länger dauern, als irgendein Abrißunternehmen für die sichtbare Mauer braucht." Peter Schneider, *Der Mauerspringer*, 3rd ed. (Darmstadt: Luchterhand, 1986), 102.

[51] "Als die DDR zusammenbrach, lebte Margarethe von Trotta in Rom und schien sich, verdientermaßen, von den deutschen Miseren vielleicht für immer abgewendet zu haben. Es brauchte den Anstoß durch einen italienischen Produzenten, der ihr einen Mauer-Film vorschlug, bis ihr die fordernde Größe der Aufgabe aufging. Erst zögerte sie. Doch nach zwei weiteren Filmen in Italien

packte sie die Mauer-Geschichte, gründlich, wie das ihre Art ist, um sie sich zu eigen zu machen. Nun thront sie darauf, eine gesamtdeutsche Betroffenheitsglucke wie noch nie." "Filmfestspiele: 'Es darf geweint werden,'" *Der Spiegel*, 6 Feb. 1995, 188.

52 "Margarethe wird immer dafür angegriffen, daß sie nicht hier war, sondern in Rom, als die Idee entstand; man streitet ihr das Recht ab, so einen Film zu machen." Schneider added that his role in the production was largely ignored. Mariam Niroumand, "Die Mauerspringer: Margarethe von Trottas Ost-West Liebestragödie *Das Versprechen* eröffnet heute abend die Berlinale; Ein Gespräch mit ihr und Co-Autor Peter Schneider," taz, 9 Feb. 1995.

53 "Ich suche meine Familie, weil ich nie eine hatte, und meine Heimat, weil ich zwar hier aufwuchs und verfolge, was hier passiert, zugleich aber immer das Gefühl habe: dies ist ja nicht mein Land." Dietmar Hochmuth, "Margarethe von Trotta: Die Balance von Erwachen und Wahn," *Regiestühle international*, ed. Fred Gehler (Berlin, DDR: Henschel Verlag, 1987), 227.

54 See Hans-Günther Dicks, "Zum Weinen? Nein, zum Heulen! Zum Festival-Auftakt: *Das Versprechen* von Margarethe von Trotta," *Neues Deutschland*, 9 Feb. 1995; Dieter Strunz, "Wenn jedes Detail stimmt, nur das Eigentliche nicht: Außer Konkurrenz; *Das Versprechen* (Deutschland)," *Berliner Morgenpost,* 10 Feb. 1995; Merten Worthmann, "Verzweifelte Bewährungsprobe: Große Gefühle, deutsche Geschichte; Der Berlinale-Eröffnungsfilm *Das Versprechen*," *Berliner Zeitung,* 10 Feb. 1995; Harald Martenstein, "Tränen kennen keine Grenzen: Margarethe von Trotta hat außer Konkurrenz den Wettbewerb der Berlinale eröffnet," *Der Tagesspiegel,* 10 Feb. 1995; Karl-Heinz Schäfer, "Schlaflos in Ost-Berlin," *Hamburger Abendblatt,* 16 Feb. 1995; Andreas Kilb, "Zahme Herzen: Margarethe von Trottas Mauerfilm *Das Versprechen*," *Die Zeit*, 17 Feb. 1995; and Frank Junghänel, "Von der Mauer verweht: In Margarethe von Trottas Film *Das Versprechen* werden große Gefühle behauptet," *Wochenpost* 8 (1995).

55 "Doch über alle Zweifel erhaben ist die politische Korrektheit: Deutsches Zeigefinger-Kino schlechthin für alle Wissensdurstigen in allen Goethe-Instituten der Dritten Welt." "Filmfestspiele: 'Es darf geweint werden,'" 190.

56 Thomas Elsaesser, "Tales of Sound and Fury: Observations on the Family Melodrama," [1972], in *Home Is Where the Heart Is: Studies in Melodrama and the Woman's Film*, ed. Christine Gledhill (London: British Film Institute, 1987), 55.

57 "Auch da wurde ein Liebespaar durch die politischen Verhältnisse getrennt, doch Manfreds Flucht in den Westen stand am Ende eines langen Ringens um das richtige, bessere Leben. Christa Wolf ließ keinen Zweifel daran, daß das Dableiben, zu dem Rita entschieden hatte, das Richtigere war, doch auch sie war unsicher, voller Widersprüche und Konflikte . . . Konrad bleibt im Osten zurück, weil er über einen offenen Schnürsenkel stolpert. Ein unglücklicher Zufall ersetzt, was bei Christa Wolf bewußte Entscheidung war." Jörg Magenau, "Poesiealbum der Geschichte: Margarethe von Trottas Film *Das Versprechen* eröffnet die Berliner Filmfestspiele," *Freitag: Die Ost-Westwochenzeitung,* 10 Feb. 1995.

58 "So begann eines der merkwürdigsten Experimente in der Geschichte. Aus einem Volk, das einmal dem Wahn erlegen war, die Welt zu beherrschen, wurden

allmählich zwei Völker. Und bald hielt nur noch die Mauer die Illusion aufrecht, daß nur eine Mauer die Deutschen trennte." Peter Schneider and Margarethe von Trotta in collaboration with Felice Laudadio, *Das Versprechen oder Der lange Atem der Liebe: Filmszenarium* (Berlin: Volk & Welt, 1995), 7. See also *Das Versprechen* [1995], dir. Margarethe von Trotta, DVD (Berlin: StudioCanal, 2008). Further references to the film script are given using the abbreviation *V* and the page number.

[59] For example, every time Rosa Luxemburg suffers a traumatic event or engages in a passionate debate, these scenes are followed by a shift to a different time frame until she learns of Kostja's death, whereupon the remainder of the film is linear until her own death.

[60] "Für die Idee und die Ausführung hatte Moskau das Copyright, der Stacheldraht wurde von westdeutschen Firmen geliefert." *V*, 7.

[61] "Was macht die Geschichte aus Individuen, die sie gewissermaßen als Geiseln genommen hat? Das Prinzip Zufall gehört selbstverständlich dazu. Ist Konrad aufgrund einer lächerlichen Lappalie — weil er im entscheidenden Moment über seine Schnürsenkel stolpert — im Osten geblieben? Wie wird das Paar mit diesem Zufall fertig, ist es überhaupt ein Zufall?" Otto Matthies, "Interview mit Margarethe von Trotta und Peter Schneider," in *V*, 142.

[62] This newscast employs footage from the NBC broadcast of *The Tunnel* on 10 December 1962 about the escape of 26 people from East Berlin on 14 September 1962 in a tunnel built by three engineering students at the Technical University in West Berlin. In total, this tunnel allowed 59 people to escape to West Berlin before it was discovered by authorities in the GDR. *The Tunnel* (Producer: Reuven Frank) won the 1962–63 Emmy Award for Program of the Year. NBC aired the program despite objections by the US State Department, which feared the broadcast would heighten tense foreign relations following the Cuban Missile Crisis. See *The Tunnel*, reported by Piers Anderton, http://www.msnbc.msn.com/id/21134540/vp/33623268#33623268. Various dramatic escapes inspired several motion pictures, including Robert Siodmak's *Escape from East Berlin* (1962), also known as *Tunnel 28*, and Roland Suso Richter's two-part television film *Der Tunnel* (Sat. 1, 23 and 24 Jan. 2001). Part 1 reached an estimated television audience of 7.31 million viewers and part two 6.75 million. *Der Tunnel* won the German Television Prize for Best TV Film and was exported to seventy-one countries. See *11 Jahre Teamworx: Ein Rückblick*, http://www.teamworx.de/nc/presse/downloads/allgemeine-infos.html?cid=35&did=893&sechash=215a8e1b.

[63] "Sie sind die Gewähr für die Unantastbarkeit unserer Grenzen und unseres Territoriums." *V*, 104.

[64] The differences between the two German states become more pronounced as the years go by, and it becomes difficult for people on opposite sides of the border to understand each other. As Sophie and Konrad age, they are played by different actors, which illustrates that their distinct political environments and distinct patterns of socialization have made them different people. The young Konrad and Sophie are played by Anian Zollner and Meret Becker. The older Konrad and Sophie are played by August Zollner and Corinna Harfouch.

[65] "Erst muß ich mich einmauern lassen, weil ich in einem besseren Land lebe. Und dann muß ich mich von meinem Vater anzeigen lassen, weil ich aus dem besseren Land abhauen will." *V*, 34.

[66] "Ich habe lernen müssen, mich in dem Leben einzurichten, das mir offenstand." *V*, 92–93.

[67] "Hierzubleiben — das war ein Wagnis, ein Abenteuer. Wir wollten hier etwas ganz Neues aufbauen." *V*, 101.

[68] "Irgendwann mußt du dein Leben, auch wenn es dir nur passiert ist, zu deinem erklären." *V*, 92.

[69] Kristie A. Foell, "History as Melodrama: German Division and Unification in Two Recent Films," in *Textual Responses to German Unification: Processing Historical and Social Change in Literature and Film*, ed. Carol Anne Costabile-Heming, Rachel J. Halverson, and Kristie A. Foell (Berlin: Walter de Gruyter, 2001), 246.

[70] "Die Bilder des Interieurs haben fast immer etwas 'zuviel,' zuviel Bedeutung der Details, der ästhetischen Konstruktion, als daß sich hier ein Leben leicht führen ließe. Ein Realismus, der sich beinahe selbst zitiert, zeigt, daß das Gewicht der Dinge und Haltungen die Menschen erdrückt. . . . [Gestalten] belauern einander in einem Licht, das übergenau ist, auch diesen Touch des 'Zuviel' hat und in dem sich die realistische Grundhaltung mit einer Aura von unerklärlicher Bedeutung umgibt." Jutta Brückner, "Für Margarethe von Trotta," in *V*, 153–54.

[71] John Blair, "Madness and Bliss as Ideological Categories in Margarethe von Trotta's *The Promise*," *The Journal of the Association for the Interdisciplinary Study of the Arts* 7, no. 1–2 (2001–2): 95.

[72] "Da ist in mir so ein . . . Haß entstanden — ich wollte unbedingt etwas dafür tun, daß so was nie wieder passiert." *V*, 94.

[73] "Die Deutschen sehen sich immer als Opfer der Geschichte, nicht als Subjekte. Sie erleiden immer alles, lamentieren. Dabei ist das, was wir heute leben, die Konsequenz unserer eigenen Geschichte. Das ist das, was leicht vergessen wird." Margret Köhler, "Beschreibung von Leben: Bemerkungen zu Margarethe von Trottas *Das Versprechen*," *Film-Dienst* 1 (3 Jan. 1995): 16.

[74] "Sie glauben also, daß wir unbescholtene Bürger einfach so einsperren, aus einer Laune heraus? . . . Wenn Sie unserem humanistischen Staat so etwas zutrauen, dann hätten wir ja schon recht, Sie zu verhaften, auch wenn sonst gar nichts wäre." Florian Henckel von Donnersmarck, *Das Leben der Anderen: Filmbuch* (Frankfurt am Main: Suhrkamp, 2006), 14–15, and *Das Leben der Anderen* [2006], dir. Florian Henckel von Donnersmarck, DVD (Munich: Buena Vista International, 2006). Further references to the film script are given using the abbreviation *LA* and the page number.

[75] AP/dpa, "*Das Leben der Anderen*: Oscar für deutsches Stasi-Drama," *Süddeutsche Zeitung*, 26 Feb. 2007.

[76] Maxim Gorky, *Days with Lenin* (Honolulu: UP of the Pacific, 2004), 52.

[77] The director recounts the film's genesis in the companion film book. See *LA*, 169–70.

[78] By the end of 2007, *Das Leben der Anderen* had reached an audience of 2,336,339 in Germany. Statistics are available at http://www.ffa.de.

[79] "Irgendwo muß der Sozialismus doch beginnen." *LA*, 59.

[80] Mary Ann Doane, "Film und Masquerade: Theorizing the Female Spectator," in *Issues in Feminist Criticism*, ed. Patricia Erens (Bloomington: Indiana UP, 1990), 50–51.

[81] "Vielleicht war das damals der falsche Jerska: freundlich und menschenlieb durch das Kraftfutter des Erfolgs . . . den ich der Gnädigkeit der Bonzen zu verdanken hatte." *LA*, 46.

[82] "Du bist so ein jämmerlicher Idealist, daß du fast schon ein Bonze bist. Wer hat denn Jerska so kaputtgemacht? Genau solche Leute: Spitzel, Verräter und Anpasser! Irgendwann muß man Position beziehen, sonst ist man kein Mensch." *LA*, 55.

[83] "Ich muß immer daran denken, was Lenin von der Appassionata gesagt hat: 'Ich kann sie nicht hören, sonst bringe ich die Revolution nicht zu Ende.' Kann jemand, der diese Musik gehört hat, wirklich gehört hat, noch ein schlechter Mensch sein?" *LA*, 77.

[84] Bertolt Brecht, *Poems, 1913–1956,* ed. John Willett, Ralph Manheim, and Erich Fried (New York: Methuen, 1976), 35. "An jenem Tag im blauen Mond September / Still unter einem jungen Pflaumenbaum / Da hielt ich sie, die stille bleiche Liebe / In meinem Arm wie einen holden Traum. / Und über uns im schönen Sommerhimmel / War eine Wolke, die ich lange sah / Sie war sehr weiß und ungeheuer oben / Und als ich aufsah, war sie nimmer da." Bertolt Brecht, "Erinnerung an die Maria A.," *Gedichte*, vol. 3 of *Werke*, 5 vols., ed. Werner Mittenzwei, 3rd ed. (Berlin, GDR: Aufbau, 1981), 68.

[85] Marc Silberman, "A Postmodernized Brecht?" *Theatre Journal* 45, no. 1 (1993): 9.

[86] "Sorgt doch, daß ihr, die Welt verlassend / Nicht nur gut wart, sondern verlaßt / Eine gute Welt!" and "Es hilft nur Gewalt, wo Gewalt herrscht und / Es helfen nur Menschen, wo Menschen sind." Bertolt Brecht, *Die heilige Johanna der Schlachthöfe*, in *Stücke* 1, vol. 1 of *Werke*, 268 and 271.

[87] "Was soll man auch schreiben in dieser BRD: nichts mehr da, woran man glauben kann, nichts mehr, wogegen man rebellieren kann. Es war schön in unserer kleinen Republik. Das verstehen viele erst jetzt." *LA*, 149.

[88] "Stell Dich mitten in den Regen" based on Wolfgang Borchert's poem "Versuch es," was set to music by the East German band Bayon. See Wolfgang Borchert, *Das Gesamtwerk*, 2 vols. (Hamburg: Rowohlt, 1949), 2:290.

[89] Andreas Kurtz and Anne Lena Mösken, "Abgeordnete im Dunkeln: Der Kulturstaatsminister lud ins Kino — die Grünen konnten sogar zwischen zwei Filmen wählen," *Berliner Zeitung,* 15 Mar. 2006.

[90] "Sie stellen sich als Opfer dar und deklarieren uns als Täter." Ingo Rößling, "Stasi-Offiziere leugnen den Terror," *Berliner Morgenpost*, 16 Mar. 2006. See also Berthold Seewald, "Sogenannte Museumsführer," *Die Welt*, 30 Mar. 2006; and Edith Siepmann, "Stasi-Debatte: Alles verlogen, Flierl muss weg!" *Spiegel Online*, 5 Apr. 2006, http://www.spiegel.de/kultur/gesellschaft/0,1518,409920,00.html.

[91] According to Knabe, he refused to allow von Donnersmarck to film at the memorial site because "Die Opfervertreter haben das kategorisch abgelehnt, weil ihre Erfahrung mit der Staatssicherheit diametral anders war. . . . [Man kann] einen Ort, in dem Menschen gelitten haben und den sie vielleicht im Kino wiedererkennen, nicht als Kulisse für einen Film missbrauchen, der so lässig mit dieser Vergangenheit umgeht." Ddp/mar, "Historiker Knabe kritisiert Stasi-Film *Das Leben der Anderen*," *Ddp Basisdienst*, 6 Apr. 2006.

[92] He conceded that it was unlikely there had been a Stasi officer like Wiesler, "aber ein Spielfilm ist keine zeitgeschichtliche Dokumentation, er kann freier mit Geschichte umgehen." Joachim Gauck, "*Das Leben der Anderen*: 'Ja, so war es!'" *Stern*, 23 Mar. 2006.

[93] "Vielleicht erzählt der Film mehr von der Sehnsucht danach. . . . *Das Leben der Anderen* zeigt in bedrängender Weise, wie auch in einer eher unblutigen Diktatur wie der späten DDR Menschen eingeschränkt und des Vertrauens zu ihren Mitmenschen beraubt werden." Robin Mishra and Hans-Joachim Neubauer, "Das gute Leben im Schlechten: Marianne Birthler, die Bundesbeauftragte, warnt davor, das DDR-Unrecht zu verharmlosen," *Rheinischer Merkur*, 25 May, 2006.

[94] "Die Grundgeschichte in *Das Leben der Anderen* ist verrückt und wahr und schön — soll heißen: ganz schön traurig. Der politische Sound ist authentisch, der Plot hat mich bewegt." Wolf Biermann, "Die Gespenster treten aus dem Schatten: *Das Leben der Anderen*; Warum der Stasi-Film eines jungen Westdeutschen mich staunen läßt," *Die Welt*, 22 Mar. 2006.

[95] "Dieser starke Charakterdarsteller verleiht den ideologisch verkrusteten Schattenrissen in der Steinhöhle meines Gemütes endlich eine menschliche Fresse, hinter der dann sogar die Reste eines Gesichts sichtbar werden. So erfahren die schablonenhaften Bösewichte meines Lebens endlich eine lebensechte Konkretion, bei der ich erkennen kann, wie sogar in jedem verwüsteten Menschenantlitz alle Farben zwischen Schwarz und Weiß aufleuchten." Biermann, "Die Gespenster treten aus dem Schatten."

[96] "Manchmal hat das Kunstwerk mehr dokumentarische Beweiskraft als die Dokumente, deren Wahrheit angezweifelt wird — von den Tätern sowieso, aber schmerzhafter noch von den bald schon gelangweilten Zuschauern." Biermann, "Die Gespenster treten aus dem Schatten."

[97] "Unter diesem Gesichtspunkt sind Filme wie *Das Leben der Anderen*, *Nikolaikirche* oder auch *Der Tunnel*, bei allen Einwänden, die man im Detail oder von Seiten der Wissenschaft erheben könnte, wichtige Momente staatspolitischer Bildung. Sie bauen eine Brücke von dem Teil des Landes, der die kommunistische Diktatur hautnah erlebt hat, zu dem Teil, der sich darunter nichts Genaues vorstellen kann." Thorsten Stegemann, "Unterm Schlussstrich kommt der Neuanfang," *Telepolis*, 19 May 2006, http://www.heise.de/tp/r4/artikel/22/22698/1.html.

[98] "Das ist das eigentlich Kuriose an diesem Film: Die Überwachung, von der er erzählt, und mit dem er die wahre Natur des Überwachungsstaats bloßlegen will, ist rein persönlich durch Eifersucht motiviert und gar keine politische. . . . Henckel von Donnersmarck erfindet sich den guten Stasi-Menschen — und man möchte schon wissen, woher das Entlastungsbedürfnis eigentlich kommt, das sich in solchen Szenarien befriedigt?" Rüdiger Suchsland, "Mundgerecht konsumier-

bare Vergangenheit: Was ist eigentlich dran am Hype um Disneys DDR-Melo *Das Leben der Anderen?*" *Telepolis*, 28 Mar. 2006, http://www.heise.de/tp/r4/artikel/22/22334/1.html.

[99] "Er entmündigt seine Zuschauer und entlässt sie mit einer historischen Lüge." Günter Jeschonnek, "Die Sehnsucht nach dem unpolitischen Märchen: Ein kritischer Kommentar zum Stasi-Film *Das Leben der Anderen*," *Deutschland Archiv* 39, no. 3 (2006): 503.

[100] Jan Schulz-Ojala sees in these three films a "seltsamen Trend einer Gesellschaft, die sich in diesem Jahrhundert neu zu definieren scheint. Die Deutschen: Seit einigen Jahren gefällt sich das einstige Tätervolk, mal wissenschaftlich und mal medial intoniert, als Opfermasse." Jan Schulz-Ojala, "Die Täterversteher: *Das Leben der Anderen, Der Untergang, Der freie Wille*; Wie neue deutsche Filme Verbrecher zu Helden machen," *Der Tagesspiegel*, 22 Mar. 2006.

[101] Jan Schulz-Ojala argues that von Donnersmarck's film "verwandelt einen Täter in eine tragische Figur, ein Opfer der Verhältnisse, einen Gutmenschen — und vermenschlicht den dazugehörigen Apparat ansatzweise gleich mit." Schulz-Ojala, "Die Täterversteher."

[102] "*Das Leben der Anderen* spielt in der düster-muffig vergangenen DDR, hat aber in seinem aus jedem Bild ablesbaren Beharren auf formaler Perfektion und mainstream-orientierter Extremgefühlsabschöpfung etwas ungemein Amerikanisches." Jan Schulz-Ojala, "Wie hältst du's mit der Million? Lola-Gala 2006: Die Filmakademie hat sich etabliert — nun muss sie sich an die Gretchenfrage wagen," *Der Tagesspiegel*, 14 May 2006.

[103] Susanne Vieth-Entus, "FU-Studie: Berliner Schüler verklären die DDR," *Der Tagesspiegel,* 10 Nov. 2007.

[104] *Die Frau vom Checkpoint Charlie* [2007], dir. Miguel Alexandre (Munich: Universum Film, 2007). *Die Frau vom Checkpoint Charlie* was broadcast in its entirety on Arte on 28 September 2007 and then on Das Erste (ARD) in two parts on 30 September and 1 October 2007. It was seen in its entirety by 1.6 million viewers on Arte. Part 1 was seen by 8.35 million on ARD, a market share of 24 percent, and part 2 by 9.12 million, a market share of 28 percent. In total the film claimed to have reached nearly 10 and 11 million viewers for parts 1 and 2. See HA, "Ferres überzeugt auch die Zuschauer," *Hamburger Abendblatt*, 2 Oct. 2007, and "ARD-Zweiteiler schlägt Jauch: Checkpoint Charlie," *Hamburger Abendblatt*, 4 Oct. 2007. The theme-related programs were equally popular. Following part 1 of *Die Frau vom Checkpoint Charlie* on 30 September 2007, Anne Will's talk show *Unrecht vergeht nicht: Der lange Schatten der DDR*, broadcast on Das Erste, featured Jutta Gallus Fleck and her daughters Claudia and Beate as well as actress Veronika Ferres, federal commissioner for the Stasi files Marianne Birthler, human rights activist Friedrich Schorlemmer, and politicians Petra Pau (the Left Party) and Peter Hintze (CDU). *Unrecht vergeht nicht* was watched by 5.87 million viewers. Peter Adler's film *Die Frau vom Checkpoint Charlie: Die Dokumentation*, broadcast on ARD on 1 October 2007 at 9:45 p.m., reached 7.38 million viewers with a market share of 26.7 percent. Statistics are available from Bavaria Films, http://www.bavaria-film.de.

[105] *Die Frau vom Checkpoint Charlie*, http://www.daserste.de/checkpointcharlie/.

[106] For use of the terms "Edutainment" and "eine gefühlsduselige Mitleidstour und dumpfe Zährenschinderei," see Lutz Kinkel, "Spektakulärer Kampf um die Töchter: Jutta Gallus, im Film gespielt von Veronica Ferres, lässt sich vor dem KSZE-Konferenz-Gebäude in Helsinki an den Fahnenmast fesseln," *Stern*, 30 Sept. 2007, and Harald Keller, "Tränen lügen doch," *Frankfurter Rundschau*, 28 Sept. 2007.

[107] "[Sie] sind weniger ein Spiegel der DDR als ein Spiegel der gegenwärtigen Fernsehästhetik. Sie sind ideologische Produkte. . . . verlogen also, wegen ihrer Anbiederei ans Publikum. Weil sie ihm keine intellektuelle Herausforderung zumuten möchten, die über die Unterscheidung von Schwarz und Weiß, Gut und Böse hinausgeht. Keine Nuance, keinen Gegenton. Es ist legitim, wenn eine Seifenoper sagt: Ich bin eine Seifenoper. Wenn sie sagt: Ich bin ein Geschichtsbild, wird es fatal." Kerstin Decker, "DDR im TV: So oder so, Geschichte wird gemacht," *Der Tagesspiegel*, 29 Oct. 2007.

[108] ". . . der Eindruck entsteht, dies müsse wieder und wieder erinnert werden, um die DDR noch einmal und noch einmal töten, delegitimieren und zugleich vor der heutigen politischen Linken warnen zu können, die sich angeblich von diesen Praktiken nicht oder nicht genug abgesetzt hat." Friedrich Schorlemmer, "Erinnern und Vergessen," *Freitag: Die Ost-Westwochenzeitung*, 12 Oct. 2007.

[109] Whereas Leander Haußmann's comedy *NVA* (2005) treats regular army troops in the National People's Army, the Border Troops of the GDR are the topic of *Drei Stern Rot* (Three stars in red, dir. Olaf Kaiser, 2002, ZDF) and *Hundsköpfe* (Dog heads, dir. Karsten Laske, 2002). *An die Grenze* received mostly positive reviews and won the Adolf-Grimme Prize. See Regina Mönch, "Mit dem Rücken zum Osten: Der erste Fernsehfilm über Gewissenskonflikte von DDR-Soldaten müht sich redlich; *An die Grenze* (Arte/ZDF)," *Frankfurter Allgemeine Zeitung*, 7 Sept. 2007, and Torsten Wahl, "Liebe am Minenfeld: Das Drama *An die Grenze* ist der bisher eindrücklichste Film über die NVA," *Berliner Zeitung*, 7 Sept. 2007.

[110] "Hier entdeckst du, wer du wirklich bist." Film dialogue. *An die Grenze* [2007], dir. Urs Egger, DVD (Cologne: Colonia Media, 2007).

[111] "Hier die Lüge, da die fette Selbstgefälligkeit — und dazwischen keine Alternative." Film dialogue.

[112] "Wenn der Utopiegedanke nicht mitgedacht wird, bleibt die DDR in der Rückschau die platte Idee idiotischer Funktionäre." Torsten Wahl, "'Jetzt gibt's was auf die Fresse.' Autor Stefan Kolditz gilt in der TV-Branche als Experte für Zeitgeschichte," *Berliner Zeitung*, 29 Oct. 2007.

[113] "Wenn man keine Wahl hat, woher weiß man dann, ob man auf der richtigen Seite steht?" Film dialogue.

[114] Starting in October 2005, the "Deaths at the Berlin Wall Research Project," supported by the Center for Contemporary Historical Research in Potsdam, began to compile life histories on all the people who died at the Berlin Wall between 1961 and 1989. According to the study, 134 people died, of whom 8 were border guards. See "Totenbuch für die 134 Opfer der Berliner Mauer," *Berliner Morgenpost*, 18 May 2008. The total number of deaths along the entire inner-German border (excluding Berlin) is generally estimated to be between 248

and 371. See Maren Ullrich, *Geteilte Ansichten: Erinnnerungslandschaft deutsch-deutsche Grenze* (Berlin: Aufbau, 2006), 86.

[115] Till Harms's documentary film *11 und 12* was broadcast on 10 October 1999 on 3 Sat. For their memoirs, see Regina Kaiser and Uwe Karlstedt, *Zwölf heißt: Ich liebe Dich; Der Stasi-Offizier und die Dissidentin* (Munich: Knauer, 2004).

[116] "Er ist zufrieden, wenn sein Chef zufrieden ist." Film dialogue, *12 heißt: Ich liebe Dich*, dir. Connie Walther, broadcast 16 April 2008, ARD.

[117] "Du bist zwar nicht für das politische System in der DDR verantwortlich, aber für deine Entscheidung." Film dialogue.

[118] Vera Linß, "Interview: Hubertus Knabe über den Film *12 heisst: Ich liebe Dich*," *RevolutionundEinheit.de: Medienmonitor und Magazin*, 10 Apr. 2009, http://www.friedlicherevolution.de/index.php?id=49&tx_comarevolution_pi4%5Bcontribid%5D=104.

3: The Wild West and East of Eden: The Red Army Faction and German Terrorism

T HE 1960s HIPPIE GENERATION produced a counterculture that has not seen its match in the decades since. Rejecting the world their parents had made, they dropped out, dropped acid, and abandoned themselves in free love and rock-and-roll. Alongside the youth who experimented in alternative lifestyles, a politically active student movement was calling for social change. International in scope, from Berkeley to Berlin, from Paris to Rio de Janeiro, students took to the streets to protest the Vietnam War, capitalism, and US imperialism, to fight for free speech, civil rights, homosexuals' rights, and women's liberation, and to save the environment. A direct outgrowth of the student movement was the rise of Marxist urban guerilla movements around the world. Splitting off from the more reform-based student organizations, groups such as the Weathermen in the United States, the Red Brigade in Italy, and the Revolutionary Movement 8th October in Brazil attacked national governments in the hope of inspiring a popular uprising and saw themselves as part of an international struggle against imperialism. In the Federal Republic of Germany it was no different. The Red Army Faction (Rote Armee Fraktion, RAF), left-wing radicals who took on the authoritarian West German state with such force and flair beginning in the late sixties, captured the nation's imagination in a series of daring exploits.[1] The contrast between the two sides in the battle for the nation's soul and its future could not have been starker. On the one side was a generation of influential old men in suits and horn-rimmed glasses, who sought to uphold the prevailing power structures built upon the pillars of capitalism, a collective amnesia of the country's National Socialist past, and complicity with other Western states that spawned the Vietnam War and colonialism. On the other side stood a generation of good-looking, trendy young men and women who brutally attacked representative individuals and institutions to draw attention to exploitation, repressed guilt, and injustice. Led by charismatic bad boy Andreas Baader, passionate doctoral student Gudrun Ensslin, and articulate journalist Ulrike Meinhof, the RAF took up arms against the state because, as Ensslin reportedly claimed: "Violence is the only way to answer violence. This is the generation of Auschwitz. There's no arguing with them."[2] The RAF's dramatically staged bank robberies, jail breaks, kidnappings, bombings, and shoot-outs rivaled the plot lines of a Hollywood action adventure. Their eventual incarceration followed by years of isolation and suicide turned the life stories of RAF leaders into a tragedy of mythic proportions that continues to fascinate the nation and serves as a cautionary tale of postwar German idealism gone wrong.

Ever since the Red Army Faction officially disbanded itself in 1998, its ghost has come to haunt the silver screen in Germany. Volker Schlöndorff's *Die Stille nach dem Schuss* was followed in quick succession by Christian Petzold's *Die innere Sicherheit* (Inner security, English title: *The State I Am in*, 2001), Andres Veiel's *Black Box BRD* (2001), Gerd Conradt's *Starbuck — Holger Meins* (2002), and Christopher Roth's *Baader* (2002).[3] There seems to be no end in sight for exhausting this topic, since the trend continues with Uli Edel's *Der Baader Meinhof Komplex* (The Baader Meinhof Complex, 2008), Roland Suso Richter's made-for-television film *Mogadischu* (2008), Connie Walther's *Schattenwelt* (Shadow world, 2009), and Andres Veiel's *Wer wenn nicht wir* (If not us, who?, 2011).

Fascination with the RAF has not been limited to motion pictures or even television,[4] but has permeated the print media, fashion, music, and the visual arts in Germany today. The fashion industry elevated the Baader-Meinhof gang to pop icons and stylized political terrorism as radical chic standing for dissatisfaction with the status quo. In 2001 the now-defunct lifestyle magazine *Tussi Deluxe* published a fashion spread featuring models in retro seventies clothing staged in familiar poses from news photos of the Frankfurt arson trial and the Hanns-Martin Schleyer kidnapping. At the turn of the millennium, German youth displayed a penchant for the RAF look, including Ray Ban Wayfarers, black turtlenecks, crushed velvet pants, and T-shirts embossed with a hand grenade, the RAF's self-stylized logo of a red star covered by a machine gun, or simply the logo "Prada-Meinhof."[5] Writing for *Der Spiegel*, Reinhard Mohr commented: "RAF goes pop. The historicizing of armed revolutionary struggle winds up in postmodern aestheticism. Politics becomes quotation, passion coolness, class conflict cult: murderers become fashionable. The myth of the struggle of 'six against sixty million' lives on."[6]

As is so typical of the youth of each subsequent generation, the desire to antagonize those in power and rebel against the establishment finds expression in music as well as fashion.[7] In 2001 singer Jan Delay debuted an album with the provocative song "The Sons of Stammheim," in which he notes: "Now people fight only about dogs and gasoline, follow Jürgen and Zlatko and no longer Baader and Ensslin." Big Brother has been transformed from the Orwellian omnipotent state apparatus to the watchful eye of reality television, where Jürgen und Zlatko become media stars for living in a so-called container in front of cameras. According to Jan Delay, with the demise of the RAF, capitalism can now thrive again unimpeded: "Finally the terrorists are gone, and order and peace and quiet reign, and one can safely drive a Mercedes again without the thing always exploding."[8]

Along with a plethora of recent novels, dramas, and autobiographies,[9] the controversial "Imagining Terror: The RAF Exhibition" (2005) in Berlin illustrates the extent to which the history of German terrorism is anything but past. In 2002 the founder and director of the Kunst-Werke Institute for Contemporary Art (KW) in Berlin, Klaus Biesenbach, proposed an exhibition on the media echo of the RAF, exploring how the prevailing perception of the RAF was developed in and through media. The idea of focusing on the impact of visual culture on historical understanding was immediately rejected by government officials, who feared that public funds would be used to glorify terrorism and contribute to a further mythologizing of the key players who have become cult figures. Reacting to the public outcry, Biesenbach returned the government subsidies and organized a charity auction on eBay in December 2004 to elicit private funds. Twelve international artists not included in the show donated their works for the auction, which collected 250,000 euros, and together with an additional 100,000 euros in private donations, they were able to finance the exhibition without state aid. By the time the exhibit was shown at the KW from 28 January to 16 May 2005, Biesenbach had taken a position as curator at the Museum of Modern Art in New York City, and so he shared the curating work with Ellen Blumenstein and playwright Felix Ensslin, terrorist Gudrun Ensslin's son. Featuring the works of some forty artists, including such contemporary masters as Joseph Beuys, Gerhard Richter, Martin Kippenberger, and Sigmar Polke, as well as countless media reports from newspapers, magazines, and television newscasts, the exhibition was intended to question the various myths surrounding the RAF. In the accompanying catalogue, Biesenbach explains:

> *Imagining Terror: The RAF Exhibition* contrasts overloaded media images to art via a kind of over-information and reprivatization and tries to provide visitors to the exhibition once again with an eyewitness state of being that they will remember. It illuminates the first generation of the RAF as the object of an image, citation, and reference machine that in the postmodern, media-driven world seems to draw a great deal of unaddressed attention. It attempts to reconstitute the complexity of content lost in media selections and to let the viewers carry out their own analysis and critical observation of this traumatic chapter of German history, and allow them to experience it, or to come closer to doing so. The in-between space and the interface between history and art can be described as the *imagining* of the RAF. Because apparently one is not allowed to speak of a *myth* in a country that consists on the one hand of the FRG, which now no longer exists, and on the other hand of the GDR, which apparently never did exist.[10]

Biesenbach ties the problem of viewing the past through mediated images to the very problem of looking at national identity and highlights the fact that national identity, like national history, is itself a constructed discourse with glaring inconsistencies and contradictions. He argues that since the FRG reunited with the former GDR in 1990, the country has changed so radically that it does not seem accurate to call it the FRG, and the GDR has been dismissed to such an extent that its validity as a separate nation has been seriously challenged. His comments also emphasize that the history of the RAF cannot be seen as merely a West German phenomenon. Considering this highly politicized content, Biesenbach's opening remarks at the gala might seem rather odd. He proclaimed: "We are here to view an art exhibition. We are here for art, not politics." Despite the seemingly contradictory nature of this statement, it does attest to the exhibition's central objective: it draws our attention to the line between representation and meaning, between art and politics, between event and mediation. Ultimately it aligns itself with art and insists that art can approach these uncomfortable places in national history with a sensitivity and logic unavailable in the realms of politics or academics.

The thirtieth anniversary of the German Autumn, the forty-five days in September and October 1977 when the nation was held captive by a terrorist drama unfolding before its eyes, triggered a series of commemorative events and various forums for reflection on this unresolved chapter in Germany history.[11] Newspapers, magazines, talk shows, film retrospectives, and book launchings competed with podium discussions featuring politicians, victims and their families, historians, and former terrorists, all vying for the public's attention and the right to determine how the past should be interpreted. The visual collective memory of German terrorism in the seventies is especially powerful and evokes probably as much indignation, fascination, and confusion today as did the original images circulating at the time. Startling depictions of homegrown terrorism ranging from the photographs of wreckage littering the street from the 1972 bombing of the Augsburg police station to the autopsy photo of Holger Meins following his hunger strike conjure up visions of the Second World War and the Holocaust and illicit questions on how and why the country unleashed this type of violence on itself. At the same time, the photograph of Andreas Baader wearing sunglasses and playing with beautiful Gudrun Ensslin's long hair at their arson trial in Frankfurt, and the ubiquitous wanted posters featuring attractive, normal-looking young people who were nonetheless criminals, have produced a certain romanticized impulse to recreate at least the look of rebellion. The iconic imagery of the RAF has been recycled with such repetitiveness that it has become embedded "in the visual memory of a generation that had no direct experience of the RAF except through the presence of images in this traumatic but predominantly iconic and therefore contradictory signification of action and violence."[12] The RAF, therefore, seems almost readymade as a screen upon which social fantasies, both fears and desires, can be projected: the desire to lash out at a repressive social order that demands conformity and promotes consumption but is oblivious to human suffering across the globe, the paranoia of a computerized police state where every detail of one's life is monitored, or the fantasies of participating as a spectator in the display of liberated sexual energy and violent impulses. Seen in this light, it is not surprising that the RAF resonates beyond its historical setting to today and speaks to a contemporary post 9/11 audience with such clarity.

Films about the RAF made since the fall of the Wall range in popularity from obscure to blockbusters with millions of viewers, but rather than gauge the impact of German terrorism on the moviegoing public by the sheer number of tickets sold, I would suggest that the persistent return of this theme over the years attests to its importance in the cultural realm. Historian Walter Laqueur noted as early as 1977 that the enduring fascination with terrorism was somewhat baffling and not necessarily commensurate with the actual number of actors and victims or the concrete impact of terrorist actions. Laqueur remarked: "If terrorism nevertheless attracted so much attention it was, of course, mainly owing to its dramatic character. It fascinated millions of people, but it directly affected the life of only a handful." The dramatic, sensational nature of terrorism meant to draw the attention of the masses to their cause has, in Laqueur's words, led terrorists to become "super-entertainers of our time."[13]

One element in this discussion that has not yet received sufficient scholarly attention is how the demise of the GDR is related to the history of the RAF. Not only did several members of the RAF find refuge in the GDR, a point only made public after 1989, but the RAF functioned to some extent even in the East as an example of youthful rebellion against conformity and authoritarianism. Filmmakers have started to explore the commonality between the failure of Communism and the failure of the RAF, two idealistic attempts to envision an alternative to Western capitalism that were themselves fraught with instances of brutality and inhumanity. Despite all their acknowledged shortcomings, especially their use of violence and coercion to try to bring about a better world, Communism and terrorism continue to stand for admirable, however misguided, attempts at perfecting human society. In a world without viable alternatives to the current political and economic system, the history of the RAF often emerges as a tale about the kind of outlaw vitality found in the Wild West of the FRG and about the utopianism East of Eden in the GDR, a tale that seems to have enduring appeal.

This chapter examines four films in depth, because they present different aspects of the current cultural preoccupation with the RAF. Christopher Roth's *Baader* is about the recycling of media images of the

Baader-Meinhof gang and tries to break through the myths surrounding the first generation of terrorists who took up arms to rally for a social revolution. Volker Schlöndorff's *Die Stille nach dem Schuss* is about the revelation that the GDR harbored terrorists and looks at how these idealistic fugitives survived under real-existing socialism. Andreas Dresen's black comedy *Raus aus der Haut* investigates the impact of the RAF on GDR youth and Eastern counterculture at the height of the German Autumn in 1977. Finally, Uli Edel's star-studded, action-packed blockbuster *Der Baader Meinhof Komplex* aspires to be a modern-day epic and provide the definitive historical reenactment of the terrorist phenomenon but gets so mired down covering ten years of history in 150 minutes that it ends up being like Cliff Notes on speed. Despite their various approaches, all of these motion pictures are fuelled by a desire to deal with the trauma of homegrown terrorism in the sixties and seventies. While the cinematic attention given the RAF immediately following the suicides in Stammheim and again after its complete demise in 1998 has been extensive, questions still linger. The RAF's idealistic but deadly agenda, their self-destruction in prison, the state's massive build-up of security to combat some thirty terrorists, and the public hysteria and paranoia surrounding the violence and abuses on both sides have not yet been adequately examined and collectively mourned. Thomas Elsaesser rightly points out that the RAF's rise and fall had an enormous impact on the nation and resulted in a loss of idealism that has not yet been processed completely. Elsaesser has argued that there is an element in the buried past "that we have not even begun to reflect upon: the lost belief in a different, changeable, 'better' world, to which our ability to act can in fact contribute, either individually or collectively."[14] The widespread acknowledgment that utopian visions of a better world can no longer be upheld in the aftermath of the German Autumn is, I would argue, accompanied by a deeply rooted desire to reverse this trend and an equally strong echo that such a national project cannot succeed. Rather than concentrating exclusively on the loss of political idealism this chapter will investigate the tensions that arise between a collective yearning for the cohesiveness and spiritual contentment that comes with the conviction that one's life is devoted to the higher order of social justice and an equally strong cynicism that sees such a project as doomed by the weight of twentieth-century German history and its failed attempts to put politically revolutionary ideas into peaceful practice.

Baader

On the twenty-fifth anniversary of the suicide of Andreas Baader, Gudrun Ensslin, and Jan-Carl Raspe in Stammheim prison, Christopher Roth's film *Baader* premiered in German cinemas. Roth, the author of the pop

Fig. 3.1. Still from Christopher Roth's Baader *(2002).*
Photo courtesy of Stiftung Deutsche Kinemathek.

novel *200 D* (2003), wrote the screenplay with Moritz von Uslar, best known for his hyper-speed star interviews and lifestyle journalism.[15] With its pop-culture pedigree, the film promised to offer a new approach and did not disappoint in that respect. *Baader*, which had already been shown at the Berlin Film Festival in February 2002 to mixed reviews, deals with the first generation of the RAF, from 1967 to 1972. Although the film won the coveted Alfred Bauer Prize for new perspectives, it also sparked heated debates and made a disappointing showing at the box office with sales of only 27,570 tickets.[16] By far the most controversial aspect was the director's choice to fictionalize Baader's death. Andreas Baader does not commit suicide in October 1977 in Stammheim maximum-security prison but dies in 1972 in a slow-motion shoot-out with police a la *Butch Cassidy and the Sundance Kid* (dir. George Roy Hill, 1969). Newspaper critics offered an array of opinions. Gernot Gricksch was shocked that "a director had the chutzpah to bend the facts so audaciously to make them fit into his filmic concept."[17] Jan Schulz-Ojala was not surprised that the film caused such a stir, since many people do not believe Baader committed suicide and Roth's blatantly fictionalized ending resonates this discomfort.[18] Rüdiger Suchsland called the film "courageous," because in contrast to conventional feature films, which offer up a deceptively clear answer to historical complexities, *Baader* puts collective memory into doubt.[19] Writing for the *Süddeutsche Zeitung*, Rainer Gansera praised precisely these fictionalized scenes because they make clear "what the truth behind the reality is," and he argued further that "the explicitly fictional passages serve the search for truth to a remarkable extent."[20] At the core of the debate is Roth's decision to play with the gray zone between collective memory and media-produced imagery. Motivated largely by the notion that "the RAF cannot be separated from its style," Roth focuses precisely on the superficial nature of Baader's personality, his constant need to stage himself as a James Dean-type bad boy, who is equally adept at hotwiring luxury cars and seducing beautiful young women, while galvanizing a generation to hit the capitalist state machinery "where it hurts."[21]

In a largely fragmented theory of cinema, Roth has argued that his goal was to concentrate on the surface imagery and ambiguities inherent in Baader's poses, in order to create an empty space where viewers could give their imagination free reign. Rather than providing a conclusive depiction of historical fact, Roth maintains that his obvious fictionalization of important events forces audiences to come to grips with competing versions of the past. Roth's jarring editing with numerous shifts in time, his extensive use of familiar media images, and his obviously ahistorical soundtrack all contributed to confusion among audiences and reviewers alike. What critics have failed to address is that Roth's ideas display a remarkable resemblance to the theoretical underpinnings of the quintessential contemporary filmic response to the RAF, *Deutschland im Herbst* (Germany in autumn, 1978). Roth has called for a form of active spectatorship, echoing but never acknowledging Alexander Kluge's theory of montage that emphasizes cuts and is constructed from an array of diverse materials, employs contrary information (*Gegeninformation*) to invoke imagination (*Phantasie*), and works on the spectator's capacity to make connections between the fragments. Moreover, like the collaborative that shunned governmental and big studio sponsorship in 1977, Roth has also promoted *Baader* as an "anti-subsidy" film made without sponsorship to avoid consumerist or undue political influence. Considering Roth's reticence to claim Kluge's influence, one must contemplate whether his approach is better characterized by a postmodern aesthetic that favors self-referentiality, intertextual citations, and irony, or further still whether Roth merely mimics Kluge in much the same way as his cinematic figures mimic movie idols and mythic heroes in a world so saturated with ideas and imagery that one must simply combine them in different ways in order to achieve something new. I will explore here this tacit connection between Roth, New German Cinema, and postmodernism and analyze the extent to which Roth's film is held captive by the very media-driven myth it serves to critique.

Working with the notion that Andreas Baader carefully fashioned his own media image, Roth has argued that it was the superficiality of this historical figure that attracted him to the subject matter:

> I tried to start from the surface, from the impact and fascination. In order to then dig deeper, to read the signs and try to craft something new. By going deeper, I don't mean going to the core in order to arrive at a fairly conclusive analysis; rather I am after the integration of poetic and lyrical moments. Not dissecting, but rather creating an openness, in which every viewer can project his own ideas.[22]

Mass media shape our understanding of the past to such an extent that it is difficult to imagine the RAF without conjuring up in our minds images that were once broadcast on television or published in newspapers and are now endlessly reproduced and recycled: the Frankfurt arson trial defendants smoking cigars and wearing sunglasses, Hanns-Martin Schleyer in front of the RAF logo, the wanted poster of Ulrike Meinhof, or the nearly naked Holger Meins screaming in protest as he is arrested. With this film, Roth wants to forge an openness for viewers to imagine the RAF in a manner different from prevailing accounts in history books or documentaries. He maintains that he never intended to produce a historically accurate record of the time or a bio-pic in the strictest sense, because in his words: "Fiction can pose more questions and irritate more than pure documentation. A feature film can rattle more at the deadlocked images of reality, it can demythologize."[23]

Roth was born in 1964 and 13 years of age when Baader committed suicide. His childhood impression of Germany as a strange, dreary, and cold land stood in stark contrast to the colorful mediated reality: "My image of Germany back then was awfully bleak: it was gray and there were these old men with big rimmed glasses who represented the state, and it always snowed. It was a strange country." He continues, "At the opposite pole were American movies and music, and then there was Andreas Baader, who for me — because I didn't understand what he had done — was simply the man with the cigarette and Ray Ban Wayfarer sunglasses, and was like a movie star."[24] Roth focuses on this media image and on the contradictions in Baader's personality — his overwhelming charm and allure on the one side and his machismo and despotic temperament on the other — and attempts to illustrate these contrasts formally by constructing a nonlinear narrative and continuously interrupting the main plot with super-8 footage, news clips, and black-and-white sequences. He also uses an asynchronic soundtrack, with Baader listening to the 1980s band Stone Roses to accentuate the disjuncture between sound and image, and thereby let viewers know that they are watching a fictional film.[25] Lastly, Roth adopts the style of films Baader admired, ranging from Sam Peckinpah Westerns to Jean Paul Melville gangster flicks and Jean-Luc Godard's *Pierrot le fou* (1965).[26] These self-reflective moments and what Roth has called "conspicuously cheeky lies"[27] are essential, because "the ending must leave everything open and call the entire narrated history into question" ensuring that "a conceptual discomfort lingers."[28]

Many of Christopher Roth's statements echo Alexander Kluge's theory of an independent avant-garde cinema providing *Gegenbilder* for the film created in the spectator's head. Kluge argues: "One can see it so: for tens of thousands of years there has been a film in human minds — stream of consciousness, day dream, experience, sensuality, consciousness. The technical invention of cinema has merely added reproducible *Gegenbilder* to this."[29] Kluge's cinematic work challenges the notion that reality is unequivocal and immutable. By constantly drawing attention to the ways in which cinematic reality is constructed, he emphasizes that our perception of reality in general is socially constructed. To this end Kluge uses stylistic effects that work at cross-purposes: editing, music, quotations versus narrative, shifts in mode, interruptions in chronology, all of which contribute to a self-reflectivity that contests narrative authority — and, by analogy, social and political authority — by undermining its very logic. The distinct relationship between images created in the editing process is essential to his artistic concept: "Each [image] has its own value, its own life. The entire information resides in the cut. I did not make the images. The world made the images, or prehistory, or the dear Lord, or the performers who have a right to their own faces. But I freely acknowledge that I've edited them together. One doesn't see the cut, but my signature resides in it."[30] Kluge has advocated a form of filmmaking that rejects the conventional dichotomy between history and fiction, because:

> When used appropriately, the musical-poetic narrative and documentary forms of film complement each other. Here, too, it is the hybrid form that mediates between montage and unabridged reproduction, between imagination and a sense of reality. Sociology and fairy tale are not, as one assumes, opposites. Rather they are poles of one and the same thing and only look different depending on whether one starts from the premise that human beings are capable of being satisfied with facts, or that they are capable of forming desires.[31]

By routinely breaking the flow of images and fashioning an empty space for viewers to dream up a film in their head, it becomes possible, Kluge asserts, "also to portray reality as the historical fiction it is."[32]

Kluge acknowledges his fascination with heterogeneity but rejects the label postmodern for his own work, because he views postmodernism as a theoretical approach that dominates materials and puts them to use to realize intentions (for example, ornamentation). Kluge defines himself as an avant-gardist who respects the autonomy of materials. Despite his rejection of postmodernism, Kluge recognizes the quandary for independent filmmakers in a media-saturated environment: "There is no avant-garde when the avant-garde has done everything. If a culture is highly developed, the avant-garde must bring its materials together in a dialogue, into a new context."[33] I would suggest that the difference between Kluge's avant-gardism and Roth's postmodernism goes well beyond the problem of originality in the current glut of information and lies in the tone of their work. Whereas Kluge's intellectually demanding films expect viewers to recognize the biases inherent in *any* narration and come to their own understanding, Roth's emphasis on the surface and citation is all about pleasure in recognition and destruction of established and petrified meanings, projects that lie at the heart of postmodernism.

Some critics have rejected Roth's approach and argue that his film lacks authenticity, but such criticism needs reevaluation. Andreas Baader's real life provided sufficient material to make him a celebrity in his own time and to ensure his legendary status today. Baader's allure owes as much to his outlaw reputation of stealing cars and seducing women as to setting department stores on fire and waging war against the establishment as an urban guerilla. Moreover, Baader's narcissism and his relentless efforts to craft his life in mythic terms make him a nearly ideal movie hero. Former '68 radical Gerd Koenen has noted that from the moment they entered the public's eye at their trial in Frankfurt, the RAF members were highly conscious of their media image:

> If you observe the images of the defendants seated, how they are smoking Castro cigars in the storm of flashbulbs, waving the little red book, kissing, or peering over the stools, it feels as if you are in a film. The call for *action* had already lent the whole thing the flavor of a road movie, as I've already pointed out. Obviously they felt themselves to be actors and stars in a self-staged film drama, for which the major media delivered the set and technical equipment and the public, both in and outside the courtroom, became extras, before whom they acted.[34]

Indeed, many in the RAF's first generation were closely aligned with the media and understood its power. The German Film and Television Academy Berlin (dffb) opened its doors in 1966, and the first class of students included future terrorist Holger Meins, who directed the film, "Die Herstellung eines Molotow-Cocktails" (Production of a Molotov cocktail, 1967). In the sixties Gudrun Ensslin starred in the underground film *Das Abonnement* (Subscription, dir. Ali Limonadi, 1967) and Andreas Baader stood for the camera in a series of provocative poses and reportedly worked briefly for the Springer Verlag's *B.Z.* Ulrike Meinhof was a renowned journalist who appeared on radio and TV as a cultural commentator, produced numerous radio programs, and wrote the script for the television film *Bambule* (Bedlam, dir. Eberhard Itzenplitz, 1970).[35] While the RAF lashed out against the mass media, and especially against the Springer press, its leadership was keenly aware of the importance of visual representation and mass communication and took great care in styl-izing its image, right down to creating its own readily recognizable logo. In the 1960s in general, theatrical gestures and the tendency toward sim-ple iconography characterized the new political style of the student move-ment. From spontaneous happenings and sit-ins to Che Guevara posters and the peace sign, pop and politics fused to define a counterculture that was as much about protesting the Vietnam War and US imperialism as about sex, drugs, and rock-and-roll.[36] And in this sense Christopher Roth's film is highly realistic, because it focuses on the synthesis between pop and politics and the extent to which the medium is the message.

Although numerous eye-witnesses and historians have depicted Andreas Baader as a charismatic but brutal man, drawn to action rather than contemplation, and utterly absorbed in fashioning his aura, many film critics reject this portrayal as inauthentic and reproach Roth's film for presenting Baader as a "poser without a program," a petty criminal who becomes a revolutionary but never quite seems to get the ideology.[37] In Roth's film Baader starts off in 1967 as a car thief who does not know who Hubert Humphrey is, let alone why the *Kommune Eins* would want to throw pudding at him. Rather than showing any interest in the intel-lectual debates, he takes joyful glee in chanting "Beat the pigs to a pulp" (Haut die Bullen platt wie Stullen) and comes across as an infantile rebel without a cause. Even as he goes underground as a terrorist, Baader cares more about cars than politics. He dictates to a young rookie, adopting the current Marxist jargon in a nearly meaningless manner: "Look at the SPD. The strategic function of the Social Democrats is to ensure the initiative of capital in crisis. Do you get it?" By contrast, Baader knows exactly what kind of car he wants and describes it passionately as he strokes the steering wheel like a lover, and he dreams of stealing a luxury BMW 2500 with inlaid wood and leather seats, and driving as fast as the wind will take him. He routinely blasts the others for their intellectual approach: "There'll be no more talking, we gotta hit 'em where it hurts!" Baader is a bully who insists upon his status as absolute leader, banishing a member for chal-lenging his authority and then rationalizing: "He isn't questioning, he's whimpering, and Marx never whimpered! The whimperer can go and for all I care Marx can get lost, too!"[38]

Moments of spectacle, desire, and domination mark the main char-acters' relationship to each other and to their cause. While still in jail, Baader watches the news of the T-shirt demonstration following Benno Ohnesorg's death and sees Gudrun Ensslin for the first time up on the silver screen. She looks like a glamorous movie star, her face captured in a soft focus black-and-white close-up as she peers directly into the camera, looking downward at the viewer. With a reaction shot of Baader looking up to her in admiration, we see that he has fallen in love with her celeb-rity image even before they meet. In their first encounter in real life this exchange of glances is replicated. A seated Baader stares up at the standing Ensslin and the two trade demure looks and smiles, in effect doubling the earlier scene. What may have been conceived as a device to highlight the constructed nature of their relationship in a staged spectacle of desire comes across as the fulfillment of destiny. With the emphasis on media imagery and desire, it is not surprising that Baader first courts Ensslin in a cinema, where they watch Klaus Lemke's slick gangster film *48 Stunden bis Acapulco* (48 hours to Acapulco, 1967). When they leave the cinema, Baader and Ensslin act out the film scenario of the hip-but-world-weary gangster and his devoted moll they have just seen. With the same mixture of ennui and rebellious nature as the characters in Lemke's movie, Baader steals a woman's purse and gives Ensslin the proceeds as he mimics revolutionary zeal: "Sure, because we're gonna clobber the world until it understands that the will to be free is stronger than the will to oppress," to which Ensslin can only reply: "That's groovy, you're groovy."[39] This scene illustrates the playful intertextuality of postmodernism that allows well-versed movie buffs to enjoy the various levels of cinematic references. *48 Stunden bis Acapulco* is itself a citation of Hollywood gangster films, so that when Baader performs the movie role, he cites a citation of a citation. And although it is 1967, Baader walks past a poster for *Liebe ist kälter als der Tod* (Love is colder than death), Rainer Werner Fassbinder's homage to the gangster film made two years later, in 1969. This nonsynchronicity, while theoretically aimed at drawing attention to Baader's self-mythologizing efforts, is so exaggerated that it contributes more to tongue-in-cheek recognition than to character development.[40]

Roth is more successful at using self-reflective techniques to address political conflicts in the film's opening. A black-and-white vignette shows the RAF members in an isolated field, waving flags, pontificating, and filming themselves, while bewildered farmers watch the spectacle. The sequence stylizes Baader and Ensslin as romantic rebels, but it also reveals the latent violence in mainstream German society. From the first shot of a young man waving a starred flag in the wind while reading Mao's little red book to the last shot of a farmer hitting a teen on the head with a pail to the approving nod of a fellow farmer, the lines are drawn between the revolutionaries and the establishment. The historical violence associated with the RAF is not visualized; rather it is the establishment that lashes out against the youth. Whereas the rebels are armed only with a flag, book, and camera, the farmers have rifles, pitchforks, and hunting dogs, implying that there is at least some merit to the RAF's claim that the Federal Republic structurally harbors repressed violence.

The group is captured in a tight shot that illustrates their fixation on image-making, art, and social change. Gudrun Ensslin, center stage, quotes Bertolt Brecht in a monotone and admonishes the listener: "If things stay as they are, you are lost. Your friend is change, your comrade in arms is antagonism. You must make something out of nothing but you should not become the mighty. Give up what you have and take what is denied to you."[41] Baader sits to her left, head lowered, smoking his cigarette, more engrossed in posing than in the message. Behind them is a Holger Meins figure aiming a camera to their left offscreen, highlighting the value they place on image-making. Placed at the film's immediate opening, this mise en abyme draws attention to the group's interest in stylizing their own self-image, but it nonetheless begs the question of who is actually filming this black-and-white art film. There is little time to contemplate this paradox, because the abstract opening with only the sound of Ensslin's voice, the wind, and tractors immediately segues into the title sequence accompanied by MC5's thunderous song "Kick out the jams!" In a montage of well-known personalities and events from the late sixties, the viewer is bombarded with news footage of Joan Baez, the Rolling Stones, Vietnam, Mao Tse Tung, Willy Brandt, the Shah of Iran, Rudi Dutschke, street demonstrations, fashion shows, logos for Ufa studios, *Tagesschau* newscast, the *Bild* newspaper, and RAF wanted posters. The actors playing the RAF are embedded in pseudo-documentary footage, and so they weave through fiction and reality, moving around in time and space at such a dazzling speed to the pulsating rhythms of rock-and-roll that the original thought-provoking opening is lost to history clips for the MTV generation. Any theoretical empty space for contemplation is swallowed up in visual and audio overload.

So what space has Roth devoted to political idealism? In contrast to the poser Baader, the dreamer Ensslin, and the oddly silent Meinhof, it is ironically the federal police commissioner Kurt Krone (modeled after the real-life Horst Herold) who becomes the voice of the political left. Although he is charged with developing a computer system to track and capture the terrorists, Krone acknowledges that much of the youth's critique is legitimate:

> Dear comrades, I would like to talk a bit about the APO, the Non-Parliamentary Student Opposition. The APO is concerned not just about their university but about social change. The APO is conspicuous because of its constant provocation. How should we react to this provocation, what should we do? [From the audience: "Shoot them dead!"] First of all we must recognize that their criticism is legitimate. There are authoritarian structures in our country. People are indeed manipulated by the *Bild* newspaper. Therefore we have to say to these young people: Yes, we need your criticism so that society does not come to a standstill. But we also have to say: Violence? No![42]

The enlightened, fatherly socialist recognizes that rebellious energy will turn into terrorism if it is not addressed seriously. Krone warns:

"Whoever feels this misery existentially will not hesitate to throw bombs into the consciousness that obviously cannot be detonated in any other way."[43] Using time-honored traditions of the Western, Roth presents Krone as the principled sheriff who understands and sympathizes with the outlaw, even though he knows that at high noon there will have to be a showdown. But Krone also functions as the pendant to Baader's fascination with the spectacle of desire, in that the police commissioner represents the spectacle of control. Krone builds up a super computer for the state to watch over every detail of its citizens' existence and contributes to a 1984 world of big brother, offering up equal portions of domination and entertainment. The ambivalent nature of the modern surveillance state is poignantly revealed in the staging of the police commissioner at work. On the one side, Krone is an efficient public servant who collects data on ordinary citizens and assembles a surveillance apparatus for the state to rein in and control its subjects. Pictured with a low-angle camera towering over the computer and examining the records in the hope of capturing the terrorists, he is the image of a dutiful enforcer of the law. On the other side, he is also depicted as a puppeteer who manipulates people and has a vast arsenal of high-tech weapons at his disposal. Perched in his second-story office overlooking a courtyard with a squadron of six riot police in full gear, Krone demonstrates to the assembled ministers the new radio technology that allows him to deploy the police at will. The old men take childish glee in maneuvering the radio-wired riot police as if they were automated toy soldiers, suggesting that conspiracy theories of mind control may have some basis in reality.

In terms of authenticity, Roth's film largely colors within the lines of known history about the RAF. The film follows Baader's arrest for grand theft auto, Benno Ohnesorg's death at the hands of the Berlin police, the Frankfurt department-store arson and the subsequent trial, the flight to Paris, military training in a PLO camp in Jordan, and the spate of bank robberies and bombings. Andreas Baader, Gudrun Ensslin, and Ulrike Meinhof are the only historical figures identified by name. Federal police commissioner Horst Herold becomes "Kurt Krone," terrorist Petra Schelm becomes "Karin Rubner," and defense lawyer Horst Mahler becomes "Kurt Wagner." Thorward Proll, Astrid Proll, and Holger Meins are identifiable but remain largely unnamed in the dialogue and have different names in the credits. While the outer contours of history are here, there is no psychological depth to the characters: audiences never learn about their motivations or inner conflicts, or even much about their goals. Voice-over commentaries that might offer insight are largely quotations from well-known pamphlets. We watch, for instance, Ulrike Meinhof transform from a respected journalist to a terrorist by simply donning a gray-streaked wig, dark sunglasses, and a chic black suit and walking directly into the camera to the pulsating music. In an urban housing development devoid of people she strides past her own wanted poster and dictates in a voice-over her now famous axiom: "The cops are pigs. The guy in the uniform is a pig not a human being."[44] With a fashionably dressed spokesperson, trendy setting, catchy slogan, pop music, high-key lighting, and rapid editing, terrorism has the look of a slick TV ad or an MTV music clip — not surprising when we remember that Roth financed *Baader* by making television commercials.

Baader's death is the only event beyond the realm of the possible and in Roth's terms a cheeky lie, but there are aspects that make it familiar and thus *unheimlich*. The slow-motion action shoot-out takes place in a historically accurate setting (the Frankfurt garage where Baader was arrested), so that the incongruity between fact and fiction is puzzling and disturbing. Roth has stated that he consciously juxtaposed the historical setting and the artificial Hollywood ending because the two opposing things produce a tension and reciprocally charge each other. The resemblance between Roth's film style, the seventies television detective series *Derrick*, and Jean Paul Melville films is intentional because "Jean Paul Melville is really another Hollywood quotation. It is almost like a quote of a quote of a quote."[45] The perceptive viewer can recognize the citation of a citation of a citation. While Roth speaks of an independent form of filmmaking, his primary concern is to generate insider recognition. How good is the counterfeit image and are there enough telltale signs of the counterfeiter's signature to see the copy as a copy? He relies so heavily on a clip aesthetic that the viewer never gets enough time or distance to ponder what lies beyond Baader's image. Roth's film serves up entrenched images in a new way and deconstructs the myth that the first generation of RAF was composed of highly sensitive intellectuals who took up weapons out of sheer desperation.[46] However, in his zeal to teach us that Baader was fascinated by movie idols and transformed his desires for sexual release, speed, and violence into political terrorism, Roth gets caught up in the frantic pace of surface imagery and nostalgia for the rebellious energy that can never be recovered. The audience is left pondering whether the RAF could have been that shallow and if one should be satisfied with the images that linger: the slow-motion shots of Baader stealing a motorcycle, dropping LSD with friends in the red glow of sunset over the Paris rooftops, and drawing two pistols only to be killed in a blaze of glory — slick images that glamorize trendy terrorism.

Roth has repeatedly stated that he uses self-reflectivity and distanciation techniques to avoid just such a glamorization of terrorism. Viewers should recognize the constructed nature of images and interrogate them rather than consume them mindlessly. This aesthetic agenda, strongly associated with Kluge and Brecht, whom Roth cites twice in the film, has long stood in opposition to German popular cinema as represented by Lemke, for example, whose primary aim is to entertain. Roth tries to position himself between these two apparently disparate traditions of spectatorship: Brechtian distanciation geared toward critical analysis and Hollywood-type seduction intent on sheer entertainment. He states: "First of all the film should entertain, that's what film is all about. It should seduce, probably also irritate, because [Baader] is an outrageously ambivalent figure. And then, naturally, it should once again interrogate this image that one has of the RAF and the time."[47] In the attempt to merge these two forms of cinema, Roth aspires to draw attention to artifice and celebrate it at the same time, an agenda that echoes Fassbinder's to some extent. Based on Roth's overriding concern with intertextuality, a closer look at how his ideas relate to those espoused by Lemke and Fassbinder should serve as the basis for understanding his endeavor to bridge art-house and mainstream cinema.

Roth's citation of Klaus Lemke's *48 Stunden bis Acapulco* points to the tradition of German popular cinema that is based on strong identification with characters, seamless story lines, continuity editing, and an emphasis on genre conventions. Roth actually worked as an editor under Lemke and considered the citation a homage to this unsung hero of German popular cinema, who was highly critical of what he saw as the overly intellectual and elitist avant-garde filmmaking of the late sixties and early seventies. Thematically Roth's film *Baader* shares much with Lemke's television film *Brandstifter* (The arsonists, ARD, 1969) starring Margarethe von Trotta as the bored student activist Anka, who decides to burn down a department store. Both directors treat the reciprocal relationship between film and rebellion, fashion and adventure, as the prevailing spirit of the '68 generation. Roth's protagonist Baader goes to the cinema and then acts out the scenario in real life. He lives in Regis Debris's Paris apartment, tries on the imprisoned revolutionary's clothing, carefully studies iconic images of Fidel Castro and Che Guevara, and reads Debris's book *Revolution in the Revolution* (1967) as if to acquire the accoutrements of rebellious identity and copy this persona.[48] Afterward Baader directs a super-8 movie on a Paris rooftop that allows him to imitate his idol and star in his own production. Lemke's protagonist, the fashion and art gallery aficionado Anka, goes to the cinema to watch a Western but is captivated by a man who claims to have a better film, and while watching his agitprop super-8 movie she starts to interact with the film and demand revolutionary action. Whereas Roth uses a montage of news footage of late-sixties pop icons and political events in the title sequence accompanied by MC5's "Kick out the Jams," Lemke embeds such contemporary news footage in the agitprop film to the sound of the Rolling Stones' "Street Fighting Man."[49] Together with Lemke, Roth regards the entertainment value of cinema as one of its highest priorities, since filmmaking is primarily about storytelling. Both appreciate genre cinema, especially gangster films and Westerns, but unlike Lemke, who rejected the New German Cinema, Roth is selective in his appreciation.

Openly acknowledging a profound admiration of Fassbinder, Roth argues that the historical figure of Baader and the enfant terrible of New German Cinema Fassbinder displayed similar personality traits, most notably charisma combined with despotism, that led both men to become cult-like leaders with a band of devoted followers.[50] Along with the brief allusion to *Liebe ist kälter als der Tod*, Roth concedes that he shares with Fassbinder a fascination with Hollywood and genre cinema, especially gangster films. Like Fassbinder, Roth is not interested in scrutinizing the biographies of terrorists to uncover their personal motivations as Margarethe von Trotta did in *Die bleierne Zeit* (1981), based loosely on the life of Gudrun Ensslin and her sister. Von Trotta's film is the closest any German film has come to exploring the social origins and personal, psychological motivations that led to terrorism. Roth's interest in Fassbinder is geared more to his pastiche of American and French gangster films. Roth's figure of Baader could easily be the protagonist of one of Fassbinder's early gangster films: the aforementioned *Liebe ist kälter als der Tod*, *Götter der Pest* (Gods of the plague, 1969), or *Der amerikanische Freund* (The American friend, 1970). As a modern outlaw, whom women idolize despite the fact that he denigrates the female sex as "cunts," Baader demands attention and recognition by conflating sexual desire and violence in the spectacle, a recurring theme in Fassbinder's oeuvre. And yet there are clear differences in the two directors' approaches. Fassbinder borrows from Hollywood gangster films but subverts the traditions in a highly stylized manner so as to deny his audience automatic fulfillment of expectations. As Gerd Gemünden has aptly argued: "The Hollywood formula is invoked in a fashion that vacillates between nostalgia and parody — a homage to past times and the awareness of the pastness of those times that cannot be recuperated."[51] Gemünden notes that Fassbinder's citations of Hollywood popular formulas always contain a disconnect — the predominance of long takes in action sequences, a slow and monotonous editing pace, characters adopting star poses but lacking the requisite charisma — that celebrate familiar gestures while undercutting them by placing them in an unfamiliar stylistic framework. This allowed Fassbinder to differentiate between imitating genre cinema and commenting on it in a postmodern manner, a distinction that is clear from his statement: "I was not trying to imitate an American gangster film but to make a film about people who have seen a lot of American gangster films."[52] Distinguishing himself from directors like Kluge, who use distanciation techniques to force the viewer to think, Fassbinder contends: "Kluge's alienation is intellectual like Brecht's, while mine is stylistic."[53] Fassbinder thus straddled the line between auteurist and popular cinema. Roth attempts much the same thing by repeatedly highlighting the filmic edifice. He uses slow motion in scenes that merge romantic notions of the desperado and terrorist action (for example, when Baader flees a bank

robbery or when he is riddled with bullets at the end), but the sheer pace
of his film with its flash editing to upbeat rock-and-roll music, could not
be further from Fassbinder's approach in a film such as *Liebe ist kälter
als der Tod*. For example, Fassbinder has Johanna (Hanna Schygulla) and
Bruno (Uli Lommel) walk around a huge supermarket with a shopping
cart, stealing items in a surreal four-minute sequence that consists of one
single meandering tracking shot accompanied by no diegetic sounds and
only a dissonant version of Richard Strauss's *Der Rosenkavalier*. Despite
their divergent stylistic choices in editing, camerawork, and soundtrack,
Roth sees a parallel in thematics and character constellations. Describing
how Baader is a prototypical movie gangster, Roth comments: "You have
this one fellow who simultaneously causes turmoil and on the other hand
then descends into loneliness, etc. Naturally it is all a big Fassbinder film.
I think he would have loved the film."[54]

Roth's appreciation of Fassbinder is also visible in the scene where
federal police commissioner Krone meets Baader. The clandestine meeting is a purely fictional encounter that allows the figures to admire each
other and philosophize about the relationship between terrorism and
the state's monopoly on power, but it also provides the director with an
opportunity to reflect upon milestones in cinematic history. The scenario
of Krone single-handedly laying a trap for public enemy number one on
an isolated highway merely to talk with him is extremely unlikely, and it
is staged using all the conventions of *Derrick* and Melville films. Sitting
together in the front seat of Baader's car both men concede that their
fates are inextricably linked. Baader remarks: "You need us in order to
rearm," to which Krone replies "and you need me in order to sharpen
the existing contradictions, to widen the gap between the state and the
masses."[55] The argument that the state needs the terrorists to justify
beefing up the police force and intelligence services, while the terrorists
need the image of a demonic police force to justify violence and engender
bourgeois sympathy, sounds like a recycled rendition of Fassbinder's *Die
dritte Generation* (The third generation, 1978). In Fassbinder's farce, the
bored young people become terrorists without an ideological platform
and are unknowingly manipulated by the head of a US computer company in order to force a confrontation with the state, so that the state
will turn to the computer company to build a surveillance system capable
of controlling the terrorists. The police commissioner foreshadows the
film's ironic twist right from the start when he reveals: "I recently had a
dream that capital invented terrorism in order to force the state to protect
it better."[56] Fassbinder uses a carnivalesque setting to comment on the
ludicrousness of the third generation's rebellion and the loss of anything
resembling social criticism or utopianism.[57] By contrast, Roth's sympathetic fatherly detective, who seems as familiar as the characters from
childhood television shows, comforts with his knowledgeable, level-headed

attitude and assures that a stable world exists where people like Krone are in charge and so justice will be served in the end (just like on television).

There are many poignant moments in Christopher Roth's *Baader* where viewers are made aware of cinematic constructs. Most notable is the scene where Ulrike Meinhof's friend refuses to aid the RAF and she confronts him with his own words: "Deeds have to follow words. You wrote that, Henry!" to which he replies: "That is fiction! My protagonist says that and he ends tragically!"[58] Baader's fictionalized death in slow motion was intended as a commentary on the death of his outlaw legend, since once he ended up in Stammheim, his life took on new meaning, and a new myth evolved around him as the victim of the system. However, Roth has Baader quote from Bertolt Brecht's play, *Die Maßnahme* (The measures taken, 1930) right before he dies, and this intertextual device is jarring. In a voice-over Baader cites Brecht: "It is terrible to kill. Not only others, but to kill ourselves. However, only with violence can this murderous world be changed, just as everyone living knows."[59] Armed with the words of one of Germany's most respected authors and a devout leftist agitator, Baader comes out shooting in a valiantly heroic, if hopelessly fatal, gesture. He dies in the arms of Krone, held reverently in a pieta-like pose, so despite the obviously fictionalized history, Roth portrays Baader as a flawed underdog whose rebellious energy was misguided but nonetheless admirable.

Die Stille nach dem Schuss

At the turn of the millennium, Volker Schlöndorff directed his third film on the legacy of the Red Army Faction, *Die Stille nach dem Schuss*,[60] in his words "closing a chapter on terrorism rather than reopening it."[61] Along with Alexander Kluge, Schlöndorff had been the driving force behind the collaborative film *Deutschland im Herbst* (1978) and together with Margarethe von Trotta he had made the film adaptation of Heinrich Böll's novel, *Die verlorene Ehre der Katharina Blum* (The lost honor of Katarina Blum, 1975). These landmark films present different models for treating terrorism and exemplify how Schlöndorff's approach to the topic has ranged from documentary to self-reflective narrative and melodrama.

Together with Kluge, Schlöndorff was responsible for filming in Stuttgart the majestic state funeral for murdered President of the Federal Union of Employers Association Hanns-Martin Schleyer and two days later the controversial and chaotic burial of RAF terrorists Gudrun Ensslin, Andreas Baader, and Jan-Carl Raspe, which frame the film *Deutschland im Herbst*. This documentary footage of the contrasting funerals delivered memorable images of the old guard maintaining the veneer of its authority and the younger generation mourning the end of an era. The polemic in this cultural revolution was poignantly illustrated in a cross-cut sequence. On the one side, we see a lingering pan around a shiny black Mercedes Benz limousine as the epitome of German prosperity, status, and quality work and long shots of armed policemen on horseback standing sentry on the hilltops among the autumnal trees. On the other side, silent masked mourners walk aimlessly over graves, fists raised high in protest, and Christiane Ensslin discusses the difficulties surrounding her attempts to bury her sister with dignity. Public protest over the internment of terrorists next to ordinary citizens in a municipal graveyard was quickly resolved by Stuttgart's mayor Manfred Rommel, who granted the grief-stricken families the right to bury their loved ones. The parallels between the mayor's personal history and the contemporary situation — the mayor's father, Field Marshal Erwin Rommel, was forced to commit suicide by the National Socialist regime and then honored with a state funeral — suggest a continuity in the struggle between state and individual. In addition to the striking imagery, the accompanying music reminds the viewer that these deaths are part of a distinctly German national history and also part of a broader human history in which dissidents have routinely clashed with the establishment. As workers fill the terrorists' graves with dirt, one hears Josef Haydn's string quartet in C major, known as the *Kaiserquartett*, whose second movement provided the melody for the German national anthem, *das Deutschlandlied*, suggesting that on the rocky road to nationhood both patriotism and insurgency have had their place in the unbroken line between the Holy Roman Empire of the German Nation and the Federal Republic of Germany. The film concludes with Joan Baez's protest song "Here's to you" about executed anarchists Sacco and Vanzetti playing, over a scene of a hippie mother and daughter leaving the funeral and walking off into the distance. The global and timeless nature of resistance is made evident in the use of an English-language song by one of America's most outspoken songwriters about a notorious clash between the state and dissenters in the early part of the twentieth century that resulted in international protests. Setting this music against the image of two new generations, both female and wearing clothing that mark them as nonmainstream, portends that the struggle will be carried on in the future, hopefully in a nonviolent fashion. The desire for peaceful activism is echoed as the music segues to the last title, which reads: "When the horror reaches a certain point, it is irrelevant who committed it: it should simply stop."[62]

Schlöndorff also directed the segment on *Antigone* based on a script by Heinrich Böll, who saw striking similarities between the ancient play and the current events in 1977. The segment features a German public television advisory board that repeatedly censors a director for his various prologues to Sophocles's *Antigone,* because regardless of how he handles the material, it is always politically suspect and potentially explosive. The story of King Creon granting the loyal warrior Eteocles, who defended the state, a ritual burial, while denying his fallen renegade brother Poly-nices the same right, was too close to home in the autumn of 1977, when a similar drama was unfolding around the burial of RAF terrorists and their victim in Stuttgart. The advisory board considered Antigone's refusal to accept the state's authority and her subsequent suicide too con-troversial and demanded that the director provide a disclaimer that would distance himself and the station from any suggestion that violence was a proper response to political conflicts. The three versions of the pro-logue are shown on a series of televisions, each version progressively more frank in its condemnation of violence and more Brechtian in its use of distancing devices, until it becomes ridiculous and the advisory board's discussion becomes ludicrous, even though it is completely serious. The self-reflective aspect of having the board watch and critique a movie in a movie as well as having Antigone played by actress Angela Winkler, who starred as Katharina Blum in Schlöndorff's 1975 terrorist film, sensitizes the viewer to the political dimensions of image making, film financing, distribution, and consumption.

Die verlorene Ehre der Katharina Blum, codirected by Schlöndorff and Margarethe von Trotta, portrays the hysteria surrounding domestic terrorism fueled by the state's misuse of power and media manipulation. Set in 1975 in Cologne during carnival week, the story revolves around Katharina Blum, a shy divorced housekeeper, who meets Ludwig Götten at a party and invites him home to spend the night with her. The next morning a phalanx of heavily armored riot police storm the apartment in search of Ludwig and arrest Katharina for harboring a fugitive. Even though Ludwig turns out to be an army deserter who stole the payroll and not a member of the notorious Baader-Meinhof gang, Katharina is belligerently interrogated by the police and slandered by the yellow press to such an extent that she becomes the victim of state-sanctioned terrorism. In the course of just a few days her life is overturned by the unscrupulous tabloid reporter Tötges, working in tacit cooperation with the equally ruthless police detective Beizmenne. Robbed of her dignity, unfairly labeled a terrorist sympathizer and a whore, and relentlessly hounded by anonymous hecklers, Katharina decides to strike back and kill Tötges in her now-ransacked apartment.

One of the first and biggest commercial successes of the New German Cinema, *Die verlorene Ehre der Katharina Blum* is marked by a realist sensibility and a strictly linear narrative framed by dated inserts that lend the highly melodramatic storyline a semi-documentary quality. The juxta-position of observant but understated camerawork and restrained acting style with the carnivalesque setting that sporadically intrudes reveals an absurd world where a seemingly normal but ultimately repressive state is out of control. From the opening scene, depicting Ludwig being secretly filmed in black-and-white footage by undercover police, to the closing scene, where cameramen swarm the grave site of the murdered reporter, the surveillance apparatus is omnipresent and inescapable. The climate of paranoia, created by a system that demands acquiescence and destroys anyone who refuses to submit, leads to a backlash of violence. Schlöndorff and von Trotta's film underscores that the structural violence inherent in the current system has a historical dimension, which is poignantly visualized in the architecture. Katharina's anonymous high-rise apartment and the sterile police station are urban spaces that breed alienation, but this estrangement is not attributed to modernity per se, rather it is the direct result of Germany's past. When Katharine leaves Konrad Beiters's house and takes the former Nazi's gun to kill Tötges, the camera lingers on two photographs of Cologne in ruins after the Second World War. The shot immediately following is Katharina's cold, imposing building surrounded by nothing but an empty dirt field, implying that there is a clear link between the fascist past and a terrorist present. Destruction of the German homeland because of the violence Germany inflicted on the world and the resulting loss of community come back to haunt the nation in a continuous cycle of self-inflicted trauma. The film concludes with an indictment of the sensationalist media and draws a parallel between the fictionalized story and the real-life terrorist drama unfolding in Germany: "Any similarity to certain journalistic practices is neither intentional nor accidental, but rather unavoidable."[63]

The director of more than thirty feature films and documentaries, Volker Schlöndorff (1939–) enjoys an international reputation as a prominent exponent of the New German Cinema who has often turned to politically charged subject matter. Indeed, the difficulty of sustaining political idealism has been a prominent theme in Schlöndorff's work from his very first short film, *Wen kümmert's* (Who cares, 1960) about an Arab and a German who consider leaving the Algerian Liberation Front and the German Democratic Republic respectively but encourage each other to return to their homeland and fight for a better future. However, unlike his more aesthetically radical colleagues such as Alexander Kluge, Rainer Werner Fassbinder, Wim Wenders, and Jean-Marie Straub, Schlöndorff tends toward a largely conventional style, an appreciation for traditional genres and literary adaptations, and a strong emphasis on storytelling over experimentation. Schlöndorff began his career in France, studying first at the celebrated Institute des Hautes Études Cinématographiques, but he left after a year to work as an assistant for leading film directors such as Louis Malle, Jean-Pierre Melville, and Alain Resnais. Rejecting the term *auteur* to describe his own work, Schlöndorff prefers to see himself as a stylist and believes that a director should remain at a safe distance from the material and not project his own personality onto a work, because this would disturb the integrity of a film's inner logic.[64] Schlöndorff has worked both inside and outside the dominant produc-

tion systems in Europe and the United States, but from the beginning of
his career he has advocated for the reform of film financing and the development of a strong national film industry in Germany. He cofounded two
production companies, Hallelujah Film in 1969 with Peter Fleishmann,
and Bioskop Film in 1974 with director Reinhard Hauff, and served from
1974 to 1978 as the SPD delegate to the administrative council of the
national film-subsidy foundation (Filmförderungsanstalt). After unification he became the head of the renowned DEFA film studios in Babelsberg and oversaw its privatization. An Oscar and Golden Palm winner for
Die Blechtrommel (The tin drum, 1979), Schlöndorff was regarded as a
significant German filmmaker, and there were high expectations for his
new film, whose subject was the startling revelations that the GDR government had given RAF terrorists political asylum in the eighties.[65]

With a screenplay by celebrated author Wolfgang Kohlhaase, who had
written the filmscripts for such DEFA classics as *Berlin: Ecke Schönhauser*
(Berlin: The corner of Schönhauser, dir. Gerhard Klein, 1966), *Ich war
19* (I was 19, dir. Konrad Wolf, 1968), and *Solo Sunny* (dir. Konrad Wolf,
1980), *Die Stille nach dem Schuss* promised to be a significant East-West
collaboration about two puzzling phenomena of postwar Germany: why
did a group of young people take up arms to protest against the smug and
repressive capitalist system that engendered the economic miracle in the
FRG and why did the other Germany in the GDR, which purported to be
a socialist alternative, turn out to be an equally repressive state governed
by petty-bourgeois values and conformism?

The film centers on Rita Vogt, an RAF-type terrorist, who starts out
happily robbing banks to protest against mindless consumption under capitalism, but her actions become increasingly violent. She masterminds a jailbreak to free her terrorist lover, and while the plan is successful, it results in
a deadly shoot-out. Rita goes into hiding in Paris where she shoots a policeman to avoid capture and then flees to the GDR. Faced with the choice of
life on the run or a stable, productive existence in the GDR, she decides
to give up militant activism and adopt a new identity in the socialist state.
Working in a textile factory, she befriends the outsider Tatjana and begins
a sexual relationship with her, but she is recognized by a coworker and
must leave abruptly and begin a new life in a new city. Now living under
another false identity, she spends the summer working in a children's camp
on the Baltic Sea and falls in love with the aspiring physicist Jochen. When
Jochen asks her to marry him and move to Moscow, the Stasi inform her
that she cannot go because of political considerations. Shortly thereafter
the Wall falls and the FRG demands the return of RAF terrorists residing in
the GDR. Rita tries to escape on a motorcycle but is shot by a border guard
as she tries to cross over into West Germany.

The premiere of *Die Stille nach dem Schuss* at the Berlin Film Festival
on 16 February 2000 was marked by scandal when former 2 June Movement

Fig. 3.2. Still from Volker Schlöndorff's Die Stille nach dem Schuss *(2000). Photo courtesy of Stiftung Deutsche Kinemathek.*

and RAF terrorist Inge Viett claimed that Schlöndorff and Kohlhaase had not only plagiarized her autobiography, *Nie war ich furchtloser* (Never was I more fearless, 1996), but they had also gotten her life story wrong. Critics, already alerted to the issue of authenticity, were nearly universal in their condemnation of Schlöndorff's film for failing to address adequately the burning question of what motivates an individual to embrace terrorism as a political strategy.[66] Schlöndorff defended the film and argued that he and Kohlhaase were more concerned with how the former terrorists survived under socialism than with their motivations for armed struggle. Moreover, they had gone through numerous script revisions starting in 1993 and had used the biographies of many RAF members including those of Inge Viett, Susanne Albrecht, and Sabine Maier-Witt. Schlöndorff emphasized that they had fictionalized much of the film's narrative because "if we stay glued too strongly to the facts, then we might as well shoot a documentary film. If one wants some distance, then one needs a fictional plotline."[67] Kohlhaase had interviewed Viett in prison years before her autobiography appeared and had also interviewed other terrorists as well as the Stasi handlers before researching the historical facts extensively in the files overseen by the BStU. Despite the decidedly negative reception in German newspapers, the film won three important awards at the Berlin Film Festival: the Silver Bear for best actress was shared by Bibiana Beglau (Rita) and

Nadja Uhl (Tatjana) and Schlöndorff won the Blue Angel for the Best European film. Ticket sales, however, were extremely modest at 137, 532 seats sold in the first full year of distribution.[68]

As many commentators have rightly noted, *Die Stille nach dem Schuss* does not dwell on the psychological motivations that led a group of disenchanted youth to embrace violence in their war against the establishment. When asked why she became a terrorist, Rita simply replies: "I was head over heels in love."[69] The idea that a woman would follow a man into armed resistance based exclusively on emotional and sexual needs rather than political conviction reinforces a gender cliché that women are irrational and driven by sentiment. It also positions Rita as a victim of male-dominated authority, whether manifest in her relationship to the aggressive terrorist leader or to the paternalistic state-security apparatus. Schlöndorff has argued that Rita's pert reference to her infatuation with Andi does not reflect her actual opinion but is a type of posturing typical of the time.[70] Rita's insolence plays down Friederike's more serious rationale for joining the terrorist group, namely that she was tired of living an idle life of luxury consisting of riding horses, playing tennis, and eating salmon. Despite the director's explanation, there is a disconnect between Rita's words and actions that is never resolved satisfactorily. It is difficult to dismiss completely her admission that her political stance is related to her emotional state, since she decides to leave the terrorist cell at exactly the moment when her relationship with Andi fails.

When Rita first arrives in her newly adopted home in the GDR, she tells Tatjana that she has always held leftist beliefs, but since she is hiding behind a false identity, this assertion is somewhat suspect. However, Rita's statements to Tatjana are compelling because their relation is pivotal to the film. Indeed, the entire story is told in a type of flashback as a letter to Tatjana, and the film's raison d'être is for Rita to clarify to her friend what she did and why. In a voice-over at the beginning of the film Rita admits: "We thought we were the greatest, Tatjana. Somehow we wanted to eradicate injustice and the state with it or the other way around. They were connected. Politics was war. Everywhere in the world."[71] It is only at the end of the film that the viewer learns that this is a voice from the grave, ironically introduced by a beggar's wish that she should live a long life. Later in Beirut, as Rita and her comrades drive along in a car, sealed off from the civil war as if in a cocoon, she explains again in a voice-over:

> We wanted to attempt the impossible, at least once in our life. We felt we were part of an international struggle. And then in Beirut we experienced how a just cause led to a murderous civil war. We wanted to bring the war into the metropolitan areas. There were endless discussions, successful and failed actions, dead bodies on both sides.[72]

This matter-of-fact tone, where political debates are given the same significance as murder victims, characterizes Rita's attitude throughout the film. Aside from her brief crying fit after breaking up with Andi and deciding to stay in the GDR, Rita never lets down her guard. Whether this is a function of her need to protect herself or an indication of her overall naive approach to life, Rita is emotionally restrained and uncompromising in her moral outlook. She shows absolutely no remorse for killing a man and describes her own culpability in murder as something passive: "It happened to me." It is only years later, after the fall of the Wall, that Rita actually sits down to write Tatjana, and paradoxically the very act of locating the beginning of Rita's letter writing as the temporal origin of her voice-over signals the end of her story and her life. In her final message Rita admits: "It is clear to me that we are caught in a false system, but the guerilla war could not lead to emancipation, because no one understood us. When I came over here, I did not merely want to hide. I was seeking another world than the one I knew. I wanted to move forward, not backward."[73] The nonsynchronicity of voice and action evident in each of Rita's voice-overs implies that she has the distance to judge her past with some insight. However, her attempts at an account taking are always filled with passive constructions and blind spots. Years of living a covert existence have taken their toll, because Rita suffers from selective amnesia and self-alienation and is blind to both social and personal inconsistencies, whether her failure to acknowledge the inner contradictions she has witnessed in GDR socialism or the discrepancy between her own belief in human dignity and her willingness to take a human life. Rita's perpetual blindness is verified in the scene where she writes to Tatjana in a notebook while the news of the fall of the Berlin Wall plays on television. Rita sits with her back to the television as she reminisces, blocking out the historical context, so that she can concentrate on her own narrative. Although Rita is oblivious to the images of the present whizzing by on the television, the camera moves into a close-up but always keeps the television set within the frame so as to highlight the mediated nature of the events. The audience sees not just footage of Willy Brandt promising that things will never be the same in the East and Trabis bringing GDR citizens over the previously fortified border, but also an abundance of young children held up high to see the celebration and one young girl carrying a Woolworth shopping bag, insinuating that the consumerism that drove Rita to terrorist action has triumphed and will govern the future in a unified Germany. Rita's reluctance to explore the past openly from the vantage point of defeat in the present seems motivated by the fear of acknowledging that her life and political engagement have all been in vain.

Just as Christopher Roth was criticized for depicting the terrorists as if they were modern-day outlaws from a Hollywood Western, Schlöndorff was disparaged for focusing on a generic storyline replete with bank robbery, jailbreak, doomed relationship between sheriff (Stasi officer Erwin) and renegade (Rita), and showdown at high noon. And like Roth, Schlöndorff was accused of trivializing militant activism as a farce worthy of the Marx Brothers. The opening scene of the film, for example, features Rita and her compatriots robbing a bank to protest the pressures of a materialistic society under capitalism. As the *International* plays in the background on a tinny-sounding child's music box, imparting an infantile tone to the entire scene, the rebels, wearing Ray Ban Wayfarers and stylish hats, brandish their guns as if playing cops and robbers, hand out chocolate desserts, and shout slogans like "property is theft" and "down with capitalism." The hand-held camera captures the action in extremely close proximity, with close-ups and tight mid-shots that never afford an overview and place the viewer in the thick of things. The editing is fast-paced, with cuts on unfinished movements that serve to highlight the unruly, chaotic nature of the terrorists' exploits. Moreover, the blue tint to the images and the extensive use of glass panes and reflective surfaces draw attention to the camera and the staged aspect of the scene. The depiction of Rita as belonging to the so-called "hash rebels" or "merry guerillas" (Spaßguerilla) met with opposition by numerous film critics, who found the staging of the bank robbery amateurish and inappropriately lighthearted. Anke Westphal regarded the scene as "a trace too casual, a hint too relaxed,"[74] while Katja Nicodemus objected strongly to the formulaic portrayal of the militants: "This beginning, which stages the RAF with the kind of titillation found in the *Berliner Zeitung* (weapons, slogans, holdup, a little sex, a little guerilla romanticism), has something oddly shameful in its superficiality."[75] Whereas these film reviewers assume that the RAF and 2 June Movement had from the beginning a clear-cut, theoretically sound political platform and were deadly serious in the execution of their actions, Schlöndorff is of the opinion that they were at least as much motivated by the thrill of deviant behavior as by saving the world. The amateurish atmosphere surrounding the bank robbery reflects the farcical nature of early terrorist actions in West Germany. Inge Viett herself remembers handing out chocolate desserts during bank robberies "to get rid of the tension," but she calls Schlöndorff's rendition a Punch and Judy show (Kasperletheater). Interestingly, Schlöndorff agrees, because he uses the exact same phrase to describe the early exploits of the 2 June Movement before they escalated to deadly force.[76]

The jailbreak, during which Rita, Friederike, and Jochen smuggle guns into a maximum-security prison and free Andi in a spray of bullets that injure a guard and kill a lawyer, clearly has theatrical aspects to it. Film critic Peter von Becker rejects the scene as an unbelievable fairy tale.[77] While the likelihood that a group of terrorists could smuggle weapons into a prison and liberate their fellow conspirators seems remote, one only has to remember Andreas Baader's infamous jailbreak to see that truth is often stranger than fiction. For *Die Stille nach dem Schuss*, Inge Viett's participation in the armed assault organized by Gabriele Rollnik to free her lover Till Meyer in 1978 from Moabit prison is even more significant. Viett describes the real-life scene as a series of mishaps that remarkably ended in success, surprising the terrorists at least as much as the guards.[78] Not only the jovial atmosphere surrounding the deadly serious terrorist actions, but also the language used in the film is alienating. The most jarring example is the political discussion in Paris, where the dialogue is stilted and the terrorists sound as if they are reciting from their own pamphlets.[79] The unnatural quality of the conversations is especially apparent when an unnamed young man steps to the forefront and gives a monologue that reads like a direct quote from Holger Meins's last prison note, in which he infamously characterizes the struggle in absolute terms: "either human being or pig / either survival at any price or struggle to the death / either problem or solution / there is nothing in between / . . . surely death comes to everyone. the question is merely, how you have lived: FIGHTING AGAINST THE PIGS as a HUMAN BEING FOR THE LIBERATION OF HUMAN BEINGS."[80] When Rita begins spouting this kind of propagandistic rhetoric, Friederike quickly reminds her friend that she is echoing Andi's texts by rote. What disturbed film critics the most, however, was that Rita shows no remorse for killing a policeman, and the audience never learns how she feels about this unspeakable deed. While it would be enlightening to know the extent to which this fictional character felt regret, and whether she absolved herself of guilt because it was an instinctive reaction of self-preservation or whether she believed the rhetoric that the pigs deserved what they got, the memoirs of terrorists like Inge Viett are equally vague about their emotional responses and soul searching. When describing how she shot Francis Violleau in a parking garage after the policeman stopped her for riding through Paris on her motorcycle without a helmet, Viett states: "I told him to split, and he stared and stared. Then I shot." What remains in her memory is the ridiculous look on his face as the bullet entered his spine, and, vividly aware of the gruesomeness of her statement, she quickly adds: "One has to be allowed to say such things." In 2000, nineteen years after she shot and paralyzed Violleau, sentencing him to life in a wheelchair, Viett was still not able to speak with him in person, let alone apologize, and was reluctant even to talk with reporters about it: "I can't deal with some things any more."[81] This inability to express grief and take some measure of responsibility for violence is rendered palpable in *Die Stille nach dem Schuss* when Rita is more upset by the fact that the Stasi killed an untrainable guard dog than by her own use of deadly force on a fellow human being.

Despite the criticism lodged against Schlöndorff and Kohlhaase that they trivialized and sensationalized the actions of terrorists like Inge Viett,

Die Stille nach dem Schuss does present a valid historical thesis on uncomfortable aspects of the past. Early terrorist acts were often chaotic and lighthearted before they evolved into more violent confrontations. Many former terrorists like Inge Viett find it difficult to delve into their own emotional struggles with guilt for the suffering they inflicted upon others. The RAF terrorists who dropped out of the struggle and found sanctuary in the GDR idealized the socialist state because they found something here that approximated their dreams of a world not governed by wealth and class privileges. While critics and audiences may want from this film a definitive explanation of the past — especially reassurances that the terrorists were always deadly serious about their unambiguous agenda, recognized their own responsibility for their actions, regretted the pain caused by their violence, and realistically evaluated the merits and blemishes of both the FRG and the GDR — documented sources tell us that history is more complex.

While the main protagonist Rita protects herself with nearly impenetrable psychological armor, her foil Tatjana wears her heart on her sleeve. Tatjana is the eastern equivalent of Rita, a young woman in her twenties who rebels against the staid, authoritarian social order. Rita considers materialism and economic exploitation as the root of social injustice in the West, but Tatjana sees the pressure to conform and become an obedient worker drone as the equally unfair form of oppression in the East. With her punk hairdo, run-down apartment resembling a squat, and disillusioned attitude, Tatjana is an outsider who runs the risk of being classified as an "asocial," an offense punishable with incarceration in the GDR. She escapes into alcohol and ecstatic dancing, looking for an intoxication that would allow her to experience a passion left unfilled by everyday life. Failing to show up for work, sitting in her bed in the late afternoon listening to Tamara Danz from the GDR band Silly sing about being under the control of hostile forces, Tatjana is the image of alienated youth. Danz's punk ballad is about being hooked up to an EKG machine that allows Dr. Frankenstein-like figures to see all her inner defects and tinker with her soul until she measures up. When Rita enters Tatjana's apartment, the viewer hears the lines: "And again I am hooked up to the wires / Like a wayward wicked child / And feel how without being asked / My soul is drained from my body / What do they know about love / What do they know about hate / About the web of dreams and desires / Through whose mesh I cannot pass."[82] The song's refrain: "I want to split but can't any more / The shit machine has sucked me dry," summarizes the futility of rebellion in the GDR, for there is no way out, and the system cripples people who are different.

For someone like Tatjana, who borders on being a drop-out, Rita is a welcome change, a bird of a different color in this dreary landscape. Tatjana is shocked that anyone from the West would choose to live in the

East, because she imagines the world beyond the Wall as a more exciting, freer society, and she dreams about leaving the GDR the first chance she gets. The prison-like atmosphere of everyday life is captured in a long shot of the factory's brick facade filled with row after row of windows with frames that resemble bars and the tiny figures of Rita and Tatjana at an open porthole. In a close-up of the two women staring out into the distance beyond their fenced-in existence, Tatjana expresses the wish to make her own choices and determine her own fate. While Rita naively believes that in the workers-and-peasants-state that the GDR claims to be, workers will display solidarity with each other and with the oppressed all over the world, Tatjana has practical experience that bears out a reality marked by mean-spirited bickering and parsimony. In the textile factory the petty coworkers routinely pick on Tatjana for being different and ostracize her. They also react with shock and anger when Rita enthusiastically signs a petition in support of Nicaragua and gives 10 marks to the cause. Faced with such obligatory and empty gestures of solidarity on a regular basis, the workers can only meet her raw enthusiasm with scornful looks and insults. Ironically, Rita's zealous belief in socialism and her willingness to conform to party expectations for public displays of camaraderie make her as much of an outsider in the GDR as Tatjana is.

Surrounded by coldness and cruelty in the workplace and bewilderment in her family, Tatjana reacts to Rita's show of concern with growing interest. Starved for affection and acceptance, she looks up to Rita as a strong and dominant personality. Indeed, Rita's concern for Tatjana has a motherly quality, since she is constantly caring for her: cooking her dinner, disciplining her alcohol use, putting her to bed, and teaching her to drive. Tatjana's impenetrable "web of dreams and desires" in a society where no one understands love takes the form of lesbian desire for Rita. Her unseen glances at Rita, their fervent and uncontrolled dancing, and mutual affection briefly and tentatively become sexual. Tatjana steals into Rita's bed one night, kisses and strokes her but leaves just as quickly, and while Rita offers no opposition, she also demonstrates no clear ardor. Rita's declaration to the Stasi that she wants to go back to Tatjana is thus somewhat puzzling. While Rita's sexual relationships to men are captured on camera and are staged as voyeuristic pleasure for the male characters (the Stasi listen to her making love to Andi, ostensibly to learn about any political pillow talk, and Jochen presents a slide show of Rita dressed in a bikini), physical affection between women is depicted as somewhat awkward and ultimately taboo. It seems to be no coincidence that just when Rita appears willing to engage in a lesbian relationship, she is forced to leave before it can be consummated. Rita and Tatjana's passionate good-bye kiss is accompanied by the punk band Silly's instrumental piece "Reprise," hinting at the deviant nature of their behavior. And while the Stasi are again listening to Rita's sexual activities, their surveillance is now to ensure that she terminate the relationship. Despite the fact that Rita leaves her, Tatjana is willing to accept the former terrorist's violent past and remains true to her. Arrested by the Stasi because she knows about Rita's true identity (or as the cynical viewer might conclude, because her asocial behavior now includes lesbian desire), Tatjana becomes the true hero of the film, because she sacrifices her own freedom and refuses to betray her friend or work for the Stasi as an informant. When the GDR state collapses, Tatjana fares no better, since she is arrested by West German authorities who seek Rita's whereabouts, an irony again signaled by the child's music box, this time playing the FRG's national anthem.

The victimization of strong, defiant women by the dominant social order is also evident in the portrayal of the third female character, Friederike Adelbach. Like Rita, the former terrorist Friederike has been given a new identity in the GDR and at first glance appears to have been successfully assimilated into the collective. When the two meet by chance in a seaside town, Friederike is in a folk choir performing Matthias Claudius's "Abendlied." Wearing a black-and-white uniform and standing in her proper place in the row, she is the picture of conformity when she sings the melancholy prayer for forgiveness, which resonates not only with her own dark past but with that of the divided nation as well: "Cold is the evening breeze. God spare us from punishment and let us sleep peacefully and our sick neighbor too."[83] Rita assumes that conformity, marriage, and motherhood have brought her friend true happiness, but she reads the situation incorrectly. Trapped in a life she does not want, confined to a bourgeois marriage as a silent, obedient wife and mother, the former terrorist is deeply unhappy and unable to run away. As a sad and silent Friederike sits behind her window on the bus with no possibility of escape from her guilty past or her cheerless present, the child's music box from the film's opening scene now plays the GDR national anthem, for, like the tinny music, socialism's promise proves to be hollow.

Despite numerous instances that challenge the official view of socialism's achievements, Rita's relentless and naive enthusiasm never falters. Looking out onto the Baltic and the GDR's watery border with the West, she gushes with excitement about spending the summer at the seashore and wonders why anyone would want to leave this paradise. Kohlhaase explains that Rita's uncompromising belief and her unadulterated acceptance of the GDR were modeled on typical attitudes voiced by former terrorists in their interviews with him. This wholehearted acceptance of everything in the GDR was not just based on the fact that they did not really have any other choice except prison in the FRG or a life in the underground. According to Kohlhaase, former terrorists like Inge Viett, Susanne Albrecht, and Sabine Maier-Witt also expressed their appreciation of a lifestyle that was not based on wealth and privilege:

As declared enemies of the so-called *Konsumterror*, the pressures of a materialistic society, the fact that things were grayer, more modest, and more orderly here did not pose a problem for them. And they were already completely demoralized regarding their own ideals. Perhaps it was actually the banality of everyday life that they liked about the GDR, that they could live a life that they did not know before. The desire for normality cannot be underestimated.[84]

Rita retains her belief in socialism as the morally correct political philosophy, but she becomes progressively more conventional in appearance and lifestyle in the course of the film. She starts out as a bank-robbing renegade with long hair, sunglasses, and tie-dyed bell bottom jeans, not just brandishing a gun but also a swagger. She even gives Großgern a lesson on how carrying a gun in your pants changes the way you carry yourself and results in a more confident stride. After arriving in the GDR for the first time with Andi, wearing blue jeans and a keffiyeh, the traditional Palestinian scarf long associated with the PLO, Rita must quickly change her looks to protect her identity. To fit in as the clean-cut factory worker Susanne Schmidt, she cuts her hair and pulls it back in a slick pony-tail and starts wearing flowery blouses and dresses. Forced to take on a second legend as Sabine Walter, Rita adopts an even more traditionally feminine role as a bespectacled secretary, wearing dresses, skirts, shorts, and a bikini that all accentuate her figure, and happily accepting Jochen's proposal to give up her job and follow him to an isolated enclave in the Soviet Union as a married woman and mother. In an ultimate gesture of domesticity, Rita is now shown watching television and ironing. Despite all of her costume changes and attempts to comply with societal expectations of feminine conformity, Rita never gives up her beliefs. After the fall of the Wall, when a co-worker renounces her allegiance to the GDR state, Rita admonishes the workers, saying that they do not know what they are losing. While they may now be able to afford consumer goods, their future is anything but certain. With a fervor bordering on bathos Rita addresses the entire cantina: "But this was a great experiment here. It was a revolution. Regardless of all the crap, all the stupidity, you were part of it. This was supposed to be a world in which money didn't determine everything. Why don't you believe in it anymore? Why don't you believe in yourselves anymore?"[85]

What sets this film apart from most post-Wall films is the depiction of the Stasi as rather sympathetic characters, if at times old-fashioned and even laughable. Rita's handler, Erwin Hull, is a practical man, who helps the RAF because it is in the state's interest to know about the enemy of its enemy. His effort to earn the terrorists' confidence by inviting them over for a beer and a barbecue comes across as a clichéd example of the GDR's backwardness. The Stasi's attention to outdated standards of decorum in an unspoiled natural setting stands in strong contrast to the experiences and expectations of the hardened revolutionaries. And yet it seems to work because both sides see something in the other that is appealing. Rita and Friederike are attracted by the prospect of returning to a normal life without violence and do not seem to recognize (or refuse to acknowledge) the significance of Erwin's claim that the GDR state is "the organized form of violence." Erwin and his subordinate Großgern ("upstart"), on the other hand, admire Rita and Friederike as "nice girls" who display the kind of strong political convictions one does not see much in the GDR populace. Even the Stasi general voices a certain affinity for the youthful revolutionaries, because like them the founding members of the Stasi fought against the fascists in Spain and against the National Socialists in their own country and see themselves as romantics. The falseness and violence lying just below the surface of the state security's romantic notions of power are best demonstrated in the scene where Erwin and the General go hunting. Dressed in traditional loden clothing and affecting the air of gentlemen, Erwin gets his finger stuck in the rifle barrel, and neither one can hit a single boar in the herd running past them. Despite their considerate manners and fatherly concern, the Stasi officers represent an authoritarian regime against which there is no recourse. Erwin reveals the frightening logic behind their caring facade: "We are for the people. That is why we are against them."[86] When Erwin learns after the fall of the Wall that the Federal Republic knew all along that RAF terrorists had taken refuge in the GDR, he is disheartened that his moral sacrifices were based on illusion. Believing in the righteousness of his actions, he had put an innocent woman in prison for merely knowing that the state harbored a Western terrorist. Thus in the end the Stasi comes across as a victim of an even more influential and clandestine power, the capitalist regime in the FRG.

Rita is a person out of time and space, whose life is told in a flashback ending in death and whose idealism has no place in the new postcold-war order. Constantly shown in vehicles, on the move, crossing borders physically, politically, and sexually, she is never at home. However, as the *Wende* approaches and the GDR begins to transform and cease to exist, the country itself becomes a place out of time and Rita's position is now completely untenable. At an ice-skating rink filled with children ice-dancing to ethereal music amid a rising fog that marks the otherworld quality of the political upheaval happening outside, Rita learns that throngs of GDR citizens are seeking asylum in the Prague embassy while the rest of the nation sleeps. When the sleeping giant awakens, there will be no room for this woman who is always transgressing borders, and she will be hunted in every direction she flees. Just as Rita's life has straddled the tenuous cord holding the two German states together, locating her in a type of ideological no-man's-land, her death takes place at the border, the empty space between legitimate realms of existence. The tinny, childlike version of the FRG's national anthem accompanies Rita on her motorcycle when she meets her death, bringing the story full circle, since Rita had shot a motorcycle policeman in Paris. After she is shot by a border guard, there is a moment of silence, as alluded to in the film's title, giving viewers time to contemplate how things got to this point. As if to answer this question, Tamara Danz's song "PS" plays in the background. Rita's most admirable quality is her uncompromising stance, but this unwillingness to bend leads to her tragic downfall, because, as Danz sings: "No one is going to bend me . . . I am too young to be weak, too blind to give up."[87]

The film concludes with Rita dead on the inner German border, snow falling silently on the empty road, and a title consisting of the enigmatic phrase: "That's exactly how it was. More or less."[88] This ending brings the question of historical accuracy and authenticity to the forefront but leaves the viewer to ponder what the historical truth is. Against claims that *Die Stille nach dem Schuss* presented history as a fairy tale, Schlöndorff responded that he had no problem with fairy tales and that one can sometimes find a truth in fiction that is missing from historical documentation. He states: "Therefore it was our opinion that this heroine deserved a tragic end. I find that in a film narrative — and to that extent cinema is also a moral institution — guilt cannot be left unatoned for when the curtain falls. It demands, as one used to say, 'divine judgment.'"[89] In response to the question of whether RAF terrorism belongs to the canon of German history and is no longer a painful national trauma, Schlöndorff responded:

> Today the left wing has really been abolished, because this utopia no longer exists. They will remain as a bolded footnote to history. One will say that there was the leaden time in the Adenauer years when nothing moved, there was the upheaval and the student revolts in '68, and there was this guerilla-type armed struggle, completely confusing and unexpected. Nothing in German history since Thomas Müntzer could have prepared for the fact that a group assaulted the state with violence and challenged it. That it was doomed to failure from the very start is another story. But it will always be said: "That happened." And we have not really digested it completely.[90]

Raus aus der Haut

Directed by Andreas Dresen, *Raus aus der Haut* (Changing skins) was made for the ORB series "Wild Hearts" and premiered on the ARD television station on 24 September 1997. It was also shown at the Berlin Film Festival in February 1998 in a series entitled New German Films. Despite its modest budget of 1.8 million DM and its limited release, the film was well received and won the main prize at the Eighth Film Art Festival in

Fig. 3.3. Screenshot from Andreas Dresen's Raus aus der Haut *(1997).*

Schwerin in 1998 as well as the Lucas prize for the best youth film at the International Children and Youth Film Festival in Frankfurt am Main in 1998.[91] The last honor might seem somewhat surprising, since *Raus aus der Haut* represents what might be every student's secret dream and every teacher's nightmare: the film tells the fictional story of two GDR high-school students who are inspired by the Red Army Faction to kidnap their school principal because they hope that this will lead to their admission to university.

Born in 1963 in Gera, the son of theater director Adolf Dresen and actress Barbara Bachmann, Andreas Dresen started making amateur movies as a teenager in the GDR. He first applied to the Film and Television Academy Konrad Wolf (HFF) in 1982 without success. He therefore volunteered as a sound technician at the Schwerin Theater, served in the National People's Army (NVA) for two years, and worked as an assistant for renowned film director Günter Reisch, until in 1986 he was finally accepted at the HFF for studies in directing. While his formative years were spent in the German Democratic Republic, Dresen's first full-length feature film, *Stilles Land* (Quiet country, 1992) was made after the *Wende* and reflects the rupture in time and shock of a world coming to an end. *Stilles Land* is a black comedy about a provincial theater staging Samuel Beckett's *Waiting for Godot* just as the GDR collapses. Beckett's enigmatic play about the passing of time, waiting for an unknowable future that never arrives, and the memory lapses that must be constantly recovered, was an apt metaphor for the existential crisis surrounding the collapse of the communist world order.

The ideological vacuum created in the aftermath of unification is a theme that links Dresen's first feature film to his persistent interest in

West German terrorism. Speaking a decade after the fall of the Wall, Dresen recounted how his own doubts about the political developments led him to consider working on various projects about disillusionment and terrorism:

> We in the East are especially jaded, weary of politics. Many have retreated into the private realm. Up until two or three years ago that was the case for me to an extent. After the *Wende* I was disappointed with a lot of things, believed — completely quixotically — in a possible reform of the GDR system. After the over-hasty reunification I had to come to terms with my own lack of orientation.[92]

At that point in 1999, shortly after he had directed *Raus aus der Haut*, Dresen planned to make a film about the 2 June Movement, the terrorist group that took its name from the day on which student Benno Ohnesorg was shot by police while protesting the Shah of Iran's visit to Berlin on 2 June 1967. Dresen's fascination with this group of radicals was based on their ingenuity and energy as much as on their grave mistakes. He maintains:

> This Berlin urban guerilla unit from the seventies functioned like the RAF . . . These people wanted to reform the system and hoped to rally many to the cause. Unfortunately their path was fatal. However, despite prison they remained true to their resolve and continued to think creatively about social change.[93]

Dresen believes that the picture painted of the 2 June Movement is generally tainted by partisan politics: "The left wing turns them into gods, the right wing into monsters. But who are these people really? I would like to tell their story fairly and without polemics."[94]

Over the next few years Dresen researched the 2 June Movement extensively, collecting more than a thousand pages of documentary material and interviewing Inge Viett and other members of the group and their victims. Based on this research he wrote and directed the play *Zeugenstand — Stadtguerilla-Monologe* (Witness stand — urban guerilla monologues), which premiered at the Deutsches Theater (Kammerspiel) on 5 June 2002. The play consists of six monologues and follows the events surounding two terrorist actions in late 1974 and early 1975 undertaken by this group. After Holger Meins's death from a hunger strike in November 1974, the group murdered Günter von Drenkmann, the presiding judge of the Court of Appeals in Berlin. In February 1975 they kidnapped CDU candidate Peter Lorenz in the middle of an election in Berlin and were able to ransom Lorenz for the release of five political prisoners. Dresen explained that he was attracted to the subject of terrorism because: "We live in a time in which there are no more utopias.

Therefore I am interested in people who still questioned this world. That was the case in '68. The experiment of dreaming of a better society certainly failed, but despite that one should deal with the failed attempts."[95] Dresen's statements about the death of utopia and the abiding, insatiable yearning for idealism echo those of Volker Schlöndorff, and despite the fact that they represent different generations and grew up in different German states, their probing of radicalism in the seventies speaks to this uncomfortable void that has prevailed in German society since unification. Moreover, the two filmmakers illustrate a remarkable mirror of how utopianism in one German state is reflected in the other, so that the Westerner Schlöndorff explores how the RAF idealized the GDR, and the Easterner Dresen examines how GDR teenagers idealized the RAF.

Raus aus der Haut takes place in 1977 in the GDR, where awkward high-school student Marcus pines for the beautiful, sophisticated Anna, who is dating drop-out rock singer Randy. When Anna brings contraband material to school, she is caught by the principal, Rottmann, who shatters her dream of becoming a physician. In an effort to save Anna, Marcus tries to steal the evidence from Rottmann's office but is caught in the act. Facing a year working in a factory before she can apply to medical school, Anna is inspired by the RAF to kidnap Rottmann and hold him prisoner until her unsuspecting teachers can recommend her for college admission. Since the student prank leaves Marcus likewise confronting an unbearable future of officer's training before applying to the university, he agrees to help her. The two teenagers kidnap the school principal and lock him up in a cellar, but through a series of mishaps they get into more trouble and even begin to sympathize with their victim. Once freed, Rottmann does not seek vengeance on his young captors. After he learns that he was replaced and forgotten despite his sacrifices for the party, Rottmann stops taking his medicine and dies of a heart attack. Although Anna and Marcus receive positive recommendations, neither is admitted to university, and Randy is arrested for seditious acts.

From the film's opening scenes, where Randy's band Feuersbrunst performs in concert Deep Purple's "Smoke on the Water" and Anna brings a Rolling Stones and Renft album to class, music is an essential component of youthful protest against the establishment in 1977. The prominent display of Western rock bands situates GDR youth culture in an international context where music connected young people across the globe in their common desire for self-expression and their need to question authority. The generational conflict that pitted an entrenched authoritarian system against a rebellious youth was an international phenomenon that found expression in fashion, hair styles, and music. Scholar Paul Kaiser contends that this deep rift in social values was the most significant common postwar phenomenon, and while a cultural revolution took place with the same vehemence in both German states, "models for

East German protest culture came almost exclusively from the West."[96] Rock bands and the fashion industry in the West set the tone and offered up the stylistic trends, but GDR youth subculture developed on its own against very different pressures than on the other side of the Wall. Western youth protested against economic exploitation under capitalism, but Eastern youth rallied against the lack of personal freedoms in a closed socialist society where they could not openly say what they wanted and could not travel freely. The Renft album Anna brings to school highlights these specific areas of discontent in the GDR, namely the lack of free speech and free movement. The Klaus Renft Combo, originally formed as a beat-music band in 1958 by Klaus Jentzsch, was repeatedly banned, then reconstituted and given awards, only to be banned again. Renft became a cult band among young people who considered their songs filled with double meanings such as "Als ich wie ein Vogel war," "Wer ehrt die Rose," and "Wandermann" as easily deciphered coded messages that captured their sense of disillusionment. In 1975 Renft was definitively disbanded and its members blacklisted, and the following year its leader Klaus Jentzsch defected to the West. In November 1976 band members Gerulf Pannach and Christian Kunert protested Wolf Biermann's expatriation and were arrested on charges of "subversive agitation." They spent nine months in Hohenschönhausen prison before being ransomed ("freigekauft") to West Germany in August 1977, just one month before the fictional events in *Raus aus der Haut* occur.[97] In the heated atmosphere following the Biermann affair, the fact that Anna brings a Renft album to school and Randy listens to their music positions them as daring rebels, admired by their classmates, distrusted by the school authorities, and suspicious to the Stasi, who consider such acts potentially seditious.

Rock-and-roll was not merely entertainment; it represented a lifestyle that rejected the SED's paternalistic oversight of every detail in one's life and demanded conformity to rigid standards of behavior. According to photographer Harald Hauswald, who grew up in the GDR, rock bands such as the Rolling Stones and Renft

> triggered in us the urge to get to know a piece of the great, wide world. Music was the bridge. When Renft played 'Child in Time,' I felt freer for the rest of the week. I traveled then in my thoughts around the world, became a part of the universe. Many in my generation had found a way out in rock and literature. Otherwise the fate of being locked up for life would not have been tolerable.[98]

Listening to Western music fanned the desire to travel beyond the borders of the GDR, but the Wall prevented these desires from ever being fulfilled. Trapped behind the iron curtain, teenagers like Marcus and Anna decorate their bedrooms with globe lights and postcards from exotic places beyond their reach and create their own realm through music and its subculture happenings. As music scholar Michael Rauhut has suggested: "The pressure of the state upgraded the event 'rock concert' to an autonomous zone, an enclave. The more strongly it restricted official spaces, the more eagerly niches were established."[99] In *Raus aus der Haut*, the opening rock concert at the local social club, where Randy imitates Deep Purple, is just such a forum for the teenagers to vent their frustrations and satisfy their yearnings. With his long, unkempt hair, tight blue jeans, sleeveless T-shirt, and electric guitar, Randy is the epitome of rebellious energy within acceptable limits. When he walks into the audience, sweeps Anna off her feet, brings her up onto the stage, kisses her passionately, and the two sing "Smoke on the Water" together, the scene is witnessed with great longing by an unnamed female classmate wearing conspicuously large eyeglasses. In its staging as both anti-establishment confrontation and vicarious sexual fantasy, Randy's musical performance allows the embedded audience to participate in a collective experience that ultimately does not disturb the social order. The next day all the teenagers (except Anna and Randy) dutifully show up for assembly on the first day of school wearing their blue FDJ shirts. Dressed in the uniform of socialist conformity, they form a perfect square around the various flags of the state to listen to the national anthem and their principal's patriotic speech. Paul Kaiser has argued that the GDR rock scene offered music fans an alternative identity based on "symbolic provocation, political resistance, and social repudiation."[100] Rather than prohibiting rock music completely, as the SED had attempted earlier without much success, by 1977 the regime was trying to promote a sanitized version of rock that could fulfill the young people's needs without threatening the state. Fearing that a total ban on rock would only deepen dissatisfaction among an already disaffected youth, the Ministry of Culture made some concessions, allowing dance clubs in 1976.[101] As long as Randy avoids singing forbidden Renft songs whose lyrics convey dissatisfaction in metaphoric language operating on multiple levels and evoke the historical circumstances surrounding the band's opposition, imprisonment, and banishment, the authorities tolerate and even promote him, because he is a rebel without a cause.

The GDR has been labeled a niche society, in which citizens were able to create enclaves where the state did not intrude on their personal lives. The limits of this strategy are shown in *Raus aus der Haut*, when Anna and Marcus try to convert their classroom, an official venue controlled by the SED state, into a private niche for subversive actions. Before their teacher arrives, Anna shares with her classmates illegal Western news materials, including a newspaper photograph of Baader and Ensslin in Paris and a copy of *Spiegel* magazine with the headline "Women and Violence," as well as Renft and Rolling Stones albums. Marcus goes one step further by placing the RAF photograph under the projector, closing the curtain to darken the room, effectively creating his own cinema and a collective rebellious act, to the glee of the entire class. When Rottmann catches them in the act of distributing forbidden media, their private interaction becomes a public gathering of political concern. As a teacher of history, a loyal SED party member, and school principal, Rottmann is aware of connections beyond the comprehension of his young students, who seem to view these media as titillating largely because they are outlawed rather than out of interest in armed resistance to the state. The mere act of looking at this material is sufficient to register their symbolic protest against the paternalistic authorities. What the adolescents most likely do not know, and what Rottmann must be keenly aware of, is that in early September 1977 the *Spiegel* magazine does not represent merely the illegal importation of foreign press materials. On 19 August 1977, economist and regime critic Rudolf Bahro illegally published a chapter of his book, *Die Alternative: Zur Kritik des real existierenden Sozialismus* (The Alternative: a critique of real-existing socialism), in *Spiegel* magazine and was arrested the next day. Bahro's study charged the Soviet Union with being a backward, ineffective, and deviant form of Marxism, and his landmark accusation of the bankruptcy of Soviet-style economic policy sent ripples throughout the entire Eastern bloc. Thus while Marcus is taken by the photograph of Baader and Ensslin because it reflects a romantic image of life in the underground and also the kind of romantic relationship he wants with Anna, Rottmann is concerned that these manifestations of Western terrorism, capitalist media, and youth subculture could encourage his students to protest against socialism.

Rottmann's fear that the spirit of Western radicalism could infiltrate the GDR is matched by Randy's delight that this flow of ideas is inevitable. When they hear the first radio news report about the RAF's kidnapping of Hanns-Martin Schleyer, Randy argues that the revolutionary impulses underscoring West German terrorism are bound to invade the GDR as well: "That'll make its way over here — simply a matter of time."[102] Just as the school authorities equate images of the Baader-Meinhof gang with Western rock-and-roll music and regard both as contraband of the same order, Randy sees terrorism as an extension of the social criticism expressed in popular music. When asked what terrorist action he would undertake, Randy jokingly proposes kidnapping First Secretary Erich Honecker and Prime Minister Willi Stoph and demanding that the prohibition against Renft be lifted so that the band could perform publicly again. Randy's wisecracking jest becomes Anna's serious plan. Even though she has no intention of violently attacking the SED state to force radical social change, she does begin to adopt terrorist tactics to get what she wants. She engages in kidnapping, manipulating the media, finding sympathizers, and going underground — if only to her grandmother's cellar.

Since terrorism is based on asymmetrical warfare, in which the terrorists' use of force can never match that of the dominant power, their isolated violent strikes are effective in symbolic terms only if they become public knowledge. Terrorism requires the media to get its message out and to communicate with those in power who can fulfill their demands. As such, terrorism is a communicative act geared toward eliciting a specific effect, and without an audience it remains ineffective. Thus the RAF tried to manipulate the press to further its cause, becoming in Walter Laqueur's terms the "super-entertainers of our time." By contrast, Anna and Marcus do not want their actions to become public, because they are not making demands for systemic changes. The teenagers simply want to change their own life and can see no legal avenues for recourse. Anna and Marcus want Rottmann out of the picture until their teachers can make their decision about university applications. However, just like the Western terrorists, these two high-school students in the GDR begin to manipulate the forms of communication at their disposal. Marcus tears up the bulletin-board newspaper as a diversion technique so that he can steal into the principal's office. Anna intercepts Rottmann's letter to her parents and clandestinely reads the correspondence. She also falsifies a letter from Rottmann to the school authorities, providing a plausible cover for his disappearance. Finally, Anna, Marcus, and Anna's grandmother read Rottmann's letters from his former lover Jutta and inspect his private photographs, in order to piece together his personal history and blackmail him into conforming to their wishes. The high-schoolers' tactics are no different than those of the dominant order they oppose (school officials make up a story about Rottmann's failing health and forge a resignation letter in his name), leading the principal to assume at one point that he is being held by the Stasi. Thus while Christopher Roth's *Baader* demonstrates how the RAF ironically adopted fascist tactics of coercion to deal with a system they viewed as fascist, Andreas Dresen's *Raus aus der Haut* shows how Marcus and Anna use Stasi techniques of surveillance and blackmail to attack a representative of GDR tyranny, thereby becoming tyrants themselves. In both cases, rather than dismantling the traditional power relations, the terrorists replicate them. What separates the two films is that Dresen's characters become acutely aware of how in this process they have turned from victims into perpetrators.

Even though *Raus aus der Haut* is a comedy obviously based on fiction, it displays a remarkable sensitivity to those aspects of terrorism that make it attractive and fatal. What starts out as an exciting adventure quickly turns uncomfortable and eventually deadly. In a voice-over Marcus raves that planning the kidnapping with Anna was exhilarating, even if she was just using him: "And also, the first few days were a lot of fun, almost like being in a detective movie. We investigated Rottmann's habits and stuff like that." He admits that there was a price to pay for this illicit thrill: "If I had known what was going to happen to me, I couldn't have enjoyed this time as much."[103] The idea that victims of an unfair system could attack their oppressor and get what they wanted is a highly appealing thought. Turning the order of things around so that justice can be served has nearly biblical significance of the same magnitude as the promise that the meek shall inherit the earth. But as Markus learns, the reality of forcing justice is brutal if not cruel. When Rottmann wakes up in a cellar confronted by a mysterious masked man and held against his will for unknown reasons, suddenly the oppressor is a victim, not just helplessly shackled to a bed but a real, vulnerable human being with a weak heart. Marcus finds the perpetrator role hard to accept and is haunted by Rottmann's penetrating look, because he sees himself in the old man's eyes and must recognize that he is now responsible for someone else's suffering. Anna tries to convince him that they are doing the right thing by quoting Che Guevara ("Try the impossible!"), but Marcus counters that the ends do not always justify the means. Although he has a Che poster above his bed and dreams of majoring in Latin American Studies and traveling to Cuba, Marcus is not a revolutionary. What sounded like a good idea has become a painful reality, and the two high-schoolers adjust their image of Rottmann as they get to know him better.

Rottmann starts out as a rigid authoritarian who demands complete compliance to school rules, socialist ideals, and the party's agenda. He represents a petrified educational system and also functions as a stand-in for the entire SED leadership, which demands obedience and disciplines noncompliance. This point is visually illustrated when Rottmann walks into his office and discovers Marcus stealing evidence. The principal is shown in a close-up poised next to the ubiquitous portrait of First Secretary Erich Honecker. The similarities between the two are striking: in double form we see a balding sixty-year-old man wearing oversized horn-rimmed glasses and a suit and tie, who could just as easily signify the hated father-generation in the FRG targeted by the RAF if it were not for the party badge in his label. In captivity Rottmann argues that he does not wield power over his helpless pupils for personal reasons but because he must teach young people to think first about the collective good. He resolves that Marcus and Anna should not be allowed to study at the university "because their desires do not conform to social exigencies."[104] As the representative of the state, it is his duty to teach the next generation that they must forego desire for the sake of idealism. The principal is not asking for something from his students that he has not done himself. His lover Jutta became disillusioned with the GDR after the Prague Spring and defected to the West. Although Rottmann loved Jutta, he decided to stay in the GDR and break off contact with her, because he believed that such a sacrifice was necessary for the perpetuation of socialist ideals. This renunciation of desire proves futile, because Rottmann learns upon his release that he was forgotten by the system he served so loyally. When he tries to explain his kidnapping without much detail in order to protect Anna and Marcus, the school officials and the Stasi refuse to believe his story, stating: "Comrade Rottmann, surely you aren't seriously trying to sell us some cops and robbers story. We aren't in the FRG, after all."[105] Despite the Stasi's claim, the predatory relationship between the state and its servants looks surprisingly analogous in East and West in 1977. Rottmann has become a victim of the system he devoted his entire life to, and his situation is parallel to that of Hanns-Martin Schleyer, who commented in his last communiqué: "I really have to ask myself in my current situation, what more has to happen for Bonn finally to make a decision? I have after all been held captive by terrorists for five and a half weeks only because I have served the state and its free democratic order for years."[106] Like the RAF hostage, the school principal feels he has been sold out by the government because he has become inconvenient. Rottmann, however, never goes so far as to blame the state openly; he just quietly leaves and accepts his fate. Although he is not killed by terrorists as Schleyer was, the results are the same. Rottmann knowingly stops taking his medicine and dies of a broken heart.

In the close quarters of her grandmother's cellar, Anna and Marcus change their attitude toward their school principal. At first they are shocked to learn that this stuffy old bachelor has a personal life and that there is someone out there who loves him. They explore his personal history by reading his love letters and scrutinizing old photographs and find a happy young man, who shared an ardent and tender love with a beautiful young woman. The story of this new couple, Wilfried and Jutta, suddenly displaces the photograph of Baader and Ensslin in Paris as the archetype of love. It remains a mere surface image that the teenagers project their own desires upon, but they never come closer to understanding the terrorists as people or their relationship. By contrast, Wilfried Rottmann's life is revealed to them through Jutta's letters, and through her eyes the teenagers begin to see a complex man who is vulnerable, passionate, and even admirable. Anna in particular is impressed with Rottmann's strength and conviction. Rather than allowing himself to be intimidated by the armed kidnappers, the old man stands by his ideals and refuses to lose his dignity. Wilfried the man is able to do something that Rottmann the history teacher never could: he teaches his young pupils about the past in a way that matters to them, through their emotions and empathy with him as a human being.

Nearly every time Rottmann tries to talk about the past in his capacity as school official and disciplinarian, the young people fail to listen. At the opening assembly, he lectures about the significance of starting the school year on 1 September, the national holiday known as the International Day of Peace, which commemorates Germany's invasion of Poland in 1939 and calls for a renewed dedication to world peace. Despite the importance of this lesson, Rottmann's voice becomes mere background noise for the students, who are more interested in discussing their summer vacations. Official versions of history fall on deaf ears. When Rottmann does not show up for class because he has been kidnapped, the consequences are even more dire: history is erased. His colleague asks a student to erase the history lesson on the blackboard, and they turn to mathematics. Rottmann tries to talk with his masked captors about being interrogated by the Soviets in a prisoner-of-war camp after the Second World War, but they remain completely silent (ostensibly because he would recognize their voices), and no dialogue about the past takes place. Rottmann tries unsuccessfully to explain to Anna how after the war everyone had to do whatever was necessary to build a new society, regardless of their individual aspirations. Happy to be alive and to have a purpose, they all contributed to a fresh start together. Anna accuses Rottmann and his generation of using history as a weapon to control the present: "Come on, if we make demands, you reproach us with how difficult it was in the beginning."[107] Personal history, lived experience that defines the individual as a human being, is more convincing because the young people can empathize, and the goal of this engagement with the past is to learn about how others have coped with external circumstances. Academic history, by contrast, remains mere noise, because it instrumentalizes people's lives in order to teach a moral and to discipline society. Even contemporary history functions in this manner. Apart from the initial radio report that inspires Anna to hatch her own terrorist-type plan, she and Marcus do not pay attention to the details of the German Autumn being reported on in the television news magazine "Aktuelle Kamera." Anna has no difficulty learning about the RAF's deeds, despite the FRG's news blackout established on 6 September 1977 to thwart the terrorists' access to the media and to potential sympathizers. Ironically, in the GDR, a country where government efforts to shield its citizenry from outside influence resulted in severe censorship, the teenagers actually seem to have more access to Western news than their counterparts in the FRG. And yet they ignore contemporary history because it has no bearing on their lives. Western terrorism functions as a seductive counterimage to the boredom of everyday life in the GDR, but without a personalized story it holds no allure beyond the fact that it is forbidden.

Randy's peaceful protest holds much more significance for the young people. He demonstrates true bravery by singing the forbidden Renft song "Als ich wie ein Vogel war" at a concert marking the GDR's national Independence Day (*Tag der Republik*). This song lends the film its title and follows the characters around as a constant reminder of their lack of power to speak freely and to change themselves and their social environment. Randy sings:

When I was like a bird, who sang in the evening,
Everyone only cried sunset.
All the birds were already there, none called out.
Voiceless I flew away, as everyone slept.
At some point everyone wants out of his skin.
At some point everyone thinks about it, even if not out loud.[108]

In the metaphors of a voiceless bird and shedding skins, this song is a strong accusation against a closed and static society and represents such a threat to the status quo that the authorities literally pull the plug. The Stasi cut off the electricity and forcefully take Randy off the stage, quickly ending any demonstration of serious discontent. The high-school concert functions as a microcosm of the nation, because it parallels a historical concert on the Alexanderplatz, which also took place on 7 October 1977. A riot broke out when the authorities cut off the electricity and demanded that the crowds disperse. Although there is some dispute over the details, apparently 3 people died and 200 were injured.[109] Most importantly, the potentially disruptive power of youth subculture was demonstrated by the fact that the young people started shouting that the Wall had to go. Deprived of the symbolic protest afforded by rock-and-roll, these young people transferred their pent-up energy and frustrations to political protest.

As the Renft song makes clear with its lament that "everyone slept" and Dresen's film illustrates so well, in 1977 the nation was not ready for change. Instead the high-school students dutifully return to their classroom and sit at their desks, half-heartedly singing the assigned "Solidarity Song" by Brecht and mouthing the words: "Forward and don't forget wherein our strength lies. When starving or eating, forward and don't forget: solidarity."[110] The indifference with which the students call for solidarity is matched by the school officials' utter disregard of it in their dealings with Rottmann. In a cross-cut between the classroom and the office where Rottmann is being interrogated by the Stasi, Brecht's poems function as a bitterly ironic commentary on the GDR socialist state. After he has been discarded and forced into retirement, Rottmann leaves the school to the sounds of Brecht's poem "In Praise of Communism." The lonely figure walking with his bicycle off into the distance is accompanied only by the words: "What's wrong with Communism anyway? It is rational. Everyone understands it. It is easy. You aren't an exploiter. You can understand it. It is good for you."[111] Rottmann's quiet suicide parallels Schleyer's execution and is covered up by the authorities, who hold a solemn funeral service to laud the principal as a loyal communist. The hypocrisy goes unchallenged, because as Marcus admits in a voice-over: "We stood there, knew better, and were silent."[112] Rottmann's death represents not merely his own personal despair but also the communal loss of innocence and faith in the system. Accordingly, the film ends on a dark note. As Marcus helps load coal into the basement where he once held Rottmann captive, he grieves in a voice-over: "We prepared ourselves for a long cold winter."[113] The screen fills with coal streaming into the cellar as clouds of black smoke rise into the shaft of light from the window. The desire for self-expression and individual freedom, which was so strongly felt at the beginning and for which the characters risked nearly everything, ends with their self-imposed hibernation in inner exile. Western domestic terrorism holds no more allure in a country where, for the time being, it is impossible to shed your skin and start anew.

Der Baader Meinhof Komplex

More than thirty years after the German Autumn, the film industry marshaled many of its greatest assets to bring a sweeping epic about the history of the RAF from 1967 to 1977 to the silver screen. With a budget of 20 million euros, *Der Baader Meinhof Komplex* (The Baader Meinhof Complex) was reportedly the most expensive German film ever made, and it is characterized by a host of superlatives. Germany's most successful and highly controversial producer, the late Bernd Eichinger, oversaw the production and also delivered the screenplay, based on Stefan Aust's famous 900-page chronicle. Uli Edel was seduced back to his homeland after nearly three decades in Hollywood to direct the ambitious project. An enormous cast of 123 speaking parts was filled by many of Germany's best-known and most respected actors, including Moritz Bleibtreu, Martina Gedeck, Johanna Wokalek, Nadja Uhl, Bruno Ganz, Michael Gwisdek, Heino Ferch, Jan Josef Liefers, Tom Schilling, Stipe Erceg, Alexandra Maria Lara, and Hannah Herzsprung. Even the premiere on 16 September 2008 in Munich was accompanied by scandals that were just the kind of ready-made publicity designed to sell tickets. At a closed press showing on 14 August 2008, Constantin Film, Germany's largest production company, required journalists to sign a contract agreeing not to print anything about the film before 17 September.[114] In case of breach of contract, a penalty of 100,000 euros would be levied, 50,000 euros each for the journalist and the publication. Many critics responded with charges that Constantin was trying to control the media, and the *Süddeutsche Zeitung* notably refused to attend the showing and canceled its plans for a large spread on the film.[115] In addition, Inge Ponto, widow of Dresdner Bank chief Jürgen Ponto, who was murdered by the RAF, sued Constantin Film for falsifying history. She objected to the staging of the attack in her home, because the filmmakers had her sitting outside on the terrace in the sunshine talking on the phone while her husband was murdered in a thunderous discharge of bullets. Contrary to this portrayal, she asserted that the killers used silencers and she witnessed her husband's shooting from the next room. Mortally wounded, he made his way over

Fig. 3.4. Still from Uli Edel's Der Baader Meinhof Komplex *(2008).*
Photo © and by permission of The Kobal Collection and G. T. Film Productions.

to her and collapsed at her feet. Eichinger's response was: "If our research had shown that Mrs. Ponto had witnessed the killing of her husband in close proximity, then naturally we would have filmed it that way. I know that this will sound cynical now, but that would have enhanced the drama of the film."[116] Inge Ponto lost the case and in protest returned her Federal Cross of Merit (*Bundesverdienstkreuz*), but she won the small concession that the DVD and television broadcast would be required to note that some scenes deviated from historical reality. These scandals did not stop viewers from buying tickets. From its general release on 25 September 2008 until the end of 2009 the film garnered 2,416,341 viewers, ranking it on par with the hit *Die Welle* (The Wave, dir. Denis Gansel, 2008) but nowhere near the six million figure of the romantic comedy *Keinohrhase* (No-Ear Rabbit, dir. Til Schweiger, 2007).[117] While Edel's film received mixed reviews in the press, it won the Bavarian film prize and was nominated for the German film prize for best motion picture, the Oscar for the best foreign language film, and the Golden Globe.

Director Uli (Ulrich) Edel, born in Neuenburg am Rhein in 1947, studied at the Film and Television Academy in Munich, where he met fellow student Bernd Eichinger. The two shared an interest in Hollywood cinema and later collaborated on several projects. Edel worked as an editor and assistant for famed director Douglas Sirk, before taking on the role of director. His break-through film *Christiane F.: Wir Kinder vom*

Bahnhof Zoo (Christiane F.: We children from the Zoo station, 1981) was followed by *Last Exit to Brooklyn* (1989),[118] winner of the Bavarian film prize and the German film prize for best direction and best feature film. Both of these early films were produced by Eichinger. Unfortunately, Edel's career in Hollywood has been checkered with critical acclaim and failure. *Body of Evidence* (1993), for instance, won the dubious Razzie award for worst actress, awarded to Madonna, and the film won a further six Razzie nominations, including nods for worst director and worst feature film. For the last two-and-a-half decades Edel has worked extensively in television, directing episodes of the popular shows *Twin Peaks, Tales from the Crypt, Homicide: Life on the Street,* and *Oz,* as well as made-for-television films such as the Golden Globe and Emmy winner *Rasputin* (1996), *The Mists of Avalon* (2001), *Julius Caesar* (2002), and *Ring of the Nibelungs* (2004).

Edel's two feature films from the eighties produced by Eichinger are especially enlightening for the current discussion. *Christiane F.: Wir Kinder vom Bahnhof Zoo* is based on journalists Horst Rieck and Kai Hermann's reportage about the Berlin teenage drug scene first published in installments in *Stern* magazine and then in book form in 1978. Shot in Berlin on original locations using amateur actors and documentary-style camerawork, the film is a harrowing reenactment of real-life drug addict and child prostitute Christiane F.'s downward spiral. What Michael Schwarze wrote about the Edel-Eichinger film in 1981 reflects many of the issues concerning their newest endeavor: "*We Children from the Zoo Station* is for the most part nothing more than a timid illustration of a bestseller. The effort at authenticity is unmistakable, but too often it seems like an escape from the necessity of translating a book into an independent world of cinematic images." Schwarze concludes: "Certainly it shows what is normally hidden, the shadow existence of junkies at subway stations, dingy toilets, but the film does not grab, doesn't move, doesn't make one feel especially affected. *We Children from the Zoo Station* is a film that lacks rage and vehemence."[119]

Last Exit to Brooklyn is a gritty social drama of life on the mean streets of Brooklyn in the 1950s and is based on Hubert Selby Jr.'s 1964 best-selling cult classic. It was filmed in the Red Hook neighborhood of Brooklyn in August 1988 but released only in 1990.[120] The film weaves Selby's six separate life stories into a comprehensive linear narrative and follows the original work fairly closely by examining the discontent and desperation of the underclass, which stands in stark contrast to the myth of American postwar prosperity. The film is set against the background of a workers' strike in the slums of Brooklyn; the characters face a brutal world, partially the result of the oppressive capitalist, conformist system and partially of their own making because of ignorance, greed, and uncontrolled, self-destructive rage. Edel's dark, hyperrealist style and gloomy sets correspond to the bleak reality of teenage pregnancy, gang-rape, union strikes, violent beatings, and vicious gay bashing. *New York Times* film critic Vincent Canby praised the film for its handling of large-scale riot scenes, where workers are attacked with water cannons, and its nearly documentary look, which produces a notable sense of authenticity. This veracity, however, comes at the cost of emotional detachment because "it sees everything at the distance of a sober-minded alien observer."[121]

Uli Edel sees the three films as variations on a theme:

> For me, *The Baader Meinhof Complex* is the third part of a trilogy about violence that Bernd and I began with *Christiane F.: We Children from the Zoo Station* and continued with *Last Exit to Brooklyn*. *Last Exit to Brooklyn* is about social violence, *The Baader Meinhof Complex* is about political violence, and *Christiane F.* is about the violence we commit against ourselves.[122]

Working in each case with a bestselling literary or journalistic text noted for its realistic and often gritty portrayal of violence, which lends the film an aura of legitimacy, Edel employs a documentary-like approach to the camerawork, reenacts the original on location, pays strict attention to historical details, blocks viewer identification with characters on an emotional level, and refuses to create a narrative perspective that results in a psychological explanation for violence. If viewers are looking for an answer to the question of what drives individuals to inflict such self-destructive rage on themselves and devastating injury to others and how to prevent such real-life horrors, then they will be sorely disappointed with this film trilogy.

In a series of interviews and press releases, Eichinger and Edel stressed that *Der Baader Meinhof Komplex* was informed by the same overarching interest in authenticity as they had practiced in early collaborations. Since Eichinger based his screenplay on Stephan Aust's eponymous book published in 1985, the film builds on the personal reputation of this celebrated journalist and eyewitness to history. Aust served as a junior editor for the literary magazine *konkret*, worked closely with its founder Klaus Rainer Röhl and his wife, columnist Ulrike Meinhof, and personally rescued their daughters from being sent to a Palestinian orphanage in 1970. His chronicle of the RAF has long served as an insider's view of the period. In addition, Aust's position as editor-in-chief of *Der Spiegel*, Germany's leading news magazine, lends the film a validity that a fictionalized screenplay would not. Eichinger intended this film to be revolutionary in form and to break with traditional notions of viewer identification and conventional narrative structure: "There are no identification figures in *Der Baader Meinhof Komplex*. . . . The speed of events turns into an undertow, a rapidly moving current, and the viewer knows: sometime soon the waterfall is coming and there has to be a violent end."[123] Referring to his approach as *Fetzendramaturgie* (shredded dramaturgy),

Eichinger sees the film as a large puzzle that viewers have to put together themselves. He adamantly rejects the idea of identification with the main characters: "I did not want to attach the story emotionally to a specific figure — whether a member of the RAF or a representative of state authority. If I had done that, I would have inevitably provided the interpretation — and that's exactly what I wanted to avoid. I wanted the film to ask questions and not provide easy answers."[124] Uli Edel concurs: "In this film I wanted to avoid everything that a filmmaker would typically do in a genre movie. . . . Authenticity was called for. Just as we did in *Christiane F.*, we followed the principles of *cinéma vérité* and not those of a fictional film."[125]

Every attempt was made to film in the original locations where historical events took place. Edel used handheld cameras and little artificial light to get a natural look, embedded historical news footage, and avoided computer-generated images or special effects, in order to render the historical events as reliably as possible. Against criticism that he overemphasizes the violent assaults, Edel counters that his team paid careful attention to details and based the number of bullets fired on evidence from police reports: "People probably won't believe how much shooting took place. In the Schleyer kidnapping, for example, 107 bullet casings were found at the scene and up to 30 entry wounds in the bodies. In the case of the Buback, 15 shots were fired and that's what I show in the film, not 20 or 30."[126]

The filmmakers aim at realism by focusing on events and are vehemently opposed to a psychological approach that would try to get at the root of personal motivation. Eichinger maintains:

> The film will not give many people what they want: explanations. I do not know what kind of person Ulrike Meinhof really was. I can only tell what she did. At the beginning she said: I could never leave my children. Then she not only left her children, she was going to send them away to a Palestinian camp forever! Because she believed that the revolution demanded such sacrifices. One cannot understand such a thing, even if one tries to fathom it. I can only write: she did it.[127]

In much the same vein, Edel notes that forty years of recycled images of the RAF have contributed to a mythologizing of the past. Rejecting the notion of identification figures and an exploration of psychological motivation because they are tools for mythologizing things that can never be verified, he states:

> We opened up the collective memory drawer and looked very closely at what is inside. This type of critical analysis is the key to making sure the film reaches the public. Without psychologizing. Ever since

Aristotle we have known that there is no such thing as characterization; a human being shows his character when he acts. We are what
we do — not what we say.[128]

A closer look at the film's opening should suffice to illustrate that
even without psychological inquiry and strong identification figures, Edel
and Eichinger's film has a clear moral to tell despite its rambling narrative
of countless events strung together without a traditional story arc. Their
main moral lesson is taught in the first ten minutes of the film and guides
the logic of the next 140 minutes, which are filled with examples demonstrating how the basic conflict intensified over the years. The film portrays
the Federal Republic as a repressive, authoritarian society that reacted to
peaceful democratic protest with excessive brutality and inspired a group
of young people to retaliate with ever-increasing bloodshed in a deadly
game of violence, which then escalated. The government, despite a few
isolated voices of reason, refused to engage in productive conversation
with the youth until it was too late. More importantly, the state never
addressed the deeper social ruptures that had given birth to the protest in
the first place. Despite their reliance on Aust's chronicle, documentary-
like camerawork, and attention to historical details, Edel and Eichinger's
film is as much a construction of the past based on selection, arrangement, and control of information as any fictionalized historical drama or
documentary film would be. Authenticity is as elusive as truth, and their
film has a moralistic perspective, even if it is not conveyed via identification or affective relationships with characters. Indeed, as I will argue
here, their film delivers a plethora of moralistic perspectives, which allows
the viewer to pick and choose which string of truth to follow. Thus they
deliver the ultimate consensus film. Rather than asking the audience to
consider individual human behavior, they see the fault for violence in
societal structures and offer up a series of competing, ambivalent morals
that cannot be easily disentangled. With its numerous threads the film
invites and in the end forces viewers to pick whichever one appeals to
them if they are ever going to make any sense of the film.

Der Baader Meinhof Komplex opens with five consecutive scenes that
seem disjointed but are linked through music, voice-overs, crosscuts, and
a contemporaneous timeframe that set the stage for both the film's central idea and the narrative logic of the entire film. In the first ten minutes there is a black screen introducing the title and filmmakers, a scene
at the beach in Sylt, a garden party in Sylt, a demonstration in Berlin
that turns into a riot, and a television talk show analyzing the riot. The
black screen and white title, scratched to indicate age, appear first and are
accompanied by Janice Joplin's a cappella rendition of "Mercedes Benz,"
a very brief scene that highlights both the dubious reliability of historical "authenticity" and the ambivalence of social protest in the decade

between 1967 and 1977. Although Joplin recorded this song in October 1970 shortly before her death from a heroin overdose, Edel uses it
as nondiegetic music to comment on the atmosphere in West Germany
three years earlier in 1967. Joplin's prayer equating material goods with
happiness and "making amends" with consumption is a satirical take on
a world governed by possessions. It also reflects a notable ambivalence of
this era. Janis Joplin blasted conformist, status-conscious greed that led
people to want a Mercedes Benz luxury car, yet she herself owned a psy-
chedelic Porsche convertible. In a similar manner, Ulrike Meinhof operates on a double standard. She chastises Empress Farah Pahlavi for saying
that "like most Persians" she vacations on the Caspian Sea, when in truth
most of her subjects live in extreme poverty and hardship. Meinhof con-
demns Farah Pahlavi's unreflected life of luxury and privilege at the same
time as she seems to suffer from much the same blind spot. Meinhof is
portrayed as likewise vacationing at the sea and enjoying a garden party
in a beautiful villa filled with fashionably dressed guests without giving
much thought to her own carefree life of bourgeois wealth and leisure.

Janice Joplin's *Mercedes Benz* forms the musical bridge from the title
sequence to the very first scene, which features Ulrike Meinhof vacationing with her husband, Klaus Rainer Röhl, and their two daughters in Sylt.
The idyllic setting at a nude beach where the children frolic in the water
is quickly revealed to be a mere illusion, for there is trouble in paradise,
both in the marriage and in the nation. Meinhof catches her husband
looking at another woman with too much interest while she is reading
in a lifestyle magazine about the Shah of Iran's visit to Berlin. Just as
her husband will prove unfaithful, the FRG will expose itself as a brutally
repressive state lurking behind a prosperous and peaceful facade.

In the second scene at the garden party in Sylt Meinhof reads her
commentary addressed to Farah Pahlavi and the scene crosscuts several
times to the Shah of Iran's visit to the opera in Berlin and the riot that
ensued on the evening of 2 June 1967. The first images outside the opera
draw the lines for a clear-cut confrontation. On the left there is a single
vertical row of policemen that continues as far as the eye can see and on
the right is an equally long row of spectators crowded between a barricade
and a wall, some people wearing a paper bag over their head with images
of the Shah and his wife, others waving Iranian and German flags. A city
bus arrives, delivering the so-called *Jubelperser*, Iranian men, including
members of the Iranian secret police, whose job it was to welcome the
Shah with enthusiastic cheering. After an unseen hand throws a bag or
two of flour and students start chanting "Shah, Shah, Charlatan!" the
Jubelperser break off the signs from their long wooden slats and attack the
defenseless demonstrators to relentless pulsating, repetitive music. The
police look on without making any moves to protect the crowd, including
old people and a woman thrown to the ground and bleeding from a head

wound. A mounted policeman strikes a young man with a nightstick and on cue an entire phalanx of policemen storms the German spectators and begin to beat them, indiscriminately and without provocation. The scene quickly turns into chaos. Storming from the right, mounted police surrounded by foot soldiers chase the unarmed young people down, beating them with nightsticks. From the left, water cannons fire into the crowds and directly into the camera. The mounted police then begin to herd the protestors from every direction and the scene develops an excessive, surreal quality as if it were a science-fiction thriller and the police were alien monsters intent upon hunting down human beings like animals. The three-minute riot sequence is shot exclusively with hand-held cameras at shoulder height, often from within the crowd. There are no crane shots that could give an overview of the situation and so the camerawork contributes to the sense of immediacy and the feeling that the viewer is placed in the middle of the action. The scene ends with Benno Ohnesorg shot dead by plainclothes detective Karl-Heinz Kurras, who in 2009 was exposed as a former spy for the Stasi.[129] With this fatal shot the pulsating musical score is replaced by the sound of rushing water, as if one were hearing it from inside Ohnesorg's head, indicating both his approaching death and the fact that history is in the making.

The scene then cuts to Ulrike Meinhof on a television talk show discussing the consequences of the riot. Meinhof calmly declares:

> In the right-wing press the guilt for the catastrophe of 2 June is placed squarely on the students' shoulders. Above all the Springer Corporation is trying in its newspaper to demonize the critical voice of students as troublemakers and hooligans. . . . The truth is that the protests of these students have exposed our state as a police state, that the police and press terror on 2 June in Berlin reached a climax, and that we understand that freedom in this state means freedom for the police nightstick.[130]

If one takes the first ten minutes of *Der Baader Meinhof Komplex* as a cohesive unit, then the rather sympathetic Meinhof's words confirm an interpretation of the riot just presented and one that matches Eichinger's own notion of the film's overall message. According to Eichinger: "The story begins in an idyll and ends in a bloodbath like in a Greek tragedy, but with the difference that here it dealt with a bitter reality."[131] Meinhof's reading of the situation seems plausible, because the audience has just seen Iranian secret police beating peaceful student protestors while the German authorities did nothing to stop it. Worse still, the German police then joined in the brutal attack, thereby exposing Germany as a police state, like Iran, where terror and assaults are used to stop democratic assembly.

There are several reasons why this ten-minute sequence deserves greater scrutiny. First, its placement at the beginning of the film in this specific order lends it a privileged position, since the viewer will begin at this stage to frame events into a logical narrative. Going from a state of innocence in a Garden of Eden to a bloodbath and ending with a refusal to demonize the students leaves only one culprit — the police are responsible for this fall from grace. Second, considering the importance historians have given to Ohnesorg's death as the single most important event that radicalized the student movement and led to the formation of the RAF, it seems valid to question the accuracy of this cinematic depiction. Finally, Edel and Eichinger advertised their desire to present the most historically accurate and objective chronicle of events. So what is historically verifiable and what is fictionalized out of expediency and in the name of artistic freedom?

The most noticeable choice of artistic freedom is the conflation of two historic events that took place on 2 June 1967 into one. The scene with Iranians attacking students, police on horseback, and water cannons took place not at the opera in the evening but miles away in Schöneberg hours earlier. According to historical accounts, a dozen Jubelperser attacked a group of about 400 student protestors earlier in the day at the Schöneberg city hall during the Shah's visit with the mayor. Police stood by and watched the attack but did nothing to stop the Iranians from injuring dozens of protestors. As things escalated, police on horseback using nightsticks and water cannons were used to control the crowd. The scene later that evening at the German Opera thus began with heightened tensions. Police were already on high alert, because less than one month earlier the *Kommune Eins* had called for a symbolic attack on US Vice President Hubert Humphrey during his planned trip to Berlin. Earlier in the week a wanted poster featuring the Shah was distributed in Charlottenburg that charged him with murder, torture, and exploitation. The wanted poster challenged Berliners to act, using language reminiscent of Nazi rhetoric against its enemies: "We ask citizens to support energetically all actions that lead to rendering this perpetrator harmless [Unschädlichmachung des Täters]."[132] According to information provided by Michael Müller, an eyewitness reporter for the *Berliner Morgenpost*, students who were angered by the demonstration in Schöneberg were more prepared for confrontation: "When the Shah, Farah Diba, and Mayor Albertz arrived at 7:56 p.m. [reporter] Michael Müller saw 'all hell break out.' From the opposite sidewalk eggs filled with paint, rotten tomatoes, and even stones started flying in the direction of the opera."[133] For more than an hour students had been calling police "fascists" and "SS henchmen," "at least two police officers were injured; one collapsed before the evacuation began and was bleeding profusely from a head wound, clearly having been hit with a rock."[134] Berlin Police Chief Erich Duensing ordered the clearing of demonstrators and specifically ordered that water cannons not be used to avoid panic. The plan was twofold. Police were to go "fox hunting"; plainclothes detectives would weed out agitators and collect their names and addresses. Using a "sausage procedure" police would start at the center and disperse the crowd on both ends. An announcement over the loudspeaker falsely claiming that a policeman had been stabbed (and not hit in the head with a rock) may well have riled the other policemen, because they started beating demonstrators and unleashed the worst police assault on civilians in the history of the FRG. It ended with a West German policeman who was secretly working as an informant for the Stasi shooting and killing an unarmed twenty-five-year-old student of German literature.

Edel and Eichinger use artistic freedom to summarize a great deal of information in the short span of ten minutes. Conflating events is commonplace and nearly unavoidable in the genre of history film. In this case it certainly does not change the outcome of events. Ohnesorg was dead, and his death at the hands of a policeman would galvanize the youth in ways that the authorities could not have foreseen. The staging of the riot, however, makes the police action seem more calculated, brutal, and unprovoked, with the result that the blame for starting the violence appears to lie on their side alone. The lack of background on how demonstrators also escalated the situation in the weeks before 2 June and throughout that day creates a scenario where the police are the sole aggressors and the students are innocent victims. Moreover, even without traditional heroes and emotional connections to main characters, a moral evolves that will color all subsequent scenes and will help viewers to frame history in an us-versus-them schemata.

Despite the filmmakers' rejection of identification figures as a structuring principle for *Der Baader Meinhof Komplex*, two characters help to frame the linear narrative and give it some consistency, if not moments of interpretation. Ulrike Meinhof functions as a terrifying example, and Horst Herold serves as a quasi-narrator and social critic.

The film introduces Ulrike Meinhof as the very first character, and she is portrayed with more personal details than any other character in the film. In the brief opening scenes in Sylt she is shown to be a wife and mother who has a successful career, a modest and almost shy woman who does not seek the limelight but when encouraged displays confidence and eloquence. Above all she is a perceptive observer, of both her husband's questionable behavior and the greater social issues unfolding in Germany. Meinhof continues to observe and comment on developments, but as the tensions grow, she begins to take small steps toward action, at first merely passing rocks to rioters after the assassination attempt on Dutschke. Her encounter with Gudrun Ensslin, however, is the fateful event that will put her on the path to terrorism. Even before they meet in person, Meinhof is seen watching Stefan Aust interviewing Gudrun's parents during the arson trial (a fictionalized scene since Aust was not the reporter who conducted this well-known interview). Gudrun's mother reveals: "I feel that she has produced something liberating with her deed, even in the family. Suddenly I feel myself freed from the narrowness and also the fear that determined my life before. She took away my fear."[135] Meinhof observes this conversation with great interest and seems fascinated by the idea that action can mean liberation. As if to see for herself the nearly magical powers of this woman who can take away fear, Meinhof is shown in the very next scene interviewing Ensslin in jail. The reporter questions the arsonist about her motivations, and Ensslin explains:

> You have to understand it as rebellion. This time we will not look on without acting, the way fascism expanded under Hitler. This time we are going to resist. We have a responsibility to history. . . . When they start knocking our people off as they did with Ohnesorg and Dutschke, then in the future we'll shoot back.[136]

In one of the strongest arguments made in the film, Gudrun maps out a critical relationship between the fascist past and the spirit of the student movement. The young people refuse to adopt a passive approach to the social and political conflicts taking place before their eyes. As children who have inherited the horrific historical legacy of the Third Reich, they refuse to behave like their parents' generation and merely watch things evolve at a safe distance. Meinhof is shocked to learn that Ensslin intends to use violence if necessary, but Ensslin reproaches the reporter for her naiveté and taunts her with the question: "Or do you really believe that you are changing anything with your theoretical jerking off?"[137] Clearly Ensslin gets under her skin, because Meinhof begins to play with her fingers nervously, revealing that this is her Achilles' heel and will remain so throughout the film. As a commentator whose job it is to watch things from a safe distance and interpret other people's deeds, Meinhof longs to act. Both Ensslin and Baader taunt others into action and will go to extraordinary lengths to demonstrate that the individual must be ready to sacrifice the most personal and sacred relationships for a higher cause. Thus once Meinhof makes the leap into the underground, her first communiqué stating "naturally one may shoot" seems to be as much a response to Ensslin as a declaration of intent to the authorities. Meinhof, however, remains reflective and submissive in her personal life; she just watches as Ensslin betrays her lover Peter Hoffmann by telling the PLO he is an Israeli spy, and arranges for her two daughters to be sent to a Palestinian orphanage. Meinhof's hysterical crying fit when arrested and her transformation into a hallucinating neurotic in solitary confinement are glimpses into her psyche that other characters are not afforded. The only comparable scene is when Ensslin is walking around Hamburg in a heightened state of paranoia. In both instances the jerky camerawork and fast-motion editing deviate considerably from the more common realistic rendering of events and poignantly demonstrate the women's delusional mental state. In the confines of Stammheim prison, faced with Ensslin's constant badgering and her own guilt, Meinhof is driven to suicide. As the most public figure among the RAF terrorists, Meinhof's development from an intellectual seduced by revolutionary violence to someone destroyed by it provides a connective tissue for the film narrative and demonstrates the personal losses inherent in succumbing to the fatal allure of terrorism.

If Meinhof is a semi-identification figure, then Horst Herold is the film's fleeting narrator and interpreter of both the state and the terrorists' agendas. Like Christopher Roth's Kurt Krone in *Baader*, the figure of the federal police commissioner (BKA) functions as the voice of reason. Although he is charged with capturing the terrorists and emphatically rejects their methods, he recognizes that there are serious social problems that need to be addressed. In conversations with his assistant Koch, an invented figure to aid dialogue based on the BKA chief's actual statements, Herold reflects on the motivations of the RAF. He prophesies at the beginning that the conflict will only intensify as long as groups like the RAF think that they need to awaken an apathetic society to injustice: "I think that groups who feel the circumstances are oppressive, and I mean here existentially oppressive, that they will not hesitate to throw bombs into the conscience of a society that from their perspective is encrusted."[138] Herold is often pictured seated alone in his office, quietly watching the news and reading terrorist communiqués. His idea to create a massive computer database encompassing seemingly insignificant details on every citizen's personal life and then turning this information into a dragnet to find the terrorists is outlined briefly but effectively. The depiction of computer-aided surveillance of the populace takes a slightly different spin here than in other films about the RAF. The threat of the loss of privacy and the intrusion of the German government into its citizens' personal life is underplayed, and the focus turns instead to the ultimate big brother, the United States. Herold and his assistant Koch give a tour of the computer room to US military and government officials and instruct them in English about the possibilities of using computer technology to combat terror. As the conflict continues, Herold notes that the state is concentrating too much attention on trying to control violent opposition instead of addressing the underlying issues: "It is not the police but the political powers that have to change the circumstances under which terrorism arises."[139] Moreover, he sees the RAF as part of a global phenomenon. As long as global systemic problems are ignored, terrorism will continue and will replace traditional warfare as the primary means to address political conflicts that lie beyond the reach of one single country. Herold concludes that the fault for terrorism cannot lie with the terrorists alone: "It is also our ignorance that fosters terrorism."[140] Herold's insights into the dynamics of terrorism are not merely a commentary on developments in Germany in the seventies but can stand as an interpretation of the underlying causes of 9/11, which might not be easily said in a contemporary setting. Eichinger's choice to have Herold and Koch present the German model for a computer-aided dragnet to exclusively American officials (in stark contrast to Christopher Roth's *Baader*, which has a similar scene but includes an ethnically diverse group of diplomats), allows for these generalized statements about the persistence of international terrorism to be read as a critique of current US policy in the so-called war on terror.

Film critics largely considered *Der Baader Meinhof Komplex* an action film that moves from one act of violence to the next with such speed that it becomes merely a series of shoot-outs, assassinations, bank robberies, kidnappings, and bombings without the benefit of a plotline. Michael Althen went so far as to call the film "polit-porn" because it consists of mere climaxes.[141] Many found the violence gratuitous, and indeed Uli Edel does not shy away from depicting bloodshed with disturbing details. He insisted that all the actors playing terrorists take lessons on how to use guns so that they could portray the sheer physical force of discharging a weapon in a convincing manner. The RAF evolves into calculating and bloodthirsty murderers. The second generation, in particular, executes its targets with a confidence and ramrod body posture that is diametrically opposed to the victims, who jerk and rebound as bullets enter their bodies, with the camera recording the assault in close proximity. The back and forth between police and terrorists, each side using excessive force to make their point and escalating the violence at each step in a fruitless attempt to get the other side's attention and change their behavior, is illustrated very well in the course of the film. We see police disciplining protestors, clubbing displaced youth in detention centers, and beating Holger Meins in an act of revenge, and prison guards callously allowing Meins to die of starvation. RAF terrorists pay back in kind by shooting leading political and economic figures in their homes and cars, blowing up police stations, US army facilities, and the Springer Corporation newspaper offices, all captured with a meticulous attention to historical and intimate details. Considering Edel and Eichinger's stated interest in providing a chronicle of events, what is missing from their depiction of escalating violence takes on heightened significance. Notably, the audience never sees Meinhof, Baader, Raspe, and Ensslin committing suicide. This may seem like a minor detail, but the question of whether the RAF leaders actually killed themselves or were executed has been a serious point of contention over the years. Gudrun Ensslin is shown planting the seed of uncertainty by telling the pastors that she has documents in her cell meant for the chancellor in case of her untimely death (documents never found). After they are discovered dead in their cells, the scene cuts to Brigitte Mohnhaupt speaking to the devastated second generation and declaring that the first generation chose death: "They aren't victims and never were. . . . They determined their situation themselves up to the last moment. That means that they did it and not that it was done to them. . . . You never knew these people. Stop seeing them like they never were."[142] For a motion picture that has placed so much value in the *act* speaking for itself, it is jarring to be confronted with the mere word. Rather than witnessing their suicide as we have watched beatings, kidnappings, murders, forced feedings, and explosions for two and a half hours, we are suddenly given an *interpretation* of events that remain unseen.

Mohnhaupt's admonishment is thus directed to the audience as much as to the second generation, coming as the last word before we see Schleyer's corpse hit the ground in a final close-up. So what are the myths viewers are supposed to reject, the preconceived ideas that have turned real-life individuals and a marginal terrorist group into a myth? Sufficient attention is given to the RAF leadership to forge some understanding of their personalities, but many of the conclusions correspond to standard arguments from history books (including Aust's). Baader was a charming adrenalin-addicted bully, who had little interest in political philosophy and was primarily in it for the action. Ensslin was a fanatic caught up in a euphoric state of "saintly self-realization," as her father put it. Together Baader and Ensslin were a force to reckon with and highly manipulative, if not cruel, but somehow alluring and compelling. Meins suffered from a Jesus complex and became a martyr for the cause. Meinhof was an intellectual seduced into the underground by the allure of concrete action and then caught up in events she could not control. Edel's film adroitly presents these characterizations of the RAF leadership, but they do not deviate from historical accounts and cannot be considered the debunking of a myth. Or are the myths a much broader confluence of events and ideas? *Der Baader Meinhof Komplex* illustrates in admirable fashion how the RAF was deeply moved by the horrors of the Vietnam War, the Palestinian independence movement, the assassination of charismatic reformers and revolutionaries across the globe, and the revolts from Paris to Mexico City to Prague, and felt justified in attacking their own government and institutions to draw attention to these injustices. They were also motivated by the public's passivity during the Third Reich and vowed not to repeat the mistakes of the past; they intended to act against injustice at any cost. Finally, they saw consumption as a form of terror against the population because it kept them preoccupied with material goods and diverted their attention away from injustice. Again, Edel conveys these political motivations via dialogue, voice-overs, and embedded news footage, but as former German Minister of the Interior Gerhart Baum wrote about the film in *Die Zeit*: "It offers absolutely no new findings, and it gives no reason whatsoever to rewrite the history of German terrorism."[143] Or are audiences supposed to reject the notion that some people joined up to gain a sense of belonging to a family, some were enticed by the thrill of holding a gun, while others sought a venue for the release of sexual and violent impulses, all motivations argued by historians and demonstrated in the film?

If there is any single myth that might be broken in this film, it is that the RAF was made up not of harmless dreamers but rather of calculated killers. According to statements made by both Edel and Eichinger this was their intention, but it is debatable whether audiences will walk away with this reading of the RAF. The very fact that the terrorists are played by the country's best and most famous actors is *unheimlich* and gives the RAF a familiarity and to some extent a sympathy that is difficult to measure, let alone overcome. Unlike Christopher Roth, who presented Baader as a hip outlaw with little interest in politics, Edel and Eichinger give ample attention to the group's political ideology and their rage over concrete international conflicts and inequalities. Thus it does more to propagate rather than demystify the image of the RAF as misunderstood intellectuals, who despite their wrong methods were idealists. The benevolent figure of Herold, who is isolated from the real world and represents moral judgment more than state authority, repeatedly stresses that the RAF are exposing significant global problems that need to be solved collectively. Moreover, the black-and-white depiction of the conflict between police and dissenters, without any room for shades of gray, established at the onset and maintained throughout the film, may well prevent such a clear-cut debunking of the myth that the RAF were misguided idealists. In the last few minutes of *Der Baader Meinhof Komplex*, the viewer is reminded of the dire consequences of the state's unwillingness to listen to youthful protest and make some concessions. More than five weeks after Schleyer's kidnapping and after the Palestinian hijackers arrive in Mogadishu, an anonymous senior government official comes to Stammheim prison to speak with Andreas Baader in person. Baader calmly explains that the spiral of violence will continue and that in retrospect the RAF first generation will appear reasonable in comparison to the convicted killers in the second and third generations. Baader's calm and reasonable demeanor when a representative of the state finally sits down to talk to him seems to be the long-awaited resolution that the film set up from the beginning. If the state had calmly addressed the youth's concerns, perhaps all the bloodshed could have been avoided.

The film ends with Bob Dylan's song "Blowing in the Wind," suggesting that like so many other existential questions, the RAF will always remain an enigma. Writing for the *Süddeutsche Zeitung*, Thomas Kniebe argues that *Der Baader Meinhof Komplex*'s refusal to take a stance is ultimately a slick marketing strategy:

Actually the political and ideological ambiguity of the film is surely intentional — a blockbuster strategy imported from Hollywood. The more intelligent big-time entertainment over there has for some time included targeted political charades — see for instance most recently *The Dark Knight*: here a morsel for the proponents of vigilantism, there a wink for the enemies of a surveillance state. Everyone gets to see what he wants to see, and in the end everything neutralizes everything else. Eichinger and Edel also do the same thing, cleverly riding the wave of the zeitgeist — only, the trend they are serving has already become stale.[144]

While I would argue that *Der Baader Meinhof Komplex* does take a stance, it could easily be overlooked considering the film's extended length, countless figures, accelerated pace, and lack of a traditional story arc. The more than two million viewers to date have been given so much material to digest in such a short period that one must wonder what won in the battle for their attention: star allure, shoot-outs, a flood of images, or history lessons?

The Fatal Attraction of Terrorism

The cinema has latched on to the history of German terrorism with such vehemence for a number of reasons. The fact that this urban guerilla movement persisted in some shape and form for three decades and its history spanned both West and East Germany gives the RAF a unique ability to function as the backdrop for an exploration of national identity. Moreover, interest in the RAF has not subsided, because many of the issues that engaged the nation in the past have not been resolved and most likely will not be in the foreseeable future. The conflicts between the state and this small oppositional group resulted in decades of destruction and ideological struggle that represents the most extreme reaction to a core of questions defining postwar national identity. If one looks somewhat objectively at the RAF's agenda, then one can see that their primary concerns are at the heart of a debate about what it means to inherit an unwanted past and forge a new identity in the present.

In the late sixties there was a deeply rooted desire to break with the past, an immediate past that was filled with collective guilt over unfathomable atrocities perpetrated in the name of the German nation, and perhaps even more unforgivable, a past in which the vast majority of people watched what was happening and did nothing to stop it. Today the National Socialist past has moved into a more distant history, but the postwar imperative "never again" continues to define one of the most cherished and ingrained national values in Germany today. Collective responsibility for peace was an idea promulgated for more than four cold-war decades by allied occupiers and by German intellectuals, teachers, religious leaders, parents, and politicians. The idea that representatives of the first generation to grow up after the Second World War would take this lesson to heart and use violence against the state to promote their concept of peace is a paradox that may never be unraveled. The universal question of whether one should ever resort to violence and take up arms against a system perceived as unjust has a special meaning in Germany and cannot be separated from national history. Uli Edel's *Der Baader Meinhof Komplex* shows particularly well how the Vietnam War profoundly affected German youth, who drew parallels between the Second World War and a far-off war in Vietnam propagated by the victorious US army occupying a foreign country — and their own country. Ironically, this youth called for exactly the kind of moral outrage that the American occupiers had tried to instill in the German population via the reeducation program starting in 1945. Gudrun Ensslin, played by Johanna Wokalek in Edel's film, captures brilliantly this rage against the father-generation with a mixture of righteous indignation, impatience, and determination to act. The fact that she is depicted as a manipulative and cruel woman does not deter from her representative quality as the voice of her generation, although it does humanize her and begins to explain how Ensslin was able to transform from a protester into a terrorist. Her statement at her trial that she participated in arson to protest against the apathy with which people accepted the Vietnam War is directed specifically at her parents. In a reaction shot taken from their seats in the courtroom, the audience sees Gudrun explain to the generation that tolerated Auschwitz: "We have learned that speaking without acting is unjust."[145]

The Red Army Faction voiced indignation over so-called *Konsumterror*, the pressures of a materialistic society, and their critique of consumption as an intentional ploy by the powers that be to divert attention from serious social problems continues to be a hallmark of the contemporary protest culture in Germany. However, serious debate about economic and social inequalities, both domestic and international, routinely occurs in mainstream media and political forums. The question of how to create a truly just economic order is anything but a marginal topic: it is at the very core of political engagement across party lines. Despite the collapse of the GDR and the discrediting of Communism as a viable state form, the abiding desire for a more equal distribution of wealth and a value system based on something other than money and status is palpable. Considering that there is no longer an alternative German state whose declared purpose is to enforce such a moral imperative, this common social value is expressed in stories about the past, which often convey nostalgia for a time when this idea was cherished and supported with greater enthusiasm. Rita's speech in Schlöndorff's *Die Stille nach dem Schuss*, where she tries to rally her coworkers to continue believing in socialism, taps into this longing for a better world and poignantly expresses people's sadness over the passing of an era.

Even if audiences do not accept the RAF's political ideology, the sheer force of their protest against the establishment is impressive, and their youth and vitality, let alone their erotic aura, make them captivating. In *Baader* Christopher Roth concentrates on the surface images and the way in which the RAF embodied a mesmerizing mixture of sexual energy, speed, and violent discharge. In contrast, Andreas Dresen approaches the RAF's alluring protest from another direction. In *Raus aus der Haut* he concentrates on how this group of terrorists stood for a model of counterculture and opposition to conformity that in the end proved to be a recipe for turning victims into perpetrators.

Although none of the films under discussion focuses primarily on the security dilemma, they do refer to the crisis instigated by terrorism that led the state to develop computer-aided surveillance systems. Recent German history is replete with examples of the government collecting information on ordinary citizens, using secret police to observe every aspect of one's private life, and disciplining dissidents. Motion pictures have explored the link between the Gestapo under National Socialism, the Stasi in the GDR, and the computer-aided surveillance system developed to combat the RAF and have addressed how these security measures may be effective as a deterrent because they contribute to a mindset of self-censure. This domestic issue is part of an international problem that has become more acute since 9/11. The fear of violence and excessive reactions to security continue to be a prominent theme in German films, regardless of their historical setting. A recent film that taps into this dilemma is Austrian director Christian Frosch's *Weiße Lilien* (White lilies, 2007), a futuristic, surreal vision of Neustadt, a fortified new city that promises total security service and delivers a nightmarish realm of control, violence, and paranoia.

The abiding interest in the history of the RAF also reflects the need for idealistic collective national heroes, strong and fearless people who were united in their belief in the attainability of social justice and were willing to risk their lives to see their plans through to completion. The fact that the RAF's admirable idealism came at the cost of murder, kidnapping, bombings, a heightened security dilemma, a loss of privacy for everyone, and mass fear is the kind of paradox that leads to mythmaking. Considering the RAF's ability to repel and attract at the same time and with equal force, it might be helpful to consider German homegrown terrorism as a type of monster and RAF films as sharing with horror films a deadly fascination with the unknowable. In many ways, horror films allow society to create the monster it needs for today, a surface on which to project a horrible vision of all that cannot be understood and that draws us into its lair, where society must face its collective demons.

Notes

[1] The origins of the Red Army Faction are generally dated with the Frankfurt department store arson on 2 April 1968. The term "Rote Armee" (Red Army) was first used in the communiqué issued after Baader's escape from prison.

[2] "Gewalt kann nur mit Gewalt beantwortet werden. Dies ist die Generation von Auschwitz — mit denen kann man nicht argumentieren!" Quoted in Stefan Aust, *Der Baader Meinhof Komplex*, 8th ed. (Munich: Goldmann, 1998), 60. Ensslin reportedly made this statement in a meeting held at the SDS building shortly after Benno Ohnesorg was shot to death by police at a demonstration against the Shah of Iran's visit to Berlin. Recently the authenticity of this statement has been called into question. Compare, for instance, Gerd Koenen, *Vesper, Ensslin, Baader: Urszenen des deutschen Terrorismus* (Frankfurt am Main: Fischer, 2005), 124.

[3] In a similar vein, Philip Gröning's controversial film *Die Terroristen* (The terrorists, 1992) depicts three terrorists who are so disturbed by the *Wende* and German reunification that they plan to assassinate Chancellor Helmut Kohl. Kohl was outraged by the film's premise and wrote an open letter condemning the filmmaker and television station for being irresponsible and promoting violence against the state. See Helmut Kohl, "Offener Brief, nach der Ausstrahlung von *Die Terroristen* von Philip Gröning im Südwestfunk in der FAZ vom 28. 11. 1992," in *Deutschland im Herbst: Terrorismus im Film*, ed. Petra Kraus, Natalie Lettenewitsch, Ursula Saekel, Brigitte Bruns, and Matthias Mersch (Munich: Münchner Filmzentrum, 1997), 100–101.

[4] Television documentary films include the five-part *Im Fadenkreuz* (In the crossfire, dir. Christian Berg and Cordt Schnibben [ARD, 1997]), Heinrich Breloer's two-part *Todesspiel* (Deadly game [ARD, 1997]), Klaus Stern's *Andreas Baader — Der Staatsfeind* (Andreas Baader: Public enemy [ARD, 2002]), and Lutz Hachmeister's *Schleyer — eine deutsche Karriere* (Schleyer, a German career [ARD, 2003]). Dennis Gansel's made-for-television film *Das Phantom* (The phantom [Pro 7, 2000]) also uses the RAF terrorist movement as the background for its fictionalized suspense story.

[5] See Reinhard Mohr, "Die Prada-Meinhof-Bande," *Der Spiegel,* 27 Feb. 2002, http://www.spiegel.de/kultur/gesellschaft/0,1518,184222,00.html.

[6] "RAF goes Pop. Die Historisierung des bewaffneten revolutionären Kampfs mündet in seine postmoderne Ästhetisierung. Politik wird zum Zitat, Leidenschaft zur Coolness, Klassenkampf zum Kult: Mörder werden Mode. Der Mythos vom Kampf der 'sechs gegen sechzig Millionen' lebt." Mohr, "Die Prada-Meinhof-Bande."

[7] Stefan Reinecke notes that this youth rebellion must be risky and provocative enough to gain attention: "Gambling with moral outrage . . . is a necessary part of the game. There is no terror pop without attention. The RAF T-shirt that is not conspicuous is only an expensive piece of material." The German original: "Die Spekulation mit moralischer Empöring ist . . . notwendiger Teil des Spiels. Kein Terrorpop ohne Aufmerksamkeit. Das RAF T-Shirt, das nicht auffällt, ist nur ein zu teures Stück-Stoff." Reinecke, "Das RAF-Gespenst: Die RAF ist verschwunden und in Pop-Inszenierungen wiedergekehrt. Dann kam der 11. September," *taz*, 5 Sept. 2002.

[8] "Nun kämpfen die Menschen nur noch für Hunde und Benzin, / folgen Jürgen und Zlatko, und nicht mehr Baader und Ensslin, / . . . Endlich sind die Terroristen weg, / und es herrscht Ordnung und Ruhe und Frieden, / und man kann wieder sicher Mercedes fahr'n, / ohne dass die Dinger immer explodieren." Jan Delay, "Die Söhne Stammheims," *Searching for Jan Soul Rebels*, Buback EFA, released 9 Apr. 2001. "Jürgen und Zlatko" refers to Jürgen Milski and Zlatko Trpkovski, the stars of the popular reality show "Big Brother," whose first season ran 28 February to 9 June 2000.

[9] A few examples of post-wall narratives that address the RAF are Friedrich Christian Delius's *Himmelfahrt eines Staatfeindes* (1992), Leander Scholz's novel *Rosenfest* (2001), and Gerhard Seyfried's *Der schwarze Stern der Tupamaro* (2004). Theater pieces include John von Düffel's *Rinderwahnsinn* (1999), Oliver Czeslik's *Stammheim Proben* (2002), and Elfriede Jelinek's *Ulrike Maria Stuart* (2006). Autobiographical works include Peter Jürgen Boock's *Mit dem Rücken zur Wand* (1994), Inge Viett's *Nie war ich furchtloser* (1996) and *Einsprüche! Briefe aus dem Gefängnis* (1996), Irmgard Möller's *RAF: Das war für uns Befreiung* (1996), Stefan Wisniewski's *Wir waren so unheimlich konsequent* (1997), Margit Schiller's *Es war ein harter Kampf um meine Erinnerung* (1999), and Birgit Hogefeld's *Versuche, die Geschichte der RAF zu verstehen* (2000).

[10] "*Zur Vorstellung des Terrors: Die RAF-Ausstellung* setzt in einer Art Überinformation und Reprivatisierung den überbeanspruchten Bildern der Medien die Kunst entgegen und versucht wieder eine erinnerbare Augenzeugenschaft für den Ausstellungsbesucher anzubieten. Sie beleuchtet die erste Generation der RAF als Gegenstand einer Bilder-, Zitier- und Referenzmaschine, die in der postmodernen mediengeprägten Welt eine hohe, unhinterfragte Aufmerksamkeit innezuhaben scheint. Sie versucht die Komplexität des in der Medienauslese verlorengegangenen Gehaltes wieder herzustellen und dem Betrachter eine eigene Analyse, kritische Betrachtung und Erfahrbarkeit dieses traumatischen Kapitels deutscher Geschichte zu erlauben oder näherzubringen. Der Zwischenraum und die Schnittstelle zwischen Historie und Kunst lässt sich als das beschreiben, was im Weiteren als die *Vorstellung* der RAF bezeichnet wird. Denn anscheinend darf man in einem Land, das zum einen aus der jetzt nicht mehr existierenden BRD und zum anderen aus der anscheinend nie bestanden habenden DDR zusammengesetzt wird, nicht von einem *Mythos* sprechen." Klaus Biesenbach, "Engel der Geschichte oder den Schrecken anderer betrachten oder Bilder in den Zeiten des Terrors," in *Zur Vorstellung des Terrors: Die RAF Ausstellung*, ed. Klaus Biesenbach (Berlin: Steidl/KW Institute for Contemporary Art, 2005), 2:13.

[11] In the strictest sense, the term "German Autumn" refers to the period starting on 5 September 1977 with the RAF's second-generation kidnapping of Hanns-Martin Schleyer, followed by the hijacking of a Lufthansa flight by the Popular Front for the Liberation of Palestine, the launching of the most extensive police dragnet across the entire West German state, the suicides of RAF leaders Andreas Baader, Gudrun Ensslin, and Jan-Carl Raspe in Stammheim prison, and the discovery of Schleyer's corpse in the trunk of a car in France on 19 October 1977.

[12] Elsaesser notes that images of the RAF have become embedded "in die visuelle Erinnerung einer Generation, die keine direkte Erfahrung mit der RAF hatte, außer durch ihre Bildgegenwart in diesen traumatischen, doch machtvoll

ikonischen und von daher widersprüchlichen Signifikanten von Handlung und Gewalt." Thomas Elsaesser, *Terror und Trauma: Zur Gewalt des Vergangenen in der BRD* (Berlin: Kulturverlag Kadmos, 2006), 23.

[13] Walter Laqueur, *Terrorism* (Boston: Little, Brown, 1977), 223.

[14] Elsaesser maintains there is a history, "die wir noch nicht einmal angefangen haben zu reflektieren; der verlorene Glauben an eine andere, eine veränderbare, 'bessere' Welt, zu der unsere Handlungsfähigkeit — entweder individuell oder kollektiv — tatsächlich beitragen kann." Elsaesser, *Terror und Trauma*, 45–46.

[15] Christopher Roth studied direction at the Film and Television Academy in Munich, worked as an editor for Klaus Lemke, and was editor-in-chief for the magazine *Elaste* (1984–86). His first film, *Loosers* (1995), failed to garner even a modest audience share, and the broadcast of his first TV film, *Candy* (1998), was delayed for several years, so Roth put his energy into producing commercials. *Baader* cost approximately 700,000 euros, and since Roth was able to finance the film based on the work he had done in commercials, he was fond of saying that media-magnet Leo Kirch inadvertently paid for *Baader*.

[16] Statistics are available at http://www.ffa.de

[17] Gernot Gricksch was shocked that "ein Regisseur die Chuzpe besitzt, sich die Fakten dermaßen hemmungslos so zurechtzuschnitzen, wo sie am besten in sein filmisches Konzept passen." Gernot Gricksch, "Abenteuer aus Wildwestdeutschland: Der Terrorist mit rauchenden Colts: Christopher Roths Jungenphantasie *Baader*," *Rheinischer Merkur*, 10 Oct. 2002.

[18] See Jan Schulz-Ojala, "Kleinbürger, überlebensgroß: Der Kampf um die Deutungshoheit: Christopher Roths irritierender *Baader*," *Der Tagesspiegel*, 17 Oct. 2002.

[19] See Rüdiger Suchsland, "'Die Freiheit nehm ich mir': Christopher Roths mutiger Film *Baader* erzählt mit schnellen Autos und rotem Lippenstift vom Terrorismus," *Frankfurter Rundschau*, 17 Oct. 2002.

[20] Rainer Gansera praised the fictionalized scenes because they made clear "was die Wahrheit hinter der Wirklichkeit ist," and he argued further that "die ausdrücklich fiktiven Passagen in erstaunlichem Maß der Wahrheitsfindung dienen." Rainer Gansera, "Bewußt wie ein Projektil: Wie Christopher Roth den Mythos von Baader zerbröselt," *Süddeutsche Zeitung*, 17 Oct. 2002.

[21] "Die RAF ist von ihrem Stil nicht zu trennen." Suchsland, "'Die Freiheit nehm ich mir.'"

[22] Roth states: "Ich versuchte, von den Oberflächen auszugehen, von der Wirkung und Faszination. Um erst dann tiefer zu graben; also die Zeichen lesen und versuchen, daraus etwas Neues zu basteln. 'Mit Tiefergehen' meine ich nicht, den Dingen auf den Grund zu gehen, um eine möglichst schlüssige Analyse zu erhalten, sondern mir geht es dabei eher um die Integration von poetischen und lyrischen Momenten. Nicht sezieren, sondern eine Offenheit schaffen, in die jeder Zuschauer seine Sachen hineinprojizieren kann." Ulrich Kriest, "'Ich sage ja nie: So war das!' Gespräch mit Christopher Roth über *Baader*," *Film-Dienst* 21 (Oct. 2002): 62.

23 "Ich glaube, daß die Fiktion mehr Fragen stellen und irritieren kann als etwa die reine Dokumentation. Ein Spielfilm kann mehr an festgefahrenen Bildern der Wirklichkeit rütteln, er kann entmythologisieren." Arnold Schnötzinger, "Keine Angst vor Geschichtsklitterung: Die Fiktion kann mehr Fragen stellen und irritieren als die reine Dokumentation, meint *Baader*-Regisseur Christopher Roth," OE1@ORF, http://www.oe1.orf.at.

24 "Mein Deutschlandsbild war halt wahnsinnig trostlos damals, es war grau und da waren diese alten Männer mit Kassenbrillen, die den Staat repräsentiert haben und es hat immer geschneit. Es war ein komisches Land ... Da gab es eben immer so als Gegenpole amerikanische Filme und Musik und dann gab's eben Andreas Baader, der für mich aber, ich habe gar nicht verstanden, was er da so gemacht hat, aber er war halt so der Mann mit der Zigarette, der Ray Ban Wayfarer Sonnenbrille, und war so wie ein Kinoheld." Interview with Christopher Roth, *Baader* [2002], dir. Christopher Roth, DVD (Munich: Universum Film, 2003).

25 For interviews where Roth discusses his approach, see Heide Platen, "'Baader war ein rührender Verlierer': Gespräch mit Regisseur Christopher Roth und Daniel Cohn-Bendit," *taz*, 15 Feb. 2002, and Ralph Eue, "Alles Feeling! Christopher Roth hat mit seinem Terroristen-Porträt *Baader* keine ernsthafte Biographie im Sinn, sondern Lust auf den Geschmack von Freiheit, Abenteuer und Gefahr," *Der Tagesspiegel*, 17 Oct. 2002.

26 After viewing Godard's film, Baader reportedly commented: "Ha! We're going to do that ourselves." (Ha! Das machen wir selber.) Quoted in Klaus Stern and Jörg Hermann, *Andreas Baader: Das Leben des Staatsfeindes*, 3rd ed. (Munich: dtv, 2007), 99.

27 Roth admits the film contains "dreiste Lügen." Platen, "'Baader war ein rührender Verlierer.'"

28 "Das Ende soll alles offen lassen und die ganze erzählte Geschichte in Frage stellen. . . . Da muß ein konzeptuelles Unbehagen bleiben." Kriest, "'Ich sage nie: So war das!,'" 63.

29 "Man kann das so sehen: seit einigen zehntausend Jahren gibt es Film in den menschlichen Köpfen — Assoziationsstrom, Tagtraum, Erfahrung, Sinnlichkeit, Bewußtsein. Die technische Erfindung des Kinos hat dem lediglich reproduzierbare Gegenbilder hinzugefügt." Alexander Kluge, *Gelegenheitsarbeit einer Sklavin: Zur realistischen Methode* (Frankfurt am Main: Suhrkamp, 1975), 208.

30 Stuart Liebman, "On the German Cinema, Art, Enlightenment, and the Public Sphere: An Interview with Alexander Kluge," *October* 46 (1998): 54.

31 "Ähnlich ergänzen einander, richtig angewendet, die musikalisch-poetisch erzählenden und die dokumentierenden Formen des Films. Auch hier ist es die Mischform, die zwischen Dokument und Fiktion, zwischen Montage und ungekürzter Wiedergabe, zwischen Phantasie und Wirklichkeitssinn vermittelt. Soziologie und Märchen sind eben nicht, wie man annimmt, Gegensätze, sie sind Pole in ein und derselben Sache, die verschieden aussieht, je nachdem, ob man von der Fähigkeit des Menschen, es mit den Fakten auszuhalten, oder von der Fähigkeit, Wünsche zu bilden ausgeht." Klaus Eder und Alexander Kluge, *Ulmer Dramaturgien: Reibungsverluste*. Arbeitshefte Film 2/3 (Munich: Hanser, 1980), 7.

[32] Kluge maintains it must be possible "die Realität als die geschichtliche Fiktion, die sie ist, auch darzustellen." Alexander Kluge, *Gelegenheitsarbeit einer Sklavin,* 215.

[33] See Liebman, "On the German Cinema," 57.

[34] "Betrachtet man die Bilder der Angeklagten auf der Bank, wie sie im Blitzlichtgewitter Castro-Zigarren rauchen, das Rote Buch schwenken, sich küssen oder über die Bänke hechten, fühlt man sich wie in einem Film. Schon der Aufbruch zur 'Tat' selbst hatte ja, wie beschrieben, Züge eines *road movie* getragen. Offentsichtlich fühlten sie sich als Akteure und Stars eines selbstinszenierten Filmdramas, dessen Bühne und technische Ausrüstung die großen Medien lieferten und zu dessen Komparsen auch das Publikum drinnen und draußen gehörte, vor dem sie agierten." Gerd Koenen, *Das rote Jahrzehnt: Unsere kleine deutsche Kulturrevolution, 1967–1977* (Frankfurt am Main: Fischer, 2002), 360. This type of observation is not isolated. Even Thorwald Proll, one of the Frankfurt defendants, recently described the proceedings as a scene from a Marx Brothers film. See Thorwald Proll and Daniel Dubbe, *Wir kamen vom anderen Stern: Über 1968, Andreas Baader und ein Kaufhaus* (Hamburg: Edition Nautlis, 2003), 33.

[35] Moreover, the Frankfurt arson defendant Horst Söhnlein and RAF terrorists Philipp Sauber and Christopher Wackernagel were actors, while Astrid Proll studied photography. For further information on the RAF's relationship to the media, see Ulrich Enzensberger, *Die Jahre der Kommune I: Berlin 1967–1969* (Munich: Goldmann, 2006), 221; Koenen, *Vesper, Ensslin, Baader,* 109–10; and Astrid Proll, ed., *Hans und Grete: Bilder der RAF, 1967–1977,* rev. ed. (Berlin: Aufbau, 2004).

[36] Stefan Reinecke writes: "The political icon is not a discovery of the 90s. The affinity for the simple image, the symbol as a feature of identity, the Che Guevara poster, has its roots in the 60s. The hip RAF retro chic is not treason against 1968 but rather its continuation: exactly in the coquettish mixture of pop and politics." The German original: "Denn die Politikone ist keine Erfindung der 90er-Jahre. Die Neigung zum einfachen Bild, zum Symbol als Identitätskennzeichen, zum Che-Guevara-Poster, wurzelt in den 60er-Jahren. Der hippe RAF-Retroschick ist nicht Verrat an 68, sondern eher dessen Fortsetzung: gerade in der ziemlich koketten Vermischung von Pop und Politik." Stefan Reinecke, "Koketter Retroschick: Interessant gescheitert: *Baader* von Christopher Roth hat berührende, dichte Szenen — aber noch mehr Löcher im Erzählgeflecht," *taz,* 16 Feb. 2002.

[37] See for example Andreas Kilb, "Identifikation eines Mannes: Der schmale Grat; Christopher Roths Versuch, mit *Baader* einen Filmclip über den bundesdeutschen Terrorismus zu drehen," *Frankfurter Allgemeine Zeitung,* 16 Oct. 2002.

[38] "Schau dir die SPD an. Die strategische Funktion der Sozialdemokraten ist die Initiative des Kapitals in der Krise zu sichern, kapiert? . . . Nix ausdiskutieren, es muß auf die Fresse gehen! . . . Außerdem zweifelt der nicht, der wimmert und Marx hat nicht gewimmert! . . . Der Wimmerer kann gehen und Marx kann meinetwegen auch abhauen!" Film dialogue.

[39] Baader exclaims: "Klar, weil wir der Welt solange auf die Fresse hauen, bis sie versteht, daß der Wille zur Freiheit stärker ist als der Wille zur Unterdrückung." Ensslin replies: "Das ist toll. Du bist toll!" Film dialogue.

[40] Another scene worth mentioning is the first "fictional" segment of the film after the title sequence. An inset title sets the stage as 1972. Baader is sitting in a car reading the headlines in the *Bild* newspaper, which claim that he is ready to give himself up, while in a voice-over he states that he has no intention of doing so. This opening scene stylistically resembles the *Derrick* television show and highlights the postmodern penchant for quotation, but there are also several layers of irony. First, Baader is shown reading the newspaper that the RAF specifically heralded as manipulative. Second, there is a clear disconnect between reality and media, since Baader reveals that his intentions are different from those reported in the paper.

[41] Ensslin quotes Bertolt Brecht: "Wenn das so bleibt, was ist, seid ihr verloren. Euer Freund ist der Wandel, euer Kampfgefährte ist der Zwiespalt. Aus dem Nichts müßt ihr etwas machen, aber das Großmächtige sollst du nicht werden. Was ihr habt, das gebt auf und nehmt euch, was euch verweigert wird." Film dialogue. Bertolt Brecht, "Wenn das bleibt, was ist" in *Gedichte 4: Gedichte und Gedichtfragmente 1928–1939*, Vol. 14 of *Werke: Große kommentierte Berliner und Frankfurter Ausgabe*, ed. Werner Hecht, 30 vols. (Frankfurt am Main: Suhrkamp Verlag, 1993) 14:343.

[42] "Liebe Genossen, ich würde gerne ein bißchen über die APO, die Außerparlamentarische Opposition der Studenten, sprechen. Der APO geht es nämlich nicht nur um ihre Hochschule, sondern um gesellschaftliche Veränderungen. Die APO fällt durch ständige Provokation auf. Wie sollen wir auf diese Provokation reagieren, was sollen wir tun? — Erschießen! — Erst mal müssen wir erkennen, daß diese Kritik berechtigt ist. Es gibt autoritäre Strukturen in unserem Lande. In der Tat werden die Menschen von der *Bild-Zeitung* manipuliert. Deshalb müssen wir den jungen Menschen sagen: Ja, wir brauchen eure Kritik, damit die Gesellschaft nicht zum Stillstand kommt. Aber wir müssen auch sagen: Gewalt? Nein!" Film dialogue.

[43] Krone warns: "Wer diese Bedrückung als existentiell empfindet, der wird nicht zögern, Bomben in das Bewusstsein zu schmeißen, das offenbar nicht anders aufgebrochen werden kann." Film dialogue.

[44] "Die Bullen sind Schweine. Der Typ in der Uniform ist ein Schwein, das ist kein Mensch." Film dialogue.

[45] "Jean Paul Melville ist auch wieder ein Hollywood Zitat eigentlich. Es ist fast so wie das Zitat des Zitates des Zitates eigentlich." Roth, "Interview."

[46] According to Anke Bergmann, Roth's film "[mythisiert] jugendlich-unbedarfte Abenteuerlust und stilisierte Coolness mit politischer Radikalität und militärischer Gewalt. Wenn *Baader* einen Mythos konsequent destruiert, dann den, dass es sich bei der ersten Generation des RAF um hochsensible Intellektuelle handelte, die aus reiner Verzweifelung zur Waffe griffen." Anke Bergmann, *RAF auf der Leinwand: Diskursanalyse anhand ausgewählter Filmbeispiele zwischen dem Deutschen Herbst und der Jahrtausendwende.* Diplomarbeit (Potsdam-Babelsberg: HFF Konrad Wolf, Studiengang AV-Medienwissenschaft, 2005), 245.

[47] "Erst soll der Film einen unterhalten, was eben Film tun soll. Der soll verführen, wahrscheinlich auch irritieren, weil es eine wahnsinnig ambivalente Figur ist. Und dann soll er natürlich noch mal dieses Bild hinterfragen, das man so hat von der RAF und von der Zeit." Roth, "Interview."

[48] According to real-life cohort Thorwald Proll, Andreas Baader's transformation from youth rebel to hardened revolutionary was highly influenced by movie idols and legendary heroes with equal elan: "At the very beginning Andreas wanted perhaps to be a Brandoesque hero, solitary, urbane, dreaming of role models, disregarding love. In the end he became more like a Sergey Nechayev hero: distrusting, unpredictable, brooding and gloomy, paying for freedom by suffering." ("Ganz zu Beginn wollte Andreas vielleicht wie ein Brandoscher Held sein, einsam, manieriert, von Vorbildern träumend, Liebe eher versäumend. Am Ende wird er eher wie ein Netschajewscher Held werden: Mißtrauisch, unberechenbar, grübelnd und düster, der Freiheit Leiden büßt er.") Proll and Dubbe, *Wir kamen vom anderen Stern*, 94–95.

[49] For an analysis of *Brandstifter* and its role in the evolution of terrorist films, see Ulrich Kriest, "Bilder aus 'bleiernen Jahren,'" in Petra Kraus et al., *Deutschland im Herbst: Terrorismus im Film*, 26–27.

[50] Eue, "Alles Feeling!"

[51] Gerd Gemünden, *Framed Visions: Popular Culture, Americanization, and the Contemporary German and Austrian Imaginations* (Ann Arbor: U of Michigan, 1998), 95.

[52] Quoted from John Hughes and Brooks Riley, "A New Realism," *Film Comment* 11, no. 6 (1975): 14.

[53] "Kluges Verfremdung ist intellektuell wie Brechts, während meine stilistisch ist." Rainer Werner Fassbinder, *Die Anarchie der Phantasie: Gespräche und Interviews*, ed. Michael Töteberg (Frankfurt am Main: Fischer, 1986), 41.

[54] "Dann gibt's diesen Einen, der immer so gleichzeitig für Aufruhr sorgt und andererseits dann aber auch in so einer Einsamkeit verfällt, usw. Es ist natürlich alles so ein riesiger Fassbinder Film. Ich glaube, er hätte den Film geliebt." Roth, "Interview."

[55] Baader states: "Sie brauchen uns, um aufzurüsten" to which Krone replies "Und ihr braucht mich, um die bestehenden Widersprüche zu verschärfen, den Riß zwischen Staat und den Massen zu vertiefen." Film dialogue.

[56] "Ich hatte da neulich einen Traum, da . . . da hat das Kapital den Terrorismus erfunden, um den Staat zu zwingen, es besser zu schützen." *Die dritte Generation* [1979], dir. Rainer Werner Fassbinder, DVD (Munich: Kinowelt Home Entertainment, 2004).

[57] For an examination of *Die dritte Generation* in relation to postmodernism, see Timothy Corrigan, "The Temporality of Place, Postmodernism, and Fassbinder Texts," *New German Critique* 63 (1994): 139–54.

[58] Meinhof states: "Den Worten müssen Taten folgen. Das hast du geschrieben, Henry!" Henry counters: "Das ist Fiktion! Das sagt die Hauptfigur in meinem Roman und der endet tragisch!" Film dialogue.

[59] "Furchtbar ist es zu töten. Aber nicht andere nur, auch uns töten wir, wenn es nottut. Da doch nur mit Gewalt diese tötende Welt zu ändern ist, wie jeder Lebende weiß." Film dialogue.

[60] *Die Stille nach dem Schuss*, dir. Volker Schlöndorff, DVD (Munich: Kinowelt Home Entertainment, 2001).

[61] Gary Crowdus and Richard Porton, "Coming to Terms with the German Past: An Interview with Volker Schlöndorff," *Cineaste* 26, no. 2 (2000): 19.

[62] "An einem bestimmten Punkt der Grausamkeit angekommen, ist es schon gleich, wer sie begangen hat: sie soll nur aufhören." Film text, *Deutschland im Herbst* (Germany in Autumn, 1978), dir. Alexander Kluge, Volker Schlöndorff, Alf Brustellin, Bernhard Sinkel, Rainer Werner Fassbinder, Katja Rupé, Hans Peter Cloos, Edgar Reitz, Maximiliane Mainka, and Peter Schubert, DVD (Munich: Kinowelt Home Entertainment, 2004).

[63] "Ähnlichkeiten mit gewissen journalistischen Praktiken sind weder beabsichtigt, noch zufällig, sondern unvermeidlich." Film text, *Die verlorene Ehre der Katharina Blum* (The lost honor of Katharina Blum, 1975), dir. Volker Schlöndorff and Margarethe von Trotta, DVD (Berlin: StudioCanal, 2008).

[64] "Je ne suis pas un auteur, je suis peut-être un styliste." Volker Schlöndorff, "Sur le tambour," *Jeune cinema* 121 (1979): 20.

[65] Noted DEFA director Heiner Carow had already taken up the topic of the GDR's granting sanctuary to RAF terrorists in the television film *Vater, Mutter, Mörderkind* (Father, Mother, Killer Child) based on a screenplay by renowned author Ulrich Plenzdorf and first broadcast on ZDF on 1 February 1993.

[66] For reviews that criticize the lack of psychological development and the extensive reliance on clichés, see Peter von Becker, "Die Geschichte der Schattenfrau: Wie die DDR weltweit gesuchte RAF-Terroristen verbarg, war eines ihrer bestgehüteten Geheimnisse. Daraus hat Volker Schlöndorff seinen neuen Film gemacht, Premiere zur Berlinale *Die Stille nach dem Schuss*," *Der Tagesspiegel*, 17 Feb. 2000; Constanze von Bullion, "RAF light und die Idylle im Osten: Terroristen in der DDR; Inge Viett streitet mit Volker Schlöndorff über seinen Film *Die Stille nach dem Schuss*," *Süddeutsche Zeitung*, 17 Feb. 2000; Frank Junghänel, "Nach drüben: Im Wettbewerb; Volker Schlöndorffs *Die Stille nach dem Schuss* arbeitet ein Stück DDR auf," *Berliner Zeitung*, 17 Feb. 2000; Peter Zander, "Die verlorene Ehre der Inge Viett: Von Terroristen, die in der DDR untertauchen; Volker Schlöndorffs Wettbewerbsfilm *Die Stille nach dem Schuss* wird vermutlich die Justiz beschäftigen — obwohl er spießig ist," *Berliner Morgenpost*, 17 Feb. 2000. When the film went into general release in September 2000, the same assessment resurfaced. See Georg Seeßlen, "Zweierlei Wahn: *Die Stille nach dem Schuss* — Volker Schlöndorffs gespaltener Film über ein gespaltenes Land," *Die Zeit*, 14 Sept. 2000; Dietrich Kuhlbrodt, "Bloß kein Fehler, Genosse General! Die DDR, ein Heimatmuseum aus Stasi-Loden, Volksgut und VEB-Betriebsfeiern: In *Die Stille nach dem Schuss* bebildert Volker Schlöndorff ein deutsches Terroristenschicksal," *taz*, 14 Sept. 2000; and Anke Westphal, "Mensch oder Schwein: Volker Schlöndorff hat drei Filme in einem gedreht; *Die Stille nach dem Schuss*," *Berliner Zeitung*, 14 Sept. 2000. By contrast, Hanns-Georg Rodek argued that the lack of emotional depth and psychological development contributed positively to the film, because otherwise Rita would have become an identification figure and run the risk of glorifying terrorism. Hanns-Georg Rodek, "Das Schweigen nach der 'Stille': Im Wettbewerb; Schlöndorffs Terroristen-Film," *Die Welt*, 17 Feb. 2000.

[67] "Wenn wir zu stark an den Fakten kleben, dann können wir gleich einen Dokumentarfilm drehen. Wenn man etwas Abstand will, dann braucht man eine fiktive Handlung." Constanze von Bullion, "Gelebte Geschichte: Eine Figur, mehrere Biografien; Volker Schlöndorff über die Vorwürfe gegen seinen Film," *Süddeutsche Zeitung*, 17 Feb. 2000.

[68] Statistics are available at http://www.ffa.de.

[69] "Ich war verknallt." Film dialogue.

[70] Kirsten von Hagen, "Im Gespräch: Volker Schlöndorff über seinen Film *Die Stille nach dem Schuss*; Das war so in der DDR," *Rheinischer Merkur*, 15 Sept. 2000.

[71] "Wir dachten, dass wir die Größten sind, Tatjana. Irgendwie wollten wir das Unrecht abschaffen und den Staat gleich mit oder umgekehrt. Beides hing ja zusammen. Politik war Krieg. Überall auf der Welt." Film dialogue.

[72] "Wir wollten das Unmögliche versuchen, wenigstens einmal im Leben. Wir fühlten uns als Teil des internationalen Kampfes. Und dann erlebten wir, wie in Beirut eine gerechte Sache zu einem mörderischen Bürgerkrieg führte. Wir wollten den Krieg in die Metropolen tragen. Es gab endlose Diskussionen, geglückte und gescheiterte Aktionen, Tote auf beiden Seiten." Film dialogue.

[73] "Es hat mir eingeleuchtet, dass wir in einem falschen System gefangen sind, aber der Guerillakrieg hat zu keiner Befreiung führen können, weil uns niemand verstanden hat. Als ich hier vorüber kam, wollte ich mich nicht einfach verstecken. Ich habe eine andere Welt gesucht, als ich kannte. Ich wollte vorwärts, nicht zurück." Film dialogue.

[74] Anke Westphal regarded the scene as "eine Spur zu lässig, einen Hauch zu entspannt." Westphal, "Mensch oder Schwein."

[75] "Dieser Anfang, der die RAF sozusagen über ihre *B.Z.*-Schlüsselreize inszeniert (Waffen, Parolen, Überfall, ein bißchen Sex, ein bißchen Guerillaromantik), hat in seiner Oberflächlichkeit etwas merkwürdig Verschämtes." Katja Nicodemus, "Von der Zelle in die Platte: Auf Schleichwegen; Volker Schlöndorffs *Die Stille nach dem Schuss*," *taz*, 17 Feb. 2000.

[76] Constanze von Bullion spoke with Inge Viett and wrote: "An die Banküberfälle der 'Bewegung 2. Juni,' wo mal Schokoküsse verteilt wurden, 'um die Spannung rauszunehmen,' erinnert sie noch. Mit dem 'Kasperltheater' in Schlöndorffs Film habe das allerdings nichts zu tun." In an interview, Schlöndorff commented: "Das ist für mich das, was man damals so die 'Spaßguerilla' nannte — im Rückblick beinahe so eine Art Kasperletheater." Compare Bullion, "RAF light und die Idylle im Osten" and Wolf Martin Hamdorf, "'Was für ein trauriges Ende!' Film und Terrorismus: Ein Gespräch mit dem Regisseur Volker Schlöndorff," *Filmforum* 25, no. 5 (2000): 13.

[77] Becher, "Die Geschichte der Schattenfrau."

[78] Inge Viett, *Nie war ich furchtloser: Autobiographie* (1996; repr., Hamburg: Nautilus, 2005), 185–95.

[79] "Die Terroristen sprechen, als rezitierten sie eigene Flugblätter." Seeßlen, "Zweierlei Wahn."

80 Shortly before his death from a hunger strike, Holger Meins wrote to fellow prisoner Jan-Carl Raspe: "entweder mensch oder schwein / entweder überleben um jeden preis oder / kampf bis zum tod / entweder problem oder lösung / dazwischen gibt es nichts . . . es stirbt allerdings ein jeder. frage ist nur, wie du gelebt hast: KÄMPFEND GEGEN DIE SCHWEINE als MENSCH FÜR DIE BEFREIUNG DES MENSCHEN." Quoted in Koenen, *Das rote Jahrzehnt*, 405–6.

81 "Ich habe zu ihm gesagt, verschwinde, und er guckt und guckt. Da habe ich geschossen. . . . Man muss so etwas doch sagen dürfen. . . . Manche Dinge kann ich nicht mehr anfassen." Bullion, "RAF light und die Idylle im Osten."

82 "Und wieder häng ich an den Drähten / Wie ein verirrtes böses Kind / Und fühle wie mir ungebeten / Die Seele aus dem Leibe rinnt / Was wissen die denn schon von Liebe / Was wissen die denn schon vom Haß / Vom Netz der Träume und der Triebe / Durch dessen Maschen ich nicht pass." The refrain states: "Ich möchte abhaun kann nicht mehr / Die Scheißmaschine säuft mich leer." Silly, "EKG," *Bataillon d'Amor*, Vocals, Tamara Danz; Lyrics, Werner Karma, CD (Amiga & BMG, 1986).

83 "Kalt ist der Abendhauch. Verschon uns Gott mit Strafen und lass uns ruhig schlafen und unseren kranken Nachbarn auch." Matthias Claudius's "Abendlied." Film dialogue.

84 "Dass es hier [in der DDR] bescheidener, grauer, ordentlicher zuging als im Westen, stellte für sie als erklärte Feinde des so genannten Konsumterrors nicht so ein Problem dar. Und sie waren ja bereits gehörig demoralisiert, was die eigenen Ideale betraf. Vielleicht war es ja gerade diese Banalität des Alltags, die ihnen an der DDR gefallen hat, dass sie hier ein Leben führen konnten, das sie bisher noch gar nicht kannten. Die Sehnsucht nach Normalität darf nicht unterschätzt werden." Claus Löser, "'Ich vestehe Inge Viett': Wie frei darf man Leben verfilmen? Ein Interview mit Wolfgang Kohlhaase, dem Drehbuchautor von *Die Stille nach dem Schuss*," *taz*, 17 Feb. 2000.

85 "Es war doch ein großer Versuch hier. Es war doch eine Revolution. Bei allem Mist, bei aller Dummheit, ihr wart doch dabei. Es sollte doch eine Welt werden, in der das Geld nicht alle Dinge regelt. Warum glaubt ihr nicht mehr daran? Warum glaubt ihr nicht mehr an euch selbst?" Film dialogue.

86 "Wir sind für die Leute, und deshalb sind wir gegen sie." Film dialogue.

87 "Und niemand kriegt und keiner kriegt / mich einfach krummgebogen . . . ich bin zu jung um schwach zu sein / zu blind um aufzugeben." Silly, "PS," *Bataillon d'Amor*.

88 "Alles ist so gewesen. Nichts war genau so." Film text.

89 "Deshalb waren wir der Meinung, dass diese Heldin ein tragisches Ende verdient. Ich finde, in einer Filmerzählung — und insofern ist auch Kino eine moralische Anstalt — kann eine Schuld nicht ungesühnt bleiben, wenn der Vorhang fällt. Sie fordert, wie man früher so sagte, ein 'Gottesurteil' heraus." Hamdorf, "Was für ein trauriges Ende!," 14.

90 "Heute ist diese Linkskomponente wirklich abgeschlossen, weil auch diese Utopie nicht mehr existiert. Die werden zurückbleiben als eine fettgedruckte Fußnote

der Geschichte. Man wird sagen, dass es die bleierne Zeit der Adenauer Jahre gab, wo sich nichts bewegte, es gab '68 den Aufbruch und die Studentenrevolte, und es gab diesen guerillaartigen Kampfteil, vollkommen verblüffend und unerwartet. Nichts in der deutschen Geschichte seit Thomas Müntzer bereitete darauf vor, dass eine Gruppe gewalttätig gegen den Staat losgeht und ihn herausfordert. Dass das von vornherein zum Scheitern verurteilt war steht auf einem anderen Blatt. Aber es wird immer heissen: 'das hat es gegeben.' Und so richtig haben wir das alles noch nicht verdaut." Hamdorf, "Was für ein trauriges Ende!,"15.

[91] Filming started in April 1997 and was completed on 16 May 1997. See Ki/jam, "Tragikomische Filmgeschichte: Ein Schuldirektor wird entführt," *Berliner Morgenpost*, 10 May 1997.

[92] "Wir im Osten sind wohl besonders abgestumpft, der Politik überdrüssig. Viele ziehen sich ins Private zurück. Das traf bis vor zwei, drei Jahren bedingt auch auf mich zu. Nach der Wende war ich von vielen Sachen enttäuscht — glaubte — völlig weltfremd — an eine mögliche Reformierung des DDR-Systems. Mit dieser eigenen Orientierungslosigkeit mußte ich nach der überstürzten Wiedervereinigung erst einmal zurecht kommen." Heidi Jäger, "'Ich spüre den Erwartungsdruck': Am 12. August kommt Andreas Dresens preisgekrönter Film *Nachtgestalten* in die Kinos," *Potsdamer Neuste Nachrichten*, 7 Aug. 1999.

[93] "Diese Berliner Stadtguerilla aus den 70er Jahren funktionierte ähnlich wie die RAF . . . Diese Leute wollten das System reformieren und hofften, viele dabei mitzureißen. Leider war ihr Weg fatal. Doch trotz Knast blieben sie ihrem Willen ungebrochen, denken weiterhin kreativ über Gesellschaftsveränderung nach. Jäger, "'Ich spüre den Erwartungsdruck.'"

[94] "Die Linken machen aus ihnen Götter, die Rechten Monster. Doch wer sind diese Menschen wirklich? Ich möchte über sie gerecht und nicht polemisch erzählen." Jäger, "'Ich spüre den Erwartungsdruck.'"

[95] "Wir leben in einer Zeit, in der es keine Utopien mehr gibt. Von daher interessieren mich Leute, die diese Welt noch befragt haben. Das war '68 der Fall. Das Experiment vom Traum einer besseren Gesellschaft ist zwar missglückt. Aber mit gescheiterten Versuchen sollte man sich trotzdem beschäftigen." Stefan Kirschner, "Experiment Stadtguerilla: Ein Filmregisseur macht Theater; Andreas Dresens Terroristen-Monologe," *Berliner Morgenpost*, 4 Jun. 2002.

[96] "Leitbilder der ostdeutschen Protestkultur [stammten] fast ausnahmslos aus dem Westen." Paul Kaiser, "Heckenscheren gegen Feindfrisuren: Das Vokabular der Macht; Asozialität, Dekadenz und Untergrund," in *Bye Bye Lübben City: Bluesfreaks, Tramps und Hippies in der DDR*, ed. Michael Rauhut and Thomas Kochan (Berlin: Schwarzkopf & Schwarzkopf, 2004), 267.

[97] In that same August 1977, Rudolf Bahro illegally published a chapter of his book *Die Alternative: Zur Kritik des real existierenden Sozialismus* in *Der Spiegel*. Bahro was arrested and sentenced on 30 June 1978 to eight years imprisonment in maximum security prison Bautzen but was ransomed to the FRG in 1979. Members of Renft had close contact with other prominent dissidents, including Robert Havemann and writer Jürgen Fuchs.

[98] "[Musik aus dem Westen] löste in uns den Drang aus, von der großen weiten Welt ein Stück mitzubekommen. Musik war die Brücke. Wenn Renft 'Child in

Time' spielten, fühlte ich mich den Rest der Woche freier. Dann reiste ich in Gedanken um den Globus, wurde Teil des Universums. Mit Rock und Literatur hatten viele meiner Generation einen Ausweg gefunden. Anders wäre das Schicksal, ein Leben lang eingesperrt zu sein, nicht zu ertragen gewesen." Harald Hauswald, "Einmal um die Welt," in Rauhut and Kochan, *Bye Bye Lübben City*, 394.

[99] "Der Druck des Staates wertete das Ereignis 'Rockkonzert' zur autonomen Zone, zur Enklave auf. Je stärker er offizielle Räume beschnitt, desto eifriger wurden Nischen erschlossen." Michael Rauhut, "Kleine Fluchten: Vom Blues einer unruhevollen Jugend," in Rauhut and Kochan, *Bye Bye Lübben City*, 59.

[100] "Symbolische Provokanz, politische Resistenz und gesellschaftliche Verweigerung — das waren die Inhaltsstoffe subkultureller Gegenidentität in der DDR." Kaiser, "Heckenscheren gegen Feindfrisuren," 269.

[101] Pedro Ramet, "Disaffection and Dissent in East Germany," *World Politics* 37, no. 1 (1984): 92.

[102] "Das greift über — nur eine Frage der Zeit." Film dialogue, *Raus aus der Haut*, dir. Andreas Dresen, DVD (Amherst, MA: DEFA Film Library, 2004).

[103] "Außerdem waren die ersten Tage ganz lustig, fast wie im Detektivfilm. Wir erforschten Rottmanns Gewohnheiten und so. Wäre mir klar gewesen, was auf mich zukam, hätte ich die Zeit nicht so geniessen können." Film dialogue.

[104] Rottmann withholds his approval, "weil ihre Wünsche nicht mit den gesellschaftlichen Erfordernissen übereinstimmen." Film dialogue.

[105] "Genosse Rottmann, du willst uns doch nicht allen Ernstes diese Räuber-Pistole auftischen. Wir sind schließlich nicht in der BRD." Film dialogue.

[106] "Ich frage mich in meiner jetzigen Situation wirklich, muß denn noch was geschehen, damit Bonn endlich zu einer Entscheidung kommt? Schließlich bin ich nun fünfeinhalb Wochen in der Haft der Terroristen und das alles nur, weil ich mich jahrelang für den Staat und seine freiheitlich-demokratische Ordnung eingesetzt habe." Quoted from Charlotte Klonk, "Bilderterrorismus: Von Meins zu Schleyer," in *NachBilder der RAF*, ed. Inge Stephan and Alexandra Tacke (Cologne: Böhlau, 2008), 210–11.

[107] "Komm, stellt man Forderungen, kriegt man einen schweren Anfang vorgehalten." Film dialogue.

[108] "Als ich wie ein Vogel war, der am Abend sang, / riefen alle Leute nur Sonnenuntergang. / Alle Vögel sind schon da, keiner das rief. / Ohne Stimme flog ich fort, als schon alles schlief. / Irgendwann will jedermann raus aus seiner Haut. / Irgendwann denkt er dran, wenn auch nicht laut." Film text.

[109] According to Anna Hahn the riot began because a group of young people were on an airshaft grate and it broke under their weight, sending ten teenagers down the shaft. Since the fire department could not get through the crowds, the police decided to cut electricity to the bands and force the crowds aside. Unaware of the circumstances, the crowd reacted with anger and violence against the police. Hahn questions whether there were any fatalities during the riot. See Anne Hahn, "Feuerwerk am hellichten Tag," *Freitag: Die Ost-Westwochenzeitung*, 31 Aug. 2007. Compare this account to a report published by the BStU, which claimed that three people died. Compare "Bei Ausschreitungen auf dem Ostberliner Alex-

anderplatz werden drei Menschen getötet und 200 verletzt," BStU, Chronik zur Geschichte der DDR und ihres Ministeriums für Staatssicherheit, http://www. bstu.bund.de/DE/Wissen/DDRGeschichte/Chronik-DDR/chronik-1970_79_ inhalt.html?nn=1768732.

[110] "Vorwärts und nicht vergessen, Worin unsere Stärke besteht, Beim Hungern und beim Essen, Vorwärts, nie vergessen: Die Solidarität!" Film text. Bertolt Brecht, "Solidaritätslied," *Gedichte*, vol. 3 of *Werke*, 5 vols., ed. Werner Mittenzwei, 3rd ed. (Berlin, GDR: Aufbau, 1981), 207.

[111] "Was spricht eigentlich gegen den Kommunismus? Er ist vernünftig. Jeder versteht ihn. Er ist leicht. Du bist doch kein Ausbeuter. Du kannst ihn begreifen. Er ist gut für dich." Bertolt Brecht, "Lob des Kommunismus." The film text differs slightly from the poem. Compare Bertolt Brecht, "Lob des Kommunismus," *Gedichte*, vol. 3 of *Werke*, 5 vols., ed. Werner Mittenzwei, 3rd ed. (Berlin, GDR: Aufbau, 1981), 162.

[112] "Wir standen dabei, wußten es besser und haben geschwiegen." Film dialogue.

[113] "Wir machten uns auf einen langen kalten Winter fest." Film dialogue.

[114] Munich-based Constantin Film is the largest production company in Germany and financed such blockbusters as *Der bewegte Mann* (The moved man, English title: *Maybe, Maybe Not*, dir. Sönke Wortmann, 1994) with 6,565,342 tickets sold as of 1997, *Der Schuh des Manitu* (The shoe of the Manitu, dir. Michael Herbig, 2001) with 11,719,160 as of December 2004, *Das Parfum: Die Geschichte eines Mörders* (Perfume: The story of a murderer, dir. Tom Tykwer, 2006) with 5,589,217 as of December 2007, and *Der Untergang* (Downfall, dir. Oliver Hirschbiegel, 2004) with 4,621,483 as of December 2005. Statistics are available at http://www.ffa.de.

[115] See Sonja Pohlmann, "Wer redet, zahlt — Medien dürfen nur eingeschränkt über RAF-Film berichten," *Der Tagesspiegel*, 13 Aug. 2008, and Hanns-Georg Rodek, "Eichinger will die Medien kontrollieren," *Berliner Morgenpost*, 14 Aug. 2008.

[116] "Hätte sich für uns aus den Recherchen ergeben, dass Frau Ponto die Tötung ihres Mannes aus nächster Nähe mitansehen musste, hätten wir das natürlich so gedreht. Das hätte — und ich weiß, das klingt jetzt zynisch — die Dramatik des Films sogar erhöht." "Ponto-Witwe ruft Gericht an," *Süddeutsche Zeitung*, 1 Nov. 2008.

[117] By the end of 2009 *Die Welle* had sold 2,672,429 tickets and by December 2008 *Keinohrhase* reached sales of 6,286,012. Statistics are available at http://www.ffa.de.

[118] *Christine F.: Wir Kinder vom Bahnhof Zoo* [1981], dir. Ulrich Edel, DVD (Ismaning: EuroVideo, 2000); *Last Exit to Brooklyn* [1989], dir. Ulrich Edel, DVD (Santa Monica, CA: Summit Entertainment, 2011).

[119] "*Wir Kinder vom Bahnhof Zoo* ist denn auch über weite Strecken nichts anderes als eine furchtsame Bebilderung eines Bestsellers. Das Bemühen, um Authentizität ist unverkennbar, doch zu oft erscheint es wie eine Flucht vor der Notwendigkeit, ein Buch in die eigenständige Welt der Filmbilder zu übersetzen. . . . Gewiß,

er zeigt, was sich sonst versteckt, die Schattenexistenz der Fixer auf U-Bahnhöfen, schmuddeligen Toiletten, doch der Film packt einen nicht, rührt einen nicht, macht einen nicht sonderlich betroffen. *Wir Kinder vom Bahnhof Zoo*: das ist ein Film, dem es an Wut und Wucht fehlt." Michael Schwarze, "Ohne Wut und ohne Wucht: Uli Edels umstrittener Film *Wir Kinder vom Bahnhof Zoo*," *Frankfurter Allgemeine Zeitung*, 4 Apr. 1981.

[120] Richard Gehr visited the set and spoke with Edel and Eichinger during the filming. See Richard Gehr, "*Last Exit to Brooklyn*," *American Film* 15, no. 8 (1990): 34–39, 48.

[121] Vincent Canby, "A Brutal, Elegiac *Last Exit*, Unrelieved by Hope," *New York Times*, 2 May 1990.

[122] "Für mich ist *Der Baader Meinhof Komplex* der dritte Teil einer Trilogie über das Thema Gewalt, die Bernd und ich mit *Christiane F. — Wir Kinder vom Bahnhof Zoo* begannen und mit *Letzter Ausfahrt Brooklyn* fortsetzten. Dort ist von sozialer Gewalt, in *Der Baader Meinhof Komplex* von politischer Gewalt die Rede. Und *Christiane F.* handelt von jener Gewalt, die wir uns selbst zufügen." Quoted in Katja Eichinger, *Der Baader Meinhof Komplex: Das Buch zum Film* (Hamburg: Hoffmann und Campe, 2008), 38.

[123] "Es gibt in *Der Baader Meinhof Komplex* keine Identifikationsfigur für das Publikum. . . . Die Geschwindigkeit der Ereignisse wird zu einem Sog, zu einem reißenden Strom, bei dem man weiß: Irgendwann kommt der Wasserfall, und es wird ein gewaltsames Ende geben." Quoted in K. Eichinger, *Der Baader Meinhof Komplex*, 24–25.

[124] "Ich wollte die Geschichte auch nicht emotional an einer bestimmten Person festmachen — sei das nun ein Mitglied der RAF oder ein Vertreter der Staatsmacht. Wenn ich das getan hätte, hätte ich die Interpretation zwangsläufig mitgeliefert, und genau das wollte ich nicht. Ich wollte, dass der Film Fragen stellt, aber nicht gleich die Antworten mitliefert." Quoted in K. Eichinger, *Der Baader Meinhof Komplex*, 24.

[125] "Ich wollte in diesem Film alles vermeiden, was man als Filmemacher sonst im Genrekino tun würde. . . . Authentizität war angesagt. Wie schon in *Christiane F.* sind wir den Gesetzen des 'Cinéma Verité' gefolgt und nicht denen des Fiktionsfilms." Quoted in K. Eichinger, *Der Baader Meinhof Komplex*, 42–43.

[126] "Es wird wahrscheinlich so sein, dass die Leute uns nicht glauben werden, wie viel da geschossen wurde. Aber bei der Schleyer-Entführung etwa wurden am Tatort 107 Patronenhülsen gefunden und in den Körpern der Toten bis zu 30 Einschüsse. Bei Buback waren es 15 Schüsse, und genau die habe ich gezeigt, nicht 20 oder 30." Quoted in K. Eichinger, *Der Baader Meinhof Komplex*, 70.

[127] "Der Film gibt manchen Leuten nicht, was sie wollen: Erklärungen. Ich weiß auch nicht, was für eine Person Ulrike Meinhof wirklich war, ich kann nur erzählen, was sie macht. Anfangs sagt sie: Ich könnte meine Kinder nie verlassen. Dann verlässt sie die Kinder nicht nur, sie würde sie sogar ins palästinensische Lager schicken, für immer weg! Da sie glaubte, die Revolution erfordere solche Opfer. So etwas versteht man nicht, auch wenn man es zu ergründen versucht. Ich kann nur schreiben: Sie hat es getan." Christopher Huber, "Bernd Eichinger: 'Wir leben in Zeiten des Terrors,'" *Die Presse*, 25 Sept. 2008.

[128] "Wir haben die kollektive Erinnerungsschublade aufgemacht und ganz genau hingesehen, was drin ist. Diese Art der Aufarbeitung ist ein Schlüssel, das soll der Film beim Publikum erreichen. Ohne Psychologisierung. Seit Aristoteles wissen wir: Charakterisierung gibt es nicht, der Mensch zeigt seinen Charakter, wenn er agiert. Wir sind, was wir tun — nicht, was wir reden." Angie Dullinger, "'Kein Schuss zu viel:' Regisseur Uli Edel über das Polit-Drama *Der Baader Meinhof Komplex*, gescheiterte Träume der 68er und den Terrorismus der RAF," *Abendzeitung*, 21 Sept. 2008.

[129] In May 2009 the startling news broke that Karl-Heinz Kurras, the officer who shot Benno Ohnesorg, was a member of the SED and a secret Stasi informer. Although there is no evidence that the GDR ordered Kurras to murder a demonstrator, the fact that this police officer was working for the Stasi puts a different spin on the history of the West German student movement. Ohnesorg's death is considered to be the event that radicalized the student movement and eventually led to the formation of the RAF. If it had been known at the time that this policeman, considered to be a representative of the capitalist, imperialist state, was in reality a communist and supporter of the GDR, at the very least the rhetoric surrounding Ohnesorg's death would have been different. See "Ohnesorg-Todesschütze gibt sich unangreifbar," *Spiegel Online*, 24 May 2009, http://www.spiegel.de/politik/deutschland/0,1518,druck-626527,00.html.

[130] "In der rechten Presse ist die Schuld an der Katastrophe vom 2. Juni den Studenten selbst in die Schuhe geschoben worden. Vor allem der Springer-Konzern versucht in seiner Zeitung, die kritischen Stimmen der Studentenschaft als Randalierer und Krawallmacher zu verteufeln . . . Die Wahrheit ist aber, dass die Proteste dieser Studenten unseren Staat als Polizeistaat entlarvt haben, dass Polizei- und Presseterror am 2. Juni in Berlin ihren Höhepunkt erreicht haben, und dass wir begriffen haben, dass Freiheit in diesem Staat die Freiheit für den Polizeiknüppel ist." Bernd Eichinger, "*Der Baader Meinhof Komplex*: Drehbuch von Bernd Eichinger. Nach dem Buch und mit Beratung von Stefan Aust. Drehbuchmitarbeit Uli Edel," in Katja Eichinger, *Der Baader Meinhof Komplex*, 139. See also *Der Baader Meinhof Komplex* [2008], dir. Uli Edel, DVD (Unterföhring: Paramount Home Entertainment, 2008).

[131] "Die Geschichte beginnt in einem Idyll und endet in einem Blutbad, wie in einer griechischen Tragödie, nur mit dem Unterschied, dass es sich hier um bittere Realität handelte." Quoted in K. Eichinger, *Der Baader Meinhof Komplex*, 25.

[132] "Wir bitten die Bevölkerung, alle Aktionen, die zur Unschädlichmachung des Täters führen, tatkräftig zu unterstützen." Quoted in Sven Felix Kellerhoff, "Berlin, 2. Juni 1967: Um 20.30 Uhr fällt der Schuss, der Deutschland verändert," *Berliner Morgenpost*, 30 May 2007.

[133] "Als der Schah, Farah Diba und Bürgermeister Albertz um 19.56 Uhr eintreffen, sieht Michael Müller, 'wie die Hölle' losbricht. Vom gegenüber liegenden Bürgersteig fliegen Farbeier, faule Tomaten und sogar Steine in Richtung Oper." Kellerhoff, "Berlin, 2. Juni 1967."

[134] "Mindestens zwei Beamte sind verletzt, einer bricht vor Beginn der Räumung zusammen und blutet heftig aus seiner Kopfwunde, wohl getroffen von einem Stein." Kellerhoff, "Berlin, 2. Juni 1967."

135 "Ich spüre, dass sie mit ihrer Tat etwas Freies bewirkt hat, sogar in der Familie. Plötzlich fühle ich mich selbst befreit von einer Enge und auch Angst, die mein Leben vorher bestimmt hatte. Sie hat mir die Angst genommen." B. Eichinger, "*Der Baader Meinhof Komplex:* Drehbuch," 154.

136 "Du musst das als Rebellion begreifen. Diesmal werden wir nicht tatenlos zuschauen, wie sich der Faschismus breitmacht wie unter Hitler. Diesmal werden wir Widerstand leisten. Wir haben eine Verantwortung vor der Geschichte. . . . Wenn die Leute von uns abknallen wie Ohnesorg und Dutschke, dann werden wir in Zukunft zurückschießen." B. Eichinger, "*Der Baader Meinhof Komplex:* Drehbuch," 155–56.

137 "Oder glaubst du vielleicht, dass ihr mit eurem Theorie-gewichse irgendwas verändert?" B. Eichinger, "*Der Baader Meinhof Komplex:* Drehbuch," 157.

138 "Ich denke, dass Gruppierungen, die die Verhältnisse als Bedrückung empfinden, und ich meine damit existenziell bedrückend, dass diese nicht zögern werden, Bomben in das aus ihrer Sicht verkrustete Bewusstsein der Gesellschaft zu schmeißen." B. Eichinger, "*Der Baader Meinhof Komplex:* Drehbuch," 161.

139 "Nicht die Polizei, sondern die politischen Mächte haben die Verhältnisse zu ändern, unter denen Terrorismus entsteht." B. Eichinger, "*Der Baader Meinhof Komplex:* Drehbuch," 199.

140 "Es ist auch unsere Ignoranz, die den Terrorismus fördert." B. Eichinger, "*Der Baader Meinhof Komplex:* Drehbuch," 227.

141 Michael Althen, "Polit-Porno: *Der Baader Meinhof Komplex,*" *Frankfurter Allgemeine Zeitung*, 24 Sept. 2008.

142 "Sie sind keine Opfer und sind es nie gewesen. . . . Sie haben ihre Situation bis zum letzten Augenblick selber bestimmt. Das heißt, dass sie das gemacht haben, und nicht, dass es mit ihnen gemacht worden ist. . . . Ihr habt die Leute nie gekannt. Hört auf, sie so zu sehen, wie sie nicht waren." B. Eichinger, "*Der Baader Meinhof Komplex:* Drehbuch," 293.

143 "Er bietet keinerlei neue Erkenntnisse, und er gibt keinerlei Anlass, die Geschichte des deutschen Terrorismus neu zu schreiben." Gerhart Baum, "Film *Baader Meinhof Komplex:* Es war kein Krieg," *Die Zeit*, 18 Sept. 2008.

144 "Tatsächlich ist die politische und ideologische Zweideutigkeit des Films sicher gewollt — eine aus Hollywood importierte Blockbuster-Strategie. Das intelligentere Groß-Entertainment enthält dort seit einiger Zeit gezielte politische Verwirrspiele, siehe zuletzt *The Dark Knight:* Hier ein Happen für die Anhänger der Selbstjustiz, dort ein Zwinkern für die Feinde des Überwachungsstaats, jeder darf sehen, was er sehen möchte, und am Ende hebt sich alles gegenseitig auf. So machen es Eichinger und Edel auch, clever auf der Höhe des Zeitgeists — nur ist der Trend, den sie bedienen, gerade schon dabei, recht schal zu werden." Tobias Kniebe, "Bang Boom Bang: *Baader Meinhof Komplex,*" *Süddeutsche Zeitung*, 24 Sept. 2008.

145 "Wir haben gelernt, dass Reden ohne Handeln Unrecht ist." B. Eichinger, "*Der Baader Meinhof Komplex:* Drehbuch," 153.

4: History Lessons: The Enduring Appeal of Utopianism and the Specter of Violence

THE PAST REMAINS IN THE PRESENT, as fragmentary impressions in the imagination, as relics and recycled imagery, and as stories that reveal lessons for today. While the history film in the narrowest sense reenacts the past, with its action taking place in an earlier time period, there are feature films set in the present that explore history in a critical fashion and deserve to be examined under the rubric of the history film. Alexander Kluge's *Die Patriotin* (The patriot woman, 1979) stands as a prominent example of a film with a contemporary setting that is heavily invested in an exploration of the past and how history is written and disseminated. The central figure in Kluge's film, high-school history teacher Gabi Teichert, is dissatisfied with the limited materials available to teach her students about German history. Determined to uncover more suitable resources, Teichert takes her shovel into the forest on an archeological dig in search of what has been buried, lost, or forgotten. Dissecting history textbooks with saws and dissolving them in liquid so that she can readily digest them, Teichert seeks new ways to make history meaningful and accessible to herself and her students.

The post-Wall films under investigation here do not feature characters who interrogate German history quite so blatantly as those in *Die Patriotin*, nor do they display the montage principles used by Kluge to encourage audiences to participate actively in the process of historiography. What they share with *Die Patriotin* is the same pedagogical fervor. They look to history for lessons and guidance on what ideas deserve to be salvaged from the dustbin of history. Unlike Kluge's avant-garde film, which tries to recover long-forgotten wishes of ordinary people and give voice to a multitude of perspectives, the post-Wall films contemplate two historical traditions to gauge their relevance for the present day.

The fall of the Berlin Wall and the demise of Communism in Europe have contributed to a growing sense that currently there is no politically viable alternative to capitalism. Living in a world in which the clear lines between bipolar superpowers have been erased and nearly every imaginable youth rebellion since 1968 has already been tried and failed to overthrow the system, what is left for an activist-minded young generation to do to eradicate social injustice? The search for a workable German legacy for the new millennium is deeply imbricated in a generational conflict that differs significantly from that of the first postwar generation, who were traumatized by the horrors perpetrated under National Socialism in the name of the German nation. The generation born between 1939 and 1943, including Andreas Baader, Gudrun Ensslin, Rudi Dutschke, Peter Schneider, Margarethe von Trotta, and Volker Schlöndorff, to name just a few, partook in a revolt against the parental generation in part to signal their unwillingness to accept the heritage of dictatorship, world war, and the holocaust. Each in his or her own way reacted against German history and worked to bring about a new social order. What happens, however, when the parent's (or grandparent's) history becomes the years of revolutionary dreams rather than Nazi terror? How does the generational conflict play out when youth in the new millennium look back on the history of those who revolted in 1968? Faced with the utopianism of their parents' generation, their dreams of a better world, and their failure to change the system as radically as they had hoped, how does today's youth deal with the recent past? For those most interested in changing the world and placing their own efforts in a historical context, it is expedient to contemplate the basic tenets of this historical rebellion. Looking to the recent past for workable models and adopting timeless values worth preserving is only half the task, because the new generation seems keenly aware that it needs to promote its own originality and creativity so as not to be merely nostalgic for the good old days.

In much the same vein, Germany has long revered its philosophers and writers as the glue holding the nation together in lieu of political unity over the centuries. German idealism and especially Kant's categorical imperative seem to offer up a sense of security and an assurance that there are absolute, universal moral values to regulate society and make sense of a world that has changed so radically in the last two decades. And yet what kind of a world would it be if everyone took the idea of absolute moral imperatives seriously and became intent on enforcing them?

Against the two-sided coin of political idealism with its call for a perfect society and its use of force to obtain such lofty goals, this chapter examines two recent films that present creative chaos as a strategy to protest against the loss of utopian dreams. Creative chaos can be understood as a form of political engagement, whereby established patterns of behavior are disrupted through playful or innovative acts in the hope of generating widespread cognition of society's failures and the need for a new social order. Hans Weingartner's *Die fetten Jahre sind vorbei* (The years of plenty are over, English title: *The Edukators*) and Marcus Mittermeier's *Muxmäuschenstill* (Quiet as a mouse) are black comedies about young people who want to teach ordinary citizens about equality and civility at home and about their global responsibility in a world beset with injustice. Weingartner's film features rebellious "educators" who break into

Berlin villas, not to steal anything but to rearrange the furnishings and jolt the residents out of their comfort zone. While their imaginative acts are intended to teach the rich that possessions cannot guarantee security, their tactics begin to resemble those used by the RAF to force societal change, including kidnapping, creating a people's prison, and destroying the sources of media control. In a postmodern society where traditions are recycled in new configurations and socialism has been discredited, the educators must come to grips with the history of the '68 generation and determine which ideas are worth saving. *Muxmäuschenstill* likewise is about a self-appointed do-gooder who oversees a network of informants, monitors suspicious individuals, films his "pedagogical measures," and archives with a zeal rivaling the Stasi. Rather than joining an organized resistance movement, Mux and his videographer become independent vigilantes, dispensing justice at will. Inspired by the noble ideals of the German Enlightenment and classicism, Mux is nonetheless a sociopath obsessed with modern media and the adrenaline rush of control. *Die fetten Jahre sind vorbei* and *Muxmäuschenstill* reflect a growing discomfort with the lack of political and moral high ground in the present and look to the past for guidance. Finding correlative paradigms in different historical periods, 1968 and the late-eighteenth century respectively, they propose creative means to redefine current German national identity in a globally responsible framework. The primary question that arises is whether the characters in these films achieve an original form of social engagement that can be viewed as acts of poetic resistance and moral righteousness or whether they succumb to the ancient pitfall of violence routinely associated with forcing others to do the right thing.

Before we turn to the two films under investigation, a brief survey will reveal that the thwarted desire for utopia, and disappointment about society's inability to mobilize for change, especially among young people, have become prominent cinematic themes in recent years. In postmillennial German cinema, the desire to improve society through innovative initiatives is addressed in satires and farces more commonly than in serious social dramas. The omnibus film *Weltverbesserungsmaßnahmen* (Measures to improve the world, dir. Jörn Hintzer, Jakob Hüfner, and Tom Schreiber, 2005), for example, consists of seven short films, each outlining a way to make the world a better place. One idea is to create a "loan siblings program," in which the long-term unemployed will serve as surrogate siblings in families with only one child. This program will solve two pressing social problems in one stroke, providing steady work for individuals faced with the reduction of welfare benefits thanks to Harz-IV and giving the multitude of spoiled only-children caused by falling birthrates the companionship necessary for socialization. While many of the measures are witty comments on contemporary society, the segments tend to run too long and seem more appropriate to a comedy ensemble television show like *Saturday Night Live*. The topic of activism by means of familiar terrorist tactics such as kidnapping and extortion has found its way into two recent satires, *Der Ärgermacher* (The troublemaker, dir. Steffen Jürgens and Bettina Schoeller, 2004) and *Die Quereinsteigerinnen* (Women switching careers, dir. Rainer Knepperges and Christian Mrasek, 2005). Both films feature apolitical individuals who have no desire to change society; instead they use commando tactics to force others to fulfill their own whimsical needs. Filmed in black and white and adopting the pseudo-documentary style of investigative reporting, *Der Ärgermacher* tells the story of a writer who steals Franz Kafka's bones and holds them for ransom, demanding that his novel be published. *Die Quereinsteigerinnen* is a farce about two women who kidnap a German Telecom executive and insist that the company replace its pink and gray public-telephone pillars with the old yellow telephone booths. Inspired by the women's free lifestyle and falling in love with one of his captors, the executive decides to drop out and join them in an uncertain, spontaneous life outside conventional society. While neither comedy purports to be a realistic commentary on contemporary issues, they do illustrate how widespread and attractive the core counterculture myth is. Despite being divested of any political content, the romantic notion of dropping out and fighting the system persists as a likeable and resilient storyline.

The most ambitious recent film attempting to inspire viewers to discuss issues of social justice, democracy, and freedom in Germany today is the omnibus film *GG 19: 19 gute Gründe für die Demokratie* (GG 19: Nineteen good reasons for democracy, dir. Harald Siebler and eighteen others, 2007). In a grand gesture to celebrate the fifty-fifth anniversary of the constitution in 2004, Harald Siebler called on scriptwriters to propose six-minute stories about the fundamental civil rights embodied in the first nineteen articles of the constitution. Four hundred and eighty-two scripts were submitted for consideration by a jury, and more than 1,500 individuals participated in making the nineteen episodes that comprise the 149-minute film. While the various segments employ a variety of stylistic means to voice concerns and hopes for human rights, most have a surreal, dream-like quality or are conceived as satires rather than realistic portrayals of everyday life. For instance, in the segment *Adrenalin Flash* (dir. Johannes von Gwinner) devoted to article 1, which guarantees the inalienable right to human dignity, a man is attacked in his home, tied up, and forced to watch on a monitor as his wife and children are tortured, only to learn that he is an unwitting contestant on a bizarre reality television show.

Die fetten Jahre sind vorbei and *Muxmäuschenstill* share with many recent German films a similar visual signature, production style, and interest in young people who have no sense of direction but are searching for meaning in an alienating environment. Both films were shot in digital video format, rely heavily on improvisation and the synergy of input between actor-cameraman-director, and aim at a semi-documentary look for a realistic portrait of a generation. The same thing can be said for *Egoshooter* (2004), directed by Christian Becker and Oliver Schwabe. This intriguing film was sponsored by Wim Wenders and Ute Schneider, who initiated the series "radical digital" to support young directors making their first or second film with digital video. The main character, Jakob, played by Tom Schilling, is a lonely, reflective adolescent living in Cologne, who uses his camera to make sense of the world. In a video diary, Jakob provides the viewer with a glimpse of the everyday life of a sympathetic but bewildered teenager searching for answers and human contact. Using both an objective camera perspective to show Jakob's daily life and also arming actor Tom Schilling with a camera to give Jakob's subjective impressions of the world around him, *Egoshooter* eschews a conventional narrative focused on character development and conflict followed by resolution. Instead it offers up a fragmentary form that captures routine events in a young man's life, such as parties, concerts, sex, and breakfast table conversations, as well as more deviant behavior like breaking into a home to destroy its contents, spray-painting graffiti, feigning to be an abandoned schoolboy and begging for money to get back home, and voyeuristically filming his brother having sex with his pregnant girlfriend. Jakob uses his camera like a vital appendage of his body and mind, as if his thoughts and actions only make sense through the camera's lens. The filmmakers borrow the term egoshooter or first-person-shooter (FPS) from the realm of computer gaming, where it refers to video games that render the virtual world through the point of view of a player who aims guns or other weapons at targets. As the film's title implies, in a world saturated with media images it is only through shooting his life as a film that Jakob can acquire an identity. The power of the media is seen as untouchable, a force that manipulates the youth and prevents them from organizing and working for social change. Jakob's friend Phillip formulates a theory that can stand for the generation's motto:

> The few things we are actually told about in the media are mere fragments. It's ridiculous. I mean, what really comes across is just disinformation. We're kept happy, supposed to get excited about some pop music, fight with each other, butt heads, and bet over who is more real. If we could honestly do something together, could organize a classic, really good youth movement, like the kind I imagine, of course with violence, I don't know, with a mass willing to use violence, ready to overthrow things a bit, we could simply get started. But you see how people out there are, nothing is happening at all. When you've mobilized them a bit, they start fighting among themselves.[1]

Without a youth movement that could offer them a morally uplifting and unifying identity, the teenagers seek collective experiences in hip-hop concerts or by lashing out in meaningless destructive behavior that can result only in an adrenalin rush, not in change.

In contrast to characters like Jakob, the young girls now populating the cinematic landscape in Germany rarely consider the promise of collective political action as a remedy for their isolation and aimlessness. The teenage female protagonists in films like Henner Winckler's *Lucy* (2006) and Christian Petzold's *Gespenster* (Ghosts, 2005) seek affection and emotional connection in their sexual partners and broken families with only fleeting success. Winkler's film features Maggie, the eighteen-year-old single mother of Lucy, who is torn between taking care of her infant daughter and pursuing normal teenager activities like going to bars, meeting up with friends, and having a boyfriend. Herself the daughter of a single mother, Maggie dropped out of school and has no training for a job or for motherhood, but longs for an intact nuclear family and something worthwhile to do. The lost soul Nina in Petzold's *Gespenster* fares no better in her search for connection and identity. In two intersecting stories, the orphan Nina looks for affection first with the charismatic street urchin Toni and then with Françoise, a woman who cannot stop mourning her dead child like the mother in the Grimms' fairytale *The Shroud*. Nina tries to fulfill Toni's every wish in the promise of love, leaving her secure group home, revealing a haunting dream about finding her soul mate in order to become a contestant on the reality show *Girlfriends*, and having sex with her, but Toni abandons Nina when more lucrative prey comes along. Desolate and now homeless, Nina is drawn to Françoise, who has been searching for her long-lost daughter Marie since the three-year-old was abducted in Berlin in 1989. While Nina hopes to be rescued by this good mother, Françoise is delusional and cannot save her. Both *Lucy* and *Gespenster* end with uncertain futures for their lonely heroines, who are suffering from the lack of a functional family life and an effective social support system.[2] Sylke Enders's *Kroko* (Crocodile, 2003), presents an equally harsh portrait of urban life for young girls, but this film focuses more on the social dimension of isolation and lack of direction. Kroko is an ice-cold proletarian glamour queen, who dominates her mother, boyfriend, and nearly everyone else with her sheer determination and attitude. This blond beauty with the slick look of Brigitte Helm's evil vamp robot in Fritz Lang's *Metropolis* (1927) runs into trouble when she is caught driving without a license; she crashes into a bike rider, seriously injuring the young man. Sentenced to sixty hours of community service in a group home for mentally disabled adolescents, Kroko is at first revolted by the idea of working with "spastics" and their hippie house leader. As she gets to know her charges, who are dependent but also spontaneous and perceptive individuals, we begin to see some chinks in her armor.

While never completely letting down her guard and remaining a largely selfish, materialistic teenager with an overgrown sense of entitlement, she does begin to see value in people who are markedly uncool. Forced to deal with others by a judicial system that aims to integrate young offenders into society, Kroko allows herself a glimpse of how her inner strength can be put to use within a social context.

While contemporary German motion pictures tend to depict the everyday lives of adolescents in a gendered pattern, with boys more cognizant of and eager for social or political group membership and girls more focused on fitting into secure familial and sexual relationships, the teenagers have many common existential problems. Along with the typical lack of control particular to their age group as minors, these young people suffer from absent and ineffectual parents, unstable living conditions often bordering on homelessness, a lack of education and job training which leads to little interest or prospects for the future, and a general lethargy that can only fleetingly be overcome through shopping, drugs, sex, or violence. Without guidance and a sense of purpose, they go through life as phantoms, never knowing in which direction they should head but acutely aware that they want out of this state of limbo.

Die fetten Jahre sind vorbei

Hans Weingartner's *Die fetten Jahre sind vorbei* taps into this prevailing sense of existing in a world without orientation because the old guideposts have been taken away and nothing new has replaced them. What separates this film from others is that it proposes underground activism as a possible solution to youthful malaise. *Die fetten Jahre sind vorbei* follows the escapades of Jan and Peter, two rebels who call themselves "the educators" (*die Erziehungsberechtigten*) and are determined to teach the rich that their sheltered and privileged life is unjust. Jan and Peter break into empty villas and playfully assemble the furniture into a neat pyramid before leaving a note stating "the years of plenty are over." After learning that Peter's girlfriend Jule is saddled with a 100,000 euro debt for crashing into a Mercedes while driving without insurance, Jan tries to convince her of the injustice of her situation and divulges the details of his clandestine "punking" actions. Intrigued, Jule persuades Jan to break into the house of the man to whom she owes the debt, but the two are interrupted when Hardenberg arrives home unexpectedly and recognizes Jule. With the help of Peter, they kidnap Hardenberg and take him to an isolated cabin in the Tyrolean Mountains. The hated capitalist turns out to be a former '68 student rebel, who, like his captors, dreamed of a better world in his youth before succumbing to the rat race. After debating the value of "poetic resistance," the young people set Hardenberg free. The next day, however, Hardenberg watches from a safe distance

Fig. 4.1. Still from Hans Weingartner's Die fetten Jahre sind vorbei *(2004). Photo courtesy of Stiftung Deutsche Kinemathek.*

while riot police break into Jan and Peter's apartment, but all they find in the empty rooms is a note stating: "Some people never change." Having absconded to Spain unharmed, the educators ride off in Hardenberg's yacht, intent upon destroying television satellites serving all of Europe and forcing complacent citizens to realize that they are willingly being anesthetized to life.

Die fetten Jahre sind vorbei was invited to compete at the Cannes Film Festival, where it premiered on 17 May 2004; it was enthusiastically received by festival crowds and rewarded with a prolonged standing ovation. The trade press celebrated Weingartner's work as the first German film in eleven years to compete at Cannes and the portent of a new era in German cinema, one characterized by well-made, original films about political topics, containing an appropriate mixture of seriousness and wit.[3] From its general cinematic release on 25 November 2004 until the end of 2005, *Die fetten Jahre sind vorbei* sold 873,935 tickets in German theaters, ranking it slightly behind the critically acclaimed *Sophie Scholl: Die letzten Tage* (Sophie Scholl: The final days, dir. Marc Rothemund, 2005) with receipts of 1,096,026 tickets, and *Alles auf Zucker* (Go for Zucker, dir. Dani Levy, 2005) with 1,038,631.[4] Along with a strong showing at the box office, *Die fetten Jahre sind vorbei* received largely positive reviews and was awarded the Silver Lola for best motion picture and the best supporting-actor prize for Burghardt Klaußner at the German Film Prize ceremonies.

Hans Weingartner came to filmmaking by an unusual and somewhat roundabout route, making amateur films as a young boy but completing an academic degree program in neuroscience before devoting himself to a career in motion pictures. Born in Feldkirch, Austria, in 1970, he began studying physics and cognitive science at the University of Vienna in 1990. Alongside his university education, he received a diploma as a camera assistant in 1994 from the Austrian Association of Cinematography in Vienna. In 1994 he moved to Berlin, where he lived in a squatter house in the Friedrichshain district while studying cognitive science at the Free University. After completing his residency in neurosurgery at the FU Steglitz clinic, he enrolled at the Academy of Media Arts in Cologne (KHM), graduating in 2001 with the film *Das weiße Rauschen* (White noise). This debut film about a schizophrenic who rejects traditional medicine and embarks on a journey of self-healing through introspection has many of the hallmarks of Weingartner's subsequent films. Influenced by the Danish Dogma movement, Weingartner wrote the script, worked with a small team on a modest budget using digital cameras, no artificial light or constructed sets, improvised much of the dialogue with the actors' input, and aimed at providing a realistic portrayal of mental illness.[5] *Das weiße Rauschen* was highly praised by critics, won the Max Ophüls Award, the First Steps Award, and the best movie debut award from the Association of Film Critics, and was released by X-Film Verleih, guaranteeing it a wide cinema distribution and DVD sales.

This film tells the story of schizophrenia from the point of view of 21-year-old Lukas. Lukas moves from the countryside to Cologne to live with his sister, and after eating hallucinogenic mushrooms, he begins to hear voices and is afflicted by bouts of paranoia and disorientation. The white noise produced by rushing water is the only respite from the voices in his head: "White noise, that is all the visions, of all the people, of all time, in one moment . . . Whoever sees white noise goes insane immediately. Except when he already is insane. Then he becomes normal."[6] After two suicide attempts, institutionalization, and the threat of life-long sedation, Lukas decides to forego traditional treatment and seek out the white noise. He is rescued by a group of hippies and travels to Spain, where he finds some peace among these nonconformists, but his sense of belonging is fleeting. The voices return, and Lukas ends up alone on the seashore listening to the waves and contemplating how he can lead a normal life. He comes to the conclusion that he must turn conventional wisdom upside down: "The trick, so to speak, consists in going backward down the path of enlightenment."[7]

The jerky handheld camera and grainy image quality that have become nearly ubiquitous among young filmmakers is well suited here to convey the sense of mental instability plaguing Lukas as he suffers from schizophrenic attacks. Especially noteworthy are the mobile cameras that

encircle him and move into extreme close-ups as if physically threatening him, the out-of-focus pov shots as he is over-medicated in the mental hospital, and the scenes where he is working in a mannequin factory,
surrounded by plastic dolls that serve as a comment on the lifeless, fake
people who comprise "normal" society. Perhaps even more impressive is
the sound track, which contains the threatening voices only Lukas can
hear and the eerily beautiful music composed by Andreas Wodraschke.

Weingartner's hands-on approach to filmmaking continued with *Die
fetten Jahre sind vorbei*. He has repeatedly taken on the dual roles of director and screenwriter and has hired the same small team, which allows for
some continuity between films.[8] In addition to directing, at various times
he has worked concurrently as cameraman, editor, producer, and even
actor, appearing in cameo performances in his films. Weingartner directed
Die fetten Jahre sind vorbei, cowrote the script with Katharina Held,
founded his own production company y3, and coproduced the film with
Antonin Svoboda from Coop 99 in partnership with the television stations SWR and Arte, which both provided help with revisions to the filmscript.[9] Along with his contemporary Andreas Dresen, whose films often
take shape during production and are largely improvised (for example,
Halbe Treppe [Grill Point, 2002] and *Wolke neun* [Cloud Nine, 2008]),
Weingartner routinely conceived much of the dialogue for *Die fetten Jahre
sind vorbei* in a spontaneous fashion shortly before the cameras started
rolling, allowed the actors to improvise their own dialogues, and planned
on filming the narrative in a strictly chronological order.[10] Again shooting
with digital cameras, using little or no artificial light, no constructed sets,
and little nondiegetic music, Weingartner aimed at a documentary-like
style in the tradition of Richard Linklater's *Slackers* (1991) for his portrait
of the young generation.

Free Rainer: Dein Fernseher lügt (Free Rainer: Your television is lying,
2007) picks up where *Die fetten Jahre sind vorbei* left off and is a satirical
critique of the television industry. Rainer starts out as a slick, cocaine-
snorting, ruthless executive producing trash-TV shows such as *Go get the
super baby*, in which contestants battle to see whose sperm will impregnate
an egg first. After he is seriously injured in a car crash, he comes to his
senses. Recognizing that he has contributed to the dumbing down of the
masses, Rainer quits his job and begins a clandestine campaign to change
viewers' habits and the industry's offerings by manipulating the official
audience-share data. Rainer bands together with the woman who tried to
kill him because his deceitful programming was responsible for her grandfather's suicide, and a sociophobic employee of the Institute for Media
Analysis who believes in countless conspiracy theories and is inspired by
his favorite book, *Brave New World*, to join in the crusade against televised soma.[11] The trio hires a group of misfits, and this unlikely guerilla
group succeeds not just in changing television for the better but in creating a

contagious positive atmosphere in Germany, where people begin to read books, venture out into the streets and parks for communal activities, and generally live better lives. The film ends with the culture saboteurs embarking on a new venture, moving to the most important test market town in Germany to manipulate the research data and influence the development of new consumer products and advertising campaigns.

Despite an impressive cast including megastar Moritz Bleibtreu, a provocative topic with great potential for a witty satire, and a previously successful scriptwriting team and technical crew, *Free Rainer* was a financial and critical flop. Making a disappointing showing at the box-office and garnering mostly negative reviews, the film quickly disappeared from the movie theaters and failed to reach, let alone inspire, its intended audience.[12] Weingartner's stated goal was to teach average Germans who reportedly watch four hours of television daily that they are being manipulated by callous and shallow television executives to consent to a vegetative state. Echoing a notion put forth by Mikhail Bakunin that the masses submit willingly to society's approved forms of intoxication to prevent any opposition, but replacing the terms "church" and "pubs" in Bakunin's formulation with "the television industry," Weingartner maintains: "In my opinion television is being used as a sedative. People had to struggle all day long in tough capitalistic competition: they had to assert themselves, were afraid of losing their jobs. Then in the evening they come home and use the boob tube like a drug to beam themselves away."[13] In contrast to the relatively limited audience share of less than a million that he reached with *Die fetten Jahre sind vorbei*, Weingartner intended *Free Rainer* for the general public and aimed at making a blockbuster to rival Hollywood fare. Working with a different audience in mind, he acknowledged: "I tried to make a film that was understandable for the broad masses and not just for a small group of the educated elite who go to art-house cinemas."[14] Dismayed by the current division in the German film industry between high-brow motion pictures catering to a select audience and low-brow pictures made for the less-educated, less-discriminating masses who frequent the multiplex theaters, Weingartner decided to make a film with a challenging topic using such crowd pleasers as action sequences, slick images, and simplistic, almost black-and-white characters in a storyline that is often embarrassingly preachy and plagued by an unbalanced tempo. The result is an uneven film in which the director reverts to the very formulaic aspects of popular filmmaking he was intent upon criticizing.

Notwithstanding differences in style, critical acclaim, and level of popularity, all three of Weingartner's films address pressing social problems and are variations on the road movie. With topics ranging from mental illness to economic inequality and media manipulation, they share the same central ideal of encouraging active nonconformity to the wisdom of mainstream society. Whether featuring an individual who objects to being sedated into normalcy or small groups of outsiders who protest against affluence and television as the collective drug of choice, these films offer pedagogical lessons on the need to change societal thinking. In contrast to a cinema of consensus (Rentschler) that avoids difficult issues and seeks common ground, Weingartner wants to contribute to what I would term a *cinema of consciousness* that challenges the status quo and is unabashedly educational. He thus straddles the fine line between popular media styles that appeal to mass audiences exactly because they deliver tried and true patterns and a message of resistance to established behavior norms, economic systems, and political structures that demand new ways of thinking. Weingartner sees himself as a diagnostician of an unhealthy culture: "My task as a filmmaker is to look at where it hurts."[15] Touching the open wounds of Germany society, he prescribes a tried and true remedy: collective action. Dissatisfied individuals can only be empowered if they band together to demand change.

Die fetten Jahre sind vorbei identifies global capitalism as the disease and the educators as the cure. Jan and Peter are masked crusaders with elements of Robin Hood, Batman, and Thomas Anderson alias Neo from *The Matrix* (dir. Larry and Andy Wachowski, 1999). Like these other fictional characters, the educators are morally righteous, perceptive individuals who can see the structure of oppressive societal behavior and are intent upon rectifying injustice wherever they encounter it. It is no surprise that Jan recognizes in Jule the same superpower demonstrated by Neo in the blockbuster film *The Matrix*, namely her ability to see the facade while others believe in a web of illusions. Whereas in the Wachowski brothers' cult classic the unsuspecting masses are content to live in a make-believe world because it shelters them from the bitter reality that they serve as human batteries for alien machinery, in Weingartner's film Jan acts like the computer hacker Neo to break society's codes, alerting the public to the numbing effect of endless consumption that keeps people trapped in a mere simulacrum of reality and prevents them from living authentic lives.[16] Jan admires Jule's acute awareness of constructs, stating: "That is the matrix. You see it and can't live in it. Neither can I."[17] The centrality of this pop-culture reference for the film and for Weingartner's general philosophy is witnessed by the director's own claim: "I see myself as the submarine in the matrix."[18] Jan and Peter's nightly break-ins are based on the counterculture principle embodied in *The Matrix* that the enlightened must awaken the cataleptic masses. According to this logic, the general public does not question the basic morality of capitalism with its asymmetrical distribution of wealth, because the system is so entrenched it seems natural. As informed individuals, Jan and Peter consider it their duty to alert others to the true nature of this phenomenon. By disarming the security system and then turning expensive furniture, high-tech entertainment systems, and exclusive decorative items into new and unexpected arrangements, they hope to shatter the protective bubble of privilege surrounding the power elites. By destroying their sense of security rather than their property, they believe that the rich will begin to realize the inherent injustice of their status. The educators' playful performance art has a deadly serious purpose: they want to strike fear in the hearts of the rich by invading their home and creating chaos in their inner sanctum. The staging of break-ins as spontaneous happenings and enjoyable if mischievous symbolic shows rather than acts of violence with terrorist goals leaves little doubt with whom the audience should identify and sympathize. The contrast between an empty palatial residence devoid of human warmth and indicative of a barren lifestyle and the likeable, energetic educators who have transformed everyday objects into artistic installations makes it eminently easier to accept the film team's characterization of the break-ins as "a symbolic action" contributing to "poetic resistance." Hans Weingartner has repeatedly maintained that the educators are not criminals but rather creative individuals who use subtle forms of humor: "At first glance they create chaos, but there is meaning in the chaos. Just like in many poems. Therefore, one could call what they are doing 'poetic resistance.'"[19] He argues further: "Breaking into these people's villas is a symbolic action. . . . To break in there, at the richest of the rich, that is symbolic. . . . I find that to do something like that has an inner poetics and beauty."[20] Actor Daniel Brühl concurred: "What I like about this poetic resistance in *The Edukators* is that it proceeds non-violently."[21] Consciousness-raising on the level of the fictional characters and the actual audience is predicated on the notion that property is theft.

Although Jan does not belong to any organized political group, he does adhere to a set of ideas associated with groups like ATTAC and popularized in books by Naomi Klein, Kalle Lasn, and Mark Dery, not to mention Theodor Adorno, Max Horkheimer, Mikhail Bakunin, and Guy Debord.[22] Jan is the ideological mouthpiece among the educators, who usually provides the ideas and the rationale for their clashes with the establishment. It is Jan who teaches Jule to become more radical, to trust her instincts, and to find an outlet for her dissatisfaction with the world. When they first meet, Jule is a young person who deeply wants to change things but does not know where to begin. She admits that there is no convincing ideology or program she can grasp on to: "The problem is simply that I can't see anything anywhere that I really believe in."[23] In contrast to Jan and Peter, she starts out on a much more conventional path to political activism by joining an anti-globalism group protesting sweatshops in the Third World. Seen handing out pamphlets and calmly trying to persuade shoppers to change their spending habits and willingly stop exploitative labor practices, Jule embraces nonviolent means to change attitudes. Even when the police forcefully drag two law-abiding protesters (one played by the director Hans Weingartner)[24] out of a shoe store and arrest them, Jule refrains from joining the other young people trying to tip over the paddy wagon.

Despite her initial restraint, Jule begins to engage in minor acts of aggression, destroying property as a protest against her powerlessness in the face of wealthy, domineering adversaries. After being evicted for falling behind in the rent, she must renovate her apartment in order to get back the deposit. However, inspired by Jan's arguments about justice, she decides to forfeit the deposit and cover the walls with graffiti and newspapers, transforming the apartment into protest art and in the process willfully damaging the callous landlord's property. As a waitress in a posh restaurant, Jule is frustrated over having to deal with arrogant, petty clientele and strikes out by keying a Mercedes Benz in the parking garage. It is no coincidence that she vents her hostility on this particular brand of luxury car, since a Mercedes changed her life, destroyed her dream of living "free and wild," and trapped her in a form of indentured servitude. Driving one day without insurance or registration, Jule was responsible for a car crash that destroyed Hardenberg's Mercedes, and she now calculates that it will take her eight years to pay off the damages. Jule accepts that she was at fault and must pay for her own mistakes, but Jan counters:

> Who says so? The cops, the district attorneys, the *Bild* newspaper? That is petty bourgeois bullshit morality. Decency. Honesty. Sense of family. You have to go to work on time. You have to pay your taxes. You shouldn't steal anything in the supermarket. We get it shoved down our throats all day long, first in school and then on the boob tube. And why? So that guys like him can buy perversely expensive cars. Shit on that kind of morality. Ruining a young woman's life, that is immoral. Or do you believe that the guy asked himself even once if perhaps he was in the wrong?[25]

Jan argues that a poor waitress driving without insurance or registration cannot be considered a transgression because the real crime here is conspicuous over-consumption. When he gets the opportunity to confront the capitalist Hardenberg personally, he formulates the conflict in familiar Marxist terms: "We are living in a dictatorship of capital. Everything you own you have stolen."[26] Jan's sense of what is right and wrong is clear-cut; the rich exploit the poor and downtrodden, a wealthy victim is an oxymoron, and a truly good person protects the weak. For instance, when a homeless man is harassed by officials for riding the streetcar without a ticket, Jan stands up for him in a show of righteous indignation. The young rebel holds himself to the highest standards of moral behavior and even considers giving up seditious activities because he betrayed Peter by falling in love with Jule. Jan's strict adherence to a personal code of decency as the prerequisite for political engagement is admirable, and this crucial personality trait not only makes him a sympathetic character; it also tends to lend credence to his ideology. Moreover, even Jan's hostage (albeit under duress) confirms the legitimacy of his cultural critique and the values he instantiates. Hardenberg praises Jan as an idealist and agrees that a higher moral justice outweighs conventional laws.

The educators recognize that the West German protest movements of the sixties and seventies attempted revolutionary action already, with little change in the socioeconomic order. In the post-cold-war, postmodern condition, where Communism is no longer an untried remedy for inequality and old revolutionary ideas are merely repackaged, they wonder how their generation can be original, let alone successful. Jule notes: "Everything has already been done and nothing worked. Why should we be able to pull it off?" to which Jan replies "Even if there have been other revolutions and they didn't quite work out in the details, the most important thing is that the best ideas have survived."[27] If one looks closely at what these young people know about recent history and what revolutionary ideas they value, it becomes clear that they have a selective memory about the '68 student movement and the Red Army Faction. While they are prolific with slogans like "Reach one, teach a hundred" and "Every heart is a revolutionary cell," they reject the type of public demonstrations popularized by student radicals, saying they are completely ineffective, and never consider working within the political system or creating an alternative forum like the APO (Außerparliamentarische Opposition). While never referring specifically to the *Spaßguerilla*, *Kommune 1*, or the *Situationiste Internationale*, the educators embrace the basic strategies of these historical groups.[28] Staging protests that are playful, imaginative pranks and utilizing the establishment's power against itself to derail it (for example, arranging property in new configurations to illustrate the absurdity of property) places them as the heir to figures like Dieter Kunzelmann, Rainer Langhans, Fritz Teufel, and Guy Debord. Invoking the vocabulary of the RAF kidnapping of Hanns-Martin Schleyer in 1977, Jan asks Hardenberg how he likes it in the people's prison (*Volksgefängnis*). Only half jokingly, Peter suggests that they take a lesson from the RAF, hang a sign around Hardenberg's neck reading "prisoner of the educators," film it all, and send it to a television station. They quickly reject the idea of ransoming or killing their captive as the RAF and the 2 June Movement had done in the past. More importantly, they vehemently refuse to see any similarity between the gradual formation of the RAF from activists staging a T-shirt demonstration to arsonists protesting consumerism to terrorists routinely using kidnapping, bombing, and murder to force change and their own development from activists staging covert break-ins with an ideological message intent on spreading fear to kidnappers and vigilantes trying to force apathetic citizens to change their decadent, unhealthy lifestyles. When Hardenberg reminds them that they are using the same methods as the RAF to frighten their enemies, they dismiss the comparison and argue that the educators are unassuming and original. Originality and creativity are vital elements in their self-defini-tion, because these qualities offer assurance that the younger generation can be unique and counteract postmodern cynicism. Although the edu-cators look to the past for guidance, there are areas of recent German history that they leave untouched. The most significant taboo seems to be the GDR, because they are completely silent about the one revolu-tion that occurred in their own country during their lifetime. Considering that their analysis of capitalism has a distinctly Marxist flavor (capital-ists exploit the worker, capitalist labor is alienating, and, echoing Pierre Joseph Proudhon, "property is theft"), the fact that they never discuss the failure of an alternative economic system in Germany suggests that their ideas might implode under intense historical scrutiny. Perhaps the most important history lesson they never contemplate is whether there might be a fine line between creative chaos and violence (such as the rela-tionship between the Kommune 1's ironic pamphlet suggesting the burn-ing of department stores to bring home the economic component of the Vietnam War and the fact that Baader and Ensslin actually carried out this jest in reality). Since the educators refuse to ransom or kill Hardenberg, eventually admitting that kidnapping him was an egocentric act of self-preservation devoid of political intent, and setting him free, their crime is sublimated from an actual offense to a mental miscalculation. Inten-tion rather than actual deed becomes the standard for evaluating whether something is a crime, and since they have consciously admitted their mis-take, it somehow disappears and they are absolved of any wrongdoing.

Hardenberg functions to a great extent as a witness to history, explaining his trajectory from a student revolutionary to a multi-mil-lionaire manager. While smoking a joint with his young captors, he reminisces about his youth in the student movement, being a leader in the Socialist German Student Union (Sozialistischer Deutscher Studen-tenbund, SDS), how he knew Rudi Dutschke personally, lived in a com-mune, and experimented with free sex. But then he followed the path of many, got married, had children, got a good job, bought a house, and slowly his determination to change the world eroded and his energy was funneled into maintaining his wealth and the status quo. Surprised by his own development and the widespread conservative transformation of the '68 generation, he admits that conformity sneaks up on you, "and suddenly you catch yourself in the voting booth putting a cross beside the Christian Democratic Union."[29] Being kidnapped by the educators is depicted as ultimately a positive thing for Hardenberg. Transported from the hectic pace of Berlin to majestic, peaceful surroundings in the Tyrolean Mountains, he is given the chance to reflect upon his life. For the first time in years he has the rare opportunity to stop working, enjoy the beauty of nature, and reminisce about a time when he still believed in changing the world and was able to have fun. Indeed, he seems to revert to his youthful persona, happily embracing the everyday activities he has not undertaken in over thirty-five years: cooking, washing his clothes, sleeping in a communal bed, smoking a joint, and telling stories by candlelight. As a hostage of the educators he is liberated to such a point that he begins to see his normal life as a prison and wonders if he should just drop it all and become a teacher in some isolated village and live a simple but authentic and happy life. The sincerity of Hardenberg's transformation and the admiration he voices for the educators' idealism is put into question by his subtle gestures and intense gaze that the young people fail to notice. Although Hardenberg seems to flourish in this space beyond his normal reality, he remains a gifted observer and strategist. Acutely aware of the group dynamic, he does not pass on the chance to influence the situation and manipulate his captors. Adopting the role of a substitute father, he tries to assume command, most notably by setting Peter against Jan with his seemingly innocent reference to Jule and Jan's budding love affair.

Apart from looking to the past for lessons on what type of activism works and what should be avoided, it is the intellectual legacy of '68 that makes the greatest impression on these young people, even if specific historical references are left unspoken. Weingartner rightly avoids citing chapter and verse of seminal philosophical writings, which would make his film a pamphlet rather than an emotionally charged and compelling story. It would be misguided, however, to assume that the educators' ideas have no antecedents because they do not belong to an organized political group with a manifesto, and because they readily admit that they do not know how to transform individual acts of defiance into a collective experience.[30] Adorno and Horkheimer's critique of the culture industry and Guy Debord's *Society as Spectacle* (1967) form the basis of the educators' thinking. Their statements and actions also demonstrate an awareness of arguments put forth by Naomi Klein in *No Label* and by *Adbusters* publisher Kalle Lasn in his book *Culture Jam*.[31] Indeed, Jan's tirade against Hardenberg sounds like a synopsis of Lasn's book, almost chapter by chapter:

> The machine is overheated. We are merely the harbingers, but your time is soon up. This whole shitty technology has made you all so comfortable, but the others are enraged. The rage of nameless children who sit around in filthy slums and watch American action films. And that is only one side of it. What do we have over here? The number of mental illnesses is rising. More and more serial killers, shattered souls, senseless violence. At some point you can no longer keep sedating them with game shows and shopping.[32]

Jan laments that with Che-Guevara T-shirts and anarchy stickers becoming the latest obligatory fashion accessory, the rebellious energy embodied in historical political iconography has been transformed into a marketable product: "What used to be subversive is now for sale in stores."[33] Overlooking the historical precedent whereby the student movement popularized the peace sign only to have this anti-authoritarian icon immediately sold on posters, stickers, and T-shirts to eager youthful consumers, making it practically de rigueur, Jan sees the fusion of pop and politics as a form of selling-out and longs for a counter-culture without purchasable products. Hans Weingartner shares this sentiment with his fictional characters, but he goes even further to argue that this transformation of icons from their original function as shorthand for political convictions to mere ornamentation is an innate strategy of the capitalist system to perpetuate itself: "The system has developed ever more insidious defense strategies to take protest, package it as a product, stick a price tag on it, and sell it back to you."[34]

Weingartner has repeatedly stated that authenticity is an important factor in his filmmaking and that he wanted *Die fetten Jahre sind vorbei* to be a document of its time. As a trained cinematographer, he considers camerawork to be a decisive tool for achieving realism: "The handheld camera style produces documentary proximity and authenticity. The camera is neutral; it observes the figure, in the middle of things to be sure but mostly with the same focal distance, very short, documentary focal distances — I don't try to manipulate things with the camera."[35] Bearing in mind Weingartner's overriding interest in realism, the film's ending is a puzzling and incongruent coda. Rewritten after the premiere at Cannes, the film released in German cinemas includes a finale that is stylistically inconsistent and jarring in its pace and glamour. In a scene rivaling a Hollywood adventure blockbuster, the trio of attractive, well-dressed heroes wearing sunglasses board Hardenberg's luxury yacht to the upbeat rhythms of pulsating music. Defiant and determined, the young rebels have undergone an outward transformation and become the epitome of radical chic (especially Jan in a light blue suit and Jule in a flowing dress and high heels). Equipped with maps and a newly acquired fashionable attitude, they speed off into the horizon to intensify their struggle against the establishment. As the credits roll over a silhouette of satellites followed by the familiar image of television static and the lingering afterglow of being unplugged, it becomes clear that the educators have succeeded in halting television transmission throughout Europe.

The question of whether the educators' actions should be considered violence or poetic resistance is addressed at numerous points in the film. Jan provides the group's definitive answer when he tells Hardenberg: "Our little break-ins are completely ridiculous compared to the violence people like you commit."[36] Defining capitalism as a state-sanctioned form of collective violence, they not only validate the moral righteousness of their behavior; they redefine it in euphemisms. Breaking into people's homes, knocking Hardenberg unconscious, tying him up, kidnapping him, threatening him with a weapon (albeit a fake one), stealing his yacht, and embarking on a plan to disable television satellites are all acts of violence. If these actions were not committed by likeable characters, it seems unlikely that audiences would accept them as harmless or nonviolent. Weingartner steers viewers toward a reading of the educators as blameless children. The final scene in the film shown at Cannes presents the trio as innocent angels draped in white peacefully sleeping in their cloud-like communal bed as a modern-day hallelujah plays. Thoroughly divested of guilt, a model of harmonious coexistence despite interpersonal conflicts, the educators are depicted as righteous guardians of justice. In a brilliantly staged cross-cut sequence where the riot police break into the educators' Berlin apartment just as the three cherubs are awakened by a knock on the door, ostensibly vulnerable to attack but thankfully safe in a Spanish hotel, the notion of who is the innocent victim and who is the perpetrator is turned upside down. Hardenberg, the original injured party, is shown to be a vindictive liar and coward waiting safely in a car while heavily armed policemen attempt to uphold the establishment's authority with a show of force well beyond that necessary to subdue the young people. It comes as a relief to learn that the dreamy, defenseless idealists have escaped the wrath of a system of privilege and inequality that has eminently more violent weapons at its disposal than the educators, who never had more than their art and a broken starter's pistol.

If we look to the audience-share figures of nearly a million viewers (not to mention robust DVD sales), it is clear that this film hit the pulse of the nation. While the success of *Die fetten Jahre sind vorbei* could be due to various factors, the educators' creative chaos received the most attention from film critics in German newspapers and can give us at least some indication of how general viewers might have viewed the political implications of playful, disruptive acts. Most reviews in the trade press were overwhelmingly positive and characterized the educators' actions as "non-violent" and "ceremonial destruction."[37] Half joking and yet ultimately telling were Michael Althen's remarks in the *Frankfurter Allgemeine Zeitung*: "Smart idea, sexy actors, great music . . . what more do you want from a German film?"[38] *Die fetten Jahre sind vorbei* took many critics by surprise, because unlike the proponents of New German Cinema, who made overtly political films with a depressing seriousness in the seventies, Weingartner openly embraced the more attractive aspects of popular filmmaking to demonstrate that political activism can be attractive and fun. With its optimism, wit, good-looking and sympathetic stars, emotional conflict over friendship and romance, sincere debate over how to improve society, and serious attempt at rapprochement between the generations, *Die fetten Jahre sind vorbei* was refreshing. The appealing aspects of this film may well have flavored its reception, for as Althen reasoned, the educators seem like inoffensive creative individuals and "their funeral pyre of consumer society comes across as an art installation rather than a revolutionary beacon."[39]

Hanns-Georg Rodek was also deeply impressed with Weingartner's ability to present both an emotionally gripping and believable ménage à trois and also "the finest three-way relationship between pop, poetics, and politicalization that German cinema has managed to produce in a long time."[40] He pointed out, however, that the educators' anti-establishment actions have reached the point where "every strategy of this kind, even if it begins as a happening, inevitably ends up at the pivotal question of violence, against things and/or people."[41] Rodek argues that Weingartner's protagonists differ from their historical antecedents in their understanding of the legitimacy and unavoidability of violence in the pursuit of revolutionary change: "Baader, Meinhof & Co. acceded to it back then, Jan, Jule & Peter — because they are less politicized — have not yet got that far in their deliberations."[42] Rodek echoed the position of other critics that the kidnapping was "forced upon them," beyond their control and accidental.[43] Rodek's assessment was one of the most compelling, but I disagree with his last statement, because this line of thinking assumes that the educators are not responsible for their choices or actions. More importantly, Rodek's last argument refuses to acknowledge that the initial step toward violence against property and a deliberate invasion of other people's privacy and security could logically escalate to violence against people. Highly sympathetic characters, moving relationships, a witty and unexpected turn of events, and a well-paced narrative, in my opinion, are all so compelling that many reviewers seem willing to believe that creative chaos is harmless in the hands of good-natured activists like Jan, Peter, and Jule. Viewers face the difficult task of separating enjoyment in watching deviant behavior that arouses awareness of injustice in fiction and advocating such action in reality because it is naively done with good intentions. Since the intention of *The Edukators* is to educate the audience, the lessons on promoting creative chaos have serious implications. Apart from the actual level of harm done to individuals in the narrative, which is admittedly minor, it is the discourse surrounding the film, and in particular the use of harmless euphemisms about violence, that is striking and disturbing. Designating terror-inducing break-ins and disruption of the media as poetic resistance and beating, kidnapping, and imprisonment as an uncontrollable mistake are hardly moves that foster awareness of the far-reaching consequences of disruptive social interaction. Here

I would concur with Michael Kohler, who writes for the *Frankfurter Rundschau*. He vehemently criticized Weingartner's romantic depiction of the educators and their violent action: "It is hard to believe how unabashedly entertaining German films about the RAF have become. After *Baader* taught us that a weapon is always carried in the Peckinpahian midsection, Hans Weingartner continues to unfold the history of FRG terrorism in the mythic world of cinema."[44]

Conflicting definitions of violence and debates about appropriate forms of dissent in a democracy are not mere theoretical abstractions that function as components of an entertaining fiction. The fact that these topics are presented in art certainly makes the contours of the debate more difficult to grasp, because the constraints of narrative continuity, visual and auditory attraction, identification with fictional characters, and the ephemeral quality of star appeal can obfuscate the issues. What should not be lost in the discussion is that Weingartner aims to provide a genuine glimpse at reality and to use art to inspire social change in the real world. According to Weingartner, motion pictures can contribute significantly to a revolutionary mindset that in turn can lead to political change. In an interview with the *Montreal Mirror*, Weingartner claimed that his film already had imitators in real life: "'In Hamburg a group of people stormed the most expensive restaurant and stole the food right off the tables — they were wearing T-shirts that say, 'Your days of plenty are numbered,' says Weingartner. 'And in Switzerland, they stormed a bank that did business with the Nazis and wrote some *Edukators* graffiti on the floor.'" He continued:

> This is something I'm really quite happy about. It's something I dreamt about while I was making the film. So I'm very proud that *The Edukators* is not just abstract art, but has somehow jumped down from the screen and become something real. Just imagine if those 40 people become thousands of people then things start to happen and you have a real revolution like in East Germany, which started out with only 25 demonstrators on the street. After two years, there were millions. The regime ordered the soldiers to shoot at them but they didn't because how can you shoot at two million people? The next day the wall came down.[45]

While the details of Weingartner's history lesson are not entirely accurate, he ironically uses the historical uprising against Marxism to justify further Marxist-inspired activism. Moreover, he aligns fictional acts of resistance with real ones, suggesting that imagined stories can spark an uprising of the same magnitude as the 1989 revolution that toppled the GDR regime. If the '68 rally cry "all power to the imagination!" holds even a grain of truth, then a closer look at the political ideology behind the educators' "poetic resistance" is clearly warranted.

Fig. 4.2. Still from Marcus Mittermeier's Muxmämuschenstill *(2004). Photo © and by permission of Schiwago Film.*

Muxmäuschenstill

Marcus Mittermeier's debut feature film *Muxmäuschenstill* (Quiet as a mouse), based on a script by Jan Henrik Stahlberg, who also starred in the title role, was a surprise hit among critics and viewers alike. The film's unique black humor, politically incorrect protagonist, largely amateur cast, and pseudo-documentary camerawork lent it an underground quality, and its unusual production history contributed further to its novel, if not subversive, status. Mittermeier and Stahlberg, two actors with no previous experience in film direction and screenwriting, applied to numerous film subsidy boards and public television stations but were unanimously refused funding. They eventually made the film for a mere 40,000 euros, using inexpensive handheld digital cameras and hundreds of untrained performers, and often shooting in Berlin and Brandenburg without the required permits, leading one critic to call it a "perfect example of the new digital guerilla filmmaking."[46] Premiering at the Max Ophüls Film Festival on 28 January 2004, *Muxmäuschenstill* was greeted with overwhelming enthusiasm and won four prizes: best motion picture, best screenplay, the people's choice, and student jury awards. Shortly afterward it appeared at the Berlin Film Festival, where it was also well received. Nominated for the German Film Prize in several categories, including best motion picture and best supporting actor (Fritz Roth), it won for best editing (Sarah Clara Weber as a first-time editor). The

German Film Prize nomination alone brought in 250,000 euros, over six times the original outlay, and helped solidify the film's reputation as an indie production that managed to become a crossover to the astonishment of an overly cautious film industry. Winning a distribution contract with X-Verleih, Mittermeier's film was assured a strong promotional campaign for the cinema run and later for DVD sales. Released in German cinemas on 8 July 2004, *Muxmäuschenstill* continued to attract attention. In its first ten days in release the film garnered 90,000 viewers, ranking it in third place after the blockbusters *Shrek 2* and *Spiderman 2*, if one takes into account the ratio of film copies to audience figures.[47] By the end of 2005, *Muxmäuschenstill* had sold 306,820 tickets, making it one of the more modestly successful German film productions in recent years.[48]

In an attempt to generate a pre-premiere buzz along the lines of the *Blair Witch Project* (dir. Daniel Myrick and Eduardo Sanchez, 1999), Mittermeier and Stahlberg created a web site at www.denunziant.com, in which they tried to recruit a network of informants like the fictional character Mux does in their film. Pretending to represent a "group of young Berliners, who are fed up with passively standing by and watching while everybody disregards the rules that we all need," they admonished their fellow citizens to accept individual responsibility for shaping society.[49] In the first three days online, some twenty people filled out application forms, agreeing to spy on their neighbors and denounce wrong-doers. Although the web site was quickly exposed as a publicity stunt, even after the film appeared in cinemas, some viewers thought that *Muxmäuschenstill* was a documentary about a real organization and inquired about becoming members of the fictional "society for public spirit."[50] Mittermeier saw these reactions as evidence "that denunciation still falls on rich soil" and Stahlberg commented: "What we saw is that our film is a lot closer to reality then we thought."[51] Mux's politically incorrect idea that contemporary German society needs a domestic spy network to police ordinary citizens was intended as a biting satire, but it resonated with at least some members of the audience as a reasonable remedy for social ills. Despite the all-too-familiar and frightening historical precedent of a public willing to inform on others to the Gestapo and later to the Stasi, the notion of moral surveillance as a practical means to maintain social order continues to have its supporters. In February 2008 Christel Wegner, a parliamentarian representing the Left party in the state of Lower Saxony and a member of the German Communist Party (DKP), made a statement on national television justifying the Berlin Wall and suggesting that Germany once again needed an official agency like the Stasi to keep tabs on the population. Wegner reasoned: "I think that . . . if one is to establish another social form, then one needs once again an agency, because one has to protect against other forces, reactionary forces, that will use the opportunity and weaken the state from within."[52] The Left party quickly removed Wegner from her seat in the state parliament, but the question of whether her remarks reflect a broader public sentiment is open to debate.

By all accounts Marcus Mittermeier and Jan Henrik Stahlberg captured the public's attention with their film, and part of the attraction may have been that these relatively unknown actors were an unlikely source of such a mordant satire of contemporary Germany. Born in 1969 in Landshut, Marcus Mittermeier studied acting in Munich at the Ruth von Zerboni Drama School, where he met fellow actor Jan Henrik Stahlberg. Known primarily for playing the lead role in the television series *Samt und Seide*, along with guest appearances on *Die Rosenheim-Cops*, *Küstenwache*, und *Der Bulle von Tölz*, Mittermeier had never starred in a motion picture, let alone directed one. His one previous experience with direction was at a regional theater, where he directed Stahlberg in a production of Büchner's *Leonce und Lena*. Jan Henrik Stahlberg was equally untested in the field of screenwriting. Born in 1970 in Neuwied, Stahlberg had studied at the Ruth von Zerboni Drama School and the Institut des Arts de Diffusion in Brussels. Working primarily in the theater, he had a minor role in *Westend* (dir. Markus Mischkowski and Kai-Maria Steinkühler, 2003) before landing his first starring role in *kein Science Fiction* (Franz Müller, 2003). These inexperienced filmmakers were seen as classic underdogs who refused to follow conventional wisdom, and it was precisely their refreshingly innovative approach that led to their success.

Mux, the former philosophy student turned vigilante, scours the streets of Berlin seeking to catch individuals who have transgressed against the norms of good behavior. With his neatly pressed white dress shirt, sports jacket, and clean-cut appearance, Mux seems to be an upstanding citizen who has taken it upon himself to restore order to a world that has lost its values. Inspired by such German thinkers and poets as Kant, Goethe, and Kleist but possessing a very narrow understanding of their ideas regarding ethics, sentiments, and governance, this modern-day moralist is ultimately a psychopath intent on forcing others to follow his own rigid notion of decency. Equipped with a video camera, a holstered Mauser pistol, and an unwavering sense of moral certitude, Mux becomes a self-appointed sheriff, judge, and avenger. No one is safe from his watchful eye; he catches people who ride the subway without a ticket, shoplifters, pet-owners who fail to pick up after their dogs, badly behaved children, exhibitionists, rapists, and murderers with equal zeal. Accompanied by his videographer, Gerd, Mux publicly takes offenders to task, punishing them in increasingly humiliating ways in order to teach them manners and obedience. Documenting crime and punishment for a planned educational video, indexing the lawbreakers to prevent recidivism, and recruiting a network of informants, Mux creates a civil service beyond state authority that brings him notoriety and public approval. Suddenly he is a media star appearing on television, launching an internet site and major advertising campaign, and opening franchises throughout Germany. Along the way Mux falls in love with Kira, a waitress in a small-town tavern, whom he venerates as a pure and innocent virgin. Claiming to be her white knight and putting her up on a pedestal, he is surprised to learn that she does not want to be saved, has no interest in being an untouchable object of adoration, and resents being called his "little mouse." When Kira turns out to be a normal young woman with sexual desires and is found *in flagrante delicto* with another man, he can no longer maintain his romantic notion of love as a balsam against wickedness. Sitting with her on a park bench at the shore of a remote lake, he executes her but lacks the courage to kill himself. Distracted and unable to perform his duties, Mux decides to appoint a successor and follow in Goethe's footsteps by reinventing himself on an Italian journey. Together with Gerd, Mux happily tours the city of Rome, where he intends to have Kira immortalized in a painting. Despite his desire to be a civilian and soak up the history and culture of Italy, Mux cannot resist the urge to edify a traffic violator. Stepping out in front of a driver speeding down a country road and signaling him to stop, Mux is hit by the car and killed. As the film's title foreshadowed, Mux and his little mouse have been silenced forever.

Muxmäuschenstill works on much the same principal as *Die fetten Jahre sind vorbei*, introducing a self-appointed do-gooder to shake up society and educate the masses in unexpected, creative ways. Mux has two pedagogical goals, to punish violators so that they will learn that crime does not pay and to present the larger community with a terrifying example as a preventive measure. However, beyond this common didactic mission, Mux and the educators part ways. Whereas Weingartner's characters remain sympathetic throughout his film, Mittermeier's protagonist begins as an admirable if odd character but turns out to be a megalomaniac and murderer. At first this straight-laced avenger carries out the kind of street justice that viewers may secretly imagine doing, but they would most likely never admit it out loud. Stopping speeders and taking away their steering wheel, making the class bully wear a pig mask and stand in the corner while pelting him with wads of paper, and forcing an offender to wear a sign reading "I peed in the public pool," are all wickedly enjoyable, if socially unacceptable, forms of wish-fulfillment. At some point, however, Mux's pedagogical measures become sadistic and deadly. He shackles a wheelchair-bound man to a signpost for crossing the street on a red light and spray paints a graffiti artist in the face, which results in the blinded teenager being run over by a train. Mux bases his crusade on a misguided reading of Kant's categorical imperative: "Act as if the maxim of your action were to become by your will a universal law of nature."[53] What in theory is the foundation of individual responsibility and moral behavior becomes in practice the exact opposite of what he set out to achieve. In his zeal to right all wrongs and restore order, Mux becomes a demagogue who disregards the rights of others. The filmmakers wanted to illustrate that this aberration originates from a distinctly German intellectual heritage. Mittermeier and Stahlberg have argued that the general lack of personal responsibility is a global problem today, but Mux's reaction is uniquely German. His ideas are rooted as much in the German philosophical traditions of the Enlightenment as in National Socialism's preoccupation with order, obedience, and duty. With his fanatic moralism Mux demonstrates that idealism taken to its extreme can result in a lunacy worse than the original undesirable condition: "Mux's fascist side is a way of painting a picture in which the block warden around the corner can play a part. . . . We do not want to show a present-day Nazi. He merely has a totalitarian side. He is not a child of the brown soup, he is a child of classicism, of unhinged Romanticism, of German persnicketiness."[54]

Just as Mux's pronunciations on the current state of affairs are a mixture of leftist and right-wing ideas, so too are his philosophical and literary models a mixture of various historical epochs. His understanding of the classics is partial at best, and he turns to literature for more than spiritual edification. He patterns his own life on famed literary figures as if these steadfast fictions could provide him with a set of ideals and a genuine personality. He does not merely venerate the Enlightenment as demonstrated by the Kant breviary on his bedside table. He is also fascinated with Romantic notions of suffering and the special lonely nature of the artist. A self-described loner who is alienated from conventional society and seeks respite in nature, Mux resembles Werther and shares with Goethe's sentimental figure not only unrequited love but also a fascination with the folk. Just as Werther admired the peasants for their simple and genuine lifestyle, Mux frequents traditional corner pubs and socializes with the lower class in his quest for authenticity. Rather than just mingling with the plebeians, Mux constantly takes the lead. He offers the beer-drinking men jobs with "meaning and responsibility" and sings an emotionally loaded version of "Sechzig Jahre und kein bißchen weise" (sixty years old and nowhere near wise), which seems more like a commentary on Germany sixty years after the Second World War than on the nostalgic crowd in the local pub. Mux's sentimental nature is revealed as utter kitsch in a scene where he bids a final farewell to his neighbor Trude. The old woman lies dying in her bed while a group of her closest friends, including Mux, keeps vigil. A grief-stricken Mux weeps as a somber requiem plays, but when the music suddenly stops, he calmly reaches for the recorder at her bedside and turns the cassette over. Staging emotion with all the accoutrements of a sappy melodrama, Mux ensures that reality conforms to his overly sentimental world outlook. Moreover, like the sensitive Werther, who poured out his emotions by reciting poetry, Mux has the propensity to formulate his feelings in lyrical form.

Despondent over the weight of responsibility he carries, Mux sits alone in the gray-blue twilight looking out at the water and muses: "My breath stinks over the Landwehr canal. Today I will not save the world. A free day for all."[55] It is easy to imagine that, as a man who wants nothing more than justice and constantly champions unconditional obedience to a higher order, he has read Kleist's *Michael Kohlhaas* and *Prinz von Homburg* as a venerable catechism on integrity and duty. Like Kohlhaas, the relentless man obsessed with righting a wrong and being vindicated publicly, or the prince of Homburg, the dreamer consumed with notions of duty and just punishment for transgressions against authority, Mux cannot live in a world where other people break the rules. Kleist's description of Kohlhaas as "one of the most upright and atrocious men of his time" is an equally fitting characterization of Mux.[56] In the end Mux shares Kohlhaas's fate; his preoccupation with justice costs him his life.

With his noble ideas and overly developed zeal bordering on insanity, Mux also resembles Don Quixote. Like Cervantes' legendary figure, Mux imagines himself to be a knight errant dedicated to fighting for justice and is accompanied by his faithful servant Gerd, who has the rotund look and dim-witted nature of Sancho Panza.[57] Equally important, Mux stylizes Kira as his Dulcinea, a pure and innocent young girl who needs to be protected. Just as Don Quixote's vision of femininity bore little relation to reality and was an ideal he gained from reading medieval courtly epics, Mux's romanticized view of the perfect woman is an unobtainable fiction he has learned from reading the German classics. His first words to Kira are "Do you know *Faust*?" and this ominous question foreshadows her tragic fate. Like Gretchen, Kira will lose her life because she had the misfortune to become involved with a man who literally believes that the eternal feminine will lead him to paradise. Mux imagines Kira as an angel, and indeed she is often lit from above, creating a halo effect, and dressed in white clothes that give her a virtuous appearance. Mux's vision is predicated on Kira remaining silent and compliant, in essence adopting the role of Mux's quiet little mouse as indicated in the film's title. He thinks that she is a naive soul who still believes the world is a good place, and even when she tells him that she has no such illusions, he continues to say that she does. When Mux goes to sleep at night surrounded by his books and accompanied by the recurring melody of "Tomorrow belongs to me" from *Cabaret* (dir. Bob Fosse, 1972) Kira appears in his dream as a beatific figure. Bathed in sunlight and radiating youth, she is captured in an extreme close-up by a wavering camera that lingers on her face, constantly losing equilibrium as if knocked off balance by her beauty, and then recovering its position of adoration. Shown in slow motion staring straight into the camera, Kira exists in a type of vacuum, making no sound and simply smiling, as a haunting melody plays in the background. The same stylized camera work, action without diegetic sound but laden with a sentimental melody, also characterizes Kira's first visit to Berlin. In a parody of an interlude from a romantic comedy, Kira and Mux tour a city filled with cheerful, upbeat rhythms but strangely devoid of urban noise. When Mux and Kira are alone, he tries to declare his love and educate her at the same time. In the measured cadence of poetry he explains:

> You are like the sun . . . on a clearing . . . and do you hear it? . . . the sound of hooves. A horse comes running by . . . with a knight riding it. And that is me . . . at a gallop. It probably sounds silly, but that is what I want to be one day . . . this knight . . . whom you can look up to. You know, many great poets and thinkers had women who inspired them . . . unique women. And I would be lying if I didn't admit that I feel the same thing when we are together. By let's not forget. You have no idea yet who is standing in front of you, do you? . . . the man of your life.[58]

Kira's function is to be Mux's muse, and when she fails to meet his expectations, he eliminates her from the picture. As if taking his cue from the real life of Heinrich von Kleist, who made a suicide pact with the terminally ill Henriette Vogel and gave her the *coup de grâce* before killing himself on the shore of the Wannsee, Mux kills the unwitting Kira at a remote lake in Brandenburg, but he does not have the courage to commit suicide. He completely misconstrues the story of Kleist and Vogel's freely chosen death. Instead of following in Kleist's footsteps, he calls on his faithful servant Gerd to help him bury the body, allowing his own crime to go unpunished.

From the film's opening scene, the act of creating images and documenting reality is problematized as a highly suspect endeavor. At the very start it is clear that the camera never simply records objective truth: images are always manipulated, edited, and controlled. Before the credits roll by, Mux is seen filming a video diary, rehearsing and reformulating his lines before he is satisfied with his performance. After several takes, he speaks directly into the camera as if he were spontaneously explaining his mission:

> I am part of a society in which we have lost our ideals, in which there is no longer a utopia of a more just society. And that's why I am here: to help with the first step, so that people regain the power to accept responsibility for their behavior.[59]

The wobbly handheld camera, familiar to audiences as a device commonly used in investigative reporting to signal that the crew is in the midst of events as they happen, promises immediacy and authenticity. In Mux's hands, however, it turns out to be a carefully staged element to simulate spontaneity.

The question of documentary objectivity is repeatedly raised by the sheer fact that *Muxmäuschenstill* does not rely exclusively on the subjective camera manned by Mux and later by Gerd but constantly moves between this filmed material and an objective camera that captures all the action and is accompanied by visual inserts, embedded television clips, and a nondiegetic soundtrack, including Mux's voice-over commentary and mood music. While Gerd's filming of Mux's pedagogical measures is consistently depicted as the raw material for a planned educational video, who captures Gerd editing and archiving the videotapes, let alone Mux's intimate relationship to Kira and all the other plot developments? The actual construction of the overarching "documentary" film remains an unresolved paradox, with some shifts between the recorded material and Mux's real world smooth and others jarring. Attention is drawn to the paradox in the scene where Gerd is shown videotaping an interview with Mux. Gerd sits on the right next to his camera, which is placed on a tripod and directed at Mux, who is seated on the far left. Gerd remains out of his own camera's visual reach and merely prompts Mux with questions. A second, unexplained, camera films Gerd filming Mux, who quickly tires of explaining his ideas and tells Gerd to turn off the camera. Gerd reaches for the off button on his camera facing the audience but hesitates and decides to let it run as he continues to probe into his boss's motives. Mux begins to speak in an unscripted manner and reveals some less than noble reasons for his behavior until he recognizes that the camera is still going and orders his apprentice to turn it off. These metafictional moments cast doubt on the reliability of modern media in general and Mux's documentary in particular.

Mux is obsessed with capturing people in the act of committing a crime, and he administers punishment while his apprentice Gerd carefully films the action as evidence. The violator's name, the date, category of crime, and index number are imprinted on the videos, which are then carefully archived to document the misconduct. This fanatic attention to detail, categorizing people according to types of transgressions and keeping meticulous records, is an integral part of Mux's fascistic personality, but equally important is his obsessive need for images of domination and control. At first Mux polices mostly traffic violations and inconsiderate behavior, but after he falls in love with Kira, and especially after their relation falters, he directs his attention to sexual crimes with ever-greater frequency. Shifting the focus from the identification and categorization of lawbreakers to voyeuristic pleasure, Mux is seized by a compulsive need to watch sexual violence and humiliation. Mux comes to the realization that he is not immune to voyeurism when he catches a shoplifter and insists the woman take off the bra she has stolen in front of him. Naked and vulnerable as she is, her shame is intensified by the staging of her punishment. In a prism of looks, Gerd watches and films Mux watching a woman forced to undress and multiplies the degrading image by having both the victim and her punisher reflected in the dressing-room mirror. Afterward Mux admits that the scene was erotically stimulating because he had humiliated the woman and there was nothing she could do but submit to his authority. Immediately following his confession, Mux begins to talk about Kira as if she were some kind of antidote against sadistic pleasure — or perhaps a logical extension of it, since he repeatedly associates sexuality with violence by naming both Kira and his pistol "his little mouse." Gerd, too, becomes caught up in the delight of seeing others suffer. He lets his camera linger on the victims rather than the offenders and masturbates while viewing the scenes of punishment he shot on video. By constantly thematizing the pleasure of looking at deviance, *Muxmäuschenstill* implicates both the media, which deliver a steady stream of visual input, and the viewers, who are never satiated and demand ever more bizarre and stimulating imagery.

As the film progresses, the editing style changes from a relatively moderate pace, giving adequate time to the identification of crimes, to a point of acceleration where each incident becomes a blur in a rapid succession of violent and largely sexual images. By rendering countless disconnected transgressions into a string of nearly indistinguishable lewd acts, the film replicates channel-switching at hyper-speed. This type of montage also characterizes Mux's diatribe against society's insatiable desire for media images at the cost of living authentic and decent lives. In a sequence introduced by a TV reporter stating that the station is going live to the Gendarmenmarkt in downtown Berlin where Mux is being interviewed by the press, the truth value of the news is brought into question, since Mux is seated at the back of the room while his entire office watches him appearing "live" on television. The "live" press conference shown on the office television segues into the Gendarmenmarkt scene itself and then into a rapid montage of clips from news commentaries, talk shows, reality TV, superstar contests, game shows, and pornography that illustrate television's mindless fare. In this minute-long sequence consisting of nearly thirty television clips, images of Arnold Schwarzenegger giving a speech next to his beaming wife Maria Shriver, a man dressed in a bodysuit made of meat cutlets that are being eaten by a pack of German Shepherds, Dieter Bohlen gleefully humiliating a contestant on *Deutschland sucht den Superstar*, and a group of naked middle-aged partyers drinking champagne in a communal hot tub underscore Mux's notion of corruption and his disgust regarding the relentless barrage of titillating images demanded by an insatiable public. Framing the montage is both Mux's fictional interview on *Tagesthemen* with real-life moderator Ulrich Wickert and an authoritative voice-over, in which Mux declares:

Everyone is talking about us. We are taking the German media by
storm. Private and public stations, they are all now reporting on us.
My ideas are being over-discussed, the manifesto is getting good ratings and supplanting the broadcast rubbish. Even if some people feel
safe behind the ratings and bask in their childish view of the world,
I shit on them all. The truth, that you have become corrupted in
your moralistic self-startup companies, the truth is stronger than
any ratings. The time when everyone complained about the lack of
standards but it was nobody's fault, those times are over. Time is
now going to play out against all of you, until the spirit of the time
becomes the spirit that you let out of the bottle.[60]

Strongly associated with Mux's point of view via the framing devices and
voice-over, the sequence ironically employs the very qualities of trash-TV
programming that Mux criticizes as debased — the stringing along of
shocking, mindless, or droning surface images without depth, insight, or
artistry. He sees his own filmmaking as an educational mission and rejects
the content of trash-TV but not the medium of film or even television.
Indeed, in his last will and testament, Mux reserves his final criticism for
populist political figures and pop-culture icons: "Enough with this public idiocy. If I am right, then all the Roland Kochs, Dieter Bohlens, and
Stefan Raabs, all the obsolete models of this republic, had better prepare
themselves for a rough ride."[61]

As Mux expands his operations, opening up new branches of the society for public spirit and hiring an army of reformed delinquents to inform
on others, he turns to the Internet to advertise, with unexpected results
that provide a biting satire. His employee Bjorn proudly presents an
Internet trailer for the proposed web site that looks like a slick TV commercial for a new cop show. The black-and-white fast-paced sequence features Mux running along the Oberbaum bridge as if he were the lead in
Tom Tykwer's cult classic *Lola rennt* (1998), shown in slow motion drawing his pistol in a rage, and dressed in a trench coat and calmly firing his
gun directly at the audience. The ticking of a clock segues into a dramatic
fast-paced musical score and a commentary spoken in the deep voice and
steady cadence of a typical television announcer: "Inside you it is ticking.
You are alone. You are afraid — but you have eyes. You have ears. And
offenders will lose their hearing and sight. Because you find offenders
simply awful."[62] The trailer ends with a spectacular car crash and bright
red explosion as the background for the title words "www.denunziant.
com" and the directive: "Denounce your neighbor!" Mux reacts with
anger and dismay that Bjorn has mistakenly substituted "denouncer" for
"informant," because as he has to explain to the clueless Bjorn, the term
"denouncer leaves a bad aftertaste in Germany."[63]

The Internet trailer and Mux's entire operation play on the prevailing fear for one's safety that is a double-edged sword: the public fears

for its safety because of (at least the perception of) rampant crime and terrorism and looks to the government for protection, but the authorities, both domestic and international, threaten to institute a system of obsessive surveillance and curtail civil rights to solve the problem. The security dilemma in Germany carries the historical weight of the Gestapo and Stasi legacies, but in a post 9/11 world the implications are global, and the collective solution might well be worse than the original problem. Mux taps into this fear of surveillance by offering ordinary people the opportunity to turn the tables. Rather than tolerating the government's clandestine oversight of its citizens, he suggests that they can be empowered to scrutinize the lives of others and transfer the state's monopoly on the use of violence to a morally upright individual. Mux argues that his plan is even good for the economy, because he transforms perpetrators into informants and actually creates jobs. Wedding his critique of the "New Economy" where everyone speculates and is greedy to his self-help employment package that will solve the security dilemma, Mux seems to offer the public exactly what it wants, because he is heralded in the press as an innovative thinker and morally upright leader. Pointing to Gerd, "the epitome of a person who has accomplished nothing in his life," as an example of how he can transform even the most pathetic loser into a productive member of society, Mux purports to have a concrete method to remedy the country's pressing social and economic problems.[64] He recognizes that Germany desperately needs a modern day hero but laments: "I am not a hero, because every country has the heroes it deserves. Michael Schumacher is a hero because he can drive around curves quickly and he doesn't pay taxes. Poor country."[65] He wants Germans to be proud, not in a jingoistic fashion reminiscent of the Nazis, but as a nation of upstanding citizens who inspire others to be good. Mux is the archetypal fool who voices commonsense wisdom in modern guise, a sociopath who prescribes a cure for the world's insanity. In this satirical look at contemporary Germany through the eyes of a lunatic, the rational need for moral responsibility taken to its logical extreme provides numerous hilarious moments but also reveals a lingering sense that a system of shared values and governance has somehow gone astray.

Common Threads

Weingartner and Mittermeier criticize turbo-capitalism and the mass media, and they present vigilantes who adopt creative chaos as a strategy to change the way people think. They develop a similar visual aesthetic by using handheld digital cameras, few or no constructed sets, and no artificial lighting, which lends their films a documentary-like air of authenticity. They both worked under similar production conditions, employing a small crew on a modest budget and relying on improvisation or amateur actors. These artistic choices, primarily the result of limited financial resources, give their films the look of an indie production and contributed largely to their reception as anti-mainstream cinema. Although they both use comedy, they embrace different comedic genres and have very different intentions for their films. Mittermeier uses satire and acknowledges that his character is a violent criminal despite his good intentions. Far from promoting a model for the audience to emulate, he wants viewers to leave the cinema and contemplate the complexities of social change and be aware of their own fascist tendencies. Confronted with a sociopath who identifies a pervasive lack of respect for the law but offers up a remedy that results in tyranny, audiences are not given an easy answer to society's problems. Conflicts are left unresolved and open to discussion.

Whereas *Muxmäuschenstill* is a cautionary tale that warns against moral vigilantism as a looming threat to civil liberties, *Die fetten Jahre sind vorbei* is a plea for change and concludes with a clear-cut answer to social problems: collective grassroots activism. Weingartner plays down the potential threat of violence inherent in the educators' playful anti-establishment happenings and emphasizes that these disturbances are a necessary means of raising awareness and changing the world. He presents a humorous look at social injustice through highly sympathetic characters and argues that moviegoers should pattern themselves after these rebels. His film combines aspects of independent and mainstream filmmaking, with its jerky mobile camera and grainy image quality juxtaposed to identification, emotional engagement, and conflict resolution, and this mixture complicates the notion that there is a stark contrast between a cinema of consensus and a cinema of consciousness. Weingartner tries to bridge the gap, openly embracing the more attractive aspects of popular filmmaking to demonstrate that political activism can be attractive and fun. He wants viewers to imitate the educators and believes that motion pictures can create a revolutionary mindset that leads to political change.

Both directors see their films as documents of the time that reflect a general malaise and discomfort with the lack of political and moral high ground. Weingartner maintains: "I think that my generation is the generation of helplessness and reorientation. Nowadays there is a new generation, in the framework of the anti-globalism movement — with which I sympathize strongly — which is developing new strategies."[66] Mittermeier concurs: "*Muxmäuschenstill* is a reflection of the new spirit of the times, the general crisis atmosphere. For a long time now Germany has found itself in a state of social upheaval. However, only when the majority is doing poorly do people begin to ask questions. We are still a "fat" country, but the economic euphoria of the 1990s is long over. What remains is the moral hangover after the soaring flight. This is what we are reacting to with our film."[67] Screenwriter Jan Henrik Stahlberg echoes these sentiments: "Since the fall of the Wall there no longer exists an alternative to the form of society we are living in now. Even the idealist Mux has no alternative to offer. He is writing a manifesto and is stuck in the first chapter. He becomes violent and a psychopath because the ventilating mechanism of a utopia is missing."[68]

Die fetten Jahre sind vorbei and *Muxmäuschenstill* conspicuously end outside Germany with the educators and Mux traveling to other countries where people are equally in need of enlightenment. Whether sailing the Mediterranean Sea intent on destroying European television satellites or campaigning against speeders on Italian country roads, these characters venture beyond their own borders, implying that national concerns over inequality, consumption, media manipulation, surveillance, and the security dilemma have broader implications in an increasingly globalized, interconnected world. Underlying these films is a lament about the current state of affairs, in which modern society, despite its laudable achievements and profound historical consciousness over past failed political regimes, still cannot guarantee safety, security, prosperity, and justice for all. Bitter history lessons delivered with black humor, a healthy dose of cynicism, and an enduring hope that some things can change.

Notes

[1] "Die paar Sachen, die sie uns wirklich in den Medien erzählen, sind so kleine Bruchstücke, das sind so lächerlich. Ich meine, was wirklich ankommt, ist so eine Disinformation. Wir werden bei Laune gehalten, sollen uns über irgendwelche Popmusik aufregen, gegenseitig streiten und die Köpfe einhauen, wetten, wer realer ist. Wenn wir ehrlich etwas zusammen tun könnten, eine klassische, wirklich gute Jugendbewegung aufbauen könnten, so eben wie ich mir vorstelle, durchaus mit einer Gewalt, weiß ich nicht, mit einer gewaltbereiten Masse, die noch dazu bereit ist, alles ein bissel umzustürzen, könnten wir einfach loslegen. Aber du siehst, wie die Leute draußen sind, es passiert einfach nichts. Wenn du sie ein bißchen mobilisiert hast, fangen sie an, sich unter einander zu verstreiten." Film dialogue, *Egoshooter* [2004], dir. Christian Becker and Oliver Schwabe, DVD (Berlin: Filmgalerie 451, 2005).

[2] Similar themes are addressed in *Polly Blue Eyes* (dir. Tomy Wigand, 2005), *Stadt als Beute* (City as prey, dir. Irene von Alberti, Miriam Dehne, and Esther Groneborn, 2005), *Bin ich sexy* (Am I sexy, dir. Katinka Feistl, 2004), *Allein* (Alone, dir. Thomas Durchschlag, 2004), and *Prinzessinnenbad* (Pool of princesses, dir. Bettine Blümner, 2007).

[3] Most critics referred to Wim Wenders's *In weiter Ferne so nah* (Faraway, so close, premiered at Cannes on 17 May 1993) as the last German film before this one to compete for the Golden Palm award, although some assign this role to the same director's English language film set in Hollywood, *The End of Violence* (German title: *Am Ende der Gewalt*, cinematic release on 27 November 1997). Compare "Sind Sie in Cannes auf dem Teppich geblieben?" *Die Zeit*, 30 Dec. 2004; Jan Schulz-Ojala, "Warum hast du meinen Sohn genommen? Deutsch-amerikanischer

Tag in Cannes: Michael Moores *Fahrenheit 911* und Hans Weingartners *Die fetten Jahre sind vorbei,*" *Der Tagesspiegel,* 18 May 2004; and "Nach sieben Jahren — ein deutscher Film für Cannes," *Frankfurter Allgemeine Zeitung,* 21 Apr. 2004. The reference to *Die fetten Jahre sind vorbei* as the German entry is somewhat clouded by the fact that Weingartner was born in Austria. The fact that he was educated largely in Germany and his film received four-fifths of its funding from German sources seems to have tipped the scales toward Germany rather than Austria.

4 Statistics are available at http://www.ffa.de.

5 Weingartner filmed *Das weiße Rauschen* based on a treatment of only 99 scenes. The 130 hours of material generated was eventually edited into a three-hour version. The final cut released in movie theaters was 104 minutes long. In a podium discussion at the Filmmuseum Potsdam on 31 January 2008, Weingartner recalled that during his years at the Academy of Media Arts in Cologne the basic tenets of the Danish Dogma movement were widely discussed and students were encouraged to experiment with this method of filmmaking. Indeed, adhering to Dogma principles could often ensure funding for student projects. Although he has used many of the Dogma techniques in his films, Weingartner notes that he never slavishly followed the 1995 manifesto, in part because he could not imagine a film without music and in part because it is in his nature to break the rules.

6 "Das weiße Rauschen, das sind alle Visionen, aller Menschen, aller Zeiten, in einem Augenblick. . . . Wer das weiße Rauschen sieht, wird sofort wahnsinnig. Außer wenn er schon wahnsinnig ist. Dann wird er normal." Film dialogue, *Das weiße Rauschen* [2001], dir. Hans Weingartner, DVD (Hamburg: Warner Home Video, 2002).

7 "Der Trick besteht darin, den Pfad der Erleuchtung sozusagen rückwärts zu gehen." Film dialogue.

8 Weingartner cowrote the screenplay for *Die fetten Jahre sind vorbei* and *Free Rainer* with Katharina Held. He cowrote the screenplay for *Das weiße Rauschen* with Toby Amann and Katrin Blum. He has worked repeatedly with composer/editor Andreas Wodraschke, cameraman Matthias Schellenberg, actor Daniel Brühl, and producer Antonin Svoboda. In this respect, Weingartner has much in common with his contemporaries Andreas Dresen and Christian Petzold who tend to work with the small teams over the years.

9 SWR's "Debüt im Dritten" is a competitive program offering young filmmakers help with their film scripts and promising the broadcast of their film in the summer following its premiere. Arte provided further assistance on the script. *Die fetten Jahre sind vorbei* was first broadcast on Arte on 24 May 2007 and on SWR on 29 August 2007. Funding came from BKM Filmförderung, MBB, Filmfond Wien, and Filmfond Cine Tirol.

10 Hanns-Georg Rodek outlines Weingartner's directorial style in his review, "Die mageren Jahre sind vorbei. Zumindest für Deutschland in Cannes: Hans Weingartner und Daniel Brühl brechen den Wettbewerbs-Bann," *Die Welt,* 23 Apr. 2004. Weingartner discusses the limitations of his intentions, especially the need to reshoot certain scenes out of chronological order in his commentary on the DVD. See *Die fetten Jahre sind vorbei* [2004], dir. Hans Weingartner, DVD (Munich: Universum Film, 2005).

[11] The Institute for Media Analysis, IMA, is a fictional agency standing in for the Gesellschaft für Konsumforschung, GfK, which is responsible for compiling data on television-audience shares and consumer marketing, among other things.

[12] In its first year in release, *Free Rainer* sold 182,050 tickets. Statistics are available at http://www.ffa.de.

[13] "Meiner Meinung nach wird Fernsehen als Betäubungsmittel verwendet. Die Leute standen tagsüber im harten kapitalistischen Wettkampf: mussten sich durchsetzen, hatten Angst um ihren Arbeitsplatz. Dann kommen sie abends nach Hause und verwenden die Glotze, um sich wegzubeamen, wie mit einer Droge." Hanns-Georg Rodek, "TV-Quoten: 'Fernsehen ist für mich wie Heroin,'" *Die Welt*, 13 Nov. 2007.

[14] In a podium discussion at the Filmmuseum Potsdam on 31 January 2008, Hans Weingartner asserted definitively: "Ich habe den Film für die Multiplexes gemacht." In an interview with *Der Spiegel* he argued in a similar fashion: "Ich habe versucht, einen Film zu machen, der auch für die breite Masse verständlich ist und nicht nur für eine kleine Bildungselite, die Arthouse-Kinos besucht." Bettina Aust, "'Fernsehen ist Lebensersatz': Medienkritiker Hans Weingartner," *Spiegel Online*, 16 Nov. 2007, http://www.spiegel.de/kultur/kino/0,1518,516833,00. html.

[15] "Meine Aufgabe als Filmemacher ist es, da hinzugucken, wo es wehtut." Aust, "'Fernsehen ist Lebensersatz.'"

[16] There are numerous references in *The Matrix* to Jean Baudrillard's theory of the simulacra. For instance, Thomas Anderson uses a hollowed-out copy of Baudrillard's *Simulacra and Simulation* to hide his hacker software. Most importantly, the film's storyline of a computer matrix designed to create a virtual dreamworld corresponds to Baudrillard's concept of the simulacra of simulation, a mechanism designed to subjugate human existence to the continued survival of the hyperreal system itself. With his citation of a citation, Weingartner aligns his project to that of the Wachowskis and Baudrillard, and draws parallels to the Hollywood filmmakers and French philosopher by having the educators struggle against a socioeconomic system that seems to offer freedom but enslaves people in order to perpetuate itself.

[17] "Das ist die Matrix. Du siehst sie und kannst in ihr nicht leben. Ich auch nicht." Film dialogue.

[18] "Ich sehe mich als U-Boot in der Matrix." "Sind Sie in Cannes auf dem Teppich geblieben?" For further reference to the matrix, see R. Gansera and F. Göttler, "Liebe in Zeiten der Matrix: Interview; Hans Weingartner," *Süddeutsche Zeitung*, 22 Nov. 2004, and Andreas Borcholte, "Anarchie und Alltag: *Die fetten Jahre sind vorbei*," *Spiegel Online*, 25 Nov. 2004, http://www.spiegel.de/kultur/kino/0,1518,329478,00.html.

[19] Hans Weingartner used the term "poetic resistance" in the press booklet distributed at the film's premiere at the Cannes Film program. He contended: "Jan und Peter als 'Die Erziehungsberechtigten' haben einen Weg gefunden, die Reichen auf kreative und subtile Art und Weise aufzurütteln. Sie brechen in deren Villen ein und bringen die Ordnung ihrer Luxusgüter durcheinander, ohne dabei etwas zu stehlen oder jemanden zu verletzen. Damit legen sie den Finger auf die

Wunde, aber mit Sinn für Humor. Auf den ersten Blick erzeugen sie Chaos, aber in dem Chaos liegt eine Bedeutung. So wie bei vielen Gedichten. Deshalb könnte man das, was sie tun, 'poetischen Widerstand' nennen." Hans Weingartner, "*The Educators: Die fetten Jahre sind vorbei*," Offizielles Programm im Wettbewerb Cannes 2004, http://www.coop99.at/DFJ/pressbookgr.pdf.

[20] Weingartner states: "Bei diesen Leuten in die Villen einzudringen ist eine symbolische Aktion. . . . Dort in die Villen einzubrechen, bei den Reichsten der Reichen, das hat Symbolcharakter. . . . Ich finde, das hat eine innere Poesie und Schönheit, so etwas zu tun." Dietmar Kammerer, "'Die private Revolte ist nie privat.' Der Regisseur Hans Weingartner hofft auf eine junge Generation, die wieder Lust hat zu kämpfen. Mit seinem neuen Film *Die fetten Jahre sind vorbei* will er selbst einen Anfang machen," *taz*, 25 Nov. 2004.

[21] Actor Daniel Brühl likewise maintains: "Was mir an der Idee dieses poetischen Widerstandes in *Die fetten Jahre sind vorbei* gefällt, ist, dass er gewaltfrei verläuft." David Sarkar, "Alles, was früher subversiv war, kann man heute im Laden kaufen! Daniel Brühl über Rebellion, den Film *Die fetten Jahre sind vorbei* und dass er sich gerne 'mehr trauen' würde." *Planet Interview*, 30 Sept. 2004, http://planet-interview.de/daniel-bruehl-30092004.html.

[22] The Association for the Taxation of Financial Transactions for the Aid of Citizens (ATTAC) was founded in France in 1998 to advocate for the worldwide institution of the Tobin tax on currency speculation, in order to create a development fund. Currently ATTAC has an estimated 90,000 members in more than fifty countries and under its motto, "The world is not for sale," their activities have expanded to include monitoring the World Trade Organization, the International Monetary Fund, and the Organization for Economic Development and Cooperation; demonstrating at G8 meetings; and championing a wide variety of projects relating to sustainable development, Third-World debt relief, environmental concerns, and social justice. To review their platform, visit the group's website at http://www.attac.org. Felix Kolb provides an excellent study of how mass-media reporting on ATTAC protests at the 2001 European Summit in Gothenburg and the 2001 G8 Summit in Genoa helped to bolster the group's reputation and increase its membership in Germany. See Felix Kolb, "The Impact of Transnational Protest on Social Movement Organizations: Mass Media and the Making of ATTAC Germany," in *Transnational Protest and Global Activism*, edited by Donatella della Porta and Sidney Tarrow (Lanham, MD: Rowman & Littlefield, 2005), 95–120.

[23] "Das Problem ist einfach, dass ich nirgendwo etwas sehen kann, woran ich wirklich glaube." Film dialogue.

[24] Weingartner also appeared briefly in *Free Rainer* as one of the television executives attending a board meeting to discuss the falling audience-share data.

[25] "Wer sagt das denn? Die Bulle, die Staatsanwälte, die Bild-Zeitung? Das ist die kleinbürgerliche Scheißmoral. Anstand. Ehrlichkeit. Familiensinn. Du musst pünktlich zur Arbeit gehen. Du musst deine Steuern bezahlen. Du darfst im Supermarkt nichts klauen. Das kriegen wir reingewürgt, den ganzen Tag, zuerst in der Schule, dann in der Glotze. Und wozu? Damit Typen wie der perversteure Autos kaufen können. Auf so eine Moral scheiß' ich. Einer jungen Frau das Leben

kaputt zu machen, das ist unmoralisch. Oder glaubst du, dass der Typ sich ein einziges Mal gefragt hat, ob er vielleicht im Unrecht ist?" Film dialogue.

26 "Wir leben in einer Diktatur des Kapitals. Alles, was du besitzt, hast du gestohlen." Film dialogue.

27 "Es war alles schon mal da und hat nicht funktioniert. Warum soll es bei uns klappen?" and "Auch wenn es andere Revolutionen schon gegeben hat und das im Einzelnen vielleicht nicht funktioniert hat, ist das Wichtigste doch, dass die besten Ideen überlebt haben." Film dialogue.

28 Founded in France in 1957, the Situationist International (SI) was a Western avant-garde, Marxist movement that sought to overcome the traditional boundaries between art, politics, and daily existence. The SI decried modern society as a monolithic spectacle and advocated creating situations that drew attention to the constructed nature of everyday life in order to bring about social change. Guy Debord, one of the Situationists' most renowned theorists, argued: "The whole life of those societies in which modern conditions of production prevail presents itself as an immense accumulation of *spectacles*. All that once was directly lived has become mere representation." Guy Debord, *The Society of Spectacle* [1967], trans. Donald Nicholson-Smith (New York: Zone Books, 1994), 12. The Munich-based group SPUR was part of the SI, and SPUR member Dieter Kunzelmann was instrumental in developing the *Kommune 1* in Berlin. Together with Fritz Teufel, who coined the term *Spaßguerrilla*, referring to playful happenings meant to expose entrenched rituals and encourage the public to reflect upon and change unjust social structures, Kunzelmann and other Kommune 1 members planned the so-called pudding assassination attempt on US Vice President Hubert Humphrey. The group planned to attack Humphrey with a variety of nonlethal projectiles, including smoke bombs, paint, flour, and the vice president's favorite dessert, pudding. Ironically, the attack never took place but produced so much publicity that it turned into a virtual event that defined the Kommune I. For an overview of this international movement, see Peter Wollen, "The Situationist International," *New Left Review* 174 (1989): 67–93. Simon Teune presents an informative overview of the Kommune I's use of humor as a political strategy in his article, "Humour as a Guerrilla Tactic: The West German Student Movement's Mockery of the Establishment," *International Review of Social History* 52 (2007): 115–32.

29 "Und plötzlich ertappst du dich in der Wahlkabine, wie du das Kreuzchen bei der CDU machst." Film dialogue.

30 Matthias Müller praises *Die fetten Jahre sind vorbei* because it "documents the present-day absence of a believable political language" (das aktuelle Fehlen glaubwürdiger Politiksprache dokumentiert) and sees the film as charming because the characters are so hapless, naive and speechless (Dabei wirken diese so behutsam, so naturbelassen, so sehnsüchtig und doch so sprachlos, allesamt Eigenschaften, die den Charme dieses Films ausmachen.). Matthias C. Müller, "*Die fetten Jahre sind vorbei*: Die Sprachnot charmanter Weltverbesserer," *Stuttgarter Nachrichten*, 25 Nov. 2004. Katja Nicodemus likewise notes that the figure of Jan "encompasses the desolation of a generation that yearns for change without wanting to fall back on the elders' ideologeme" and whose rage with the system "comes from the deepest reaches of his soul but is bereft of its own language" (umgibt die

Verlorenheit einer Generation, die sich nach Veränderung sehnt, ohne auf die Ideologeme der Älteren zurückgreifen zu wollen. . . . [Es] kommt aus tiefster Seele, doch es fehlt die eigene Sprache.). Katja Nicodemus, "Denn sie wissen, was sie tun: Hans Weingartners Film *Die fetten Jahre sind vorbei* sucht mit seinen Helden nach der Revolution von morgen," *Die Zeit*, 25 Nov. 2004. The fact that the educators do not belong to a group was often seen as positive, because it implied that they were spontaneous and authentic; see for instance Dietrich Kuhlbrodt, "Für alle Fälle Magerquark: Die 3 von der Wohngemeinschaft und der böse Mercedesfahrer; Hans Weingartners globalisierungskritische Digitalvideofabel *Die fetten Jahre sind vorbei* probt den poetischen Widerstand," *taz*, 25 Nov. 2004; and Tobias Kniebe, "Generation Nix: Hans Weingartner ergründet die Jugend in seinem Film *Die fetten Jahre sind vorbei*," *Süddeutsche Zeitung*, 24 Nov. 2004. Kniebe notes that individual acts of rebellion hold a special interest, because they demonstrate that the characters will not be caught up in a political movement that could lead to the type of dictatorship that plagued twentieth-century Germany.

31 Compare Kalle Lasn's prognosis: "*America is no longer a country. It's a multitrillion-dollar brand.* America ™ is essentially no different from Mc Donald's, Marlboro or General Motors. It's an image 'sold' not only to the citizens of the U.S.A., but to consumers worldwide. . . . We will strike by smashing the postmodern hall of mirrors and redefining what it means to be alive. We will reframe the battle in the grandest terms. The old political battles that have consumed humankind during most of the twentieth century — black versus white, Left versus Right, male versus female — will fade into the background. The only battle still worth fighting and winning, the only one that can set us free, is The People versus The Corporate Cool Machine." Lasn argues that one must adopt the tactics of the Situationalists and adopt strategies of "*détournement* — a perspective-jarring turnabout in your everyday life," akin to the creative chaos practiced by the educators. Kalle Lasn, *Culture Jam: How to Reverse America's Suicidal Consumer Binge — and Why We Must* (New York: Harper Collins, 2000), xii, xvi, and xvii.

32 "Die Maschine ist heiß gelaufen. Wir sind nur die Vorboten, aber eure Zeit ist bald vorbei. Diese ganze Scheiß-Technik hat euch bequem gemacht, aber die anderen, die haben die Wut. Die Wut von irgendwelchen Kindern, die in dreckigen Slums herumsitzen und amerikanische Aktionfilme gucken. Und das ist nur die eine Seite. Was ist denn hier? Die Zahl der psychischen Krankeiten steigt nach oben. Immer mehr Serienkiller, gestörte Seelen, sinnlose Gewalt. Die könnt ihr irgendwann nicht mehr mit Gameshows und Shopping betäuben." Film dialogue.

33 "Was früher subversive war, kannst du heute im Laden kaufen." Film dialogue.

34 "Zudem hat das System immer perfidere Verteidigungsstrategien entwickelt, den Protest zu nehmen, zum Produkt zu verpacken, ein Preisschild draufzukleben und zurückzuverkaufen." Frank Arnold, "'Ich suche die Herausforderung': Gespräch mit Hans Weingartner über Politik, Liebe und seinen neuen Film," *epd Film* 12 (2004): 24.

35 "Der Handkamerastil erzeugt dokumentarische Nähe und Echtheit. Die Kamera ist neutral, sie beobachtet die Figuren, mittendrin zwar, aber meist mit derselben Brennweite, sehr kurze, dokumentarische Brennweiten — ich versuche nicht, mit der Kamera zu manipulieren." Arnold, "'Ich suche die Herausforderung,'" 25.

[36] "Das bißchen Einbrechen von us, das ist komplett lächerlich gegen die Gewalt, die Leute wie du ausüben." Film dialogue.

[37] For references to nonviolence, see Tobias Kniebe, "Mit Hans Weingartner in Cannes: Der Welt wird nichts erspart," *Süddeutsche Zeitung*, 21 May 2004; Thomas Klingenmaier, "*Die fetten Jahre sind vorbei*: Revolte gegen den Wohlstand," *Stuttgarter Zeitung*, 25 Nov. 2004; and Dominik Kamalzadeh, "Revolution auf der Almhütte: Hans Weingartners *Die fetten Jahre sind vorbei* fragt nach den politischen Möglichkeiten der jüngsten Generation," *Der Standard*, 25 Nov. 2004.

[38] "Smarte Idee, sexy Schauspieler, super Musik . . . Was will man mehr vom deutschen Film?" Michael Althen, "Wildes, freies Leben: *Die fetten Jahre sind vorbei*," *Frankfurter Allgemeine Zeitung*, 24 Nov. 2004.

[39] "Tatsächlich wirken ihre Scheiterhaufen der Konsumgesellschaft, zu denen sie die Möbel auftürmen, eher wie Kunstinstallationen denn wie ein revolutionäres Fanal." Althen, "Wildes, freies Leben."

[40] "[Es ist] das schönste Beziehungsdreieck aus Pop, Poesie und Politisierung, welches das deutsche Kino seit langem zustande gebracht hat." Hanns-Georg Rodek, "Die Außenseiterbande: Pop, Poesie und Politisierung: *Die fetten Jahre sind vorbei* kommt morgen ins Kino," *Die Welt*, 24 Nov. 2004. For a similar assessment, see Andreas Kilb, "Die netten Jahre sind vorbei: Doppelgesicht; Filme von Hans Weingartner und Michael Moore beim Festival in Cannes," *Frankfurter Allgemeine Zeitung*, 18 May 2004; Marc Peschke, "Die Rebellen sind ratlos: Hans Weingartners Film *Die fetten Jahre sind vorbei* erzählt, wie schwer es ist, einen Alt-68er zu entführen," *Handelsblatt*, 19 Nov. 2004; Ralf Schenk, "Einen treffen, Hundert erziehen: Das deutsche Kino ist mit Hans Weingartners *Die fetten Jahre sind vorbei* auf einem guten Weg," *Berliner Zeitung*, 24 Nov. 2004; Knut Elstermann, "Da kommt noch was! Jetzt im Kino: *Die fetten Jahre sind vorbei* von Hans Weingartner," *Neues Deutschland*, 25 Nov. 2004; and Jan Schulz-Ojala, "Denn sie wissen, was sie tun: Sauna aus, Alarm an; Hans Weingartners Film über unser Lebensgefühl, *Die fetten Jahre sind vorbei*, kommt ins Kino," *Der Tagesspiegel*, 25 Nov. 2004.

[41] "Jede solche Strategie, auch wenn sie als Happening beginnt, landet unweigerlich bei der Gretchenfrage nach Gewalt, wider Gegenstände oder/und Menschen." Rodek, "Die Außenseiterbande."

[42] "Baader, Meinhof & Co. haben sie damals bejaht, Jan, Jule & Peter sind — weil viel weniger politisiert — in ihren Überlegungen noch nicht so weit." Hanns-Georg Rodek, "Wie gerecht ist die Weltordnung? Die Wettbewerbsfilme von Michael Moore und Hans Weingartner in Cannes sind so politisch wie eindrucksvoll," *Die Welt*, 18 May 2004. Claudia Schwartz agrees that the educators are "not the RAF, but rather politically disoriented young people with an indeterminate feeling of injustice in their belly" (nicht die RAF, sondern politisch desorientierte junge Leute mit unbestimmtem Ungerechtigkeitsgefühl im Bauch). Claudia Schwartz, "Die große Generationenverstörung im deutschen Film: Hans Weingartner zeigt *Die fetten Jahre sind vorbei*," *Neue Zürcher Zeitung*, 3 Dec. 2004.

[43] "Doch die Entscheidung wird ihnen aufgezwungen, als sie bei einer Aktion vom Villenbesitzer überrascht werden und ihn — um Zeit zum Nachdenken zu

gewinnen — erst einmal entführen." Rodek, "Wie gerecht ist die Weltordnung?" See also Kamalzadeh, "Revolution auf der Almhütte."

[44] "Es ist kaum zu glauben, wie unverschämt unterhaltsam die deutschen Filme zur RAF mittlerweile geworden sind. Nachdem uns *Baader* lehrte, dass die Waffe stets in Peckinpah'schen Zentrum getragen wird, spinnt auch Hans Weingartner die Geschichte des bundesdeutschen Terrorismus in die Mythenwelt des Kinos fort." Michael Kohler, "Vorrecht der Jugend: Geschichte und Klassenkampf wiederholen sich als Burleske; Hans Weingartners *Die fetten Jahre sind vorbei*," *Frankfurter Rundschau*, 25 Nov. 2004. For negative assessments of the film based on various aspects of its political stance, see also Ulrike Frick, "Parolen von damals: Hans Weingartners kleiner Schlaumeier-Film," *Münchner Merkur*, 24 Nov. 2004; Ekkehart Krippendorff, "Wohlstandsgefängnis: *Die fetten Jahre sind vorbei*; Die Alt-68er, die erwachsen werden mussten in dieser Gesellschaft," *Freitag: Die Ost-Westwochenzeitung*, 26 Nov. 2004; and Juli Zeh, "Sixties würzig, Sixties light: *Die fetten Jahre sind vorbei*; Die Cabinet-Generation wird politisch, aber deshalb noch lange nicht erwachsen," *Freitag: Die Ost-Westwochenzeitung*, 26 Nov. 2004.

[45] Sarah Rowland, "Revolutionary Remodeling: *The Edukators* Director Hans Weingartner and Actor Daniel Brühl Explain Why Rearranging Furniture Is a Great Way to Protest," *Montreal Mirror*, 28 Jul.–3 Aug. 2005.

[46] Hanns-Georg Rodek called it a "Paradebeispiel des neuen, digitalen Guerilla-Filmemachens." Hanns-Georg Rodek, "Ich muxe, du/er/sie muxt, wir muxen," *Die Welt*, 5 Jul. 2004.

[47] According to Frank Junghänel, *Muxmäuschenstill* ranked third at the box office if one takes into account that it was distributed with 68 film copies in comparison to *Shrek 2* with 867 copies. Frank Junghänel, "Herr Mux geht ins Kino: Tolle Kritiken, volle Säle; Jan Henrik Stahlberg, Autor und Akteur des Überraschungsfilms *Muxmäuschenstill* — über Idole, Jusos und Harald Schmidt," *Berliner Zeitung*, 19 Jul. 2004.

[48] *Muxmäuschenstill* ended the year with 292,506 tickets sold, thus achieving an audience share that was considerably stronger than the average German production but not comparable to mega-hits of that year such as *(T)raumschiff Surprise — Periode 1* (Dreamship surprise: Period 1, dir. Michael Herbig, 2004) with 9,137,506; *7 Zwerge: Männer allein im Wald* (7 dwarfs, men alone in the forest, dir. Sven Unterwaldt, 2004) with 6,486,540, and *Der Untergang* (Downfall, dir. Oliver Hirschbiegel, 2004) with 4,521,903. Statistics are available at http://www.ffa.de.

[49] They represented themselves as a "Gruppe von jungen Berlinern, die die Schnauze voll haben, untätig dabei zuzusehen, wie sich alle über die Regeln, die wir brauchen, hinwegsetzen." The campaign web site is no longer in service, but a web site at Schiwago films provides an archive of the original. See Denunziant.com, FAQs, http://www.schiwagofilm.de/denunziant/html/index2.htm. For details on the Internet presence, see Sascha Lehnartz, "Vendetta gegen Schwimmbad-Pinkler: Um für ihren Film *Muxmäuschenstill* zu werben, haben dessen Macher im Internet zum Denunziantentum aufgerufen — mit erstaunlichem Erfolg," *Frankfurter Allgemeine Zeitung*, 8 Feb. 2004.

[50] Hanns-Georg Rodek writes: "Some viewers who took everything for documentation inquired in all seriousness about where one could apply to the Mux

Corporation." The German original: "Einige Zuschauer, die alles für eine Doku-mentation hielten, haben allen Ernstes nachgefragt, wo man sich bei der Mux-AG bewerben könne." Rodek, "Ich muxe."

[51] Mittermeier saw these reactions as evidence "daß Denunziantentum immer noch Nährboden hat" and Stahlberg commented that "Was wir gesehen haben, ist, daß unser Film viel näher an der Realität ist, als wir dachten." Lehnartz, "Ven-detta gegen Schwimmbad-Pinkler."

[52] "Ich denke, . . . wenn man eine andere Gesellschaftsform errichtet, dass man da so ein Organ wieder braucht, weil man sich auch davor schützen muss, dass andere Kräfte, reaktionäre Kräfte, die Gelegenheit nutzen und so einen Staat von innen aufweichen," quoted in Björn Hengst and Philipp Wittrock, "Eklat in Nie-dersachsen: Linken-Abgeordnete hat Sehnsucht nach der Stasi," *Spiegel Online*, 14 Feb. 2008, http://www.spiegel.de/politik/deutschland/0,1518,535427,00. html.

[53] Immanuel Kant, *Groundwork of the Metaphysics of Morals*, ed. and trans. Mary Gregor (Cambridge: Cambridge UP, 1988), 31. The German original: "Der kat-egorische Imperative ist also nur ein einziger und zwar dieser: handle nur nach derjenigen Maxime, durch die du zugleich wollen kannst, daß sie ein allgemeines Gesetz werde." Immanuel Kant, *Grundlegung zur Metaphysik der Sitten*, in *Werke*, 9 vols. (Berlin: Walter de Gruyter, 1968), 4:421.

[54] "Das Faschistoide an Mux ist das Mittel, um ein Bild zu zeichnen, an dem der Blockwart um die Ecke mitspielen kann. . . . Wir wollen keinen Nazi von heute zeigen. Er hat nur das Totalitäre in sich. Er ist kein Kind der braunen Suppe, er ist ein Kind der Klassik, der verstörten Romantik, der deutschen Pingeligkeit." Andreas Körner, "Provokation ist hohl: Kino-Gesprächsstoff; Marcus Mittermeier und Jan Hendrik Stahlberg zu *Muxmäuschenstill*," *sz-online, Sachsen im Netz*, 8 Jul. 2004, http://www.sz-online.de/freizeit/artikel.asp?id=631612. See also Hanns-Georg Rodek, "Man muss Stellung beziehen: Marcus Mittermeier und Jan Henrik Stahlberg über ihre Groteske *Muxmäuschenstill*," *Die Welt*, 8 Jul. 2004.

[55] "Mein Atem stinkt über den Landwehrkanal. Ich werde heute nicht die Welt verändern. Ein freier Tag für alle." Film dialogue. *Muxmäuschenstill* [2004], dir. Marcus Mittermeier, DVD (Hamburg: Warner Home Video, 2005).

[56] Michael Kohlhaas is described as "einer der rechtschaffensten zugleich und entsetzlichsten Menschen seiner Zeit." Heinrich von Kleist, *Michael Kohlhaas*, in *Sämtliche Werke und Briefe*, 2 vols., ed. Helmut Sembdner (Munich: Hanser, 1961), 2:9.

[57] "Mux is a modern Don Quixote, whose senseless attack against trivial reality is only tolerable with a large portion of humor. Our humor occasionally borders on bad taste, but that too is part of the concept to unsettle the viewer, to draw him out of his shell." (Mux ist ein moderner Don Quichotte, dessen sinnloses Anren-nen gegen die triviale Realität nur mit einer großen Portion Humor zu ertagen ist. Bei uns gerät der Humor bisweilen an die Grenzen des guten Geschmacks, aber auch das gehört zum Konzept, den Zuschauer zu verunsichern, ihn aus der Reserve zu locken.) Alexandra Wach, "Schiefe Welt, schräger Gang: Gespräch mit Marcus Mittermeier über *Muxmäuschenstill*," *Film-Dienst* 14 (8 Jul. 2004): 10.

58 "Du bist wie die Sonne . . . auf einer Lichtung . . . und hörst du es . . . das Getrappel. Ein Pferd kommt angelaufen . . . mit einem Ritter darauf. Und das bin ich . . . im Gallop. Hört's sich vielleicht albern an, aber das will ich einmal sein . . . dieser Ritter . . . zu dem du dann hochgucken kannst. Weißt du, viele große Dichter und Denker, die hatten Frauen, die sie inspirierten haben . . . einzartige Frauen. Und ich würde lügen, wenn ich nicht zugeben würde, dass ich das gleiche empfinde, wenn wir zusammen sind. Du weißt noch gar nicht, wer vor dir steht, oder? . . . der Mann deines Lebens." Film dialogue.

59 "Ich bin Teil der Gesellschaft, in der wir unsere Ideale verloren haben, in der es keine Utopie mehr gibt von einer gerechteren Gesellschaft. Und dafür bin ich da: beim ersten Schritt zu helfen, dass die Menschen die Kraft wiederfinden, für ihr Verhalten Verantwortung zu übernehmen." Film dialogue.

60 "Wir sind in aller Munde. Wie ein Sturm erfassen wir die deutschen Medien. Die privaten, die öffentlichen, alle berichten jetzt über uns. Meine Ideen werden überdiskutiert, das Manifest macht Quote und verdrängt den öffentlichen Schwachsinn. Macht sich auch so mancher noch sicher fühlen hinter den Quoten, sich über sein kindisches Weltbild freuen, ich scheiß' euch allen in den Hals. Die Wahrheit, dass ihr korrupt geworden seid, in euren moralischen Ich-AG, die Wahrheit ist stärker als jede Quote. Die Zeiten, wo alle sich über die Niveaulosigkeit beklagen, aber keiner die Schuld trägt, die sind vorbei. Die Zeit spielt ab jetzt gegen euch, bis der Zeitgeist noch der Geist ist, die ihr aus der Flasche gelassen habt." Film dialogue.

61 "Es reicht mit dem öffentlichen Schwachsinn. Wenn ich Recht habe, können sich all die Roland Kochs, Dieter Bohlens und Stefan Raabs, all die Auslaufmodelle dieser Republik, warm anziehen." Film dialogue.

62 "In dir tickt es. Du bist allein. Du hast Angst, aber du hast Augen. Du hast Ohren und Straftätern wird Hören und Sehen vergehen. Denn Straftäter findest du einfach nur noch ätzend. . . . . Denuziere deinen Nächsten." Film dialogue.

63 "Denunziant hat in Deutschland einen fahlen Beigeschmack." Film dialogue.

64 Gerd is described as "der Inbegriff eines Menschen, der es in seinem Leben zu nichts gebracht hat." Film dialogue.

65 "Ich bin kein Held, denn jedes Land hat die Helden, die es verdient. Michael Schumacher ist ein Held, weil er schnell um die Kurven fahren kann und keine Steuer zahlt. Armes Land." Film dialogue.

66 "Ich glaube, meine Generation ist die Generation der Ratlosigkeit und der Umorientierung. Da kommt jetzt eine neue Generation, im Zuge der Anti-Globalisierungsbewegung — mit der ich sehr stark sympathisiere —, die neue Strategien entwickelt." Arnold, "'Ich suche die Herausforderung,'" 24.

67 "*Muxmäuschenstill* ist eine Reflexion des neuen Zeitgeistes, der allgegenwärtigen Krisenstimmung. Deutschland befindet sich schon länger im gesellschaftlichen Umbruch. Doch erst, wenn es den meisten schlechter geht, fangen sie an, Fragen zu stellen. Wir sind zwar noch immer ein 'fettes' Land, aber die wirtschaftliche Euphorie der 1990er-Jahre ist längst vorbei. Geblieben ist jedoch ein moralischer Kater nach dem Höhenflug. Darauf reagieren wir mit unserem Film." Wach, "Schiefe Welt, schräger Gang," 9.

[68] "Aber seit dem Fall der Mauer existiert keine Alternative mehr zu dem Gesell-schaftsbild, in dem wir jetzt leben. Auch der Idealist Mux hat keine Alternativen zu bieten. Er schreibt ein Manifest und bleibt im ersten Kapitel stecken. Er wird gewalttätig und zum Psychopathen, weil ihm das Ventil der Utopie fehlt." Martin Schwickert, "Nicht wackeln! Marcus Mittermeier und Jan Henryk Stahlberg über ihr Regie-Debut," *Ultimo auf draht*, http://www.ultimo-bielefeld.de/kr-film/i-mux.htm#seitoben.

Epilogue

TWENTY YEARS AFTER THE FALL OF COMMUNISM, forty years after the student revolution, and sixty years after the founding of the Federal Republic, Germany has been afloat in anniversaries that beckon contemplation of the nation's development since the end of the Second World War. Cinema has contributed to these commemorations with films that scrutinize postwar German history and the yearning for a just civil society. By telling stories about a shared past, cinema functions as a public forum for debates on national history: where the divided nation has been, what struggles it has won and lost, and what dreams the country has for itself. Not only does cinema satisfy the pressing need to understand how the nation became what it is now, but by focusing on a common past it helps to create a shared identity and sense of purpose, a collectivity that seems elusive in the present.

In a 2008 interview for *Deutschland Radio*, director Christian Petzold maintained that despite all the new technological advances that provide people with an insular mediated experience, the collective aspect of cinema would win out in the end: "Cinema is in essence the story of a community. Cinema belongs to the city. In essence, cinema belongs to the public realm." Petzold acknowledged that in the near future cinema would most likely have a difficult time competing with computers and the Internet, but he argued that it would survive: "I believe that people will not endure individuality. I believe that they like to dream collectively once in a while."[1] Cinema's affinity to collective dreaming and its ability to examine social issues through the lens of fantasy make it a viable and vital institution to mediate conflicts in the process of imagining the nation.

The collective experience of watching a film together in a public space gives viewers the opportunity to participate in a vision of reality that transcends the individual. Cinema holds utopian potential as a vehicle to overcome a myriad of boundaries and connect disparate individuals into something larger than the self. In the post-cold-war era, in which common political beliefs seem beyond reach, old ideals have lost their familiar contours, technological advances in communication make physical proximity unnecessary, and human encounters are increasingly mediated, there is a feeling that the collective has changed beyond recognition. How does the nation stay connected both politically and interpersonally? Has the increasing shift in viewing formats — from films projected onto large screens in theaters designed for large audiences watching the same thing at the same time in the same place to individualized viewing of films via DVDs, television broadcasts, and the Internet — resulted in a loss of connection among people? Or have these new modes of watching films expanded the possibilities of connecting through digital means to an even larger, more diverse public less dependent on geographic space, time, and the linearity of a single performance? At stake here is whether cinema can continue to function as a medium of social contact and shared vision as it develops into a more atomized form of production and consumption.

It is the precarious status of the collective, both in regard to the experience of cinema and to the larger social experience of nation that lies at the heart of the post-Wall history films discussed in this book. Films about postwar German history form an appealing genre in part because they locate the all-too-elusive collective in the past. As such the history film can recuperate the collective on two levels: by assembling a shared national history that connects audiences today and by presenting examples from recent times in which the collective existed and can be brought back to life again on the screen. In motion pictures about the GDR and Western terrorism, filmmakers reanimate groups of like-minded people with common values and goals who demonstrated the kind of solidarity that many viewers see as missing in society today. Turning to the past, one can momentarily evoke a sense of unity and singularity of purpose, but in many ways these history films are about both triumphs and losses. Stories about the GDR feature characters who fought against the system and wanted out, gained their freedom and rebuilt insular lives with family and friends, while those who stayed and tried to contribute to the betterment of humanity were routinely blocked by obdurate bureaucrats or corrupt, self-serving officials. In stories about terrorism, a group of idealists and thrill-seekers in equal measure took up arms to fight injustice, and while many held on to their beliefs and paid with imprisonment or death, others, in their zeal to fight a malicious system, began to adopt the type of brutality and despotic mindsets that they had originally fought against. In both histories, people were empowered and chose their fate, but in the end the collectives fell apart. Taken together these history films depict a postwar past populated by individuals who displayed civil courage and most often triumphed over adversity, but a collective that ended prematurely, before it could realize its utopian vision of the future.

What should be clear from this study is that no single film can tell history in a definitive fashion. At best a history film can provide a unique perspective, granting audiences a glimpse at another time, shaping human lives into stories that reveal what it might have felt like to live in the past and what historical constraints and options helped determine the paths people took to create the world they lived in, the world the audience has inherited. As a genre that integrates competing discourses and agendas into a coherent, if complex, system, the history film can provide valuable material to help us understand the past and, equally important, how cinema constructs the past the public needs for the present.

Over the last two decades history films about postwar Germany have placed great emphasis on the struggles of individuals against an iniquitous system and on the collective mission of bringing about a fair social order. The themes of utopianism and dissent span both East and West Germany and in many cases disregard the political, philosophical, and geographical boundaries between the two countries to tell a common history. In films about the GDR we find decent, average citizens who want to escape (Martin Schulz, Heiko, Tommy, Christiane and Robert Kerner, Wanda Brenner, Sophie Sellmann, Sara Bender), who become victims of a corrupt bureaucracy that either destroys their initiative or robs them of their creativity (Hans-Peter Dallow, Daniel Brenner, Konrad Richter, Georg Dreyman), and who are driven to suicide (Harald, Albert Jerska, Christa-Marie Sieland, Wilfried Rottmann). In the filmic world of the GDR, border guards do not shoot at defectors fleeing over the border (Alexander Karow), Stasi interrogators fall in love with their prisoner (Jan Kohlfeld), and even Stasi captains save their surveillance targets by planting misinformation (Gerd Wiesler). The heroes in this modern saga are overwhelmingly rebels who fight against injustice in all its forms. The most common figure is the courageous person who refuses to be held captive behind a wall, risking imprisonment and possible death to gain liberty. Those who stay are convinced socialists who fall prey to a regime demanding the type of compliance and conformity that depletes the human spirit. One-dimensional villains with no redeeming qualities exploit the vulnerable or mindlessly serve the powers that be (Müller, Peter Koch, Anton Grubitz, Brunno Hempf). The rather clear-cut divide between upstanding heroes and self-serving scoundrels is symptomatic of mainstream cinema. However, such a simplistic opposition of good and evil does more than merely define the storyline for popular movies. Increasingly, it contributes to a prevalent discourse on national history as more and more people learn about the past in the cinema and as motion pictures are endlessly reproduced.

Films about the Red Army Faction and its corollaries also emphasize utopianism and political dissent as defining attributes of a national struggle, but they tend to romanticize the attractive elements of resistance against the status quo. The anti-heroes in this national narrative are young, alluring, and dynamic revolutionaries, who embrace violence in an effort to force change. Andreas Baader, Gudrun Ensslin, Ulrike Meinhof, Rita Vogt, Friederike Adelbach, and even Mux are charismatic, doomed figures who pay for their civil disobedience with imprisonment or death. The punk Tatjana, educators Jan, Peter, and Jule, and teenage rebels Anna, Marcus, and Randy never reach the level of violence perpetrated by RAF terrorists and thus fare better in the end. All of these figures populate stories that highlight the adrenaline rush of fighting against the system and the emotional rewards found in belonging to a collective that serves a higher order. The sheer energy of terrorism is captured in scenes that nearly glow with the stylized beauty of destruction and deviant behavior: Baader and his friends on a Paris rooftop at sunset, Rita and Andi in costumes happily robbing a bank, the educators riding off in their speedboat to blow up television towers, and a bare-chested hippie with arms wide open shouting "Hiroshima, Vietnam, Dresden" as the Springer publishing house burns.

For all their flaws, the history films under consideration here capture significant historical lessons on the dual legacies of the GDR and homegrown terrorism, the attempt to better humanity on the one side and the force employed to achieve such noble goals on the other. Rather than expecting everything from a single film, it is more productive to look at each film as providing a piece of the puzzle. When assembled together into a whole, they can give a multifaceted picture of the past, one that is constantly evolving. Many of the DEFA films made between 1989 and 1992, for instance, are remarkable films that exhibit a surrealism that for all its flights of fantasy is arguably the most realistic depiction of the GDR's dual legacy. Herwig Kipping's *Das Land hinter dem Regenbogen* illustrates brilliantly the fervor and dogma of Stalinism that led to self-destruction but never quite extinguished the desire to find utopia, a world filled with goodness and caritas just beyond the horizon. Peter Kahane's *Die Architekten* captures the frustration of the last generation to inherit socialism, optimists filled with the desire to contribute to a better world, who were constantly thwarted in their efforts and thus defected or through their collective dissatisfaction inadvertently brought down the very system they wanted to build. Margarethe von Trotta's *Das Versprechen* depicts the pain of division and forced separation of an entire nation in a story that examines both an individual promise to overcome insurmountable hurdles and an unfulfilled collective promise to create a more egalitarian system for all. Florian Henckel von Donnersmarck's *Das Leben der Anderen* illustrates the resilient belief in socialism among a group of people who continued to work for their goals despite the omnipresent Stasi surveillance system that destroyed vulnerable individuals in its drive to eradicate opposition to the party line.

History films offer equally important insights into the dual legacy of terrorism, the admirable civic courage of young people who refused to sit back passively and witness injustice, but also the carnage their action produced and the unexpected result that they ended up adopting a mindset that mimicked or even surpassed the brutal system they sought to bring down. Christopher Roth's *Baader* takes up the persistent recycling of media images of the RAF and tries to deconstruct the myths associated with the first generation of the Baader-Meinhof gang. While Roth's film is not completely successful in distancing itself from the myths it seeks to critique, it does present an alternative version of events that forces viewers to acknowledge that historiography is neither an exact science nor value-free and that different versions of the past compete for our endorsement. Volker Schlöndorff's *Die Stille nach dem Schuss* and Andreas Dresen's *Raus aus der Haut* demonstrate that the history of German terrorism transcends traditional state borders and should be reassessed as part of a pan-German history. Schlöndorff's film examines the fate of an RAF terrorist who idealized the Marxist struggle against tyranny and then experienced first-hand the conformity and complacency of real-existing socialism in the GDR. Although the main character remains oblivious to the contradictions inherent in her elected homeland, the film highlights the ambivalent legacy of both Western terrorism and Eastern socialism. Dresen's film reveals the impact of the RAF and Western counter-culture on GDR youth, but his story focuses on how adopting terrorist methods to fight against the establishment turns the righteous victim of oppression into a perpetrator of violence. What separates his film most distinctly from other history films is that his characters recognize their transformation, renounce such methods of civil disobedience, and regret their actions. Uli Edel's *Der Baader Meinhof Komplex* presents with epic breadth the history of the RAF from 1967 to 1977. His film outlines many of the grievances the RAF lodged against the political and socioeconomic system. It also underscores that the government's unwillingness to tackle large structural issues and their refusal to work together with those discontented members of society who sought change played a significant role in the escalation of violence.

History films concerned primarily with memory are equally valuable for understanding the need to uncover what has been forgotten in the transition to a unified Germany if one is to build a common future. *Berlin Is in Germany*, *Führer Ex*, and *Good Bye, Lenin!* examine the collective amnesia afflicting the nation following the *Wende*. Hannes Stöhr's *Berlin Is in Germany* and Winfried Bonengel's *Führer Ex* dwell on the trauma of being held captive and deprived of freedom. They both argue that the GDR was a prison state that needs to be forgotten so that history does not become in Nietzschean terms the gravedigger of the present. Wolfgang Becker's *Good Bye, Lenin!*, by contrast, displays a much more ambivalent and nuanced stance toward the GDR, demonstrating that there is at least as much that needs to be preserved as forgotten. *Good Bye, Lenin!* poignantly captures the dual legacy of the GDR: its dreams of a perfectible world and its mistakes along the way. What distinguishes it from Stöhr and Bonengel's films is that it makes a strong case for remembering and preserving the utopian ideals at the core of GDR history. Moreover, Becker's film illustrates that writing history is as much about the kind of lessons we need for today as about uncovering what happened in the past. Embracing an openly fictitious version of history, *Good Bye, Lenin!*

exposes the authentic wishes that remain hidden behind the real events that never matched the desired outcome.

History films reveal that the past is anything but over, mastered, and departed. Hans Weingartner's *Die fetten Jahre sind vorbei* and Marcus Mittermeier's *Muxmäuschenstill* demonstrate that the past persists in many shapes and these traces of bygone days continue to impact the present in often surprising ways. Both films scrutinize Germany history in search of a workable intellectual heritage that can offer direction for a society in need of useable models of civic engagement. Weingartner's film examines the legacy of '68, the period in recent history that has come to symbolize the prototype of a mass movement for social change. Mittermeier's film, by contrast, looks to German idealism and the pillars of German literary history, to find paradigms of moral certitude that can offer the foundation for responsible citizenship and social harmony. Looking to history for pedagogical lessons applicable to contemporary circumstances, both films use a contagious black humor but are utterly earnest in their search for utopian solutions and creative ways to jar the masses into collective action.

This body of filmic work on the German past shares certain fundamental ideas. Two of the most critically acclaimed and popular German films made in the last decade, *Good Bye, Lenin!* and *Das Leben der Anderen*, celebrate the power of fantasy and art to change the world. Inextricably linked to this belief in the power of imagination is an incongruous stance toward utopia that is remarkably compelling. Both films mourn the GDR's demise and concomitant loss of utopia yet cling to the undying belief that there is a socialist solution that will bring about a better world. Alex's rocket bearing the GDR national emblem rising into the heavens to release his mother's ashes, and reformed Stasi officer Wiesler finding a book on humanity dedicated to him in the Karl Marx Bookstore can stand as signs that despite all evidence to the contrary the seeds of socialist idealism are anything but dead. While the collective no longer exists, exemplary individuals keep the dream alive. Thus instead of referring to the death of utopia, it would be more accurate to refer to a phantom utopia. Since the GDR failed, there has been widespread skepticism toward Marxism as a practical solution to inequity. Yet faced with globalization, cultural homogenization, and turbocapitalism, the ghosts of utopia linger and refuse to give up their spirit completely. The films examined here are filled with images that embody this ambivalence and haunt the mind's eye after the screen fades to black. This phantasmagoria features a village walking past the colossal Karl Marx statue into a vast desert landscape in search of the land beyond the rainbow, Lenin bidding farewell as he rides off into the sunset over the Karl-Marx-Allee, a starry-eyed yet desperate Rita asking workers why they no longer believe in socialism, and massive amounts of coal being loaded into the basement to prepare for a long period of hibernation. Each of these scenes gives expression to the contradictory impulses of a phantom utopia, dead but undead, filled with utter despair but still somehow fanning the enduring embers of hope.

In view of the finality of bygone days, it is not too surprising that most of these history films end with death. In *Baader, Der Baader Meinhof Komplex, Die Stille nach dem Schuss, Führer Ex, Muxmäuschen-still, Das Leben der Anderen, Raus aus der Haut*, and *Good Bye, Lenin!*, the main protagonists are shot by the authorities, are beaten to death by thugs, are run over by cars in a form of moral execution, commit suicide, or die of a broken heart. What is striking about these films is how many end in either a protracted shot of stasis or a freeze frame. *Die Stille nach dem Schuss, Der Baader Meinhof Komplex, Die Architek-ten, Raus aus der Haut*, and *Die fetten Jahre sind vorbei* conclude with a lingering shot of a dead body, an anguished man collapsed on the ground, coal and black smoke filling the basement, and a motor boat on a vast sea traveling into the horizon. *Das Versprechen, Baader, Good Bye, Lenin!, Das Leben der Anderen*, and *Führer Ex* conclude with images frozen in time that become etched in the viewer's memory. These pro-tracted shots of stasis and freeze frames are stylistic devises that reify phantom utopia. In their suggestion of both the finality of death or despair and the endurance of hope in the static but continuing image, they blur the boundaries between past, present, and future. Laura Mul-vey maintains it is the inconsistency between the objectives of narrative and material image that lend the freeze frame its potential to tell two stories at once. Mulvey points out that "while the freeze frame brings finality to narrative, the sequence of individual frames can, as suggested by the system of pattern and repetition in the flicker film, lead to infin-ity. One direction finds a form to express 'the end' through metaphor. The other direction represents the aspiration to stories without end, a ceaseless metonymy."[2] Garrett Stewart has likewise argued that the freeze frame and prolonged shots of stasis have the potential to facilitate "transfiguration of a death moment into a vision of continuance beyond the threshold of narration."[3] The abundance of history films that end in a lingering stasis suggests that the past is anything but dead and gone. There is no definitive cut to mark a clear break, no dissolve to let the past fade into history. Instead we have a traumatic postwar German past that endures in the present and demands attention long after the story is over. The ideological conflicts and the human toll left in the wake of postwar division, the Stasi police state, and homegrown terrorism con-tinue to shape the present. In the coalescence of static, frozen endings and narrative closure, contemporary German history films have found the stylistic means to render the tension inherent in a phantom utopia that refuses to be exorcized.

Notes

[1] "Das Kino ist im Grunde genommen Erzählung eines Gemeinwesens. Und Kino gehört zur Stadt, und Kino gehört im Grunde genommen zum öffentlichen Raum. Ich glaube aber, die Menschen halten die Individualität so nicht aus. Ich glaube, daß sie gerne im Kollektiv ab und zu mal träumen gehen." "Christian Petzold, Regisseur, beurteilt die Zukunft des deutschen Kinos," *Deutschland Radio*, 25 Apr. 2008, http://www.tagesschau.de/multimedia/audio/audio16946.html.

[2] Laura Mulvey, *Death 24x a Second: Stillness and the Moving Image* (London: Reaktion Books, 2007), 81.

[3] Garrett Stewart, *Framed Time: Toward a Postfilmic Cinema* (Chicago: U of Chicago P, 2007), 82.

Works Cited

Althen, Michael. "Polit-Porno: *Der Baader Meinhof Komplex.*" *Frankfurter Allgemeine Zeitung*, 24 September 2008.

———. "Wildes, freies Leben: *Die fetten Jahre sind vorbei.*" *Frankfurter Allgemeine Zeitung*, 24 November 2004.

Altmann, Rick. *Film/Genre*. London: British Film Institute, 1999.

"Amnesia Patients Stuck in Present." *BBC News*, 15 January 2007. http://news.bbc.co.uk/go/pr/fr/-/2/hi/health/6263421.stm.

An die Grenze [2007]. Directed by Urs Egger. DVD. Cologne: Colonia Media, 2007.

Anderson, Benedict. *Imagined Communities: Reflections on the Origins and Spread of Nationalism*. Rev. ed. London: Verso, 1991.

Angelopoulou, Alexia. "Nun ist Schluss mit diesem Thema: Mit *Führer Ex* hat Regisseur Winfried Bonengel seinen ersten Kinofilm abgedreht." *Stuttgarter Nachrichten*, 5 December 2002.

AP/dpa. "*Das Leben der Anderen*: Oscar für deutsches Stasi-Drama." *Süddeutsche Zeitung*, 26 February 2007.

"ARD-Zweiteiler schlägt Jauch: Checkpoint Charlie." *Hamburger Abendblatt*, 4 October 2007.

Arendt, Hannah. *On Violence*. New York: Harcourt, Brace & World, 1970.

Arnold, Frank. "'Ich suche die Herausforderung': Gespräch mit Hans Weingartner über Politik, Liebe und seinen neuen Film." *epd Film* 12 (2004): 24–25.

Ash, Mitchell G. "Becoming Normal, Modern, and German (Again?)." In *The Power of Intellectuals in Contemporary Germany*, edited by Michael Geyer, 295–313. Chicago: U of Chicago P, 2001.

Ash, Timothy Garton, ed. *Wächst zusammen, was zusammengehört? Deutschland und Europa zehn Jahre nach dem Fall der Mauer: Vortrag im Rathaus Schöneberg zu Berlin, 5. November 1999*. Schriftenreihe der Bundeskanzler-Willy-Brandt-Stiftung 8. Berlin: Bundeskanzler-Willy-Brandt-Stiftung, 2001.

ATTAC. http://www.attac.org.

Aust, Bettina. "'Fernsehen ist Lebensersatz:' Medienkritiker Hans Weingartner." *Spiegel Online*, 16 November 2007. http://www.spiegel.de/kultur/kino/0,1518,516833,00.html.

Aust, Stefan. *Der Baader Meinhof Komplex*. 8th ed. Munich: Goldmann, 1998.

Baader [2002]. Directed by Christopher Roth. DVD. Munich: Universum Film, 2003.

Barber, Benjamin R. *Jihad vs. McWorld.* New York: Ballantine Books, 1996.

Bathrick, David. "Anti-Neonazism as Cinematic Practice: Bonengel's *Beruf Neonazi.*" *New German Critique* 67 (1996): 133–46.

Baum, Gerhart. "Film *Baader Meinhof Komplex*: Es war kein Krieg." *Die Zeit,* 18 September 2008.

Bavaria Films. http://www.bavaria-film.de.

Becker, Peter von. "Die Geschichte der Schattenfrau: Wie die DDR weltweit gesuchte RAF-Terroristen verbarg, war eines ihrer bestgehüteten Geheimnisse. Daraus hat Volker Schlöndorff seinen neuen Film gemacht, Premiere zur Berlinale *Die Stille nach dem Schuss.*" *Der Tagesspiegel,* 17 February 2000.

Behrens, Jan C., Thomas Lindenberger, and Patrice G. Poutros, eds. *Fremde und Fremd-Sein in der DDR: Zu historischen Ursachen der Fremdenfeindlichkeit in Ostdeutschland.* Berlin: Metropol, 2003.

"Bei Ausschreitungen auf dem Ostberliner Alexanderplatz werden drei Menschen getötet und 200 verletzt." BStU, Chronik zur Geschichte der DDR und ihres Ministeriums für Staatssicherheit. http://www.bstu.bund.de/DE/Wissen/DDRGeschichte/Chronik-DDR/chronik-1970_79_inhalt.html?nn=1768732.

Berdahl, Daphne. "'(N)Ostalgie' for the Present: Memory, Longing, and East German Things." *Ethnos: Journal of Anthropology* 64, no. 2 (1999): 192–211.

Berghahn, Daniela. "East German Cinema after Unification." In *German Cinema since Unification*, edited by David Clarke, 79–104. London: Continuum, 2006.

Bergmann, Anke. *RAF auf der Leinwand: Diskursanalyse anhand ausgewählter Filmbeispiele zwischen dem Deutschen Herbst und der Jahrtausendwende.* Diplomarbeit. HFF Konrad Wolf, Studiengang AV-Medienwissenschaft, Potsdam-Babelsberg, 2005.,

Berlin Is in Germany [2001]. Directed by Hannes Stöhr. DVD. Berlin: Absolut Medien, 2003.

Berlin Is in Germany. Presseheft. N.p., n.d.

Betts, Paul. "The Twilight of the Idols: East German Memory and Material Culture." *Journal of Modern History* 72 (2000): 731–65.

Biermann, Wolf. "Die Gespenster treten aus dem Schatten: *Das Leben der Anderen*; Warum der Stasi-Film eines jungen Westdeutschen mich staunen läßt." *Die Welt,* 22 March 2006.

Biesenbach, Klaus. "Engel der Geschichte oder den Schrecken anderer betrachten oder Bilder in den Zeiten des Terrors." In *Zur Vorstellung des Terrors: Die RAF-Ausstellung,* 2 vols., edited by Klaus Biesenbach, 2:11–15. Berlin: Steidl/KW Institute for Contemporary Art, 2005.

Blair, John. "Madness and Bliss as Ideological Categories in Margarethe von Trotta's *The Promise.*" *Journal of the Association for the Interdisciplinary Study of the Arts* 7, no. 1–2 (2001–2): 91–101.

Blum, Martin. "Remaking the East German Past: Ostalgie, Identity, and Material Culture." *Journal of Popular Culture* 34, no. 3 (2000): 229–53.

Bodewein, Lena. "In der Zeitmaschine: Mit *Berlin is in Germany* starten ORB und ZDF die zwölfteilige Ostwind Reihe." *Der Tagesspiegel*, 9 March 2003.

Boehlke, Michael, and Henryk Gericke, eds. *Too Much Future: Punk in der DDR*. Rev. ed. Berlin: Verbrecher Verlag, 2007.

Borchert, Wolfgang. *Das Gesamtwerk*. Hamburg: Rowohlt, 1949.

Borcholte, Andreas. "Anarchie und Alltag: *Die fetten Jahre sind vorbei*." *Spiegel Online*, 25 November 2004. http:/www.spiegel.de/kultur/kino/0,1518,329478,00.html.

Bordwell, David. "The Art Cinema as a Mode of Film Practice." In *The European Cinema Reader*, edited by Catherine Fowler, 94–102. London: Routledge, 2002.

Boxoffice Mojo. Market-share figures. http://www.boxofficemojo.com.

Boym, Svetlana. *The Future of Nostalgia*. New York: Basic Books, 2001.

Brauck, Markus, and Matthias Mattusek. "'Phantastischer Gedächtnisverlust:' Gespräch mit dem Schriftsteller und einstigen Marxisten Hans Magnus Enzensberger." *Spiegel Online*, 3 November 2008. http://www.spiegel.de/spiegel/0,1518,587872,00.html.

Brecht, Bertolt. *Die heilige Johanna der Schlachthöfe*. In *Stücke* 1, volume 1 of *Werke*, 153–274. Edited by Werner Mittenzwei.

———. *Gedichte*. Volume 3 of *Werke*. Edited by Werner Mittenzwei.

———. *Gedichte 4: Gedichte und Gedichtfragmente 1928–1939*. Vol. 14 of *Werke: Große kommentierte Berliner und Frankfurter Ausgabe*. 30 vols. Edited by Werner Hecht. Frankfurt am Main: Suhrkamp Verlag, 1993.

———. *Poems, 1913–1956*. Edited by John Willett, Ralph Manheim, and Erich Fried. New York: Methuen, 1976.

———. *Werke*. 5 vols. Edited by Werner Mittenzwei. 3rd ed. Berlin, GDR: Aufbau, 1981.

Brockmann, Stephen. *Literature and German Reunification*. Cambridge: Cambridge UP, 1999.

———. "Martin Walser and the Presence of the German Past." *German Quarterly* 75, no. 2 (2002): 127–43.

Brückner, Jutta. "Für Margarethe von Trotta." In Schneider and von Trotta, *Das Versprechen oder Der lange Atem der Liebe: Filmszenarium*, 150–59.

Bühler, Philipp. "Wiedergänger von Franz Biberkopf: Eine Parabel über Ost und West und ein sehr guter Film: *Berlin is in Germany* von Hannes Stöhr." *Berliner Zeitung*, 1 November 2001.

Bullion, Constanze von. "Gelebte Geschichte: Eine Figur, mehrere Biografien: Volker Schlöndorff über die Vorwürfe gegen seinen Film *Die Stille nach dem Schuss*." *Süddeutsche Zeitung*, 17 February 2000.

———. "RAF light und die Idylle im Osten: Terroristen in der DDR; Inge Viett streitet mit Volker Schlöndorff über seinen Film *Die Stille nach dem Schuss*." *Süddeutsche Zeitung*, 17 February 2000.

Bundesarchiv-Filmarchiv, ed. *Filmobibliografischer Jahresbericht 1990 (und Überläufer)*. Berlin: Henschel, 1994.

Bundesministerium für innerdeutsche Beziehungen, ed. *DDR Handbuch.* 2nd rev. ed. Cologne: Verlag Wissenschaft & Politik, 1979.

Burgoyne, Robert. *Film Nation: Hollywood Looks at U.S. History.* Minneapolis: U of Minnesota P, 1997.

———. "Prosthetic Memory/Traumatic Memory: *Forrest Gump* (1994)." In *The History on Film Reader*, edited by Marnie Hughes-Warrington, 137–42. London: Routledge, 2009.

Calle, Sophie. *The Detachment / Die Entfernung.* Berlin: G + B Art International, 1996.

Canby, Vincent. "A Brutal, Elegiac Last Exit, Unrelieved by Hope." *New York Times*, 2 May 1990.

Carnes, Mark, ed. *Past Imperfect: History According to the Movies.* New York: Henry Holt, 1995.

Christiane F.: Wir Kinder vom Bahnhof Zoo [1981]. Directed by Ulrich Edel. DVD. Ismaning: EuroVideo, 2000.

"Christian Petzold, Regisseur, beurteilt die Zukunft des deutschen Kinos." *Deutschland Radio*, 25 April 2008. http://www.tagesschau.de/multimedia/audio/audio16946.html.

Clarke, David. "Representations of East German Masculinity in Hannes Stöhr's *Berlin is in Germany* and Andreas Kleinert's *Wege in die Nacht.*" *German Life and Letters* 55, no. 4 (2002): 434–49.

Claus, Peter. "Wunden eines 'Versagers': Ab heute in den Kinos; *Die Architekten*, ein DEFA-Film von Peter Kahane und Thomas Knauf." *Junge Welt*, 21 June 1990.

Cohen, Roger. "Call for 'Guiding Culture' Rekindles Political Debate in Germany." *New York Times*, 5 November 2000.

Cooke, Paul. *Representing East Germany since Unification: From Colonization to Nostalgia.* Oxford: Berg, 2005.

Cormican, Muriel. "Thomas Brussig's Ostalgie in Print and on Celluloid." In *Processes of Transposition: German Literature and Film*, edited by Christiane Schönfeld and Hermann Rasche, 251–68. Amsterdamer Beiträge zur neueren Germanistik 63. Amsterdam: Rodopi, 2007.

Corrigan, Timothy. "The Temporality of Place, Postmodernism, and Fassbinder Texts." *New German Critique* 63 (1994): 139–54.

Crowdus, Gary, and Richard Porton. "Coming to Terms with the German Past: An Interview with Volker Schlöndorff." *Cineaste* 26, no. 2 (2000): 18–23.

Dalicow, Bärbel. "Traurige Feste: Festival des jungen deutschen Films in Potsdam." *Filmspiegel* 15 (1990): 15.

Das dicke DDR Buch. Berlin: Eulenspiegel, 2002.

Das Land hinter dem Regenbogen [1992]. Directed by Herwig Kipping. DVD. Amherst, MA: DEFA Film Library, 2009.

Das Leben der Anderen [2006]. Directed by Florian Henckel von Donnersmarck. DVD. Munich: Buena Vista International, 2006.

Das Leben ist eine Baustelle [1997]. Directed by Wolfgang Becker. DVD. Munich: Universum Film, 2001.

Das Versprechen [1995]. Directed by Margarethe von Trotta. DVD. Berlin: StudioCanal, 2008.

Das weiße Rauschen [2001]. Directed by Hans Weingartner. DVD. Hamburg: Warner Home Video, 2002.

Davidson, John E. "Overcoming Germany's Past(s) in Film since the Wende." *Seminar: A Journal of Germanic Studies* 33, no. 4 (1997): 307–21.

Dazlak-Skinhead [1997]. Directed by Helke Sander. DVD. Essen: Sunny Bastard, 2007.

Ddp/mar, "Historiker Knabe kritisiert Stasi-Film *Das Leben der Anderen*." *Ddp Basisdienst*, 6 April 2006.

DDR 1989/90 Documente. http://www.ddr89.de/.

DDR Ferner Osten: Würfelrallye und Ratespiel mit "Ach, Ja!" Effekt. Autorenkollektiv Eike Bochmann und Peter Zehrt. Berlin: Inkognito, n.d.

Debord, Guy. *The Society of Spectacle* [1967]. Translated by Donald Nicholson-Smith. New York: Zone Books, 1994.

Decker, Gunnar. "Vielfalt statt Einfalt: Zum Ost-West-Kinoerfolg von *Good bye, Lenin!*" *Neues Deutschland*, 8 March 2003.

———. "Wege durchs Labyrinth: *Berlin is in Germany* von Hannes Stöhr." *Neues Deutschland*, 1 November 2001.

Decker, Kerstin. "Das wahre Ende der DDR: Wolfgang Beckers wundersame Komödie *Good Bye, Lenin!*" *Der Tagesspiegel*, 28 February 2003.

———. "DDR im TV: So oder so, Geschichte wird gemacht." *Der Tagesspiegel*, 29 October 2007.

———. "Staatsende, letzter Akt: Hannes Stöhrs melancholische Komödie um einen herzensguten Ex-Knacki, *Berlin is in Germany*." *Der Tagesspiegel*, 1 November 2001.

De Graaf, John, David Wann, and Thomas H. Naylor. *Affluenza: The All Consuming Epidemic*. San Francisco: Berrett-Koehler Publishers, 2001.

Delay, Jan. *Searching for Jan Soul Rebels*. Label: Buback EFA, released 9 April 2001.

Denunziant.com. http://www.schiwagofilm.de/denunziant/html/index2.htm.

Der Ärgermacher [2004]. Directed by Steffen Jürgens and Bettina Schoeller. DVD. Cologne: Alive Vertrieb und Marketing, 2005.

Der Baader Meinhof Komplex [2008]. Directed by Uli Edel. DVD. Unterföhring: Paramount Home Entertainment, 2008.

Der Kick [2006]. Directed by Andres Veiel. DVD. Mainz: ZDF Theaterkanal edition, 2006.

Der Tangospieler. Directed by Roland Gräf. 35 mm. Babelsberg: DEFA Studio, 1991.

Der Verdacht. Directed by Frank Beyer. 35 mm. Babelsberg: DEFA Studio, 1991.

Derrida, Jacques. *Points: Interviews, 1974–1994*. Edited by Elisabeth Weber. Translated by Peggy Kamuf & Others. Stanford, CA: Stanford UP, 1995.

Deutschland im Herbst [1978]. Directed by Alexander Kluge, Volker Schlöndorff, Alf Brustellin, Bernhard Sinkel, Rainer Werner Fassbinder, Katja

Rupé, Hans Peter Cloos, Edgar Reitz, Maximiliane Mainka, and Peter Schubert. DVD. Munich: Kinowelt Home Entertainment, 2004.

Dicks, Hans-Günther. "Zum Weinen? Nein, zum Heulen! Zum Festival-Auftakt: *Das Versprechen* von Margarethe von Trotta." *Neues Deutschland*, 9 February 1995.

Die Architekten [1990]. Directed by Peter Kahane. DVD. Berlin: Icestorm Entertainment, 2005.

Die bleierne Zeit [1981]. Directed by Margarethe von Trotta. Berlin: Studio-Canal, 2008.

Die dritte Generation [1979]. Directed by Rainer Werner Fassbinder. DVD. Munich: Kinowelt Home Entertainment, 2004.

Die fetten Jahre sind vorbei [2004]. Directed by Hans Weingartner. DVD. Munich: Universum Film, 2005.

Die Flucht [1977]. Directed by Roland Gräf. DVD. Berlin: Icestorm Entertainment, 2007.

Die Frau vom Checkpoint Charlie [2007]. Directed by Miguel Alexandre. DVD. Munich: Universum Film, 2007.

Die Frau vom Checkpoint Charlie. http://www.daserste.de/checkpointcharlie/.

Die Patriotin [1979]. Directed by Alexander Kluge. DVD. Cologne: Alive Vertrieb und Marketing, 2007.

Die Quereinsteigerinnen [2005]. Directed by Rainer Knepperges and Christian Mrasek. DVD. Munich: Sunfilm Entertainment, 2007.

Die Stille nach dem Schuss [2000]. Directed by Volker Schlöndorff. DVD. Munich: Kinowelt Home Entertainment, 2001.

Die Terroristen [1992]. Directed by Philip Gröning. VHS. Berlin: Filmgalerie 451, 1992.

Die verlorene Ehre der Katharina Blum [1975]. Directed by Volker Schlöndorff and Margarethe von Trotta. DVD. Berlin: StudioCanal, 2008.

Dk. "Die vergessenen *Architekten*: Mehr als Trafo-Stationen und Einheitsblocks durften sie nicht bauen; Die Defa setzte den Architekten des Sozialismus ein filmisches Denkmal." *Sächsische Zeitung*, 17 November 1990.

Doane, Mary Ann. "Film und Masquerade: Theorizing the Female Spectator." In *Issues in Feminist Criticism*, edited by Patricia Erens, 41–57. Bloomington: Indiana UP, 1990.

Dullinger, Angie. "'Kein Schuss zu viel:' Regisseur Uli Edel über das Polit-Drama *Der Baader Meinhof Komplex*, gescheiterte Träume der 68er und den Terrorismus der RAF." *Abendzeitung*, 21 September, 2008.

Durth, Werner, Jörn Düwel, and Niels Gutschow. *Architektur und Städtebau der DDR*. 2 vols. Frankfurt am Main: Campus, 1998.

Dyer, Richard. "Feeling English." *Sight and Sound* 4, no.3 (1994): 16–19.

Eder, Klaus, and Alexander Kluge. *Ulmer Dramaturgien: Reibungsverluste*. Arbeitshefte Film 2/3. Munich: Hanser, 1980.

Egoshooter [2004], Directed by Christian Becker and Oliver Schwabe. DVD. Berlin: Filmgalerie 451, 2005.

Eichinger, Bernd. "*Der Baader Meinhof Komplex*: Drehbuch von Bernd Eichinger. Nach dem Buch und mit Beratung von Stefan Aust. Drehbuchmitarbeit Uli Edel." In *Der Baader Meinhof Komplex*, by Katja Eichinger, 125–293.

Eichinger, Katja. *Der Baader Meinhof Komplex: Das Buch zum Film*. Hamburg: Hoffmann & Campe, 2008.

"'Eine Abbildung der Realität in ihrer Härte:' Ein Gespräch mit Peter Kahane über seinen Film *Die Architekten*." In *Filmkunst und Gesellschaftskritik: Sozialethische Erkundungen*, edited by Walter Lesch, Charles Martig, and Joachim Valentin, 187–98. Film & Theologie 7. Marburg: Schüren, 2005.

Eldridge, David. *Hollywood's History Films*. London: I. B. Tauris, 2006.

11 Jahre Teamworx: Ein Rückblick. http://www.teamworx.de/nc/presse/downloads/allgemeine-infos.html?cid=35&did=893&sechash=215a8 e1b.

Elsaesser, Thomas. "Tales of Sound and Fury: Observations on the Family Melodrama" [1972]. In *Home Is Where the Heart Is: Studies in Melodrama and the Woman's Film*, edited by Christine Gledhill, 43–69. London: British Film Institute, 1987.

———. *Terror und Trauma: Zur Gewalt des Vergangenen in der BRD*. Berlin: Kulturverlag Kadmos, 2006.

Elstermann, Knut. "Da kommt noch was! Jetzt im Kino: *Die fetten Jahre sind vorbei* von Hans Weingartner." *Neues Deutschland*, 25 November 2004.

Elterlein, Eberhard von. "*Berlin is in Germany*: Du sollst du selbst bleiben." *Die Welt*, 1 November 2001.

Enzensberger, Ulrich. *Die Jahre der Kommune I: Berlin, 1967–1969*. Munich: Goldmann, 2006.

Erler, Peter, and Hubertus Knabe. *Der verbotene Stadtteil: Stasi-Sperrbezirk Berlin-Hohenschönhausen*. 2nd ed. Berlin: Jaron Verlag, 2005.

Eue, Ralph. "Alles Feeling! Christopher Roth hat mit seinem Terroristen-Porträt *Baader* keine ernsthafte Biographie im Sinn, sondern Lust auf den Geschmack von Freiheit, Abenteuer und Gefahr." *Der Tagespiegel*, 17 October 2002.

Evans, Owen. "Taking Stock of the *Wende* on Screen: Michael Klier's *Ostkreuz* and Hannes Stöhr's *Berlin is in Germany*." *German as a Foreign Language* 1 (2006): 60–75.

Fassbinder, Rainer Werner. *Die Anarchie der Phantasie: Gespräche und Interviews*. Edited by Michael Töteberg. Frankfurt am Main: Fischer, 1986.

Festenberg, Nikolaus von. "Sandmännchen rettet die DDR: Wolfgang Beckers wunderbare Kinophantasie *Good Bye, Lenin!* wehrt sich mit viel Ironie gegen den unerbittlichen Lauf der Geschichte." *Der Spiegel* 6, 3 February 2003, 120.

"Filmfestspiele: Es darf geweint werden." *Der Spiegel* 6, 6 February 1995, 188–90.

Finger, Evelyn. "Die unsinkbare Republik: Wolfgang Beckers Tragikomödie *Good Bye, Lenin!* kennt viele Arten von Gelächter." *Die Zeit*, 6 February 2003.

Finke, Klaus. "Utopie und Heimat: Peter Kahanes Film *Die Architekten.*" In *DEFA-Film als nationales Kulturerbe?* Beiträge zur Film- und Fernsehwissenschaft 58, edited by Klaus Finke, 53–60. Berlin: Vistas, 2001.

Fischer, Jaimey. "German Historical Film as Production Trend: European Heritage Cinema and Melodrama in *The Lives of Others.*" In *The Collapse of the Conventional: German Film and Its Politics at the Turn of the Twenty-First Century*, edited by Jaimey Fisher and Brad Prager, 186–215. Detroit: Wayne State U, 2010.

Fischer, Joschka. "Identität in Gefahr!" In *Grüne Politik: Eine Standortbestimmung*, edited by Thomas Kluge, 20–35. Frankfurt am Main: Fischer, 1984.

Flierl, Bruno. *Gebaute DDR: Über Stadtplaner, Architekten und die Macht; Kritische Reflexionen, 1990–1997*. Berlin: Verlag für Bauwesen, 1998.

Foell, Kristie A. "History as Melodrama: German Division and Unification in Two Recent Films." In *Textual Responses to German Unification: Processing Historical and Social Change in Literature and Film*, edited by Carol Anne Costabile-Heming, Rachel J. Halverson, and Kristie A. Foell, 232–52. Berlin: Walter de Gruyter, 2001.

Fredrich, Silke, and Anja Wunsch. "Parteichefin entschlossen: Merkel; 'Alles für Wachstum, Arbeit, Wohlstand.'" *RP Online*, 6 December 2004. http://www.rp-online.de/politik/deutschland/Merkel-Alles-fuer-Wachstum-Arbeit-Wohlstand_aid_71166.html.

Frick, Ulrike. "Parolen von damals: Hans Weingartners kleiner Schlaumeier-Film." *Münchner Merkur*, 24 November 2004.

Führer Ex [2002]. Directed by Winfried Bonengel. DVD. Munich: Universum Film, 2003.

Fulbrook, Mary. *Anatomy of a Dictatorship: Inside the GDR, 1949–1989*. Oxford: Oxford UP, 1995.

Galenza, Ronald, and Heinz Havemeister, eds. *Wir wollen immer artig sein . . . Punk, New Wave, HipHop, und Independent-Szene in der DDR, 1980–1990*. Rev. ed. Berlin: Schwarzkopf & Schwarzkopf, 1999.

Galle, Birgit. "Hier zartes Klopfen, dort hartes Hämmern — aber wer wird es hören: Zu den DEFA-Premieren *Die Architekten* und *Karla.*" *Neues Deutschland*, 23 June 1990.

Gansera, R., and F. Göttler. "Liebe in Zeiten der Matrix: Interview; Hans Weingartner." *Süddeutsche Zeitung*, 22 November 2004.

Gansera, Rainer. "Bewußt wie ein Projektil: Wie Christopher Roth den Mythos von Baader zerbröselt." *Süddeutsche Zeitung*, 17 October 2002.

Gauck, Joachim. "*Das Leben der Anderen*: Ja, so war es!" *Stern*, 25 March 2006.

Gaus, Günter. "Nischengesellschaft," in *Wo liegt Deutschland: Eine Ortsbestimmung*, 156–233. Hamburg: Hoffmann & Campe, 1983.

Gehr, Richard. "Last Exit to Brooklyn." *American Film* 15, no. 8 (1990): 34–48.

Gemünden, Gerd. *Framed Visions: Popular Culture, Americanization and the Contemporary German and Austrian Imaginations.* Ann Arbor: U of Michigan, 1999.

German Bundestag. http://www.bundestag.de/htdocs_e/bundestag/members17/bygroup.html.

German Federal Film Board (Filmförderungsanstalt, FFA). Marktdaten. http://www.ffa.de.

Gespenster [2005]. Directed by Christian Petzold. DVD. Berlin: Indigo, 2006.

"Gespräch mit dem Regisseur Peter Kahane." In *Die Architekten: Presseinformation.* Berlin: Progress Film-Verleih, n.d.

GG 19: 19 gute Gründe für die Demokratie [2007]. Directed by Harald Siebler. DVD. Hamburg: Filmsortiment.de, 2008.

Good Bye, Lenin! [2003]. Directed by Wolfgang Becker. DVD. Hamburg: Warner Home Video, 2003.

Good Bye, Lenin! http://www.79qmddr.de/intro.php.

Gorky, Maxim. *Days with Lenin.* Honolulu: UP of the Pacific, 2004.

Gossing, Heide. "Begrabene Träume: *Architekten*, neuer DEFA-Film von Peter Kahane." *Ostsee Zeitung*, 6 September 1990.

Grass, Günter. "Writing after Auschwitz (1990)." In *Two States — One Nation?*, translated by Krishna Winston and A. S. Wensinger, 94–123. New York: Harcourt Brace Jovanovich, 1990.

Gricksch, Gernot. "Abenteuer aus Wildwestdeutschland: Der Terrorist mit den rauchenden Colts; Christopher Roths Jungenphantasie *Baader*." *Rheinischer Merkur*, 10 October 2002.

Grimberg, Steffen. "In einem fremden Land: Mit *Berlin is in Germany* starten ORB und ZDF ihre ambitionierte Filmreihe 'Ostwind.'" *taz*, 9 March 2003.

HA. "Ferres überzeugt auch die Zuschauer." *Hamburger Abendblatt*, 2 October 2007.

Habermas, Jürgen. "Yet Again: German Identity; A Unified Nation of Angry DM-Burghers?" *New German Critique* 52 (1991): 84–101.

Hagen, Kirsten von. "Im Gespräch: Volker Schlöndorff über seinen Film *Die Stille nach dem Schuss*; Das war so in der DDR." *Rheinischer Merkur*, 15 September 2000.

Hahn, Anne. "Feuerwerk am hellichten Tag." *Freitag: Die Ost-Westwochenzeitung*, 31 August 2007.

Halbwachs, Maurice. *The Collective Memory.* Translated by Francis J. Ditter and Vida Yazdi Ditter. New York: Harper & Row, 1980.

Halle, Randall. "Unification Horror: Queer Desire and Uncanny Visions." In Halle and McCarthy, *Light Motives: German Popular Film in Perspective*, 281–303.

Halle, Randall, and Margaret McCarthy, eds. *Light Motives: German Popular Film in Perspective.* Detroit: Wayne State UP, 2003.

Hamdorf, Wolf Martin. "'Was für ein trauriges Ende!' Film und Terrorismus: Ein Gespräch mit dem Regisseur Volker Schlöndorff." *Filmforum* 25, no.5 (2000): 12–15.

Hamdorf, Wolfgang. "*Berlin is in Germany*." *Film-Dienst* 22 (23 October 2001): 22.

Hassabis, Demis, Dharshan Kumaran, Seralynne D. Vann, and Elanor A. Maquire. "Patients with Hippocampal Amnesia Cannot Imagine New Experiences." *PNAS* 104, no. 5 (2007): 1726–31.

Hasselbach, Ingo, and Winfried Bonengel. *Die Abrechnung: Ein Neonazi steigt aus.* Berlin: Aufbau Taschenbuch, 2001.

Haufler, Daniel. "Die DDR ist eine Baustelle: In Wolfgang Beckers Wettbewerbsbeitrag *Goodbye, Lenin!* wird der sozialistische Osten Deutschlands neu erfunden." *taz*, 10 February 2003.

Hauswald, Harald. "Einmal um die Welt." In Rauhut and Kochan, *Bye Bye Lübben City: Bluesfreaks*, 392–400.

Hein, Christoph. "Dritte Welt überall. Ostdeutschland als Avantgarde der Globalisierung: Wo das Kapital flieht, kommt der Nationalismus zurück." *Die Zeit*, 30 September 2004.

Hell, Julia, and Johannes von Moltke. "Unification Effects: Imaginary Landscapes of the Berlin Republic." *Germanic Review* 80, no. 1 (2005): 74–95.

Hengst, Björn, and Philipp Wittrock. "Eklat in Niedersachsen: Linken-Abgeordnete hat Sehnsucht nach der Stasi." *Spiegel Online*, 14 February 2008. http://www.spiegel.de/politik/deutschland/0,1518,535427,00.html.

Hensel, Jana. *Zonenkinder.* Reinbek bei Hamburg: Rowohlt, 2002.

Herold, Roland. "Die verratene Generation: Erster DEFA-Film nach der Wende; Peter Kahanes *Architekten*." *Sächsisches Tageblatt*, 29 June 1990.

Higson, Andrew. *English Heritage, English Cinema: Costume Drama since 1980.* Oxford: Oxford UP, 2003.

Hillman, Roger. "*Goodbye Lenin* (2003): History in the Subjunctive." *Rethinking History* 10, no. 2 (2006): 221–37.

Hochmuth, Dietmar. "Eine Suche ohne Ende: Gespräch mit Peter Kahane; Interview 1993." In *DEFA NOVA: Nach wie vor? Versuch einer Spurensicherung*, Heft 82, edited by Dietmar Hochmuth, 108–22. Berlin: Freunde der deutschen Kinemathek, 1993.

———. "Margarethe von Trotta: Die Balance von Erwachen und Wahn." In *Regiestühle international*, edited by Fred Gehler, 225–58. Berlin: Henschel Verlag, 1987.

Hodgin, Nick. "*Berlin is in Germany* and *Good Bye Lenin!* Taking Leave of the GDR?" *Debatte: Review of Contemporary German Affairs* 12, no. 1 (2004): 25–45.

Hoff, Peter. "Der ultimative Ost-Zoo: Nicht nur ein Fernsehabend im Zeichen der (N)Ostalgie." *Neues Deutschland*, 25 August 2003.

Hopp, Helge. "Die Heimat kann sehr kalt sein: Mit *Berlin is in Germany* starten ZDF und ORB ihre Filmreihe 'Ostwind.'" *Die Welt am Sonntag*, 9 March 2003.

Hoyer, Gisela. "Liebesgeschichte in Mauer-Schatten: Trottas neuer Film *Das Versprechen* unterwegs nach L.A. in Leipzig voraufgeführt." *Leipziger Volkszeitung*, 29/30 October 1994.

Huber, Christopher. "Bernd Eichinger: 'Wir leben in Zeiten des Terrors.'" *Die Presse*, 25 September 2008.

Hughes, John, and Brooks Riley. "A New Realism." *Film Comment* 11, no. 6 (1975): 14.

Hughes-Warrington, Marnie. *History Goes to the Movies: Studying History on Film*. London: Routledge, 2007.

Huntington, Samuel P. *The Clash of Civilizations and the Remaking of World Order*. New York: Simon & Schuster, 1996.

Huyssen, Andreas. "After the Wall: The Failure of German Intellectuals [1991]." In *Twilight Memories: Marking Time in a Culture of Amnesia*. New York: Routledge, 1995.

Jäger, Heidi. "'Ich spüre den Erwartungsdruck': Am 12. August kommt Andreas Dresens preisgekrönter Film *Nachtgestalten* in die Kinos." *Potsdamer Neuste Nachrichten*, 7 August 1999.

Jarausch, Konrad H., ed. *Dictatorship as Experience: Towards a Socio-Cultural History of the GDR*. New York: Berghahn, 1999.

Jarausch, Konrad H., and Volker Gransow. *Uniting Germany: Documents and Debates, 1944–1993*. Oxford: Berghahn, 1994.

Jeschonnek, Günter. "Die Sehnsucht nach dem unpolitischen Märchen: Ein kritischer Kommentar zum Stasi-Film *Das Leben der Anderen*." *Deutschland Archiv* 39, no. 3 (2006): 501–4.

Junghänel, Frank. "Herr Mux geht ins Kino: Tolle Kritiken, volle Säle; Jan Henrik, Autor und Akteur des Überraschungsfilms *Muxmäuschenstill* — über Idole, Jusos und Harald Schmidt." *Berliner Zeitung*, 19 July 2004.

———. "Nach drüben: Im Wettbewerb; Volker Schlöndorffs *Die Stille nach dem Schuss* arbeitet ein Stück DDR auf." *Berliner Zeitung*, 17 February 2000.

———. "Von der Mauer verweht: In Margarethe von Trottas Film *Das Versprechen* werden große Gefühle behauptet." *Wochenpost* 8 (1995).

Kahlschlag [1993]. Directed by Hanno Brühl. DVD. Remscheid: Kinder- und Jugendfilmzentrum, 2005.

Kaiser, Paul. "Heckenscheren gegen Feindfrisuren: Das Vokabular der Macht; Asozialität, Dekadenz und Untergrund." In Rauhut and Kochan, *Bye Bye Lübben City*, 267–82.

Kaiser, Regina, and Uwe Karlstedt. *Zwölf heißt: Ich liebe dich: Der Stasi-Offizier und die Dissidentin*. Munich: Knauer, 2004.

Kamalzadeh, Dominik. "Revolution auf der Almhütte: Hans Weingartners *Die fetten Jahre sind vorbei* fragt nach den politischen Möglichkeiten der jüngsten Generation." *Der Standard*, 25 November 2004.

Kammerer, Dietmar. "'Die private Revolte ist nie privat.' Der Regisseur Hans Weingartner hofft auf eine junge Generation, die wieder Lust hat zu kämpfen. Mit seinem neuen Film *Die fetten Jahre sind vorbei* will er selbst einen Anfang machen." *taz*, 25 November 2004.

Kant, Immanuel. *Groundwork of the Metaphysics of Morals*. Edited and translated by Mary Gregor. Cambridge: Cambridge UP, 1988. Original German, *Grundlegung zur Metaphysik der Sitten*. In *Werke*, 9 vols., 4:385–464. Berlin: Walter de Gruyter, 1968.

Kapczynski, Jennifer. "Negotiating Nostalgia: The GDR Past in *Berlin Is in Germany* and *Good Bye, Lenin!*" *Germanic Review* 82, no.1 (2007): 78–100.

Kapferer, Norbert. "'Nostalgia' in Germany's New Federal States as a Political and Cultural Phenomenon of the Transformation Process." In *Political Thought and German Reunification: The New German Ideology*, edited by Howard Williams, Colin Wight, and Norbert Kapferer, 28–40. New York: St. Martin's, 2000.

Kaspar, Frank. "Entlassen in eine fremde Freiheit: Die außergewöhnliche Filmreihe 'Ostwind' dokumentiert den Wandel nach dem Fall der Mauer; *Berlin is in Germany* (ZDF/ORB)." *Frankfurter Allgemeine Zeitung*, 8 March 2003.

Kaufman, David. "The Nazi Legacy: Coming to Terms with the Past." In *Modern Germany: Politics, Society and Culture*, edited by Peter James, 119–34. New York: Routledge, 1998.

Keller, Harald. "Tränen lügen doch." *Frankfurter Rundschau*, 28 September 2007.

Kellerhoff, Sven Felix. "Berlin, 2. Juni 1967: Um 20.30 Uhr fällt der Schuss, der Deutschland verändert." *Berliner Morgenpost*, 30 May 2007.

———. "Millionenquoten für Geschichte: Historische Ereignisse als Rahmen von fiktiven Dramen werden zum Erfolgsrezept deutscher Filmemacher." *Die Welt*, 22 March 2006.

Ki/jam. "Tragikomische Filmgeschichte: Ein Schuldirektor wird entführt." *Berliner Morgenpost*, 10 May 1997.

Kilb, Andreas. "Identifikation eines Mannes: Der schmale Grat: Christopher Roths Versuch, mit *Baader* einen Filmclip über den deutschen Terrorismus zu drehen." *Frankfurter Allgemeine Zeitung*, 16 October 2002.

———. "Die netten Jahre sind vorbei: Doppelgesicht; Filme von Hans Weingartner und Michael Moore beim Festival in Cannes." *Frankfurter Allgemeine Zeitung*, 18 May 2004.

———. "Zahme Herzen: Margarethe von Trottas Mauerfilm *Das Versprechen*." *Die Zeit*, 17 February 1995.

Kinderspiele. Directed by Wolfgang Becker. 16 mm. Berlin: FFG Film- und Fernsehgesellschaft, 1992.

Kinkel, Lutz. "Spektakulärer Kampf um die Töchter: Jutta Gallus, im Film gespielt von Veronica Ferres, lässt sich vor dem KSZE-Konferenz-Gebäude in Helsinki an den Fahnenmast fesseln." *Stern*, 30 September 2007.

Kirschner, Stefan. "Experiment Stadtguerilla: Ein Filmregisseur macht Theater; Andreas Dresens Terroristen-Monologe." *Berliner Morgenpost*, 4 June 2002.

Klärner, Andreas. "'Zwischen Militanz und Bürgerlichkeit': Tendenzen der rechtsextremen Bewegung am Beispiel einer ostdeutschen Mittelstadt." In Klärner and Kohlstruck, *Moderner Rechtsextremismus in Deutschland*, 44–67.

Klärner, Andreas, and Michael Kohlstruck, eds. *Moderner Rechtsextremismus in Deutschland*. Hamburg: Hamburger Edition, 2006.

———. "Rechtsextremismus: Thema der Öffentlichkeit und Gegenstand der Forschung." In Klärner and Kohlstruck, *Moderner Rechtsextremismus in Deutschland*, 7–43.

Klaus, Georg, and Manfred Buhr. *Philosophisches Wörterbuch*. 2 vols. Leipzig: VEB Bibliographisches Institut, 1964.

Kleist, Heinrich von. *Sämtliche Werke und Briefe*, 2 vols. Edited by Helmut Sembdner. Munich: Hanser, 1961.

Klingenmaier, Thomas. "*Die fetten Jahre sind vorbei*: Revolte gegen den Wohlstand." *Stuttgarter Zeitung*, 25 November 2004.

Klonk, Charlotte. "Bilderterrorismus: Von Meins zu Schleyer." In *Nach-Bilder der RAF*, edited by Inge Stephan and Alexandra Tacke, 197–215. Cologne: Böhlau, 2008.

Kluge, Alexander. *Gelegenheitsarbeit einer Sklavin: Zur realistischen Methode*. Frankfurt am Main: Suhrkamp, 1975.

Knabe, Hubertus. "Das Aufarbeitungskombinat: Merkwürdige Vorschläge zur Neuorganisation des DDR-Gedenkens." *Die Welt*, 8 May 2006. In Sabrow, Eckert, Flacke, et al., *Wohin treibt die DDR-Erinnerung: Dokumentation einer Debatte*, 191.

———, ed. *Gefangen in Hohenschönhausen: Stasi-Häftlinge berichten*. Berlin: List Ullstein, 2007.

Knauf, Thomas. *Die Architekten*. DEFA Studio für Spielfilme, Gruppe "Babelsberg." Produktion: Herbert Ehler. Unpublished film script, 17 July 1989. D II /8.

Kniebe, Tobias. "Bang Boom Bang: *Baader Meinhof Komplex*." *Süddeutsche Zeitung*, 24 September 2008.

———. "Generation Nix: Hans Weingartner ergründet die Jugend in seinem Film *Die fetten Jahre sind vorbei*." *Süddeutsche Zeitung*, 24 November 2004.

———. "Mit Hans Weingartner in Cannes: Der Welt wird nichts erspart." *Süddeutsche Zeitung*, 21 May 2004.

Koehler, John O. *Stasi: The Untold Story of the East German Secret Police*. Boulder, CO: Westview, 1999.

Koenen, Gerd. *Das rote Jahrzehnt: Unsere kleine deutsche Kulturrevolution, 1967–1977*. Frankfurt am Main: Fischer, 2002.

———. *Vesper, Ensslin, Baader: Urszenen des deutschen Terrors*. Frankfurt am Main: Fischer, 2005.

Koepnick, Lutz. "'Amerika gibt's überhaupt nicht': Notes on the German Heritage Film." In *German Pop Culture: How "American" Is It?*, edited by Agnes Mueller, 191–208. Ann Arbor: U of Michigan P, 2004.

———. "Reframing the Past: Heritage Cinema and Holocaust in the 1990s." *New German Critique* 87 (2002): 47–82.

Kohl, Helmut. "Fernsehansprache von Bundeskanzler Kohl anlässlich des Inkrafttretens der Währungs-, Wirtschafts- und Sozialunion, 1. Juli 1990." Konrad Adenauer Stiftung. http://www.helmut-kohl.de/index.php?msg=555.

———. "Offener Brief, nach der Ausstrahlung von *Die Terroristen* von Philip Gröning im Südwestfunk in der *FAZ* vom 28. 11. 1992." In Kraus, *Deutschland im Herbst: Terrorismus im Film*, 100–101.

Köhler, Horst. "'Das sind neue Gründerjahre': Köhler-Rede im Wortlaut." *Spiegel Online*, 23 May 2004. http://www.spiegel.de/politik/deutschland/0,1518,301109,00.html.

Köhler, Margret. "Beschreibung von Leben: Bemerkungen zu Margarethe von Trottas *Das Versprechen*." *Film-Dienst* 1 (3 January 1995): 14–16.

Köhler, Marlene. "Kommt jetzt die unterhaltsame und gut erzählte DEFA-Film-Geschichte? Zu ersten Eindrücken vom 6. Spielfilm-Festival der DDR." *Mitteldeutsche Zeitung*, 29 May 1990.

Kohler, Michael. "Vorrecht der Jugend: Geschichte und Klassenkampf wiederholen sich als Burleske; Hans Weingartners *Die fetten Jahre sind vorbei*." *Frankfurter Rundschau*, 25 November 2004.

Kohlstruck, Michael, and Anna Verena Münch. "Hypermaskuline Szenen und fremdenfeindliche Gewalt: Der Fall Schöberl." In Klärner and Kohlstruck, *Moderner Rechtsextremismus in Deutschland*, 302–36.

Kolb, Felix. "The Impact of Transnational Protest on Social Movement Organizations: Mass Media and the Making of ATTAC Germany." In *Transnational Protest and Global Activism*, edited by Donatella della Porta and Sidney Tarrow, 95–120. Lanham, MD: Rowman & Littlefield, 2005.

Kombat Sechzehn [2005]. Directed by Mirko Borscht. DVD. Berlin: Indigo, 2009.

Konrad, György. "Rückblick auf die Beglückung." In *Glück, Stadt, Raum in Europa, 1945 bis 2000*, edited by Romana Schneider and Rudolf Stegers, 8–11. Basel: Birkhäuser, 2002.

Koppold, Ruppert. "Das kann doch jedem passieren: Winfried Bonengels *Führer Ex*." *Stuttgarter Zeitung*, 5 December 2002.

Körner, Andreas. "Provokation ist hohl: Kino-Gesprächsstoff; Marcus Mittermeier und Jan Hendrik Stahlberg zu *Muxmäuschenstill*." *sz-online, Sachsen im Netz*, 8 July 2004. http://www.sz-online.de/freizeit/artikel.asp?id=631612.

Korzilius, Sven. *"Asoziale" und "Parasiten" im Recht der SBZ/DDR: Randgruppen im Sozialismus zwischen Repression und Ausgrenzung*. Cologne: Böhlau Verlag, 2005.

Kovach, Thomas A., editor and translator, and Martin Walser. *The Burden of the Past: Martin Walser on Modern German Identity: Texts, Contexts, Commentary*. Rochester, NY: Camden House, 2008.

Kraus, Petra, Natalie Lettenewitsch, Ursula Saekel, Brigitte Bruns, and Matthias Mersch, eds. *Deutschland im Herbst: Terrorismus im Film*. Munich: Münchner Filmzentrum, 1997.

Kriest, Ulrich. "Bilder aus 'bleiernen Jahren.'" In Kraus et al., *Deutschland im Herbst: Terrorismus im Film*, 22–35.

———. "'Ich sage nie: So war das!' Gespräch mit Christopher Roth über *Baader*." *Film-Dienst* 21 (8 October 2002): 62–63.

Krippendorff, Ekkehart. "Wohlstandsgefängnis: *Die fetten Jahre sind vorbei*; Die Alt-68er, die erwachsen werden mussten in dieser Gesellschaft." *Freitag: Die Ost-Westwochenzeitung*, 26 November 2004.

Kroko [2003]. Directed by Sylke Enders. DVD. Berlin: Absolut Medien, 2004.

Kronenberg, Volker. "Patriotismus in Deutschland: Eine Nation auf der Suche nach sich selbst." *Die politische Meinung* 421 (2004): 31–34.

Kuhlbrodt, Dietrich. "Bloß kein Fehler, Genosse General! Die DDR, ein Heimatmuseum aus Stasi-Loden, Volksgut und VEB-Betriebsfeiern: In *Die Stille nach dem Schuss* bebildert Volker Schlöndorff ein deutsches Terroristenschicksal." *taz*, 14 September 2000.

———. "Für alle Fälle Magerquark: Die 3 von der Wohngemeinschaft und der böse Mercedesfahrer; Hans Weingartners globalisierungskritische Digitalvideofabel *Die fetten Jahre sind vorbei* probt den poetischen Widerstand." *taz*, 25 November 2004.

Kühnel, Wolfgang. "Hitler's Grandchildren? The Reemergence of a Right-Wing Social Movement in Germany." In *Nation and Race: The Developing Euro-American Racist Subculture*, edited by Jeffrey Kaplan and Tore Bjørgo, 148–74. Boston: Northeastern UP, 1998.

Kurtz, Andreas, and Anne Lena Mösken. "Abgeordnete im Dunkeln: Der Kulturstaatsminister lud ins Kino — die Grünen konnten sogar zwischen zwei Filmen wählen." *Berliner Zeitung*, 15 March 2006.

Lammert, Norbert, ed. *Verfassung, Patriotismus, Leitkultur: Was unsere Gesellschaft zusammenhält*. Hamburg: Hoffmann & Campe, 2006.

Landsberg, Alison. *Prosthetic Memory: The Transformation of American Remembrance in the Age of Mass Culture*. New York: Columbia UP, 2004.

Landy, Marcia, ed. *The Historical Film: History and Memory in Media*. New Brunswick, NJ: Rutgers UP, 2001.

Laqueur, Walter. *Terrorism*. Boston: Little, Brown, 1977.

Lasn, Kalle. *Culture Jam: How to Reverse America's Suicidal Consumer Binge — and Why We Must*. New York: Harper Collins, 2000.

Last Exit to Brooklyn [1989]. Directed by Ulrich Edel. DVD. Santa Monica, CA: Summit Entertainment, 2011.

Lehnartz, Sascha. "Vendetta gegen Schwimmbad-Pinkler: Um für ihren Film *Muxmäuschenstill* zu werben, haben dessen Macher im Internet zum

Denunziatenum aufgerufen — mit erstaunlichem Erfolg." *Frankfurter Allgemeine Zeitung*, 8 February 2004.

Letztes aus der Da Da eR [1990]. Directed by Jörg Foth. DVD. Amherst, MA: DEFA Film Library, 2009.

Liebman, Stuart. "On the German Cinema, Art, Enlightenment, and the Public Sphere: An Interview with Alexander Kluge." *October* 46 (1998): 23–59.

Linß, Vera. "Interview: Hubertus Knabe über den Film *12 heißt: Ich liebe Dich*." RevolutionundEinheit.de: Medienmonitor und Magazin, 10 April 2009. http://www.friedlicherevolution.de/index.php?id=49&tx_comarevolution_pi4%5Bcontribid%5D=104.

Löser, Claus. "'Ich verstehe Inge Viett': Wie frei darf man Leben verfilmen? Ein Interview mit Wolfgang Kohlhaase, dem Drehbuchautor von *Die Stille nach dem Schuss*." *taz*, 17 February 2000.

Lucy [2006]. Directed by Henner Winckler. DVD. Berlin: Filmgalerie 451, 2007.

Maaz, Hans-Joachim. *Behind the Wall: The Inner Life of Communist Germany*. Translated by Margo Bettauer Dembo. New York: W. W. Norton, 1995.

Magenau, Jörg. "Poesiealbum der Geschichte: Margarethe von Trottas Film *Das Versprechen* eröffnet die Berlinale." *Freitag: Die Ost-Westwochenzeitung*, 10 February 1995.

Maihorn, Klaus. "Mutiges Menetekel — zu spät." *Wochenpost*, 6 July 1990.

Manuel, Frank E., and Fritzie P. Manuel. *Utopian Thought in the Western World*. Cambridge, MA: Belknap, 1979.

Markovits, Inga. "Two Truths about Socialist Justice: A Comment on Kommers." *Law & Social Inquiry* 22, no. 3 (1997): 849–78.

Martenstein, Harald. "Tränen kennen keine Grenzen: Margarethe von Trotta hat außer Konkurrenz den Wettbewerb der Berlinale eröffnet." *Der Tagesspiegel*, 10 February 1995.

Matthies, Otto. "Interview mit Margarethe von Trotta und Peter Schneider." In Schneider and von Trotta, *Das Versprechen oder Der lange Atem der Liebe: Filmszenarium*, 140–45.

McAdams, A. James. *Judging the Past in Unified Germany*. Cambridge: Cambridge UP, 2001.

McGee, Laura Green. "'Ich wollte ewig einen richtigen Film machen! Und als es soweit war, konnte ich's nicht!' The End Phase of the GDR in Films by DEFA Nachwuchsregisseure." *German Studies Review* 26, no. 2 (2003): 315–32.

Mennel, Barbara. "Political Nostalgia and Local Memory: The Kreuzberg of the 1980s in Contemporary German Film." *Germanic Review* 82, no. 1 (2007): 54–77.

Mensching, Steffen, and Hans-Eckardt Wenzel. *Letztes aus der Da Da eR*. DEFA-Studio für Spielfilme, "Nachswuchsgruppe." Produktionsleitung: Manfred Renger. Unpublished film script, 19 March 1990. Version D I/5.

Merkel, Ina. "From Stigma to Cult: Changing Meanings in East German Consumer Culture." In *The Making of the Consumer: Knowledge, Power and Identity in the Modern World*, edited by Frank Trentmann, 249–70. Oxford: Berg, 2006.

———. *Utopie und Bedürfnis: Die Geschichte der Konsumkultur in der DDR*. Cologne: Böhlau, 1999.

Mintz, Steven, and Randy W. Roberts, eds. *Hollywood's America: United States History through Its Films*. 4th ed. Malden, MA: Wiley-Blackwell, 2010.

Mishra, Robin, and Hans-Joachim Neubauer. "Das gute Leben im Schlechten: Marianne Birthler, die Bundesbeauftragte, warnt davor, das DDR-Unrecht zu verharmlosen." *Rheinischer Merkur*, 25 May 2006.

Mittman, Elizabeth. "Fantasizing Integration and Escape in the Post-Unification Road Movie." In Halle and McCarthy, *Light Motives: German Popular Film in Perspective*, 326–48.

Mohr, Reinhard. "Die Prada-Meinhof-Bande." *Der Spiegel*, 27 February 2002. http://www.spiegel.de/kultur/gesellschaft/0,1518,184222,00.html

Mönch, Regina. "Mit dem Rücken zum Osten: Der erste Fernsehfilm über Gewissenskonflikte von DDR-Soldaten müht sich redlich; *An die Grenze* (Arte/ZDF)." *Frankfurter Allgemeine Zeitung*, 7 September 2007.

Monk, Claire. "The British Heritage-Film Debate Revisited." In *British Historical Cinema: The History, Heritage and Costume Film*, edited by Claire Monk and Amy Sargeant, 176–98. London: Routledge, 2002.

Müller, Matthias C. "*Die fetten Jahre sind vorbei*: Die Sprachnot charmanter Weltverbesserer." *Stuttgarter Nachrichten*, 25 November 2004.

Mulvey, Laura. *Death 24x a Second: Stillness and the Moving Image*. London: Reaktion Books, 2007.

Muxmäuschenstill [2004]. Directed by Marcus Mittermeier. DVD. Hamburg: Warner Home Video, 2005.

MZ. "Mauern für die Phantasie: *Architekten* beim nationalen DDR-Filmfestival in Ost-Berlin." *Frankfurter Allgemeine Zeitung*, 6 June 1990.

"Nach sieben Jahren — ein deutscher Film für Cannes." *Frankfurter Allgemeine Zeitung*, 21 April 2004.

Naughton, Leonie. *That Was the Wild East: Film Culture, Unification, and the "New" Germany*. Ann Arbor: U of Michigan P, 2002.

Neale, Steve. "Art Cinema as Institution." In *The European Cinema Reader*, edited by Catherine Fowler, 103–20. London: Routledge, 2002.

———. *Genre and Hollywood*. London: Routledge, 2000.

Nicodemus, Katja. "Denn sie wissen, was sie tun: Hans Weingartners Film *Die fetten Jahre sind vorbei* sucht mit seinen Helden nach der Revolution von morgen." *Die Zeit*, 25 November 2004.

———. "Die unbestimmte Wut auf alles: Winfried Bonengels *Führer Ex* gelingt das Kunststück eines unpolitischen Neonazi-Films." *Die Zeit*, 5 December 2002.

———. "Von der Zelle in die Platte: Auf Schleichwegen; Volker Schlöndorffs *Die Stille nach dem Schuss*." *taz*, 17 February 2000.

Nietzsche, Friedrich Wilhelm. "On the Uses and Disadvantages of History for Life." In *Untimely Meditations*, edited by Daniel Breazeale, translated by R. J. Hollingdale, 57–123. Cambridge: Cambridge UP, 1983. Original German, "Vom Nutzen und Nachtheil der Historie für das Leben." In *Unzeitgemäße Betrachtungen II: Vom Nutzen und Nachtheil der Historie für das Leben*, vol. 1 of *Sämtliche Werke: Kritische Studienausgabe*, 243–334.

———. *Sämtliche Werke: Kritische Studienausgaben*. Edited by Giorgio Colli and Mazzino Montinari. 15 vols. Munich: dtv, 1980.

Niroumand, Mariam. "Die Mauerspringer: Margarethe von Trottas Ost-West Liebestragödie *Das Versprechen* eröffnet heute abend die Berlinale; Ein Gespräch mit ihr und Co-Autor Peter Schneider." *taz*, 9 February 1995.

Nord, Cristina. "Das Leben besteht aus Klischees: Warum das Indoktrinieren keine Rolle spielt; Ein Gespräch mit dem Regisseur Winfried Bonengel." *taz*, 5 December 2002.

———. "Scheitel und Falte im rechten Winkel: Nah dran an der Exploitation; Winfried Bonengels Spielfilmdebüt *Führer Ex* will zeigen, wie aus einem jungen, unpolitischen Mann ein strammer Nazi wird." *taz*, 5 December 2002.

Ntoubandi, Faustin Z. *Amnesty for Crimes against Humanity under International Law*. Leiden, The Netherlands: Martinus Nijhoff Publishers, 2007.

"Ohnesorg-Todesschütze gibt sich unangreifbar." *Spiegel Online*, 24 May 2009. http://www.spiegel.de/politik/deutschland/0,1518,druck-626527,00.html.

Osang, Alexander. "Zu Gast im Party-Staat." *Der Spiegel*, 8 September 2003, 212–22.

Peschke, Marc. "Die Rebellen sind ratlos: Hans Weingartners Film *Die fetten Jahre sind vorbei* erzählt, wie schwer es ist, einen Alt-68er zu entführen." *Handelsblatt*, 19 November 2004.

Platen, Heide. "Baader war ein rührender Verlierer: Gespräch mit Regisseur Christopher Roth und Daniel Cohn-Bendit." *taz*, 15 February 2002.

Platzangst. Directed by Heike Schober and René Zeuner. 35 mm. Brandenburg: Sonnensegel, 2003.

Plowman, Andrew. "Westalgie? Nostalgia for the 'Old' Federal Republic in Recent German Prose." *Seminar: A Journal of Germanic Studies* 40, no. 3 (2004): 249–61.

Pohlmann, Sonja. "Wer redet, zahlt — Medien dürfen nur eingeschränkt über RAF-Film berichten." *Der Tagesspiegel*, 13 August 2008.

"Ponto-Witwe ruft Gericht an." *Süddeutsche Zeitung*, 1 November 2008.

Professor Edward Said in Lecture: The Myth of the "Clash of Civilizations." Northampton, MA: Media Education Foundation, 1998.

Proll, Astrid, ed. *Hans und Grete: Bilder der RAF, 1967–1977*. Rev. ed. Berlin: Aufbau, 2004.

Proll, Thorwald, and Daniel Dubbe. *Wir kamen vom anderen Stern: Über 1968, Andreas Baader und ein Kaufhaus.* Hamburg: Edition Nautlis, 2003.

Ramet, Pedro. "Disaffection and Dissent in East Germany." *World Politics* 37, no.1 (1984): 85–111.

Rauhut, Michael. "Kleine Fluchten: Vom Blues einer unruhevollen Jugend." In Rauhut and Kochan, *Bye Bye Lübben City*, 51–67.

Rauhut, Michael, and Thomas Kochan, eds. *Bye Bye Lübben City: Bluesfreaks, Tramps und Hippies in der DDR.* Berlin: Schwarzkopf & Schwarzkopf, 2004.

Raus aus der Haut [1997]. Directed by Andreas Dresen. DVD. Amherst, MA: DEFA Film Library, 2004.

Reiermann, Christian. "Wie Angela Merkel ihre wichtigste Rede vorbereitete: Zwischen Reformdebatte und patriotisch-pathetischer Tünche." *Welt Online*, 5 December 2004. http://www.welt.de/print-wams/article119007/Wie_Angela_Merkel_ihre_wichtigste_Rede_vorbereitete.html.

Reimitz, Monika, Wolfgang Thiel, and Hans-Jürgen Wirth. "Muß denn Leben Sünde sein? Notizen, Assoziationen und Interpretationen zu Gesprächen mit Hausbesetzern und Punks." In *Zwischen Resignation und Gewalt: Jugendprotest in den achtziger Jahren*, edited by Marlene Bock, Monika Reimitz, Horst-Eberhard Richter, Wolfgang Thiel, and Hans-Jürgen Wirth, 11–42. Opladen: Leske + Budrich, 1989.

Reinecke, Stefan. "Koketter Retroschick: Interessant gescheitert; *Baader* von Christopher Roth hat berührende, dichte Szenen — aber noch mehr Löcher im Erzählgeflecht." *taz*, 16 February 2002.

———. "Das RAF-Gespenst: Die RAF ist verschwunden und in Pop-Inszenierungen wiedergekehrt; Dann kam der 11. September." *taz*, 5 September 2002.

Rentschler, Eric. "From New German Cinema to the Post-Wall Cinema of Consensus." In *Cinema and Nation*, edited by Mette Hjort and Scott Mackenzie, 260–77. London: Routledge, 2000.

Resik, Cornelia. "*Die Architekten*." *Sächsische Zeitung*, 13 July 1990.

Robb, David G. "Wenzel & Mensching: A Carnivalesque Clowns' Act Spanning the GDR and United Germany." *German Studies Review* 23, no. 1 (2000): 53–68.

Rodek, Hanns-Georg. "Die Außenseiterbande: Pop, Poesie und Politisierung; *Die fetten Jahre sind vorbei* kommt morgen ins Kino." *Die Welt*, 24 November 2004.

———. "Eichinger will die Medien kontrollieren." *Berliner Morgenpost*, 14 August 2008.

———. "Die mageren Jahre sind vorbei. Zumindest für Deutschland in Cannes: Hans Weingartner und Daniel Brühl brechen den Wettbewerbs-Bann." *Die Welt*, 23 April 2004.

———. "Ich muxe, du/er/sie muxt, wir muxen." *Die Welt*, 5 July 2004.

————. "Man muß Stellung beziehen: Marcus Mittermeier und Jan Henrik Stahlberg über ihre Groteske *Muxmäuschenstill*." *Die Welt*, 8 July 2004.

————. "Das Schweigen nach der *Stille*: Im Wettbewerb; Schlöndorffs Terroristen-Film." *Die Welt*, 17 February 2000.

————. "TV-Quoten: 'Fernsehen ist für mich wie Heroin.'" *Die Welt*, 13 November 2007.

————. "Wie gerecht ist die Weltordnung? Die Wettbewerbsfilme von Michael Moore und Hans Weingartner in Cannes sind so politisch wie eindrucksvoll." *Die Welt*, 18 May 2004.

Rosenstone, Robert A. "Film Reviews." *The American Historical Review* 97, no. 4 (1992): 1138–41.

————. *History on Film / Film on History*. Harlow, UK: Pearson Education, 2006.

Ross, Gordon Charles. "The Swastika in Socialism: Right-Wing Extremism and Militant Nationalism in the GDR." In *East Germany: Continuity and Change*, edited by Paul Cooke and Jonathan Grix, 81–94. German Monitor 46. Amsterdam: Rodopi, 2000.

Rößling, Ingo. "Stasi-Offiziere leugnen den Terror." *Berliner Morgenpost*, 16 March 2006.

Rost, Andreas. *Tacheles: Alltag im Chaos; Ein Fotobuch*. Interviews by Annette Gries and Heinz Havemeister. Berlin: Elefanten Press, 1992.

Roth, Christopher. "Interview with Christopher Roth." On *Baader* DVD.

Rowland, Sarah. "Revolutionary Remodeling: *The Edukators* Director Hans Weingartner and Actor Daniel Brühl Explain Why Rearranging Furniture Is a Great Way to Protest." *Montreal Mirror*, 28 July–3 August 2005.

Rusch, Claudia. *Meine freie deutsche Jugend*. Frankfurt am Main: Fischer, 2003.

Saage, Richard. *Utopieforschung: Eine Bilanz*. Darmstadt: Primus, 1997.

Sabrow, Martin, Rainer Eckert, Monika Flacke, Klaus-Dietmar Henke, Roland Jahn, Freya Klier, Tina Krone, Peter Maser, Ulrike Poppe, and Hermann Rudolph. *Wohin treibt die DDR-Erinnerung: Dokumentation einer Debatte*. Göttingen: Vandenhoeck & Ruprecht, 2007.

Sadowski-Smith, Claudia. "Ostalgie: Revaluing the Past, Regressions into the Future." *GDR Bulletin* 25 (1998): 1–6.

Sarkar, David. "Alles, was früher subversiv war, kann man heute im Laden kaufen! Daniel Brühl über Rebellion, den Film *Die fetten Jahre sind vorbei* und dass er sich gerne 'mehr trauen' würde." *Planet Interview*, 30 September 2004. http://planet-interview.de/daniel-bruehl-30092004.html.

Saunders, Anna. "Normalizing the Past: East German Culture and *Ostalgie*." In Taberner and Cooke, *German Culture, Politics, and Literature into the Twenty-First Century*, 89–103.

Schäfer. Karl-Heinz. "Schlaflos in Ost-Berlin." *Hamburger Abendblatt*, 16 February 1995.

Schenk, Ralf. "Einen treffen, Hundert erziehen: Das deutsche Kino ist mit Hans Weingartners *Die fetten Jahre sind vorbei* auf einem guten Weg." *Berliner Zeitung*, 24 November 2004.

Schindhelm, Michael. "Der Terror der Zeit: Warum die Nostalgie um sich greift — in Ost wie in West." *Die Zeit*, 31 October 2001.

Schlöndorff, Volker. "Sur le tambour." *Jeune cinema* 121 (1979): 18–20.

Schmetterlinge. Directed by Wolfgang Becker. 16 mm. Berlin: Deutsche Film- und Fernsehakademie, 1988.

Schneider, Peter. *Der Mauerspringer*. 3rd ed. Darmstadt: Luchterhand, 1986.

Schneider, Peter, and Margarethe von Trotta in collaboration with Felice Laudadio. *Das Versprechen oder Der lange Atem der Liebe: Filmszenarium*. Berlin: Volk & Welt, 1995.

Schnötzinger, Arnold. "Keine Angst vor Geschichtsklitterung: Die Fiktion kann mehr Fragen stellen und irritieren als die reine Dokumentation, meint *Baader*-Regisseur Christopher Roth." OE1@ORF. http://www.oe1.orf.at.

Schorlemmer, Friedrich. "Erinnern und Vergessen." *Freitag: Die Ost-West-wochenzeitung*, 12 October 2007.

Schroeder, Klaus. *Der SED-Staat: Partei, Staat und Gesellschaft, 1949–1990*. Munich: Carl Hanser, 1998.

Schulz-Ojala, Jan. "Denn sie wissen, was sie tun: Sauna aus, Alarm an; Hans Weingartners Film über unser Lebensgefühl, *Die fetten Jahre sind vorbei*, kommt ins Kino." *Der Tagesspiegel*, 25 November 2004.

———. "Kleinbürger, überlebensgroß: Der Kampf um die Deutungshoheit; Christopher Roths irritierender *Baader*." *Der Tagesspiegel*, 17 October 2002.

———. "Die Täterversteher: *Das Leben der Anderen, Der Untergang, Der freie Wille*; Wie neue deutsche Filme Verbrecher zu Helden machen." *Der Tagesspiegel*, 22 March 2006.

———. "Warum hast du meinen Sohn genommen? Deutsch-amerikanischer Tag in Cannes: Michael Moores *Fahrenheit 911* und Hans Weingartners *Die fetten Jahre sind vorbei*." *Der Tagesspiegel*, 18 May 2004.

———. "Wie hältst du's mit der Million? Lola-Gala 2006: Die Filmakademie hat sich etabliert — nun muß sie sich an die Gretchenfrage wagen." *Der Tagesspiegel*, 14 May 2006.

Schwartz, Claudia. "Die große Generationenverstörung im deutschen Film: Hans Weingartner zeigt *Die fetten Jahre sind vorbei*." *Neue Zürcher Zeitung*, 3 December 2004.

Schwarze, Michael. "Ohne Wut und ohne Wucht: Uli Edels umstrittener Film *Wir Kinder vom Bahnhof Zoo*." *Frankfurter Allgemeine Zeitung*, 4 April 1981.

Schwickert, Martin. "Nicht wackeln! Marcus Mittermeier und Jan Henryk Stahlberg über ihr Regie-Debut." *Ultimo auf draht*. http://www.ultimo-bielefeld.de/kr-film/i-mux.htm#seitoben.

Seeßlen, Georg. "Zweierlei Wahn: *Die Stille nach dem Schuss* — Volker Schlöndorffs gespaltener Film über ein gespaltenes Land." *Die Zeit*, 14 September 2000.

Seewald, Berthold. "Sogenannte Museumsführer." *Die Welt*, 30 March 2006.

Seitz, Axel. "Wen provoziert diese Leere? Auf der Leinwand gesehen: *Die Architekten*." *Norddeutsche Zeitung*, 4 July 1990.

Siepmann, Edith. "Stasi-Debatte: Alles verlogen, Flierl muß weg!" *Spiegel Online*, 5 April 2006. http:/www.spiegel.de/kultur/gesellschaft/0,1518,409920,00.html.

Silberman, Marc. "A Postmodernized Brecht?" *Theatre Journal* 45, no. 1 (1993): 1–19.

———. "Post-Wall Documentaries: New Images from a New Germany?" *Cinema Journal* 33, no. 2 (1994): 22–41.

Silly. *Bataillon d'Amor* [1986]. Vocals: Tamara Danz. Lyrics: Werner Karma. CD. Berlin: Amiga & BMG, 1994.

"Sind Sie in Cannes auf dem Teppich geblieben?" *Die Zeit*, 30 December 2004.

Sonnenallee [1999]. Directed by Leander Haußmann. DVD. Munich: Highlight Film and Entertainment, 2003.

Stalinallee: Ein Spiel auf Ehre und Gewissen: Für 2–6 Spieler. Berlin: Karl-Marx-Buchhandlung Kundel & Lenzner, 1999.

"Stalins Rache: Ein Berliner Konzertveranstalter will, hinter Mauer und Stacheldraht, eine Mini-DDR bauen: Ossi-Park." *Der Spiegel*, 18 October 1993, 88–89.

Stau: Jetzt gehts los [1992]. Directed by Thomas Heise. VHS. Bonn: Landesfilmdienst Nordrhein Westfalen, 1993.

Stegemann, Thorsten. "Unterm Schlussstrich kommt der Neuanfang." *Telepolis*, 19 May 2006. http://www.heise.de/tp/r4/artikel/22/22698/1.html.

Stern, Klaus, and Jörg Hermann. *Andreas Baader: Das Leben des Staatsfeindes*. 3rd ed. Munich: dtv, 2007.

Stewart, Garrett. *Framed Time: Toward a Postfilmic Cinema*. Chicago: U of Chicago P, 2007.

Stewart, Janet. "Das Kunsthaus Tacheles: The Berlin Architecture Debate of the 1990s in Micro-Historical Context." In *Recasting German Identity: Culture, Politics, and Literature in the Berlin Republic*, edited by Stuart Taberner and Frank Finlay, 51–66. Rochester, NY: Camden House, 2002.

Strunz, Dieter. "Wenn jedes Detail stimmt, nur das Eigentliche nicht: Außer Konkurrenz; *Das Versprechen* (Deutschland)." *Berliner Morgenpost*, 10 February 1995.

Suchsland, Rüdiger. "Die Freiheit nehme ich mir: Christopher Roths mutiger Film *Baader* erzählt mit schnellen Autos und rotem Lippenstift von Terrorismus." *Frankfurter Rundschau*, 17 October 2002.

———. "Mundgerecht konsumierbare Vergangenheit: Was ist eigentlich dran am Hype um Disneys DDR-Melo *Das Leben der Anderen*?" *Telepolis*, 28 March 2006. http://www.heise.de/tp/r4/artikel/22/22334/1.html.

Sylvester, Regine. "Leidenschaft und Überlebenskämpfe: Drehreport über den neuen DEFA-Film *Die Architekten* von Thomas Knauf (Autor), Peter Kahane (Regie), Andreas Köfer (Kamera)." *Filmspiegel* 9 (1990): 4–5.

Taberner, Stuart, and Paul Cooke, eds. *German Culture, Politics, and Literature into the Twenty-First Century: Beyond Normalization*. Rochester, NY: Camden House, 2006.

Tacheles. http://www.tacheles.de.

Teune, Simon. "Humour as a Guerrilla Tactic: The West German Student Movement's Mockery of the Establishment." *International Review of Social History* 52 (2007): 115–32.

Theweleit, Klaus. *One + One: Rede für Jean-Luc Godard zum Adornopreis*. Berlin: Brinkmann & Bose, 1995.

Tibi, Bassam. *Europa ohne Identität*. Munich: Bertelsmann, 1998.

Toplin, Robert B. *Reel History: In Defense of Hollywood*. Lawrence: UP of Kansas, 2002.

Töteberg, Michael, ed. *Good Bye, Lenin! Ein Film von Wolfgang Becker: Drehbuch von Bernd Lichtenberg, Co-author Wolfgang Becker*. Berlin: Schwarzkopf & Schwarzkopf, 2003.

"Totenbuch für die 134 Opfer der Berliner Mauer." *Berliner Morgenpost*, 18 May 2008.

The Tunnel, reported by Piers Anderton, http://www.msnbc.msn.com/id/21134540/vp/33623268#33623268.

Ullrich, Maren. *Geteilte Ansichten: Erinnnerungslandschaft deutsch-deutsche Grenze*. Berlin: Aufbau, 2006.

Veiel, Andres. *Der Kick: Ein Lehrstück über Gewalt*. 2nd ed. Munich: Goldmann, 2008.

Verfehlung [1992]. Directed by Heiner Carow. DVD. Amherst, MA: DEFA Film Library, 2009.

Vieth-Entus, Susanne. "FU-Studie: Berliner Schüler verklären die DDR." *Der Tagesspiegel*, 10 November 2007.

Viett, Inge. *Nie war ich furchtloser: Autobiographie*. 1996. Reprint, Hamburg: Nautilus, 2005.

Von Donnersmarck, Florian Henckel. *Das Leben der Anderen: Filmbuch*. Frankfurt am Main: Suhrkamp, 2006.

Wach, Alexandra. "Schiefe Welt, schräger Gang: Gespräch mit Marcus Mittermeier über *Muxmäuschenstill*." *Film-Dienst* 14 (8 July 2004): 10.

Wahl, Torsten. "'Jetzt gibt's was auf die Fresse': Autor Stefan Kolditz gilt in der TV-Branche als Experte für Zeitgeschichte." *Berliner Zeitung*, 29 October 2007.

———. "Liebe am Minenfeld: Das Drama *An die Grenze* ist der bisher eindrücklichste Film über die NVA." *Berliner Zeitung*, 7 September 2007.

Walser, Martin. "Erfahrungen beim Verfassen einer Sonntagsrede." Deutsches Historisches Museum, Lebendiges virtuelles Museum Online. http://

www.hdg.de/lemo/html/dokumente/WegeInDieGegenwart_redeW-
alserZumFriedenspreis/index.html.

———. "Experiences with Composing a Sunday Speech." In *The Burden of the Past: Martin Walser on Modern German Identity: Texts, Contexts, Commentary*, ed. and trans. Thomas A. Kovach, 85–95. Rochester, NY: Camden House, 2008.

———. "Über den Leser — soviel man in einem Festzelt darüber sagen soll." In *Ansichten, Einsichten: Aufsätze zur Zeitgeschichte*, vol. 11 of *Werke*, 12 vols., edited by Helmuth Kiesel and Frank Barsch, 564–71. Frankfurt am Main: Suhrkamp, 1997.

Weber, Klaus. "Sozialpsychologie des Rechtsextremismus. Rechtsextremismus bei Jugendlichen: Symposium Dokumentation," 8 May 2005, 29–34. http://www.kjr-m.de/publikationen/pdf/rechtsextremismus2005.pdf.

Weingartner, Hans. *"The Educators: Die fetten Jahre sind vorbei. Offizielles Programm im Wettbewerb Cannes 2004."* http://www.coop99.at/DFJ/pressbookgr.pdf.

Weltverbesserungsmaßnahmen [2005]. Directed by Jörn Hintzer, Jakob Hüfner, and Tom Schreiber. DVD. Ismaning: EuroVideo, 2006,

Wesely, Kathrin. "Anrührendes Porträt eines Ossies, der nach zehn Jahren Knast in die ihm fremde Welt entlassen wird." *Schwäbisches Tagblatt*, 3 November 2001.

Westphal, Anke. "Mensch oder Schwein: Volker Schlöndorff hat drei Filme in einem gedreht; *Die Stille nach dem Schuss*." *Berliner Zeitung*, 14 September 2000.

———. "Was unterging, taucht nicht mehr auf: *Good Bye, Lenin!* von Wolfgang Becker legt heiter Distanz ein — das macht traurig." *Berliner Zeitung*, 8 February 2003.

White, Hayden. *The Content of the Form: Narrative Discourse and Historical Representation*. Baltimore: Johns Hopkins UP, 1990.

———. *Metahistory: The Historical Imagination in Nineteenth-Century Europe*. Baltimore: Johns Hopkins UP, 1973.

Wiedemann, Dieter. "Wo bleiben die Kinobesucher? Daten und Hypothesen zum Kinobesuch in der neuen deutschen Republik." In *Medien der Ex-DDR in der Wende*, edited by Peter Hoff and Dieter Wiedemann, Beiträge zur Film- und Fernsehwissenschaft 40, 81–99. Berlin: Vistas, 1991.

Wiezorek, Christine. "Rechtsextremismusforschung und Biografieanalyse." In Klärner and Kohlstruck, *Moderner Rechtsextremismus in Deutschland*, 240–56.

Winkler, Thomas. "Leise Überraschungen: Ein bisschen staunend und ein bisschen zurückgelehnt; In Hannes Stöhrs Film *Berlin is in Germany* spielt Jörg Schüttauf einen DDR-Bürger, der zehn Jahre nach dem Fall der Mauer aus dem Gefängnis entlassen wird." *taz*, 31 October 2001.

"Wir brauchen eine neue Sprache für die Erinnerung: Das Treffen von Ignatz Bubis und Martin Walser." *Frankfurter Allgemeine Zeitung*, 14 December 1998.

Wirsching, Andreas. *Abschied vom Provisorium, 1982–1990*. Munich: Deutsche Verlags-Anstalt, 2006.

Wolle, Stefan. *Die heile Welt der Diktatur: Alltag und Herrschaft in der DDR, 1971–1989*. 2nd ed. Munich: Econ Ullstein, 2001.

Wollen, Peter. "The Situationist International." *New Left Review* 174 (1989): 67–93.

Worthmann, Merten. "Verzweifelte Bewährungsprobe: Große Gefühle, deutsche Geschichte; Der Berlinale-Eröffnungsfilm *Das Versprechen*." *Berliner Zeitung*, 10 February 1995.

Yoder, Jennifer A. *From East Germans to Germans? The New Postcommunist Elites*. Durham, NC: Duke UP, 1999.

Zander, Peter. "Die verlorene Ehre der Inge Viett: Von Terroristen, die in der DDR untertauchen; Volker Schlöndorffs Wettbewerbsfilm *Die Stille nach dem Schuss* wird vermutlich die Justiz beschäftigen — obwohl er spießig ist." *Berliner Morgenpost*, 17 February 2000.

Zeh, Juli. "Sixties würzig, Sixties light: *Die fetten Jahre sind vorbei*; Die Cabinet-Generation wird politisch, aber deshalb noch lange nicht erwachsen." *Freitag: Die Ost-Westwochenzeitung*, 26 November 2004.

Ziegler, Helmut. "Aus dem Schlamm: ORB und ZDF starten das Projekt Ostwind mit dem Film *Berlin is in Germany*." *Berliner Zeitung*, 9 March 2003.

12 heißt: Ich liebe Dich [2008]. Directed by Connie Walter. Broadcast 16 April 2008, ARD.

Index

Das Abonnement (1967), 183
Adamski (1994), 94n96
Adorno, Theodor, 265, 269
Akin, Fatih, 14
alaska.de (2000), 65
Alexandre, Miguel, 150–53
Allein (2004), 286n2
Alles auf Zucker (2005), 260
Alte Liebe (1984), 63
Das alte Lied (1992), 94n96
Der amerikanische Freund (1970), 190
amnesia, 23–26, 30, 34, 37, 40, 41, 55, 62, 65, 72, 73–74, 75, 77–78, 80, 81, 173, 199, 301
An die Grenze (2007), 150, 153–55, 156, 157
anamnesis, 23, 30, 34, 81
anarchy, 49, 53, 55, 270
Die andere Frau (2004), 125
Andreas Baader — Der Staatsfeind (2002), 237n4
Apfelbäume (1992), 94n96
Die Architekten (1990), 103, 110–21, 158, 300, 303
Arendt, Hannah, 53
Der Ärgermacher (2004), 256
asocials, 47, 50, 54, 202, 204
ATTAC, 265

Baader (2002), 12, 174, 177, 178–92, 214, 230, 231, 233, 236, 273, 299–300, 303
Baader, Andreas: death of, 178, 179, 188, 192, 231, 238n11; media image of, 174, 176, 180–81, 183, 188, 208 fig. 3.3, 212, 213, 216; personality of, 180–81, 184, 190, 232, 243n48; RAF leader, 173, 187, 200, 254, 268

Der Baader Meinhof Komplex (2008), 12, 174, 178, 219–34, 235, 301, 303
Bahro, Rudolf, 213, 247n97
Bakunin, Mikhail, 263, 265
Bambule (1970), 183
Baudrillard, Jean, 288n16
Becker, Christian, 257
Becker, Jens, 94n96
Becker, Wolfgang, 27, 36, 62–77, 301
Berg, Christian, 237n4
Berlin: Ecke Schönhauser (1966), 196
Berlin Is in Germany (2001), 34, 35–44, 45, 61, 77, 78, 80, 153, 301
Beruf Neonazi (1993), 46, 56
Der bewegte Mann (1994), 249n114
Beyer, Frank, 104, 107, 108–9, 110
Biermann, Wolf, 141, 147–48, 211
Biesenbach, Klaus, 175–76
Bin ich sexy (2004), 286n2
Black Box BRD (2001), 174
Blair Witch Project (1999), 275
Die bleierne Zeit (1981), 125, 128, 134, 190
Blümner, Bettine, 286n2
Boehlke, Michael, 89n62
Böll, Heinrich, 192, 193
Bonengel, Winfried, 45–61, 80, 301
Borchert, Wolfgang, 142, 145, 146
Borscht, Mirko, 58
Brandstifter (1969), 189
Brandt, Willy, 5, 125, 186, 199
Brecht, Bertolt, 104, 139, 142–44, 145, 185–86, 188–89, 190, 192, 194, 218
Breloer, Heinrich, 237n4
Der Brocken (1992), 94n96
Brückner, Jutta, 132
Brühl, Hanno, 58

Buck, Detlev, 94n96, 109
Büld, Wolfgang, 109
Butch Cassidy and the Sundance Kid (1969), 179

Cabaret (1972), 279
Calle, Sophie, 24–26
capitalism: and alienation, 48, 263, 268; and consumerism, 3, 13, 55–56, 75, 154, 196, 266; as counterpole to Communism, 6, 29, 34, 65, 69, 74, 75, 126, 145, 146, 177, 206, 213, 251n129, 268; and oppression, 221, 264, 268, 271, 284, 302; protest against, 173, 174, 180, 196, 200, 211, 253; relation of fascism to, 1, 4, 31, 133, 173; self-preservation of, 191, 270; transition for Easterners to, 38–39, 43, 44, 70, 105
Carow, Heiner, 104, 107, 108, 244n65
Christiane F.: Wir Kinder vom Bahnhof Zoo (1981), 220–22, 223
Cold War, 1, 5, 6, 30, 103, 125, 134, 152, 154, 235
Conradt, Gerd, 174

Danz, Tamara, 202, 207
Dazlak-Skinhead (1997), 59
Debord, Guy, 265, 267, 269, 290n28
DEFA (Deutsche Film Aktiengesellschaft), 14, 15, 103, 104–10, 110–21, 196, 300
Dehne, Miriam, 286n2
Delay, Jan, 174–75
Derrida, Jacques, 30
Das deutsche Kettensägenmassaker (1990), 94n96
Deutschland im Herbst (1978), 180, 192–94
dissent: and FRG, 18n7, 134, 185–86, 189, 193, 200, 229, 233, 299–303; and GDR, 31–32, 41, 45, 46, 48–50, 72, 80, 100, 107–9, 132–34, 137–39, 141, 145, 157, 202, 210–13, 299–303; and look of rebellion, 176, 270; as plotline in

national narrative, 7, 13, 80, 273, 299; and post-unification Germany, 145, 253–54, 259, 266, 270, 273, 285; as reaction to conformity, 107, 177, 212, 236, 263–64, 268, 299, 301; and youth culture, 48–50, 109, 174–77, 210–13
Drei Stern Rot (2002), 171n109
Dresen, Andreas, 12, 15, 178, 207–19, 236, 262, 301
Die dritte Generation (1979), 191
Durchschlag, Thomas, 286n2
Dutschke, Rudi, 186, 228–29, 254, 268
Dziuba, Helmut, 94n97

Edel, Uli, 12, 174, 178, 219–34, 235, 301
Ediths Tagebuch (1983), 63
Egger, Urs, 150, 153–55
Egoshooter (2004), 257–58
Eichinger, Bernd, 219–34
The End of Violence (1997), 286n3
Enders, Sylke, 15, 258–59
Engelchen (1996), 94n97
Ensslin, Gudrun, 173, 174, 175, 176, 178, 183, 187, 190, 192, 208 fig. 3.3, 212, 213, 216, 238n11, 254, 268
Enzensberger, Hans Magnus, 3, 4
Escape from East Berlin (1962), 166n62
Ete und Ali (1985), 112

Farocki, Harun, 14
Fassbinder, Rainer Werner, 14, 15, 185, 189, 190–91, 195
Federal Republic of Germany (FRG): and post-unification, 3, 14, 17, 24, 36, 38, 40, 43–44, 45, 46, 55–56, 59–60, 67, 68, 99, 105, 145, 174; power structures in, 151, 225, 228; relation of fascism to, 31–32, 49, 124, 133–34, 173; and right-wing extremism (*see* Neo-Nazis); self-image of, 1–3, 31–33, 175–76, 177; and student movement (*see* '68 student movement); and terrorism (*see* RAF); unification of,

1–2, 5, 7, 24, 28, 31, 32, 43, 55, 65, 68, 75, 76, 94n96, 94n97, 99, 157, 208–10, 237n3; and *Wende* (see *Wende*); and *Westalgie*, 29; youth culture in, 48, 88n62, 173, 174, 177

Feistl, Katinka, 286n2

feminine gender roles, 115–16, 140–41, 198, 203–5, 259, 279

Die fetten Jahre sind vorbei (2004), 254, 255, 256, 259–73, 277, 285, 286, 302, 303

Feuertheater (1984), 63

Fiebeler, Carsten, 89n62

Fischer, Joschka, 6, 18n7

Die Flucht (1977), 119

Flüstern und schreien (1988), 89n62

Fosse, Bob, 279

Foth, Jörg, 15, 104–5, 107

Die Frau vom Checkpoint Charlie (2007), 150–53, 154, 157

Free Rainer: Dein Fernseher lügt, 262–63

Friedrich Schiller: Der Triumph eines Genies (1940), 131

Frosch, Christian, 236

Führer Ex (2002), 34, 45–62, 77–81, 153, 301, 303

Gansel, Denis, 220, 237n4

Geißendörfer, Hans W., 63

German Democratic Republic (GDR), 175–76, 235, 268, 273, 298–302; Berlin Wall, 1, 2, 5, 7, 30–31, 35, 39, 49, 50, 53, 55, 65, 66–67, 74–75, 78, 110, 111 fig. 2.3, 117, 119, 121–35, 144, 149, 155, 199, 211, 218, 273, 299; collective memory of, 23–30, 33; dual legacy of, 33–34, 300, 301; escape from (*Republikflucht*), 33, 34, 39–40, 41, 43, 46, 50, 61, 65, 71, 72–73, 77–78, 80, 109, 118, 119, 121, 124, 126, 128, 132, 150, 153, 155, 215, 299, 300; as experiment gone wrong, 4, 27, 80, 146, 205; as prison state, 13, 27, 33, 34, 37–38, 43, 50, 54, 55, 60–61,

78, 80, 105, 108, 203, 301; and RAF, 177, 178, 196, 199, 202–6, 208–19, 244n65; relation of fascism to, 1, 31–32, 124, 133; and right-wing extremism (*see* Neo-Nazis); self-image of, 1–3, 24, 27; 17 June 1953, 67, 106–7, 113, 126; surveillance (*see* Stasi); *Wende* (see *Wende*)

Gespenster (2005), 258

GG 19: 19 gute Gründe für die Demo-kratie (2007), 256

Gies, Hajo, 150

Glowna, Vadim, 94

Go Trabi Go (1991), 94n96, 109

Godard, Jean-Luc, 181, 240n26

Good Bye, Lenin! (2003), 27, 34, 62–77, 79–81, 149, 301, 302, 303

Gorbachev, Mikhail, 72, 77, 144

Götter der Pest (1969), 190

Gräf, Roland, 104, 107–8, 119

Grass, Günter, 5, 6

Groneborn, Ester, 65, 286n2

Gröning, Philip, 237n3

Günther, Egon, 159n10

Habermas, Jürgen, 17n1

Hachmeister, Lutz, 237n4

Halbe Treppe (2002), 262

Halbwachs, Maurice, 25, 29, 30

Hasselbach, Ingo, 45, 46, 48, 49, 57, 58, 61, 62

Haußmann, Leander, 27, 171n109

Heimweh nach drüben (2007), 150

Hein, Christoph, 40, 105, 107

Heise, Thomas, 58

Helden wie wir (1999), 94n96, 109

Heller Wahn (1983), 128

Hensel, Jana, 26, 147

Herbig, Michael, 249n114, 293n48

heritage film, 10–12

Die Herstellung eines Molotow-Cocktails (1967), 183

Herzog, Werner, 14, 15

Herzsprung (1992), 94n96

Heuss, Theodor, 17

Hill, George Roy, 179

Hintzer, Jörn, 255

Hirschbiegel, Oliver, 149, 249n114, 293n48
historiography, 7–9, 13, 27, 47, 253, 301
history film, 8–13, 16, 110–11, 149–50, 154, 228, 253, 298–303
Hochhäusler, Christoph, 15
Holocaust, 5, 6, 31, 46, 134, 173, 176, 235, 254
Honecker, Erich, 47, 54, 72, 137, 155, 213, 215
Höntsch, Andreas, 160n11
Horkheimer, Max, 265, 269
Hüfner, Jakob, 255
Hundsköpfe (2002), 171n109
Hunger auf Leben (2004), 162n27

Ich habe gelebt und gelebt und gelebt: Die DDR Schriftstellerin Brigitte Reimann (1990), 162n27
Ich liebe, mein Gott — ich liebe: Das kurze Leben der Brigitte Reimann (1999), 162n27
Ich war 19 (1968), 196
Im Fadenkreuz (1997), 237n4
Imboden, Markus, 162n27
In weiter Ferne so nah (1993), 286n3
Die innere Sicherheit (2001), 174
Itzenplitz, Eberhard, 183

Jana und Jan (1992), 94n97
Johnson, Lyndon B., 125
Jopp, Vanessa, 65
Jürgens, Steffen, 256

Kahane, Peter, 15, 104, 110–21, 158, 300
Kahlschlag (1993), 58
Kaiser, Olaf, 171n109
Kant, Immanuel, 254, 276, 277, 278
Kasten, Ulrich, 162n27
Katzenspiele (1982), 63
Keglevic, Peter, 110
kein Science Fiction (2003), 276
Keinohrhase (2007), 220
Kennedy, John F., 125, 126
Khrushchev, Nikita, 125, 126
Der Kick (2006), 91

Kinderspiele (1992), 63–64
Kipping, Herwig, 15, 104, 106–7, 300
Klein, Gerhard, 196
Klein, Naomi, 265, 269
Kleist, Heinrich von, 276, 279, 280
Klier, Michael, 86n42, 94n97
Klooss, Reinhard, 109
Kluge, Alexander, 14, 63, 180, 182–83, 188, 190, 192, 195, 253
Knabe, Hubertus, 100, 146, 147, 157
Knauf, Thomas, 110, 120
Knepperges, Rainer, 256
Kohl, Helmut, 5, 31, 237n3
Köhler, Horst, 7
Kohlhaase, Wolfgang, 196–97, 201, 204
Kombat Sechzehn (2005), 58–59
Kommune 1, 184, 227, 267, 268, 290n28
Kroko (2003), 258–59
Kunzelmann, Dieter, 267, 290n28

Das Land hinter dem Regenbogen (1992), 104, 106, 300
Landsberg, Alison, 16
Lang, Fritz, 258
Langhans, Rainer, 267
Laqueur, Walter, 177, 214
Laske, Karsten, 171n109
Lasn, Kalle, 265, 269
Last Exit to Brooklyn (1989), 221–22
Das Leben der Anderen (2006), 102, 103, 135–49, 155, 156, 158, 300, 302, 303
Das Leben ist eine Baustelle (1997), 64
Die Legende von Paul und Paula (1972), 108
Lemke, Klaus, 185, 188–89
Letztes aus der Da Da eR (1990), 104, 105–6
Levy, Dani, 93n94, 260
Liebe ist kälter als der Tod (1969), 185, 190–91
Limonadi, Ali, 183
Lola rennt (1998), 283
Lucy (2006), 258
Die Luftbrücke: Nur der Himmel war frei (2005), 110

Maisch, Herbert, 131
Marxism, 2–4, 34, 39, 53, 57, 65, 69,
   74–75, 133, 145, 153, 177, 213,
   218, 235, 253, 267, 273, 297, 302
masculine gender roles, 50–53, 60
The Matrix (1999), 264, 288n16
Matrix Reloaded (2003), 63
Die Mauer — Berlin '61 (2006), 110
Meinhof, Ulrike, 173, 181, 183, 187,
   222, 223
Melville, Jean Paul, 181, 188, 191,
   195
Mensching, Steffen, 105–6
Merkel, Angela, 7
Metropolis (1927), 258
Milosevic, Tamara, 91n81
Miraculi (1992), 160n11
Mischkowski, Markus, 276
Misselwitz, Helke, 22n42, 36, 94n96,
   94n97
Mittermeier, Marcus, 254, 274–84,
   285, 302
Mogadischu (2008), 174
Mrasek, Christian, 256
Müller, Franz, 276
Muxmäuschenstill (2004), 254–55,
   256, 274–84, 285–86, 299, 302,
   303
Myrick, Daniel, 275

National Socialism: and atrocities, 1, 2,
   4–7, 123, 125, 134, 253–54; and
   authoritarian mindset, 32, 54, 227,
   278; and capitalism, 4, 31, 69, 133;
   and GDR, 31, 49, 53–54, 113,
   133–34; and heritage film, 11–12;
   and historiography, 101, 149;
   legacy of guilt, 2, 4–7, 31–32, 125,
   133–34, 195, 229, 232, 253–54;
   and Neo-Nazis, 57; and postwar
   division, 1, 5, 134; and '68 student
   movement, 13, 18n7, 229; and surveillance, 236; as utopia, 4
nationalism, 1, 2, 6, 7, 32, 55, 105,
   193
Neo-Nazis, 32, 45–62, 74, 78, 79,
   278
Nietzsche, Friedrich, 1, 73–74, 301

Nikolaikirche (1995), 110, 148
nostalgia, 27, 34, 74, 75, 80, 188,
   190, 235

Ohnesorg, Benno, 184, 187, 209,
   226, 227, 228, 229, 237n2
Ostalgie, 26–30, 65, 67, 80, 102
Ostkreuz (1991), 94n97
Ostpunk — Too Much Future (2006),
   89n62
Ottinger, Ulrike, 14

*Das Parfum: Die Geschichte eines Mör-
   ders* (2006), 136
Die Patriotin (1979), 253
Peckinpah, Sam, 181, 273
Peterson, Sebastian, 109
Petzold, Christian, 15, 174, 258, 297
Das Phantom (2000), 237n4
Pierrot le fou (1965), 181
Platzangst (2003), 58
Plenzdorf, Ulrich, 108, 109, 244n65
Polly Blue Eyes (2005), 286n2
Prager Botschaft (2007), 150
Prague Spring, 107, 126, 127, 128,
   130, 132, 159n10, 215, 232
Prinzessinnenbad (2007), 286n2
punks, 45–50, 58, 65, 78, 79, 88n54,
   88n62, 110, 133, 202, 203, 299

Die Quereinsteigerinnen (2005), 256

Raus aus der Haut (1997), 12, 178,
   207–19, 236, 301, 303
Red Army Faction (RAF): and anti-
   capitalism, 13, 177, 191, 196, 198,
   200, 202, 204–5, 211, 225, 232,
   235; and death of leaders, 178,
   179, 187, 192–94, 230, 231–32;
   and German Autumn, 176, 178,
   192–94, 217; and media, 17, 175–
   77, 180–81, 183–84, 185, 186,
   212–14, 217; as model for contemporary activism, 255, 267–68, 273;
   motivations of, 123, 173, 190, 197,
   198, 201, 202, 223, 230, 232–33;
   myths surrounding, 174, 175, 178,
   183, 188, 223, 232–33, 236;

Red Army Faction (RAF)—*(cont'd)*
and national narrative, 174, 177,
178, 193, 207, 234, 298–303; and
National Socialism, 13, 173, 195,
214, 227, 229, 232, 234, 235,
236; and Neo-Nazis, 61–62; and
pop culture, 174–75, 183; and
relation to GDR, 177, 178, 196,
199, 202–6, 208–19, 244n65; and
2 June Movement, 196–97, 200,
209, 267; self-image of, 180–81,
183–84, 185, 186; and surveillance, 177, 178, 187, 191, 194–95,
203–4, 214, 230–31, 234, 236;
and utopianism, 3–4, 17, 177, 178,
186, 191, 198, 205, 207, 209–10,
236; and violence, 173, 177, 184–
87, 191, 192, 194, 195, 196, 198,
222, 224–28, 229, 230, 231, 233,
235, 236
Rentschler, Eric, 14–15, 42, 152,
264
Richter, Roland Suso, 49, 110, 150,
174
Rosa Luxemburg (1986), 125
Rosenstraße (2003), 125
Der rote Kakadu (2006), 110
Roth, Christopher, 12, 174, 177,
178–92, 199–200, 214, 230, 231,
233, 236, 300–301
Rothemund, Marc, 260

Sabrow Commission, 100–102, 103
Sanchez, Eduardo, 275
Sander, Helke, 59
Sanders-Brahms, Helma, 63, 94n96
Schattenwelt (2009), 174
Schlingensief, Christoph, 94n96
Schlöndorff, Volker, 12, 36, 49, 174,
178, 192–207, 210, 235, 254,
301
Schmetterlinge (1988), 63
Schneider, Peter, 121, 122, 123, 124,
126, 254, 257
Schnibben, Cordt, 237n4
Schnitzler, Gregor, 89n62
Schober, Heike, 58
Schoeller, Bettina, 256

Schoen, Hartmut, 110
Schreiber, Tom, 255
Schübel, Rolf, 91n81
Schubert, Katharina, 162n27
Der Schuh des Manitu (2001),
249n114
Schumann, Dieter, 89n62
Schwabe, Oliver, 257
Schweiger, Til, 220
Schwestern oder die Balance des Glücks
(1979), 128
7 Zwerge: Männer allein im Wald
(2004), 293n48
Siebler, Harald, 256
Silly, 202, 203
Siodmak, Robert, 166n62
Sirk, Douglas, 131, 220
Situationist International, 267
'68 student movement, 2, 4, 7, 13,
17, 18n7, 29, 122, 189, 207,
210, 253–55, 259, 267–69, 273,
302
socialism: belief in, 74, 137–39, 141,
144, 145, 158, 199, 203, 204,
205, 235–36, 300, 302; bureaucracy, 104, 156, 158; collapse of,
28, 65, 104, 105, 121, 255; corruption in, 137–38, 144, 145;
and humanism, 31, 137–38, 146,
153; oppression in, 73, 104, 108,
156, 158, 300, 301; and planned
economy, 49, 68, 116, 146; protest
in, 132–33, 138, 144, 213; real-
existing socialism, 27, 71, 104,
116, 122, 153, 155, 178, 213,
301; and renunciation of desire,
118, 137, 146, 215; and social
justice, 145, 158, 300; solidarity in,
44, 70, 137–38, 153; Soviet influence on, 6, 126, 128, 130, 132,
134, 144, 213; as state system in
GDR, 26, 73; and totalitarianism,
27, 65; unfulfilled promise of, 3,
26, 65, 70, 74, 75, 104, 118, 121,
130, 146, 204, 300
Socialist Unity Party of Germany
(Sozialistische Einheitspartei
Deutschlands, SED), 3, 33, 34,

76, 100, 101, 107, 113, 120, 137, 213, 215, 251n109
Solo Sunny (1980), 196
Sonnenallee (1999), 27, 65, 109, 149
Sophie Scholl: Die letzten Tage (2005), 260
Stadt als Beute (2005), 286n2
Stahlberg, Jan Henrik, 274, 275, 276, 278, 285
Stalin, Joseph, 39, 94n95, 106, 113, 141, 142, 148
Starbuck — Holger Meins (2002), 174
Stasi (Ministry for Security, MfS): coercion by, 54, 107–8, 137, 214; Hohenschönhausen prison, 33, 100–101, 135, 141, 146–47, 155–57, 211; informant for, 33, 53, 54, 107–8, 137, 149, 204, 226, 228, 275, 299; interrogation by, 65, 72, 128, 135, 155–56, 218; motivation for joining, 134, 137; and RAF, 197, 200, 201, 203–6; resistance to, 129, 137–38; Stasi Romeo, 123, 150–51; surveillance by, 33, 100–101, 118–19, 135–49, 203, 214, 236, 255, 284, 299, 300; as tool in police state, 2, 75, 100–101, 121, 129, 135, 137–38, 140–41, 206, 214, 216, 275, 303; as victim, 141, 148–49, 158, 206; and youth rebellion, 49, 211, 218
Stau — jetzt gehts los! (1992), 58, 59
Stein (1991), 159n10
Stein von Kamienski, Nikolaus, 150
Steinkühler, Kai-Maria, 276
Stelzer, Manfred, 109
Stern, Klaus, 237n4
Die Stille nach dem Schuss (2000), 12, 49, 174, 178, 192–207, 235, 301, 303
Stilles Land (1992), 94n96, 208
Stöckl, Ula, 94n96
Stöhr, Hannes, 35–44, 45, 61, 80, 301
Stoph, Willi, 213
Der Straß (1991), 160n11
Straub, Jean-Marie, 195

Superstau (1991), 109
Syberberg, Hans-Jürgen, 63
Szabo, Istvan, 63
Der Tangospieler (1991), 107–8
Die Terroristen (1992), 237n3
Teufel, Fritz, 267
Theweleit, Klaus, 15
Timm, Peter, 94n96, 109
Die Todesautomatik (2007), 150
Todesspiel (1997), 237n4
(T)raumschiff Surprise — Periode 1 (2004), 293n48
Der Tunnel (2001), 110, 148
The Tunnel (1962), 166n62
Tykwer, Tom, 14, 64, 93n94, 136, 283

Ulbricht, Walter, 107, 113, 125
Eine unheilige Allianz (1992), 46
Unser kurzes Leben (1981), 162n27
Der Untergang (2004), 149, 249n114, 293n48
Unterwaldt, Sven, 293n48
utopia: as alternative space, 48, 66, 110, 297; loss of, 3, 13, 17, 26, 27, 65, 69, 77, 104, 145, 178, 207, 209–10, 280, 286, 302; and Marxism, 4, 69, 106–7, 145; and National Socialism, 4; and phantom utopia, 302–3; as plotline in national narrative, 7, 13, 177, 297–303; rejection of, 48; and social justice, 3–4, 17, 29, 61, 77, 104, 106–7, 154, 177, 178, 209–10, 254–55, 297–303; and violence, 61, 154, 178, 207, 209–10, 254–55, 299–301

Vater, Mutter, Mörderkind (1993), 244n65
Veiel, Andres, 91, 174
Der Verdacht (1991), 107, 108–9
Verfehlung (1992), 107, 108
Vergiß Amerika (2000), 65
Die verlorene Ehre der Katharina Blum (1975), 192, 194–95
Das Versprechen (1995), 103, 110, 121–35, 138, 158, 300, 303

victims: empowerment of, 150, 152,
    157; and overcoming victimization,
    41, 43, 44; perpetrator becomes
    victim, 141, 148, 149, 155, 206,
    215, 232; sympathy with, 210;
    victim becomes perpetrator, 61–62,
    64, 78, 141, 214, 215, 236, 271,
    301; victim of GDR state, 28, 34,
    41, 43, 49, 50, 61–62, 80, 102,
    123, 131, 134, 141, 146–48,
    150–52, 155–58, 216, 299; victim
    of Holocaust, 5, 6, 31; victim of
    male authority, 144, 198, 204,
    282; victim of RAF, 176, 177, 194,
    199, 209, 231; victim of right-wing
    extremism, 58–59; victim of state
    oppression, 12, 192, 194, 228; vic-
    tim of violence, 51, 63, 64
48 Stunden bis Acapulco (1967), 185,
    189
Von Alberti, Irene, 286n2
Von Donnersmarck, Florian Henckel,
    135–49, 158, 300
Von Gwinner, Johannes, 256
Von Praunheim, Rosa, 14
Von Trotta, Margarethe, 110, 121–35,
    138, 158, 189, 190, 192, 194,
    195, 254, 300
Vorspiel (1987), 112

Wachowski, Larry, and Andy
    Wachowski, 264, 288n16
Walser, Martin, 5–6
Walther, Connie, 49, 88n54, 150,
    155–57, 174
Das war der wilde Osten (1992), 109
Warneke, Lothar, 162n27
Was tun, wenn's brennt (2002), 89n62
Weingartner, Hans, 15, 254, 259–73,
    277, 284–86, 302
Weiß, Ulrich, 160n11

Weiße Lilien (2007), 236
Das weiße Rauschen (2001), 261–62
Die Welle (2008), 220
Weltverbesserungsmaßnahmen (2005),
    255–56
Wende (transitional period 1989–90),
    13, 23, 30, 34, 36, 43, 46, 55,
    56, 69–70, 73–74, 77, 103, 104,
    110–11, 114, 119–20, 206, 208,
    237n3, 301
Wendeloch (films made 1989–92), 15,
    103, 104–10
Wenders, Wim, 14, 195, 257, 286n3
Wenzel, Hans-Eckardt, 105
Wer wenn nicht wir (2011), 174
Westend (2003), 276
White, Hayden, 2, 8
Wie Feuer und Flamme (2001), 49,
    65, 88n54, 110
Wigand, Tomy, 286n2
Winckler, Henner, 258
Wir können auch anders (1993),
    94n96, 109
Wir sind wieder da (1991), 46
Wolf, Konrad, 196
Wolke neun (2008), 262
Wortmann, Sönke, 249n114
Das Wunder von Berlin (2008), 49,
    150, 156

Zahavi, Dror, 110
*Zeugenstand — Stadtguerilla-Mono-
    loge*, 209
Zeuner, René, 58
Zur falschen Zeit am falschen Ort
    (2005), 91
Zwei Tage Hoffnung (2003), 110
2 ½ Minuten (1997), 91
12 heißt: Ich liebe Dich (2008), 150,
    155–57